The

New Testament

A New Translation

Based on the Oldest Manuscripts

by

Johannes Greber

Translation

www.holyspiritanswers.com

CONTENTS

Dear Friend:

Translations of the Bible, and of the New Testament in particular, are manifold in the world. They always will be, because the Word of God will live forever! It is an actual fact that no other book on earth has undergone so many changes at the hands of copyists and translators as has the Holy Scripture — both the Old Testament and the New. The discrepancies in the documents available to us are by no means confined to trifles — in many cases touch the very foundations of the Christian Churches of today.

The New Testament, as interpreted by the scholarly Pastor Johannes Greber, has as its source the oldest manuscripts in the world, made available to Pastor Greber for study and translation through the courtesy and cooperation of theological experts and museums the world over. This is an absolutely independent translation, without restriction to the dogma of any Church.

The task was not simple. Many contradictions between what appears in the ancient scrolls and the New Testament, as we have grown to know it, arose and were the subject of his constant prayers for guidance — prayers that were answered, and the discrepancies clarified to him,. by God's Spirit World.

At times he was given the correct answers in large illuminated letters and words passing before his eyes. Other times he was given the correct answers during prayer meetings. His wife, a medium of God's Spiritworld was often instrumental in conveying the correct answers from God's Messengers to Pastor Greber.

The author recognized the crying need for a translation dressed in present day language, and not as it was spoken centuries ago. According to his own statement, he considered it a sin against the Truth to hand people of our day translations of the Bible which date from earlier centuries and appear to the modern reader peculiar and hard to comprehend which therefore does not absorb his mind, but only tires him.

The result of Johannes Greber's efforts is a translation in plain, yet beautiful language, so natural and clear a child would have no trouble in understanding it. It is a work freed of all doctrinal prejudices and disbeliefs, revealing to the reader a new world of simple beauty and true understanding of God's Will. We would like to share this with you . . . and with all the world!

Introduction

THROUGHOUT CHRISTENDOM the Bible is looked upon as the "word of God"—as the truth which God has revealed. All Christian denominations have made it an article of faith that the books of the Old and the New Testament of which the Bible is composed, were inspired by the "Holy Ghost." These creeds teach that the "Holy Ghost" not only impelled the authors of those books to write them, but imparted the contents to them in strict accordance with the truth, and also guarded the writers against any error in setting them down. Many churches even go so far as to maintain that not only the contents, but the very words themselves were inspired by the "Holy Ghost."

This doctrine is an expression of the belief that the truth can have only one source, namely God, and that hence only those things that are derived from a divine revelation can be true.

As for the truths which are taught by the Christian denominations, these are based chiefly upon the writings of the New Testament. Flawless and unassailable evidence must therefore be produced to prove that the contents of these texts were indeed revealed by God.

There are various ways in which God can manifest Himself. It may be that one of His spirits speaks to a human being, who then and there writes down the message word for word. Such were the messages from God that were received by Moses. He heard the voice of God's spirit speaking to him in the sacred tabernacle out of the cloud that overhung the ark of the covenant, and wrote down the words. Again, one of God's spirits may bring the message not in spoken words, but in the form of the letters of the alphabet. In such a case one letter after another is spelled out, and in this way words and sentences are formed. So it was with the messages that were sent by means of the high priest's breast-plate.—Again, one of God's spirits may make use of a mortal's vocal organs in order to speak, or his hand in order to write. This was often so with the prophets of the Old Testament.—Then, also, a spirit of God may so thoroughly imbue a man or a woman with thoughts to be expressed in speech or in writing, that this person's own thoughts are utterly eliminated, and he speaks or writes only as the spirit prompts. This is called "inspiration." Many of God's messages were delivered through the prophets of the Old Testament in this manner.

We distinguish between two kinds of "inspiration." In one case, only the thoughts are inspired in a person by a spirit of God, and these thoughts are written down in the person's own words and in his own human style of expression. In the case of the other kind of "inspiration" not only the thoughts are imparted, but the very words in which these thoughts are to be uttered. This is nothing more nor less than "dictation" on the part of God's spirit. "Inspiration" of this kind is known as "literal" or "verbal" inspiration.

There are in addition a great many other ways in which God may make His will known.

Nothing further is needed to prove that manifestations of God which are effected by one or another of the methods mentioned, contain the pure truth and must be accepted as "the word of God."

Into which group, now, do the writings of the New Testament fall?

All Christian churches teach that the narratives and epistles of the New Testament were imparted to their respective authors by the "Holy Ghost" through inspiration. Many churches even contend that it was through "verbal" inspiration, that is to say, by way of "dictation."

What proof have the churches for this doctrine?

There are only two ways in which it could be proved, one being an express statement on the part of the authors of the New Testament to the effect that the contents of their records and epistles had been imparted, or in fact dictated to them, by the Spirit of God. The only other proof that we could consider would be an express assertion, made at any time or in any place by the Spirit of God, to the effect that the books of the New Testament are "inspired" writings. No other possible method of proof exists.

Do the authors themselves say that their writings were imparted to them by the "Holy Ghost"? They, if any one, must have known whether they were writing the story of their personal experiences and observations freely and of their own accord, or whether they were only being employed as "instruments" by God's Spirit. If they wrote their accounts on their own impulse in a purely human style, they would, quite naturally, make no special mention of the fact. If, however, they acted merely as "instruments of God's Spirit," they were in duty bound to acknowledge the fact and give the credit to God. They were obliged to do what the writers of the Old Testament had done. Whenever these announced or recorded a revelation from God, they repeatedly emphasized the fact that it was a divine revelation. So often that it becomes almost wearisome, we read, "Thus says Jehovah," or "God spoke."

Of the books of the New Testament, only one, *The Revelation of John,* was communicated by an angel. What is more, John stresses this fact in the very opening sentence of his book. The authors of all the other books of the New Testament say nothing about the operation of any supernatural influence upon the writing of their reports. Luke, on the contrary, expressly states in the first few lines of his gospel that he has compiled his story in quite the ordinary human way. He writes: "Many before me have undertaken to write the story of the well-established events that happened among us. Their accounts agree with what we are told by those who were eyewitnesses from the beginning, and who appeared in public to proclaim the truth. Having looked carefully into all of the facts from the very outset, I have also decided to write them down in historical order and to send my account to you, most noble Theophilus, in order that you may convince yourself of the truth of that which you have learned by word of mouth." His account, therefore, contains the things that were told to him by eyewitnesses, and not those that were imparted to him by the "Holy Ghost." He tells the same story that many others before him had written down. He is familiar with their writings. He re-examines these one by one and arranges everything in its chronological order, having looked carefully into all of the facts from the very outset; only then does he write his own account. He is therefore doing merely what any conscientious historian would do. If, on the other hand, he had been engaged only in setting down the knowledge imparted to him by the "Holy Ghost," what need would there have been for any painstaking research or for arrangement in chronological sequence or for a careful investigation of all of the facts from the very outset? In that case he would have been spared the duty of making any personal investigation. The same is true of his *Acts of the Apostles.* It would be foolish to speak of these two writings of Luke as "inspired" by the "Holy Ghost."

Again, the apostle John declares that he himself witnessed the events that he relates, and that for this reason his story is authentic. In the introduction to his *First Epistle* he writes: "I am writing to you to tell you of him who is the Word of

Life; of the events in his career from the beginning; of that which we ourselves heard from him; of that which we saw with our own eyes; of that which we observed in him, and which was so close to us that we could touch it with our hands. In this way we learned beyond a doubt that in him the true life was made manifest. We saw it before our eyes and therefore can bear witness to it." He also denies any kind of "inspiration" by the "Holy Ghost" in connection with his gospel and his epistles.

The same thing is true of the gospels of Matthew and Mark, and of the various epistles. All of these epistles deal with contemporary matters, and were occasioned by inquiries and reports that were sent in by Christian congregations. The teachings, explanations, exhortations, and warnings contained in these epistles are such as would be addressed by any pastor to distant flocks.

The foregoing implies no denial of the fact that a spirit from God carried to the apostles those Christian truths that appear here and there in their epistles. But there is nothing to prove that these truths were withheld from them until they were actually engaged in committing their epistles to writing. On the contrary, the members of the Christian congregations are expressly reminded in some of these passages that these truths have already been proclaimed to them in the past by word of mouth. At all events, the apostles do not say that their epistles were inspired by the Holy Ghost.

It is therefore obvious to every honest student of the Bible that the authors of the books of the New Testament say nothing about having received their writings through "inspiration by the Holy Ghost," with the exception of John in *The Revelation.* As for the gospels and epistles of Luke and John, the proof that they were written without any supernatural aid or intervention is their own statement to that effect.

It follows that the Christian churches cannot produce from the New Testament itself any proof of their doctrine of inspiration.

Neither has God's Spirit at any time declared the books of the New Testament to be "inspired writing." The only two ways by which the New Testament could possibly be proved to be inspired, are therefore eliminated from consideration.

Hence only this fact remains: The authors of the New Testament writings wrote of their own choice and on the basis of their purely human knowledge, with the exception of *The Revelation of John.* Some wrote as eye- and ear-witnesses of that which they describe; others had made careful investigation among such as had been eye- and ear-witnesses of the facts that they report.

Their accounts therefore justly laid claim to trustworthiness as long as the reports of their own hands were extant. They contained the truth. Whether a truth is obtained by purely human ways or by inspiration of God's Spirit does not in any way affect the truth; for truth remains truth, regardless of the manner by which it comes to us.

One very weighty reason for believing that the books of the New Testament, as we have them to-day, do not owe their existence to any divine inspiration, is found in the following fact: If, as the Christian churches contend, the New Testament as an inspired work were the source of the divine truth, that same source would naturally contain all of the truths that Christ wished to reveal to mankind. The fact is, however, that Christ while he was on earth had many important truths which he could not reveal to his disciples because they were unable to bear them. Had he disclosed them, his disciples would have lost faith in him; but it was his intention that the spirits of truth, whom he meant to send to them later, should initiate them into all these truths. If, then, it was the "Holy Ghost" who, as the spirit of truth promised by Christ to his disciples, inspired the authors of the New Testament, he would also have revealed to them those important truths which at an earlier date had been beyond the apostles' strength to bear. For according to what is taught by all denominations except the Catholic, there are no sources other than the New Testament from which we can learn those truths that Christ promised.

But does the New Testament contain a single one of those mighty truths that Christ never revealed because they were too weighty to be borne? Not one. And yet, according to Christ, many such truths existed. As for the four gospels, the truths not revealed by Christ cannot be found there, if only for the reason that these gospels deal merely with the things that Christ did and taught while he was on earth.

Let us for a moment admit as a fact the unproved and unprovable "inspired nature of the New Testament"—a statement which could apply only to the text as originally written down. But we no longer possess a single such original manuscript of the New Testament. What we have to-day consists of about three thousand incomplete copies and fragments of copies, no two of which agree. In fact, each individual manuscript can be read in more ways than one, many of its words having been altered by marks subsequently superimposed on them. Often one and the same word has been repeatedly changed. Consequently, no one can say what part of the copies agrees with the original manuscripts of the authors of the New Testament.

It is an actual fact that no other book on earth has undergone so many changes and falsifications at the hands of the copyists as has the Bible, both the Old Testament and the New. With respect to falsifications of the Old Testament, God Himself announces through the prophet Jeremiah: "You think yourselves wise and believe that you are in possession of the truth. Yes, but the pen of the falsifying copyists has turned the truth into a lie."

The same thing can be said of the text of the New Testament. Even the well versed scholar cannot say for certain, with reference to those three thousand copies, which are the words, sentences, or chapters that have been intentionally or accidentally left out, overlooked, misread, misinterpreted, capriciously altered, or deliberately falsified by the copyists. Furthermore, not one of the scribes who made the copies that we have to-day had access to the original text, but only to copies of still earlier copies.

The discrepancies in the documents available to us are not by any means confined to trifles, but in many cases touch the very foundations of the various Christian denominations of to-day. There are many passages, moreover, in which the gospels contradict each other even when reporting the same facts.

As though it were not enough that the old copies available to us conflict in matters of the greatest importance to the doctrines held by the creeds of to-day, the situation is made worse by the translations of the text into our modern languages. Often the translators have failed to understand the Greek text and have assigned to its words, sentences, or phrases a meaning which they either do not have at all, or at least not in their context. Faulty translation is responsible, for instance, for the doctrine of eternal damnation, for the term "the Holy Ghost" as a divine personage, and for the whole doctrine of a Trinity.

Dr. Eugene Huehn is therefore right when he says in his *Hilfsbuch zum Verstaendnis der Bibel* (*Guide to the Interpretation of the Bible*): "Those of us who are acquainted only with our standardized New Testament would never suspect that there are many thousand different versions in existence. Competent judges estimate that the number of discrepancies exceeds the number of words in the New Testament. Under the circumstances, the church of to-day would be not a little embarrassed if called upon to uphold the doctrine of 'inspiration'."

Any unprejudiced observer of the situation must ask with Pilate, "What is the truth?" For if the copies of the New Testament in our possession essentially differ from each other in matters of the utmost importance to the creed of the Christian church, and if in addition they have been incorrectly translated into modern speech, no dogma remains in support of which we could refer to the Bible with a feeling of certainty.

This view is confirmed by no less an authority than St. Jerome. About the year 370 A.D. he translated the whole Bible into Latin. Damasus, who was Pope at that time, had asked him to make this translation, and Jerome, in a letter to Damasus, reports on his work in connection with the new version. He writes that it would be a dangerous presumption to attempt to issue a Bible which would reproduce the correct text, since the existing copies of the original documents were scattered all over the world and no two of them were alike. He was now called upon to judge between them. If he were to produce a Bible at this time, it would be unlike any of the others that had preceded it. As a result he would be called an irreverent forger for having altered words and sentences, or having omitted something here, inserted something there, or tried to improve on the original elsewhere. And then he adds a remark that strikes a fatal blow at all who hold the Bible as we have it to-day to be the unadulterated word of God. He says: "Even those who condemn me as an impious forger must admit that we can no longer speak of such a thing as 'truth' where there are variations in that which is said to be true. (*Verum non esse quod variat etiam maledicorum testimonio conprobatur.*)" What he means to say is this: If the writings which are supposed to contain the truth contradict one another as to the truth, no one can call me a "perverter of the truth;" for in my case one can no longer speak of "truth," nor, therefore, of any "perversion" of it.

In his letter Jerome goes on to state how the many discrepancies between the copies of the original text can be explained. Some copyists, he says, were deliberate, criminal forgers. Others were conceited enough to attempt to improve on the text, but in their inexperience merely succeeded in impairing it. Still others dozed while they copied, and so left out, misread, or misplaced words and passages.

But what Jerome says of copying in general, and of copyists, is quite as true of his own version of the Bible; for he himself did exactly what all other translators and copyists had done before him. He too, following his own personal opinion, added material in his new Bible, altered passages and words, and made omissions, as he himself admits. And we may be sure that such changes as he made were not unfavorable to the doctrines then being taught by the papacy. Subsequently, still further changes were introduced into Jerome's translation, which is known as the "Vulgate;" and then, by decree of the Council of Trent, it was declared that the Vulgate contained "the inspired word of God." We are not told to whom the inspiration of the Vulgate with all of its additions, omissions, and subsequent alterations was vouchsafed, whether to Jerome himself, or to some one else. Thus, for example, Jerome's Vulgate does not contain the passage which is of such importance to the Catholic Trinitarian doctrine and which appears in the first Epistle of John: "There are three in heaven to bear witness—", for not a single manuscript to which he had access contained this passage. Nevertheless, it was inserted in the Vulgate that was examined by the Council of Trent, and consequently this spurious matter is held to be inspired, even though it does not occur in a single manuscript that antedates the fifteenth century. Since even Catholic theologians regarded the passage as spurious, the Index Congregation on January 15th, 1897, at the instance of the Pope expressly declared that it constituted an "integral part" of the New Testament and that in consequence it was to be considered as having been inspired by the "Holy Ghost."—There was evidently no intention of surrendering this falsified proof for the doctrine of the union of "three persons in one Godhead," seeing that no other evidence for it is to be found in the Bible.

The opinion is often expressed by people in general that God was obliged to preserve the original documents of the New Testament unaltered and to protect them against falsification. The fact that God did not do so has been established above. As a matter of fact, God does not forcibly intervene in any course of action upon which men, even forgers, may decide to embark. He did not prevent the gross falsification of the writings of the Old Testament, and He likewise left those of the New Testament to their fate at the hands of mankind.

We shall now go a step further and assert that it was not Christ's intention that his teachings should be written down at all, or that documents of any sort should be looked upon as the source of the truth. Had he intended his teachings to be recorded in writing he would have clearly said so. A written record of this kind, according to the belief of most of our denominations, would have been of supreme importance to all succeeding generations as the sole source of the truth. Are we asked to believe that Christ remained silent concerning a matter on which the diffusion of his gospel would depend for all time to come? The truth is that he did not say one word about setting down his doctrines in writing, neither in his sermons nor in his talks with his disciples. He sends them forth to teach, to heal the sick, to drive out evil spirits—but not to write books.

Moreover, he would certainly not have entrusted the task of recording his teachings to his disciples, but would have performed it himself. Besides, it would have been an easy matter for him to dictate his doctrine in full to a scribe, for in his day there were many men who made their living by writing; and even in those times shorthand writing for taking down dictation had been invented.

But he thought it to no purpose to record his doctrine in writing, for he knew the vicissitudes to which all writings are subject. He, too, recognized the force of the eternally true saying: *Habent sua fata libelli*—"Written matter is the sport of fate." It may be destroyed or falsified, and later generations will be in no position to judge whether that which they have before them is the original text of a manuscript, or a forgery. Moreover, writings on behalf of a good cause may be falsified to serve an evil one, and untruths can be circulated under the guise of truth. If, according to God's own word, truth was turned into lies in the Old Testament by the pen of the falsifying copyists, is it not certain that the same fate would have befallen Christ's writings? Have we not seen what was done with the text of the New Testament in the course of the centuries? It has become a book in which every one seeks and finds evidence to support his own particular doctrine. As many as two hundred and six different Christian sects have been counted, each differing from the rest in one tenet or another, yet each of them citing the New Testament to prove that its own creed is the true one. Could an all-knowing God have willed that a book in which every man can find substantiation for his erroneous views, should serve as the source of unalloyed truth? The very thought is sacrilege, implying, as it does, that God gave to mankind, starving for the truth, a stone instead of bread.

Where, then, can we find the unsullied fountain of truth, from which no error can flow?

INTRODUCTION

It has been plainly indicated by Christ. The words in which he directs us to that source are the same in all the manuscripts of the New Testament. They are the words that Christ spoke a few hours before he departed from this earth: "And I will pray to the Father, and He will give you another helper to be with you for ever—the spirits of the truth; and they will teach you all things."

God's spirits of truth as the sole source of the truth—that is the legacy that Jesus bequeathed to us in his last hours.

In speaking as he did, Jesus proclaimed no new doctrine. His doctrine is as old as mankind. As long as man has been on earth, God's spirit-messengers have been the only bearers of the truth. Such messengers spoke with Cain, Abel, and Enoch. Abraham constantly communicated with them. Three of them, materialized as human beings, came to him with messages from God. They went into Lot's house, and saved Lot and his family. The people of Israel used to inquire of God, Who answered them through His messengers by methods perceptible to the human senses. God's messenger spoke to Moses out of the burning bush, led him to Egypt, and through the desert. It was this messenger's voice that Moses heard coming from the cloud that travelled before the people, and later, from the cloud that gathered over the ark in the tabernacle. Of Moses we are told that he announced to the people only the things that had been said to him by this voice, which spoke to him "as one friend speaks to another." On Mount Sinai it was God's voice that resounded as He gave the people His laws. Later there were a great number of so-called "prophets" through whom God transmitted His messages.

At the threshold of the New Testament we again find God's messengers. An angel from God appears to Zacharias, to Mary, and to Joseph, and delivers God's messages to them. John the Baptist is commanded by one of God's envoys to administer baptism. The same messenger tells him of the sign by which he may recognize the Messiah. While Christ is being baptized in the Jordan, the Spirit of God speaks to him. The same Spirit leads him into the desert, where angels of God visit him and attend him after he has passed his test.

Christ's life on earth is an unbroken communion with God's world of spirits. With the aid of a spirit sent by God, Jesus exorcizes evil spirits and heals the sick. Through his contact with God's messengers he learns from his Father the doctrines that he must preach to the people.

Again and again he confesses that he is not speaking on his own authority, but is proclaiming only that which was imparted to him by his Father. As far as there was need, his Father instructed him through spirit-messengers who were constantly descending and rising above the Son of man. "You will see God's messengers ascending and descending above the Son of man."—"The things that I have heard from Him, I speak to all the world."

It was his wish that all who preached the gospel should draw anew from the same source from which he himself had drawn. First and foremost, his apostles. They were not merely to repeat their own conception of what they had heard from Christ, for people are prone to be inaccurate when repeating the words of others. For that reason even the apostles were to be instructed anew by the spirits of truth concerning the things which they had learned from the human discourse of Christ, in order that they might be guarded against errors arising from misunderstanding. Through God's spirits they were to receive confirmation of the gospel that Christ had preached, and also to be taught the new truths that Christ had been constrained to withhold because the apostles were not yet ready to receive them.

The correctness of this conclusion we find confirmed by Christ's own words: "And I will pray to the Father, and He will give you another helper to be with you for ever—the spirits of the truth."—"I have yet many things to say to you, but you cannot bear them now. But when these spirits of truth come, they will guide you into all the truth."—"But the helpers, the holy spirits whom the Father will send in my name, will teach you all things and bring to your remembrance all that I have said to you."

According to these words the spirits of truth had a twofold task to perform. First they were to keep the faithful in mind of that which Christ had taught them and to confirm their belief in the same. After that, however, their duty was to continue the instruction begun by Christ and to reveal those things which, for the reasons already given, he had withheld from his disciples. Moreover, God's spirits were to remain with them for all time, since the danger of error was a constant menace because of the powers of evil and human weakness. In short, it was not Christ's wish that later generations should be dependent on the religious traditions handed down to them by their forbears; for such traditions, after having passed through human agencies, could not be warranted as true. There could be no way of knowing what part of them came from the divine fountain of truth, and what part from human error.

Thus, true to the promise of Christ, God's messengers were constantly coming as spirits of truth after his earthly death. It is they whom the apostles invoke again and again when they call upon men to believe their teachings. In Paul's writings especially we continually find references to these bearers of the truth. "The things that I said and preached I did not lay before you in fascinating words of human wisdom, but it was *God's spirits* and God's power that spoke through me. For your faith was not to be based on human wisdom, but on a divine power."—"But to us God has revealed them through *His spirit-world.*"—"Now we have not received one of the evil spirits that rule the world, but *a spirit that comes from God.*"—"We preached about this, not with words taught by human wisdom, but in such words as *a spirit of God* teaches us; thus we deliver the spirit's message in the same words in which the spirit gave it to us. True, a worldly-minded man does not accept what comes from a spirit of God, for he looks upon communication with God's spirit-world as madness."—"You are an epistle of Christ, written not with ink but *with a spirit of the living God.*"—"For I make known to you, brothers, as touching the gospel which was preached by me, that it is not the work of man. I neither received it from man nor was it taught to me by man, but it came to me *through a revelation of Jesus Christ.*"

It was not only the apostles who were taught by God's spirits, but also the early Christian communities as well, inasmuch as messengers from God spoke to them through so-called "prophets." The word "prophet" means the same as an "instrument" of God. Such instruments were to be found in all of the Christian congregations of early times. Hence Paul writes that the "mysteries of Christ have now been revealed to his holy apostles and to the prophets, *by a spirit of God.*"

Through these "mediums" or instruments of the good spirits the faithful could at all times ascertain whether a doctrine were true and how it was to be interpreted. For this reason Paul writes to the Philippians: "And if in any matter you are of a different opinion, God will make it clear to you." They were free to inquire of God when they were gathered for worship, and they received their answer from God's spirits who spoke through mediums.

Again, such prophets or mediums are frequently mentioned in the *Acts of the Apostles* as transmitting messages from God brought by His spirits.

In the Old Testament God calls upon men to come to *Him* in their search for the truth: "Inquire of Me," He said, and through His spirit-messengers He revealed the truth. By his own admission, Christ, as a mortal, learned the truth from God's spirits. He promises his apostles to initiate them into the whole truth through spirits of truth. The apostles bear witness that this promise was fulfilled in their case and in that of the Christian congregations; therefore that they received their doctrine from God's spirits.

But from what source does Christianity of to-day draw the truth? Can the Christian divines of the various sects say of themselves that a spirit of God is speaking through them? Can they like Paul contend that they did not learn their doctrine from men and acquire it by human instruction, but by a revelation of Christ? They cannot. They are in the employ of their respective churches. They have learned the creed of those churches through human instruction in schools, seminaries, and universities. What they have absorbed is human wisdom, professional wisdom, together with all of its errors, and this is what they teach their congregations. Of spirits as envoys of God and as bearers of the truth they know nothing. They too think it foolishness, as Paul says, to believe that in this day any doctrine should be taught by a spirit of God,—when there are so many learned theologians, doctors, and professors. It is as though Christ had said, "I will send you high priests, popes, bishops, clergymen, professors, and doctors of divinity." A man like Moses had to communicate with God's world of spirits and to "inquire of God" in order to find the truth. The same was true of the great prophets and even of Christ, as well as of the apostles and the Christians of the early centuries of the era. But to-day such a thing is considered antiquated and outmoded.

As a matter of fact it was precisely the learned clergymen and the professors of "sacred theology" who introduced the doctrines against which Paul warns us when he says: "Let no man beguile you with the wisdom and the vain deceit that belongs to men and to the powers of the spirits of the world, but not to Christ."—"Some of the men have lost sight of this goal and are beating the air with their interpretations, wishing to be regarded as versed in the truth although they do not understand the meaning of the terms which they use or the things of which they speak with so much assurance."—"They are the men who cause divisions; worldly-minded men *who have not received a holy spirit.*"

For sixteen hundred years the world of God's spirits has been excluded from the Christian churches. The leaders of the churches have "extinguished the holy spirits." But wherever God's spirits are forced to give ground, others appear, the very ones of which Paul writes to Timothy: "God's spirits expressly declare that in times to come many will fall away from the faith and turn to spirits and doctrines of deceit."

Thus from the time at which communion with the world of God's spirits as the only road to the truth was abandoned, the most diverse and far-reaching errors crept into the Christian religion. Century by century matters grew worse. Truth after truth was tainted and rendered unpalatable by error. And what was the result? To-day we have a Christianity split asunder by countless sects, each preaching things that are not true, and each believing its own creed to be the one and only true gospel of Christ. And yet we wonder that a religion so adulterated and frayed should have ceased to exert any influence on mankind. Give back to the people the religion of the early Christians! Take from their shoulders the spiritual burdens that you have imposed by man-made teachings and the craving for power, and restore to them their freedom to commune with God's bearers of the truth. Then you will see how great an influence Christianity can exert on the people of to-day also. For it is only the truth, not falsehood, that creates power.

INTRODUCTION

The Catholic Church tries to explain the division into sects on the ground that all of the other Christian creeds seceded from her, whose faith alone was the true one. But it was precisely that church which drove God's spirit-world from the Christian faith. It was that church which, leagued with the temporal powers, destroyed all who believed otherwise than was prescribed by the authority of the pope. In the name of Catholic Christianity, the blood of hundreds of thousands has flowed.

It is true that the Catholic Church has succeeded in creating a human substitute for the divine spirits which were active in the early days of the Christian era. It has instituted an office vested with infallibility. That was the simplest way of solving the problem of providing an authentic source of the truth. Now Christ was spared the task of sending spirits of truth to groping humanity, as he had promised to do. Moreover, there was no longer any need of the fulfillment of his promise to be with the faithful always, "even to the end of the world." Was there not a pope, a "vicar of Christ" on earth? Where there is a vicar, he whom that vicar represents surely need not appear.

Thanks to the doctrine of an "infallible vicar of Christ on earth," the dispensation of the truth was placed wholly in the hands of erring, sinful men, to the exclusion of God's messengers of truth. Thus the gates were thrown open to human caprice and worldly ambition. True, the Catholic Church maintains that the "Holy Spirit" also acts through the papal office, but if we study the procedure of selecting the pope, and the history of the papacy, we shall soon realize that God's spirits can have little voice in the matter. Were not some of the popes instruments of hell rather than vicars of Christ in their deeds and in their whole manner of living?

To surmount this objection, however, a curious explanation has been devised. A distinction is drawn between the pope as a man and the pope as a vicar of Christ. It is maintained that even the worst of men, as soon as he becomes pope, may represent Christ and acquire infallibility. In other words, he might be an instrument of Satan and at the same time the vicar of Christ. Could man utter a greater blasphemy? Are we to believe that God entrusts His precious gifts, such as those on which salvation depends, to a servant of the evil one? Ordinary common sense should teach any one that this is unthinkable. God's spirits are sent only to the God-fearing, and remain with them only so long as they keep their faith. This is illustrated by the story of King Saul. As long as that king obeyed God, he was in daily communion with the world of God's spirits and could inquire of God whenever he wished to be enlightened on any matter. God always answered him through His spirits. But when Saul broke faith with God, further access to the world of God's spirits was denied him. Answers were no longer returned to the questions which he addressed to God, and instead of divine messengers, evil spirits took possession of Saul. The gifts with which he had been endowed were taken from him.

No man who is evil, not even if he is the pope, can ever be the bearer of God's sacred gifts. Consequently, the evil popes, at least, never possessed the gift of infallibility; and so the whole dogma of papal infallibility collapses of its own weight.

Only God chooses those to whom He sends the spirits of truth. No human choice can make any man the channel through which the truth is conveyed. Not even Christ chose his apostles at his own discretion, for the *Acts of the Apostles* expressly states that he made his choice through a holy spirit. It follows that God would certainly not invest a human office, such as the papacy, with infallibility. God alone is infallible; even His spirits are not. They are infallible only when they bring a message from God.

INTRODUCTION

Whoever, then, seeks to know what is true and what is untrue in the Bible as we have it to-day, can find out only in the way in which all God-fearing people in the past have sought the truth, namely by communicating with God's spirit-world. He must accept the invitation which God extends to each one of us through the prophet Jeremiah: "Ask Me and I will answer you and show you great and mighty things, which you did not know before." God's answer will come through His spirits, for "God's spirits are His servants, sent to serve all who earnestly desire salvation." The assurance that God will send us His messengers in answer to our prayers was given to us by Christ when he said: "If you, then, being evil, know how to give good gifts to your children, how much more will your Father in heaven *give a holy spirit to those who ask Him for it.*"

I myself was a Catholic priest, and until I was forty-eight years old had never so much as believed in the possibility of communicating with the world of God's spirits. The day came, however, when I involuntarily took my first step toward such communication, and experienced things that shook me to the depths of my soul. After I had taken the first step, I could not stop. I must go forward, I must have enlightenment. On I went, treading carefully, and bearing in mind the words of the apostle Paul: "Test all things, keep that which is good." It was only the good that I sought. I wanted the truth. I was ready to accept it, come what might. I knew that God does not desert an earnest, interested seeker, and that, in the words of Christ, He will not offer a humble suppliant a stone instead of bread. I also realized the grave consequences of my step. My position as a clergyman, my entire material existence, my whole future in the worldly sense were threatened with ruin if I proceeded further. I knew that I was bound to undergo abuse, ridicule, persecution, and suffering to excess. But the truth meant more to me. And on the path that I followed I found the truth.

My experiences are related in a book that has appeared in both German and English and bears the title, *Communication with the Spirit-World: Its Laws and Its Purpose.* (*Der Verkehr mit der Geisterwelt, seine Gesetze und sein Zweck*). Many of the readers of this book who have sought to communicate with God's spirit-world have had experiences similar to my own and found the same truths that I found.

I availed myself of this contact with the source of truth to seek enlightenment above all in regard to the text of the Bible as we know it to-day; for on the occasion of my first experience with the world of divine spirits my attention had been called to the fact that the books of both the Old and the New Testament contained a great deal of spurious matter which had given rise to the many erroneous ideas prevailing in the Christian churches of our day. Subsequently I learned about these falsifications in detail.

This led me to a close study of the manuscripts of the New Testament. I found that the text of *Codex D* (*Codex Bezae Cantabrigiensis*), which unfortunately has several gaps, most nearly approaches the truth. It was consequently the one that I used as the basis for my translation.

In the rare instances in which a text pronounced correct by the divine spirits can be found in none of the manuscripts available to-day, I have used the text as it was given to me by those spirits. But in my Explanation I have always been careful to indicate which passages are derived from this source.

In my German translation I made it my chief concern to reproduce the exact meaning of the Greek text in good but simple German, so that people of limited education may be able to understand every sentence without difficulty. The translation of the German original into English was made by a professional translator, corrected by a committee of American clergymen who are perfectly versed in both languages, and thoroughly revised by a teacher, so that not only the exact meaning of the German text is found in the English translation but also the same simplicity of language.

May this book of truth deliver many from the burden of error and guide them to the road that leads to God. Christ says, "The truth will make you free." It delivers us from everything in the way of man-made ordinances and human error that has crept into religion; it frees us from a man-made Christianity and takes us back to the true Christianity of Christ.

May God's spirits of truth enlighten the hearts of my readers and bestow on them the spiritual gifts promised by Christ to all who believe in him.

I dedicate this book with heartfelt love to the One who said, "I am the way, the truth, and the life."

Good Friday, 1937 JOHANNES GREBER.

The Gospel according to
MATTHEW

CHAPTER 1.

1 THE following are the ancestors of Jesus, the Messiah, the proof
of his descent from David and Abraham:
2 Abraham was the father of Isaac, Isaac was the father of Jacob,
3 Jacob was the father of Judah and his brothers. Judah was the
father of Phares and Zerah, by their mother Tamar. Phares was
4 the father of Esrom, and Esrom the father of Aram. Aram was the
father of Aminadab, Aminadab the father of Naason, and Naason
5 the father of Salmon. Salmon was the father of Boaz by Rahab;
6 Boaz was the father of Obed, by Ruth. Obed was the father of Jesse;
Jesse was the father of King David. David was the father of Sol-
7 omon, whose mother had been Uriah's wife. Solomon was the father
of Rehobóam, Rehoboam the father of Abijah, and Abijah the father
8 of Asa. Asa was the father of Jehoshaphat, Jehoshaphat the father
9 of Joram, Joram the father of Uzziah. Uzziah was the father of
Jotham, Jotham the father of Ahaz, and Ahaz the father of Hezekiah.
10 Hezekiah was the father of Manasseh, Manasseh the father of Amon,
11 and Amon the father of Josiah. Josiah was the father of Jechoniah
12 and his brothers in the time of the Babylonian captivity. After the
Babylonian captivity Jechoniah had a son called Shealthiel, the
13 father of Zerubbabel. Zerubbabel was the father of Abiud, Abiud
14 the father of Eliakim, and Eliakim the father of Azor. Azor was the
father of Zadok, Zadok the father of Achim, Achim the father of
15 Eliud, Eliud the father of Eleazar. Eleazar was the father of
16 Matthan, Matthan the father of Jacob. Jacob was the father of
Joseph, the husband of Mary, who bore of his seed Jesus, the
Messiah.

17 Thus the generations from Abraham to David are fourteen, from
David to the Babylonian captivity fourteen, and from the Babylonian
captivity to the Messiah, fourteen.

18 The human birth of the Messiah came about as follows: His
mother, Mary, was betrothed to Joseph, but before they lived together it was found that she was with child through the intervention
of a holy spirit. Joseph, being a God-fearing man and unwilling to

expose her to public shame, resolved to break the betrothal secretly.
20 But while he was thinking how best to proceed, he saw, in a state
of clairvoyance, an angel of the Lord, who said, "Joseph, son of
David, do not scruple to accept Mary as your wife, for she has con-
21 ceived through the intervention of a holy spirit. But the son whom
she will bear is of your seed; therefore you shall name him and call
him 'Jesus' (Redeemer). For it is he who will redeem his people
from their sin of apostasy."
22 All this took place so that in this case also the words spoken by
23 the Lord through the prophet Isaiah should be fulfilled: "Behold,
the young woman will conceive and bear a son who will be called
'Immanuel,'" meaning "God with us."
24 When the apparition had vanished, Joseph did as the angel of the
25 Lord had bidden, and accepted Mary as his wife. But he did not
live with her as a husband until she had born of his seed her first
son, to whom he gave the name "Jesus."

CHAPTER 2.

1 When Jesus was born in Bethlehem in the land of Judaea, during
the reign of King Herod, there came certain Magi from the east to
2 Jerusalem and inquired, "Where is he, the newly-born king of the
Jews? For we have seen his star rise before us and have followed
it, in order to render him our homage."
3 When King Herod heard this he became frightened, and all Jeru-
4 salem with him. He summoned all the chief priests and scribes of
the people, and from them sought to learn where that king was to be
5 born who had been anointed by the Lord as the Redeemer. They
answered, "At Bethlehem, in the land of Judaea; for so it is written
6 by the prophet: 'And you, Bethlehem, in the land of Judaea, are not
the least among the princely cities of Judah, for from you will come
a king who will shepherd my people of Israel.'"
7 Then Herod summoned the Magi secretly, and inquired of them
8 the precise time at which the star had appeared to them, and sent
them to Bethlehem, saying, "Go and seek carefully for the child, and
when you have found him, bring me word at once, that I too may
9 go to render him homage." After this they took leave of the king
and went their way; and behold, the star which they had seen rise
before, again preceded them to guide them to the place where the
10 child lay, and there it stood still. When the Magi saw the star stand-
11 ing still, they were filled with an unspeakable joy. Entering the
shelter they found the child with his mother Mary, and knelt down
12 to pay homage to him. Then they opened their treasures and

gave him as gifts gold, frankincense, and myrrh. Being warned by
a spirit-borne message not to return to Herod, they departed for their
homes by a different way.
13 After they had left, Joseph, in a clairvoyant state, saw an angel
of the Lord, who said, "Arise, take the child and his mother and flee
into Egypt. Stay there until I bring you further word, for Herod intends to seek the child and kill him."
14 When the apparition had vanished, Joseph took the mother and
15 the child that same night and fled into Egypt. He stayed there until
the death of Herod. Thus was fulfilled in this case also the word
spoken by the Lord through the prophet: "Out of Egypt have I
called my son."
16 When Herod saw that the Magi had tricked him he was greatly
enraged, and sent out his men to kill all children in Bethlehem and
in the country round about, who were two years old and less, according to the precise time that he had learned from the Magi.
17 Thus here also was fulfilled the word that the Lord had proclaimed
18 through the prophet Jeremiah: "An outcry was heard in Rama,
lamentation and weeping and great mourning; Rachel weeps for her
children and will not be comforted, because they are no more."
19 After Herod's death there appeared to Joseph in Egypt one of the
20 Lord's angels, whom he saw by clairvoyance, and who said, "Arise,
take the child and his mother and go into the land of Israel, for they
21 who sought the child's life are dead." Then Joseph rose, and tak-
22 ing mother and child, returned to the land of Israel. But when he
heard that Archelaus was king in Judaea in his father Herod's place,
he was afraid to go there, and heeding the warning brought by a
23 spirit-message, went instead into the land of Galilee. There he settled in a town called Nazareth. So were fulfilled the words of the
prophet: "He will be called a Nazarene."

CHAPTER 3.

1 The time came when John the Baptist appeared, preaching in the
barren mountain-country of Judaea and admonishing his hearers,
2 "Change your hearts, for communication with God's spirit-world is
3 at hand." It was he of whom the prophet Isaiah had foretold: "The
voice of a man is heard crying in the barren mountain-country,
'Prepare the way for the lord to reach you; make even the paths by
4 which he will come.'" John wore a garment of camel's hair, and a
leather belt about his waist, and lived on locusts and wild honey.
5 The people of Jerusalem and Judaea and the region about the Jordan
6 flocked to him in crowds, to be baptized by him through immersion

in the Jordan, thereby to testify publicly to their faith in his teaching and to confess that they were sinners.
7 Seeing that many Pharisees and Sadducees came to oppose him
in his baptism, John responded to them with the words: "You brood
of vipers! Who has driven you into the folly of thinking that you
8 can escape the impending judgment? For you also must change
9 your hearts, and let your deeds bear witness thereto. Do not seek to
appease your conscience by saying, 'We have Abraham for our
father.' For I assure you, God can raise up children to Abraham
10 out of these rocks. The axe is already laid to the roots of the trees.
Every tree that fails to bear good fruit shall be hewn down and
11 thrown root and branch into the fire. I can immerse you only in
the waves of water as an outward sign of your change of heart. But
after me will come one mightier than I, in comparison to whom I
am not even worthy to untie his sandals. He will immerse you in
12 the power-waves of a holy spirit and of fire. He has his winnowing-
fan in his hand and will thoroughly clean his threshing floor. The
grain he will gather into his bins, but the chaff he will burn in a
fire which cannot be quenched until all chaff is consumed."
13 One day Jesus also came out from Galilee to the Jordan to be
14 baptized by John. John, however, offered objection, saying, "Do you
15 come to me, when it is I who should be baptized by you?" But
Jesus answered, "Let it be as I say, for it behooves us both to do
16 what is right in the eyes of God." Thereupon John consented. While
Jesus was immersed a powerful light gleamed forth out of the water,
striking fear into all who saw it.
When his baptism was ended, Jesus immediately stepped out of
the water. At that instant the heavens opened, and he saw the Spirit
17 of God descend like a dove and light upon him; and he heard a
voice from heaven calling, "You are my beloved son, in whom was
my delight."

CHAPTER 4.

1 Thereafter Jesus was led by the spirit-world into the wilderness
2 to be tempted by the devil. He fasted there for forty days and forty
nights, until he was nearly dead with hunger.
3 Then the tempter came near him and said, "If you are a son of
4 God, speak the word that will turn these stones into bread." But
Jesus answered, "It is written: 'Man shall not seek to preserve the
life that is only sustained by partaking of earthly food, but the life
that rests on obedience to every commandment that God causes to
5 be proclaimed.'" Then the devil took him up into the holy city, set

6 him upon the pinnacle of the temple, and said, "If you are a son of
God, throw yourself down; for it is written: 'He will command his
angels for your sake to bear you up in their hands, lest you dash
7 your feet against a stone.'" Jesus answered, "But it is also written:
'You shall not tempt the Lord your God.'"
8 Once more the devil took him with him and led him up onto a
a very high mountain, showing him all the kingdoms of the universe
9 with their magnificence, and saying, "All this will I give you, if you
10 prostrate yourself before me and acknowledge me as your lord." At
that Jesus cried out to him, "Get out of my sight, Satan! For it is
written: 'Only the Lord your God shall you acknowledge as your
lord, and Him alone shall you serve.'"
11 Now the devil left him. And behold, angels came and brought
food to Jesus.
12 When Jesus learned that John had been thrown into prison, he
13 withdrew to Galilee, and leaving Nazareth he went to live in Capernaum, a town which lies on the lake in the neighborhood of Zabulon
14 and Nepthalim. Thus were fulfilled the words of the prophet Isaiah:
15 "The land of Zabulon and the land of Nephthalim that lies by the
16 lake, the land beyond the Jordan, the Galilee of the Gentiles, the
people who sit in darkness, have seen a great light; and a light has
appeared to them who dwell in the land and shadow of the spiritual
death of separation from God."
17 From that time Jesus began his ministry of teaching, warning his
hearers, "Change your hearts, for communication with God's spirit-
world is at hand."
18 One day as he was walking by the Lake of Galilee, he saw two
brothers throwing their net into the water, for they were fishermen.
One of them was Simon, also called Peter; the other was Simon's
19 brother Andrew. Jesus said to them, "Come, go with me, and I will
20 make you fishers of men." And they left their net at once and
21 went with him. Somewhat further he saw two other brothers, James
the son of Zebedee, and his brother John, sitting in a boat with their
22 father and mending their nets. Jesus called them to him, and they
straightway left the boat and their father and followed him.
23 Jesus now went about through all Galilee and taught in the synagogues there, proclaiming the gospel of the kingdom of God, and
healing all manner of sickness and infirmity that he found among
24 the people. His fame spread through all Syria, and every one who
was afflicted with any kind of sickness and pain, as well as the possessed, and such as suffered epilepsy or complete paralysis in consequence of being possessed, were brought to him; and he healed them.

25 On this account he was followed by great throngs from Galilee and
from the region of the Ten Towns, as well as from Jerusalem and
Judaea and from the country east of the Jordan.

CHAPTER 5.

1 When he saw these crowds, Jesus ascended the nearest hill and
2 seated himself, his disciples taking their places beside him. Then he
began to preach the following sermon:
3 "Fortunate are they whose spirits feel helplessly poor before
God; for God's spirit-world will communicate with them.
4 "Fortunate are the gentle; for they will have their just share of
earthly happiness.
5 "Fortunate are they who lament their estrangement from God;
for they will be comforted.
6 "Fortunate are they who have the greatest desire to please God;
for their longing will be satisfied.
7 "Fortunate are the merciful; for they will obtain mercy for themselves also.
8 "Fortunate are the pure in heart; for they will experience the
nearness of God in their lives.
9 "Fortunate are the peacemakers; for they will be called children
of God.
10 "Fortunate are they who are persecuted for the sake of the right;
for God's spirit-world will communicate with them.
11 "Fortunate are you when men revile and persecute you and speak
12 evil of you because you do God's will. Be glad and rejoice, for great
is your reward in the beyond. So too did men persecute God's instruments who lived before you.
13 "You are the salt of the earth; but if salt becomes tasteless, how
shall its saltiness be restored? It is thenceforth fit for nothing but
to be thrown into the street and trodden underfoot.
14 "You are the light of the world. A town built on a mountain-top
15 cannot be hidden. When men make a light they do not put it under
a cover but on a stand, so that it may give light to all in the household.
16 So shall your light shine before men, that they may see your good
deeds and thereby be led to honor and praise your heavenly Father.
17 "Do not think that I have come to abolish that which you have
been taught by the Law of Moses and by the prophets. No, I have
18 come not to abolish, but to fulfill. And I assure you most positively
that until the moment when heaven and earth change their present
form, not the smallest letter nor the smallest part of a letter in the
19 Law shall be altered. Everything must first be fulfilled. And who-

ever abolishes a single one of those commandments, even though it
be the smallest, and teaches others to do so, will be ranked as the
least in the beyond. But whoever observes the whole Law and
20 teaches men to do likewise, will be exalted in the beyond. I tell you
that unless you do God's will better than the scribes and the Pharisees, you will not be able to enter into communication with God's
spirit-world.

21 "You have heard that our forefathers were told, 'You shall
not kill'; and again, 'Whoever kills shall be subject to condemna-
22 tion.' But my message to you is this: Whoever is angry with his
brother without cause already stands condemned; whoever calls his
brother a fool, shall answer for it to the High Council; and whoever calls his brother an outcast of God, shall be condemned to the
fire of suffering.

23 "If when you are offering your gift at the altar, you remem-
24 ber that your brother has a grievance against you, leave your gift
at the altar, first go and make peace with your brother, and then
25 come back and offer your gift. To him who has cause for complaint
against you, manifest your good will without delay so long as the
way to reconciliation with him is open; otherwise he may deliver
you to the judge, and the judge deliver you to the officer for pun-
26 ishment. Then you would be thrown into prison, from which, I assure you, you will not be released until you have paid to the last
cent.

27 "You know the law, 'You shall not commit adultery.' I, however,
28 teach you that whoever so much as looks at a woman with lustful
29 desire, has already committed adultery in his heart. If, therefore,
your good eye is the cause of this sin, tear it out and throw it aside;
30 for it is better for you that you lose one of your members than that
your whole body be thrown into the fire of suffering.

31 "Another precept reads: 'Whoever wishes to divorce his wife shall
32 give her a letter of divorce.' But I say: Whoever divorces his wife
unless it be on the ground of adultery, causes her to become a harlot.

33 "Again, you have heard that the men of olden times were told:
'You shall not break a promise made under an oath, but shall ful-
34 fill that which you have promised before the Lord.' But I say to
you: If you make a promise, you shall not swear at all, either by
35 heaven, for it is God's throne; nor by the earth, for it is his foot-
36 stool; nor by Jerusalem, for it is the city of the great king. Nor
shall you swear by your head, because you cannot make a single
37 hair white or black. But if you say 'yes' making a promise, it shall
remain a 'yes' and may not be changed into a 'no.' For such as fail

to keep their word may expect an abundant measure of trouble from
38 those who are injured by the broken promise. Though you have
39 heard it said, 'An eye for an eye, and a tooth for a tooth,' I teach
you not to resist as an enemy him whom you have injured by
the breaking of a promise; but if such a one strikes you on one
40 cheek, turn the other cheek toward him also. And if he sues you at
law for your pledged undergarment, give him also the promised
41 coat. And if he forces you to carry his belongings one mile as agreed
42 upon, then rather accompany him two miles farther. If any one asks
of you that which you have promised, give it; and when one comes
to you to receive a promised loan, do not turn your back on him.
43 "You have heard that it has been said: 'You shall be kindly disposed to him who is dear to you, but need not be concerned about
44 him with whom you are at odds.' But I say to you: Be kindly disposed even to those with whom you are at odds; reason with those
who call down evil upon you; do good to those who care nothing
45 about you, and pray for those who insult and persecute you, for
thereby you will prove yourselves to be children of your heavenly
Father. He also lets His sun rise over the wicked and the good, and
46 His rain fall on the godly and the ungodly. If you love only those
47 who love you, what special reward have you a right to expect? Do
not the tax-collectors do the same? And if you greet only your
friends, are you doing anything unusual? Do not the godless do
48 the same? Your love, therefore, should embrace all, just as the
love of your heavenly Father is extended to all.

CHAPTER 6.

1 "Take care not to perform your good deeds openly for men to
see, or else you will not be rewarded for them by your heavenly
Father.
2 "Thus, when you give alms, do not trumpet it out as the hypocrites in synagogues and frequented places do, in order to gain
recognition among men. That, I assure you, will be their only
3 reward. When you give alms, do not let your left hand know what
4 your right hand is doing, so that your benevolence may remain
hidden; and your Father, who sees even those things that pass in
secret, will reward you openly.
5 "When you pray, do not imitate the hypocrites who like to stand
at prayer in synagogues and on street-corners, that no one may fail to
6 see them. That, I assure you, will be their only reward. Rather, when
you pray, go to your room, close the door, and pray to your Father
in secret; and your Father, who sees even that which happens in

7 concealment, will reward you. Do not, like the idolaters, chatter
thoughtlessly when you are praying; for they think they will be
8 favorably heard if they use many words. Do not, therefore, imitate
them. Your Father knows of your needs before you open your lips
9 to pray. Let your prayers be in the following manner:
10 "Our Father in heaven, hallowed be Thy name. Thy spirit-world
11 come to us. Thy will be done in the beyond and on earth. Give us
12 this day our bread for to-morrow. Forgive us our offences, as we
13 too forgive those who have offended against us. Be Thou, O Lord,
our guide in the time of temptations, and deliver us from the Evil
14 One.—For as soon as you forgive your fellow-men their offences,
15 your heavenly Father will likewise grant you forgiveness. But if
you do not forgive the sins of your fellow-men, your heavenly
Father will not forgive your sins either.

16 "When you fast, do not wear a gloomy look as the hypocrites do,
who affect suffering in order to let people see that they are fasting;
17 that, I assure you, will be all their reward. Rather, when you fast,
18 anoint your head and wash your face, so that none shall see that
you are fasting. Only your Father shall see it in secret, and He,
Who sees even the most secret acts, will reward you.

19 "Do not amass for yourselves treasures on earth, where moths
and rust will consume them, and where thieves break in and steal;
20 but gather for yourselves treasures in the beyond, where they will
not be consumed by either moths or rust, and where thieves cannot
21 break in and steal. For where your treasures are, there also will
your heart be.

22 "The light of the body is the eye. Now if your eye is sound, your
23 whole body will be encompassed with the light of the eye; but if
your eye is seriously diseased, your whole body will be shrouded
in darkness. If, then, that which is to serve you inwardly as light is
enveloped in darkness, how great must be the darkness within you!

24 "No one can serve two masters at the same time; for he will
either neglect one and be faithful to the other, or he will hold to the
one and care nothing about the other. You cannot be servants of
God and slaves of money at the same time.

25 "Therefore I say to you: Do not be worried about your bodily
subsistence, or the clothing needed to cover you. Is not life more
precious than food, and the body more precious than clothing?
26 Look at the birds of the air! They neither sow nor reap, nor gather
into barns, and yet your heavenly Father feeds them. Are you not
27 worth as much as they? Who among you with all his worry
28 can prolong his allotted time of life by a single span? And why

should you trouble over clothing? Consider the lilies of the field,
29 how they grow; they neither toil nor spin, and yet I say to you that
Solomon in all his glory was not so splendidly arrayed as one of
30 them. If, then, God so clothes the flower of the fields, which blooms
to-day and to-morrow is thrown into the furnace, will He not do the
31 same for you, O men of little faith? Therefore do not ask with a
troubled heart, 'What shall we eat?' or 'What shall we drink?' or
32 'What shall we do for clothing?' For these are matters which trouble
only those who have no faith and no trust in God. Your heavenly
33 Father knows your need of all these things. Strive first, therefore,
to get on the way to God, and to do His will. Then you will be
34 granted everything else in addition. So do not be troubled about the
morrow; for the morrow will bring cares of its own. To-day's own
trouble is quite enough for to-day.

CHAPTER 7.

1 "Do not condemn others, so that you yourselves may not be con-
2 demned; for the judgment that you pass upon others will be passed
upon you, and by the same standard by which you measure others,
you too will be measured.

3 "How is it that you see the splinter in your brother's eye and yet
4 do not see the beam in your own? Or how dare you say to your
brother, 'Let me take the splinter out of your eye,' while the beam
5 remains in yours? Hypocrite! Take the beam out of your own eye
first; then you can see to take the splinter out of your brother's eye.

6 "Do not throw to the dogs that which is sacred, or cast your pearls
before swine, lest they crush them under their feet and then turn
on you and tear you to pieces.

7 "Ask for the truth, and it will be given to you; seek God, and
you will find Him; knock at the gate of God's spirit-world, and it
8 will be opened to you. For whoever asks for the truth, receives it;
whoever seeks God, finds Him, and to him who knocks at the gate
of God's spirit-world it is opened.

9 "Is there a single one among you who, if his child asks him for
10 bread, will give him a stone? Or offer a serpent if he has asked for
11 a fish? If you, then, sinful men though you are, nevertheless are
disposed to give only good gifts to your children, how much more
will your heavenly Father give only that which is good to those who
ask Him for it?

12 "In all things treat your fellow-men as you would have them treat
you. This is the whole substance of what is taught by the Law and
the prophets.

13 "Enter by the narrow gate, for the way leading to the gate of
perdition is wide and provided with spacious pleasure-grounds, and
14 many are there who travel that way. How narrow and toilsome in
contrast is the path that leads to the narrow gate of spiritual life;
and few are they who find it.
15 "Beware of communication with evil spirits. They come to you
16 in sheep's clothing, but at heart they are ravenous wolves. By their
fruit you will know them. Can grapes be gathered from thorn-
17 bushes, or figs from thistles? So, too, a sound tree will bear good
18 fruit, and a diseased tree, bad fruit. A sound tree cannot bear bad
19 fruit, nor a diseased tree, good fruit. A tree that does not bear good
20 fruit is cut down and thrown into the fire. Therefore by their fruit
you will know them.
21 "Not every one who says to me, 'Lord, lord,' will enter into communication with heavenly spirits, but only those who do the will of
22 my heavenly Father. Many will say to me on that day, 'Lord, lord,
did we not eat and drink, calling upon your name? Did we not
speak in your name as instruments of the spirit-world? Did we not
invoke your name when we attempted to cast out evil spirits? Did
23 we not by virtue of your name perform many miracles?' Then I shall
say to them, 'I never knew you. Begone from me, you evil-doers!'
24 "Whoever hears these words of mine and acts according to them,
25 is like the wise man who had built his house upon rock. And though
the cloudburst came and the torrents raged and the gale beat against
the house, it did not fall; for its foundations stood on rock.
26 "And whoever hears these words of mine but does not act according to them, is like the fool who had built his house on sand.
27 The cloudburst came and the torrents raged, the gale beat against
the house, and it fell with a mighty crash."
28 When Jesus had ended this sermon, the people were lost in won-
29 der at his words; for he preached like a man endowed with a higher
power and quite differently from the scribes.

CHAPTER 8.

1 Then Jesus descended the hill, followed by a great crowd, and
2 was met by a leper who threw himself down before him and im-
3 plored, " Lord, if you will, you can cleanse me." Jesus stretched out
his hand, touched him, and said, "I will. Be clean." And he was in-
4 stantly freed from his leprosy. But Jesus admonished him, "Be careful to say nothing of this to any one, but show yourself to the priest
and offer the gift that Moses commanded to be given in testimony
of cleansing from leprosy."

5 As he entered Capernaum there came to him a captain entreating,
6 "Lord, my servant is lying sick with paralysis at my home, and is
7 in great pain." Jesus answered, "I will go there myself and cure
8 him." But the captain said, "Lord, I am not worthy that you should
come under my roof. Speak only one word, and my servant will be
9 well. For I too am a man subject to superiors and have soldiers
under me, and when I say to one of them 'Go,' he goes, and to another 'Come,' he comes, and to my servant 'Do this,' he does it."

10 When Jesus heard these words he was amazed and said to those
about him, "I tell you truly that in no one in Israel have I found
11 such faith. And I assure you that many will come from the east and
from the west to sit with Abraham, Isaac, and Jacob at the feast in
12 the kingdom of heaven. But the 'children of the kingdom' will remain outside and will be consigned to the darkness, where there will
13 be loud wailing and gnashing of teeth." Then Jesus turned to the
captain with the words, "Go back to your house. As you have believed, so it shall be done to you." And his servant was cured the selfsame hour. When the captain arrived at his home, he learned that at that very hour the servant had been healed.

14 From here Jesus went to the house of Peter, where he found
15 Peter's mother-in-law sick in bed with a high fever. He took her by
the hand, and the fever left her, and she rose and waited on him.

16 In the evening they brought to him many who were possessed.
At one word from him, the spirits left them. Moreover, he healed
17 all those who were suffering from other ailments. So were fulfilled
the words spoken by Isaiah the prophet: "It is he who took away our infirmities and removed our diseases."

18 Then when Jesus again found himself pressed by a great crowd,
19 he gave orders to cross over to the other shore of the lake. There a
scribe came to him and said, "Master, I will follow you wherever
20 you go." To this Jesus answered, "Foxes have burrows, and the
birds of the air have nests, but the Son of man does not even own
21 so much as a place on which to lay his head." Another of his followers said to him, "Lord, give me leave to go first to bury my
22 father." But Jesus answered, "Come with me, and let the spiritually
dead bury their spiritually dead."

23 When Jesus had embarked, followed by his disciples, a great
24 storm arose on the lake, dashing the waves over the vessel while he
25 lay asleep. Then his disciples went to his side and waked him call-
26 ing, "Lord, help us, for we are sinking!" But he replied, "Why do
you lose heart so easily, you men of little faith?" Then rising, he

27 rebuked the storm and the waves, and there was a great calm. At
this the men exclaimed in amazement, "What kind of man is this?
Even the wind and the waves obey him."

28 He now landed on the other shore in the country of the Gadarenes,
where he was met by two possessed men who had just come forth
from the tombs. They were so violent that people dared not travel
29 by that path. On seeing him they cried aloud, "What do you want
of us, you Son of God? Have you come here to torture us before the
30 appointed time?" It happened that a large herd of swine was feed-
31 ing at some distance, and so the demons entreated him, "If you in-
32 tend to drive us out, allow us to enter that herd of swine." He
answered, "Enter them!" Then the demons left the possessed men
and went into the swine; and the whole herd, dashing downhill
into the lake, was drowned in its waters.

33 The herdsmen fled, and on arriving at the town, related every-
34 thing, including what had befallen the possessed men. The whole
town went out to meet Jesus, and on finding him, earnestly besought
him to leave the neighborhood.

CHAPTER 9.

1 Accordingly Jesus took a boat in which he crossed the lake and
2 reached his home in Capernaum, where a man lying in bed with
paralysis was brought to him. When Jesus saw the confident faith
of the people, he said to the paralytic, "My son, be of good cheer,
3 your sins will be forgiven." Hearing these words, some of the scribes
4 thought to themselves, "This fellow is a blasphemer!" But Jesus
read their thoughts and said, "Why do you think evil in your hearts?
5 Which is more easily said: 'Your sins are forgiven' or 'Get up and
6 walk'? But now you shall see that the Son of man has the power to
7 forgive sins on earth." Then he turned to the sick man, saying, "Get
up. Take your bedding and go to your home." The man rose and
8 went to his house. When the people saw this they were awed and
praised God, Who had given such power to men.

9 As Jesus left his house, he passed by the tax-office and saw a tax-
collector named Matthew sitting there. To him he turned and said,
"Come with me." And he rose and went with him.

10 Later, while Jesus was reclining at table in Matthew's house, a
great many tax-collectors and other people of bad reputation came
11 and joined Jesus and his disciples at their meal. Seeing this, the
Pharisees asked of the disciples, "Why does your master eat with

12 tax-collectors and notorious sinners?" Jesus, who had overheard
these words, said, "It is not the healthy who need a physician, but
13 the sick. Go and learn the meaning of the words, 'I require of
you mercy, and not sacrifice.' For I have not come to call back the
faithful to God, but those that have strayed from Him."

14 It was at that time that the disciples of John came to Jesus to ask
him, "Why do we and the Pharisees fast so often, while your dis-
15 ciples do not fast at all?" Jesus answered them, "The guests at a
wedding cannot well be expected to fast while the bridegroom is still
with them. The time is coming, however, when the bridegroom will
be taken from them, and then they will have their share of fasting.

16 "No one puts a new piece of cloth on an old garment, for the
17 patch will tear the cloth and leave the rent worse than it was. And
one does not put new wine into old skins; otherwise the new wine
will burst the skins, and both the wine and the skins will be lost.
New wine is put into new skins, and then both are preserved."

18 While he was speaking an official approached him, and throwing
himself on his knees, implored him, "My daughter has just died,
but if you will come and lay your hand on her, she will come back
19 to life." Jesus rose and followed him, and so did the disciples. At
20 that moment a woman who for twelve years had suffered from an
issue of blood, came up behind him and touched the hem of his robe,
21 thinking, "If I only touch his robe, I shall be helped." Jesus turned,
22 and seeing her, said, "My daughter, be of good cheer. Your confident faith has brought you healing." And from that hour on her
health continued to improve until she was completely cured.

23 When Jesus entered the official's house he found there flute-players
24 and a large and noisy assemblage. "Go away," he said, "for the girl
is not dead, but asleep." They laughed at him, but the crowd was
25 ushered out. Then he stepped beside the dead girl and took her
26 hand, and she instantly rose. The news of this spread through the
entire neighborhood.

27 While Jesus was on his way from this house, he was followed by
two blind men who called to him, "Son of David take pity on us!"
28 When he reached his own home, the blind men also entered with
him, and he asked them, "Do you firmly believe that I can help
29 you?" They answered, "Yes, lord." At that he touched their eyes
30 and said, "According to your faith, it shall be done to you;" and
their sight was restored. Jesus strictly charged them to let no one
31 know of what had happened, but as soon as they were out of the
house they told the story to every one in the district.

32 No sooner were they gone than there was brought to him a man
33 rendered dumb by a spirit with which he was possessed. Jesus drove
out the evil spirit, and the man recovered his speech. At this the
people were overcome with amazement and said, "Such things have
34 never before been seen in Israel." But the Pharisees said, "It is
because he is in league with the prince of devils that he can drive
out evil spirits."

35 In this way Jesus travelled through all the towns and villages,
and taught in their synagogues, preaching the gospel of the kingdom
of God, and healing all diseases and infirmities.

36 But as often as he looked at the crowds he was moved to compassion for them, for they were harassed in spirit and bewildered,
37 like sheep without a shepherd. And so he would say to his disciples,
38 "The harvest-field is large, but the laborers are few. Pray therefore
to the Lord of the harvest to send laborers into His harvest-field."

CHAPTER 10.

1 One day Jesus called twelve of his disciples to him and gave them
the power to drive out evil spirits and to heal sickness and infirmity
2 of every kind. The names of these twelve apostles are: first, Simon,
also called Peter, and his brother Andrew; then James, the son of
3 Zebedee, and his brother, John; Philip and Bartholomew; Thomas,
and the tax-collector Matthew; James the son of Alpheus, and Leb-
4 baeus, surnamed Thaddeus; Simon the Canaanite, and Judas Iscariot,
the same who later betrayed Jesus.

5 These twelve Jesus sent out, giving them the following instruc-
6 tions: "Do not travel the ways that lead to the Gentiles, and visit no
Samaritan town. Go rather to the lost sheep of the house of Israel.
7 On your travels preach that communication with God's spirit-world
8 is at hand. Heal the sick, raise the dead, cleanse lepers, drive out
evil spirits. You have received your gifts without payment, and you
9 shall dispense them without payment. Do not try to obtain gold or
10 silver or copper for your purses, and carry no bag on your journeys,
nor two undergarments, nor shoes, nor a staff; for the workman is
11 worthy of his maintenance. When you enter a town or a village, inquire whether there is any one living there who is ready to receive
12 your message, and stay with him until you leave. When you enter his
house, use the greeting, 'Peace be with this house;' and if the house
13 is worthy, your wish will be fulfilled. But if it is not worthy, your
good wishes will reflect their blessing upon your own heads. And
14 wherever you find no one who will receive you or hear your mes-

15 sage, leave that place and shake its dust from your feet. For truly,
it will be more tolerable for the people of Sodom and Gomorrha on
the day of judgment, than for such a place.
16 "I am sending you out like sheep into the midst of wolves; therefore be wise as serpents and as guileless as doves.
17 "But beware of men; for they will bring you up before the courts
18 and flog you in their synagogues, and because of me you will be
taken before governors, to testify to them and to the Gentiles on be-
19 half of the truth. When you are delivered to them, do not be concerned as to how you shall speak or what you shall say, for when
20 the time comes, the right words will be given to you. For it is not
you who will speak then, but a spirit from your Father who will
speak through you.
21 "Brother will deliver up brother to death, and the father his
child; children will testify against their parents and cause them to
22 be put to death. On my account you will be hated by all men; but
he who holds out to the end will be saved.
23 "If you are persecuted in one place, flee to another, and if you
are persecuted in that place also, flee to a third; for I assure you
that you will not yet have been in all the towns of Israel before the
day when the Son of man comes.
24 "The disciple is not above his teacher, nor the servant above his
25 master. It is enough for the disciple to fare as well as his teacher,
and for the servant to share his master's lot. If they call the master
of the house Beelzebub, how much worse names will they call those
26 of his household? But do not fear them, for there is nothing so
well hidden that it will not be revealed, and nothing so secret that
27 it will not be known. What I confide to you in the darkness of the
night, preach in broad daylight; and what you learn from me in
private, make known from the housetops.
28 "Do not fear those who can indeed kill the body, but who cannot
kill the soul. Fear only Him Who has the power to deliver both
29 body and soul to destruction in hell. Are not two sparrows sold for
a cent? Yet not one of them falls to the ground unless your Father
30 wills it. And as for you, the very hairs of your head are numbered.
31 So have no fear. Do you think you are of less value than sparrows?
32 Every one who acknowledges me before men I shall acknowledge
33 before my Father in heaven; but every one who disowns me before
men, I shall also disown before my Father in heaven.
34 "Do not think that I have come to bring peace on earth by force;
I have not come to bring peace alone, but also the sword of dissen-
35 sion. For my coming may well sow discord between the son and his

36 father, between the daughter and her mother, between the daughter-
in-law and her mother-in-law; and on account of me enmity will
37 arise against a man among the inmates of his own household. He
who prefers his father or mother to me, is not worthy of me; and he
38 who prefers his son or daughter to me, is not worthy of me. He who
will not take up his appointed cross and follow me, is not worthy of
39 me. Whoever covets a life of worldly ease will forfeit the spiritual
life, and whoever forsakes worldly pleasures for my sake will find
the spiritual life.
40 "Whoever receives you, receives me, and whoever receives me, re-
41 ceives Him Who sent me. He who receives any one through whom
God's spirits manifest themselves, because he recognizes him to be
an instrument of God, will also receive the same reward that is due
an instrument of God; and he who receives a godly man because of
42 his godliness, will also receive a godly man's reward. And whoever
gives so much as a cup of water to one of those who are looked upon
as of the lowest standing, because he sees in him one of my disciples, will assuredly not want for his reward."

CHAPTER 11.

1 These were the admonitions that Jesus gave to his twelve apostles as they set out. He himself then went from there into the various
towns to preach the gospel of salvation.
2 At that time John, in prison, heard of the works of Jesus, and
3 sent two of his disciples to inquire of him, "Are you he who is to
4 come, or are we to wait for another?"—"Go back and tell John,"
5 answered Jesus, "of what you hear and see: blind men recover their
eyesight, lame men their ability to walk, lepers are cleansed, the
deaf are restored to hearing, the dead are raised, and the poor ac-
6 cept the glad tidings; and fortunate is he who permits nothing to
separate him from me."
7 When John's disciples had left, Jesus began to address the people
thus concerning John: "What was it that you expected to see when
8 you went out into the desert? A reed, shaken by the wind? If not, why
did you go? Was it to see a man dressed in finery? Finely dressed
9 people are found in the palaces of kings.—What then did you go
out to see? A messenger of God? Be assured, he is an especially
10 great messenger of God, for it is he of whom it is written: 'Behold,
I send my messenger before you; he shall prepare the way for you.'
11 I can testify to you that among those born of women, not one has
appeared who was greater than John the Baptist. Yet the One who
12 came after him is greater in God's spirit-world than he. From the

days of John the Baptist until now, men have been violently sup-
pressing communication with God's spirit-world, and those who have
external power are uprooting from the hearts of the people their
13 belief in such spirit-communication. And yet before John every
messenger of God, and the Law of Moses as well, predicted the
14 coming of God's spirit-world; and if you will believe it, John is the
15 Elijah who was to return from God's spirit-realm. Let him who
rightly understands my words, heed them.

16 "To whom now shall I compare this people? They are like chil-
17 dren who sit in the public squares and sing to each other, "We have
whistled for you, but you have not danced; we have sung dirges, but
18 you have not mourned.' For when John came and did not eat the
usual food or drink the usual drink, people said of him, 'He is pos-
19 sessed by the devil.' Then came the Son of man, eating and drinking
as others do, and now they say of him, 'Look at this glutton and
lover of wine, this friend of tax-collectors and mistresses.' Nevertheless, the wisdom preached by both of them has been vindicated by
their deeds."

20 Against those towns which had witnessed the greater number of
his miracles, but still had not changed their inner attitude, he di-
21 rected the following threat: "Woe to you, Chorazin! Woe to you,
Bethsaida! If the miracles that were worked within your walls
had been performed in Tyre and Sidon, they would have repented
22 long ago in sackcloth and ashes. Therefore I tell you, it will go
more lightly with Tyre and Sidon on the day of reckoning than with
23 you. And you, Capernaum, who were exalted to heaven by those
miracles, must be brought down to hell; for if the miracles that were
performed in you had been performed in Sodom, that city would
24 without doubt be standing to-day. And so I tell you all, it will be
more tolerable with the people of the region of Sodom on the day
of reckoning, than with you."

25 Then Jesus exclaimed, "I praise Thee, Father, Lord of heaven and
earth, that Thou hast hidden these things from the men called
learned and wise, and hast revealed them to those who are con-
26 sidered fools. Yes, Father, for so Thou hast ever done.

27 "All things have been put into my charge by my Father; and no
man knows the Son so well as does the Father, or knows the Father
so well as does the Son and all to whom the Son thinks fit to reveal
28 Him. Come to me, all you who are weary and burdened, and I will
29 refresh you. Take up my yoke and learn from me, for I am gentle
and lowly of heart; and you will find rest for your souls, for my
30 yoke is easy and my burden is light."

CHAPTER 12.

1 Once on a Sabbath it happened that Jesus was passing through
fields of grain, and his disciples, being hungry, began to pick the
2 ears and to eat the grains. When the Pharisees saw this they reproached him, saying, "Look! Your disciples are doing something
3 that is forbidden on the Sabbath." To this Jesus answered, "Are
you ignorant of what David did when he and his companions were
4 hungry? How he entered the house of God and ate the shewbread
which neither he nor his men could lawfully eat, but only the
5 priests? And do you not know besides the law that on the Sabbath
the priests in the temple may break the Sabbath without thereby
6 committing sin? But I tell you, here stands one who is greater
7 than the temple. If you knew the meaning of the words, 'It is mercy
I ask for, and not sacrifice,' you would not have condemned these
8 innocent men. For the Son of man is lord even over the Sabbath."

9 From this place he went to the synagogue of the town, in which
10 he found a man who had a withered arm. Now they asked Jesus,
"Is it lawful to heal on the Sabbath?" For they hoped to find
11 grounds for an accusation against him. Jesus answered, "If one of
you had only one sheep, and this fell into a pit on the Sabbath,
12 would he not exert his full strength to lift that sheep out? Is not a
man worth as much as a sheep? Therefore it is lawful to do good
13 on the Sabbath." And he said to the man, "Stretch out your arm."
The man did so, and his arm was restored and as sound as the other.
14 Seeing this, the Pharisees withdrew and deliberated upon a way to
destroy Jesus. But he was aware of it and left the neighborhood.

15 Great crowds of people followed him, and all those among them
16 who were sick he cured, but he enjoined them not to let it be known
17 publicly. In this he fulfilled the words of the prophet Isaiah: "Be-
18 hold, this is my servant whom I have chosen, my beloved, to whom
my heart cleaves. I will place my spirit-world at his disposal, and
he will proclaim to the nations that the day of decision has come
19 for them. He will not wrangle nor make an outcry; nor will any one
20 hear his voice in the streets. He will not break the reed that is
bruised nor quench the smouldering wick, until in the final issue his
21 victory is complete; and on his name the nations will build their
hope."

22 One day there was brought to him a possessed man who was both
blind and dumb. Jesus healed him, restoring to him his eyesight and
23 his speech. At this the people were exceedingly amazed, exclaiming,
24 "May not this man after all be the son of David?" When the Phar-

isees heard this they replied, "If this fellow drives out demons, he
does it only with the help of Beelzebub, the prince of demons."
25 Reading their thoughts, Jesus turned to them with the words, "Every
kingdom that is divided against itself suffers desolation; and no city
26 or house that is divided against itself can stand. If one devil could
drive out another, the kingdom of Satan would be divided against
27 itself; how then could it stand? And if I am in league with Beelzebub to drive out the evil spirits, with whose help do your own
28 people drive them out? They shall therefore be your judges. But
if I drive out the demons with the help of one of God's spirits, then
29 indeed God's spirit-world has already come to you. How could
any one enter a strong man's house and rob him of his goods without first binding the strong man? Only so can he plunder the
house.

30 "He who is not for me, is against me, and he who does not
31 gather with me, scatters. For this reason I say: Men will be pardoned for every sin and blasphemy, but for blaspheming God's
32 spirit-world there will be no pardon. If any one speaks a word
against the Son of man he will be pardoned; but whoever speaks
against the holy spirit-world cannot expect pardon in this age or
33 the next. Either call the tree good, and consider its fruit good
also; or call the tree evil, and hold its fruit to be bad; for by its
34 fruit a tree is known. O brood of vipers! How could you who
are evil speak what is good? For that which fills the heart will
35 rise to the lips. A good man will bring only good things out of his
store of good, while a bad man out of his store of evil can bring
forth only what is evil.

36 "But I tell you, for each unfounded judgment that men render
37 they shall give account on the day of judgment. For according to the
reasons that you had for your judgments, you will be declared either
guilty or innocent."

38 Then certain of the scribes and Pharisees answered him, "Master,
39 we wish that you would show us a miracle as a sign." But Jesus told
them, "An evil and a godless people demand a miracle as a sign;
but they will receive none other than that which was given to the
40 prophet Jonah. For as Jonah was three days and three nights in the
belly of the monster-fish, so will the Son of man be three days and
41 three nights in the centre of Satan's realm. The people of Nineveh
will appear as witnesses when this nation one day stands before
God's judgment-seat, and will cause their condemnation. For they
repented at the preaching of Jonah; and here stands one who is
42 greater than Jonah. The queen of the south will appear as a wit-

ness when this nation is judged, and will cause their condemnation.
For she came from the ends of the earth to hear the wisdom of a
Solomon; and here stands one who is greater than Solomon.
43 "When the evil spirit has gone out of a man, it wanders through
44 desolate spheres, searching for rest but finding none. Then it says
to itself, 'I will go back to my former home which I left;' and when
45 it comes it finds the house vacant, clean, and in good order. Then
it goes and brings with it seven other spirits, even more wicked than
itself, and if they succeed in entering they settle there; and the last
state of such a man will be still worse than the first. So it will be
with this corrupt nation."

46 While he was still speaking to the people, his mother and his
brothers came and stood behind the crowd, trying to reach him,
47 in order to talk with him. Some one said to him, "Over there
are your mother and your brothers, who would like to speak to you."
48 But Jesus answered the man who had brought him the message,
49 "Who is my mother, and who are my brothers?" Then he added,
pointing to his disciples, "Look, these are mother and brothers to
50 me. For whoever does the will of my heavenly Father, is to me
brother, sister, and mother."

CHAPTER 13.

1 One day Jesus went out of doors and sat down by the shore of the
2 lake. Very soon a great crowd gathered about him, so that he was
forced to find a seat in a boat, while the people stood on the shore.
3 Then he gave them an address that touched on various truths in
4 the form of parables. He said: "A sower went out to sow, and as he
sowed, some seed fell on a path trodden across the field, and the
5 birds came and picked it up. Some of the seed fell on rocky parts of
the field where there was little soil; to be sure, it sprouted quickly,
6 because it could not root deeply into the ground; but as the heat of
the sun grew stronger day after day, the seed was scorched and
7 withered, because it had only surface-roots. Some fell among sprouting thistle-seeds, and as the latter sprang up they choked the growing
8 seed. But the rest of the seed fell on fertile soil and yielded, some a
9 hundredfold, some sixtyfold, and some thirtyfold. Let him to whom
it is given to understand the meaning of my words, heed them."

10 Then the disciples turned to him and asked, "Why do you speak
11 to the people in parables?" He replied, "To you it has been given
to understand the mysterious operation of God's spirit-world, but
12 not to them. He who holds fast to that gift of understanding will

have it increased to abundance. But from him who does not hold
13 fast, even that gift that he once had will be taken. My reason for
speaking to the people in parables is this: These are people who are
destined to look, and yet not to see; to listen, and yet not to hear
14 and understand, and therefore not to change their hearts. In them
you see fulfilled the words of the prophet Isaiah: 'Go and say to
these people, "You shall listen and yet not understand; you shall
15 look, and yet not see. For the hearts of these people are not open;
their spiritual hearing is dull, and their spiritual eyes are closed.
Thus they will not be able to see aright the things that they see, and
hear aright the things that they hear, and arrive at a true understanding in their hearts, so that they might change their inner atti-
16 tude and that I might be able to heal them."' But you are fortunate,
17 because your eyes do see and your ears do hear correctly. For I tell
you, many prophets and godly men wished to see what you now
see, and did not see it; and to hear what you now hear, and did not
18 hear it. To you, therefore, I shall explain the parable of the sower
as follows:

19 "To every one who hears the truth concerning the beyond, but
does not permit it to penetrate, the Evil One comes and quickly takes
away that which was sown in his heart. In his case the seed has
fallen upon the path trodden across the field.

20 "The rocky places on which the seed fell are like the man who
hears the word of truth, and for the moment does accept it joy-
21 fully, but in whom it takes no root, because he is a superficial and
unstable man. If later he suffers hardship or persecution because of
his acceptance of the truth, this causes him to fall away immediately.

22 "The seed that fell among the sprouting thistles symbolizes a
man who hears the truth, but in whose case the cares of daily life
and the passion for worldly riches choke the truth and render it
unfruitful.

23 "Lastly, the seed that fell on fertile soil represents a man who not
only hears and accepts the word of truth, but who lives accordingly,
and thereby yields fruit, one man a hundredfold, another sixtyfold,
and a third thirtyfold."

24 The second parable addressed to the people was this: "With the
truth concerning the beyond it is as with a man who sowed good
25 seed on his field. While all of the household were asleep, his enemy
26 came and sowed weeds among his grain, and stole away. When the
27 seed came up and began to head, the weeds also appeared. Then the
householder's men came to him and asked, 'Master, did you not sow

good seed in your field? Where then do these weeds come from?'
28 He answered, 'Some enemy has done this.' They asked, 'Shall we go
29 and root up the weeds and throw them in a heap?' 'No,' he answered, 'for while you are rooting up the weeds, you would root up
30 grain also. Just let both grow until the harvest. When the harvest comes I will tell the reapers: First of all gather the weeds and tie them into bundles and burn them; but bring the grain into my barn.' "

31 He gave them another parable: "The truth concerning the beyond is like a mustard seed that a man took and sowed in his field.
32 Though it be the smallest of all seeds, when it is full grown it surpasses all other plants and becomes a tree so large that the birds of the air come and nest in its branches."

33 Another parable was the following: "The truth concerning the beyond is like yeast which a woman took and mixed with three measures of flour, until the whole mass was leavened."

34 All this Jesus told the people in parables; indeed, he preached
35 no sermon without illustrating with parables; and thus were fulfilled the words of the prophet: "I will speak in parables and so reveal the secrets kept hidden since the creation of the universe."

36 He now dismissed the people and went back to his home. There his disciples came up to him saying, "Explain to us the parable
37 of the weed sown in the field."—"The sower of the good seed,"
38 answered Jesus, "is the Son of man; the field is the universe; the good seeds are the children of the kingdom of heaven; the weeds
39 are the children of the Evil One; the enemy who sowed the weeds is the devil; the harvest-time is the end of an age; the reapers are mes-
40 sengers sent by God. Just as the weeds are gathered and burned in
41 the fire, so will it be at the end of every age. The Son of man will send out his spirit-messengers, and they will sort out from his king-
42 dom all evil-doers and everything that leads to sin, and throw them into the furnace of suffering. And there will be wailing and gnash-
43 ing of teeth. Then the godly will shine like the sun in their Father's kingdom. Let him who understands the meaning of my words, heed them.

44 "The truth concerning the beyond is like a treasure that was buried in a field. Some one found it and buried it again, and rejoicing in his find, went home and sold everything that he had, and bought that field.

45 "Whoever hears the truth concerning the beyond must do as a
46 merchant did who sought to acquire choice pearls. When he had

found an especially valuable pearl, he went and sold all that he
had and bought the pearl.
47 "Again, in the beyond it is similar to fishing with a drag-net.
The drag-net is thrown into the sea, and fish of every kind are caught.
48 When it is full it is drawn to the side of the vessel, and the fishermen sit down and gather the perfect fish into tubs, throwing the im-
49 perfect ones back into the sea. So too will it be at the end of every
age. The spirit-messengers will go out and pick the evil from
50 among the godly, and throw them into the furnace of suffering; and
51 there will be wailing and gnashing of teeth. Have you understood
all this?" The disciples answered, "Yes." Then Jesus continued,
52 "You see, a teacher who has acquired his knowledge in the school
of God's spirit-world may be compared to the head of a family
who out of his rich storehouse of truth brings forth new things and
old."
53 After Jesus had related these parables he went on to his native
54 village, Nazareth, and preached in the synagogue there. His words
impressed his hearers so deeply that they asked of one another,
55 "Where did he get all this wisdom and power of eloquence? Is he
not the carpenter's son? Is not his mother's name Mary, and are
56 not his brothers named James, John, Simon, and Judas? Do not his
57 sisters all live here, too? How has he come by all this?" And so
they turned away from him; but Jesus said to them, "By no one is
a messenger of God so little honored as by his own townsmen and
58 his own family." And because the people did not believe in him he
could not perform many miracles there.

CHAPTER 14.

1 At about that time reports concerning Jesus reached the tetrarch
2 Herod, who said to his courtiers, "Surely this is John the Baptist
whom I had beheaded, risen from the dead. That is why such mir-
3 aculous powers are working through him." For Herod had ordered
John to be arrested, fettered in chains, and thrown into prison. This
he had done at the bidding of Herodias, his brother Philip's wife,
4 because John had charged him, "It is not lawful for you to have
5 her." For this reason Herod would rather have had John put to
death; but he feared the people, who looked upon John as a messenger of God.
6 Now when Herod was celebrating his birthday, the daughter of
7 Herodias danced before the guests and pleased Herod so greatly
that he promised her under oath to grant any favor that she might
8 ask. The girl, with whom her mother had schemed beforehand, re-

plied, "Then order that the head of John the Baptist be brought to
9 me." The king was startled, but mindful of his oath and of his guests
10 he commanded that her wish be carried out. He therefore sent his
11 executioners to the prison and had John beheaded. His head was
placed on a dish and brought to the girl, who took it to her mother.
12 John's disciples took the body away and buried it, and then they
went to Jesus and reported what had happened.
13 When Jesus heard their story he took a boat and went to a solitary
place in order to be entirely alone. But the people heard of his
departure, and pouring out of the towns, made their way to the place
14 on foot. When he came out of his retreat and saw the crowds before
him, he was moved to compassion for them and healed their sick.
15 In the meantime evening had come on, and now one of his disciples
approached him and said, "This is an uninhabited region, and
the hour is late. Send the people away, so that they may go to the
16 villages to buy food." Jesus answered, "They need not go away; you
17 can give them something to eat." They protested, "We have only
18 five loaves and two fish between us."—"Bring them to me," he re-
19 plied. Then he ordered the people to sit down on the grass, took the
five loaves and the two fish, looked up to heaven, uttered a prayer,
and broke up the loaves. After this he gave the food to his disciples,
20 and they distributed it among the people. All had enough to satisfy
their hunger. What was left over was gathered up and filled twelve
21 baskets. Of those who had eaten, the men only, not counting the
women and the children, numbered about five thousand.
22 Jesus now urged his disciples to embark at once and to make for
23 the opposite shore, leaving him to dismiss the people. When all had
left he climbed the hill to pray there in quietness and solitude.
24 Darkness fell, but he still lingered in this lonely place. The boat
was already far out on the lake, struggling hard against the waves,
25 for there was a head-wind. Not until about three o'clock in the
morning did Jesus set out, walking over the surface of the lake
26 toward his disciples. When they saw him walking thus over the lake
they were frightened, for they thought that it was a ghost; and they
27 cried out in terror. Instantly they heard Jesus calling to them,
28 "Courage! It is I. Do not be afraid." Peter called back to him,
29 "Master, if it is you, let me come to you across the water."—"Come,"
answered Jesus. Then Peter stepped from the boat and walked over
30 the water toward Jesus; but when he felt the violence of the storm
he became frightened, and beginning to sink, cried out, "Lord, save
31 me!" At once stretching out his hand, Jesus drew him up and said,
"O man of little faith and confidence, why did you doubt?"

32 Together they stepped into the boat, and the storm died down
33 immediately. But the men in the boat fell upon their knees before
him and exclaimed, "Truly, you are a son of God!"

34 After reaching land, they went to Gennesaret. When the inhabi-
35 tants of the village recognized him, they sent messengers throughout
36 the country, and all the sick were brought to him. They begged for
permission to touch only the tassel of his robe. And all who did so
were healed.

CHAPTER 15.

1 One day certain scribes and Pharisees came from Jerusalem to
2 see Jesus, and asked him, "Why do your disciples not observe the
traditions of their ancestors? For they do not wash their hands be-
3 fore meals." He answered, "Why do you break God's command-
4 ments for the sake of your traditions? For God has commanded:
'Honor your father and your mother,' and further: 'Whoever curses
5 his father or his mother, shall suffer death.' You, however, maintain: Whoever says to his father or his mother, 'I will dedicate to
God as a gift to the treasury of the temple that which I should contribute to your support,' has no need to honor his father or his
6 mother. Therewith you have rendered God's commandment of no
7 effect for the sake of your traditions. Hypocrites that you are!
8 Aptly was it said of you through Isaiah by a spirit of God: "These
people do homage to Me with their lips, but their hearts are widely
9 separated from Me. Their ways of worshipping Me are futile, for
10 the doctrines of their religion are man-made ordinances.'" Then,
calling the people nearer to him, he said, "Listen carefully, and
11 remember what I now say to you: Not everything that enters the
mouth necessarily indicates a man's inner attitude; but whatever
comes out of his mouth expresses his true intention."

12 His disciples now came to him and said, "Do you know that the
13 Pharisees are shocked at your words?" But he answered, "Every
plant that was not planted by my heavenly Father will be torn
14 up. Let these blind men go their way. They are such guides as cannot see the path themselves; and if one blind man leads another,
15 both will fall into the ditch." Peter now begged him, "Explain that
16 parable to us." He answered, "Are you, too, still without under-
17 standing? Do you not see that whatever goes into the mouth is received by the stomach and expelled from the body by the natural
18 channels? But whatever issues from the mouth, comes from the
19 heart, and reveals a man's inner attitude. Out of the heart arise

evil thoughts, murder, adultery, fornication, theft, slander, and blas-
20 phemy; and these are the things that relate to a man's inner attitude; but eating with unwashed hands has no bearing whatever on
his inner condition."

21 From there Jesus went into the region of Tyre and Sidon. There
22 a Canaanite woman from a nearby district repeatedly called, "Lord,
son of David, take pity on me! My daughter is dreadfully tormented
23 by an evil spirit." But he did not answer a word. Then his disciples
turned to him and entreated him, "Get rid of her! She persists in
24 screaming after us." He answered, "I have been sent only to the
25 stray sheep of the house of Israel." But the woman drew nearer,
threw herself upon her knees before him, and implored, "Lord, help
26 me!" But he said to her, "It is not right to take bread from the chil-
27 dren, and throw it to the dogs."—"True, lord," she answered, "but
the dogs eat only of the crumbs that fall from their master's table."
28 On hearing this Jesus said to her, "Woman, your faith is great. Your
wish shall be granted." And from that hour her daughter was well.

29 Jesus next came to the region of the Lake of Galilee, and climbing
30 a hill sat down there. The people came to him in great numbers,
bringing with them their lame, blind, crippled, deaf, and many af-
31 flicted with other ailments, and laying them at his feet. He cured
them all. The people were amazed when they heard the dumb speaking and saw the maimed with their limbs sound again, the lame
walking, and the blind seeing. All praised aloud the God of Israel.

32 Jesus now called his disciples and said, "I pity these people, for
they have been with me for three days and have no food left. I am
unwilling to send them away hungry, for they may become faint on
33 the road." But the disciples protested, "Where, in an uninhabited
34 place like this, can we find enough bread to feed so many?" Jesus
35 asked them, "How many loaves have you?" They answered, "Seven,
36 and a few fish." Thereupon He ordered the people to be seated on
the ground; then taking the seven loaves and the fish he uttered a
prayer, broke up the loaves, and gave them to his disciples, who
37 divided them among the people. Every one had enough to eat.
38 What was left over was gathered up and filled seven baskets. Of
those who were fed, the men only, not counting the women and
39 the children, numbered about four thousand. Then he dismissed the
people, and embarking, made his way to the district of Magadan.

CHAPTER 16.

1 Here he was met by Pharisees and Sadducees, who tried to put
2 him to the test, urging him to show them a sign in the sky. But

he answered them, "If the sky is red at sunset, you predict fair
3 weather; but if it is red and murky in the morning, you say, 'It will
rain to-day.' The signs of the sky, then, you are able to read, but the
4 signs of the coming of a new era you do not understand. A wicked
and apostate people demands a sign; but it will receive no other
than that which was vouchsafed to the prophet Jonah." With these
words he turned his back on them and went away.

5 When the disciples landed on the farther shore they found that
6 they had forgotten to bring bread, and after Jesus warned them,
7 "Beware of the leaven of the Pharisees and the Sadducees," they discussed his words with each other, thinking that he referred to their
8 failure to provide bread. Aware of the subject of their discussion,
Jesus said to them, "You men of little faith! Why do you worry
9 over having brought no bread? Do you not yet possess true understanding? Have you already forgotten how five thousand people
were fed with five loaves, and how many basketfuls you gathered
10 of what was left? And can you no longer remember the seven
loaves that were enough for four thousand, and how many basket-
11 fuls then also were left? How could you so misunderstand me as to
think that I meant every-day bread when I warned you against the
12 leaven of the Pharisees and the Sadducees?" Then only did they
realize that his warning alluded, not to the leavening in the bread
of the Pharisees and the Sadducees, but to their doctrine.

13 When Jesus entered the region of Caesarea Philippi he asked of
his disciples, "Who do the people say that I, as the son of man,
14 am?" They answered, "Some say you are John the Baptist; others,
that you are Elijah; still others, that you are Jeremiah or one of the
15 other prophets." Then he asked them further, "But you, who do you
16 say I am?" Simon Peter replied, "You are the Messiah, the Son of
17 God, of the Deliverer." Jesus turned to him, saying, "Fortunate are
you, Simon, son of Jonah, that it was not your own human mind
18 that told you this, but my heavenly Father. And now I for my
part would say something to you. Your name is Cephas, meaning
rock. Upon such a rock I will build my congregation, and the
19 strongest Powers of Darkness will not conquer it. I will give you the
key to understanding the laws of the beyond: All fetters with which
you bind yourself on earth, you will have to carry in the beyond
also; and from all fetters from which you release yourself on earth,
20 you shall be released in the beyond also." Then he gave his disciples the strict order to tell no one that he was the Messiah.

21 From that day on Jesus began to make it known to his disciples
that he must go to Jerusalem, where it would be his lot to suffer

many things at the hands of the elders, the high-priests, and the
scribes, and in the end to be put to death by them; but that on the
22 third day he would be brought back to life again. On hearing this
Peter took him aside and attempted to dissuade him. "Lord," he said,
23 "may God prevent these things! They must never happen to you!"
Then Jesus turned upon Peter with the words, "Out of my sight,
Satan! You seek to divert me from my divinely appointed mission.
For your thoughts do not express the will of God, but merely your
purely human feelings."

24 Then Jesus said to his disciples, "Whoever wishes to walk in my
footsteps must sacrifice his purely human inclinations, and take up
the cross destined for him. Only then can he be a follower of mine.
25 For he who seeks to make sure of his physical well-being will lose
the spiritual; but he who is willing to suffer the loss of his physical
26 well-being for my sake will find the spiritual. For what can it
profit a man to gain the whole world, if he thereby loses his spiritual
well-being? Or what ransom can a man pay for his spiritual well-
27 being, once it is lost? For the Son of man will come in the glory
of his Father, attended by his spirit-messengers, and will reward
every one according to his deeds.

28 "I tell you, some of those who stand here will not taste of bodily
death until they have seen the Son of man come in the glory of his
royal power."

CHAPTER 17.

1 Six days later Jesus took with him Peter, James, and John the
brother of James, and led them up on a high mountain where they
2 were alone. There his human form was transfigured before their eyes,
His face shone like the sun, and his garments glistened like snow.
3 And Moses and Elijah appeared to them and conversed with Jesus.

4 Then Peter said to Jesus, "Lord, how wonderful it is to be here!
If you are willing, I shall make three shelters of leafy boughs, one
for you, one for Moses, and one for Elijah."

5 While he was still speaking, a brightly radiant cloud spread
above them, and out of the cloud came a voice calling, "This is my
beloved Son, in whom was my delight. Hearken to him!"

6 When the disciples heard these words they were so overwhelmed
7 by terror and awe that they fell upon their faces. Then Jesus, step-
ping to their side, touched them and said, "Get up, and have no
8 fear!" When they opened their eyes, they saw no one but Jesus.

9 While on their way down the mountain, Jesus instructed them,

"Tell no one of what you saw here, until the Son of man has risen
from the dead."
10 The disciples then asked him, "But why do the scribes say that
11 Elijah must come first?" He answered, "Elijah comes repeatedly
12 and helps to lead everything back to God. And I can inform you
that Elijah has already come once; however, the leaders of the people did not recognize him, but mistreated him as much as lay in
13 their power." Then the disciples understood that he was speaking
of John the Baptist. "So also," Jesus continued, "will the Son of
man suffer at their hands."
14 Scarcely had they rejoined the waiting crowd when a man ap-
15 proached Jesus and knelt before him with the entreaty, "Lord, have
pity on my son. He suffers from epilepsy and is in a very bad condition. He often falls into the fire, and sometimes into the water.
16 I have taken him to your disciples, but they could not cure him."
17 At that Jesus exclaimed, "Oh, these people who have no faith and
confidence in God and are of an utterly perverse disposition! I wonder how long I must be with you? How much longer must I have
patience with you? Bring him here to me!"
18 Then Jesus sternly commanded the evil spirit, and it went out of
the boy, and he was well from that very hour.
19 Later the disciples approached Jesus when he was alone and
20 asked him, "Why was it that we could not drive out the spirit?" He
answered, "Because you have no trust in God. For I assure you that
if your confidence in God were even as small as a mustard seed, and
you would say to this mountain, 'Move from here to there,' it would
move; indeed, nothing whatever would be impossible for you."
22 As they journeyed from place to place in Galilee, Jesus said to
the disciples, "Soon the Son of man will be handed over to men.
23 They will put him to death, but on the third day he will be raised
again." At this they were deeply grieved.
24 In Capernaum the collectors of the temple-tax approached Peter
25 with the question, "Does your master pay no temple-tax?" Peter
replied, "Certainly he does." When Jesus entered his house he
asked, before Peter could speak, "Simon, what do you say: From
whom do the kings of the earth collect tribute or taxes, from their
26 sons or from their subjects?"—"From their subjects," answered
27 Peter. "The sons, then, are exempt," said Jesus. "But in order that
we may give no ground for complaint, go to the lake and throw out
a hook and line. Take the first fish that you catch and open its
mouth; in it you will find a silver coin. Take it, and give it to
them in payment of the tax for me and for you."

CHAPTER 18.

1 At this time the disciples went to Jesus and asked him, "Who will
2 reach the higher planes in the beyond?" By way of answer Jesus
3 called to him a child, placed it among them, and said, "I tell you
that unless you change and become like children, you will not be
4 admitted to the higher spheres of the beyond. Whoever is humble,
5 like this child, will enter the higher planes of the beyond. And
whoever cares for such a child—though it be but a single one—
6 leading it to me, cares for me. But whoever leads away from me but
a single one of these little ones who believe and trust in me—it
would be better for him if a millstone were hung around his neck
and he were drowned in the lowest depth of the ocean.
7 "Woe to the world for leading men away from me! True, such
8 misleading must be; but woe to him who is the cause of it! If, then,
your hand or your foot causes you to leave me, cut it off and throw
it from you; for it is better for you to go into the spiritual life
maimed or lame, than to be thrown into the fire of suffering with
9 both hands and both feet. And if your eye causes you to leave me,
tear it out and throw it aside, for it is better for you to go into
the spiritual life with only one eye, than to be thrown into the fire
of suffering with both.
10 "See to it that you are not careless of your behavior in the
presence of even a single one of these little ones who believe and
trust in me; for I say to you, the spirits of God who are set over
them can at all times appear before the face of my heavenly Father
11 to make their report. For the Son of man has come to save that
which was lost.
12 "What would you say: If a man has a hundred sheep, and one of
them strays, will he not leave the ninety-nine on the hills and hunt
13 for the strayed? And if he succeeds in finding it, then he will be
happier over it than over the ninety-nine that did not stray, will
14 he not? So too it is the will of your heavenly Father that not even
a single one of these little ones shall be lost.
15 "If your brother has wronged you, go to him and talk the matter over with him face to face; if he will listen to you, you will have
16 won your brother. But if he will not listen, take one or two others
with you so that he may have the unanimous verdict of two or three
17 witnesses. If he is unwilling to listen to these also, lay your case
before the congregation. And if he declines to abide by its verdict,
18 regard him as an unbeliever and a hardened offender. For I say
to you, with whatever you fetter yourselves on earth, you will be
fettered in the beyond also; and from all fetters from which you

release yourselves on earth, you will be released in the beyond also.
19 And further, if only two of you on earth join in prayer for any-
20 thing, it will be granted them by my heavenly Father. For where-
ever two or three come together to serve me or my cause, I am in
their midst."
21 Then Peter went to him and asked, "Master, how often shall I
forgive my brother if he repeatedly wrongs me? As often as seven
22 times?" Jesus answered, "I tell you, not only seven times, but
23 seventy times seven. For the procedure in the beyond is similar to
that of a certain king who wished to settle his accounts with his
24 officials. The first to come before him owed him ten million dollars,
25 and because he could not pay this debt, his lord ordered him to be
sold, together with his wife and children and all his property, there-
26 with to pay on his debt. Then the official fell on his knees and
pleaded, 'My lord, please have patience with me, and I will repay
27 you in full.' The lord took pity on him, gave him his freedom, and
also remitted the debt.
28 "But as this official went out, he met a subordinate who owed him
29 twenty dollars. Seizing him by the throat, he cried, 'Pay what you
owe me!' Then the subordinate threw himself at the other's feet
and entreated him, 'Please be patient with me, I will repay you in
30 full.' The other would not listen to him, however, but went out and
had him placed in prison until the debt was paid.
31 "The other officials had witnessed what had happened and were
greatly distressed over it. They came and laid the case before their
32 lord, who summoned the official again and received him with the
words, 'You scoundrel! I cancelled all of your debts, because your
33 pleading touched my heart. Should you not then have had mercy
34 with your subordinate, as I had with you?' Justly incensed, his lord
turned him over to the officers of the law until he paid him the debt
in full.
35 "So too will my heavenly Father deal with every one of you who
does not sincerely forgive his brother."

CHAPTER 19.

1 When Jesus had ended these discourses he went from Galilee into
2 the region of Judaea on the farther bank of the Jordan. Great numbers of people followed him, and there he cured all those among
them who were sick.
3 Again the Pharisees approached him with the intention of trapping him and asked, "Would you say that the law permitting a man
4 to divorce his wife on any pretext is right?" He answered them,

"Do you not know that in the beginning the Creator made male
and female, designating each particular man for one particular
5 woman, and said: 'Because of this, a man shall leave his father and
mother and firmly hold to his designated wife, and both shall be
6 as one living being?' They are thus to be regarded not as two, but
as a single, inseparable unit. Therefore, what God has joined to-
7 gether in pairs, man shall not separate." To this they retorted,
"Why then did Moses allow a wife to be given a letter of divorce
8 and then dismissed?" He answered, "It was only because of your
hard-heartedness that Moses allowed you to dismiss your wives; but
9 this was not so in the beginning. And so I say that whoever divorces
his wife except for unchaste conduct, and marries another, commits
adultery."

10 Then his disciples said to him, "If that is the law governing relations between men and women, it would seem better not to marry
11 at all." To this he answered, "What I am about to tell you will not
be clear to every one, but only to those to whom it is given to un-
12 derstand me. Some men are unfit from birth to reproduce; others
have been made unfit by their fellow-men, and still others have
made themselves unfit, thinking it to be for the sake of the kingdom
of heaven.—Let him who understands the meaning of my words,
heed it."

13 There were now brought to him some little children, so that he
might lay his hands on them and pray for them. The disciples
14 spoke roughly to the people who brought the children, but Jesus
reproved them, saying, "Let the children be, and do not hinder them
from coming to me; for God's spirit-world is open to him who is
15 like them." Then he laid his hands on the children and went on his
way.

16 Now there came to him one who asked, "Master, tell me the good
17 I must do in order to attain to the future life." He replied, "Why do
you ask me about goodness? There is only One who is good. But if
you wish to enter into life, you must keep the commandments."—
18 "Which commandments must I keep?" asked the other. Jesus answered, "The commandments: 'You shall not kill; you shall not
19 commit adultery; you shall not bear false witness; you shall honor
your father and your mother, and you shall love your neighbour as
20 yourself.'" In response the young man said, "I have kept all these
21 from my childhood. What more must I do?"—"If you are ready to
do that which you are still lacking," said Jesus, "then go and sell
all that you have, and give the proceeds to the poor; so you may

expect riches in the beyond. Then come back and be my follower."
22 When the young man heard this he went sadly away, for he owned
a great deal of property.
23 Then Jesus turned to his disciples and said, "Truly, it will be
hard for a rich man to enter into communication with God's spirit-
24 world. I might go further: it is easier for a camel to pass through
the eye of a needle, than for a rich man to enter God's spirit-realm."
25 At these words the disciples asked in consternation, "What hope
26 is there, then, for any rich man to be saved?" Looking at them
earnestly, Jesus answered, "With men, this is indeed impossible, but
with God all things are possible."
27 Peter now turned to him and said, "But see, we have left everything and followed you. What reward shall we have for this?"
28 Jesus answered him, "I will tell you. You who have followed me
will, in the new life to come, when the Son of man sits on the
throne in his glory, likewise sit on twelve thrones and judge the
29 twelve tribes of Israel. And whoever for my sake has left his brother
or his sister, his father or his mother or his children, his houses or
his lands, will be recompensed with values a hundred times higher
and obtain the future life that is prepared for him according to a
30 divine law. And many who were among the first, will then be last,
and many who were among the last, will be first.

CHAPTER 20.

1 "Under the laws of the beyond it is the same as with a householder who went out early one morning to hire laborers to work in
2 his vineyard. He agreed with them to pay each man a dollar for his
day's work, and then he sent them to his vineyard.
3 "At nine o'clock in the morning he went out again and met others
4 standing idly about the market-place, and said to them, 'You too go
to my vineyard. I will pay you fair wages.' They also accepted the
work.
5 "At noon and at three o'clock in the afternoon he went out again
and did as before.
6 "When at last he went out once more at five o'clock in the afternoon, he found still others without work, and asked them, 'Why are
7 you idling here all day long?' They answered, 'Because nobody has
hired us.' He said to them, 'Go to my vineyard as quickly as you
can.'
8 "When evening came, the owner of the vineyard said to his steward, 'Call the workmen and pay them their wages. Begin with those
9 who came last, and end with those who came first.' Thus those who

had been hired at five o'clock were the first to be paid, and each man
10 received a dollar. Then those who had been the first to go to work
thought they would receive more, but each of them also received
11 only one dollar. They took the money, but grumbled to the house-
12 holder, 'These men who came last have worked only one hour, and
you have given them the same wages that you gave us, although we
13 had to bear the burden and heat of the whole day.' But he said
to one of them, 'My friend, I do you no injustice. Did you not agree
14 with me for a dollar a day? Take what you agreed to take, and go.
It is my desire to pay this last-comer just as much as I have paid
15 you. Have I not the right to do as I please with my own money?
16 Or do you consider my kindness something wrong?'—So the first
will be last, and the last, first."

17 Jesus now journeyed up toward Jerusalem. On the way he took
18 his Twelve aside and said to them, "We are now going to Jerusalem.
There the Son of man will be handed over to the high priests and
19 the scribes. They will sentence him to death and deliver him to the
pagans to be scoffed at and scourged, and at last to be crucified.
And on the third day he will rise again."

20 One day the mother of Zebedee's children came to him with her
21 sons and knelt before him in supplication. He asked her, "What is
it that you wish?" She replied, "Give orders that of these two sons
of mine, one shall sit at your right hand and one at your left in your
22 kingdom." Jesus answered her, "You do not know what you ask.
Can you drink the cup that I shall drink?"—"We can," was the reply.
23 "You shall indeed drink my cup," returned Jesus, "but the places
at my right hand and at my left are not mine to give, for they will
be bestowed upon those to whom they are allotted by my Father."

24 When the other ten disciples heard of this they were indignant
25 with the two brothers, but Jesus called them nearer and taught them
as follows: "You know that temporal rulers force their will upon
their subjects, and that their officials let the people feel their power.
26 This must not be so among you. Any one of you who wishes to be
27 reckoned among the great must rather be your servant, and he
28 among you who wishes to be the foremost, must toil for you; just as
the Son of man himself has not come to be served, but to serve
others, and to give his life as ransom for the many. Strive, therefore,
to perfect yourselves in that which men regard as lowly, and to
divest yourselves of that which men regard as great. If, for example,
you come to a house and are invited to stay for a meal, do not re-
cline in the place of honor. For there may be among the guests some
one more highly honored than you; then it would be the duty of the

host to ask you to move lower down, and you would be put to shame.
But if you take the lowest place, and there comes a guest of less
importance than you, your host will say to you, 'Please move higher
up.' And that will be an honor for you."
29 On leaving Jericho they were followed by a great throng. Two
30 blind men sitting by the wayside, when they heard that Jesus was
31 passing, cried aloud, "Son of David, take pity on us!" The people
threateningly told them to be quiet, but they cried all the louder,
32 "Son of David, take pity on us!" Then Jesus stood still, called them
to him, and asked, "What is it that you want me to do for you?"—
33 "Lord," they answered, "open our eyes that we may see."—"Do you
truly believe that I can do this?" asked Jesus. "Yes, lord," they answered, "and indeed we should like very much to see you, too."
34 Jesus took pity on them and touched their eyes, and immediately
they were able to see, and followed him.

CHAPTER 21.

1 As they drew nearer to Jerusalem they reached Bethphage by the
2 Mount of Olives. Here Jesus sent out two of the disciples, telling
them, "Go to the village before you. Right at the entrance you will
find an ass tied together with her colt. Untie both, and bring them
3 to me. If any one protests, say to him, 'The lord needs them,' and
he will at once let you have them."
4 Thus was fulfilled the word of the prophet: "Say to the daughter
5 of Sion, 'Behold, your king comes to you in all meekness, riding
upon an ass, the colt of a beast of burden.'"
6 The disciples went away and did as Jesus had directed, bringing
7 back with them the ass and her colt. Then they laid their cloaks on
8 the colt, and Jesus sat on it. Most of the people spread their cloaks
on the road, while others cut twigs from the trees and strewed them
9 on his path. The throngs in the lead and those that followed him,
called out, "Hosanna to the son of David! Blessed be he who comes
in the name of the Lord! Hosanna in the highest!"
10 When he entered Jerusalem the whole city was stirred, and men
11 asked each other, "Who is this?" The crowds answered, "This is
the prophet Jesus from Nazareth in Galilee."
12 Then Jesus went into the temple of God and drove out all who
trafficked there, overturned the tables of the money-changers and the
13 crates of the dealers in doves, and said to them, "My house shall be
called a house of prayer, but you have turned it into a robbers' den."
14 The blind and the lame were now brought to him in the temple,
and he healed them.

15 The high priests and the scribes were eyewitnesses of these miracles and had to hear besides how the children cried aloud in the
temple, "Hosanna to the son of David!" This aroused their dis-
16 pleasure, and they turned upon Jesus with the question, "Do you
hear what they are calling?"—"Indeed I do," he answered. "But have
you never read: 'Out of the mouths of infants and sucklings have
you brought forth your praise'?"
17 With these words he left them standing there and went out of the
city to Bethany, where he passed the night.
18 Early on the following morning he returned to the city. On the
19 way he felt hungry, and seeing a lone fig tree by the roadside, went
to it and found that it bore nothing but leaves. Then he said to the
tree, "As long as this age endures, no more fruit shall grow upon
you." And at once the tree withered.
20 When the disciples saw this, they exclaimed in wonder, "How
21 could that fig tree wither so suddenly?" Jesus answered, "If you
have confident faith and do not doubt, you will not only be able to
do what was done to this fig tree, but you need only say to this
22 mountain, 'Rise and plunge into the sea,' and it will be done. In
fact all that you ask in prayer you will receive, if you have confident faith. Let the fig tree serve as a lesson."
23 He now went back into the interior of the temple to address the
people, at which the high priests and the elders hurried in and demanded of him, "What is your authority for these acts of yours, and
24 who gave you such authority?" Jesus answered, "I will ask you a
question also, and only one. If you can answer it, then I too will
25 tell you by what authority I act as I do. My question is: The baptism of John — whence was it? From heaven or from men?" They
considered among themselves and reasoned, "If we say 'From heaven'
26 he will retort, 'Why, then, did you not believe in the Baptist?' and
if we say 'From men' we shall have trouble with the people, for they
27 all regard John as a messenger of God." Therefore they answered,
"We do not know." Jesus replied, "Then neither will I tell you by
what authority I act as I do."
28 Now he asked, "What is your opinion of the following case?
A man had two sons. He went to the first and said, 'Son, go to work
29 in the vineyard to-day.' He answered, 'Yes, father, I will go,' but
30 he did not go. The father made the same request to the second son,
who answered, 'I do not wish to go;' but later he regretted his an-
31 swer and went. Which of the two did as his father wished?" They
answered, "The second." Then Jesus said to them, "Be assured that
the tax-collectors and the harlots will enter the spirit-world of God

32 before you. For John came to show you the way to God, and you
would not believe him. But the tax-collectors and harlots did believe
him. When you saw this you even became angry because those
people believed in him.
33 "Hear now another example: A householder planted a vineyard,
fenced it in, dug a wine-press, built a watch-tower, let his vineyard
out to grape-growers, and went abroad.
34 "At the approach of the picking season he sent his servants to the
35 tenants to receive, as agreed, his share of the harvest. But the
grape-growers seized the servants, maltreated one, killed another,
and stoned a third.
36 "Then he sent other servants, a greater number than at first, but
these met with the same treatment.
37 "At last he sent his son to them, for he said to himself, 'Surely
38 they will not dare to harm my son.' But no sooner did the grape-
growers see the son than they said to one another, 'This is the heir.
39 Come, let us kill him and seize his inheritance.' So they laid hold of
him, drove him out of the vineyard and killed him.
40 "Now, when the lord of the vineyard returns, what do you think
41 he will do to these grape-growers?" They answered, "He will treat
them as criminals and cause them to die a terrible death. But the
vineyard he will entrust to such as will deliver the fruits to him at
the required time as his share of the harvest."
42 Then Jesus continued, "Have you never read in the Scriptures:
'The stone that the builders rejected as unfit has become the corner-
stone. He was made this by the Lord, and in our eyes he is a divine
43 wonder'? And so I tell you, communication with God's spirit-
world will be taken from you and given to people who produce
fruit worthy of such communication."
45 When the chief priests and the Pharisees heard these parables
46 they knew only too well that it was they whom he meant. They
would therefore have liked to seize him, but they feared the people;
for the people took him to be a messenger of God.

CHAPTER 22.

1 There were still other parables in which Jesus spoke to them in
2 answer to their questions. Thus he said: "Taking part in communication with God's spirits is like the wedding-feast given by a king in
3 honor of his son. He sent out his servants to invite to the wedding
those whom he had chosen for his guests, but they did not care to
4 come. Then he again sent servants to tell the guests, 'The breakfast
is prepared. My steers and fat cattle have been slaughtered, and

5 everything is ready. Make haste to come to the wedding.' But they
disregarded the invitation, and each man went about his work, one
6 to his estate, another to his place of business. The rest seized his
7 servants, and abused and killed them. Then the king, greatly enraged, sent his soldiers and had these murderers put to death and
8 their city burned. After this he said to his servants, 'The wedding
feast is prepared, but those who were invited were unworthy of it.
9 Go now to the cross-roads and invite all whom you meet.' The
10 servants went out on the highways and brought every one whom they
found, high and low, and the banquet-hall was filled with guests."

15 The Pharisees now withdrew and consulted on the best manner of
16 trapping him with a question. At length they sent to him their
scholars, together with the adherents of Herod, and had them put
this question to him: "Master, we know that you are always truthful,
and that you teach the true way to God without regard to any one,
17 for you do not consider the high rank of men. Tell us therefore your
18 opinion: Should we pay the head-tax to Caesar or not?" Jesus saw
through their evil intentions and answered, "Why do you hypocrites
19 try to set a trap for me? Show me a piece of tax-money." They gave
20 him a denarius. "Whose likeness and inscription are these?" he
21 asked. "Caesar's," they replied. "Then," he continued, "pay to
Caesar what you owe him, and give to God what you owe to God!"
22 Abashed by this answer, they turned away and left him.

23 On the same day the Sadducees, who deny the resurrection, came
to him and tried to put him into a quandary by telling him the fol-
24 lowing story: "Master," they said, "Moses decreed that if a man
dies childless, his brother shall marry the widow, in order to assure
25 posterity to the deceased brother. Now there were among us seven
brothers. The first married, and died childless, and left his wife to
26 his brother. So too with the second and third, until at length all
27 seven had married her in turn. Last of all the woman died. To
28 which one of the seven will she belong in the resurrection? For she
29 had been married to them all." Jesus answered, "You are altogether
mistaken, because you know neither the Scriptures nor the laws of
30 God's creation. For in the resurrection no man need seek a wife, nor
any woman a husband. The same law operates in their case as in
31 the case of the spirits in heaven. But as regards the resurrection of
32 the dead, do you not remember what was spoken by God: 'I am the
God of Abraham, the God of Isaac, and the God of Jacob'? Surely
33 He is not a God of the dead, but of the living." When the masses of
the people heard this, they marvelled at his doctrine.

34 It came to the ears of the Pharisees that he had silenced the Sad-

35 ducees. Nevertheless, they again approached him, and one of them,
36 a jurist, put him to the test with the question, "Master, of all the
commandments, which do you hold to be especially important?"
37 Jesus answered him, "'You shall love the Lord your God with all
38 your heart, with all your soul, and with all your mind.' That is the
39 important commandment that comes first of all; but there is a
40 second equal to it: 'You shall love your neighbor as yourself.' In
these two commandments the whole doctrine of the Law and the
prophets is comprised."

41 One day when the Pharisees had again come to Jesus, he asked
42 them, "What is your opinion of the Messiah? Whose son is he?"
43 They answered, "David's."—"Then," continued Jesus, "how could
44 David, inspired by a holy spirit, call him 'lord,' saying: 'The Lord
said to my lord, "Sit at my right until I have put your foes beneath
45 your feet"'? If David calls the Messiah 'lord,' how then can the
46 Messiah be the son of David?" To this question not one of them
could find an answer.

CHAPTER 23.

1 One day Jesus addressed the people and his disciples in these
2 words: "The scribes and the Pharisees sit in the seat of Moses, but
you need not observe and accept as true everything that they teach;
3 still less need you imitate their deeds, for they themselves do not
4 live according to their own teachings. They bind together burdens
too heavy for any one to carry, and lay them on the people's shoulders; but they themselves are not willing even to lift a finger to
5 them. Whatever they do they do for the sake of being seen by the
people. That is why they wear their phylacteries very wide, and
6 the tassels of their mantles very long. At banquets they always like
to seek the foremost places, and in the synagogues the seats of honor.
7 They lay stress on being greeted by the people in public places, and
8 on being addressed by them as 'master.' But you must not let yourselves be addressed as 'master,' for but One is your Master, and you
9 are all brothers. And call no one on earth 'father,' for but One is
10 your Father, He who is in heaven. Nor let yourselves be called
11 'teacher,' for but One is your teacher—the Messiah. He who is
12 greatest among you shall be your servant, for whoever exalts himself will be humbled, and whoever humbles himself will be exalted.

13 "Woe to you, scribes and Pharisees, hypocrites that you are!
You close the door of God's spirit-world to men. You yourselves do
not enter; but you will not even let in those who would like to enter.

14 "Woe to you, scribes and Pharisees, hypocrites that you are!
Your greed devours the estates of widows in payment for the long
prayers which you profess to offer on their behalf. Because of such
a practice the sentence of your punishment shall be the harder.
15 "Woe to you, scribes and Pharisees, hypocrites that you are! You
travel by land and sea to make one convert, and when you have won
him, you make of him a child of hell, twice as vile as yourselves.
16 "Woe to you, blind guides that you are! How dare you contend
that he who swears by the temple to keep a promise is not bound
by his oath, while he who swears by the gold of the temple must
17 keep his word? You blind fools! Which is greater, the gold or
18 the temple by which that gold is sanctified? Again, how dare you
contend that an oath by the altar has no force, while an oath by the
19 gift lying on the altar is binding? You blind men! Which has a
20 higher value, the gift or the altar that sanctifies the gift? Whoever, then, swears by the altar, swears at the same time by all that
21 lies on it; whoever swears by the temple swears at the same time by
22 Him who lives therein, and whoever swears by heaven swears by
the throne of God and by Him who sits thereon.
23 "Woe to you, scribes and Pharisees, hypocrites that you are!
You pay the tithe on mint, dill, and anise, but you ignore the
weightier provisions of the Law: that men shall not judge unfairly,
that men shall show mercy, and that men shall have faith and confidence in God. The one should be observed without neglecting the
24 other. Blind guides that you are! You are careful to strain out gnats
through a sieve, but do not stop at swallowing camels.
25 "Woe to you, scribes and Pharisees, hypocrites that you are!
You do indeed keep clean the outside of the cup and the dish, but
26 within they are full of greed and immorality. Blind Pharisee! First
of all clean the inside of the cup; then its outside will also remain
clean.
27 "Woe to you, scribes and Pharisees, hypocrites that you are!
You are like whitewashed tombs. Outwardly a tomb appears beautiful in its adornment of flowers, but within it is filled with dead
28 men's bones and corruption. So you also appear to men to be outwardly God-fearing; but inwardly you are filled with hypocrisy and
godlessness.
29 "Woe to you, scribes and Pharisees, hypocrites that you are!
You build monuments over the graves of the prophets and adorn
30 the tombstones of God's faithful. And you do not weary of saying,
'Had we lived in the days of our forefathers, we should not, like
31 them, have been guilty of the blood of God's messengers.' Thereby

you at least admit that you are the sons of those who murdered God's
32 messengers. Nor are you any better than they. So fill up the
33 measure of your father's guilt! You snakes! You brood of adders!
How do you think to escape the judgment that will condemn you to
34 hell? For mark! I shall send you messengers and sages and
teachers; some of them you will kill and crucify, others you will
35 flog in your synagogues and persecute from city to city. So will all
the innocent blood shed on earth, from the blood of Abel to the blood
of Zechariah, the son of Barachiah, whom you murdered between
36 the temple and the altar, be upon your heads. Be assured that all
37 these things will be avenged upon this nation. Jerusalem, Jerusalem! You that murder the prophets and stone those who are sent
to you! How often have I tried to gather your children about me
38 as a hen gathers her chicks; but you would not have it so. And so
39 your dwellings in heaven must remain empty. For I tell you that
from now on you will not see me again until the day on which you
say, 'Blessed is he who comes in the name of the Lord!' "

CHAPTER 24.

1 One day Jesus wandered out into the open country. From the
path he had taken the temple was visible in the distance, and his
2 disciples called his attention to its beauty. Jesus answered them,
"To-day you look upon it with wonder; but I say to you that not
one stone will be left upon another; everything will be demolished."
3 Then he sat down upon the Mount of Olives, and when his
disciples were alone with him they begged of him, "Tell us, when
will these things happen? And what will be the sign of your return
4 and of the end of this age?" Jesus answered, "Take care to let no
5 one mislead you in this matter; for many will come in my name,
6 saying, 'I am the Messiah,' and they will mislead many. And you
will hear of wars and rumors of wars; but do not be alarmed, for
such things must happen from time to time, and they do not signify
7 that the end has come. Nation will rise against nation, and kingdom
against kingdom. There will be plagues and famines and earth-
8 quakes, now in one place, now in another. All this will be but the
9 beginning of the sufferings. Then men will inflict great hardships
on you and kill you, and you will be hated by all unbelievers for
10 my name's sake. Many will turn their backs on the truth and will
11 betray and spitefully persecute one another. So too, instruments of
the evil spirit-world will appear in great numbers and mislead many.
12 And because ungodliness will gain the upper hand, the love of the
13 majority of the people will grow cold; but he who endures to the

14 end will be saved. And this gospel of the kingdom of God will be
preached throughout the universe, so that all unbelievers may learn
to know the truth, and then the end will come for this nation.
15 "And so when you see in the holy place the horror of desecration foretold by Daniel the prophet — and let every one who can
16 read consult this passage — then shall all in Judaea flee to the hills.
17 Let him who is then on the roof not go down to take any of his be-
18 longings out of the house, nor let him who is in the field go back to
19 get his clothes. But woe to the women with child and to those with
20 babes at the breast. Pray that your flight may not be in winter or on
21 the Sabbath. For this will be the beginning of a time of great tribulation, such as has never been from the beginning of the world, nor
22 shall ever be again thereafter. And were it not that these days will
be shortened, no man could be saved; but for the sake of the elect,
23 the number of these days will be lessened. And should any one then
say to you, 'Look, here is the Messiah,' or, 'That is he,' do not be-
24 lieve it. For there will arise false Messiahs and false prophets, and
they will work great signs and miracles to lead even the elect astray
wherever possible.
25 "Remember, I have told you this beforehand.
26 "Should they tell you then that the Messiah is in the desert, do
not go there; should they declare that he is in this house or another,
27 do not believe it. For such will not be the manner of Christ's return; rather will it be like lightning flashing in the east and throw-
28 ing its gleam into the western sky. — Where dead bodies lie, there
will the vultures gather.
29 "Immediately after this time of affliction the sun will grow dark
for the victims, and the moon will lose its brightness; for them the
light of the stars in the sky will disappear, and the powers of the
30 low spheres of the beyond will tremble in terror. For then will the
sign of the Son of man appear in the beyond, and all spirits of the
earthly spheres will lament. They will see the Son of man coming at
31 the head of his heavenly hosts with great might and glory. He will
send out his spirit-messengers to the sound of trumpets, and they
will gather from the four winds, from one end of the beyond to the
other, those whom he has designated.
32 "May that which you see in the fig tree serve as a lesson to you.
When the sap rises in its branches and bursts into leaf you know
33 that summer is near. So too when you see that which I have just
told, you may at once know that the fulfillment is close at hand.
34 "I tell you, this nation will not pass away until all this has been
35 fulfilled. The sky and earth will pass away, but my words will

36 never pass away unfulfilled. The day and the hour of fulfillment
are known to no one, neither to the angels of heaven nor to the
Son, but to my Father alone.
37 "As it was in the days of Noah, so will it be at the time of the re-
38 turn of the Son of man. Before the days of the flood, the people
gave themselves over to eating and drinking, men seeking intercourse with women, and women with men, until the hour at which
39 Noah went into the ark. They were aware of nothing until the flood
came and swept all away. So too will it be each time that the Son
40 of man returns. Two men will be working in the field; one will be
41 taken and the other left. Two women will be grinding at the mill;
42 one will be taken and the other left. Be watchful, therefore, for you
43 do not know the day on which your lord will come. But so much
will be clear to you: if the householder knew at what hour of the
night the thief would come, he would stay awake and find means of
44 keeping his house from being entered. And so be ready yourselves!
For the Son of man will come at an hour at which you do not
expect him.
45 "Who, then, is the wise and faithful servant whom his master put
in charge of the household to deal out to each his due allowance?
46 Fortunate is that servant whom the master on his return finds at his
47 allotted task! I tell you, he will put him in charge of all his posses-
48 sions. But if the servant is of the base kind, he will think in his
49 heart, 'My master will be a long time coming,' and begin to abuse
50 his fellow-servants and to feast and to carouse with drunkards. Then
that servant's master will come on a day on which he did not expect
51 him and at an unforeseen hour, and will have the servant cut to
pieces and put where he belongs, among the hypocrites; and there
will be loud wailing and gnashing of teeth.

CHAPTER 25.

1 "In the selection of those who may enter into communication with
God's spirit-world it will be as it was with the ten bridesmaids who
2 took their lamps and went out to meet the bridal pair. Five of them
3 proved to be careless, and five prudent. For although the careless
4 ones took their lamps, they took with them no oil; the prudent ones,
however, took oil in vessels in addition to the lamps.
5 "As the arrival of the bridal pair was delayed, they all grew tired
6 from their long wait, and fell asleep. At midnight the cry was suddenly heard, 'The bridegroom has arrived! Come out quickly to meet
7 him!' Then all the young women rose and trimmed their lamps;
8 and the careless ones said to the prudent, 'Please give us some of

9 your oil, for our lamps are about to go out.' But the prudent ones
answered, 'That will not do, for the oil would not be enough for us
and for you also. You had better go to the shopkeeper and buy what
10 you need.' And while they went to buy oil, the bridegroom came.
The bridesmaids who were ready to greet him went with him to the
11 wedding, and the doors of the hall were immediately shut. Later the
other bridesmaids also came and cried, 'Lord, lord, open the door
12 to us!' But he answered, 'I do not know you.'—Therefore be on
13 your watch, for you do not know the day and the hour when the Son
of man will come.

14 "A man who was setting out on a journey summoned his servants
15 to him and put his property under their care. One servant was given
five thousand dollars; another, two thousand, and another one thousand, each according to his personal ability. Then he left.

16 "The man who had received five thousand dollars immediately
began to trade with the money and made a profit of another five
17 thousand dollars. He who had received two thousand dollars like-
18 wise gained another two thousand. He who had received the one
thousand dollars dug a hole in the ground and put his master's
money in it.

19 "Long afterwards the master returned, and settled with his
20 servants. The first in turn was he who had received the five thousand
dollars. He brought this together with the other five thousand, and
said, 'Master, you entrusted me with five thousand dollars, and I
21 have made five thousand more.' His master then said to him, 'Well
done, good and faithful servant! You have shown yourself trustworthy in small matters; therefore I will put you in charge of great
ones. Come and share the happiness of your master.'

22 "Then he who had received the two thousand dollars came forward and said, 'Master, you entrusted me with two thousand dol-
23 lars. Here I have made two thousand more.' His master said to him
also, 'Well done, good and faithful servant! You too have shown
yourself trustworthy in small matters; therefore I will put you in
charge of great ones. Come and share the happiness of your master.'

24 "The last to come forward was he with the one thousand dollars.
He said, 'Master, I knew you to be a hard man, who hopes to reap
where he has not sown, and to gather where he has not strewed.
25 And so I was afraid, and I buried your thousand dollars in the
26 ground. Here is your money back again.' His master answered,
'Worthless and lazy servant that you are! Then you knew that I
hope to reap where I do not sow, and to gather where I do not

27 strew? Ought you not, in that case, to have deposited my money in
the banks, so that I should at least have had my interest on it when
28 I came back? Therefore take the one thousand dollars away from
29 him and give it to the one who has the ten thousand dollars.' For
to him who has achieved much, more shall be given, so that he may
have in abundance; but from him who has achieved nothing, even
30 that which he had at first shall be taken. And as for the useless
servant, throw him out into the darkness, where there will be wailing and gnashing of teeth.

31 "Each time that the Son of man comes in his glory, and all the
hosts of spirits with him, he will seat himself on the throne of his
32 power. All sorts of spirits will be gathered before him, and he will
separate them as a shepherd separates the sheep from the goats.
33 He will place the sheep on his right hand, and on his left hand the
34 goats. Then to those on his right hand the King will say, 'Come, all
of you who have the blessing of my Father, and receive as your heritage the kingdom that has been held in readiness for you since the
35 foundation of the universe. For I was hungry, and you gave me
food; I was thirsty, and you gave me drink; I was a stranger, and
36 you gave me shelter; I was naked, and you clothed me; I was sick,
and you visited me; I was in prison, and you came to me.'

37 "Then the godly will answer him, 'Lord, when did we see you
38 hungry and give you food? or thirsty and give you drink? When
did we see you as a stranger and give you shelter? Or when did we
39 see you naked and cover your nakedness? Or when did we see you
sick or in prison and go to you?'

40 "Then the King will answer them, 'Everything that you have done
for the least of these brothers of mine, you have done for me.'

41 "And to those on his left hand he will say, 'Begone from me,
accursed that you are, into the fire of suffering that lasts through
undesignated periods of time and is ordained by my Father for the
42 devil and his spirits. For I was hungry, and you gave me no food;
43 I was thirsty, and you gave me no drink; I was a stranger, and found
no shelter with you; I was naked, and you did not cover my nakedness; I was sick and lay in prison, and you did not come to visit me.'

44 "Then these also will answer him, 'Lord, when did we see you
hungry, or thirsty, or as a stranger, or naked, or sick, or in prison,
and did not minister to your needs?'

45 "And he will answer them, 'Everything that you have failed to do
46 to one of the least of these, you have failed to do to me.' Then they
will begin to serve a new period of suffering; but God's faithful
will enter upon their heavenly life."

CHAPTER 26.

1 When Jesus had finished these instructions, he turned to his dis-
2 ciples. "You know," he said to them, "that the feast of the Passover
falls on the day after to-morrow. It is then that the Son of man will
3 be handed over to be crucified." At this very time the chief priests
and elders were meeting in the palace of the high priest, Caiaphas,
4 to lay plans for seizing Jesus by trickery, in order to kill him. All
5 agreed that this could not be done during the feast of the Passover,
since it might cause a riot among the people.

6 Jesus had gone into the house of Simon the leper in Bethany, and
7 while he was reclining at table there, a woman came in to him
bearing an alabaster jar of precious ointment, which she poured
upon his head.

8 When the disciples saw this they were indignant, for they thought,
9 "Why such waste? This ointment might have been sold at a good
price, and the money given to the poor."

10 Observing their frame of mind, Jesus asked them, "Why do you
11 find fault with this woman? She has done me a good service. For the
12 poor you will have with you always, but me you will not. With this
ointment that she has poured on my body, she thought to anoint me
13 for burial. Be assured that throughout the whole world, wherever
the gospel is preached, men will also tell what this woman did and
thus honor her memory."

14 Judas Iscariot, one of the Twelve, now went to the chief priests
15 and asked them, "What will you pay me for delivering him into
16 your hands?" They weighed out to him thirty pieces of silver, and
from that hour he sought a favorable opportunity to betray Jesus.

17 On the first day of the unleavened bread the disciples went to
Jesus and asked him, "Where shall we prepare the feast of the
18 Passover for you?" He told them, "Go into the city to a certain
man, and say to him, 'The Master sends you word: My time is at
hand. I will keep the Passover at your house with my disciples.' "
19 The disciples did as Jesus had directed, and prepared the Passover.

20 When evening had come, he reclined at table with his twelve.
21 During the course of the meal he suddenly exclaimed, "One of you
22 is going to betray me." At this they asked him in consternation,
23 one after another, "Master, surely it is not I?" He answered, "He
24 who dipped his hand into the dish with me will be my betrayer. The
Son of man will indeed travel the path of his destiny, as it is written in the Scriptures, but woe to him by whom the Son of man is

betrayed! It would be better for him if he had never been born."
25 Then Judas, his betrayer, also asked him, "Master, surely it is not
I?" Jesus answered, "Yes, it is you."
26 During the meal, Jesus took bread, offered a prayer, and breaking the bread, gave it to his disciples with the words, "Take and eat
27 this. It is the symbol of my body." Then he took a cup, gave thanks,
28 and passed it to the disciples, saying, "Drink of it, all of you. For
this is the symbol of my blood, the blood of the new covenant, to be
shed on behalf of the many, for the forgiveness of the sins of apos-
29 tasy. But I tell you that I shall not again drink of the fruit of the
vine until the day on which I drink of it in my Father's kingdom in
a form unknown to you."
30 They now joined in a hymn of praise, left the room, and went to
31 the Mount of Olives. On the way Jesus said to them, "This night
you will fall away from me, for it is written: 'I will smite the shep-
32 herd, and then the sheep of the flock will be scattered.' But after
33 my resurrection I will go before you into Galilee." To this Peter
answered, "All the rest may fall away from you, but I never!"—
34 "I tell you," replied Jesus, "that this very night, before the cock
35 crows, you will disown me three times." Peter answered, "Though
I must die with you, I shall never disown you." The other disciples
all gave him the same assurance.
36 Accompanied by them Jesus now reached a place called Gethsemane, and said to his disciples, "Sit here, while I go over yonder to
pray."
37 He took with him only Peter and the two sons of Zebedee. Over-
38 come by a feeling of deepest despondency and loneliness, he turned
to them with the words, "I am so unutterably sad at heart that I
wish I were dead. Do stay by my side and watch with me."
39 Then walking a little farther he fell on his face and prayed, "My
Father, if it be possible let this cup pass from me; yet be it not as
40 I will, but as Thou wilt." Then going back to the three disciples,
he found that they had fallen asleep. He said to Peter, "So you had
not even strength enough to keep watch with me for just one hour?
41 Be on your guard and pray, that you may not fall in the time of
temptation. The spirit is indeed willing, but the flesh is weak."
42 A second time he went out and prayed, "My father, if this cup
may not pass from me without my drinking it, let Thy will be done."
43 On coming back he found the disciples asleep again, for their eyes
44 had fallen shut from weariness. Without waking them he went back
45 and offered the same prayer as before. Then he went to the disciples
and said, "Another time you may sleep and rest, but now the hour

has come for the Son of man to be delivered into the hands of the
46 apostates. Rise and let us go. See, my betrayer is already close at
hand."
47 While he was still speaking, Judas, one of the Twelve, suddenly
came upon them accompanied by a great mob armed with swords
and clubs, by order of the chief priests and elders of the people.
48 His betrayer had agreed upon this signal with them: "He whom I
49 shall kiss is the man. Seize him." Going up quickly to Jesus, there-
50 fore, he kissed him and exclaimed, "Greetings, Master!"—"Friend,"
answered Jesus, "what are you here for?" Then they came nearer
and laid hands on Jesus and arrested him.
51 One of the followers of Jesus drew his sword and struck at the
52 high priest's servant, cutting off his ear; but Jesus said to him, "Put
up your sword; for he who wields the sword shall die by the sword.
53 Do you think that if I should pray to my Father now, He would
54 not send me more than twelve legions of angels? But how then
could the words of the Scriptures be fulfilled, according to which
all this must happen?"
55 Then Jesus turned to the crowd and said, "You have come
here armed with swords and clubs to take me as you would take a
robber. Yet every day I sat in the temple and taught, and you did
56 not seize me. But all this has happened as it did in order that the
Scriptures might be fulfilled."
At this all the disciples forsook him and fled.
57 Those who had seized Jesus led him to the high priest Caiaphas,
58 around whom the scribes and the elders had gathered. Peter followed him at a distance as far as the palace of the high priest, went
inside, and sat down there among the servants to await the outcome.
59 The chief priests and all the Council tried to secure false testi-
60 mony on which they could sentence Jesus to death, but found none,
even though many false witnesses appeared. At length two men
61 came and testified, "This man has declared, 'I can tear down the
temple of God, and rebuild it in three days.'"
62 On hearing this, the high priest rose and asked him, "Have you
nothing to answer to the testimony of these witnesses?" But Jesus
63 remained silent. Then the high priest addressed him, saying, "Under oath, by the living God, tell us whether you are the Messiah,
64 the Son of God." And Jesus answered, "Yes, I am he. And I hereby solemnly state that hereafter you will see the Son of man sitting at the right hand of the Almighty, and coming at the head of
65 the spirit-hosts of heaven." Then the high priest tore his robes, exclaiming, "He has uttered blasphemy! What further need have we

of witnesses? You yourselves have all heard his blasphemy. What
66 is your verdict?" They replied, "He deserves the death-sentence."
67 Then they spat in his face and struck him with their fists. Others
68 slapped him and taunted him, saying, "Show your prophetic powers, you Messiah! Name him who struck you!"

69 Meanwhile Peter was sitting in the courtyard, and a maid went up
70 to him and said, "You were also with Jesus the Galilean." But he
denied it before all, and said, "I do not understand how you can
71 say such a thing." Then he went out into the vestibule, and there
another maid saw him and pointed him out to the bystanders, say-
72 ing, "This fellow was with Jesus of Nazareth." But he denied it
73 again, and said with an oath, "I do not know that man." After a
while the people about him drew close to Peter and said, "Surely
you are one of his followers. Why, the very way you speak betrays
74 you." At that he began to curse himself and swear, "I do not know
75 the man." A moment later a cock crowed. Then Peter remembered
that Jesus had said to him, "Before the cock crows, you will disown
me three times."

CHAPTER 27.

1 At daybreak all the chief priests and elders of the people formu-
lated the charge against Jesus in order to carry out the death-sen-
2 tence. Then they had him bound and led away and handed him over
to the governor, Pontius Pilate.

3 When the traitor Judas learned that Jesus had been condemned
to death, he felt remorse for his act. He then took the thirty pieces
4 of silver back to the chief priests and the elders, and confessed, "I
sinned when I betrayed innocent blood." But they answered, "How
5 does that concern us? It is your affair." At this he threw the silver
upon the temple floor, ran away out of the city, and hanged himself.

6 The chief priests took up the pieces of silver saying, "It is unlawful to put these into the temple treasury, for this is blood-money."
7 Accordingly, they resolved to use the money to buy a potter's field
8 in which to bury strangers, for which reason that piece of ground
received the name of "The Field of Blood," which it still bears.
9 This was in fulfillment of the words of Jeremiah the prophet: "And
they took thirty pieces of silver, the price of him whose price had
10 been set thereat by the children of Israel, and gave them for the
potter's field, as the Lord had designated."

11 Jesus was now taken before the governor, who asked him, "Are
12 you the king of the Jews?" Jesus answered, "Yes, I am he." But to

the charges of the chief priests and the elders he made no answer.
13 Then Pilate asked him, "Do you not hear all these charges they are
14 bringing against you?" But to the governor's great astonishment,
Jesus did not answer a single one of even his questions.
15 Now it was the custom at festivals for the governor to set free
16 one prisoner whom the people might select. At this time there was
17 in confinement a notorious criminal named Barabbas. Pilate therefore asked the throng, "Whom shall I release to you, Barabbas, or
18 Jesus, the alleged Messiah?" For he knew that Jesus had been
delivered to him only out of envy.
19 While Pilate was still sitting on the judge's bench, his wife sent a
messenger to him to say, "By no means have anything to do with
that God-fearing man, for I suffered severely last night in my dreams
on his account."
20 In the meantime the chief priests and the elders incited the people
to demand that Barabbas be released and Jesus put to death.
21 When the governor asked them once more, "Which of the two
22 shall I set free?" they cried out, "Barabbas." Then Pilate continued,
"What shall I do then with Jesus, the alleged Messiah?" To this
23 all answered, "Let him be crucified!" Then Pilate asked, "What
crime has he committed?" But they shouted all the louder, "Let
him be crucified!"
24 When Pilate saw that he could accomplish nothing, but that the
uproar was increasing, he called for some water and washed his
hands in the sight of the people, saying, "I am innocent of the blood
25 of this righteous man. Do as you like." The people, as one man,
answered, "Let his blood be upon us and our children!"
26 Pilate then released Barabbas, but Jesus he struck with a scourge
to signify that he was condemned to death, and delivered to be
crucified.
27 The governor's soldiers took Jesus with them to the barracks and
28 assembled the whole detachment around him. They stripped him of
29 his clothes and dressed him in a purple robe, wove a crown of
thorns which they set on his head, and placed a stick in his right
hand. Then they knelt down before him and taunted him, "Hail,
30 king of the Jews!" Then they spat in his face, and taking the stick
31 from him, struck him over the head with it. After subjecting him to
these insults, they took off the robe and dressed him again in his
own clothes. Later they led him away to the crucifixion.
32 On the way they met a man from Cyrene, Simon by name, whom
33 they forced to carry the cross for Jesus. So they reached the place
34 called Golgotha, meaning, "the place of the skulls." There they

offered him wine mixed with gall, but after he had tasted of it, he
35 would not drink it. Then they crucified him and divided his gar-
36 ments among them by lot, and afterward sat down by him to keep
watch.

37 Above his head some one had placed an inscription purporting
to give the grounds on which he was put to death. It read: *This is*
Jesus, the King of the Jews.

38 Together with him two robbers were crucified, one on his right
hand and one on his left.

39 The passersby reviled him, and some, wagging their heads, called
40 out, "And you are the one who wanted to pull down the temple and
rebuild it in three days! Now save yourself! If you are a son of
God, come down from the cross."

41 In like manner the chief priests, the scribes, and the elders said
42 tauntingly, "He helped others, but cannot help himself! He, the
king of Israel! Let him come down from the cross now; then we too
43 will believe in him. He trusted in God; let God deliver him now if
He is well pleased with him. For he said — did he not? — 'I am a
44 son of God.'" And the robbers who were crucified with him also
abused him in the same manner.

45 Beginning at noon darkness fell upon the whole land and lasted
46 until three o'clock in the afternoon. At that hour Jesus cried out in
a loud voice, "Eli, Eli, lama sabachthani?" that is to say, "My God,
47 my God, why hast Thou forsaken me?" When some of the by-
48 standers heard this, they said, "He is calling upon Elijah," and one
of them, running up at once, took a sponge which he soaked in
49 vinegar, fastened to a pole, and offered to Jesus to drink. But the
others said, "Let be! We will see whether Elijah will really come to
50 save him." But Jesus cried out once more in a loud voice, and gave
up his spirit.

51 At that moment the curtain in the temple was torn in two from
top to bottom, the earth quaked, and the rocks were shattered.
52 Tombs were laid open, and many bodies of those buried there were
53 tossed upright. In this posture they projected from the graves and
were seen by many who passed by the place on their way back to
the city.

54 When the centurion and his men who were standing guard over
Jesus, saw the earthquake and the other happenings, they were terri-
fied and felt constrained to acknowledge, "This is truly the son of
a god."

55 Many women were looking on from a distance. They had followed Jesus out of Galilee and had dedicated themselves to his ser-

56 vice. Among them were Mary Magdalene, and Mary the mother of
James and Joseph, as well as the mother of Zebedee's sons.
57 Late in the afternoon came a rich man from Arimathaea, named
58 Joseph, who had also been a disciple of Jesus, and went to Pilate
and requested of him the body of Jesus. Pilate directed that it be
59 delivered to him. Taking the body, Joseph wrapped it in fresh linen
60 and laid it in the new tomb that he had ordered to be hewn for
himself out of rock. Then he had a large stone rolled before the
61 entrance to the tomb, and went away. Mary of Magdala and the
other Mary were present while this was done, and sat opposite to
the tomb.
62 On the next day, which follows the day of preparation for the
Sabbath, the chief priests and the Pharisees went together to Pilate,
63 and said, "Sir, we remember that while he was alive this impostor
64 asserted that he would rise again after three days. Direct, therefore, that the grave be well guarded until the third day, so that
his disciples do not come and steal the body and say to the people
that he has risen from the dead. In that case the latter fraud would
65 be worse than the first." Pilate answered them, "You shall have a
66 guard. Go and make it as secure as you can." So they went and
placed a seal on the stone and made the tomb secure with the aid of
a guard.

CHAPTER 28.

1 After the Sabbath was over, at the dawn of the first day following,
Mary of Magdala and the other Mary went out to visit the grave.
2 The earth suddenly began to quake violently, for an angel of the
Lord who had come down from heaven and drawn near, rolled
3 away the stone and seated himself upon it. His appearance was
4 radiant as a lightning-flash and his robe as white as snow. Overcome
with fear of him the guards trembled and fell down as though dead;
5 but the angel spoke to the women, saying, "You need have no fear.
6 I know that you have come to seek Jesus who was crucified. He is
not here. He has risen, as he foretold. Come nearer and see the
7 place where the lord has lain. Then go quickly and tell the disciples
that he has risen from the dead and will go before you into Galilee.
It is there that you will see him. Mark well what I have told you."
8 Fearing yet rejoicing, they hurried from the grave to carry the
9 message to the disciples. On their way Jesus met them and said to
them, "Greetings to you." They went up to him and kneeling before
10 him, embraced his knees; and Jesus said, "Go and tell my brothers
to go into Galilee, for there they will see me again."

11 In the meantime some of the tomb-guards arrived in the city and
12 reported to the chief priests everything that had happened. The
priests summoned the elders and conferred with them. As a result
13 it was decided to distribute money freely among the soldiers and to
instruct them, "Spread this story: 'His disciples came during the
14 night while we were asleep and stole his body.' And if the story
should come to the ears of the governor, we will satisfy him and
15 arrange it so that you will have nothing to fear." They took the
money and did as they had been instructed; and this is the story that
is current among the Jews to this very day.
16 The eleven disciples went into Galilee to the mountain to which
17 Jesus had directed them. When they saw him they fell down before
18 him. Some of them, however, were in doubt. But Jesus, drawing
nearer, spoke to them and said, "All power has been given to me in
19 the beyond and on earth. Go, therefore, and make all unbelievers
my disciples, baptizing them by immersion as a symbol of their faith
20 in the Father and in the Son and in the holy spirit-world. And teach
them to observe all the commandments that I gave to you. You
have my solemn promise: 'I will be with you always, until the end
of the ages.' "

The Gospel according to
MARK

CHAPTER 1.

1 I BEGIN the gospel of Jesus the Messiah, the Son of God, with the
2 words written by the prophet Isaiah: "See, I send my messenger
3 before you. He shall prepare the way for you. His voice resounds
in the barren mountain-country, calling, 'Prepare the way for the
lord's coming! Make even the paths leading back to our God!'"
4 This messenger was John. He baptized among the poor people
in the mountains, and in his preaching he pointed out that the immersion in water symbolized a change of heart whereby they ob-
5 tained deliverance from the sin of apostasy. From all Judaea and
Jerusalem the people flocked out to him and were baptized by immersion in the River Jordan, in public testimony of their faith in his
teachings and in acknowledgment of their sins.
6 John wore a garment of camel's hair and a leather belt around
7 his waist, and lived on locusts and wild honey. In his sermons he
proclaimed, "After me will come one who has a higher power than
I. In comparison to him I am not even worthy to stoop and untie
8 his sandals. I have only immersed you in waves of water; but he
will immerse you in the power-waves of a holy spirit."
9 One day Jesus also came to John from Nazareth in Galilee and
10 received baptism from him by immersion in the Jordan. At the instant that he stepped from the water he saw the heavens open and
11 the Spirit of God descending upon him in the form of a dove, and
heard a voice from above calling, "You are my beloved son; with
you I was well pleased."
12 The Spirit of God immediately aroused in him the irresistible
13 desire to go into the wilderness. There he remained for forty days
and during this time was exposed to the temptations of Satan. He
was surrounded by wild beasts; but God's angels also came, and
they befriended him.
14 After John had been imprisoned, Jesus came to Galilee and
preached the gospel of the coming of God's spirit-world. The sub-
15 stance of his preaching was this: "The periods of time provided by
God have now come to a close, and communication with God's spirit-
world is within reach. Change your hearts and accept these glad
tidings with faith."

16 One day when Jesus was walking by the shore of the Lake of
Galilee, he saw Simon and his brother Andrew throwing out their
17 nets; for they were fishermen. He said to them, "Come with me!
18 I will make you fishers of men." They immediately left everything
19 and went with him. After he had gone a little farther he saw James,
the son of Zebedee, and his brother John. They were also sitting
20 in a boat, mending their nets. Immediately he called them to him,
and they left their father Zebedee in the boat with the hired men,
and followed him.

21 They went to Capernaum, and on the first Sabbath after their
22 arrival he entered the synagogue and taught. The people were deeply
impressed by his sermon, for he spoke like one invested with a
higher authority, and not at all like the scribes.

23 There happened to be present in the synagogue a man who was
24 possessed by an evil spirit, which suddenly cried out, "What is it
that you want of us, Jesus of Nazareth? Have you come to destroy
us? I recognize you, I know who you are—the Holy One of
25 God!" Jesus sternly ordered him, "Be silent, and leave him!" and
26 the evil spirit, after tossing the man to and fro, went out of him with
27 a loud cry. All were amazed, and asked one another, "What is this?
A new sort of preaching in which a higher power is active! He
28 commands even demons, and they must obey him." His reputation
quickly spread throughout the whole surrounding region of Galilee.

29 Leaving the synagogue he went straight to the house of Simon
30 and Andrew, with James and John accompanying him. Simon's
mother-in-law was in bed, sick with a fever. This was at once made
31 known to Jesus, and he went to her and laid his hand upon her.
Through his healing power she was cured, so that the fever instantly
left her, and she set about waiting on them.

32 When the sun had gone down and dusk had set in, all the sick
33 and possessed were brought to him. The whole town had gathered
34 before the house, and every one was crowding about the door. He
healed many who were suffering from diseases of the most various
kinds, and drove out many evil spirits. But he did not allow the evil
spirits to make it known that they recognized him as the Messiah.

35 Very early in the morning, when it was still quite dark, he rose,
36 left the house, and went to a secluded place to pray. Simon and his
37 companions hurried after him to look for him, and when they found
38 him they said to him, "Every one is asking for you." He answered,
"Let us go to the nearby villages and towns, for I wish to preach
there also. That is why I went away this morning."

39 So he went about through all Galilee, preaching in the synagogues and driving demons out of the possessed.

40 It was at this time that a leper came to him with the entreaty,
"Oh, if you were only willing to cleanse me! For you have the
41 power to do so." Moved by an irresistible impulse, Jesus stretched
42 out his hand, touched him, and said, "I am willing. Be clean!" In-
43 stantly the leprosy vanished, and the man was clean. Following the
44 same impulse, Jesus urged him to go away at once, and directed
him, "Tell no one anything of this, but go quickly, show yourself to
the priest, and make the offering for your purification prescribed
45 by Moses as evidence of cleansing from leprosy." But no sooner
had the man left than he began to tell the story at length and to
spread it everywhere. For this reason Jesus could no longer enter
any town by daylight, but was obliged to remain outside in the less
frequented places; and even there the people flocked to him from
all sides.

CHAPTER 2.

1 After some time he returned to Capernaum, where his home-
2 coming was quickly noised about. Immediately there gathered such
a press of people that even the space before the door was not large
3 enough to hold them. While he was preaching God's word to them,
4 a group of people brought a paralytic to him. Four men carried him
in a litter, but because of the crowd they could not make their way
to Jesus. They therefore uncovered the roof above the place where
Jesus sat and lowered through the opening the litter in which the
5 sick man lay. When Jesus saw their confident faith he said to the
sick man, "Son, your sins shall be taken from you!"

6 It happened that several scribes were sitting near by, and these
7 thought to themselves, "How can that man talk so? What he says
is blasphemy! For who but One — and that is God — can take away
8 sins?" Through the spirit in attendance upon him Jesus at once
knew that they were entertaining these thoughts, and so he asked
9 them, "Why do you harbor such thoughts in your hearts? Which is
easier to say to the sick man, 'Your sins shall be taken away' or
10 'Rise, take up your bed and go home'? But you shall see now that
the Son of man does have authority to take away sins on earth."
11 Then he said to the sick man, "Rise, take up your bed and go home!"
12 The man stood up, at once picked up his bed, and went out in full
sight of every one. All were lost in amazement and praised God,
saying, "Nothing like this was ever seen before."

13 Then he walked along the shore of the lake, followed by the great
14 throng of people, to whom he delivered an address. On going a little
farther he saw James, the son of Alphaeus, sitting in the toll-booth,
and said to him, "Come with me!" And he instantly rose and went
15 with him. Jesus partook of a meal in his house, where many tax-
collectors and others of evil reputation were with Jesus and his disciples at table; for there were a great many of them among his fol-
16 lowers. When the scribes and the Pharisees saw him eating in the
company of tax-collectors and notorious sinners, they turned to his
disciples and asked them, "Why is it that he eats and drinks with
17 tax-collectors and notorious sinners?" Overhearing the question,
Jesus answered, "It is not the healthy who need a physician, but the
sick. I have not come to call back to God His faithful ones but
those estranged from Him."
18 Just at this time the disciples of John and those of the Pharisees
were keeping a day of fasting, and certain persons came to Jesus
and asked him, "Why is it that the disciples of John and those of the
19 Pharisees fast, while your disciples do not?" To this Jesus answered,
"The wedding-guests cannot be expected to fast while the bride-
20 groom is among them. But the time will come when the bridegroom
is taken from them, and then they will have their share of fasting.
21 No one sews a piece of new cloth on an old garment, else the new
patch will tear loose again from the old garment, leaving the rent
22 worse than before. Neither does any one put new wine into old
skins, for the wine would burst the skins, and both the wine and the
skins would be lost."
23 One day — it was on a Sabbath — Jesus was walking through
some grain-fields, and his disciples began to pick the ears in pass-
24 ing. Seeing this the Pharisees said to him, "Why do they do what is
25 unlawful on the Sabbath?" He answered, "Have you never read
what David did when he had nothing to eat, and he and his com-
26 panions were hungry? He went into the house of God and ate the
shew-bread, which only the priests were allowed to eat, and gave
27 some of it to his followers also. I tell you, the Son is lord both of
man and of the Sabbath."

CHAPTER 3.

1 On another occasion Jesus came into a synagogue and found
2 there a man with a totally withered arm. His enemies watched intently to see whether he would heal him in spite of the Sabbath, so
3 that they might bring charges against him on these grounds. Turning to the man with the withered arm he said, "Rise, and stand here

4 in the midst of the congregation." Then he put the question to them,
"May one do good on the Sabbath, or should one do evil? May one
5 save life, or should one destroy it?" No one answered. Looking
around at them one after another in deep emotion, pained to find
their hearts as withered as the man's arm, he said to him, "Stretch
6 out your arm." He did so, and his arm was sound again. The Pharisees immediately left and consulted with the followers of Herod as
to how they might put him out of the way.

7 Together with his disciples Jesus withdrew to the lake, followed
8 by a great throng of people from Galilee. Crowds also flocked to
him from Judaea and Jerusalem, from Idumaea, and from the region
east of the Jordan, as well as from Tyre and Sidon, for they had
9 heard what he was doing. On account of the press of people Jesus
ordered his disciples to have a boat in readiness for him at all
10 times, to enable him to withdraw from the throng. For because of
the many whom he had cured, every one who suffered from an ailment of any sort endeavored to get near enough to touch him.
11 Whenever the evil spirits saw him, those by whom they were possessed fell down before him and cried aloud, "You are the Son of
12 God!" But each time he strictly forbade them to make known the
full significance of his identity.

13 Then he went up on a mountain and called to him those whom he
14 had chosen for himself, and they went to him. There were twelve
whom he designated as his constant companions, and these he in-
15 tended to send out to preach the gospel. They were also to be invested with power to heal disease and to drive out demons from the
16 possessed. The names of these twelve were: Simon, to whom he gave
17 the name of Peter; James, the son of Zebedee, and John, the brother
of James (the last two he named Boanerges, that is, Sons of Thun-
18 der); Andrew, Philip, Bartholomew, Matthew, Thomas, James the
19 son of Alphaeus, Thaddaeus, Simon the Canaanite, and Judas
Iscariot, who betrayed him.

20 When he returned home, there again gathered so large a crowd
that they did not even have the opportunity to take a bit of bread.
21 His relatives, having heard of his doings, had set out to take him
22 home by force; for they said, "He has lost his wits." And the scribes
who had come down from Jerusalem asserted that he was possessed
by the devil and was driving out devils in league with the prince of
23 devils. Jesus therefore summoned them to him and gave them
several examples. "How could it be possible," he said, "for one
24 devil to drive out another? For if a kingdom is disunited, it can
25 have no stability; and if a household is torn by dissension, it cannot

26 last. If, therefore, Satan would rise against his own kind and thus
call forth dissension in his ranks, he would have no further support,
27 and his reign would come to an end. Furthermore, no one can enter
a strong man's house and rob him of his belongings without first
having bound the strong man; only then can his house be pillaged.
28 "I give you my solemn assurance that the sons of men will find
pardon for all their sins and even for all their blasphemies, be these
29 ever so many. But whoever utters a blasphemy against the holy
spirit-world receives no pardon for it, but incurs a sin that bur-
30 dens him for ages." Jesus spoke of this because they had said that
he was working his miracles as the instrument of an evil spirit.
31 It was then that his mother arrived with his brothers and sisters.
They stood outside and sent some one to call him, for he was sur-
32 rounded by a throng of people. He was told, "Your mother and your
brothers and sisters are standing outside, waiting to speak to you."
33 But he answered, "Who is my mother, and who are my brothers and
34 sisters?" And looking around at the circle of those who sat about
35 him, he said, "See, these are my mother, brothers, and sisters. For
whoever does the will of God is brother, sister, and mother to me."

CHAPTER 4.

1 At another time when he had begun to preach by the shore of the
lake, such a crowd of people surged around him that he was forced
to step into his boat. He sat down in it and had it pushed a short
distance away from the land, while the people lined the shore along
2 the water's edge. He laid his doctrine before them in parables, and
3 in this way made many truths clear to them. Among other things
4 he said, "Listen: A sower went out to sow. Some of the seeds he
scattered fell upon a hard-trodden path, and the birds came and
5 picked them up. Some seeds fell upon rocky parts of the field where
there was little top soil. These sprouted quickly because they could
6 not sink deep into the earth; but as the sun's heat grew stronger day
by day, they were scorched, and because they were not rooted deeply
7 enough they died away. Others fell among sprouting thistle-seeds
8 which grew up and choked them, and they did not bear. But still
others fell on good soil, sprouted, headed, and grew steadily, some
9 yielding thirty, some sixty, and some a hundredfold." He ended with
the words, "Let him who understands the parable, take it to heart!"
10 Later, when he was alone with his disciples, they asked him to
11 tell them the meaning of this parable, and he answered, "To you is
granted the gift of understanding the mysterious laws of God's
spirit-realm. But to those who have no communication with His

12 spirit-world everything is presented only in parables, so that they
may look again and again, and yet not see, and hear again and
again, and yet not understand, and hence that they may not be converted and obtain forgiveness."
13 Then he continued, "Do you not understand this parable? Then
14 how can you hope to understand any parables? The sower is any one
15 who sows the word of God. Those with whom the seed falls on the
hard-trodden path are the ones into whose hearts the seed of truth
is indeed sown; but they no sooner hear the truth than the devil
comes and takes away the word of truth that was sown in their hearts.
16 Those with whom the seed falls on rocky ground are the ones who
hear the word of truth and immediately receive it with joy, but in
whom it does not take sufficient root, because they lack stability.
17 No sooner do they suffer tribulation and persecution because of the
18 truth, than they turn their backs upon it. With others the seed falls
among sprouting thistles. They are those who hear the word of
19 truth, but in whom the daily cares and disappointments of life, and
the worldly desires that arise on every hand, choke the truth and
20 will not let it bear fruit. Lastly, the good soil on which the seed
falls stands for those who hear the word of truth, take it to heart,
and shape their lives accordingly. Then they bear fruit, thirty, sixty,
and even a hundredfold."
21 He said to them further, "Is a candle lighted to be put under a
bushel-measure or under a bed? By no means, it is set in a candle-
22 stick. For whatever is hidden shall be brought to light, and what-
23 ever was shrouded in mystery shall be revealed. Let him who understands my words, heed them."
24 Then he added, "Mark well what I am about to tell you: The
same measure you give to others will be given to you; indeed it will
25 be even fuller. For if any one makes good use of a gift from God,
that gift will be increased; but from him who fails to make use of
his gift, even that which he has will be taken."
26 And he further said to them, "With the operation of God's spirit-
27 world it is as with a man who sows seed in his field. He lies down
28 to sleep and rises again, following the round of day and night. The
seed sprouts and grows without his knowing how it happens. Of its
own accord the earth brings forth fruit: first the blade, then the
29 ears, which in time fill up with grain. When the grain is ripe, the
man takes his sickle to it, for the harvest time has come.
30 "To what," he continued, "can the operation of God's spirit-world
31 best be likened, and by what example illustrated? I shall compare
it to a mustard-grain. When it is scattered over the field, it is the

32 smallest of all grain sown, but after the sowing it quickly grows tall
and becomes the largest of all plants, sending out branches so large
that the birds of the air can nest under their shade."
33 It was by many such parables that he sought to make the divine
truths clear to them in a manner best suited to their understanding.
34 He never taught them a truth except in parables; but when he was
alone with his disciples, he explained everything to them.
35 That same day when dusk had set in, he said to his disciples, "Let
36 us cross to the other side of the lake." They sent the people home
and took him aboard the boat without making any further prepara-
37 tions. Other boats also joined theirs. Then a furious storm arose,
and the waves broke into the boat, so that it began to fill with water.
38 Jesus was lying in the stern of the boat, asleep on a cushion. They
woke him up calling to him, "Master, is it nothing to you if we
39 sink?" At that he rose, spoke sternly to the wind, and said to the
waves, "Silence! Be still!" At his words the storm subsided, and
40 there was a great calm. Then he turned to them with the question,
41 "Why are you so afraid? Are you still without faith?" But a great
fear had come over them, and they asked one another, "Who can
this man be, that even the storm and the seas obey him?"

CHAPTER 5.

1 Then they landed on the farther shore of the lake in the region
2 of the Gerasenes. Scarcely had he stepped out of the boat when he
3 was approached by a man who was possessed by an evil spirit. He
lived in the tombs, and as yet no one had been able to bind him, not
4 even with a chain. Indeed there had been many attempts to subdue
him by chaining him hand and foot; but he had always broken the
chains and snapped the fetters, and nobody was strong enough to
5 overpower him. Day and night he hovered about the tombs and the
mountains, shrieking like a beast and gashing himself with stones.
6 On seeing Jesus in the distance he came running up, and throwing
7 himself down before him cried aloud, "What do you intend to do
with me, Jesus, you Son of God the Highest? I implore you in the
8 name of God not to torment me." For Jesus was about to order the
9 evil spirit to go out of the man. Then Jesus asked him, "What is
your name?" He answered, "My name is Legion, for there are many
10 of us." And he earnestly begged him not to send them out of the
neighborhood.
11 As it happened, a large drove of swine was feeding there on the
12 hillside, and the demons pleaded, "Send us to the swine so that
13 we may enter them." Jesus at once sent them, and the evil spirits

went out of the man and entered the swine, whereupon the whole
drove — some two thousand head — dashed down the steep slope
into the lake, and all were drowned.
14 The herders fled and carried the news into the village and the surrounding homesteads, and the people came to see with their own
15 eyes what had happened. They found Jesus, and with him the man
who had been possessed by the legion of evil spirits, quietly seated,
16 clothed, and in his right mind. At the sight of him they became
frightened, and those who had witnessed the occurrence told them
17 what had happened to the madman and the swine; and the people
pressed Jesus to leave the neighborhood.
18 While Jesus was getting into his boat, the man who had been
19 possessed entreated to be allowed to remain with him. This, however, Jesus would not permit, but said to him, "Go home to your people and tell them of the great things the Lord has done for you, and
20 how he has taken pity on you." So the man went and began to
spread about the neighborhood of the Ten Towns the news of the
great things that Jesus had done for him. And all who heard him
were amazed.
21 Jesus now crossed back in his boat to the opposite shore. He had
no sooner landed than again the people gathered about him in great
22 numbers. It was while he was standing by the water's edge that there
came to him one of the heads of the synagogue, Jairus by name, and
23 falling down before him, implored, "My daughter is at the point of
death. Come and lay your hands on her, so that she may recover and
24 live." Jesus went with him, followed by a large crowd which pressed
25 closely upon him. In the crowd there was a woman who for twelve
26 years had been afflicted with an issue of blood. She had suffered
much under the treatment of numerous physicians, and had spent all
her fortune in this way without obtaining relief; on the contrary,
27 her ailment had grown worse. Having heard of the cures effected by
Jesus, she had joined the crowd. Approaching him from behind,
28 she touched his robe, thinking, "If I can touch only his clothes, I
29 shall be helped." Instantly the issue of blood ceased, and from her
physical condition she realized that she had been cured of her ail-
30 ment. Jesus, who at the same moment had perceived that healing
power had gone out from him, turned about in the crowd and asked,
31 "Who touched my clothes?" His disciples answered, "You see the
crowd pressing around you, and still you ask, 'Who touched me?' "
32 But he kept looking about for the one who had done it. The woman,
33 knowing that she had done it secretly, became frightened and began
to tremble, for she understood what had happened to her; and com-

34 ing to him, she fell at his feet and confessed everything. He said to
her, "Daughter, your faith has saved you. Go your way in peace,
and remain free of your complaint."
35 In the meantime people had come from the household of the
leader of the synagogue and told him, "Your daughter is dead. Why
36 need you trouble the master any further?" Hearing this, Jesus
turned to the head of the synagogue and said, "Do not be concerned,
37 only have faith." He allowed no one to go with him except Peter,
38 James, and John the brother of James. They came to the house of the
head of the synagogue and found there the greatest confusion, for
39 every one was weeping and lamenting. On entering the house he
asked, "What is this confusion, and why do you weep? The girl is
40 not dead, she is only sleeping." They laughed at him, but he ordered
them all out of the house, and together with the child's father and
mother and the disciples who were with him, went into the room
41 where the girl lay. Then taking the child by the hand he said,
"Talitha cum," which means, "Little girl, I say to you, awake."
42 At once she rose and walked about. She was a girl twelve years
43 of age. Every one was lost in amazement, but Jesus strictly enjoined
them to let no one hear what had occurred. He also told them
to give the child something to eat.

CHAPTER 6.

1 From there he went to his own town of Nazareth, accompanied by
2 his disciples. On the following Sabbath he taught in the synagogue
for the first time. Many of his hearers were astounded at his doctrine and asked one another, "Where did he learn all these things?
What sort of knowledge does he command that he is able to perform
3 such miracles? Is he not the son of the carpenter and of Mary, and
the brother of James, Joses, Judas, and Simon? Do not his sisters
4 also live in our town?" And they did not believe in him; but Jesus
said to them, "A messenger of God is nowhere less honored than in
5 his own country, in his own home, and by his own kin." He could
not perform a single miracle there, except that he laid his hands on
6 a few sick people and healed them. Again and again he marvelled
at their unbelief.
7 He also visited the surrounding villages and preached there.
Then he called the twelve disciples to him and sent them out in pairs,
8 at the same time giving them power over the evil spirits. He directed
them to take with them nothing but a staff; no bread, no bag, and no
9 money in their belts. They were told to wear sandals, but not to put
10 on two undergarments; and he instructed them further, "If you are

11 received in any house, let it be your home until you leave the place;
but if no one will take you in or listen to you, go away and shake the
12 dust of the place from your feet as testimony against them." So
they set out and preached the need of conversion. They also drove
13 out many evil spirits, and healed great numbers of sick people by
anointing them with oil.

14 King Herod received word of this, for the fame of Jesus had
spread everywhere. Some maintained that John the Baptist had risen
from the dead, and that hence these miraculous powers were active
15 in him. Others thought that he was Elijah, and still others took him
16 for one of the earlier prophets. But Herod, when he heard these
different opinions expressed, would say, "John, whom I beheaded,
17 has risen again." For Herod had sent out servants and had John
arrested and thrown into prison in chains. He had done this at the
bidding of Herodias, whom Herod had married, although she was
18 his brother Philip's wife. John had reproached him for this, saying,
19 "It is not lawful for you to have your brother's wife." For this
reason Herodias bore him a grudge, and would willingly have had
20 him killed. But she could find no way of accomplishing her end, for
Herod stood in awe of John, whom he had come to recognize as a
God-fearing and holy man and had taken under his protection. He
also practised much of what he heard from John and took pleasure
in listening to him.

21 One day, nevertheless, Herodias achieved her purpose. It was
Herod's birthday, which he celebrated by giving a banquet to his
dignitaries and higher officers and the leading people of Galilee.
22 The daughter of Herodias entered the banquet-hall and danced, and
so pleased were Herod and his guests that the king said to the
23 girl, "Ask of me what you like, and I will give it to you." This
promise he confirmed with the oath, "I will give you whatever you
24 ask of me, even if it should be half of my kingdom." She hurried
out to inquire of her mother, "What shall I ask?" Her mother an-
25 swered, "The head of John the Baptist." She went back to the king
26 and said, "Give me the head of John the Baptist on this dish." At
this the king was aghast, but on account of his oaths and his guests
27 he was unwilling to break the word that he had pledged her. He
therefore immediately sent one of his bodyguards with orders to
bring John's head. The man went and had John beheaded in the
28 prison. He returned with the head on the dish and gave it to the girl,
29 and the girl took it to her mother. When John's disciples heard the
news they came and took his body away and buried it.

30 The apostles returned to Jesus and told him of everything they

31 had done and taught. Then he said to them, "Come, let us go to
some place where we shall be alone, so that you may rest a
little." For so many people were coming and going that they had
32 not even time to eat. So they went away with him in his boat; but
33 the people had seen them leave, and many guessed where they were
bound. Crowds therefore flocked to the place on foot from every
village, and arrived there as soon as he did.

34 When Jesus went ashore and saw a great multitude before him,
he was deeply moved on their behalf, for they were like sheep without a shepherd. He began to preach at once and instructed them in
35 various truths. Meanwhile the day was far advanced, and his disciples went to him and said, "This is a deserted place, and it is late
36 in the day. Send the people away, so that they may go to the nearest
37 farms and villages and buy something to eat." He answered, "Furnish them with food yourselves." They retorted, "Do you want us
to go and buy forty dollars' worth of bread to supply their wants?"
38 He asked them, "How many loaves have you on hand? Go and see."
39 They looked, and told him, "Five loaves and two fish." He then
40 directed that all should sit down in groups on the green grass, and
41 they seated themselves by hundreds and by fifties. Then he took the
five loaves and the two fish, looked up to heaven, and pronounced a
blessing. Breaking up the loaves, he gave them to his disciples to
serve out to the people, and he also ordered them to divide the two
42 fish among all. Every one ate his fill. The leavings of the bread and
43 the fish that they gathered up were enough to fill twelve baskets.
44 Of those who had eaten, the men alone numbered five thousand.

45 Immediately afterwards he urged his disciples to take to their
boat and cross over before him to Bethsaida on the opposite shore,
leaving him to dismiss the people.

46 When he had sent the people away he climbed the hill to engage
47 in prayer. It was already late in the evening, and the boat was but
halfway to its destination. He himself remained on shore, all alone.
48 He could see the men straining at the oars, for there was a head-
wind. At about three o'clock in the morning he walked over the lake
49 toward them, but apparently intended to pass them by. When they
saw him walking over the lake they thought it was a ghost and cried
50 out, their limbs trembling in fear. But he immediately called to
51 them, "Take courage, it is I. You have nothing to fear." Then he
stepped into the boat with them, and the wind abated. They were be-
52 side themselves with amazement; they had not yet learned the lesson
taught by the miracle of the loaves, for their hearts were not yet
ready to accept it.

53 They landed near Genezareth, and on going ashore Jesus was at
54 once recognized by the people, who hurried in every direction, seek-
55 ing to bring all of the sick to him in litters. For they had fallen into
the habit of taking their sick to the places at which Jesus was said to
56 be staying. Wherever he stopped, in villages, towns, or farms, the
people laid their sick in the open, and begged him to allow them
only to touch the tassels of his robe; and all who touched him were
made well.

CHAPTER 7.

1 One day while some of the Pharisees and scribes who had come
2 from Jerusalem were with him, they saw that some of his disciples
ate their bread with "unclean hands"—that is, without ceremonial
3 washing. For the Pharisees, like all Jews, never partake of a meal
until they have thoroughly washed their hands in observance of the
4 traditions handed down to them by their ancestors. On coming home
from the market they will not eat until they have washed in this
manner. Besides this there are many other rules that they observe
for tradition's sake, such as those pertaining to the cleaning of drink-
5 ing-cups, jars, kettles, and beds. The Pharisees and scribes therefore
asked him, "Why do your disciples not observe the traditions of
their ancestors in their daily habits? For they eat bread without
6 washing their hands." He answered them by saying, "Isaiah, as
God's messenger, described you hypocrites exactly when he said:
'These people show me their love only with their lips, but their
7 hearts have entirely forsaken me. Their ways of worshipping me are
8 futile, for the doctrines they teach are but human precepts.' God's
commandment you set aside, but man-made customs you are scrupu-
lous to observe. You are careful to clean your jars and your cups,
9 and to observe many other like formalities." And he continued,
"You understand very well how to set aside God's commandment so
10 that you may hold to your traditional precepts. Thus, Moses has
commanded, 'Honor your father and your mother,' and, 'Whoever
11 curses his father or his mother shall be put to death.' But you maintain that if any one says to his father or his mother, 'Whatever you
have hitherto been receiving from me for your support shall here-
12 after be "Corban"'—meaning a gift to the treasury of the temple—
he is relieved of all further duty to help his father or his mother.
13 By these man-made ordinances that you pass on to your successors,
you nullify God's commandment. And there are many other similar
14 examples that I might cite." Then calling the people nearer to him,
he said to them, "Listen attentively, and understand my words cor-

15 rectly: Nothing that goes into a man from the outside can defile
him. It is only that which comes out of a man from within that can
16 make him 'unclean.' Whoever has true understanding will know
what I mean."

17 When he had withdrawn from the people and gone home, his dis-
18 ciples asked him the meaning of his parable. He answered, "Are
you still without understanding, too? Do you not see that nothing
19 that goes into a man from the outside can defile him? For it goes
not into his heart, but into his stomach, and from there it is eliminated in the natural way by which the body is purged of all food.
20 On the contrary, that which comes out of a man can indeed make
21 him 'unclean;' for from within, from the hearts of men, come evil
22 designs: unchastity, theft, murder, adultery, greed, spite, deceit,
23 licentiousness, envy, blasphemy, pride, folly. It is from within that
all these evils come and make man 'unclean.'"

24 From there he came to the region of Tyre, where he went indoors
to avoid being seen by any one; but his arrival could not be kept
25 secret. Among those who heard of it was a woman whose little daughter was possessed by an evil spirit. She came into the house and
26 threw herself at his feet; and although she was a heathen, a Phoeni-
cian, she begged him to drive the evil spirit out of her daughter.
27 But he answered her, "Let the children first eat their fill, then it will
be time to think of the dogs; for it is not fitting to deprive the chil-
28 dren of their bread and throw it to the dogs." She replied, "That is
true, lord; but even the dogs under the table eat of the children's
29 crumbs." And he said to her, "For the sake of these words, go home
30 in peace; the evil spirit has gone out of your daughter." She hurried
home and found her daughter resting easily in bed. The evil spirit
had gone out of her.

31 Now he again left the region of Tyre and went by way of Sidon
to the Lake of Galilee, and thence up into the region of the Ten
32 Towns. Here they brought him a deaf-mute, on whom they asked
33 him to lay his hands. He took the deaf-mute aside from the crowd
so that he might be alone with him, moistened his fingers with saliva
and put them into the deaf man's ears, and likewise touched his
34 tongue with saliva. Then looking up to heaven, he sighed in sup-
35 plication and said, "Ephphatha," which means, "Be opened." Instantly the man's organs of hearing were released, and his tongue,
36 which had been tied, was loosed, and he could speak plainly. Jesus
enjoined all those present to tell no one of this; but the more he
37 forbade it, the more they spread the story far and wide. The people
were beside themselves with wonder, and said, "Everything that he

does is crowned with the highest success. He even makes the deaf
hear, and the dumb speak."

CHAPTER 8.

1 One day there was again a great crowd around him, and the
people had nothing to eat. Calling his disciples to him, Jesus said,
2 "I pity the people. They have been with me now for three days and
3 have nothing to eat. I will not let them go home without food, for
fear that they will grow faint on the way; for some of them have
4 come a long distance." The disciples answered, "How can bread be
5 supplied for so many people in this uninhabited place?"—"How
6 many loaves have you?" asked Jesus. They answered, "Seven."
Ordering the people to be seated on the ground, he took the seven
loaves, asked a blessing, and broke the bread. Then he gave it to his
7 disciples to distribute, and they served it out to the people. They had
in addition a few fish, which Jesus also blessed and ordered to be
8 distributed. Every one there ate his fill, yet the leavings, when gath-
9 ered from the ground, amounted to seven basketfuls. The people
present numbered some four thousand. When they had eaten he sent
them away.

10 Immediately afterwards he took a boat with his disciples and
11 landed in the region of Melegada. Here he was met by the Pharisees,
who sought to engage him in conversation. Wishing to put him to
12 the test, they called upon him for a sign in the sky. He sighed from
the depth of his soul and answered, according to the direction of his
spirit-guide, "Why do people of this kind ask for a sign? I assure
13 you that such people will never be given a sign." With these words
he left them, and taking his boat, crossed to the other side.

14 The disciples had forgotten to take bread and had on board with
15 them only a single loaf. When he now warned them, "Be sure to be
on your guard against the leaven of the Pharisees and the adherents
16 of Herod," they thought to themselves, "He probably says this be-
17 because we have brought no bread with us." Jesus, knowing their
thoughts, asked, "Why are you concerned over having brought no
bread? Have you not yet attained insight and understanding? Are
18 your hearts still dull to the truth? You have eyes to see with, and
19 yet do not see? You have ears to hear with, and yet do not hear?
Have you forgotten how many basketfuls of leavings you gathered
20 up, when I broke bread for the five thousand?"—"Twelve," they replied. "And when I broke the seven loaves for the four thousand,
how many basketfuls of leavings did you gather then?"—"Seven,"

21 was the answer. He said to them, "How is it that you still cannot
draw the right conclusions from this?"

22 Then they reached Bethany, where a blind man was brought to
23 him, and he was entreated to touch his eyes. Taking the blind man
by the arm, he led him to the outskirts of the village. Here he
moistened the blind man's eyes with saliva, laid his hands on him,
24 and asked, "Can you see anything?" The man looked up and said,
25 "I see people, but they look like trees moving about." Then Jesus
again laid his hands on the man's eyes. He was now healed and
could see clearly, being able to distinguish even distant objects.
26 Jesus sent him home, saying, "Go home, and tell no one in the village about it."

27 After this Jesus and his disciples went to Caesarea Philippi. On
the way he asked the disciples, "Who do people say that I am?"
28 They answered, "Some say that you are John the Baptist; others,
29 Elijah; still others, one of the earlier prophets." Then he asked
them, "And who do you say that I am?" Peter answered, "You are
30 the Messiah." Jesus then gave them strict orders not to tell any one
what they knew about him.

31 From now on he began to prepare them for the knowledge that
the Son of man would have to undergo much suffering; that he would
be expelled from the community by the elders, the chief priests, and
the scribes, and killed, but that on the third day he would be raised
32 again. He spoke of this quite openly. Peter took him aside to remon-
33 strate with him, but he turned and looked at his disciples inquiringly,
then rebuked Peter sharply, saying, "Out of my sight, Satan! You
are allowing yourself to be guided not by divine inspiration, but by
purely human emotions."

34 He then bade the people come nearer to his disciples, and addressed them in these words: "Whoever wishes to travel by my path
must renounce his worldly inclinations. He must learn to bear the
35 cross allotted to him. Then only will he be able to follow me. For
he who covets mere worldly happiness will forfeit true happiness.
But he who by following the gospel loses worldly happiness, will
36 attain true happiness. What will it profit a man to gain the wealth
37 of the whole world if he thereby forfeits true happiness? And with
38 what worldly wealth could he redeem his lost happiness? If any one
is ashamed of me and of my teachings before this apostate and sinful people, the Son of man will also be ashamed of him, when he
comes in the glory of his Father with God's holy messengers."

CHAPTER 9.

1 Then he continued, "I assure you, some of those who stand here
will not taste death until they with their own eyes have seen God's
spirit-world in all its might."

2 Six days later Jesus took with him Peter, James, and John, and
led them to an isolated place on a high mountain where they were
3 entirely alone. There he was transfigured before their eyes. His
garments became radiant and of a snowy whiteness such as no
4 bleaching on earth can equal. And there appeared to them Elijah,
5 accompanied by Moses, and both spoke with Jesus. Then Peter
turned and said to Jesus, "Master, we feel so happy here! Let us
make three shelters of leafy boughs: one for you, one for Moses,
6 and one for Elijah." For he was in such a frame of mind that he
could not properly express his emotions, all three of the disciples
7 being overcome by an indescribable feeling of awe. Presently a
bright cloud came and gathered about them, and out of the cloud
they heard a voice saying, "This is my beloved Son. Heed him."
8 When they looked around in the direction of the voice they saw no
9 one but Jesus standing beside them. While they were making their
way down the mountain he directed them to tell no one of what they
had witnessed, until the Son of man should have risen from the dead.
10 These last words perplexed them exceedingly, and they discussed
among themselves the meaning of the phrase "risen from the dead."
11 Finally they asked him, "What real truth is there in the assertion of
12 the Pharisees and the scribes that Elijah must come first?" He answered, "Whenever Elijah comes he helps to restore everything to
God again. I tell you that Elijah has already come, and they did
him all the harm they could, as was foretold of him in the Scrip-
13 tures. In the same manner it is also written in the Scriptures concerning the Son of man that he must suffer much and be executed
as a criminal."

14 When he rejoined the other disciples, he saw a great crowd gath-
15 ered around them, and certain scribes arguing with them. As soon
as the people saw him they showed their pleasure by running up
16 and greeting him cordially. He asked them, "What is going on be-
17 tween you and my disciples?" One man stepped forward and said,
"Master, I have brought my son to you. He is possessed by a spirit
18 that makes him dumb. Whenever the spirit lays hold of him it
tosses him to and fro. The boy foams at the mouth and gnashes his
teeth, and falls down unconscious. I begged your disciples to drive
19 out the spirit, but they could not." Jesus answered, "Oh, these un-

believing people! How much longer must I be among you? How
much longer must I have patience with you? Bring him here to
20 me!" They brought the boy to him, and when the spirit in him saw
Jesus, the boy went into convulsions and fell down, foaming at the
21 mouth and writhing on the ground. Jesus asked the boy's father,
22 "How long has he had this affliction?"—"Ever since he was a little
child," replied the father, "and the spirit has often thrown him into
the fire and into the water, to kill him. Have pity on us, lord, and
23 help us, if you can." Jesus answered, "As for your words, 'If you
can,' I say to you, have firm confidence! For all things are possible
24 to him who confidently believes." The boy's father immediately
cried out, in tears, "I do believe! Help me to overcome my lack of
25 confidence!" Then Jesus, seeing the crowd thicken, spoke sharply
to the evil spirit, saying, "Spirit, you who have made your victim
deaf and dumb, I command you: Come out of the boy and never
26 return into him!" With a loud cry the spirit came out of the boy,
who fell into violent convulsions and lay as though lifeless, so that
27 the people exclaimed, "He is dead!" But Jesus took him by the hand
and raised him, and he stood erect, fully recovered.

28 Afterwards when Jesus had gone indoors and was alone with his
disciples, they asked him, "Why could we not drive out that spirit?"
29 He answered, "Spirits like that one can be driven out only by
prayer."

30 From there they journeyed on, wandering through Galilee and
31 seeking to keep their presence unknown, for he wished to devote
himself wholly to teaching his disciples. He now told them that the
Son of man would be delivered into the hands of men who would
32 kill him, but that after three days he would rise again. They did not
understand the full meaning of his words, nor did they have the
courage to ask him for any further explanation.

33 Then they went back to Capernaum, and when he had arrived at
his house he asked his disciples, "What were you discussing with
34 each other on the way?" They were silent, for they had disputed as
35 to which was the greatest among them. Seating himself, Jesus called
36 all twelve to him. Then, taking a child, he set it in their midst and
37 put his arm about it, and said, "Whoever befriends such a child and
leads it to me befriends my cause; and whoever befriends my cause
befriends in reality not my cause but that of Him Who sent me."

38 It was on this occasion that John said to him, "Master, we saw
some one driving out evil spirits as a follower of your teaching, but
because he does not belong to our circle we forbade him to do so."
39 Jesus answered, "Do not forbid him; for whoever performs a mir-

acle as a follower of my teaching will scarcely speak evil of me.
40 Such a one is not against us, but for us. And so if one of my fol-
41 lowers gives you a cup of water because you adhere faithfully to me
42 as the Messiah, he shall certainly not go unrewarded. But whoever
causes one of these little ones who believe in me to be estranged from
me, might better have a millstone hung about his neck and be
43 thrown into the sea. And if your own hand threatens to separate you
44 from me, cut it off. It is better for you to go into the spiritual life
maimed, than having both hands, to be thrown into the depths, where
there is a fire that will not be quenched until everything that is evil
45 is consumed. And if your foot threatens to separate you from me,
46 cut it off; it is better for you to go into life lame, than having both
47 feet, to be thrown into the abyss. And if your eye threatens to separate you from me, tear it out. It is better for you to enter God's
48 kingdom with but one eye, than to have both eyes and be compelled
to enter into the depths, where the worm of anguish that torments its
victims cannot be killed and the fire of suffering cannot be quenched,
49 until all that is impure is destroyed. Just as every sacrifice offered to
God must be salted, so every one who is being prepared for God
50 must be seasoned with the salt of suffering. Salt is good; but if it
loses its power, what else is there with which its saltiness can be restored? Keep in your hearts the true understanding of the salt of your
own suffering; then you will also have peace with your fellow-men."

CHAPTER 10.

1 From here he went into the region of Judaea beyond the Jordan.
Again the people flocked to him, and again he taught them accord-
2 ing to his custom. At this time certain Pharisees asked him, "Is it
lawful for a man to divorce his wife?"—for they wished to set a
3 trap for him. He asked them in reply, "What did Moses say to you
4 on this matter?" They responded, "Moses said that a man might
5 draw up a bill of divorce and send his wife away."—"It was only
because of the hardness of your hearts," answered Jesus, "that Moses
6 laid down this rule for you. But in the beginning God Himself cre-
7 ated male and female in pairs, one for the other. For this reason a
man will leave his father and mother, and live inseparably with his
8 wife. The two are as closely united as if they were but one being.
In fact they are therefore to be regarded not as two, but as one living
9 unit. What God has so joined together, man shall not sever."

10 At home the disciples questioned him again concerning this mat-
11 ter, and he told them, "Whoever divorces his wife and marries an-

12 other commits adultery against his first wife; and any woman who
leaves her husband and marries another man also commits adultery."
13 One day some little children were brought to him that he might
lay his hands on them and bless them, but his disciples sharply re-
14 buked those who had brought the children. Jesus saw this and was
greatly displeased. "Let the children come to me," he said, "and do
not hinder them; for communication with God's spirit-world is
15 granted to such as have the soul of a child. Rest assured that whoever does not seek that communication with a childlike heart will
16 never be able to find it." Then he called the children to him, laid
his hands on them, and gave them his blessing.
17 As he was setting out again, a man came running toward him and
knelt down, asking, "Good master, what must I do to attain the life
18 hereafter?" Jesus answered him, "Why do you call me 'good'? No
19 one but God is good. You know the commandments: You shall not
kill, or commit adultery, or steal, or give false testimony, or de-
fraud any one of his own, and you shall honor your father and
20 your mother." The man answered, "Master, I have observed all these
21 things from my youth." With a look of deep affection, Jesus said
to him, "There is still one thing lacking. Go sell all you have, give
the proceeds to those who are really poor, and you will have treasure
22 in the beyond. Then come back and follow me." At this answer the
man became very downcast and went away disappointed; for he had
a great fortune.
23 Jesus looked at his disciples one after the other and said, "How
hard it is for the wealthy to enter into communication with God's
spirit-world! It is easier for a camel to pass through a needle's eye
than for a rich man to enter God's kingdom."
24 The disciples showed great amazement at these words, but Jesus
repeated, "Children, how hard it is for those who trust in money and
25 possessions to come into contact with God's spirit-realm! It is actually easier for a camel to pass through a needle's eye than it is
for the rich to enter into communication with God's spirit-world."
26 This stirred them even more, and they said to one another, "What
27 rich man can be saved, then?" Looking earnestly at them Jesus said,
"With men this is indeed impossible, but with God it is possible."
28 Then Peter spoke up and said, "But we are among those who have
29 left everything to follow you." Jesus interrupted him with the words,
"I assure you that no one ever left home, brother or sister, mother
or father or children or lands for my sake and for the message of
salvation, without being rewarded a hundredfold even in this life.
30 And in addition, every one who has had to abandon home, brothers,

sisters, mother, father, children, or possessions, because of persecu-
31 tion, will gain eternal life in the beyond. Many who were among the
first will then be among the last, and many who were among the
last will be among the first."

32 They were now on the road to Jerusalem, with Jesus walking in
their lead. The disciples were oppressed by a foreboding of evil,
those who followed them by a feeling of fear. Then he once more
called the Twelve nearer to him and began to speak to them of what
33 was before him. "See," he said, "we are now going up to Jerusalem.
There the Son of man will be delivered to the chief priests and the
scribes, who will sentence him to death and hand him over to the
34 unbelievers. They will mock him, spit upon him, scourge him, and
put him to death; but on the third day he will rise again."

35 Then James and John, the sons of Zebedee, approached him and
36 said, "Master, there is one wish that we ask you to grant us." Jesus
37 asked them, "What is it that you wish?" They answered, "Grant
that when you reach the highest honor one of us may sit at your
38 right hand and one at your left." But Jesus answered, "You do not
know what you are asking. Can you drink the cup that I must drink,
39 or receive the baptism that I shall receive?"—"We can," they replied. "You will, indeed, drink the cup that I must drink and receive the baptism that I shall receive," Jesus continued; "but the
40 seats at my right and my left hand are not mine to give, but will
41 be bestowed upon those for whom they are destined." When the
other ten disciples heard of the request, they were greatly incensed
42 at James and John. But Jesus called them to him and said, "You
know that the kings of nations, under the pretext of ruling their
subjects, treat them as slaves, and that their governors exploit the
43 people. This must not be so among you. He who wishes to be great
44 among you must rather be your servant, and he among you who
45 wishes to be first must minister to all. For even the Son of man
has not come to be served, but to serve others, and to give his life
as a ransom for the many."

46 Presently they came to Jericho, and as Jesus was leaving the town,
attended by his disciples and a great crowd, they passed a blind
man who was sitting by the roadside, begging. It was Bartimaeus,
47 the son of Timaeus. When he heard that Jesus of Nazareth was
passing, he called aloud, "Jesus, son of David, have pity on me!"
48 The crowd roughly told him to keep still, but he called all the
49 louder, "Son of David, have pity on me!" Jesus stopped and commanded that he be brought to him, whereupon the people called
50 to the blind man and said, "Courage! Get up quickly! He is sending

for you!" The blind man threw off his cloak, sprang to his feet, and
51 went toward Jesus. "What is it that you want of me?" asked Jesus.
"Dear lord and master," answered the other, "I want to be able to
52 see."—"Go," said Jesus, "your confident faith has cured you." Instantly the man was able to see, and he followed Jesus on his travels.

CHAPTER 11.

1 Now they drew near Jerusalem, and reached Bethany on the
Mount of Olives. From there Jesus sent ahead two of his disciples,
2 telling them, "Go into the village over yonder. As you enter it you
will find tethered there an ass's colt which no one has yet ridden.
3 Untie it and bring it to me. If any one asks you, 'Why are you
untying the colt?' say to him, 'The lord has need of it and will send
4 it back shortly.'" They went ahead and found a colt tethered out-
5 side the door of the stable, close to the street. As they untied it some
of the bystanders asked them, "What are you doing? Why are you
6 untying the colt?" They answered as Jesus had directed them, and
7 the people let them have the colt. This they brought to Jesus, laying
8 their cloaks on it, and he mounted it. Many spread their garments
as a carpet in the road, while others broke twigs from the trees and
9 strewed them in the highway. Those who led the procession and
those who followed in the rear shouted, "Blessed is he who comes in
10 the name of the Lord! Blessed is the kingdom of our father David,
that is now coming to us! Hosanna in the highest!"
11 In this manner he entered the city of Jerusalem and went into the
temple. He looked closely at everything there, and late that evening
he went to Bethany, accompanied by the Twelve.
12 In the morning they again set out from Bethany. On the way he
13 felt hungry, and noticing a fig tree in full leaf at some distance, he
went toward it to see whether he might find some fruit on it. But
when he came nearer he found only leaves, for it was not the season
14 for figs. Then Jesus exclaimed to the tree, "Never again in this age
shall any one eat of your fruit." The disciples heard him say this.
15 After they had reached Jerusalem he went into the temple and
began to drive out all those whom he found buying and selling there.
He had the tables of the money-changers and the benches of the
16 dealers in doves put out, and would not allow any one to carry even
17 a utensil through the temple. He then upbraided them, saying, "It is
written: 'My house shall be known to all nations as a house of prayer,
18 but you have made it a robbers' den.'" The chief priests and the
scribes heard of these actions of Jesus, and sought a way to destroy

him; for they feared his influence, because his teachings were mak-
19 ing a deep impression on the people. On this account he used to
wait until it was late in the evening before he left the city.
20 Early on the following morning as they passed the fig tree, they
21 saw that it had withered to the roots. Peter, remembering the incident of the day before, said to Jesus, "Look, master, the fig tree that
22 you cursed is withered." Jesus answered, "If only your faith and
23 trust in God were what it should be! For believe me when I tell you
that if any one should say to this mountain, 'Rise, and throw yourself
into the sea,' without harboring any doubt in his heart, but in the
firm belief that his words would come true, it would happen as he
24 said. I therefore say to you: Whatever you ask in prayer will be
yours, if you will only hold the firm belief that you will receive it.
25 And when you stand up to pray, you must first forgive any one who
is in need of your forgiveness. Then your heavenly Father will also
26 forgive you your offences. If you, however, do not forgive others,
neither will your heavenly Father forgive you your trespasses."
27 They then went back to Jerusalem. As he was walking about in
the temple, the chief priests, scribes, and elders of the people ap-
28 proached him and asked, "At whose bidding are you doing all this?
29 Who has authorized you to act as you do?" Jesus replied, "I
wish to ask you one question, and if you can answer it, I will tell
30 you by what authority I do all these things. Did John baptize at
31 the bidding of God, or at the bidding of men? Answer me." They
said to themselves, "What shall we answer? If we say that John
baptized at God's bidding, he will retort, 'Then why did you not
32 believe in him?' That means we shall have to say, 'At the bidding
of men.'" But this they dared not, for fear of the people, because
33 all looked upon John as a messenger of God. They therefore answered Jesus, "We do not know."—"Then," replied Jesus, "I will
not tell you by what authority I act."

CHAPTER 12.

1 He then began to speak to them in parables again. "A man
planted a vineyard," he said, "built a fence around it, dug a cellar
for the wine-vats, and put up a watch-tower. Then he leased it to
2 tenant grape-growers and went abroad. When the rent was due, he
sent one of his servants to the tenants to receive his part of the yield
3 of the vineyard as payment, but they laid hands on him, maltreated
4 him, and sent him back empty-handed. He then sent a second servant,
5 whom they beat on the head and wounded and insulted. The third
servant whom he sent they killed. He sent many others, some of

6 whom were beaten, others killed. There was now only one left for
him to send, his beloved son, and in the end he sent him also, think-
7 ing, 'They will surely respect my son.' But the tenants said to one
another, 'He is the heir. Come, let us kill him, and the inheritance
8 will be ours.' They seized him, put him to death, and threw his body
9 out of the vineyard. Now what will the owner of the vineyard do?
He will come and put the tenants to death, and will lease his vine-
10 yard to others. Have you not read in the Scriptures: 'The stone
that the builders rejected as unfit has become the corner-stone; he
11 was made this by the Lord, and in our eyes he is a divine wonder'?"
12 On this occasion they tried to lay hold of him, for they knew that
the parable was aimed at them. But they feared the people, and so
they let him alone and went away.

13 They next sent to him certain Pharisees and partisans of Herod
14 to entrap him with a question. These men came to him with a question which the Pharisees had craftily framed in this manner: "Master, we know that you always speak the truth without regard to persons, for you do not consider the high rank of men, but teach the
way to God in strict accordance with the truth. Tell us this: Is it
right to pay the head-tax to Caesar or not? Should we pay it or
should we refuse it?"

15 Jesus, seeing through their hypocrisy, answered, "Why are you
16 trying to set a trap for me? Let me see a denarius." They handed
him the coin. "Whose likeness and inscription are these?" he
17 asked. "Caesar's," they replied. Jesus answered, "Then pay to
Caesar what you owe him, and give to God what you owe to God."
This answer left them utterly confounded.

18 Then certain of the Sadducees, who teach that there is no resur-
19 rection, approached him and related the following story: "Master,
Moses made the rule that a man must marry his deceased brother's
widow if she is childless, and by her beget descendants to the de-
20 ceased. Now it happened that there were seven brothers among us.
21 The first married, but died childless. And so the second brother
made the widow his wife, but he also died childless; so likewise the
22 third. And such was the case with all seven: none of them left
23 children. Last of all the woman died also. Of the seven, whose wife
will she be in the resurrection? For all seven had married her."
24 Jesus answered, "Does not your whole manner of putting the question show at the outset that your views are utterly mistaken, because you understand neither the Scriptures nor the operation of
25 the laws ordained by God? For no man who has risen from the dead
26 need seek a wife, nor any woman a husband. The same law operates

with them as with the angels in heaven. But as for the fact that there
really is a resurrection of the dead, have you not proof in the book
of Moses in the story of the burning bush, which you have surely
read? I mean the passage where God said to Moses, 'I am the God
27 of Abraham, the God of Isaac, and the God of Jacob.' For God is no
God of the dead, but of the living. You are therefore laboring under
a serious error."

28 A scribe who was standing near by and had overheard this explanation, was unable to blind himself to the fact that Jesus had
given his opponents a striking answer. He now approached him and
asked, "Master, which is the most important commandment of all?"
29 Jesus answered, "The most important of all is: 'Hear, O Israel!
30 The Lord our God is the only Lord. Therefore you shall love the
Lord your God with all your heart, with all your soul, with all
31 your mind, and with all your strength.' The second in importance,
but inseparably united with the first, is the commandment: 'You
shall love your neighbor as yourself.' No other commandment is
32 greater than these two." The scribe replied, "Master, you have well
stated the truth that there is but One Who is God, and that there is
33 no other God but Him; moreover, that it is worth far more than all
of the burnt-offerings and other sacrifices, to love the Lord with all
our hearts, with all our conviction, and with all our strength, and
34 our neighbors as ourselves." When Jesus heard him speak so sen-
sibly, he said to him, "There is not much lacking to enable you to
enter into communication with God's spirit-world."

After that no one dared ask him any further questions.

35 One day as he was teaching in the temple, Jesus asked this question: "How can the scribes contend that the Messiah is David's son?
36 For David himself under the influence of a holy spirit spoke the
words: 'The Lord said to my lord, "Sit at my right hand until I have
37 made your enemies a foot-stool under your feet."' David himself
calls the Messiah 'lord'; how then can the Messiah be David's son?"

38 The common people enjoyed hearing Jesus talk in this way.
Going on with his teaching, he added, "Beware of the scribes who
are given to going about in long robes and who covet recognition
39 in the market-places; who take the foremost seats in the places of
40 prayer, and the seats of honor at banquets; who out of greed appro-
priate to themselves the belongings of widows and orphans, under
the pretext of offering long prayers on their behalf. So much the
heavier will be their punishment."

41 One day as he was sitting in sight of the alms-box he observed
42 how the people were dropping large sums of money into it. Then

came a widow who dropped in only two mites, together equal in
43 value to a cent. Calling his disciples to him Jesus said, "Truly, this
poor widow has sacrificed more than all the others who dropped
44 their gifts into the alms-box. For they gave out of their abundance;
but she, needy as she is, has offered all that she had, the very last
that was left to her for her support."

CHAPTER 13.

1 As they were going out of the temple, one of his disciples said to
him, "Look, master, what huge stones these are, and what a massive
2 building this temple is!" Jesus answered, "Yes, take a good look at
this mighty structure! For be assured, not one of these stones will
be left upon another. Everything will be torn down. But another
temple, not built by human hands, will arise — and arise within a
period of three days.
3 He then went to the mount of Olives, and as he sat there his eyes
fell upon the temple lying opposite. Peter, James, John, and Andrew,
4 being for the moment alone with him, asked him, "Tell us, when
will your prediction come true, and what sign will announce the com-
5 ing of the day of fulfillment?" Then Jesus began to teach them of
6 this matter, saying, "Take care to let no one deceive you. For some
will come calling themselves by my name, and saying, 'I am the
7 Messiah,' and many will be misled by them. Should you hear of
wars or rumors of wars, do not be alarmed on that account, for such
things are bound to happen from time to time; but they do not by
8 any means signify the fulfillment. It is not uncommon for one nation to rise against another, or for kingdom to rise against kingdom.
And even if in one part of the world or another there are earthquakes and famines, these are only forewarnings of the day that will
9 bring with it the real disaster. Moreover, you yourselves will first
be arraigned before the Jewish courts, and flogged in the synagogues.
You will be taken into the presence of governors and kings because
you are followers of mine, and you will testify before them and be-
10 fore the spirit-people of all spheres on behalf of the truth. For first
the gospel will have to be proclaimed to all the people in all the
11 spirit-realms. And when you are taken into custody and arraigned
before the court, have no anxiety beforehand as to what you shall
say there. Speak only that which will be given to you in that hour;
for it will not be you who speak then, but the holy spirit-world that
12 will speak through you. The time is coming when brother will deliver brother to death, and the father his child. Children will appear
13 against their parents and will be the cause of their execution. And

you will invite the hatred of all, because you are called by my name.
But only he who remains steadfast to the end will be saved.
14 "As soon, however, as the day comes on which you see appalling
horror and desecration in a place where otherwise such things
could not possibly happen, then let all who remember my words
realize the meaning of what is going on before their eyes. Then let
15 the people of Judaea flee to the mountains. Let no one who is on the
house-top seek safety within the house, or so much as enter it to
16 take away anything, and let no one who has gone into the fields
17 turn back to get his cloak. Woe to the women who await motherhood
18 in those days, and to those with babes at their breasts! Pray to God
19 that these things may not happen in winter, for it will be a time of
terrible suffering, such as has not been known since the creation of
20 the world and will never occur again. And if the Lord had not
lessened the number of those days, not a creature would escape
alive. But for the sake of the elect whom He has chosen, He has
21 lessened the number of those days. If any one then says to you,
22 'See, here is the Messiah,' or, 'That is he,' do not believe it. For
mediums of the evil spirit-world will arise, and they will show signs
and work miracles, hoping to deceive even the elect so far as pos-
23 sible. Be on your guard! I have told you everything beforehand.
24 "But when this time of tribulation is past, then, for the victims,
25 the sun will grow dark and the moon lose its brightness; for them
the stars will disappear from the sky, and the evil powers of the
26 beyond will be greatly disturbed. For then they will see the Son of
man coming with great might and glory at the head of the hosts of
27 heaven, and he will send out his spirit-messengers to gather from
the four winds, from one end of the beyond to the other, those who
are so designated.
28 "Learn the lesson taught by the fig tree. When its twigs become
29 tender and break into leaf, you know that summer is at hand. So too
when those things come to pass of which I have spoken, you may be
30 assured that the fulfillment of my prophecy is close at hand. You
may take my word for it that this nation will not complete its present
31 course until all these things have been fulfilled. Sky and earth will
some day pass away, but my words will not pass away unfulfilled.
32 But the exact day and hour when all this will take place, no one
knows, not the angels of heaven, nor even the Son, but the Father
alone.
33 "Take heed and watch, for you do not know when this hour of
34 destiny will come. As a man who sets out on a journey gives directions to his servants at the time of his departure, assigning to each

one his task, and enjoining his gate-keeper to keep strict watch, so
35 you also must be watchful; for you do not know when the master of
the house will come, whether in the evening, at midnight, at cock-
36 crow, or in the morning. And if he comes unexpectedly, let him not
find you asleep. Therefore I again say to you, 'Watch.'"

CHAPTER 14.

1 It was now only two days until the feast of the Passover. The chief
priests and the scribes were busily trying to contrive some way of
2 laying hold of Jesus so that they might put him to death, although
they were all agreed that on the day of the festival itself everything
that might provoke an uprising among the people would at all costs
have to be avoided.
3 Jesus was in Bethany at the house of Simon the leper. While he
was reclining at table, there came to him a woman carrying an
alabaster flask filled with fragrant oil, and breaking the flask she
4 poured its contents on his head. At this his disciples became indig-
5 nant and said, "Why this waste of ointment, which might have been
sold for more than sixty dollars and the money given to the poor?"
6 In this manner they sought to vent their anger on the woman. But
Jesus reproved them, saying, "Let her alone. Why do you censure
7 her? The woman has performed for me an act of great love. As for
the poor, you have them with you at all times, and can show them
kindness whenever you like; but you will not have me with you
8 always. She did all that lay in her power; she anointed my body
9 beforehand for the day of my burial. Be assured that wherever
throughout the whole world the gospel is preached, this woman's
deed will also be told, and her memory thus honored."
10 Judas Iscariot, one of the Twelve, went to the chief priests and
11 declared his readiness to deliver Jesus into their hands. Highly
pleased, they promised to give him money for his services. He now
sought a favorable opportunity to deliver Jesus to them by treachery.
12 On the first day of unleavened bread—the day on which the
Passover lamb is killed—his disciples asked him, "Where do you
13 wish us to go to prepare the Passover lamb for you to eat?" He
sent out two of them with the instructions, "Go into the city. There
14 you will be met by a man carrying a jar of water. Follow him into
the house that he enters, and say to the owner of the house, 'The
master sent us to ask you, "Where is the guest-chamber for me, in
15 which I may eat the Passover lamb with my disciples?"' He will
then show you a large upper room furnished with tables and cushions, and ready for use. There make your preparations."

16 The two disciples set out and reached the city. There they found
everything as Jesus had told them, and prepared the feast of the
17 Passover. At nightfall Jesus came in with the Twelve, and all re-
18 clined at table and ate. Suddenly Jesus exclaimed, "One of you will
19 betray me — one who is sharing this meal with me." Deeply pained,
one after another asked him, "Surely, master, it is not I?" and,
20 "Nor I, surely?" He answered, "It is one of these twelve; and
it is the one who is dipping his fingers into the same dish with me.
21 The Son of man must indeed travel his appointed road, as it is
written of him in the Scriptures; but woe to that man by whom he
is betrayed. It would be better for him if he had not been born in
the flesh."

22 During the meal Jesus took up a loaf, blessed it, broke it into
pieces, and passed it around among the disciples with the words,
23 "Take this; it is the symbol of my body." Then taking up a cup,
he blessed it and passed it to those who were with him, and all drank
24 of it. And he said to them, "This is the symbol of the blood of
25 my covenant, that is shed for many. You have my solemn assurance that I shall not again offer a drink of the fruit of the vine,
until that day on which I drink it in God's spirit-world — and drink
it in a form as yet unknown to you."

26 After singing a hymn of praise, they went out of the city to the
27 Mount of Olives. On the way, Jesus said to them, "All of you will
forsake me, for it is written: 'I shall strike down the shepherd, and
28 the sheep will scatter.' But after I have risen, I shall go before you
29 into Galilee." Peter protested, "Even if they all turn from you,
30 I will not." But Jesus answered, "You may take my word for it
that on this very night, before the cock has crowed twice, you will
31 disown me three times." — "Though I must die with you, I will not
disown you," Peter protested anew; and the others did likewise.

32 From there they went to a place called Gethsemane, where he
33 said to his disciples, "Sit down here, until I have prayed." He then
took with him Peter, James, and John. Suddenly he was overcome
by a feeling of dreadful fear and utter loneliness, and turning to
34 the three disciples he said, "I am so unspeakably sad at heart that I
35 wish I were dead. Wait here and watch." Then, going a little farther, he threw himself upon the ground and prayed that if it were
36 possible he might be spared this hour. "My Father," he prayed, "for
37 Thee all things are possible. Let this cup pass from me. Nevertheless, may thy will, not mine, be done." Returning to the three, he
found them asleep. He aroused Peter with the words, "What Simon?
38 Asleep? Were you unable to stay awake a single hour? Watch and

pray, that you may not fall a victim to temptation. The spirit is
39 willing, but the flesh is weak." Then he went away and repeated his
40 prayer. When he came back to them he found them sleeping again,
for in their weariness they could not keep their eyes open, nor could
41 they think of any excuse to offer. When he came to them for the
third time he reproved them, saying, "There will be other times
when you can sleep and rest. Now there is no reason for it, and this
is not the proper time. For now the Son of man is being delivered
42 into the hands of apostates. Get up, let us be going. My betrayer is
close at hand."

43 Hardly had he spoken when Judas Iscariot, one of the Twelve,
appeared, accompanied by a mob of men armed with swords and
clubs, who had been sent out by the chief priests, scribes, and elders.
44 His betrayer had arranged with them the following signal: "He
whom I shall kiss is the man. Lay hold of him, and see to it that
45 you carry him safely off." He now stepped up to Jesus, exclaiming,
46 "Master!" and kissing him; and the men laid hands on him and
47 arrested him. Some one drew a sword and struck at the high priest's
48 servant, cutting off his ear. Jesus turned to the crowd and said,
"You have come here to arrest me, armed with swords and clubs
49 as though it were to be a fight with a robber. I was among you
daily in the temple, teaching, and yet you never laid hands on me;
but it was destined that I should be taken on this day, in order that
50 the Scriptures might be fulfilled." Then all his disciples forsook him
51 and fled. One youth, however, remained near him and followed the
52 armed mob, clad only in a linen cloth. The men also seized him in
order to arrest him, but he left his linen cloth in their hands and fled
in his undergarment.

53 They took Jesus before the high priest, around whom had gath-
54 ered all of the chief priests, scribes, and elders. Peter had followed
at a distance and sat down among the servants in the inner court of
the high priest's palace to warm himself by the fire.

55 The chief priests and the whole Council sought evidence against
Jesus to warrant condemning him to death, but they could find
56 none. Many indeed testified falsely against him, but their statements
57 did not agree. Thus certain witnesses appeared and falsely testified,
58 "We heard him say that he would destroy the temple built by man,
and within three days would put up another, not built by man."
59 But their testimony also conflicted.

60 Then the high priest rose, stepped forward, and asked Jesus,
61 "Have you no answer to make to this testimony?" But Jesus remained silent and gave no answer at all. Again the high priest asked

62 him, "Are you the Messiah, the Son of the Most High?" Jesus answered, "Yes, I am he. And you will see the Son of man, surrounded
by the hosts of heaven, sitting at the right hand of the Almighty."
63 Then the high priest tore his clothing and exclaimed, "What need
64 have we of any further witnesses? You yourselves have heard the
blasphemy. What is your verdict?" All agreed that he was guilty
65 and condemned him to death. Some at once began to spit in his face
and beat him with their fists, exclaiming, "Now show that you are
a prophet!" The servants also struck at him repeatedly and slapped
him in the face.

66 Meanwhile Peter was sitting below in the courtyard. One of the
67 maids passed by, and seeing him warming himself, looked at him
more closely and said, "You are the same one who was with the
68 Nazarene—this Jesus." But he denied it, protesting, "I know
nothing of this, and I cannot understand how you come to say such
a thing." And he immediately rose and went out to the entrance of
69 the outer court. At that instant a cock crowed. But there the same
70 maid saw him again and told the by-standers, "This fellow is one of
that lot." Once more Peter denied it, but presently those near him
71 insisted, "You are certainly one of them, for you are a Galilean."
Then he began to curse, and to declare with oaths, "I do not know
72 the man of whom you speak." For the second time a cock crowed.
Now Peter remembered what Jesus had said to him; and he burst
into tears.

CHAPTER 15.

1 At daybreak the chief priests conferred with the elders, the
scribes, and all the High Council, after which they had Jesus
bound and led away into the inner court, where they delivered him
2 to Pilate. He asked Jesus, "Are you the King of the Jews?" and
3 Jesus answered, "Yes, I am he." And when the chief priests had
4 brought charge after charge against Jesus, Pilate asked him again,
"Have you no answer to make? Listen to all these things they are
5 saying against you." But to Pilate's great amazement Jesus still
answered nothing.

6 Now it was Pilate's custom to release on every feast-day one
7 prisoner whom the people might choose. At this time there was in
prison a man named Barabbas. He had taken part in a riot and had
been arrested along with the other rioters, who had committed a
8 murder. The crowd, which was continually increasing, demanded
9 that the usual favor now be granted. Pilate asked them, "Shall I
10 release the King of the Jews to you?" For he well knew that the
11 chief priests had delivered him merely out of envy. But the chief

priests had by their art of persuasion induced the people to demand
12 the release of Barabbas. "And what," asked Pilate, "do you want
13 me to do with the king of the Jews?" The whole crowd shouted, "Let
14 him be crucified!"—"Why, what wrong has he done?" Pilate
15 asked. But they shouted all the louder, "Let him be crucified!" Then
Pilate released Barabbas, and striking Jesus with his scourge to
signify that he was condemned to death, he delivered him to be
crucified.

16 The soldiers took Jesus to the garrison grounds and assembled
17 the whole detachment. They threw a purple robe over his shoulders,
18 and put a crown of thorns upon his head. Then they saluted him as
19 king with the cry, "Hail, king of the Jews!" At the same time they
20 struck him on the head with a cane and spat in his face. They then
took off the purple robe, dressed him again in his own clothes, and
led him away to be crucified.

21 They compelled a certain Simon of Cyrene, the father of Alexander and Rufus, who was returning from the fields and chanced to
22 pass there, to carry the cross for Jesus. Then they led him to the
place of execution called Golgotha, a name meaning "the place of
23 skulls." Here they offered him wine spiced with myrrh, but he would
24 not drink of it. After he had been crucified, they divided his garments among them, casting lots to decide what share each man
25 should receive. It was nine o'clock in the morning when they placed
26 a guard over him. The charge against him, as stated by the superscription read: *This is the King of the Jews.*

27 At the same time they crucified two robbers with him, one at his
29 right hand and one at his left. The passers-by jeered at him, tossing
their heads and calling out, "So you are the man who was going to
30 pull down the temple and build it again in three days! Come down
31 from the cross and save yourself!" The chief priests and the scribes
likewise said scoffingly to each other, "He has helped others, but
32 he cannot help himself. Let this Messiah, this King of Israel, come
down from the cross so that we may see it and believe in him." Even
the two who were crucified with him hurled insults at him.

33 At noon darkness fell upon the whole land and lasted until three
34 o'clock in the afternoon. At three o'clock Jesus cried out in a loud
voice, "Eli, Eli, lama dsaphthani?" which means, "My God, my
35 God, why hast Thou forsaken me?" When some of the by-standers
36 heard this, they said, "He is calling Elijah." One of them ran and
soaked a sponge in wine mixed with vinegar, put it on a staff, and
offered it to Jesus to drink, saying, "Let us see whether Elijah will
come to take him down."

37 But Jesus uttered a loud cry and expired.
38 At that instant the curtain of the temple was torn in two from
top to bottom.
39 When the centurion who stood near by heard this cry and saw
that Jesus had breathed his last, he exclaimed, "This man was certainly the son of a god!"
40 There were also some women looking on from the distance.
Among them were Mary of Magdala, and Mary the mother of the
41 younger James and of Joses, and also Salome. While Jesus lived in
Galilee these women were with him constantly. Standing beside
them were many other women who likewise had come with him to
Jerusalem.
42 In the last hours before sunset, the time when preparations are
made for the coming Sabbath, and which is therefore called the
"Pre-Sabbath," Joseph of Arimathaea boldly went to Pilate to ask
43 that the body of Jesus be given to him. Joseph was a highly respected member of the High Council, and all his life had eagerly
44 awaited the coming of God's spirit-world. Pilate could scarcely believe that Jesus was already dead, and therefore sent for the centurion to inquire of him whether the condemned man had actually
45 died. On receiving the centurion's confirmation, he allowed Joseph
46 to have the body. Joseph bought linen, took Jesus down from the
cross, wrapped him in the linen, and laid him away in a tomb that
had been hewn out of rock. Then he rolled a stone before the en-
47 trance to the tomb and went away. Mary of Magdala and Mary the
mother of James saw the place where he was laid.

CHAPTER 16.

1 These women had gone away and bought fragrant spices with
2 which to anoint the body. Early in the morning of the day after
3 the Sabbath, they set out for the grave. It was just at sunrise. As
they walked they asked each other, "Who will roll away the stone at
4 the door of the tomb?" for it was a very large one. But when they
came to the grave they found that the stone had already been rolled
5 away, and on entering the tomb they saw a youth sitting at the right,
6 clad in a long white garment. They were terror-stricken, but he said
to them, "Do not be afraid! You are looking for Jesus, the crucified.
He has risen, he is not here. See, this is the place where they laid
7 him. Go back quickly and give his disciples, including Peter, the
following message: 'Behold, I go before you into Galilee. There you
8 will see me again, as I promised.'" They hurried out of the tomb
and ran away as fast as they could, for they were filled with awe and

terror. Neither of them said a word to the other, so tongue-tied were
they with fright.
9 Among the first to whom Jesus appeared, after his resurrection in
the early morning hours of the day after the Sabbath, was the same
10 Mary of Magdala out of whom he had driven seven demons. She
carried the tidings to those who had been his companions and who
11 were now mourning and weeping for him. When they heard that he
12 was alive and had appeared to her, they would not believe it. Later
he showed himself in other than ordinary human form to two of
13 them while they were walking about the country-side. They also came
back and reported it, but the others would not believe them either.
14 Afterwards he appeared to the eleven as they were at table. He
sharply reproved them for the unbelief and the obstinacy they had
shown in refusing to credit what they had heard from those who had
seen him with their own eyes after he had risen from the dead. Seeking a defence against his reproof, they excused themselves by answering, "This age, with its lawlessness and its unbelief, is wholly under the rule of Satan, who, by means of his world of evil spirits, prevents God's truth from asserting its power. But show us the way that you know of winning God's approval." It was thus that they spoke to Christ. And he answered them, "The course of Satan's rule is now at an end. A new and wonderful reign is at hand. On behalf of all who had committed the sin of apostasy I was delivered to the Prince of Death, in order that these deserters might turn again to the truth and no longer remain apostate, but attain to the everlasting heavenly glory of the spirit, which will be the heritage of those who do God's will."
15 Then he charged them with their mission, saying, "Go out into
16 the whole universe and preach the gospel to all creation. He who
believes and is baptized will be saved, but he who does not believe
17 will be punished as he deserves. And these are the signs of the truth
that will be given to those who believe: In my name they will drive
18 out evil spirits; they will speak foreign tongues; they will be able
to handle serpents without danger, and if they drink anything
deadly, it will not harm them; they will lay their hands on the sick,
and they will recover."
19 After the lord Jesus had spoken these words he was taken up into
20 heaven, and sat at the right hand of God. But his disciples went out
and preached everywhere; and the lord stood by them with his
power and confirmed the truth of their message by the wonders that
accompanied their sermons.

The Gospel according to LUKE

CHAPTER 1.

1 MANY before me have undertaken to write the story of the well-
2 attested events that happened among us. Their accounts agree
with what we have been told by those who were eyewitnesses from
the beginning, and who appeared in public to proclaim the truth.
3 Now I too have looked carefully into all of the facts from the
very outset, and have decided likewise to write them down in historical order and to send my account to you, most noble Theophilus,
4 in order that you may be fully convinced of the truth of that which
you learned by word of mouth.
5 In the days of Herod, the king of the Jews, there lived a priest
named Zacharias, who belonged to the order of Abijah. His wife
6 was descended from Aaron, and was named Elizabeth. Both led a
life pleasing to God, for they obeyed all His commandments and
7 ordinances. They had no children, the joys of motherhood having
hitherto been denied to Elizabeth; and both she and her husband
were advanced in years.
8 One day it was the turn of the priestly order to which Zacharias
9 belonged to hold divine service. As usual, the officiating priest was
chosen by lot, and on this occasion the lot fell to Zacharias. He
therefore went into the temple of the Lord to burn incense there,
10 while the people, as was their custom, stood outside, engaged in
prayer.
11 Presently there appeared to him an angel of the Lord, standing
12 at the right of the altar of burnt-offerings. On seeing him Zacharias
13 was startled and began to tremble, but the angel said, "Have no
fear, Zacharias, your prayer has been heard. Your wife Elizabeth
will bear of your seed a son, to whom you are to give the name of
14 John. He will bring you great joy and gladness, and many others
15 will also rejoice at his birth. He will be great in the sight of the
Lord. He will drink neither wine nor other strong drink, and a great
16 number of holy spirits will be about him from his very birth. He
will lead many of the children of Israel back to the Lord their God.
17 It is he who shall go before Him in the spirit and the power of
Elijah, in order to bring about repentance among parents and chil-

dren alike, to turn unbelievers into believers, and so to prepare for
the Lord a people armed with all the weapons of goodness."
18 Zacharias asked the angel, "What proof have I that your message
is true? I am an old man, and my wife is also well on in years."
19 The angel answered, "I am Gabriel, one who is admitted to the
presence of God, and I have been sent to speak to you and bring
20 you this good news. But as punishment for doubting my words,
which will nevertheless come true at the appointed time, you will
be struck dumb. Not a word will you be able to speak until the day
on which my promise is fulfilled."

21 Meanwhile the people outside waited for Zacharias, wondering
22 at the length of his stay in the sanctuary. When at last he came out
he was unable to speak, and they knew that he must have seen a
vision in the temple. He now tried to make himself understood by
signs, and henceforward remained speechless.

23 When the days of his service as priest were over, he went back
24 to his home. Soon afterwards his wife Elizabeth conceived and went
25 into seclusion for five months. "This mercy," she used to say, "has
been shown me by the Lord at the moment when He deigned to lift
from me the reproach that rested upon me in the eyes of the people."
26 In the sixth month after this event the angel Gabriel was sent by
27 the Lord into a town of Galilee called Nazareth, to a young woman
who was betrothed to a man belonging to the house of David. His
28 name was Joseph, and the young woman's Mary. The angel entered
and greeted her with the words, "Hail, favored one! The Lord is
29 with you. You are blessed among women." Startled at this saluta-
30 tion, she began to ponder on its meaning, but the angel continued,
"Have no fear, Mary, for you have found favor in the sight of God.
31 You will conceive and bear a son whom you shall call Jesus. He
32 will be great, and will be called a Son of the Highest. The Lord
33 God will give him the throne of his forefather David. He will rule
over the house of Jacob until days to come, and his reign will have
34 no end." Then Mary asked the angel, "How can this be, when I
35 have had relations with no man?" The angel replied, "A holy
spirit will come upon you, and the power of one who is very high
will overshadow you. Therefore the child, divinely consecrated, will
36 be called a 'son of God.' Know also that your relative, Elizabeth,
has conceived in spite of her advanced age, and awaits a son; and
37 this is the sixth month with her who was said to be barren. For
38 God promises nothing that is not fulfilled." And Mary said, "I
consider myself a servant of the Lord. Let it be with me as you have
said." And the angel left her.

39 A few days later Mary set out and hurried into the hill-country
40 to a village of Judah, where she entered the house of Zacharias and
41 greeted Elizabeth. At the instant that Elizabeth heard Mary's greeting, the child leaped in her womb, and she was overwhelmed by
42 the full power of a holy spirit, and cried out, "Blessed are you
43 among women, and blessed is the fruit of your womb. Who am I
to deserve the happiness of having the mother of my lord come to
44 me? For when your greeting sounded in my ears, the child within
45 me leaped for joy. Happy is she who has believed that the promise
given her by the Lord will be fulfilled."

46 At this Mary exclaimed, "My soul praises the Lord, and my
47 spirit exults in God, my Savior. For the Lord has looked with favor
48 upon the lowliness of His servant, and henceforth all generations
49 will call me blessed; for the Almighty has done great things for me.
50 Yes, holy is His name! His mercy will be bestowed from generation
51 to generation on those who reverence Him. He has ruled with a
52 mighty arm, scattering the overbearing, driving the proud from their
53 thrones, and exalting the lowly in heart. He has satisfied the hungry
with possessions, and the wealthy He has sent away empty-handed.
54 He has befriended His servant Israel and has not forgotten to show
55 him mercy. For so, indeed, He promised our forefathers, Abraham
and his offspring, for all time."

56 Mary stayed with Elizabeth for three months, and then went back
to her home.

57 When Elizabeth's time of confinement came, she gave birth to a
58 son, and her neighbors and relatives, hearing that the Lord had
59 shown her this great mercy, rejoiced with her. On the eighth day
they came to circumcise the child, thinking to name him Zacharias
60 after his father. But his mother protested, "No, he shall be called
61 John!"—"But," they objected, "there is no one in your whole
family who bears that name!"

62 Then the father was asked by signs what name he wished the child
63 to have. He motioned for a tablet and wrote on it, "His name is
64 John." From that very moment his tongue was freed. All were
65 astonished when he opened his lips and praised God. A sense of
awe came over every one who lived in this region, and throughout
66 the hill-country of Judaea people spoke of these happenings. All
who heard of them were deeply impressed, and said to one another,
"What will this child be when he grows up? For the hand of the
Lord is over him."

67 His father, Zacharias, was filled with the overwhelming power of
68 a holy spirit, and exclaimed, "Blessed be the Lord, the God of

Israel! For He has looked graciously upon His people and brought
69 them redemption. He has raised up a mighty deliverer for us in the
70 house of His servant David, as He proclaimed of old through the
71 lips of His prophets when they said: 'He will save us from our
72 enemies and deliver us from the hand of those who hate us. Thus He
chooses to show mercy to our fathers, mindful of His holy covenant
73 and of the oath which He swore to our forefather Abraham, to save
74 us out of the hands of our enemies and to grant us strength to serve
75 Him fearlessly, piously, and uprightly, all the days of our lives.'
76 And you, little child, will be called a messenger of one who is very
high, for you will go before the lord to prepare the way for him.
77 You shall carry to his people knowledge of the redemption, which
consists in deliverance from the sin of their apostasy, and which is
78 owing to the loving mercy of our God. By His love and mercy the
79 sun has risen again for us from on high, and a light has shone down
upon us which shall illumine those who sit in the darkness and in
the shadow of the kingdom of death, and so guide their feet back to
the path of peace."

80 As the child grew into a youth, the powers of God's spirit-world
became daily more manifest in him; and until he appeared publicly
before the people of Israel, he continued to live in the barren mountain-district of his home.

CHAPTER 2.

1 The time came when the emperor Augustus decreed that a census
2 should be taken throughout the whole Roman empire. This census
was the first of its kind. In Syria it was taken by Quirinius, who was
3 governor there at that time. The people all presented themselves for
4 registration, each man in the place belonging to his own tribe. Thus
Joseph, among others, went from his place of residence, Nazareth
in Galilee, up into the district of the tribe of Judah to the town of
David called Bethlehem; for he was of the tribe and lineage of
5 David. He too intended to have himself enrolled in the census-list,
6 together with Mary, his wife, who was with child. When they ar-
7 rived there the time of her delivery came, and she brought forth
her first-born, a son, and wrapped him in swaddling-clothes and
laid him in a manger; for they had not been able to find room at
the inn.

8 Meanwhile some shepherds in this district were spending the
9 night in the open, watching their flocks. Presently an angel of the
Lord appeared over them, and a wonderful radiance shone all about
10 them. They were terror-stricken, but the angel reassured them, say-

ing, "Have no fear. I have exceedingly joyful news for you, news
11 that affects all the people. For to-day in the town of David the
12 Redeemer has been born. He is the Messiah sent by God. And this
shall be the proof for you: You will find an infant wrapped in
swaddling-clothes, lying in a manger."
13 Suddenly there appeared beside the angel a great host of spirits
14 from the beyond, praising the Lord with the words, "Glory to God
on high, and peace on earth in the hearts of men of good will."
15 Scarcely had the angels and the spirits who had once lived as
human beings vanished from their sight and gone back into the
spirit-realm, when the shepherds said to one another, "Let us hasten
to Bethlehem to see whether the news that the Lord has sent us is
really a fact."
16 They hurried away and found Mary and Joseph, and the newborn
17 babe lying in the manger. Having thus assured themselves of the
truth, they related the message that they had received concerning the
18 importance of the child. Those who heard them could not wonder
19 enough at the story told by the shepherds. Mary was also greatly
20 impressed, and she pondered on it deeply. The shepherds went back
to their flocks, glorifying and praising God for the things that they
had heard and with their own eyes had seen confirmed.
21 After eight days the infant was circumcised. He was given the
name of Jesus, as the angel had directed before the child had been
conceived.
22 Forty days later, when the time of purification prescribed by the
Law of Moses was ended, the child was taken to Jerusalem to be
23 dedicated to the Lord; for it is written in the Law of the Lord:
24 "Every first-born male child shall be dedicated to the Lord." At
the same time the parents wished to offer the sacrifice that is commanded by the Law of the Lord: a pair of turtle doves or two young
pigeons.
25 At that time there was living in Jerusalem one Simeon, a man
wholly after God's heart, who was awaiting with great longing some
26 consolation for Israel. He was under the guidance of a holy spirit,
which had revealed to him among other things that he would not
27 die until he had seen the Messiah sent by the Lord. Directed by this
spirit, he entered the temple at the moment at which the parents
were bringing in the child Jesus to fulfill the requirements of the
28 Law concerning him. Simeon took the child in his arms and praised
29 God with the words, "Now, O Lord, Thou callest Thy servant away
30 in peace, according to Thy word; for my eyes have seen Thy salva-
31 tion, which Thou hast prepared before the eyes of all nations as a

32 light that will make manifest and lead back to glory those who
belong to Thy true people Israel."
33 The father and the mother of the infant were amazed at the words
34 which they thus heard spoken of him. Simeon blessed them, and
turning to Mary, the child's mother, he said, "Through this child
many in Israel are destined to fall and many others to be raised;
35 for his method of procedure will provoke opposition, and the sword
of inner discord will pierce even your own soul. Thus the true
character of many will be revealed."

36 There also lived in those days a certain Anna, a prophetess, the
37 daughter of Phanuel of the tribe of Aser. She was now very old, for
after her girlhood she had been married only seven years, after
which had followed eighty-four years of widowhood. She never
went outside of the temple, but served God there with prayer and
38 fasting, day and night. She also came upon the infant at this
moment, praised God, and told the news to all those in Jerusalem
who were awaiting the Redemption.

39 When the parents had done everything required of them by the
Law of the Lord, they returned into Galilee to their own town of
40 Nazareth. The child grew, and day by day the powers of God's
spirit-world were seen to gain strength within him. The fullness of
wisdom came to him, and the delight of God rested upon him.

41 It was the custom of his parents to go to Jerusalem every year
42 for the feast of the Passover. Now when the boy was twelve years old
and they again went to Jerusalem for the feast of unleavened bread,
43 they took him with them. After the festival was over, they set out
for home, but the boy Jesus stayed behind in Jerusalem without the
44 knowledge of his parents. Supposing him to be somewhere in the
caravan of worshippers, they had completed their first day's journey
before they began to inquire for him among their relatives and
45 acquaintances. As they could not find him, they went back to Jeru-
46 salem to look for him there, and after three days they found him in
the temple, sitting among the teachers of the Law, listening to them
47 and asking them questions. Every one who heard him was amazed
at the understanding that he manifested and at the answers that he
48 gave. When his parents saw him they were dumbfounded, and his
mother said to him, "My boy, why have you done this to us? Your
49 father and I have been looking for you in anxiety and grief." He
answered, "What need had you to look for me? Could you not realize that I must be where my Father's affairs are being dealt with?"
50 But they did not fathom the meaning of his words.

51 He went back to Nazareth with them, and was always a dutiful

52 son. His mother treasured all these incidents in her memory. As he
ripened in years, Jesus grew in wisdom and became day by day
dearer to God and man.

CHAPTER 3.

1 In the fifteenth year of the reign of the emperor Tiberius, when
Pontius Pilate was governor of Judaea, Herod tetrarch of Galilee,
his brother Philip tetrarch of Ituraea and the district of Trachon-
2 itis, Lysanias tetrarch of Abylene, and Annas and Caiaphas the high
priests, a message from God was conveyed to John, the son of Zach-
3 arias, who was living in a barren mountain-district. After this John
travelled throughout the region that borders on the Jordan, preaching baptism by immersion as an outward symbol of faith in his
teaching and of a change of heart whereby one might obtain forgiveness for the sins of apostasy.

4 John's coming had been foretold through the prophet Isaiah, in
the words of the Scriptures: "I hear some one calling with a loud
voice in a barren mountain-district, 'Prepare the way for the lord!
5 Smooth the paths over which he will come to you! Every hollow
shall be filled, and every mountain and hill shall be levelled. That
which is crooked shall be made straight, and the paths that are
6 rough shall be evened. And all creation will see the salvation that
comes from God.' "

7 Those people whom he saw evading baptism he rebuked with
the words, "You brood of serpents! Who has beguiled you into the
8 folly of thinking that you can escape the judgment to come? You
too have to change your hearts and to give evidence of the change
by your deeds. Do not seek to quiet your consciences by saying,
'We have Abraham for our father'; for I tell you that God can raise
9 up children for Abraham out of the rocks before your eyes. The
axe has already been laid to the roots of the trees, and every tree
that fails to bear good fruit will be uprooted and thrown into the
fire."

10 The crowd asked him, "Then what must we do to be saved?"
11 And he answered, "Let every one who has two changes of clothing
give one to him who has none; and let every one who has food for
12 his daily needs likewise share it with others." Tax-collectors also
came to be baptized, and they asked him, "Master, what shall we
13 do to obtain salvation?" He answered them, "Do not collect more
14 money from the people than you have a right to."—"And we,"
some soldiers asked him, "what shall we do for the salvation of our

souls?" — "Do violence to no one," he answered; "practise no extortion on false pretexts, but be content with your pay."
15 The people fell to conjecturing about John's identity, and the
16 thought came to all that perhaps he might be the Messiah. Reading
what was passing through their minds, John addressed his entire
audience in these words: "I baptize you by immersion in waves of
water as an outward sign of your faith in my teaching and as a
symbol of your change of heart. But after me will come one who
is mightier than I, one whose very sandal-straps I am not even
worthy to undo. He will immerse you in the power-waves of a holy
17 spirit and of fire. His winnowing shovel is in his hand, and he will
clean his threshing-floor thoroughly, gathering the grain into granaries, but burning the chaff with a fire that cannot be quenched until all chaff is consumed."

18 In this and in similar sermons he framed the gospel that he preached to the people.

19 John had reproved Herod the tetrach for having married his
brother Philip's wife, and had severely censured him for all the
20 other wicked things he had done. But Herod now crowned all his
evil deeds by sending John to prison.

21 One day, after the crowds had been baptized, Jesus also came to
receive baptism. While he was still at prayer, the heavens opened
22 and John saw the Holy Spirit of God descend upon Jesus in the visible shape of a dove, and a voice came from the heavens, saying, "You are my beloved son; with you I was well pleased."

23 When Jesus first began to appear in public, he was about thirty
years of age. He was regarded as a son of Joseph. Joseph was a son
24 of Jacob, who was a son of Matthan, who was a son of Eleazar, who
25 was a son of Eliud, who was a son of Achim, who was a son of
26 Zadok, who was a son of Azor, who was a son of Eliakim, who was
27 a son of Abiud, who was a son of Zerubbabel, who was a son of
Shealthiel, who was a son of Jechoniah, who was a son of Josiah,
28 who was a son of Amos, who was a son of Manasseh, who was a son
29 of Hezekiah, who was a son of Ahaz, who was a son of Jonathan,
30 who was a son of Uzziah, who was a son of Amasiah, who was a son
of Joas, who was a son of Ochosiah, who was a son of Joram, who
31 was a son of Jehoshaphat, who was a son of Asa, who was a son of
Abiud, who was a son of Rehoboam, who was a son of Solomon,
32 who was a son of David, who was a son of Jesse, who was a son of
Obed, who was a son of Boaz, who was a son of Sala, who was a son
33 of Naason, who was a son of Aminadab, who was a son of Aram,
who was a son of Esrom, who was a son of Phares, who was a son

34 of Judah, who was a son of Jacob, who was a son of Isaac, who was
a son of Abraham, who was a son of Thara, who was a son of
35 Nachor, who was a son of Saruch, who was a son of Ragau, who
was a son of Phalec, who was a son of Heber, who was a son of Sala,
36 who was a son of Cainan, who was a son of Arphaxad, who was a
37 son of Sem, who was a son of Lamech, who was a son of Mathusala,
who was a son of Enoch, who was a son of Jared, who was a son of
38 Maleleel, who was a son of Cainan, who was a son of Enos, who was
a son of Seth, who was a son of Adam, who was a son of God.

CHAPTER 4.

1 Completely under the influence of a holy spirit, Jesus returned
from the Jordan, and by the same spirit he was led about in the
2 wilderness, where for forty days he was constantly tempted by
Satan. During this time he had nothing to eat, and at length he
3 was nearly dead of hunger. Then the devil said to him, "If you are
4 a son of God, command these stones to turn into bread." To this
Jesus answered, "It is written: 'Man shall not seek to preserve the
life that depends solely on earthly bread for its subsistence, but the
life that is obtained through observance of every one of God's commandments.' "

5 The devil then took him to the top of a high mountain, showing
6 him for a moment all the kingdoms of the universe, and saying to
him, "I will give you all of this realm of power in its full glory, for
7 it is mine to bestow, and I may give it to whom I will. If you will
fall down before me and acknowledge me as your lord, it shall be
8 yours." Jesus answered him in the words of the Scriptures: "Before
God alone shall you fall down, Him only shall you acknowledge
as your Lord."

9 Then the devil took him to Jerusalem, set him on the pinnacle of
the temple, and said to him, "If you are a son of God, throw your-
10 self down from here; for it is written: 'He will commisison His
11 angels to watch carefully over you; yes, they shall bear you in their
12 hands lest you strike your foot against a stone.' " Jesus answered,
"But the Scriptures also say: 'You shall not tempt the Lord your
God.' "

13 When the devil had exhausted all of his powers of temptation,
he withdrew from him to bide his time.

14 Under the powerful influence of God's spirit-world, Jesus went
15 back to Galilee. His fame spread throughout the region, and he
preached in the synagogues, winning high praise from all.

16 Among the places that he visited was Nazareth, where he had

grown up, and as was his custom, he went to the synagogue there
on the Sabbath. To show that he wished to read something from
17 the Scriptures, he stood up, and some one gave him the scroll of the
prophet Isaiah. On opening it he chanced upon a passage which
18 read: "A spirit of the Lord is upon me, for He has anointed me to
bring joyful news to the poor. He has sent me to proclaim deliverance to captives and recovery of sight to the blind, to free the op-
19 pressed, and to announce the Lord's year of pardon."

20 Closing the scroll he gave it back to the attendant and sat down,
while the eyes of every one in the synagogue rested expectantly upon
21 him. He began his address with the words, "The passage from the
Scriptures which you have just heard has been fulfilled to-day."
22 They all agreed with him, and amazed at the words that flowed from
the lips of this divinely favored speaker, they asked each other, "Is
23 not this Joseph's son?" — "No doubt," he continued, "you will now
come at me with the proverb, 'Physician, cure yourself,' and say,
'Do here in your own town all the things that you are said to have
24 done in Capernaum.' But let me tell you this: No prophet is favor-
25 ably regarded in his own town. To prove it I shall recall to you
that in the days of Elijah there were surely many widows in Israel;
at the time, I mean, when no rain fell from heaven for three years
and six months, and consequently a great famine prevailed in the
26 land. Nevertheless, Elijah was not sent to any of them, but to a
27 widow in Serepta in the district of Sidon. And surely there were
many lepers in Israel in the days of the prophet Elisha, and yet not
one of them was cleansed of leprosy, but only the Syrian, Naaman."

28 At these words all of his hearers in the synagogue were filled
29 with rage. They sprang to their feet, drove him out of town and
dragged him to the brow of the hill near which the town was built,
30 intending to hurl him down. But he quietly passed through their
midst and disappeared.

31 From there he went to the town of Capernaum, which lies in
Galilee on the lake of that name in the district of Zabulon and
Nephthalim. On the Sabbath it was his custom to preach in the
32 synagogue. He always moved his hearers deeply, for his speech was
33 felt to be inspired by a higher power. One day a man possessed by
an evil spirit was in the synagogue, and the spirit cried out in a loud
34 voice, "What do you want of us, Jesus of Nazareth? Have you come
to destroy us in this way? I know who you are: the Holy One of
35 God." Jesus sternly commanded the spirit, "Say no more, and come
out of him!" Then the demon threw the man upon the ground in
their midst with a fearful scream and left him without doing him the

36 least harm. All were paralyzed with fright, and said to one another, "What power and authority there are in his word! He has
37 only to command the evil spirits, and they go." His reputation
quickly spread throughout the entire region.
38 From the synagogue he went to the house of Simon and Andrew,
where Simon's mother-in-law lay sick with a high fever. They
39 begged him to help her, and so he went to her side, leaned over
her, and exorcised the fever. She was immediately rid of it, so that
she was able to get up and wait on them.
40 After sunset every one who had a sick person in his household
brought the patient, whatever his sickness, to Jesus, who laid his
41 hand on each one and cured him. Demons were also driven out of
many a sick person, shrieking as they went and exclaiming, "You
are the Son of God!" Although they knew that he was the Messiah,
they were not allowed to say so, because Jesus strictly forbade them.
42 Early on the following morning he rose and went to a secluded
place, but the people looked for him until they found him, and clung
43 to him, fearing that he might leave them. But he persuaded them,
saying, "I must preach the gospel of the kingdom of God in other
44 towns also, for that is why I was sent." After that he preached in
the synagogues of Galilee.

CHAPTER 5.

1 One day as he was standing by the Lake of Gennesaret, while the
2 people crowded about him to hear the word of God, he saw two
boats on the shore; the fishermen had landed and were washing
3 their nets. One of the boats belonged to Simon Peter, and into this
one Jesus stepped, asking him to push off some distance from the
shore. Then he sat down in the boat, in a place from which he could
conveniently preach, and addressed the people.
4 After his sermon was ended, he said to Simon, "Pull farther out
5 on the lake and throw out your nets for a haul." — "Master," answered Simon, "we have toiled all night and have caught nothing,
6 but I will gladly do as you say." On throwing out their nets they
at once caught so many fish that the nets threatened to give way,
whereupon they beckoned to their companions in the other boat to
7 come to their aid. The others rowed up, and both boats were so
8 filled with fish that they nearly sank. When Simon Peter saw this
he fell upon his knees before Jesus and exclaimed, "I beg of you,
9 lord, leave me, for I am a sinful man." For he was awed at the haul
10 of fish they had made. With Simon were James and John, the sons
of Zebedee. Jesus turned to them and said, "Come, now. You shall

11 no longer catch fish, but I will make you fishers of men." At these
words, they abandoned everything as soon as they reached the shore,
and went with him.

12 On one occasion while he was in a certain town, he met a man
who was covered all over with leprosy. As soon as the man saw
Jesus, he threw himself down before him, and called out, "Lord, if
13 you will, you can make me clean." Stretching out his hand, Jesus
touched him and said, "I will, be clean." Instantly the man was rid
14 of his leprosy, but Jesus strictly ordered him to tell no one of the
matter, and directed him, "Go and show yourself to the priest, and
also make the offering prescribed by Moses as evidence of your
cleansing." But no sooner had the man left than he told every one
about it, and in this way the story spread through the neighborhood like wildfire. Consequently Jesus could no longer show himself in any town during the daytime without being besieged by
15 crowds. He therefore returned to Capernaum again. His reputation
grew constantly, and the people flocked to him from all sides to hear
16 him speak and to be cured of their ailments; but again and again
he withdrew to unfrequented places and devoted himself to prayer.

17 One day the Pharisees and the teachers of the Law were listening
to his sermon, together with great numbers of people who had come
from all the towns of Galilee and Judaea to have their sick healed.
18 One party of men brought with them on a litter an invalid who was
paralyzed. They tried to carry him into the house to lay him at the
19 feet of Jesus, but they could not force their way in to him because
of the crowd. They therefore climbed upon the roof, stripped off the
tiling above the place where Jesus was sitting, and lowered the
litter with the paralyzed man into the midst of the group that was
20 gathered around him. When Jesus saw their faith he said, "My dear
21 man, your sins shall be taken from you." Then the Pharisees and
the scribes thought to themselves, "Who is this man that he dares
utter such blasphemy? For who can take away sins but God alone?"
22 Jesus knew their thoughts and put this question to them: "What
23 absurd notions are you harboring? Which is easier to say, 'Your
24 sins shall be taken away from you,' or 'Arise and walk'? You shall
see now that the Son of man has authority to take away sins on
earth." And turning to the paralytic he said, "I tell you, rise, take
25 your bedding, and go home." In full sight of every one the man
immediately rose, picked up his bedding, and went home praising
26 God. They were all filled with awe and said to one another, "We
have experienced unbelievable things to-day."

27 Afterwards Jesus walked along the shore of the lake, followed by

the crowd. He addressed the people again, and proceeded on his
way. Then he saw Levi, the son of Alphaeus, sitting in a toll-booth,
28 and said to him, "Come with me." Immediately he abandoned every-
29 thing and went with him. Levi gave a great banquet for him in his
house, and there were many tax-collectors and other guests at table
30 with them. The Pharisees and the scribes belonging to their party
then went to his disciples in great indignation and asked, "Why do
31 you dine with these tax-collectors?" Jesus himself answered their
question. "It is not the healthy," he said, "who need a physician,
32 but the sick. I have not come to call God's faithful but the wicked
to repentance."

33 Again they found fault with him, saying, "John's disciples fast
rigorously and keep set hours for prayer, and so do the disciples of
34 the Pharisees. But your disciples do none of these things." Jesus
answered, "You cannot expect the wedding-guests to fast while the
bridegroom is with them. But days of fasting will come for them
35 also. For the days when the bridegroom has been taken from them
36 will be their days of fasting." He then made this further comparison: "No one," he said, "cuts a patch from a new garment and sews
it on an old one. That would ruin the new garment and make a
37 patch that still would not match the old. Nor should new wine be
put into old skins; otherwise the new wine will burst the old skins
38 and be lost, and the skins themselves will be ruined. New wine
39 should be put into new skins; then both will keep. Furthermore, no
one who is accustomed to drink old wine is likely to care for the
new; for he will say, 'The old is good enough.' "

CHAPTER 6.

1 One day—it was the first Sabbath after the second day of the
Passover—Jesus was walking through grain fields, and his disciples
began to pick the ears, rubbing them between their hands and eating
2 the kernels. Some Pharisees called this to his attention and asked,
"Why is it that your disciples are doing that which is unlawful on
3 the Sabbath?"—"Have you never read," he replied, "what David
4 did when he and his followers were hungry? He went into the house
of God and took the shewbread and ate some of it, also giving some
to his companions, although only the priests are allowed to eat it?"

5 On the same day he saw a man at work before the Sabbath was
over, and said to him, "My dear man, if you know what you are
doing, you are indeed fortunate. If you do not, you are one of those
whom the Law condemns as transgressors."

6 On another Sabbath he again came into the synagogue, where he
7 found a man whose arm was totally withered. The scribes and the
Pharisees were watching to see whether he would heal him in spite
of the Sabbath, and thereby give them grounds for bringing charges
8 against him. Although he knew their intentions, he turned to the
man with the withered arm and said, "Rise, and step into the midst
9 of the congregation." The man rose and stepped forward, and
Jesus, addressing those who were present, said, "I ask you to tell me
whether it is lawful to do good on the Sabbath, or to do evil; to
10 save life, or to allow it to be lost." But they were silent. Looking
around at them in anger, he said to the man, "Stretch out your
arm." The man did so, and his arm was as sound as the other. In
conclusion Jesus said, "The Son of God is lord over man as well as
11 over the Sabbath." This enraged his adversaries beyond all bounds,
and they deliberated among themselves as to how they might put
him out of the way.

12 One day he went up on a hill to pray, and spent the whole night
13 there in prayer. At daybreak he called his disciples to him, and from
14 them he chose these twelve, whom he also called apostles: first
Simon, whom he also named Peter, and Simon's brother, Andrew;
then James and his brother John, whom he called "Boanerges,"
15 meaning "Sons of Thunder"; then Philip and Bartholomew; then
Matthew and Thomas, the latter being called "the Twin"; then
James the son of Alphaeus, and Simon, known as "the Zealot";
16 then Judas, the brother of James, and Judas Iscariot, who turned
traitor to him.

17 He came down the hill with them, and finding a level place,
stopped to rest. There gathered about him a great number of his
disciples and a large crowd of people who had come from all parts
18 of the country of the Jews and from other regions to hear him and
to be cured of their diseases. Those who were possessed by evil
19 spirits were also healed. Every one there sought an opportunity
merely to touch him, for a power flowed out from him and healed
all.

20 Then he turned his eyes upon his disciples and said:

"Fortunate are you who feel helplessly poor before God; for
God's spirit-world will communicate with you.

21 "Fortunate are you who now long for the truth; for your longing
will be appeased.

"Fortunate are you who now lament your estrangement from
God; for you will be filled with joy.

22 "Fortunate are you if men hate you and exclude you from their
society, revile you, and defame you, because you are known as fol-
23 lowers of the Son of man. When that day comes, rejoice and exult,
for your reward in the beyond will be great. Such too was the treatment accorded God's mediums by their forefathers.

24 "But woe to you who set your hearts on earthly riches; for therewith you have all that is due you.

25 "Woe to you who have more than your fill in this life; for in
another life you will suffer hunger.

"Woe to you who are heard laughing scornfully at others in this
life; for in another life you will weep and wail.

26 "Woe to you if your fellow-men flatter you; for so in former
times were the mediums of the low spirit-world flattered.

27 "On the other hand I wish to say to you who are listening to my
words: Be kindly disposed to those who are not kindly disposed to
28 you; be thoughtful to those who are inconsiderate of you; reason
29 with those who curse you; pray for those who harm you; if any one
strikes you on one cheek because you deserve it, offer him the other
also; and let him who takes away your undergarment because you
30 have pledged it have your promised cloak as well. If any one
asks you for that which you promised, give it to him; and if any
one lawfully takes what is yours, do not ask him to give it back.
31 Treat your fellow-men as you wish them to treat you. If you love
32 only those who love you, what reward can you claim? Even the
33 wicked love those who love them. And if you do good only to those
34 who do good to you, what reward can you claim? For the wicked
do the same. And if you give only to those from whom you expect
gifts in return, what reward can you claim? For even the godless
present gifts to their own kind in expectation of receiving gifts from
35 them in return. But I repeat, be kindly disposed to those who are
not kindly disposed to you; do good and give to others, hoping for
nothing in return. Then your reward will be great, and you will
prove yourselves children of the Highest. For He also is kind to the
36 ungrateful and to the wicked. Be merciful, as your Father also is
37 merciful. Do not judge others, lest you yourselves be judged; do
not condemn others, lest you yourselves be condemned. Pardon
those who have injured you, and you too will be pardoned for your
38 wrong-doing. Give, and it will also be given to you; and what is
more, good measure, pressed down, shaken, and filled to overflowing
will be poured into your lap. For by the same standard with which
you measure out to others, measurement will be made to you."

39 Making use of a parable, he continued, "Can one blind man lead
40 another? Will not both fall into a ditch? The disciple is not above
his master. Every disciple, even the most advanced, will at best be
41 like his master. Why take note of the splinter in your brother's
42 eye when you do not see the beam in your own? Or how can you
say to your brother, 'Let me take the splinter out of your eye,' so
long as the beam still remains in your own? Hypocrite! First take
the beam from your own eye; then you can see to take the splinter
from your brother's.
43 "No sound tree bears rotten fruit, neither does a diseased tree
44 bear sound fruit. It is by its fruit that a tree is known. Figs are not
45 picked from thistles, nor are grapes gathered from brambles. A
good man brings forth only that which is good out of the storehouse
of goodness within his heart; a wicked man out of his store of evil
brings forth only evil. For that with which the heart is filled, will
46 rise to the lips. Why do you call me 'Lord, lord,' and still do not do
47 as I say? Whoever comes to me and listens to my words and acts
48 according to them — I will show you whom he resembles. He is like
a man who built a house. When he dug for its foundations, he dug
deep, so as to lay them on rock. Then when the flood came and the
waters beat against his house they could not shake it, for it was
49 founded on rock. But he who hears my words and does not act
according to them is like a man who built his house without foundations. When the flood beat against it the house fell, and it became
a great heap of ruins."

CHAPTER 7.

1 After he had ended this sermon, Jesus returned to Capernaum.
2 There a centurion's servant, who was very dear to his master, lay
3 mortally ill. When the centurion heard that Jesus had come, he sent
certain Jewish elders to him, begging him to come to his house and
4 save his servant. The elders came to Jesus and laid the centurion's
plea before him, urging in its support, "This man deserves to have
5 you grant his appeal, for he loves our people and has even built
6 the synagogue for us." Jesus went with them and had nearly reached
the house when he was met by friends of the centurion, who had
been sent out with the message, "Lord, do not trouble yourself for
7 my sake, for I am not worthy to have you come under my roof. It
will be enough if you only give the command, and my servant will
8 be cured. For I too am a man under my superiors' orders and have
soldiers under me who are subject to my commands, and when I

say to one of them 'Go,' he goes, and to another 'Come,' he comes,
9 and to my servant 'Do this,' he does it." When Jesus heard this he
was amazed, and turning to those about him, he said, "Truly, no-
10 where in Israel have I found such faith." When the messengers returned to the centurion's house, they found his servant fully restored
to health.

11 On another occasion Jesus entered a town called Nain, attended
12 by his disciples and a great crowd of people. As he approached the
town gate, a dead man was just being carried out. He was the only
son of his mother, a widow. Many of her fellow-townsmen accom-
13 panied her to attend the burial. When Jesus saw her he was deeply
14 moved, and turned to her, saying, "Do not weep." Then, going close
to the bier, he touched it with his hand, and the bearers stood still.
He then called out loudly, "Young man, young man, I say to you,
15 rise!" The dead man sat up and began to speak, and Jesus gave him
16 over to his mother. All who were there trembled with emotion in
every limb, and praised God, saying, "A great messenger of God
has risen among us, and God has again become the leader of His
people."

17 The news of this event spread throughout the country of the Jews
18 and through all the neighboring regions, and in time it also reached
19 John the Baptist. Summoning two of his disciples, he instructed
them, "Go and ask him, 'Are you he who is to come, or shall we
20 look for another?'" When the men came to Jesus, they did as they
had been bidden, saying, "John the Baptist has sent us to you to
ask, 'Are you he who is to come, or shall we look for another?'"
21 Jesus was just then engaged in healing many people of their ailments and painful infirmities, driving out evil spirits, and restoring
22 sight to the blind. He therefore answered, "Go back and tell John
of everything that you have seen with your own eyes and heard with
your own ears: the blind regain their eyesight; the lame can walk
again; lepers are cleansed; the deaf hear; the dead are raised; the
23 message of salvation is preached to the poor; and fortunate is he
whose faith in me remains unshaken."

24 When John's messengers had gone, Jesus began to speak to the
people concerning John's personality. "What," he asked them,
"were you expecting to see when you went out into the wilderness?
25 A reed swaying in the wind? Or why did you go? To see a man
clad in finery? Men who wear gorgeous garments and live in
26 splendor are to be found only in the palaces of kings. Then why did
you go? To see a messenger of God? I assure you most solemnly, he
is an especially great messenger of God; for of all God's messengers

who are born of woman, there is none greater than John the Baptist.
27 It is he of whom it is written: 'Behold, I send my messenger before
28 you, and he shall prepare the way for you.' But I emphasize that
the one who was born after him is greater than John in God's spirit-
29 world. Inasmuch as the people who heard John's sermons, even the
tax-collectors, received baptism from him, they acknowledged him
30 as a messenger of God. Only the Pharisees and the teachers of the
Law refused to be baptized by him and therewith defeated God's
31 purpose for themselves. To what shall I compare men of this kind?
32 What are they like? They are like children sitting in a public
square, and singing by turns, 'We piped merrily for you, and you
did not dance; we sang mournful songs, and you did not weep.'
33 For John the Baptist came, neither eating bread nor drinking wine,
34 and you said, 'He is possessed by the devil.' Then came the Son of
man, who eats and drinks like any one else, and you say, 'Look at
that glutton, that tippler, that friend of tax-collectors and harlots.'
35 And yet the wisdom that was preached by both has been abundantly
justified in the eyes of all who have accepted it."

36 One of the Pharisees invited him to a meal, and so Jesus went to
37 his house and reclined at table. Now there lived in this town a
woman known as a harlot. When she heard that Jesus was at table
at the Pharisee's house, she took with her an alabaster jar filled with
38 ointment, and stepped close to his feet from behind him. Bursting
into tears and so wetting his feet, she dried them with her hair, and
39 then kissed them and anointed them with the ointment. His host,
the Pharisee, on seeing this, thought to himself, "If this man were
really a messenger of God, he would know what kind of a woman it
40 is who is touching him, for she is a harlot." Jesus, however, turned
to him and said, "Simon, I have something to say to you."—"Speak,
41 master," replied Simon. "A certain money-lender had two debtors,"
Jesus went on. "One of them owed him a hundred dollars, the other
42 ten. But since neither one was able to pay, he remitted the debts of
both. Which of the two, do you think, will love him the more?"
43 Simon answered, "I think he to whom the larger debt was remitted."
44 —"You have judged rightly," Jesus replied. Keeping his eyes fixed
on the woman he said to Simon, "Do you see this woman? I came
to your house, and you gave me no water for my feet. But she wet
45 them with her tears and dried them with her hair. You gave me no
kiss of greeting, but this woman has kissed my feet again and again
46 ever since she came here. You did not even anoint my head with
47 common oil, but she has anointed my feet with costly oil. Therefore,
48 I tell you, much will be forgiven her." And to the woman he said,

49 "Your sins shall be taken away from you." At these words the
other guests thought to themselves, "Who is this man who will even
50 take away sins?" Then he said to the woman, "Your faith and confidence have saved you. Go in peace."

CHAPTER 8.

1 In the days that followed he journeyed through the country from
town to town and from village to village, teaching in the public
2 squares and proclaiming the gospel of the kingdom of God. He was
accompanied by his twelve disciples and by certain women whom
he had rid of evil spirits and of other infirmities. Among these
were Mary called Magdalene, out of whom seven demons had been
3 driven; Joanna, the wife of Herod's agent Chuza; Susanna, and
many others, who provided for his wants out of their own means.
4 One day he was surrounded by an immense throng, which was
still further swelled by the people who poured out of the nearest
town. It was on this occasion that he delivered the following par-
5 able: "A sower went out to sow his seed, and as he sowed, some seed
fell on a hard-trodden path where it was trampled underfoot and
6 eaten by the birds. Some fell on rocky places in the field and no
7 sooner sprouted than it withered for lack of moisture. Other seed
fell among sprouting thistles that shot up with it and choked it.
8 Still other seed fell upon good soil, grew, and yielded a hundredfold."
When he had finished he called out, "Let all who understand this,
9 take heed." Then his disciples asked him the meaning of the par-
10 able, and he said, "To you it is given to understand the mysteries of
the kingdom of God, but the others must be shown in parables, so
that they may look and yet not see; hear, and yet not understand.
11 The meaning of the parable is this. The seed is the word of God.
12 Those with whom the seed fell upon the hard-trodden path are the
ones who hear the word of God, but the devil promptly comes and
takes it out of their hearts, so that they will not believe and be
saved.

13 "Those with whom the seed fell on rocky soil are the ones who at
first accept the word of truth joyously, but in whom it takes no root.
For a time they believe, but when they are put to the test, they fall
away.

14 "Those with whom the seed fell among thistles are such as have
heard the word of truth but are so taken up with their worldly cares,

with money-making, and with the pleasures of every-day life that
the word of God is completely choked and cannot bear fruit.
15 "Those with whom the seed fell upon good soil are they who,
having heard the word of God, treasure it in good hearts, and by
patient endeavor bring it to maturity.
16 "No one lights a lamp only to cover it with a vessel or to set it
under a bed, but he puts it on a stand so that all who enter the room
17 may see the light. Indeed, there is nothing hidden that will not be
laid bare, nor is there a secret that will not be generally known and
18 brought to light. Be careful, now, how you construe my words. For
to him who faithfully holds fast to God's gift more will be given;
but from him who does not hold fast, even the gift that he once had
will be taken."
19 His mother and his brothers came and tried to reach him, but
20 because of the dense crowd this was impossible. Some one brought
him word, "Your mother and your brothers are back there and are
21 trying to reach you." But he answered, "I consider as my mother
and my brothers only those who hear the word of God and obey it."
22 One day, acting on his own impulse, he went on board a boat. His
disciples embarked with him, and he said to them, "Let us cross to
23 the other side of the lake." So they put off from the shore. During
the voyage he fell asleep. Suddenly a violent storm swept over the
24 lake, filling the boat with water and endangering their lives. The
disciples went to him and aroused him, calling, "Lord, lord, we are
sinking!" At once he rose and spoke severely to the storm and the
waves, and there was a calm, and the surface of the lake became
25 smooth. Then he said to the disciples, "Where are your faith and
confidence in God?" Trembling and astonished they asked one another, "Who can he be? He has but to command the wind and the
waves, and they obey."
26 They then steered for the country of the Gerasenes, which lies
27 opposite Galilee. Scarcely had he landed when he was met by a man
who for a long time had been plagued by evil spirits. He wore no
clothes and did not live in any human habitation, but in the tombs.
28 On seeing Jesus he uttered a loud shriek and called out, "What do
you intend to do with me, Son of the Highest? Do not torture me,
29 I beseech you!" For Jesus was about to command the evil spirit to
leave the man. More than once it had taken possession of him, and
at such times the people had tried to bind him in chains and to put
him into confinement, but he had always broken the chains and had
30 been driven into the wilderness by the demon. Jesus now asked
him, "What is your name?" He answered, "My name is Legion";

31 for there were many demons in him. These now repeatedly implored
32 Jesus not to send them into the abyss. As it happened, a herd of
swine was feeding on the slope of the mountain, and into this herd
the demons begged to be allowed to enter. Jesus granted their plea;
33 and the demons, leaving the man, passed into the swine, whereupon
the whole herd dashed madly down the slope into the lake and was
34 drowned. When the herders saw this, they fled and carried the news
35 to the village and to the farms, and when the people came out of the
village to see with their own eyes what had happened, they found
the man who had been possessed sitting at the feet of Jesus, clothed
36 and in his right mind. At this they grew frightened, and those who
had witnessed it told them how the possessed man had been cured.
37 When they heard the story, both the people from the village and
those from the rural district of Gerasa asked Jesus to leave their
part of the country, for they were seized with great terror. Jesus
38 therefore returned to his boat and was about to put off, when the
man from whom the demons had been driven begged to be allowed
39 to go with him. But Jesus sent him home, saying, "Go home and
tell your people of the great favor that God has shown you." The
man left, and as he passed through the village, he told every one of
the great things that Jesus had done for him.

40 When Jesus returned, the people welcomed him joyfully, for all
41 had been eagerly awaiting him. Among those who came to meet
him was a man named Jairus, who at that time was the head of the
synagogue. He fell down before Jesus and implored him to come
42 to his house, for his only daughter, a girl about twelve years of age,
lay at the point of death. While Jesus was on his way to the house,
43 a great press of people crowded about him, among them a woman
who for twelve years had suffered from an issue of blood and whom
44 no one had been able to cure. Making her way to him, she touched
45 his cloak, and instantly the issue of blood ceased. Jesus had felt
that power went out from him, and asked, "Who touched me?" But
no one admitted having done it. Peter and the others near by said,
"Master, the people are pushing against you from all sides and are
46 constantly touching you." But Jesus insisted, "Some one touched
47 me purposely, for I felt power going out from me." The woman,
who now saw that she could not escape detection, came forward
trembling, fell at his feet, and confessed before all the people why
48 she had touched him and how she had been instantly cured. "My
daughter," Jesus said to her, "your faith and confidence have saved
you. Go in peace."

49 He was still speaking when messengers came from the house of the

head of the synagogue with the news, "Your daughter is dead. You
50 need not trouble the master any further." When he heard this, Jesus
said to the head of the synagogue, "Do not lose heart. Only have
51 confidence, and she will return to life." On reaching the house he
let no one enter it with him except Peter, James, and John, and the
52 child's parents. Every one was weeping and mourning for the dead
girl, but he said, "Do not weep, for she is not dead, she is only
53 sleeping." But they laughed at him, for they knew only too well that
54 the child was dead. Taking her by the hand, he said to her, "Awake,
55 my child!" In an instant her spirit returned into her body and she
56 stood up. He then ordered that food be given her. Her parents were
lost in wonder, but he forbade them to speak to any one of what
had taken place.

CHAPTER 9.

1 On another occasion he called together his Twelve and gave them
power and authority over evil spirits of all kinds, and to cure
2 disease. He then sent them out to proclaim the coming of God's
3 spirit-world and to heal the sick. The rules that he bade them observe were these: "Take nothing with you on your travels, neither
4 staff nor bag, bread nor money, nor change of clothing. Whenever
you are received in a house, let that house be your home until you
5 leave. If in any place you are denied shelter, leave that place and
6 shake its very dust from your feet in testimony against it." Thus
prepared they set out, going from village to village, preaching the
gospel and healing the sick everywhere.

7 Meanwhile Herod the tetrarch also had heard of the deeds of
8 Jesus and was thereby greatly troubled. For some people said that
in Jesus John had risen from the dead. Others, to be sure, maintained that in him Elijah had reappeared; still others believed that
9 one of the ancient prophets had come back. Herod said more than
once, "So much is certain: I myself have had John beheaded. Then
who can this man be, of whom I hear such wonderful things?"
And he sought an opportunity of becoming personally acquainted
with Jesus.

10 When the apostles returned they related to their master all that
they had done and experienced on their travels. He then took them
to a place called Bethsaida, for he wanted to be alone with them.
11 But scarcely had the people noticed his departure when they followed close at his heels. He received them kindly nevertheless, spoke
to them about the kingdom of God, and cured all who were in need

12 of healing. As the day began to wane, the Twelve appealed to him,
"Send the people away, in order that they may seek food and shelter
in the villages and farms of the surrounding districts; for we are in
13 an uninhabited region here." He answered, "Give them food yourselves." But they protested, "We have only five loaves and two fish.
That means that we should have to go and buy the necessary food
14 for all these people." For they numbered some five thousand men.
But he directed his disciples, "Have the people sit down in groups
15 of about fifty." They did as he directed them. Then he took the
16 five loaves and the two fish, looked up to heaven, prayed fervently,
pronounced a blessing, and taking the food, gave it to the disciples
17 to divide among the people. Every one ate his fill, and of the leavings that remained, twelve basketfuls were gathered up.

18 One day when he was alone with his disciples he asked them,
19 "Who do the people say that I am?" They answered, "John the
Baptist. There are, of course, some who say that you are Elijah,
and others who maintain that one of the ancient prophets has come
20 back again in your person." He asked them further, "And you, who
do you say that I am?" Peter replied, "You are the Messiah, the
21 son of God." Jesus strictly forbade them to tell this to any one,
22 and added, "The Son of man will have to endure great suffering;
it will be his lot to be excluded from the community by the elders,
the chief priests, and the scribes, and to be put to death by them,
and on the third day to be raised from the dead."

23 Then he admonished them all, "Whoever wishes to travel my
road must be strong enough to say 'No' to his worldly desires, and
24 to take up his cross day after day and to walk in my foot-steps. For
whoever is anxious to secure his earthly welfare only, will suffer
25 the loss of his spiritual welfare. But whoever is willing to sacrifice
his earthly welfare for my sake, will preserve his spiritual welfare.
For what advantage does a man have if he gains the whole world,
but entirely loses or seriously damages his soul's true happiness?
26 If any one is ashamed of me and mine, the Son of man will also be
ashamed of him when he comes in his own glory and in the glory
27 of his Father and his holy angels. I speak truthfully when I say to
you that some who stand here will not taste death until they have
seen the Son of man come in his glory."

28 About eight days after this discourse he took with him Peter,
29 James, and John and went up on the mountain to pray. As he
prayed, a change came over his countenance, and his garments as-
30 sumed a radiant whiteness. Two men conversed with him. They
31 were Moses and Elijah, who appeared in celestial glory and spoke

32 with him of the death which he was to suffer in Jerusalem. Peter
and his companions were in a condition similar to a deep sleep, and
when full consciousness returned to them they saw him in his
celestial glory, and likewise the two who were standing with him.
33 When these were about to bid him farewell, Peter said to Jesus,
"Master, we feel so happy here! If you are willing, I will put up
three shelters of leafy boughs, one for you, one for Moses, and one
34 for Elijah." For he scarcely knew what to say at this moment. He
was still speaking when a bright cloud gathered overhead, and as it
35 slowly closed about them, they were filled with awe. Out of the
cloud came a voice which called to them, "This is my Son, my beloved, with whom I was well pleased. Give heed to his words."
36 At the sound of the voice Jesus was alone again. Of that which they
had seen the disciples maintained deep silence and spoke of it to no
one during the lifetime of Jesus.

37 On the next day he again came down from the mountain. Very
38 soon a large crowd had gathered around him, and a man called to
him out of the throng, "Master, I beg of you, do something for my
39 son. He is my only child. At times an evil spirit overpowers him,
and then he suddenly bursts out screaming. It tosses him to and fro
until he foams at the mouth. It will not let go of him except with
40 a struggle that saps all his strength. I have already asked your dis-
41 ciples to rid him of the spirit, but they could not."—"Oh, this
unbelieving and God-estranged people!" exclaimed Jesus. "How
much longer must I be among you and have patience with you?
42 Bring your son to me." As the boy approached him, the demon
again tossed him to and fro and distorted his features; but Jesus
reprimanded the evil spirit severely, and it went out of the boy,
43 whom he then gave back to his father cured. Every one was awed
by the mighty power of God, and while those who were present were
seeking for words to express their wonder at the deeds of Jesus, he
44 turned to his disciples with the admonition, "Let the words that you
hear the people now speak continue to echo in your ears. For the
45 Son of man will soon be delivered into the hands of men." But they
did not understand the significance of his words. It was so obscure
to them that they did not for a moment suspect what he meant; but
they shrank from asking him for a fuller explanation of his words.

46 Often the disciples fell to wondering which of them was the
47 greatest. Seeing their thoughts, Jesus took a child and set it beside
48 him, and then said to his disciples, "He who befriends such a child
in order to lead it to me, befriends my cause; and he who befriends
my cause befriends the cause of Him Who sent me. For he who in

49 his own eyes is the lowliest among all of you, is truly great." Then
John spoke out and said, "Master, we saw some one driving out evil
spirits in your name, and we tried to hinder him because he would
50 not join us."—"Do not hinder him," replied Jesus, "for such a one
is not against you, he is for you."
51 The time was now approaching when he was to be taken from
this earth. From now on, therefore, the one goal that he kept in view
52 was Jerusalem. He sent out messengers into a village of the Samar-
53 itans to find lodging for him there, but because he intended to go
on to Jerusalem, the inhabitants of the village refused to take him
54 in. When the disciples James and John heard of this, they asked
him, "Master, are you willing for us to call down fire from heaven
55 to consume those people, as Elijah did in a like case?" But he
looked at them gravely and gave them a severe rebuke. "Do you
56 not know," he said, "of which spirit you are the children? The Son
of man has not come to destroy souls, but to save them." And they
went to another village.
57 As they were on their way, a man came to him and said, "I will
58 follow you wherever you go." Jesus answered, "Foxes have dens,
and the birds of the air have nests, but the Son of man does not even
59 possess so much as a place on which to lay his head." To another
he said, "Go with me." When the man replied, "Let me first go and
60 bury my father," Jesus told him, "Let the spiritually dead bury their
own spiritually dead; but you go and preach of God's kingdom."
61 Yet another said, "Lord, I will gladly follow you, but first let me
62 bid farewell to my family." Jesus answered, "No one who looks
behind him, once his hand is on the plow, is a fit instrument for the
kingdom of God."

CHAPTER 10.

1 Jesus appointed seventy-two others, whom he sent ahead two by
two into all those towns and villages which he himself intended to
2 visit. "The harvest is large," he told them, "but few indeed the
number of the laborers. Pray therefore to the Lord of the harvest
3 that he will send laborers into the harvest-field. And now go. Remember that I am sending you out like lambs into the midst of
4 wolves. Take with you no purse nor bag, nor an extra pair of shoes.
Do not make visits to friends or acquaintances on your journeys.
5 When you enter a dwelling, pronounce the greeting, 'Peace be with
6 this house,' and if but one of its inmates is deserving of peace, your
wish will be fulfilled for him; if not, the power of your blessing will
7 be turned back upon you yourselves. Stay at one and the same

house. Eat and drink what is offered to you, for a laborer is worthy
8 of his wages. Do not, therefore, go from house to house. If you
come to a town in which you are well received, eat what is set before
9 you, heal the sick whom you find there, and preach to its inhabitants
10 that communication with the spirit-world is near at hand. But if
you come to a town where you are refused food and shelter, go out
11 into the open country near by and say, 'We shake the very dust of
your streets from our feet. Let it remain with you, but this one
thing never forget: communication with God's spirit-world is at
12 hand.' Believe me, when the day comes for selecting those who may
enter the kingdom of God, it will go more lightly with Sodom than
13 with such a town. Woe to you, Chorazin! Woe to you, Bethsaida!
If the miracles that have been worked within your walls had happened in Tyre and Sidon, they would long since have sat penitent
14 in sackcloth and ashes. And so it will go more lightly with Tyre
15 and Sidon than with you. And you Capernaum, have you not been
exalted to the sky by these miracles? But you will be thrust down
to the abyss.

16 "Whoever listens to you, listens to me. Whoever turns you away,
turns me away. But whoever listens to me, listens to Him Who has
sent me."

17 When at length the seventy-two returned, they joyfully related,
"Master, even the evil spirits obey us when we command them in your
18 name!" He answered, "I saw Satan fall like lightning from heaven.
19 I have given you power to tread on serpents and scorpions, yes,
power over the whole host of the enemy. Nothing, therefore, can do
20 you harm. Nevertheless, it is not because the spirits obey you that
you should rejoice, but rather because your names are recorded in
heaven."

21 At that instant a holy spirit so filled his heart with joy and rap-
ture, that he exclaimed, "I praise Thee, Father, Lord of heaven and
earth, that Thou hast hidden these things from those who are called
wise and prudent, and revealed them to those whom men call fools.
22 Yes, Father, for so it was ordained in Thy plan of salvation." Then
turning to his disciples, he said, "Everything has been committed
to me by the Father. No one knows who the Son is but the Father;
and who the Father is, no one knows except the Son and him to
23 whom the Son will reveal it. Fortunate are they whose eyes see the
things that you see, and whose ears hear the things that you hear.
24 For believe me, many kings and messengers of God longed to see
the things that you see, and did not see them; and to hear the things
that you hear, and did not hear them."

25 Then a certain expert in the Law stepped forward to put Jesus
to the test, and asked him, "Master, what must I do to gain the
26 future life?" Jesus asked him in turn, "What is written in the Law
27 concerning this matter? How do the words read?" The other replied, "You shall love the Lord your God with all your heart, with
all your soul, and with all your strength, and your neighbor as your-
28 self." — "You have given the right answer," replied Jesus; "do this,
29 and you will live." But he, professing to be eager for further in-
30 struction, asked again, "And who is my neighbor?" Jesus answered
the question with the following story: "A certain man travelling
from Jerusalem to Jericho fell into the hands of robbers who stripped him, beat him until he was bloody, left him lying half dead, and
31 then escaped. A priest who happened to come that way saw him
32 lying there, but passed him by. A Levite also came to the same
33 place; he too saw the man, and likewise passed him by. Then a
Samaritan who was making a journey also approached him. When
34 he saw the man lying there he was moved to pity, and he went to
his side, poured wine and oil into his wounds, and bound them up.
Then he set the man on his own mule, led him to an inn, and took
35 care of him. On the following day he took out two silver coins and
gave them to the landlord with the request,' Take care of him when
I have gone, and if you should be put to further expense on his
36 account, I will repay you when I come back.' Which of the three do
you think showed himself to be the neighbor of the man who had
37 fallen into the hands of the robbers?" He answered, "The one who
took pity on him." — "Then go and do the same," answered Jesus.
38 Jesus continued his travels and came to a village where a woman
39 named Martha took him into her home. She had a sister called
40 Mary, who sat at the feet of Jesus and listened to him, while Martha,
busy with preparing a bounteous meal, constantly hurried away
from his side. Finally she went to Jesus and said, "Lord, are you
content to see my sister allowing me to do all the work of waiting
41 on you? Tell her to lend me a hand." But the lord answered her,
"Martha, Martha, you are giving yourself much trouble and work
42 in order to prepare an elaborate meal, when a few dishes, or even
one, would have been sufficient. Mary has chosen the good part,
which can never be taken from her."

CHAPTER 11.

1 Once Jesus went to a certain place to pray. When he had ended
his prayer, one of his disciples said to him, "Lord, teach us to pray,
2 as John also taught his disciples." He answered, "When you pray,

do not babble unthinkingly as others do; for many people believe
that their prayers will be granted by reason of the number of words
that they use. You may pray as follows: 'Our Father Who art in
Heaven, hallowed be Thy name. Thy spirit-world come to us. Thy
3 will be done in the beyond and on earth. Give us this day our bread
4 for to-morrow. Forgive us our sins as we forgive those who have
sinned against us. And do not withdraw Thy hand from us, lest we
fall victims to temptation, but deliver us from the Evil One.' "

5 Then he continued, "Suppose that one of you had a friend, and
went to him at midnight with the request, 'My dear friend, lend me
6 three loaves of bread, for a friend of mine has just stopped at my
7 house on a journey, and I have nothing to offer him.' The man to
whom you went would answer you from within, 'Do not trouble me
now. The door is locked, and my children and I are in bed. I can-
8 not possibly get up now to give you the bread.' Let me tell you that
although he may not get up and give him the bread out of friendship, yet in the end he will yield to his insistent request, and will
9 rise and give him as much as he needs. So I tell you, ask for the
truth, and it will be granted to you; seek God, and you will find
Him; knock at the gate of God's spirit-world, and it will be opened
10 to you. For whoever asks for the truth receives it; whoever seeks
God finds Him; and to any one who knocks at the gate of God's
11 spirit-world, it will be opened. Again, is there a father among you
12 who would give his son a stone if he asked for bread? Or a serpent
13 if he asked for a fish? Or a scorpion instead of an egg? If you,
then, prone as you are to evil, are still careful to give nothing but
good gifts to your children, how much more readily will your
heavenly Father give a holy spirit to those who ask for it."

14 He had scarcely finished speaking when some one brought him a
posessed man who was dumb. Jesus drove out the demon, and the
man who had been dumb was once more able to speak. The people
15 wondered greatly at this, but some of them said, "It is with the help
of Beelzebul, the chief of the devils, that he drives out the evil
16 spirits." Others again, wishing to put him to the test, called upon
17 him for a sign in the sky. Jesus read their thoughts, and said to
them, "Every country that is swept by civil war is laid waste, and
18 one house falls after another. And so if Satan were at war with his
own kind, how could his kingdom still endure? You say that I drive
19 out the demon's with Beelzebul's help. But even assuming that he
does help me drive out the demons, will you tell me, then, with whose
help your own people seek to drive them out? Let them be the true
20 judges of your accusation. But if it is by God's spirit-powers that I

drive out the demons, then indeed the spirit-world of God has al-
21 ready come into contact with you.—When a strong man, armed to
22 the teeth, guards his palace, his goods are safe. But if he is attacked
and overpowered by one stronger than he, the victor will strip him
23 of the armor in which he trusted and divide the spoils. He who is
not with me is against me, and he who does not gather with me
scatters.

24 "Whenever an evil spirit has gone out of a man, it roams through
desolate places, seeking rest. If it finds none, it says to itself, 'I will
25 go back to the house from which I came.' If, on arriving there, it
26 finds the place well swept and in good order, it goes and fetches
seven other spirits, more wicked than itself, and if it can force an
entrance, it will make its home there; and the last state of such a
man will be worse than the first."

27 At these words a woman in the crowd called out, "Fortunate are
28 the womb that bore you and the breasts that nursed you!"—"No,"
he answered, "only they are fortunate who hear the word of God
and faithfully observe it."

29 Then as the people continued to gather in ever greater numbers,
he addressed them anew: "This is a people that gives me great
difficulties. It asks for miraculous signs, but none shall be given to
it other than the miraculous sign made manifest through Jonah.
30 For as Jonah became a miraculous sign to the people of Niniveh
31 so shall the Son of man be a miraculous sign to this people. As
Jonah was for three days and three nights in the belly of the great
fish, so will the Son of man remain in the same manner in the depths.
When this people is judged, the men of Niniveh will appear to
testify against it and will bring about its condemnation; for they
repented at the preaching of Jonah, and yet here stands one who is
32 greater than Jonah. The queen of the south will also appear to
testify against the men of this nation and bring about its condemnation; for she came from the ends of the earth to hear the wisdom of
Solomon, and yet here stands one who is greater than Solomon.

33 "No one lights a lamp only to put it in a hidden corner or to
cover it with a bushel measure. He puts it on a stand so that all
34 who come in may see its light. The light of the body is the eye.
When your eye is sound, the beam of its light falls on all parts of
your body; but if your eye is seriously diseased, every part of your
35 body is shrouded in darkness. You have such a light within your
36 soul also; should it turn to darkness, how dreadful then must be
your spiritual darkness."

37 A Pharisee asked Jesus to dine at his house, and he went there

38 and took his place at the table. It offended the Pharisee that Jesus
did not wash before the meal, and because of this he was inwardly
39 disturbed. And so the lord said to him, "You hypocritical Pharisees,
you may indeed keep the outside of cup and platter clean, but in-
40 side they are full of greed and malice. You fools! Did not He Who
41 made the outside make the inside as well? But if you would practise mercy so far as you are able, then you would find everything
clean.

42 "But woe to you Pharisees! You may indeed give the tithe of mint
and rue and of all other herbs, but to do that which is truly right
and to love God are things of which you know nothing.

43 "Woe to you Pharisees! You love to have the seats of honor in
the synagogues, to be greeted in public by every one, and to occupy
the foremost places at banquets.

44 "Woe to you scribes and Pharisees! You are like graves that
have been levelled and disguised, so that men walk over them un-
aware of what lies underfoot."

45 At this a teacher of the Law spoke up and said, "Master, by such
46 speeches you give offence to us also." — "Surely," answered Jesus,
"my words apply to you teachers as well; for you load your fellow-
men down with intolerable burdens to which you yourselves will
47 not lay a finger. Woe to you! You erect monuments for God's mes-
48 sengers, and it was your own forefathers who killed them. Do you
seek thereby to show that you do not approve of the deeds of your
ancestors, since in spite of the fact that they killed these messengers,
you erect monuments in their memory?

49 "Again and again I shall send mediums of God's spirit-world and
apostles to them; some they will kill, others they will subject to the
50 most terrible persecution. I do this in order that all of the blood
of these messengers that has been shed since the foundation of the
51 world may be charged to this people, from the blood of Abel to the
blood of Zechariah, the son of Barachiah, whom they put to death
between the burnt-offering altar and the sanctuary. Yes, you may
believe me when I tell you that it will be charged to this people.

52 "Woe to you teachers of the Law! You have hidden the key
of the door of the truth. You have not entered by that door yourselves, nor have you admitted those who tried to enter."

53 When he hurled these words at them the scribes and the Pharisees began to assail him before all the people with the utmost
54 bitterness, and to overwhelm him with questions, hoping to provoke him into some utterance that could be used as grounds for
bringing a charge against him.

CHAPTER 12.

1 In the meantime great throngs had gathered from far and near,
so that the people crowded and pushed against each other. Jesus
turned first of all to his disciples and said to them, "Beware of the
2 leaven of the Pharisees—hypocrisy! For there is nothing so carefully covered but that its cover will be stripped from it sooner or
3 later, and nothing so securely hidden but that it will be found. So
also every word that you have uttered in private will come to the
ears of the public, and that which you have whispered into each
other's ears behind closed doors will be proclaimed from the house-
4 tops. But to you who are my friends, I wish to say this: Do not fear
those who, while they may kill the body, cannot kill the soul or do
5 you any other harm. I will show you who it is whom you have to
fear. It is He Who has power to kill, and afterwards to send the
6 dead into the abyss. Truly, it is He Whom you should fear.—Are
not five sparrows bought for two cents? Yet not one of them has
7 been forgotten by God. Even the hairs of your head are numbered. And so have no fear. Are you by chance less valuable than
sparrows?

8 "Again I say to you, whoever acknowledges me before men will
also be acknowledged by the Son of man before the angels of God;
9 but whoever disowns me before men will also be disowned be-
10 fore the angels of God. And every one who speaks a word against
the son of man will find pardon, but he who utters blasphemy
against the holy spirit-world can expect no pardon, either in this
age or in the next one.

11 "When men drag you into the synagogues and before the authorities and those in office, do not consider beforehand with fear
and trembling how you shall speak in your defence or what you
12 shall say, for the holy spirit-world will inspire you at the right
moment with the words that you are to speak."

13 A man in the crowd now made the request, "Master, tell my
14 brother to share his inheritance with me." But Jesus answered, "My
15 good man, who has appointed me as arbitrator between you?" And
he added the warning, "See to it that you guard yourselves against
greed of every kind, for no one's living depends upon the surplus
that he possesses."

16 In explanation of this saying he related the following parable:
17 "A rich man's land had yielded its owner a bountiful harvest, and
he thought to himself, 'What shall I do, for I have no room where
18 I can store my crop?' Finally he said, 'I will do this: I will tear

down my barns and build larger ones, and store in them all of my
19 harvest. Then I will say to my soul, "Soul, you are amply provided
20 for; take your ease!"' But God said to him, 'You fool! This very
night your soul will be demanded of you. Then who will enjoy the
things that you have stored up?'"
22 He now turned to his disciples, and continued, "Therefore I tell
you, do not be troubled as to whether you will have enough to eat
to sustain life, or whether you will have clothing enough to cover
23 your bodies. Life means more than food, and the body means more
24 than clothing. Think of the birds of the air. They neither sow nor
reap; they have neither storehouses nor barns, and yet God sends
25 them food. Surely, you are worth as much as the birds! Who
26 among you can add even a moment to the span of his life? So, too,
27 in all other things. Why, then, do you distress yourselves? Consider the lilies that neither toil nor spin; and yet I tell you that not
even Solomon in all his glory was so splendidly clad as one of them.
28 Now if God so clothes the flowers of the field that are growing to-
day, and to-morrow are thrown into the furnace, He will do at least
29 as much for you, men of little faith! And so do not be uneasy
as to what you will eat or drink or what you will wear, and do not
30 let yourselves be tossed to and fro between hope and fear. For only
those who go through life without faith and confidence in God are
troubled over such matters. Your Father well knows that you have
31 need of all these things. Rather be concerned about communication
with His spirit-world. Then all else will be given to you as well.
32 "Fear nothing, then, little flock, for in the Father's plan of salva-
33 tion the kingdom of heaven is destined to be given to you. Sell the
goods that are yours to dispose of, and give away the proceeds as
alms. Do not provide yourselves with purses, which wear out with
age, but with an inexhaustible treasure-chest in the beyond, where
34 no thief can enter and no moth can destroy. For where your treasures are, your heart will be also.
35 "Keep your loins girded and your lamps burning. Be like men
36 who await their master's home-coming from the wedding, ready to
37 open the door to him at the first sound of his knocking. Fortunate
are those servants whom their master finds awake on his return. I
tell you, he will tuck up his robe, lead them to the table, and serve
38 them with his own hands. Whether he comes in the early hours of
the evening or at midnight or at three o'clock in the morning, if he
finds them awake, he will deal with them as I have said; and happy
39 indeed will such servants be! So much you must see for yourselves:
If a householder knew at what hour the thief would come, he would

40 remain awake and keep his house from being entered. So hold yourselves ready, also. For the Son of man will come at an hour at which
he is not expected."
41 "Lord," asked Peter, "is this parable meant only for us, or for
42 every one else too?" The lord answered, "Who do you suppose is
meant by that faithful, that wise and good steward, whom his master
will set over his domestic servants in order to provide for all their
43 needs at the proper time? Fortunate, to my mind, is that steward
whom his master on his return finds faithfully performing his tasks.
44 Truly, the master will give him charge over all his property. But
45 should the steward think to himself that his master's home-coming
will be delayed, and should he begin to beat the menservants and
the maidservants, and to eat as he pleases and drink until he is
46 drunk, his master will come on a day on which he does not expect
him and at an unforeseen hour. He will separate the body and the
soul of that servant and drive him out among the unfaithful.
47 "A servant who knows his master's wishes and does not follow
48 them will receive many lashes; but a servant who does not know the
master's wishes, and in his ignorance commits acts deserving punishment, will receive but few lashes. For of him to whom much was
given, more will be demanded in return, and from him who received much help, far greater services will be required.
49 "I have come to hurl fire upon the earth; and what could I long
50 for more earnestly than that it were already in full blaze! But I
have yet to be immersed in a baptism, and until this has been accom-
51 plished I shall find no rest. You think perhaps that I came to
bring only peace on earth? No, I tell you, I am bringing discord
52 as well. For henceforth a household of five will be divided on account of me; three will be ranged against two and two against
53 three; the father against the son and the son against the father; the
mother against the daughter and the daughter against the mother;
the mother-in-law against the daughter-in-law and the daughter-in-
law against the mother-in-law."
54 Then, turning once more to the people, he continued, "When you
see a cloud rising in the west you say, 'We shall have rain,' and the
55 rain comes. When you mark that the wind is in the south, you pre-
56 dict hot weather, and again your prediction comes true. Hypocrites!
57 You can read the signs of earth and sky. Why, then, can you not
read the signs spelled by the events of the times occurring before
your eyes? Why can you not reason these things out for yourselves?
58 "If you must go before the court with your opponent, take pains,
on your way there, to come to an understanding with him, lest he

persuade the judge to condemn you, and the judge deliver you to the
59 officer, and the officer throw you into prison. Be assured that you
will not be released until you have paid to the last cent."

CHAPTER 13.

1 Among his hearers were several who told of the Galileans whom
Pilate had caused to be put to death while they were slaughtering
animals for sacrifice, so that their blood mingled with that of the
2 slain beasts. On hearing this, Jesus said, "Do you infer from this
that those Galileans were greater sinners than the rest of the in-
3 habitants of Galilee? By no means, I tell you! All of you will in
4 time come to some such end, unless you repent. Or do you think
that the eighteen who were crushed to death by the tower of Siloam
5 when it fell, were more sinful than any one else in Jerusalem? By
no means, I tell you! All of you will some day die a similar death,
unless you change your hearts."

6 Then he related this parable: "A man had planted a fig tree in
his vineyard, and went to see whether it bore fruit, but he found
7 none. He therefore said to the gardener, 'For the past three years I
have been coming to look for fruit on this fig tree and have never
found any. Take your axe and cut down the tree. It is a waste of
8 ground to let it stand.' But the gardener pleaded, 'Sir, let it stand
for this year at least. I will once more dig up the soil around it
9 and spade in a basketful of manure. Perhaps then it will bear next
year; if not, you can have it cut down.'"

10 One day — it was on a Sabbath — he was preaching in the syna-
11 gogue. There was a woman present who for eighteen years had been
possessed by a spirit which had sapped all her strength. She sat
12 bent over, and was quite unable to straighten herself. When Jesus
saw her, he said to her, "My dear woman, you shall be freed from
13 your infirmity!" Then he laid his hands on her, and at once she
14 sat erect and praised God. The head of the synagogue was very
indignant because Jesus performed this cure on the Sabbath, and
he said to the people, "There are six days on which men should
work. Come and be healed on those days, but not on the Sabbath."
15 The lord answered him, "You hypocrite! Does not every man here
untie his ox or his ass from the stall on a Sabbath, and lead it to
16 water? And should not this woman, this daughter of Abraham
whom Satan has kept in bondage these eighteen years, be freed from
17 her bonds, merely because this is the Sabbath?" At these words all
his opponents were shamed into silence; but the great mass of the
people rejoiced at the glorious deeds he had done.

18 Then he continued, "What does the coming of God's spirit-world
19 resemble, and to what shall I compare it? It is like a grain of
mustard that a man took and planted in his garden, where it grew
20 into a tree, and the birds of the air nested in its limbs." And again
he said, "With what else shall I compare the coming of God's spirit-
21 world? It is like leaven which a woman mixed with three measures
of meal, until the whole was leavened."

22 So he journeyed from town to town and from village to village,
preaching as he went, and always taking the way that led to
Jerusalem.

23 One day some one asked him, "Lord, are there but a few who will
24 be saved?" He answered, "Do your utmost to enter by the narrow
gate, for many, I warn you, will seek to enter and will not succeed.
25 Then, when the master has come and locked the door, and you stand
outside, knocking at it and calling, 'Lord, lord, open for us,' he will
26 tell you, 'I do not know where you come from.' And if you then
say, 'We have eaten and drunk at the same table with you, and you
27 have preached in our public squares,' he will reply to you, 'I can
only tell you that I have never known you; away with you, there-
28 fore, you evil-doers, all of you!' When you see Abraham, Isaac,
and Jacob and all the messengers of God in God's kingdom, while
you yourselves are kept out, there will be wailing and gnashing of
29 teeth among you. They will come from the east and from the west,
from the north and from the south, and will take their places at the
30 feast in the kingdom of God; and some of them who were among
the last will be with the first, and others who once were with the
first, will be among the last."

31 It was at this time that several Pharisees came to him with the
warning, "Get away from here and go somewhere else, for Herod
32 means to kill you." He said in answer, "Go back to that fox and tell
him that I am engaged in driving out evil spirits; that to-day and
to-morrow I shall be busy healing the sick, and shall not be through
33 with my work until the day after; but that to-day, to-morrow, and
on the following day I shall be forced to journey on, for it would
not do for a messenger of God to suffer death elsewhere than in
34 Jerusalem. O Jerusalem, Jerusalem! You who destroy God's instruments and stone those who are sent to you! How often have I been
willing to gather your children around me as a hen gathers her
35 brood under her wings; but you would not have it so. Now the
heavenly dwelling that has been prepared for you must once more
remain empty. But I assure you that you will see me no more until

the day comes on which you will exclaim, 'Praised be he who comes
in the name of the Lord!' "

CHAPTER 14.

1 One Sabbath he came to dine at the house of one of the leaders
of the Pharisees' party. All those present were watching him closely.
2 Near him was a man who suffered from dropsy, and Jesus asked the
3 teachers of the Law and the Pharisees, "May one heal on the Sab-
4 bath or not?" But no one answered. Then he stretched out his hand
5 to the sick man, cured him, and sent him home. But to the rest he
said, "Is there any one among you who, if his sheep or his ox should
fall into a well, would not pull the beast out at once, even if it were
6 on a Sabbath?" Again they made no answer.
7 When he saw that the guests chose the foremost places for them-
8 selves he reproved them with the following example: "When some
one invites you to a wedding, do not take a place at the first table,
for it might happen that a guest more distinguished than you had
9 been invited, and your host would come to you and say, 'Let this man
have your place.' Then you would have to get up and shamefacedly
10 move to the lowest place. When you are invited anywhere, take
rather the lowest place at the table. Then it may be that your host
will come and say to you, 'My dear friend, move higher up,' and
you will be all the more honored in the eyes of your fellow-guests.
11 For he who exalts himself will be humbled, and he who humbles
himself will be exalted."
12 Then he said to his host, "When you give a luncheon or a dinner,
do not ask your friends and your brothers, your relatives and your
rich neighbors, for they would feel bound to ask you in return, and
13 you would be repaid in kind. When you issue invitations, ask the
14 poor and the halt, the lame and the blind, and you will reap a
blessing, for they cannot repay you. Your recompense will come on
the day when the faithful return to God again."
15 At these words, one of his table-companions remarked, "For-
16 tunate is he who may share the feast in the kingdom of God!" Jesus
answered him in this parable: "A certain man once gave a great
17 dinner, to which he asked many guests. When the hour for dinner
had come, he sent out his servant to tell those whom he had invited,
18 'Come, everything is ready.' But they all without exception begged
to be excused. The first one sent word, 'I have bought a piece of
land and am absolutely obliged to go to inspect it. Please con-
19 sider me excused.' The second offered as an excuse, 'I have bought
five yoke of oxen and am about to try them, and so I cannot

20 come.' A third said, 'I married only a few days ago and cannot
21 leave my home.' The servant went back and reported this to his
master. The master was very indignant and sent his servant out into
the streets and alleys of the city with orders to bring in the poor
22 and the maimed, the blind and the lame. Presently the servant reported, 'Sir, your orders have been carried out, but there are still
23 vacant seats.' Then the master said, 'Go out once more, this time
upon the highways and byways outside of the city, and urge all
whom you meet there to come, so that every place in my hall may
24 be filled. But as for those who were asked first, you may be sure
that not one of them will taste of my meal.'"

25 Great crowds of people always accompanied him. One day he
26 said to them, "If any one wants to come to me, he must not consider
his father or his mother, his wife or his child, his brother or his
sister, or even his own life; otherwise he cannot be my disciple.
27 And whoever is not ready to take up his allotted cross and so fol-
28 low in my footsteps, does not belong to my disciples. For which one
of you, intending to build a tower, will not first sit down and count
the cost, to make sure that his means will allow him to finish it?
29 For if he had laid the foundation and could not finish the building,
30 all who saw it would begin to scoff at him, and say, 'That man be-
31 gan to build and could not finish.' Or suppose that a king is
forced to make war on another king. Will he not at once sit down
and consider whether with ten thousand men at his command he
can successfully go into battle against an enemy who is advancing
32 upon him with twenty thousand? And finding that he cannot, will
he not send envoys to the enemy while that enemy is still far off,
33 and ask on what terms he will make peace? So, likewise, none of
you can be my disciple, unless he is able to renounce all that belongs to him.

34 "Salt is good, but if it should lose its strength, how can it be
35 turned into salt again? It is thenceforth good for neither the land
nor the dung-hill, but can only be thrown away. Let him who understands my words profit by them."

CHAPTER 15.

1 Those who pressed most closely around Jesus to listen to his
words were the tax-collectors and others who were publicly looked
2 upon as sinners. This led the Pharisees and the scribes to grumble
at every opportunity, "That man associates with sinners and takes
3 his meals with them." Jesus met their censure with this parable:

4 "Let us suppose that one of you had a hundred sheep, and that he
lost one of them. Would he not leave the ninety-nine in the pasture
5 and hunt the missing one until he found it? And having found it,
6 would he not joyfully take it on his shoulders? And when he came
home, would he not call together all his neighbors and friends, and
say to them, 'Rejoice with me, for I have found the sheep that was
7 lost'? Believe me, so also will there be more joy in heaven over
one sinner who repents than over ninety-nine faithful souls who
need no change of heart.

8 "Or again, let us suppose that a woman has ten pieces of silver
and loses one. Will she not light a lamp, and sweep out the whole
9 house, and search carefully until she finds it? And when she has
found it, will she not call together her friends and neighbors and
say, 'Rejoice with me, for I have found the piece of silver that I
10 lost'? You may be sure that there will be the same joy among the
angels of God over the conversion of one sinner."

11 By way of a third example, he said, "A man had two sons. The
12 younger said to his father, 'Father, give me my share of the property.' The father did so, and divided his property between the two.
13 Soon afterwards the younger son gathered his belongings together
and went to a foreign country, where he squandered his means in
14 loose living. When he had spent everything, a terrible famine came
upon that country, and for the first time in his life, he suffered ex-
15 treme want. After long wandering to and fro, he hired himself out
to a citizen of the country, who sent him to his farm to tend the
16 swine. He would gladly have allayed his hunger with the pods on
17 which the swine were fed, but even these were denied him. Then he
began to reflect on his condition, and said to himself, 'All of my
father's day-laborers have bread and to spare, while I here am dying
18 of hunger. I will set out and return to my father, and confess my
fault. "Father," I will say, "I have sinned against heaven and against
19 you. I am no longer worthy to be called your son. Treat me as you
20 would one of your day-laborers."' And so he set out for his father's
home. While he was still far from the house his father saw him
coming, and pitying him deeply, he ran to meet him and threw his
21 arms about him and kissed him. 'Father,' stammered the son, 'I
have sinned against heaven and against you; I am no longer worthy
to be called your son. Treat me as you would one of your day-
22 laborers.' But the father gave orders to his servants, 'Hurry and get
the best garment and put it on him. Put a ring on his finger and
23 shoes on his feet. Bring the fattened calf and kill it, and let us eat
24 and be merry! For this son of mine was dead and has come back

to life; he was lost and has just been found.' And there was great
joy among them.
25 "His older son was out in the field. As he was on his way home
and drew near the house, he heard music and the sound of dancing.
26 Calling one of the servants he asked what this meant. The servant
27 answered, 'Your brother has come home, and your father, overjoyed to have him safe and sound again, has ordered the fattened
28 calf to be killed.' This made the older brother very angry, and he
would not go into the house. Then his father came out and pleaded
29 with him, but he answered, 'Father, all these years I have served
you and have never yet disobeyed an order of yours. Yet you never
gave me so much as a kid that I might hold a banquet for my
30 friends. But when this son of yours who has squandered all his
money on harlots comes home, you have the fattened calf slaugh-
31 tered for him!'—'My dear son,' said the father, 'you are always
32 with me, and all that I have is yours. Why, then, should we not
rejoice and be glad when this brother of yours who was dead, has
come back to life?—was lost, and has been found again?'"

CHAPTER 16.

1 Another parable that he told his disciples was the following:
"There once was a rich man whose steward, as his master learned,
2 was defrauding him in the management of his property. The master
therefore summoned the steward and said to him, 'What is this that
I hear of you? Make out the accounts of your stewardship at once,
3 for I cannot keep you as my steward any longer.'—'What shall I
do?' thought the steward, 'when my master dismisses me? I am not
strong enough to work as a laborer with a hoe, and I am ashamed
4 to beg. But there has just occurred to me a very good plan by which
I shall be accepted at several houses as soon as I am deprived of
5 my position.' He immediately sent for his master's debtors one by
one, and asked the first, 'How much do you owe my master?'—
6 'A hundred casks of oil,' answered the debtor. 'Here,' said the
steward, 'take your old account and write out a new one for fifty
7 casks.' Then he asked another, 'How much do you owe my master?'
This one answered, 'A hundred measures of wheat.' To him the
steward said, 'Take back your old note and write out a new one for
8 eighty measures.' And the master felt bound to admit that his
steward had shown great shrewdness in this dishonest transaction.
—From this you may see that the men of this world are more far-
sighted in their dealings with their fellows than are the children of
9 light. And so I give you this advice: Make friends with those riches

which in themselves are worthless, so that you will be received in
the tents of the beyond as soon as your stay in this world is over.
10 "Whoever is faithful in the smallest matters is faithful in great
ones as well, and he who is dishonest in the smallest is dishonest
11 also in great matters. If, then, you have not proved yourselves
honest in administering even those goods which in themselves are
12 worthless, who will entrust you with the true riches of God? And
if you have failed to prove yourselves honest in administering another's goods, who will entrust you with the goods that are your
own?
13 "No servant can serve two masters at once, for he will either
loathe his duty to the one, and perform it cheerfully for the other,
or he will hold to the first and slight the second. You cannot be
servants of God and slaves of money at the same time."
14 The Pharisees, who were ruled by avarice, also heard all these
15 things, and they sneered at him. It was to them that he now addressed
the words, "You give the appearance before others of being perfect
in the eyes of God; but God knows your hearts. And the things that
are great in men's eyes are loathsome in the eyes of God.
16 "The Mosaic Law and the messengers of God until and including
John the Baptist foretold the communication with God's spirit-
world as joyful news; but since then violence has been done to all
who tried to enter into communication with God's spirit-world.
17 Nevertheless, heaven and earth shall sooner pass away than shall
remain unfulfilled one letter of that which the Law of Moses foretold.
18 "Any man who divorces his wife and marries another woman
commits adultery; and any one who marries a woman who has forsaken her husband likewise commits adultery."
19 Then, to carry home to them the truth that he was about to proclaim, he gave them this parable: "There once was a rich man
named Phineas who wore purple and fine linen and lived in luxury
20 all his days. A poor man by the name of Lazarus, who was all cov-
21 ered with sores, lay before the other's door and would gladly have
allayed his hunger with the crumbs that fell from the rich man's
table. But there was no one to give them to him. Only the dogs
22 had pity on him, and they came and licked his sores. In time the
poor man died and was carried by the angels to Abraham's bosom.
The rich man also died and was buried in the abyss of the beyond.
23 When he raised his eyes, he saw, far away, Abraham, and resting
24 by his side, Lazarus. Then he called imploringly, 'Father Abraham,
have pity on me, and send Lazarus to me, that he may dip the tips

of his fingers in water, and cool my tongue; for I suffer great tor-
25 ment in this heat.' But Abraham answered him, 'My son, remember
that while you lived on earth you enjoyed all the good that you
could have desired, while Lazarus had to suffer his woe in the same
measure. He is now finding his consolation here, and you there
26 your torment. But aside from all this, there is a great gulf fixed
between you and us, so that those who might wish to pass from our
27 side to yours, could not, nor can they come to us from there.' Then
Phineas begged, 'I beseech you, Father Abraham, at least send him
28 to my father's house, for I still have five brothers there, whom he
ought to warn earnestly, lest they also come to this place of torment.'
29 Abraham answered, 'They have Moses and the messengers of God;
30 let them heed them.' But the other protested, 'No, they will not,
Father Abraham. But if some one should come to them from the
31 dead, they would be converted.'—'If they will not heed Moses and
the messengers of God,' answered Abraham, 'neither will they believe if one of the dead rises and comes to them.'"

CHAPTER 17.

1 He further said to his disciples, "The world cannot be rid of the
seductions that lead away from God, but woe to him who is the cause
2 of them! It would be better for him if a millstone were hung around
his neck and he were sunk in the sea, than that he should cause one
3 of these lowly people to sin. Let every one, therefore, watch himself. If your brother sins against you, rebuke him, and if he repents,
4 forgive him. And though he may sin against you seven times on one
day, and come to you seven times to say that he is sorry, you should
forgive him each time."

5 The apostles entreated the lord, "Let the faith within us in-
6 crease!" He answered, "If you had faith no greater than a mustard
seed, and said to this mountain, 'Move from here to yonder,' it
would move; and to this mulberry tree, 'Transplant yourself from
here into the sea,' it would obey you.

7 "Suppose that one of you had a servant, hired to plow or to look
after your cattle. When that servant came in from the field would
8 he say to him, 'Come and take your place at the table'? Would he
not rather say, 'Get my supper ready for me; then tie on an apron
and wait on me until I have eaten and drunk. Afterwards you may
9 eat and drink'? Surely he owes the servant no thanks for doing as
10 he was bidden. The same thing is true in your case also. When
you have done all those things that I have told you to do, say, 'We

are servants and deserve no thanks, for we have only done our
duty.' "
11 On his journey to Jerusalem Jesus passed through Samaria and
12 Galilee. One day he approached a village near which ten lepers
13 were staying. Keeping at a distance from him they called out loudly,
14 "Jesus, dear master, have pity on us!" When he saw them he said
to them, "You shall be healed! Go and show yourselves to the
priests." While they were on their way to the priests, they were
15 cleansed of their leprosy. One of them, when he saw that he had
been cleansed, came back immediately and loudly praised God;
16 then he fell on his face before Jesus and thanked him. And that man
17 was a Samaritan. Then Jesus said, "Were not all ten made clean?
18 Where are the nine? Of all that were healed, not one has come
19 back to praise God but this foreigner." To the Samaritan he turned
and said, "Rise and go home. Your faith has helped you."
20 One day he was asked by the Pharisees, "When will God's spirit-
world come to us?" He answered them, "God's spirit-world does not
21 come so that you can stand on the street and gape at it; and you
must not believe those who might say to you, 'See, here it is,' or,
22 'There it is.' For God's spirit-world is in your midst." And turning
to his disciples he continued, "The time will come when you will
long to have but a single one of these days that you are now spending with the Son of man; but you will not see your wish fulfilled.
23 If, therefore, any one should say to you later on, 'See, here is the
Son of man,' or, 'See, there he is,' do not go where they direct you,
24 and give no heed to their words. For when the Son of man reappears
it will be as when lightning flashes and lights the whole vault of the
25 sky with its beam. But before that time comes he must suffer much,
and be rejected by this people.
26 "In the eras when the Son of man returns, it will be each time as
27 it was in the days of Noah. There was eating and drinking, men
sought wives, and women husbands; suddenly the day came on
which Noah went into the ark, and the flood broke forth and destroyed all.
28 "Again, it will be as it was in the days of Lot, when men also
thought only of eating and drinking, of buying and selling, of plant-
29 ing and building. Then came the days of Lot's flight from Sodom;
30 fire and brimstone rained from heaven and destroyed all. So it will
be on the day on which the Son of man will appear, divested of his
31 mortal frame. On that day, let no one who is on the housetop and
whose belongings are still inside, go down to fetch them; and let
no one who is out in the field turn back to save what he has left in

32 his house. Remember Lot's wife! Whoever tries to save his life
33 will lose it, and whoever is ready to lose his life will save it. I tell
34 you that on such a night, of two men lying in one bed, one will be
35 taken and the other left. Of two women grinding at the same hand-
36 mill, one will be taken and the other left. Of two men in the same
37 field, one will be taken and the other left." Upon this the disciples
asked him, "Lord, what will become of those who are left?" He answered, "Wherever there are dead bodies the vultures will gather."

CHAPTER 18.

1 To teach them to pray steadfastly and not to weary of prayer,
he told them the following parable:
2 "In a certain city there lived a judge who felt neither fear of
3 God nor regard for man. In the same city lived a widow who again
and again went to that judge to beseech him, 'See that justice is
4 finally done to me against my opponent.' For a long time the judge
gave no heed to her, but at last, on giving the matter thought, he
said to himself, 'Although I have no fear of God nor regard for man,
5 yet I will see to it that this widow receives justice; for she tires me
with her endless complaints, and in the end she may fly into a rage
6 and lay hands on me.'—Did you mark what that unjust judge said?
7 And will not God also see that justice is done to His chosen ones
who cry to Him day and night, even though He may bide His time
8 in sending help? You may be sure that He will soon have justice
done to them. But will the Son of man who has come down here
find on earth the necessary faith?"
9 By way of reproof to those who presume upon their own upright-
10 ness and despise their fellow-men, he told this parable: "Two men
went up into the temple to pray, one of them a Pharisee, the other
11 a tax-collector. The Pharisee stood proudly erect and prayed to
himself, 'I thank Thee, O God, that I am not like other men: I am
neither a robber nor a cheat nor an adulterer, nor am I like that
12 tax-collector. Twice a week I fast, and I pay the tithe of all I re-
13 ceive.' But the tax-collector stood in the doorway, not even daring
to raise his eyes to heaven, and beat his breast, and prayed, 'God be
14 merciful to me, a sinner!'—Believe me, this man went back to his
house with a heart more pleasing in the sight of God than that of
the Pharisee. For he who exalts himself will be humbled, and he
who humbles himself will be exalted."
15 It often happened that the people brought their little children to
Jesus that he might lay his hands on them, and whenever the dis-

16 ciples saw this they treated the people roughly. But Jesus reprimanded the disciples, calling to them, "Let the children come to me,
and do not hinder them. For it is to those who have the heart of a
17 child that communication with God's spirit-world is granted. I
stress it once more: Whoever is not ready to receive communication
with God's spirit-world with a childlike heart will never gain entrance to that spirit-world."

18 On one occasion a certain man of authority asked him, "Good
19 master, what must I do to share in the life hereafter?" Jesus answered him, "Why do you call me 'good'? None is good but One,
20 and that is God. But as to your question, you know the commandments: you shall not commit adultery; you shall not kill; you shall
not steal; you shall not give false testimony, and you shall honor
21 your father and your mother."—"I have kept all of these from my
22 youth," replied the other. Upon this Jesus said to him, "There is
but one thing lacking: sell all you have and give the proceeds to
the very poor, and you will have treasure in the beyond. Then come
23 back and follow me." At these words the man became extremely
24 discouraged, for he was very rich. Seeing how downcast he was,
Jesus said, "How hard it is for the wealthy to enter into communi-
25 cation with God's spirits! Truly, it is easier for a camel to go
through a needle's eye than for a rich man to enter into communica-
26 tion with God's spirits." His hearers asked, "What rich man can
27 be saved, then?" Jesus answered, "Things that are impossible to
28 men are nevertheless possible to God." Then Peter spoke out and
said, "Remember, we are among those who left all that they had and
29 followed you." Jesus said to him, "Be assured that no one has yet
left home or wife, brothers, parents, or children in this life for the
30 sake of entering into communication with God's spirits, without receiving in return far more in this world, and in the beyond the life
hereafter."

31 Then, taking the Twelve aside, he said to them, "We are now
going up to Jerusalem, where all the things written by the prophets
32 concerning the Son of man are to be fulfilled. He will be delivered
33 to the unbelievers and will be derided and spit upon; they will
scourge him and put him to death, and on the third day he will rise
34 again." But they could not grasp all these things; the significance
of his words remained hidden from them, and they did not understand what he meant.

35 As he approached Jericho a blind man was sitting by the way-
36 side, begging. When he heard so many people going past him, the
37 blind man asked what it meant and was told that Jesus of Nazareth

38 was passing by. Then he cried out at the top of his voice, "Jesus,
39 Son of David, have pity on me!" The people nearest to him angrily
told him to keep still, but he cried all the louder, "Son of David,
40 have pity on me!" Jesus stopped and ordered that the man be
41 brought to him. When he had come nearer, he asked him, "What is
it that you want me to do for you?"—"Lord," replied the blind
42 man, "I should like to have my sight back."—"You shall have it
back," answered Jesus; "your faith and confidence have brought
43 you healing." At that instant the blind man's sight was restored. He
followed Jesus, praising God, and all the people who had seen what
occurred joined him in his praise.

CHAPTER 19.

1 Jesus then reached Jericho and passed through the city. A man
2 named Zacchaeus lived there, a head tax-collector who was very
3 wealthy. He was eager to see close at hand what kind of a man
Jesus was, but on account of the great crowd he could not do so,
4 for he was short of stature. He therefore ran on ahead of the others
and climbed up into a fig tree so that he could see him better, for
5 Jesus was to pass that way. When Jesus reached this place he
looked up, and seeing Zacchaeus, called to him, "Make haste and
6 come down, for I must come to your house to-day." Zacchaeus
hastily climbed down out of the tree and joyfully took Jesus into
7 his home. When the by-standers saw this, they all murmured, saying, "He has gone to the house of a notorious sinner and is staying
8 there as his guest." But Zacchaeus went up to the lord and said to
him, "See, lord, I herewith give half of my property to those who
have nothing, and if I have taken more than my due from any one
9 I will restore it fourfold." Jesus answered him, "To-day salvation
10 has come to this house; for he also is a son of Abraham. The Son
of man has indeed come to seek and to save what was lost."

11 Since they were listening intently to his words, he went on with
his teaching; and as he was now near Jerusalem and the people
12 thought that God's spirit-world was about to appear, he spoke to
them in the following parable: "A certain man of the high nobility
set out for a distant country to be crowned there as king and then
13 to return. Calling to him ten of his servants he gave them twenty
dollars each, and instructed them, 'Trade with the money while I
14 am gone.' But his fellow-citizens hated him and sent envoys after
15 him to say, 'We will not have this man as our king.' When he
returned after having been invested with the royal office, he sum-

moned the servants to whom he had given the money, in order to
16 learn to what use they had put it. The first one came and said,
17 'Lord, your money has increased tenfold.'—'You excellent servant,'
answered his master, 'because you have shown yourself so trust-
18 worthy in a small matter, I will give you ten cities to govern.' The
second came and said, 'Lord, your money has increased fivefold.'
19 To him he said, 'And you shall have five cities to govern.' The third
20 came and said, 'Lord, here is your money. I have kept it well
21 wrapped up in a cloth, for I feared you because you are an exceedingly stern man who expects to gain money without laying it out,
22 and to reap where you did not sow.'—'You are a worthless fellow,'
replied the master, 'and I will judge you by your own words. You
knew me to be a stern man, expecting to gain money where none
23 was invested and to reap where I did not sow. Then why did you
not leave my money with a bank, so that I could have collected it
24 with interest on my return?' Turning to those about him he said,
'Take the twenty dollars from him and give it to the man who has
26 the two hundred; for I tell you that to him who makes good use of
his gifts, more will be given, but from him who does not use his
27 gifts, even that which he had will be taken. As for my enemies who
would not have me as their king, bring them here and kill them
before my eyes. But throw this worthless servant into the uttermost
darkness, where there will be wailing and gnashing of teeth.'"

28 After concluding this discourse, Jesus continued on his way to
29 Jerusalem. As he drew near Bethphage and Bethany, which lie at the
foot of what is called the Mount of Olives, he sent ahead two of his
30 disciples, instructing them, "Go into the village that lies before you.
Right at the entrance you will find standing tethered an ass's colt on
31 which no one has ever ridden. Untie it and bring it here. If any one
should ask you to explain, say to him, 'The lord has need of it.'"
32 They went and found everything as he had told them. While they
33 were untying the colt, the people who owned it asked, "Why are you
34 untying our colt?" and they answered, "The lord has need of it."
35 Then they took the colt to Jesus, and after laying their cloaks on its
36 back, they let him mount. As he rode forward the people spread
37 their garments in the road as a carpet for the colt's hoofs. When he
had reached the beginning of the descent from the Mount of Olives,
the whole host of his disciples burst into praises of God for all the
38 wonders they had witnessed, shouting, "Praised be he who comes in
the name of the Lord! Praised be the king! Peace in the lower-
39 spirit-realm, and joy in heaven's highest spheres!" At this, some of
the Pharisees who had mingled with the crowd protested, "Master,

40 tell your disciples to stop this!" But he answered, "Let me tell you
that if they were silent, the very stones would cry out!"
41 As he drew near Jerusalem and saw the city before him, he wept
42 over it, breaking into the lament, "If you had but known — and on
the day appointed for you — the grace of God which was to have
brought you peace! But now, unhappily, it is hidden from you!
43 And so the days will come when your enemies will cast up a ram-
part against you, surrounding you and hemming you in on every
44 side. Yes, they will level you to the ground and dash your children
to the earth, and within your borders they will not leave one stone
upon another, to punish you for allowing to pass unheeded the
moment at which the merciful eye of God was turned upon you."
45 He then went into the temple and drove out those who were buying and selling there, overturned the tables of the money-changers
46 and the stands of the dealers in doves, and said to them all, "It is
written: 'My house shall be a house of prayer, but you have made
it a den of robbers.' "
47 Thereafter he taught in the temple daily, but the chief priests and
48 the scribes and other leading people sought his life. As yet they
found no good opportunity for carrying out their design, for all the
people were always gathered closely about him to listen to his
words.

CHAPTER 20.

1 One day as he was again teaching in the temple and explaining
the gospel of God, some of the chief priests, scribes, and elders of
2 the people came to him and asked, "Tell us what authority you have
for doing these things, and who it is who gave you the right to be-
3 have as you do." He answered, "I will ask you one question which
4 you first have to answer me: Was the baptism that John adminis-
5 tered derived from heaven or from men?" They debated the question among themselves and agreed, "If we say, 'From heaven,' he
6 will ask, 'Why, then, did you not believe him?' And if we say,
'From men,' all the people will stone us, for they are convinced that
7 John was a messenger of God." They therefore answered that they
8 did not know whence it was derived. "Then neither will I tell you,"
returned Jesus, "what authority I have for doing these things."
9 Now he turned once more to the people, and told them this parable: "A man once planted a vineyard, let it out to some grape-
10 growers, and went abroad for a long time. On the date when the
rent was due, he sent a servant to the grape-growers to have them
deliver in payment his share of the crop, as agreed. But the grape-

11 growers beat him and sent him away empty-handed. The owner
then sent another servant, but him they also beat and abused and
12 sent back empty-handed. He sent still a third, whom they also
13 beat until he bled and sent away empty-handed. Then the owner of
the vineyard said to himself, 'What shall I do? I will send my son,
14 my beloved; it may be that they will respect him.' But no sooner
did the grape-growers see the son, than they put their heads together
and whispered to one another, 'That is the heir. Let us kill him; then
15 the inheritance will be ours.' So they drove him from the vineyard
and killed him. Now what will the owner of the vineyard do to
16 them? He will come and put those grape-growers to death and let
the vineyard to others."—"God preserve us from this!" exclaimed
17 his hearers. But Jesus, looking gravely at them, said, "What then is
the meaning of the words of the Scriptures: 'The stone that the
18 builders rejected has become the corner-stone. He who falls upon
this stone will lie shattered on the ground, but he upon whom the
19 stone falls will be ground to pieces?'" Upon this the chief priests
and the scribes sought to lay hands on him in that very hour, for
they saw clearly that the parable had been aimed at them; but they
were afraid of the people.

20 In the hope of trapping him they sent out spies, who acted the
part of law-abiding citizens, to ensnare him in his own words and
21 then to deliver him into the hands of the governor. These men put
their question to him thus: "Master, we know that you speak and
teach in all sincerity, having no regard whatsoever for men but
22 truthfully preaching the way to God. Tell us then, is it right that
23 we should pay the head-tax to Caesar or not?" Seeing through their
24 evil intentions, Jesus said to them, "Show me a tax coin. Whose
likeness and inscription does it bear?" They answered, "Caesar's."—
25 "Then give to Caesar," he replied, "what belongs to Caesar, and to
26 God, what belongs to God." So they failed to catch him with this
question before the people, and utterly disconcerted by his answer,
they held their peace.

27 Soon afterwards some of the Sadducees, who deny the resurrection, came up to him and laid the following case before him:
28 "Master, Moses gave us the law that if a brother should die leaving
a wife but no children, his brother shall marry the widow, and by
29 her raise posterity to his deceased brother. Now there were seven
30 brothers, and the first one took a wife and died childless. And so
31 the second brother married the woman; then the third, and thus all
seven one after the other, each of them dying without leaving chil-
32 dren. Finally the woman died also. Whose wife will she be on the

33 day of the resurrection? For she had been married to each of the
34 seven." Jesus answered them, "Among the children of this world,
35 men seek wives and women husbands. But among those who have
been found worthy to attain that other world and the resurrection
from the dead, men have no need to seek wives, nor women hus-
36 bands. It is no longer their lot to die, but they are like the angels,
37 because they are children of the resurrection. But the fact that the
dead are really raised was shown even by Moses in the story of the
bush, inasmuch as he calls the Lord the God of Abraham, the God
38 of Isaac, and the God of Jacob. He is not a God of the dead but of
39 the living, for through Him all will come back to life again." At
this reply several of the scribes exclaimed, "Master, you have com-
40 pletely routed them with your answer!" And thenceforth they did
not dare to ask him any further questions.
41 He now asked them, "How can any one say that the Messiah is a
42 son of David? Does not David himself say in the Book of Psalms:
43 'The Lord says to my lord, "Sit at my right hand until I have laid
44 your foes at your feet"'? David therefore calls the Messiah his lord;
how, then, can he be David's son?"
45 Then, addressing his disciples, but in such a way that all the
46 people could hear him, he said, "Beware of the scribes who enjoy
going about in long robes and being saluted in public; who covet
the foremost seats in the synagogues and the places of honor at
47 banquets; who in their greed seek to devour the property of widows,
under the pretext of saying long prayers on their behalf in return
for pay. So much the heavier will be the punishment they will have
to undergo."

CHAPTER 21.

1 One day he was looking on while the rich dropped their offerings
2 into the alms-box. Among them he saw a poor widow dropping in
3 two mites, together worth a cent. This prompted the remark, "That
4 destitute widow has given more than any one else; for all the others
gave to the alms-fund out of their abundance, while she, poor as she
is, has given the last she had toward her own support."
5 To some who spoke admiringly of the temple, decorated with
6 beautiful stone-work and votive offerings, he said, "The days are
coming when of all that you see here, this whole masonry, not one
stone will be left upon another, but everything will be torn down."
7 —"Master," they inquired of him, "when will this be? And what
8 signs can you give us of your return?" He answered, "Take care
not to be misled, for many will come in my name, saying, "I am the

9 Messiah,' and, 'The time is at hand.' Do not run after them. And
if later you hear of wars and uprisings, do not be afraid. For all
these things are bound to happen first, but they do not by any
10 means signify the end. Moreover, nation will rise against nation,
11 and kingdom against kingdom. Violent earthquakes will come, and
in some countries famines and plagues, fearful sights and strange
12 signs from heaven will be seen. But before all these things happen,
men will lay hands on you and persecute you. They will hale you
into synagogues and prisons, before governors and kings, for my
13 name's sake, and there you will have the opportunity to testify on
14 my behalf. But at such times — and take my words well to heart —
you will have no need of meditating beforehand on the manner of
15 your defence, for I will endow you with an eloquence and a wisdom
which all your adversaries will be unable to resist or to gainsay.
16 You must, it is true, be prepared for betrayal even by parents and
brothers, relatives and friends, and they will be the cause of the
17 death of one or another of you; for you will be hated by all men
18 for being called by my name. But not a hair of your head shall
19 perish. By your steadfastness you will gain permanent possession
of your spiritual life.

20 "When you see Jerusalem surrounded by armies, you shall know
21 that the destruction of the city is at hand. Then the people of Judaea
shall flee to the mountains, and the inhabitants of the capital shall
not seek to leave it, nor shall the country-folk seek safety in the city.
22 For those days will be the days of retribution, on which everything
23 that is written in the Scriptures will be fulfilled. Woe to the women
who are with child on that day, and to the women with babes at their
breasts; for there will be great tribulation throughout the land, and
24 a fearful judgment will fall upon its people. Many will die by the
edge of the sword, and the rest will be led as captives among all
nations. Jerusalem will be trodden under the feet of the unbelievers
until they shall have completed their work of destruction.

25 "And there will be signs to be seen in the sun, the moon, and the
stars. The spirits of the earthly spheres will be driven together in
droves, as will also the spirits confined to the trackless sea and the
26 streams of water, while among living people many will perish from
fear and dread of the things which will come upon the world. In-
27 deed even the lower powers of the beyond will tremble. Then they
will see the Son of man appear in the midst of a mighty host of
28 spirits, in great power and radiant glory. And so when all these
things begin to come about, lift up your hearts and your heads, for
your redemption is drawing near."

29 He ended with this analogy: "Look at the fig tree and at all the
30 other trees. When they burst into bud you know that summer is
31 near. So also when you see these things taking place you shall know
32 that God's spirit-world is at hand. Mark my words, this people will
33 not pass away until all these things have been fulfilled. The sky
and the earth will pass away, but my words will not pass away
34 unfulfilled. See to it, however, that your hearts are not dulled with
gluttony and drunkenness and worldly anxieties, lest that day come
35 upon you unawares; for it will come like a cast-net over all who
36 dwell in the earthly spheres. Be watchful at all times, therefore,
and pray that you may be found worthy to be spared the doom to
come; then you will be able to stand the test before the Son of man."
37 By day Jesus used to preach in the temple, but toward nightfall
he always went to the hill known as the Mount of Olives to pass the
38 night there. All the people would flock to him in the temple early
in the morning to listen to him.

CHAPTER 22.

1 Meanwhile the festival of unleavened bread, which is called the
2 Passover, drew near. The chief priests and the scribes sought ways
3 and means to destroy Jesus, but they feared the people. Then Satan
entered into Judas, surnamed Iscariot, who was one of the Twelve,
4 and he went and discussed with the chief priests a way by which he
5 could deliver Jesus into their hands. They were highly pleased at
6 this, and agreed to pay him a certain sum of money for it. He declared himself satisfied with this reward and from now on sought
a favorable opportunity to betray Jesus without the knowledge of
the people.
7 The day of the Easter season on which it was the custom to kill
8 the Passover lamb was now at hand, and Jesus sent out Peter and
John with the instructions, "Go and prepare the Passover for us, so
9 that we may celebrate the feast." They asked him, "Where shall we
10 prepare the meal?" He replied, "As you enter the city, you will be
met by a man carrying a water-jar. Follow him into the house
11 that he enters and say to its owner, 'The master sends us to ask
you, "Where is the guest-chamber where I may eat the Passover with
12 my disciples?"' He will then show you a large upper room fur-
13 nished with tables and cushions. Prepare everything there." They
went and found everything as he had said, and made ready for the
meal.
14 When the hour had come, Jesus reclined at the table with his
15 disciples, and turned to them with the words, "I have deeply longed

16 to eat this Passover with you before my suffering. For I assure you
that this is the last meal I shall share with you until that which will
17 be partaken of in a new form in my Father's kingdom." Then, taking up a cup, he gave thanks to God and said, "Take this cup and
18 share it among you, for I tell you that from this time on I shall
drink no more of the fruit of the vine until that day on which God's
19 spirit-world has come to you." Next he took bread, gave thanks,
broke it and gave it to them, saying, "This is the symbol of my
21 body. Unhappily I must tell you that the hand of him who is plot-
22 ting my betrayal is at the same table with mine. It is true that the
Son of man must travel the path of his destiny, but woe to him by
23 whom he is betrayed!" The disciples now fell to inquiring and con-
24 jecturing which of them could be capable of such a deed, and in
25 their zeal they disputed as to which of them was the greatest. To
end their discussion Jesus said, "The kings of nations call themselves absolute masters over their subjects, and their officials cause
26 themselves to be styled 'benefactors'. Among you this must not be.
The greatest of you must look upon himself as the least, and the
27 chief as a servant. Have not I who am here at table with you done
this to a far greater degree? For I walked among you not as one
28 who is served, but as your servant. You also, profiting by the example I have set you in service, have progressed in this direction.
In the heavy trials that beset me, you have stood by me faithfully.
29 And inasmuch as my Father appointed me as king, I ordain that in
30 my kingdom you shall eat and drink at my table, and sit upon
31 thrones to judge the twelve tribes of Israel." Then addressing Peter,
he said, "Simon, Simon, Satan has sought and obtained leave to
32 shake your hearts as wheat is shaken in a sieve. For you, however,
I have prayed that your faith may not completely break down;
and when you have been converted, strengthen your brothers!"—
33 "Lord," answered Peter, "by your side I am ready to go both into
34 prison and to my death." But Jesus said, "I tell you, Peter," the
cock will not crow to-day before you have three times denied that
35 you know me." Then he continued, "When I sent you out without
money or a bag or shoes, did you ever want for anything?" They
36 answered, "No."—"But now," he went on, "let him who has a
purse, take it, and also his bag, and let him who has none sell his
37 cloak and buy a sword. For I tell you, the words of the Scriptures,
'He was reckoned among the criminals,' must now be fulfilled in
38 me. And then my destiny will have come to an end."—"Lord,"
they answered, "we have two swords here." He replied, "Enough
of this."

39 He then went out to the Mount of Olives, as was his custom, but
40 this time his disciples went with him. When they reached the place
to which he was in the habit of going he said to them, "Pray that
41 you may not yield to temptation." He then went about a stone's
42 throw from them, knelt down, and prayed, "Father, not my will,
but Thine, be done! If, therefore, it be Thy will, let this cup pass
43 from me." Then an angel appeared from heaven and strengthened
44 his vital force. Dread fear came over him, while he continued to
pray with the utmost fervor, and his sweat became like drops of
45 blood falling down to the ground. When he had ended his prayer,
he rose and went to his disciples. Finding that they had fallen
46 asleep from overwhelming grief, he aroused them with the words,
"What? Sleeping? Get up and pray, that you may not fall victims
to temptation!"

47 He was still speaking to them when a great mob of people appeared. At its head was one of the Twelve, the man called Judas
Iscariot. He went up to Jesus as though to kiss him, according to
the signal which he had pre-arranged: "The one I shall kiss is the
48 man." But Jesus said to him, "Judas, would you betray the Son of
49 man with a kiss?" When the companions of Jesus saw what was
50 taking place, they asked, "Lord, shall we use our swords?" and
one of them did actually strike, his blow cutting off the right ear of
51 the high priest's servant. But Jesus said to them, "Let it go no further." And he stretched out his hand toward the servant, replaced
52 his ear, and healed it. He then turned to the chief priests, the captains of the temple-guards, and the elders who had surrounded him,
and said to them, "You have come armed with swords and clubs,
53 as though to take a robber. Yet day after day I was among you in
the temple, and then you never laid a hand on me. But an hour like
this suits you, and in the dark you are strong."

54 They then took him prisoner and led him to the house of the
55 high priest, while Peter followed at a distance. A fire was kindled
in the middle of the court-yard, and after all had gathered around
56 it, Peter sought a place among them in order to warm himself. A
maid who saw him sitting by the fire, looked closely at him and exclaimed, "That man was with him also!" But Peter denied it, pro-
57
58 testing, "Woman, I do not even know him." Soon afterwards some
one else made the same statement, and again Peter protested, "Man,
59 that is not true." About an hour later still another man said, "I say
with all certainty, this fellow was also with him, for he too is a
60 Galilean."—"Man," exclaimed Peter, "I do not understand how
61 you can say such a thing." At that moment a cock crowed. Then

the lord turned around, and his eye fell upon Peter; and Peter immediately remembered that the lord had said to him, "Before the
cock crows to-day you will have three times denied that you know
62 me." And he went outside and wept bitterly.
63 Meanwhile the men who had Jesus in custody abused him, blind-
64 folding him and asking, "Who was it who struck you? If you are a
65 prophet, now is the time to prove it." And they hurled many other
insults at him.
66 At daybreak the gathering of the elders of the people, the chief
priests, and the scribes, met and ordered him to be taken before the
67 High Council. There they said to him, "If you are the Messiah, say
so!" He answered, "Even if I should tell you that I am he, you
68 would not believe me; and if I should question you, you would not
69 answer me, neither would you set me free. It is now only a little
while before the Son of man will sit at the right hand of the power-
70 ful God." At this they all shouted, "Are you the Son of God then?"
71 He answered, "I am."—"Why need we hear any witnesses?" they
rejoined. "Have we not heard it from his own lips?"

CHAPTER 23.

1 The whole gathering now rose and led Jesus before Pilate, bring-
2 ing the following charges: "We have found that this fellow is stirring up our people and inciting them to pay no more taxes to
Caesar; further that he declares he is the Messiah and a king."—
3 "Are you the king of the Jews?" asked Pilate. "I am," answered
4 Jesus. Then Pilate said to the chief priests and the people, "I find
5 no fault in this man." But they grew more and more turbulent and
repeated, "He is stirring up the whole nation and spreading his
doctrines wherever there are Jews. He began in Galilee, and now
6 he has made his way as far as this city." When Pilate heard the
7 word Galilee, he asked, "Is this man a Galilean?" And when he
learned that Jesus actually belonged under Herod's jurisdiction he
8 sent him to Herod, who was in Jerusalem at that time. Herod was
greatly pleased to see Jesus. For a long time he had wanted to know
him because of the many things he had heard about him; moreover,
he hoped that Jesus would perform some miracle in his presence.
9 He began by asking Jesus a number of questions, but Jesus an-
10 swered not a one, while the chief priests and the scribes stood by
and presented their charges against him in the most vehement man-
11 ner. Herod and the dignitaries about him now turned from Jesus
in contempt and made him an object of general derision by dressing

12 him in a purple robe and sending him back to Pilate. On that same
day Herod and Pilate, who previously had not been on good terms
with each other, became fast friends.
13 Pilate now called together the chief priests and the members of
14 the High Council, as well as the people, and said to them, "You
have brought this man before me as an agitator. I have examined
him in your presence, as you yourselves know, but I have not found
15 him guilty of a single one of your charges. Neither has Herod, to
whom I sent you. You see for yourselves that he has done nothing
16 to merit the death-penalty. I will therefore give him a severe warn-
17 ing and set him free." For it was a fixed rule that he had to release
18 one prisoner at every festival. But they all shouted with one accord,
19 "Away with this man! Release Barabbas." Barabbas was a man
who was in prison for taking part in a riot in the city, and for
20 murder. Pilate, who had firmly resolved to release Jesus, appealed
21 to them a second time, but they shouted, "Crucify him, crucify him!"
22 For the third time Pilate asked, "What wrong has this man done?
I have not found him guilty of anything calling for death. I will
23 therefore give him a severe warning and set him free." But they
persisted in demanding amid a great uproar that Jesus be crucified.
In the end their shouting, together with that of the priests, pre-
24 vailed, and Pilate pronounced the sentence, "Let the request of the
25 accusers be granted. The prisoner who is being held for murder
and whose release is demanded, is free. Let Jesus be delivered to
his accusers, to be executed in accordance with the sentence they
desire."
26 He was then led away to be executed. On the way they stopped
a certain Simon of Cyrene who chanced to be coming in from the
fields, and laid the cross on his shoulder so that he might carry it
27 after Jesus. There followed a vast crowd of people, among them
28 women who lamented and wept for him. Jesus turned to them and
said, "Daughters of Jerusalem, do not weep and lament for me.
29 Weep rather for yourselves and for your children, for the days are
coming when men will exclaim, 'Fortunate are the barren and the
women who never became mothers and the breasts that have no need
30 to nurse.' Men will say to the mountains, 'Fall on us,' and to the
31 hills, 'Cover us.' For if these things happen when the wood is green,
what will happen when it is dry?"
32 Together with Jesus two criminals were taken out to be put to
death.
33 After they had reached the place of execution, known also as the
"Place of the Skulls," they proceeded with the crucifixion. They also

crucified the two criminals, one on his right hand and one on his
34 left. Then they divided his clothes among themselves by drawing
35 lots, while the people stood and stared. The members of the High
Council called to him in derision, "You have saved others, now save
yourself, if you are the Son of God, the Messiah, the chosen One."
36 The soldiers also made sport of him, going to the cross to offer him
37 vinegar to drink, and saying, "Hail, King of the Jews," while they
38 set a crown on his head — a crown of thorns. Above him was placed
an inscription written in Greek, Latin, and Hebrew, which read:
This is the King of the Jews.

39 One of the criminals hanging by his side abused him. "Do you
call yourself the Messiah?" he said. "If you are, save yourself and
40 us!" But the other rebuked him sharply, saying, "Have you no fear
41 of God? This man is suffering the same death as we are. In our
case it is just, for we are receiving the due reward of our deeds.
42 But he has done no wrong." Then turning to Jesus he pleaded,
43 "Oh, think of me on the day of your coming!" And Jesus said to
him who had reproached his companion, "Take courage, for on this
very day you will be with me in paradise."

44 When it was about noon, darkness fell upon the whole land and
45 lasted for three hours, while the sun was hidden in an eclipse. Then
46 Jesus cried out in a loud voice, "Father, into Thy hands I commend
my spirit!" After these words he died. At that instant the curtain
47 of the temple was torn. The centurion praised God loudly and said,
48 "Surely, this was an upright man." And the people who had come
out to witness the sight and who had seen everything that took place,
beat their breasts and their foreheads and went back to their homes.
49 But all those who loved Jesus stood in the distance looking on,
among them some women who had followed him from Galilee.

50 Now there was a man named Joseph who came from the Jewish
town of Arimathaea and who was a member of the High Council.
51 He was a good and a God-fearing man who was awaiting the coming
of the kingdom of God, and who had been opposed to the decision
52 and course of action taken by the High Council. He now went to
53 Pilate to beg for the body of Jesus. Taking it from the cross, he
wrapped it in fine linen and laid it away in a tomb which was hewn
in the rock and which had never before been used for burial. After
laying away the body, Joseph caused the entrance to the tomb to be
closed with a stone so large that twenty men could scarcely roll it
54 into place. This was done in the hours of the so-called "Pre-Sab-
55 bath," shortly before the actual Sabbath began. At the burial were
present two women who had followed Jesus from Galilee and who

56 now saw the tomb and the interment of the body. They then went
back to the city and on their way provided themselves with spices
and fragrant ointments. They spent the Sabbath resting.

CHAPTER 24.

1 On the first day after the Sabbath they went out to the tomb at
dawn and took with them the things that they had previously pro-
2 vided. Several other women went with them. On their way to the
tomb they discussed who should roll the stone from the grave for
them, but when they arrived they found that the stone had already
3 been rolled away. They went into the tomb but did not find the
4 body, and as they paused there, perplexed, two men in radiant gar-
5 ments suddenly stood beside them. Seized with terror, they bowed
their faces to the ground, but the men said to them, "Why do you
6 seek the living among the dead? Do you remember the words that
7 he spoke to you while he was still in Galilee, telling you that the
Son of man must be delivered into the hands of men and be cruci-
8 fied, but that on the third day he must rise again?" Then they
9 remembered his words, and they hurried back to relate to the Eleven
as well as to all the others everything that they had experienced.
10 The women who carried the tidings to the apostles were Mary
Magdalene and Joanna, and Mary the mother of James, and the
11 other women who had gone with them. But the apostles regarded
their tale as imaginary and they would not believe them.

13 On the same day two of their number went out to a village
14 named Emmaus, which lies about seven miles from Jerusalem. As
they walked they conversed about the events that had taken place,
15 and in the midst of their conversation and discussion, Jesus himself
16 suddenly came toward them and joined them; but their eyes were
17 prevented from recognizing him. "What is all this that you are
discussing so earnestly on your way," he began, "and seem so de-
18 pressed about?" One of them named Cleopas answered, "Are you
the only stranger in Jerusalem who does not know what has hap-
19 pened there during the last few days?"—"What can it be?" he
asked. "Why," they answered, "all about Jesus of Nazareth, who
was a messenger of God mighty in word and deed before God and
20 before all the people; and how our chief priests and the High
Council delivered him up in order that the sentence of death which
they had passed upon him might be confirmed, and afterwards cru-
21 cified him. But we had hoped that it was he who would bring salva-
22 tion to Israel. True, that was only three days ago, and some women

have aroused great hopes in us, for they went out to his grave early
23 this morning and did not find his body there. When they came back
they told us that angels had appeared to them and announced that
24 he was alive. When we heard this, some of our companions went
out to the grave and found everything as the women had stated, but
25 him they did not see."—"What short-sighted men you are," he
answered, "and how hard it is for you to understand the sayings of
26 the prophets! Was not the Messiah destined to suffer all these
27 things in order that he might enter into his glory?" And beginning
with Moses he now explained to them all those passages in the
28 writings of the prophets which related to the Messiah. By this time
they had nearly reached the village for which the two were bound.
29 He made a pretence of wanting to go farther, but they urged him,
"Stay with us, for it is late in the day and evening is coming on."
30 He therefore followed them to their lodgings, and as he reclined at
table with them he took bread, returned thanks, broke the bread,
31 and gave it to them. In the moment that they received the bread
from his hands their eyes were opened and they recognized him.
32 But he vanished from their sight. "Was there not a veil over our
hearts while he spoke to us on the way and explained the text of the
33 Scriptures?" they asked one another. And saddened by his disappearance they set out at that very hour and went back to Jeru-
34 salem. There they found the Eleven and the others gathered, and
were told by them that the lord had in truth risen and had appeared
35 to Simon. They in their turn related at length everything that had
happened to them on their walk, and how they had recognized the
lord as he broke the bread.

36 While they were still speaking, Jesus himself suddenly stood
37 among them. They huddled together in terror, thinking that it was
38 a ghost that they saw, but he said to them, "Why are you so disturbed, and why do such foolish thoughts arise in your minds?
39 Look at my hands and my feet, and see for yourselves that it is I.
Touch me, and you will know that a phantom cannot have flesh and
41 bones as you see that I have." And when they in their joyful excitement still hesitated to believe, he asked them, "Have you any food
42 here?" They gave him a piece of broiled fish, and he ate it in their
43 presence. Then he said to them, "The words that I spoke to you
44 while I was with you were these: 'Everything that is written concerning me in the Law of Moses, in the writings of the prophets, and
45 in the Psalms must be fulfilled.'" And now he opened their minds
46 to the understanding of these writings, and made it clear to them
that in accordance therewith the Messiah was bound to suffer and

47 on the third day to rise again; moreover, that the gospel of repentance and forgiveness of the sins of apostasy would be preached in
48 his name to all nations, beginning with Jerusalem. "You," he said,
49 "can bear witness to these things. And so I will send down upon you
that which I have promised you. Wait here in this city until you
have been endowed with power from on high."
50 Then, after having led them to the outskirts of Bethany, he lifted
51 his hands and blessed them. As he pronounced the blessing, he
52 vanished from their sight. With joyous hearts they went back to
53 Jerusalem, where they passed most of their time in the temple,
praising God.

The Gospel according to JOHN

CHAPTER 1.

1 IN the beginning was the Word, and the Word was with God; and
2 the Word was a god. This was with God in the beginning. Every-
3 thing came into being through the Word, and without it nothing
4 created sprang into existence. In it is life, and that life was the light
5 of mankind. The light shines in the realm of darkness, but the darkness would have none of it.
6 There was one who came into the world as a man, sent by the
7 Lord. His name was John. He came as a witness, to testify to the
light, in order that through him all men might be led to believe in
8 the light. He himself was not the light, but was sent simply to tes-
9 tify that the light would appear; for he who is the true light which
10 shines upon all men was then about to be born into the world. It
is true that he was always in the world, for through him the world
11 came into being; but the world did not acknowledge him. He came
12 into his own, and his own people would not receive him. But to all
who did accept him he granted the privilege of becoming children
13 of God, only asking that they believe in his name as in the name of
one who came into being not by way of descent, nor in consequence
of the natural instinct of the flesh, nor through the will of any man,
14 but through God. And the Word became flesh and for a short time
dwelt among us. We saw his glory, a glory such as befits the only
Son who was brought into being by the Father and is full of grace
and truth.
15 John testified to him and raised his voice on his behalf. It was
John who proclaimed, "There is one who will come after me who
16 was before me; for he came into being sooner than I. Out of his
abundance of life we have all received life, and blessing after bless-
17 ing. While the Law was given to us by Moses, grace and truth have
18 come to us through Jesus the Messiah. No human being has ever
seen God; it is the only-begotten Son, resting upon the Father's
bosom, who has brought us knowledge of Him."
19 The leading Jews of Jerusalem sent priests and Levites to John to
20 ask him, "Who are you?" Frankly and without any concealment he
21 confessed, "I am not the Messiah."—"Who are you then?" they
asked again. "Are you Elijah?"—"No," he answered.—"Are you

22 the prophet?"—"No," he repeated.—"But who are you?" they
insisted; "for we must take an answer to those who sent us. Who
23 do you profess to be?" He replied, "I am he whose voice is heard
calling in the barren mountain-country, 'Make smooth the way for
24 the lord,' as the prophet Isaiah foretold." The men who had been
25 sent, partisans of the Pharisees, now asked him, "Why do you baptize, then, if you are neither the Messiah, nor Elijah, nor the
26 Prophet?"—"I immerse you in water only," answered John, "but
27 among you there is one whom as yet you do not know. He will come
after me, although he came into being before me. He is one whose
very shoe-laces I am not worthy to undo. He will immerse you in
28 the fiery waves of a holy spirit." This meeting took place in Bethany
beyond the Jordan, where John was baptizing.

29 On the next day he saw Jesus coming toward him, and exclaimed,
"See, there is the Lamb of God, who takes away from the world the
30 sins of apostasy! It is he of whom I said yesterday, 'After me will
come one who came into being before me; for he existed before I
31 did.' Even I did not know him. But in order that Israel might learn
32 to know him, I have come baptizing by immersion in water." Then
John continued, "I saw the Spirit in the shape of a dove descend
33 from heaven and hover above him. As I have said, he was personally unknown to me, but the One who sent me to baptize by immersion in water had told me, 'He upon whom you see the Spirit descend and above whom it hovers, is he who baptizes by immersion
34 in the fiery waves of a holy spirit.' This I witnessed with my own
eyes, and therefore testified that he is the Son of God."

35 On the following day John was again standing in the same place
with two of his disciples, while Jesus walked to and fro near by.
36 Turning his eyes upon him John said, "See the Lamb of God!" Upon
37 hearing these words the two disciples followed Jesus. He turned,
38 and seeing them coming toward him, asked, "What is it that you
wish?" They answered, "Rabbi" (which means "master"), "where
39 do you live?"—"Come and see," he replied. And they went with
him and saw where he lived. It was then about noon, and they
passed the rest of the day with him.

40 One of the two who had heard what John said and followed Jesus
41 was Simon Peter's brother, Andrew. First of all he found his brother
Simon and told him, "We have found the Messiah,"—which means
42 "the anointed." He then took Simon to Jesus, and when Jesus saw
him he said, "You are Simon, the son of John; but from this day
you shall be called 'Cephas,'"—which means "rock."

43 On the following day Jesus intended to set out for Galilee, and

44 meeting Philip, he said to him, "Come with me." Philip was from
45 Bethsaida, the home of Andrew and Peter. Philip met Nathanael
and told him the good news: "We have found him of whom Moses
spoke in the Law, and the prophets in their writings. His name is
46 Jesus, and he is a son of Joseph of Nazareth." Nathanael replied,
"Can anything good come out of Nazareth?"—"Come and see,"
47 said Philip. When Jesus saw Nathanael coming toward him he exclaimed, "Here is an Israelite such as he ought to be, a man in whom
48 there is no flaw!"—"How do you know me?" Nathanael asked.
Jesus answered, "I saw you even before Philip called to you, while
49 you were sitting under the fig tree."—"Master," cried Nathanael,
50 "you are indeed the Son of God,—the King of Israel!"—"You
believe in me," returned Jesus, "because I told you that I saw you
51 under the fig tree; but you will see greater things than that. For I
solemnly assure you that hereafter you will see the heavens open and
the messengers of God ascending and descending above the Son of
man."

CHAPTER 2.

1 Two days later there was a wedding at Cana in Galilee. The
2 mother of Jesus was present, and Jesus and his disciples had also
3 been invited. Suddenly it was found that they lacked wine, for the
supply that had been provided for the wedding had given out. Turn-
4 ing to Jesus his mother said to him, "There is no more wine." Jesus
answered, "Woman, why need you concern yourself with my affairs?
5 The time for me to act has not yet come." His mother then said to
the servants, "If he should give you any orders, carry them out at
6 once." Standing near by were six stone water-jars, such as were
customarily used by the Jews for purification. Each jar held some
7 two or three bucketfuls. Jesus now gave orders to fill these jars with
8 water, and they were at once filled to the brim. He then said, "Draw
some, and take it to the master of ceremonies." This was also done.
9 The master of ceremonies tasted the water which had been turned
into wine, without knowing where it came from, although those who
had served it of course knew very well. He now called the bride-
10 groom and said to him, "Usually the good wine is served first, and
the poorer wine only after the guests have been drinking. But you
have kept the good wine until now."

11 Thus at Cana in Galilee Jesus performed the first of his miracles
and so manifested the power with which he was endowed; and his
disciples believed in him.

12 Afterward he went down to Capernaum, together with his mother,

his brothers, and his disciples. Here he stayed only a short time,
13 because the Jewish Passover was at hand, and Jesus went up to
14 Jerusalem to attend the festival. There in the temple he found men
engaged in selling cattle, sheep, and doves. Money-changers were
15 also sitting there. He braided a whip out of strips of leather, and
drove all of them, together with their sheep and cattle, out of the
temple. He scattered the coins of the money-changers upon the
16 ground, and overturned their tables. To the dealers in doves he
said, "Take your things away from here! Do not turn my Father's
17 house into a market!" His actions brought to the minds of his disciples the words of the Scriptures: "Zeal for Thy house consumes
18 me." Some of the leaders of the Jewish people now asked him,
"How can you prove to us that you are authorized to do these
19 things?" He answered, "Tear down this temple, and within three
20 days I will rebuild it."—"It took forty-six years to erect this
temple," exclaimed the Jews, "and are you going to rebuild it in
21 three days?" But he was speaking of the temple of his body. Afterward, when he had risen from the dead, his disciples remembered
this saying, and then they believed the Scriptures and the words that
Jesus had spoken at this time.

23 During the Passover Jesus remained in Jerusalem, and many
came to believe in his name when they saw the miracles that he per-
24 formed. But Jesus himself placed no confidence in them, because he
25 knew the true inner nature of every one; nor had he need of making
inquiries concerning any one, for he knew what went on in the heart
of a human being.

CHAPTER 3.

1 Among the Pharisees there was a man named Nicodemus, one of
2 the leaders of the Jews. He came to Jesus by night and said to him,
"Master, we know that you are a teacher sent by God; for no one
can perform such miracles as you perform, unless God Himself is
3 with him." Jesus gave him the answer, "Believe me, unless a man
4 is born from above he cannot see the kingdom of God."—"How can
a man be born when he is old?" asked Nicodemus. "Can he possibly enter his mother's womb a second time and be born again?"
5 —"I can only repeat," said Jesus, "that no one can enter God's
6 spirit-world unless he is born into it by a spirit of God. Whatever is
born of the flesh is flesh, and whatever is born of the spirit is spirit.
7 You need not wonder, therefore, at my saying that you must be born
8 from above. The spirit-world of God dispenses life where it chooses;
you hear its voice, but you do not know where it comes from or

where it goes. This is also the case with every one who is born as a
9 spirit-child." — "How can that be?" asked Nicodemus. "What,"
10 replied Jesus, "you are a teacher of Israel, and do not understand?
11 That which I am telling you is the truth, for the things that we know
thoroughly are the things that we teach, and the things that we have
seen are the things to which we bear witness. To be sure, you do
12 not accept our testimony. If you would not believe me when I spoke
to you of earthly matters, how will you believe me if I speak to you
13 of heavenly matters? No one has ascended to heaven unless he came
down from heaven. Thus the Son of man also has come down from
14 heaven; and as Moses once lifted up the serpent in the wilderness,
15 so must the Son of man again be lifted up, in order that every one
16 who believes in him may share with him the life hereafter. For God
so loved the world that He gave His only-begotten Son, in order
that those who believe in him may not perish, but have life here-
17 after. God did not send His Son into the world to condemn the world
18 but in order that through him the world might be saved. He who
believes in him will not be condemned; but he who does not believe
is already condemned. He is condemned for not believing in the
19 name of the only-begotten Son of God. In this lies the condemnation: that the light came into the world and that men loved the dark-
20 ness better than the light; for their deeds were evil. For every evil-
doer hates the light and shrinks from going where the light shines,
21 for fear that his works will be branded as evil. But he who accepts
the divine truth as the guiding star of his life gladly walks in
the brightly illuminated paths of the light, so that all his doings
may be seen to be in accord with the will of God."

22 After this Jesus went with his disciples into the country of Judaea,
23 where he stayed for a short time and administered baptism. At the
same time John was baptizing at Aenon near Salim, because water
was plentiful there. The people used to go there to be baptized by
24 him, for at that time John was not yet imprisoned. Thus it came
25 about that among some of John's disciples there arose a certain
jealousy, which was still further aggravated by ill-disposed Jewish
leaders. The question at issue was who should administer baptism
26 as the symbol of inner purification. These disciples now went to
John and said to him, "Master, the man who was with you on the
other side of the Jordan and on whose behalf you testified, is now
administering baptism himself, and everybody is going to him."
27 John answered, "No human being can assume authority unless it
28 has been conferred upon him from heaven. Can you yourselves not
bear witness that I said, 'I am not the Messiah, but have been

29 sent only as his forerunnner'? He who has the bride is the bridegroom. But the bridegroom's friend, standing beside him and hearing his words, rejoices with all his heart at the bridegroom's exulta-
30 tion. Such joy is now mine to overflowing. That man's star must
31 rise; mine must set. For he comes from on high, as one who is
above all. He who springs from the earth is earthly, and speaks
32 according to an earthly point of view; but he who comes from
heaven bears witness to that which he himself has seen and heard.
33 Unfortunately, no one is willing to accept his testimony. But every
one who has accepted it as true has received confirmation in his own
34 experience that God is the truth. For he who was sent by God
speaks only as God has directed him. To that end God gives him
the aid of His spirit-world, and indeed in an extraordinary measure.
35 The Father loves the Son, and for this reason has placed everything
36 in his hands; whoever, therefore, believes in the Son, obtains the
life hereafter, while he who will not listen to the Son will not see
life, but will undergo the penalty prescribed by divine law."

A short time later John was thrown into prison.

CHAPTER 4.

1 It came to the knowledge of Jesus that the Pharisees had heard
that he was gaining more disciples and baptizing more converts than
2 John — though Jesus himself did not baptize, but allowed his dis-
3 ciples to baptize in his stead. He thereupon left the district of
4 Judaea and returned to Galilee. His road took him through Samaria,
5 and on his journey he came to the Samaritan town of Sychar. This
town lies near the field that Jacob once gave to his son Joseph.
6 Jacob's Well was there also, and Jesus, tired from his journey, sat
7 down beside it to rest. It was about noon. Presently a Samaritan
woman came to draw water, and Jesus said to her "Please give me
8 a drink"; for his disciples had gone into the town to buy food.
9 "How is it," asked the Samaritan woman, "that you, a Jew, ask me,
a Samaritan, for a drink of water?" For the Jews were not on good
10 terms with the Samaritans. Jesus answered her, "If you understood
the favor that God wishes to show you, and if you knew who it is that
has asked you for a drink of water, you would have asked him first,
11 and he would have given you living water." — "Lord," she answered, "you have no bucket with which to draw, and the well is
12 deep. Where can you get the living water? Surely you are no
greater than our forefather Jacob, who gave us this well and who
13 himself drank from it, he and his children and his cattle." — "Who-
14 ever drinks of this water will be thirsty again," said Jesus; "but

whoever drinks of the water that I shall give him will never again
know thirst. Rather will the drink that I give him become a spring
15 in him which will flow until the life hereafter." — "Lord," said the
woman, "give me that water, so that I may never be thirsty again,
16 nor need to come here to draw water." — "Go and call your hus-
17 band," said Jesus, "and then come back." — "I have no husband,"
she answered.—"You are right in saying that you have no husband,"
18 Jesus replied to her, "for you have had five husbands, and the man
with whom you are now living is not your husband. In so far you
19 have spoken the truth." — "Lord," she exclaimed, "I see that you
20 are a prophet. Then answer me this: Our forefathers worshipped
God on this mountain that you see before you, but you Jews declare
that Jerusalem is the place where men should worship God." —
21 "Woman, believe me," said Jesus, "the hour is coming when you
will not pay the homage due to God either on this mountain or in
22 Jerusalem. You still worship something which you do not know;
we are worshipping what we do know, for the redemption will come
23 from the Jews. The time is coming, in fact it is already here, when
the true worshippers will worship the Father under the guidance of
a spirit and of the truth. For only such worshippers does the Father
24 care to have. God is a spirit, and those who worship Him must
therefore be under the guidance of a spirit of God and of the divine
25 truth when they come to do Him homage." To this the woman replied, "I know that the Messiah whom people call God's anointed
will come some day. When he comes, he will tell us everything."
26 Jesus said to her, "I am he — I, who am now speaking to you."

27 At that moment his disciples returned. They were astonished to
find him talking with the woman, but all shrank from asking him,
"What do you want of her?" or "Why are you speaking with her?"
28 Meanwhile the woman left her water-jar and hurried back to the
29 town, calling to all whom she met, "Come! There is a man out there
30 who told me everything that I ever did. Can he be the Messiah?"
And all of the people streamed out of the town and went to him.

31 In the meantime his disciples had begged him again and again,
32 "Master, eat something." But he answered, "I have food to eat of
33 which you know nothing." Then the disciples asked themselves,
34 "Could any one else have brought him food?" — "My food," Jesus
said, "is to do the will of Him Who sent me, and to finish His work.
35 Do you not have the saying, 'Four more months, and then the harvest'? But listen to what I tell you. When you look about you and
observe the fields, you can tell that they are now ripe for the har-
36 vest. The reaper is receiving his wages and gathering the crop for

the life hereafter, so that sower and reaper may rejoice together.
37 For in this case also the saying holds true, 'One man sows and an-
38 other reaps.' I have sent you to reap where you did not toil. Others
have done the work, and you need only gather in the fruit of their
labor."
39 Many of the Samaritans in that town believed in him because of
the woman's testimony that he had told her everything that she had
40 ever done. And so when the Samaritans came to him they urged him
41 to stay among them, and he remained there for two days. As a re-
42 sult of his preaching the number of converts greatly increased, and
they used to say to the woman, "Now we believe, not because of
what you told us, but because we ourselves have heard him and
know that he is truly the Redeemer of the world—the Messiah."
43 At the end of the two days Jesus left the Samaritans and went on
44 to Galilee. Although he himself had said that a messenger of God
45 is not honored in his own country, when he reached Galilee the
people there received him well; but this was only because they had
witnessed all the miracles that he had performed in Jerusalem dur-
46 ing the Easter festival; for they also had attended the festival. He
now went once more to Cana in Galilee, where he had turned water
into wine.
At that time there lived in Capernaum a royal official whose son
47 had fallen ill. When he heard that Jesus had returned to Galilee
from Judaea, he sought him out and begged him to come down and
48 heal his son, for he was at the point of death. Jesus said to the
official, "Unless you men see signs and wonders, you will not be-
49 lieve." But the official implored, "Lord, come before my child dies."
50 —"Go," said Jesus, "your son is well." The man trusted the words
51 of Jesus and went home. On his way there his servants met him with
the joyful news that his son was well. He asked them at what time
52 the boy had begun to mend. "The fever left him yesterday at about
53 one in the afternoon," they told him. Then the father remembered
that it had been at that very hour that Jesus said to him, "Your son
54 is well." He and his whole household became believers. This was
the second miracle that Jesus performed in Galilee, and occurred
after his return from Judaea.

CHAPTER 5.

1 Jesus again went up to Jerusalem to a later Jewish festival. Near
2 the sheep gate of the city there is a pool called "Bethesda" in the
3 Hebrew tongue, and around the pool there are five porticoes. In
these porticoes great numbers of sick people used to lie: blind men,
4 cripples, consumptives, and paralytics, waiting for the moment at

5 which the water was moved. Among them was a man who had been
6 sick for thirty-eight years. Jesus saw him lying there, and knowing
that he had been patiently waiting for a long time, asked, "Do you
7 wish to be well?" — "Lord," replied the sick man, "I have no one
to put me into the pool when the water is moved, and before I can
8 crawl into it by myself, some one else is there before me." — "Stand
9 up," said Jesus, "take your bedding and leave." At once the man
became well, picked up his bedding, and went away.

10 This happened on a Sabbath. The Jews therefore called out to the
man who had been cured, "This is the Sabbath, and you should not
11 be carrying your bedding." He answered them, "The man who cured
12 me told me to take up my bedding and go home." — "Who is the
man," they asked, "who told you to take up your bedding and go
13 home?" But he who had been cured did not know who it was, for
Jesus had gone away unobserved in the crowds that thronged about
the place.

14 Soon afterwards Jesus met the man in the temple and said to
him, "You have been healed, but you must sin no more, or some-
15 thing worse may befall you." The man hastily left and told the
Jews that it was Jesus who had made him well.

16 Whenever Jesus performed such a cure on the Sabbath, the Jewish
17 leaders would attack him. But he would say to them, "My Father
works day in and day out, and in the same way I do my work also."
18 Because of these words his Jewish enemies sought more intently than
ever to take his life, for they now held him guilty not only of pro-
faning the Sabbath, but also of making himself equal to God by
19 calling God his true father. In reply to this charge he said to them:
"I solemnly assure you that the Son of man can do nothing of himself, but the Father must first show him how he is to do it; and the
20 Son can do only that which the Father shows him. For the Father
loves the Son and shows him all the deeds that He Himself performs.
Indeed, He will show the Son things that he is to do which are far
greater than those he has heretofore accomplished, so that you will
21 be astonished. Thus, as the Father raises the spiritually dead out
of the depths and gives them back spiritual life, so will the Son of
man dispense this spiritual life to all on whom it is to be bestowed.
22 Moreover, the Father judges no one, but has left it to the Son to
23 judge, so that the honor due the Son shall be given to him by all,
just as they are to give the Father the honor due to Him. He who
withholds honor from the Son will withhold it also from the Father,
24 by Whom the Son was sent. I assure you that he who listens to my
word and believes in Him Who sent me will receive life in the be-

yond. He need no more appear before the judgment-seat, but by his
faith has passed from the realm of the spiritually dead into the
25 realm of spiritual life. Believe me, the hour will come and has in
fact already begun, when the spiritually dead will hear the voice of
the Son of man, and when those who listen to it will receive spiritual
26 life. For as the Father Who has lived from eternity carries spiritual
life within Him, so likewise He has conferred upon the Son the gift
27 of bearing spiritual life within him. He has also given him authority
to sit in judgment over mankind, because he has become a son of
28 man. Do not wonder, then, that the hour is coming when all who
are in the caverns of darkness will hear his voice and come forth.
29 For those who have done good, this will be a restoration to spiritual
life, but for those who have done evil, a summons before the judge.
30 I have not the power to do anything of myself; I make my decisions
according to the directions that are transmitted to me through clairaudience, and therefore my decisions always correspond to the will
of God; for it is not my will, but the will of Him Who sent me, that
I carry out.

31 "Were I to testify on my own behalf, my testimony would not be
32 valid. There is another who testifies for me, and you know that his
33 testimony on my behalf is true. You yourselves sent delegates to
John, and at that time he gave truthful evidence concerning me.
34 Not that I rely on the testimony of men, but I mention this merely
for the sake of guiding you in all safety along the road to your
35 salvation, even though I might justly appeal to John's evidence. For
he was indeed the light of truth, which burned brightly, and for a
short time you also were willing to rejoice in that light of truth.
36 But I have weightier evidence than that of John, namely the deeds
which my Father has given me the power to perform. These very
deeds that I am accomplishing are the best proof that the Father has
37 sent me. Moreover, the Father Who sent me has testified for me in
His own person. True, at that time you did not hear His voice nor
38 see the form out of which He spoke; neither will you trouble yourselves to recall His words, for you reject all faith in him whom the
39 Father has sent. Instead, you search the Scriptures and think that
therein you have the life hereafter; and yet it is the very Scriptures
40 that testify for me. But you are unwilling, once for all, to come to
41 me and receive spiritual life out of my hand. I seek no honor from
42 you men, but I know that in your hearts there is no love of God.
43 I have come to you in my Father's name, but you will have nothing
to do with me. If some one else had come to you without a higher
commission, but on his own initiative, him you would have received.

44 How can you attain to faith if you accept honor from your equals,
but feel no desire for the honor that comes from the only God?
45 Do not think that I am going to accuse you to the Father, for you
already have an accuser in Moses—him on whom you have built
46 all your hope. If you had believed Moses, you would also believe
47 me; for I am he of whom Moses wrote. But if you put no faith in
his writings, how are you to believe my words?"

CHAPTER 6.

1 After this Jesus crossed to the other side of the Sea of Galilee,
2 not far from Tiberias. A great throng of people followed close behind him, for they had again and again witnessed his marvellous
cures of the sick.

3 Jesus climbed a hill, and sat down with his disciples. The Pass-
4 over, the principal festival of the Jews, was at hand, and as Jesus
5 looked about him and saw the vast crowds, he said to Philip, "Where
6 shall we find food, so that these people may eat?" He said this only
to test Philip, for he himself knew exactly what he intended to do.
7 Philip answered, "Forty dollars' worth of bread will not be enough,
8 even if every one gets only a small piece." Then one of the disciples,
9 Andrew, the brother of Simon Peter, remarked, "There is a boy here
who has five loaves of barley-bread and two fish. But what is that
10 among so many?" Jesus now said to them, "Make the people sit
down." There was a thick growth of grass in the place, and the
people sat down, the men among them alone numbering some five
11 thousand. Then Jesus took the loaves, gave thanks, and had the
bread distributed to the seated multitudes. Every one also had as
12 much of the fish as he wanted. When all had eaten, Jesus said to
his disciples, "Gather the leavings so that nothing may be wasted."
13 Everything was gathered up, and the leavings from the five barley-
14 loaves filled twelve baskets. When the people saw the miracle that
he had performed, they exclaimed, "This really is the messenger of
15 God who is to come into the world." Aware that they meant to
come and take him by force and proclaim him king, Jesus withdrew
to the hillside unaccompanied, and there devoted himself to prayer.

16 Toward evening his disciples went down to the lake and got into
17 their boat in order to cross over to Capernaum. Darkness suddenly
18 covered them, and Jesus had not yet come back. A violent storm
19 arose, churning the lake to its very depths. After they had rowed
for about an hour, the disciples saw Jesus walking over the lake
20 toward their boat. They were seized with a great fear, but he called
21 to them, "Do not be frightened, it is I." They offered to take him

into the boat, but at that moment they had already reached the shore,
and at the very spot for which they were bound.
22 Next morning the people were still on the farther shore. On the
evening before they had seen that there was no other boat near except the one that the disciples had used, and that Jesus himself
had not gone into the boat with them but that his disciples had gone
23 away without him. Boats coming from Tiberias now landed near
the place at which the bread had been distributed on the day before,
24 and the people, not seeing either Jesus or his disciples in the neighborhood, made use of these boats to cross to Capernaum in search
25 of him. When they found him there after crossing the lake, they
26 asked, "Master, when did you come here?" Jesus answered, "You
are looking for me not because you saw the miracle, but because
27 you had your fill of bread to eat. Do not strive for the food that
perishes, but for the food that will endure until the life hereafter.
Such is the food that the Son of man gives you. For God the Father
28 has chosen him for this task and set His seal on him." — "What are
the works that we must do to please God, then?" they asked him.
29 "The work that is pleasing in the sight of God," he answered, "con-
30 sists in believing in him whom God has sent." Again they asked,
"What sign can you work before our eyes in order that we may be-
31 lieve in you? How great is your power? Our forefathers had
manna in the wilderness, as the Scriptures tell: 'He gave them
32 bread out of heaven to eat.' " — "I tell you," answered Jesus, "that
it was not Moses who gave you the true bread of heaven, but that
33 it is my Father who gives you the true bread of heaven. The true
'bread of God' is he who comes from heaven and dispenses spiritual
34 life to the world." — "Lord," they said, "give us this bread for all
35 time." To this Jesus answered, "I am the bread of life. He who
enters into communion with me will never know hunger, and he
who builds his faith upon me will never thirst. You ask me for a
36 sign, but I have told you that you have seen such signs, and yet you
37 will not believe. All that the Father gives to me will enter into communion with me, and I will not reject any one who seeks such com-
38 munion with me. I have not come from heaven to do my own will,
39 but to do the will of the Father by Whom I am sent. The will of the
Father Who sent me is this: Of all that He has given to me I must
40 lose nothing, but restore everything to Him on the last day. Therefore it is also the will of my Father that every one who comes to
know the Son and believes in him shall have the life hereafter, and
that on his last day I shall lead him on high."
41 The Jewish leaders now began to express their displeasure at

42 Jesus for saying, "I am the bread that came from heaven."—"Is
this not Jesus the son of Joseph," they asked, "and do we not know
who his father and mother are? How can he say then that he came
43 from heaven?"—"Do not murmur to one another," Jesus said to
44 them. "No one can enter into communion with me unless he is inspired to do so by my Father, Who has sent me so that on his last
45 day I may lead him on high. For it is set down in the writings of
the prophets: 'And they will all be taught by God.' Every one,
therefore, who listens to the inner voice that comes from the Father
46 and who gives heed to it, enters into communion with me. Not that
any human being has seen the Father; only those who have been
47 near to God have seen Him. But I say to you with all certainty that
48 only he who believes in me will have the life hereafter. I am the
49 bread of life. Your fathers ate manna in the wilderness, and yet they
50 died the spiritual death of separation from God. He who stands
here is the bread from heaven of which all may eat and so escape
51 spiritual death. I am the living bread that has come down from
heaven. He who eats of this bread will have spiritual life in the
hereafter. And the bread that I give for the spiritual life of the
world is my flesh."

52 His last words brought on an angry debate among the Jews, and
53 they exclaimed, "How can this man give us his flesh to eat?" Jesus
answered them, "Once more I tell you, unless you eat of the flesh
of the Son of man and drink of his blood, you will have no spiritual
54 life within you. But whoever eats of my flesh and drinks of my
blood will have spiritual life in the hereafter, and on his last day
55 I shall lead him on high. For my flesh is really food and my blood
56 is really drink. He who eats of my flesh and drinks of my blood
will remain in communion with me and I with him, as the Father is
one with me and as I am one with the Father. Trust me when I say
to you that unless you receive the body of the Son of man as the
bread of life, you do not have spiritual life, which lies only in com-
57 munion with him. Just as I was sent by the Father Who is the source
of spiritual life, and as I owe my life to my Father alone, so will
58 he who receives me within himself owe his spiritual life to me. This
is the bread that has come down from heaven. It is not like the
bread that your forefathers ate and yet died the spiritual death of
separation from God. Whoever eats of this bread, will have spiritual
life for ever."

59 These words were spoken by Jesus as he taught one Sabbath in
60 the synagogue at Capernaum. Even many of his disciples who heard
them said disapprovingly, "This is a hard speech. Who can listen

61 to it?" Knowing that his disciples had found fault with his words,
62 Jesus said to them, "Does my doctrine offend you? What will you
say, then, when you see the Son of man ascend to the place where
63 he was before? It is the spirit that gives life; the earthly flesh is as
nothing. The words that I spoke to you concern the spirit and
64 spiritual life. But there are some among you who have no faith."
For Jesus knew from the very beginning who those were that would
65 remain unbelievers, and also who was to be his betrayer. He added,
"For this reason I said to you that no one may enter into communion
with me unless this gift of mercy has been bestowed upon him by
my Father."

66 From that hour on, many of his disciples withdrew from him and
67 no longer accompanied him on his journeys. And so Jesus said to
68 the Twelve, "Do you also wish to leave me?"—"Master," said
Simon Peter, "to whom should we go? For you alone possess the
69 knowledge that will lead us to the life hereafter. We therefore have
70 the belief and conviction that you are the Holy One of God." Jesus
answered, "It is not I myself who have chosen you twelve; and yet
71 one of you is a devil." He meant Judas, the son of Simon of Cariot,
for this man was later to betray him. He was one of the Twelve.

CHAPTER 7.

1 After this Jesus went from place to place in Galilee. He would
not go into Judaea, because his Jewish enemies there were seeking
2 his life. As the Jewish Festival of the Tabernacles drew near, his
3 brothers said to him, "Go from here to Judaea, so that your fol-
4 lowers there may see the things that you are doing. For no one
works secretly, but every one tries to gain public recognition. If you
5 are going to do these things, do them before all the world." At that
6 time not even his own brothers believed in him. "My time has not
yet come," answered Jesus, "although for you one time is as good as
7 another. The world has no cause to hate you; but it hates me be-
8 cause I proclaim that its deeds are evil. Go up to the festival if you
like. I myself shall not go now, because my time has not yet come."
9 Sending them off with these words, he remained behind in Galilee;
10 but after his brothers had left for the festival he also set forth. He
did not, however, go in any one else's company, but made the jour-
11 ney alone. The Jewish leaders were looking for him at the festival
12 and inquiring, "Where is he?" Among the masses of the people
there was also much talk concerning him, some saying, "He is a
13 good man," while others said, "No, he is an agitator." But no one
dared to speak openly of him for fear of his enemies among the Jews.

14 The week of festivities was nearly half over when Jesus went into
15 the temple and gave discourses there. His Jewish opponents asked
in amazement, "Where did this man get his knowledge of the Scrip-
16 tures? He has never studied." Jesus answered them, "That which
17 I teach does not come from me, but from Him Who sent me. Any
one who strives to do His will learns of himself whether my doctrine
18 is from God or whether I am teaching my own opinions. Whoever
proclaims his own opinions seeks his own glory, but whoever seeks
the glory of him who sent him will faithfully deliver the sender's
message; therefore nothing can be found in him that is not genuine.
19 Did not Moses bring you a message in the form of the Law? And
yet not one of you observes it faithfully. What reason have you for
20 wanting to kill me?" — "You are mad!" they shouted at him. "Who
21 wants to kill you?" — "Yes," insisted Jesus, "because of one single
thing I did that has driven you quite beside yourselves, you want
22 to kill me. And yet I did nothing but what Moses did when he prescribed circumcision and decreed that you are to circumcise even on
the Sabbath. And I might mention, by the way, that circumcision
did not originate with Moses, but was handed down from your fore-
23 fathers. Now if a male child must be circumcised on the Sabbath
so as not to break the Law of Moses, why do you vent your spite
24 against me for healing men, body and soul, on the Sabbath? Do
not be so superficial in your judgment, but judge a case by its
25 merits." Then some of the people of Jerusalem said, "Is this not
26 the man whom they are trying to kill? Yet here he is, speaking in
the open, and no one dares to say a word against him. Have the
27 leaders of the people found out that he is indeed the Messiah? To
be sure, we know where this man comes from; but when the Messiah
28 appears, no one will know where he comes from." Then Jesus, who
was preaching in the temple, called out to them, "True, you know
me and know where I come from; you know that I did not come of
my own accord; you also know that it was the true God Who sent
29 me. You do not know Him, of course; but I know Him, because it
30 was from Him that I came, and it was He Who sent me." They now
made repeated attempts to arrest him, but no one dared lay hands
on him; for his hour had not yet come.

31 Among the common people many came to believe in him, for
they reasoned to themselves, "Can the Messiah, when he does come,
32 perform more miracles than this man has performed?" The Pharisees heard how the people were thus expressing their opinion of
him among themselves, and they and the chief priests therefore sent
33 out servants to seize him. Jesus said, "I shall be with you for only

34 a little while longer; then I shall go to Him Who sent me. You
will seek me but you will not find me, for you cannot follow me to
35 the place where I shall then be." Upon this the Jews asked one another, "Where is he going that we shall not be able to find him?
Is he perhaps going to the Jews who live scattered among the Greeks,
36 and preach to the Greeks? Or what else does he mean by saying,
'You will seek me but you will not find me,' and 'You cannot follow
me to the place where I shall be'?"

37 On the last day of the festival, the so-called "great day," Jesus
stood before them and repeatedly called out in a loud voice, "If any
38 one is thirsty, let him come and drink, with faith in me. Then, according to the words of the Scriptures, fountains of living water will
39 gush from within him." He was alluding to the spirits of God which
those who believed in him were to receive; for so far no spirit of
God had come to them, because Jesus had not yet entered into his
40 glory. The people who heard these sayings of Jesus expressed many
41 different opinions, some saying, "This is surely the Prophet," and
others, "He is the Messiah." Still others said, "It is certainly not
42 from Galilee that the Messiah will come. Do not the Scriptures say
that the Messiah shall be a descendant of David and come from
43 Bethlehem, the city of David?" Thus the people differed in their
44 opinions of him. Certain ones among them were eager to seize him,
but none dared lay hands on him.

45 So it was that the servants went back to the chief priests and the
Pharisees without him. "Why have you not brought him?" they
46 asked the servants. — "No man ever spoke as he did," they replied.
47 —"Have you too allowed yourselves to be duped?" the Pharisees
48 asked them. "Is there a single one among the leading people or
among the Pharisees who has come to believe in him? Not a man;
49 it is only the common herd, which understands nothing of the Law.
Curse it!"

50 Nicodemus, one of the prominent people, now took them to task.
51 It was the same Nicodemus who at one time had visited Jesus. "Does
our Law allow this man to be condemned," he asked, "before he has
52 been tried and found guilty?" — "Are you also from Galilee?"
they replied sneeringly. "Look through the Scriptures and you will
53 find that Galilee has never produced a prophet." Then they separated and went to their homes.

CHAPTER 8.

1 Jesus went to the Mount of Olives, and at daybreak returned to
2 the temple. The people came to him from all sides, and he sat down

3 among them and taught them. The scribes and Pharisees now
brought him a woman who had been caught in adultery, and placed
4 her face to face with him. Then the priests, thinking to set a trap
for him and thus furnish grounds for a charge against him, said,
5 "Master, this woman was caught in the very act of adultery. Now the
Law of Moses decrees that such women should be stoned. What
6 have you to say?" Jesus stooped down and traced letters with his
7 finger in the dust on the floor. When they insistently demanded an
answer, he rose and said to them, "Let him among you who has
8 never committed that sin throw the first stone." Then, stooping
9 down again, he continued tracing letters on the floor. When they
heard these words the Jewish leaders stole away one by one, from
the oldest to the youngest, leaving Jesus alone with the woman who
10 was standing before him. Then Jesus rose and asked the woman,
"Where have they all gone? Was none of them willing to begin
11 the stoning?" She answered, "Not one, lord." — "Nor do I condemn
you to death," said Jesus. "Go back to your home, and from now
on give up your sinful life."

12 On another occasion he said to his hearers, "I am the light of the
world. He who follows in my footsteps will not go astray in the
13 darkness, but will have the light of spiritual life." To this the
Pharisees objected, "You are testifying on your own behalf, and
14 therefore your testimony is worthless." Jesus answered them, "Even
though I do testify on my own behalf, my testimony is true; for I
know where I came from and where I am going. But you do not
15 know where I came from or where I am going. You judge by outward appearances only; I judge no one according to such a stand-
16 ard. When I do judge, my judgment is true, for in such cases I do
not depend upon my judgment alone but also upon the judgment
17 of Him Who sent me. Your own Law provides that the testimony of
18 two men shall be accepted as true. I am one witness on my own
behalf, and the other who testifies for me is the Father Who has
19 sent me." — "Where is your father?" they asked. "You know my
Father as little as you know me," he answered. "If you knew me you
20 would also know my Father." This dispute with them took place
while he was sitting near the alms-box, addressing the people; but
no one dared lay hands on him, because his hour had not yet come.

21 In another discourse he said, "I shall go away from you, and
you will search for me, but in your sins of apostasy you will die the
death of separation from God. You cannot go where I am going."
22 The Jews then asked each other, "Does he mean to kill himself, that
23 he says, 'You cannot go where I am going'?" He answered, "You

are from below, and I am from above. You belong to the realm of
24 this world; I do not. That is why I said to you that in your sins of
apostasy you would die the death of separation from God. For if
you do not believe that I am what I profess to be, you will suffer
25 separation from God through your sins of apostasy." They asked
him, "Who are you, then?"—"Have I not told you from the first
26 who I am?" answered Jesus. "But as for who you are, that is a point
on which I might say much and pass many a true judgment. For He
Who has sent me speaks only the truth, and I speak to the world
only that which I have heard from Him."
27 They did not understand how he could presume to call God his
28 father to their faces. He therefore added, "When you have prepared
for the Son of man the fate that will raise him to heaven, then you
will know that I really am what I have professed to be, and that I
do nothing of myself, but only speak as my Father has taught me.
29 And He Who sent me remains in communication with me. He has
had no reason to abandon me, for I always do what pleases Him."
30 As a result of this discourse, many came to believe in him; but
31 to those of the Jews who had been converted he addressed the warning, "You belong to my true disciples only if you hold fast to my
32 teaching; only then will you know the whole truth, and the truth
33 will make you free." At this, his opponents called out, "We are
descendants of Abraham and have never been subject to any one.
34 How can you say that we shall be made free?" Jesus replied, "Every
35 one who commits the sin of apostasy is a slave. The slave does not
remain in his master's household for all time, but the son does.
36 Now if the Son releases you from servitude for ever, you will be
37 free. I know that you are descended from Abraham. In spite of this
you seek to kill me, because your hearts are not receptive to my
38 teaching. I speak only that which I have heard from my Father.
In the same way you too should do as you were taught by your
39 father." They replied, "Abraham is our father."—"If you were
Abraham's children," returned Jesus, "you would do as Abraham
40 did. But you are the ones who want to kill me—a man who has
told you only the pure truth—truth that I received from God. This
41 was not Abraham's way. You have an altogether different father,
and it is his work that you do."—"We are not illegitimate children," they retorted; "we have only one father, and that is God."—
42 "If God were your father," Jesus answered, "you would love me;
for I came to you from God and am here on His errand. I did not
43 come of my own accord; it is He Who sent me. Why is it that you
do not understand what I am trying to say and cannot even bear to

44 listen to my teaching? It is because you are the offspring of your
true father, the devil, and therefore mean to carry out his wishes.
He was a murderer from the beginning. He has no foundation in the
truth, for his whole being is untruth. When he lies, he is merely
expressing his own nature. For he is the lie incarnate and the father
45 of all liars. Now because I, on the contrary, teach the truth, you
47 will not believe me. For only he who comes from God listens to the
words of God. That is the reason why you do not listen to them;
48 for you do not belong to God." Then his enemies among the Jews
retorted, "Were we not right in saying that you are a Samaritan and
49 possessed by an evil spirit?"—"I am possessed by no evil spirit,"
answered Jesus; "but I honor my Father, and you dishonor me.
50 True, I am not seeking my own glory; but there is One Who will
51 intercede for my glory and judge those who dishonor me. And I
can assure you that whoever follows my teaching will never see
52 death."—"Now we know beyond doubt," exclaimed his Jewish
enemies, "that you are possessed by an evil spirit. For Abraham
died, and the prophets died, and yet you dare to tell us, 'Whoever
53 follows my teachings will never taste death.' Are you greater, perhaps, than Abraham, who was obliged to die? And the prophets
54 were obliged to die, too. How great do you profess to be?" Jesus
answered, "If I were to speak in my own praise, my boasting would
be worthless. He Who will determine my true greatness is my
55 Father, Who you say is your God. You do not know Him at all,
but I know Him. And if I were to say that I did not know Him, I
should be a liar, as you are. But I do know Him, and I hold to His
56 word. Your father Abraham rejoiced that he could foresee the day
of my coming; he has now seen that day and been filled with glad-
57 ness."—"How can that be?" the Jews exclaimed. "You are not yet
fifty years old, and do you mean to tell us that Abraham has seen
58 you?"—"I am speaking the truth," Jesus answered; "I am older
59 than Abraham." At this they gathered up stones with which to kill
him, but Jesus was made invisible before their eyes and left the
temple.

CHAPTER 9.

1 As he passed along, he saw a man sitting there who had been
2 blind from birth. His disciples asked Jesus, "Master, for whose sins
3 was that man born blind? His own, or his parents'?" Jesus answered, "He is blind because of neither his own sins nor his parents',
but in order that the miraculous works of God might be manifested
4 in him. While the daylight lasts, I must do the work of Him Who

5 sent me, for the night is coming when no one can work. As long as
6 I am in the world, I am the light of the world." After these words
he spat upon the ground, made a clay with the saliva, and rubbed
7 it on the man's eyes, saying, "Go and wash yourself in the pool of
Siloam,"—a name meaning "gusher." The man went and washed
himself, and came back seeing.

8 His neighbors and all who had formerly known him as a blind
beggar, asked in astonishment, "Is not this the man who used to sit
9 and beg?" Some said, "Yes, that is he," and others, "No, it is some
one who looks like him." Finally the man himself spoke up and
10 said, "Yes, I am the one you mean."—"How did you receive your
11 sight?" they asked. He told them, "The man called Jesus made
some clay, rubbed it on my eyes, and told me to go to the pool of
Siloam and wash. I went there, washed, and came back seeing."—
12 "Where is this man?" they asked.—"I do not know," he answered.

13 Then they took the man who had been blind to the Pharisees.
14 It happened that the day on which Jesus had made the clay and
15 restored sight to the blind man was a Sabbath. The first question
that the Pharisees asked the man was also how he had been made to
see. He told them, "He rubbed some clay on my eyes, then I
16 washed, and now I can see." Then some of the Pharisees said, "That
man cannot come from God. He does not keep the Sabbath." But
others objected, "How could a sinful man work such mircales?"
17 Thus dissension arose among them. They now asked the man who
had been blind, "What do you think of him for being able to restore your sight?"—"He is a messenger of God," was his brief
18 answer. Now the Jewish leaders would not believe that he had been
blind and had been made to see. At last they sent for his parents,
19 and asked them, "Is this your son, who you declare was born blind?
20 How is it that now he can see?"—"That he is our son we know,"
answered the parents; "and we also know that he was born blind.
21 But how he came to receive his sight we do not know, nor do we
know who opened his eyes. Ask him. He is old enough to tell you
22 about it." The parents spoke as they did out of fear of the Jewish
leaders, who had already agreed to put a ban on all who acknowl-
23 edged Jesus as the Messiah. That was why the parents said, "He is
old enough. Ask him."

24 And so the Pharisees again sent for the man who had been blind,
and said to him, "Give God the praise. We know that that man is a
25 sinner."—"Whether or not he is a sinner I do not know," he replied; "but I do know that I came into the world blind and that now
26 I can see." Once more they asked him, "What did he do to you?

27 How did he open your eyes?" — "I have already told you that," he
answered, "and you would not listen. Why do you want to hear it
28 again? Are you too thinking of becoming his disciples?" At this
they hurled abuse at him. "Be his disciple yourself!" they exclaimed.
29 "We are disciples of Moses. We know that God spoke to Moses, and
that He does not listen to sinners. But as for this fellow, we do not
30 know where he comes from." — "It is indeed very strange," replied
the man, "that you should not know where this man is from in spite
31 of the fact that he has opened my eyes. We all know that God does
not listen to a sinner, but only to a man who fears Him and does
32 His will. Now since the world began, no one has ever been known
33 to give sight to a person who was born blind. Therefore unless this
man came from God, he could not have done such a thing." —
34 "What!" they shouted at him, "are you trying to teach us, you mis-
begotten offspring of sin?" And they drove him out of their congregation.

35 Jesus learned that he had been put under the ban, and when he
36 met him he asked, "Do you believe in the Son of God?" — "Lord,"
answered the man, "who is he? I should be very glad to believe in
37 him." Jesus said to him, "You have seen him, and it is he who is
38 speaking to you now." — "Lord," answered the man, "I do believe,"
39 and he fell at his feet. "I have come into the world," continued
Jesus, "to pronounce a judgment under which those who have been
considered blind shall be reckoned among those who see, and those
who have thought of themselves as seeing shall be numbered among
40 the blind." Some of the Pharisees who were standing near by and
listening to his words asked him, "Shall we perhaps be reckoned
41 among the blind?" Jesus answered them, "If you were really blind,
your blindness would not be held against you as a sin. But you
declare that you can see, and so your sins remain."

CHAPTER 10.

1 "You may be sure that any one who does not enter the sheepfold
by the door but climbs into it by some other way, is to be considered
2 a thief and a robber. But the one who goes in through the door is
3 the shepherd of the sheep. The keeper opens the gate to him, and
the sheep obey his voic. He calls his sheep by name and leads them
4 out. When he has led out all that belong to him he walks before
them, and the sheep follow at his heels; for they know his voice.
5 But they will not follow a stranger one step; on the contrary they
will flee from him, because they do not know the voice of strangers."

6 By this parable Jesus sought to make his teachings clear, but his

7 hearers did not understand what he meant. He therefore continued,
8 "I am the door that leads to the sheep. Those who came before me
9 were thieves and robbers, and the sheep would not heed them. I am
the door. Whoever enters the sheepfold through me will be saved.
10 He will go in and out, and find pasture. The thief comes only to
steal, to kill, and to destroy. I have come in order that they may
11 have food, and have it in abundance. I am the good shepherd. A
12 good shepherd risks his life for his sheep. The hired man cannot
be considered a shepherd at all, for the sheep are not his property.
If he sees a wolf coming he abandons the sheep and runs away, and
13 the wolf falls upon them and scatters them. For he is only a hired
14 man, and the sheep mean nothing to him. But I am the good shep-
15 herd. I know my sheep and they know me, just as the Father knows
16 me and I know the Father. I give my life for the sheep. And I have
still other sheep that do not belong to my present fold. I must
gather them also, and they will listen to my voice, and then there
17 will be one flock and one shepherd. The Father loves me dearly,
18 because I lay down my life in order to take it up again. No one can
take it from me by force, but I give it up of my own free will. I
have the power to lay it down, and I have the power to take it up
again. This power I have received from my Father."

19 These words again brought on violent dissension among the Jews.
20 Many of them said, "He is possessed by an evil spirit and has gone
21 quite out of his mind. Why do you listen to him at all?" Others,
however, protested, "These are not the words of one who is possessed. Besides, can a man who is possessed restore sight to the
blind?"

22 In Jerusalem the Festival of the Dedication of the Temple was
23 being celebrated. It was winter. As Jesus walked back and forth in
24 what was known as the Hall of Solomon, his Jewish enemies crowded
about him and asked, "How much longer are you going to leave us
25 in doubt? Tell us plainly, are you the Messiah?"—"I told you so
long ago," answered Jesus, "but you will not believe me. And yet
the deeds that I do at my Father's bidding are the best evidence that
26 I am he. But, as I have repeatedly told you, because you are not my
27 sheep you do not believe me; for my sheep listen to my voice, I
28 know them well, and they follow me closely. I give them the life
hereafter.They shall no longer be in danger of perishing, for no one
29 will snatch them from my hand. My Father Who gave them to me
is greater than all. There is no one strong enough to take anything
30 from His hand; and I and my Father are closely united."

31 Again his Jewish enemies took up stones, intending to kill him,

32 but Jesus faced them and said, "I have performed many marvellous
deeds to demonstrate to you the power that I have received from the
Father. For which of these deeds do you mean to stone me?"—
33 "It is not because of any good deed that we mean to stone you,"
answered his adversaries, "but because of blasphemy; for you, a
34 mere man, call yourself a god." Jesus answered, "Is it not written
35 in the Law: 'I said, "You are gods"?' If the Scriptures call those
'gods' to whom a message from God was sent — and surely the Scrip-
36 tures are true — how can you call it blasphemy if I, whom the
Father consecrated and sent upon earth as His envoy, say that I
37 am a son of God? Either I do not perform the work of my Father,
38 in which event you need not believe in me; or I do perform it, in
which case you must at least believe in the deeds, even though you
will not believe my words. For it is by my deeds that you should
know that the Father is in communion with me and that I am in
39 communion with the Father." Then they attempted to seize him,
but he escaped their hands.

40 He now went back into the country east of the Jordan to the
place where John had administered his first baptism, and there he
41 remained. Many came to him, and the people often spoke of the
fact that John had not performed a single miracle, but that every-
42 thing he had said of this man was true. Thus many of the people
of that neighborhood also came to believe in him.

CHAPTER 11.

1 A man named Lazarus fell ill. He lived in Bethany, the home of
2 his sisters Mary and Martha. Mary was the woman who had anointed
the lord with ointment and dried his feet with her hair, and it was
3 her brother Lazarus who, as we have said, was sick. The sisters
therefore sent messengers to Jesus to tell him, "Lazarus, of whom
4 you are so fond, is very sick." On hearing this, Jesus said, "This
sickness will not end in his death but will serve to glorify God, and
thereby the Son of God will also be glorified."

5 Jesus loved Martha and her sister and Lazarus dearly; neverthe-
6 less, he remained two days more in the place at which he was stay-
7 ing. Only then did he say to his disciples, "Come, let us go back
8 into Judaea." — "Master," his disciples protested, "only a short
time ago the Jews wanted to stone you; do you mean to go back
9 there again?" Jesus answered them, "Are there not twelve hours in
the day? A man who walks in the daytime does not stumble, because
10 he can see well by the light of this earth; but a man who walks at
11 night may easily stumble, because then there is no light." After

these words he added, "Our friend Lazarus has fallen asleep, but I
12 am going to awaken him from his sleep." — "Lord," they answered,
13 "if he has fallen asleep, he is on the way to recovery." Jesus had
meant the sleep of death, but his disciples thought that he was
14 speaking of natural sleep. He therefore told them plainly, "Lazarus
15 is dead; and for your sakes I am glad that I was not there, so that
you may believe. But now let us go to him."

16 Then Thomas, who was known as "the Twin," said to his fellow-
17 apostles, "Yes, let us all go and die with him." When Jesus reached
Bethany he heard that Lazarus had already lain in his grave four
18 days. As Bethany was only an hour's walk from Jerusalem, many
19 people from that city had gone out to the house of Martha and
20 Mary to condole with them on the death of their brother. Now when
Martha heard that Jesus was coming, she went out to meet him,
21 while Mary sat at home. "Lord," said Martha to Jesus, "if you had
22 been here, my brother would not have died; but even so, I know that
23 God will grant you anything that you ask of Him." Jesus answered,
24 "Your brother will rise again." To this Martha replied, "I know
25 that he will rise at the resurrection on the last day." Jesus said to
her, "I am the resurrection and the life. He who believes in me will
26 live even though he has died; and whoever possesses life and
holds to his faith will never die again. Do you believe that?" —
27 "I do, lord," she answered, "for I have learned to believe that you
are the Messiah, the Son of God, who was to come into the world."
28 She then hurried away, and calling her sister Mary, whispered to
29 her, "The master is here and has sent for you." When Mary heard
30 these words, she hastily rose and went to him, for Jesus had not
gone into the town but was waiting at the place where Martha had
31 met him. On seeing her get up and go out so quickly, the Jews who
had gone to her house to console her followed at her heels, for they
32 thought that she was going to the grave to mourn. As soon as Mary
came to the place where Jesus was waiting for her and saw him, she
fell at his feet and exclaimed, weeping, "Lord, if you had been here,
33 my brother need not have died." When Jesus saw that she was
weeping, and that the Jews who were with her were likewise in
tears, he was so affected by the power of a spirit of God that he
34 trembled. "Where have you laid him?" he asked. They answered,
35 "Come and see." Then Jesus wept. At this the Jews said to one an-
36 other, "See how he loved him!" But some of them said, "Could not
37 this man who restored sight to the blind have prevented Lazarus
from dying?"

38 As Jesus was walking toward the grave he was again inwardly

shaken. The grave had been hewn out of rock, and its entrance was
39 closed by a large stone which Jesus directed to be moved aside.
Martha, the sister of the dead man, said to him, "Lord, he probably
smells of decay, for he has already been dead for four days."—
40 "Have I not told you," Jesus answered, "that you shall see the
glorious power of God, if you have confident faith?"

41 In the meantime the stone had been moved aside, and Jesus,
raising his eyes to heaven, prayed, "Father, I thank Thee that Thou
42 hast heard me. I knew that Thou hearest me always, but I have
spoken these words of thanksgiving because of the people about me,
43 that they may believe that Thou hast sent me." Then he called in a
44 loud voice, "Lazarus, come out!" At once the dead man came from
the tomb, bound hand and foot in cloth wrappings and his face
covered with a handkerchief. "Take off those wrappings," said
Jesus, "and let him move about."

45 Many of the Jews who had come to see Mary and had witnessed
46 this event, now believed in Jesus. Others, however, immediately
47 went to the Pharisees and told them what Jesus had done. The chief
priests and the Pharisees called together the High Council and said,
"What shall we do to prevent this man from performing such great
48 miracles? If we allow this to go any further, every one will believe
in him, and the Romans will come and take both land and people
49 away from us." One of them, Caiaphas, who was the high priest for
50 that year, said, "You do not understand this matter at all, nor do
you realize that it is much better for you to have one man die for the
51 people than for the whole nation to perish." He did not say this
out of his own consciousness, but as the high priest for that year
he unknowingly prophesied that Jesus would die for the people;
52 and not merely for the people, but also that the widely scattered
children of God might be gathered again into one great community.
53 From this day on they plotted to bring about his death. Accordingly
54 Jesus no longer showed himself in public among the Jews, but withdrew into the district of Samphuris near the desert, to a town called
Ephraim. There he stayed for some time with his disciples.

55 With the approach of the Jewish Passover many people went up
to Jerusalem from the country before the festival began, to perform
56 the rites of purification. They also inquired about Jesus, and among
the crowds of people assembling near the temple he became the
topic of conversation. One would ask another, "What do you think?
57 Will he come to the festival?" For the chief priests and the Pharisees had given orders that any one who knew where Jesus was to be
found should make it known, so that he might be arrested.

CHAPTER 12.

1 Six days before the Passover Jesus reached Bethany, where
Lazarus, who had died but whom he had raised again from the
2 dead, was living. In honor of Jesus they gave a dinner, at which
Martha waited on the guests and Lazarus was the only one who
3 shared the same table with him. Then Mary took a pound of pure
and very costly ointment of spikenard, anointed the feet of Jesus
with it, and dried them with her hair. The whole house was filled
4 with the fragrance of the ointment. At this, one of the disciples,
5 Judas of Cariot, who was later to betray him, said, "Why was not
this ointment sold for sixty dollars, and the money given to the
6 poor?" He said this, not because he cared for the poor, but because
he was a thief; for he had charge of their money and used to pilfer
7 a part of what they took in. "Let her alone," said Jesus; "let her
anoint me for the day of my burial."

9 The news that he was there quickly spread, and great numbers of
Jews hurried to the place, not only because of Jesus but in order
that they might see Lazarus, whom Jesus had raised from the dead.
10 The chief priests therefore resolved to put Lazarus to death also,
11 for it was on his account that many of the Jews went to the place
and came to believe in Jesus.

12 On the following day the crowds that had come to the Passover
13 heard that Jesus was on his way to Jerusalem. They took palm-
branches and went out to meet him, shouting again and again,
"Hosanna! Blessed be he who comes in the name of the Lord—
14 the king of Israel!" Jesus had found an ass's colt and had mounted
15 it, as was foretold in the Scriptures: "Fear not, daughter of Zion.
16 Behold, your king is coming, mounted on an ass's colt." Those who
were with him did not think of these words at first. Only after Jesus
had entered into his glory did they understand that this passage
17 referred to him and had also been fulfilled in him. The great crowds
who had seen and heard him when he called Lazarus from the grave
18 and raised him from the dead, everywhere testified to the fact; and
it was just because they heard that he had performed this miracle
19 that so many now went out to meet him. The Pharisees therefore
said to one another, "You see, you can do nothing! All the world
is running after him!"

20 There were several Greeks among those who had gone up to Jeru-
21 salem to perform their religious duties at the festival. They went to
Philip, because he came from Bethsaida in Galilee, and said to him,
22 "Sir, we should like to see Jesus." Philip went to Andrew and told
him of it, and together they went and laid the request before Jesus.

23 Jesus answered them, "The hour has come for the Son of man to b
24 glorified. Believe me, unless a kernel of wheat is buried in th
ground and dies, it will always be but one kernel. But if it dies
25 many kernels then spring from it. He who loves his life on eart
will lose his life in the beyond; but he who hates this life and th
ways of the world will secure for himself life in the beyond as th
26 true life of the future. If any one wishes to serve me he must trave
by my road, for where I am, there my servant shall be also. And i
27 any one serves me, my Father will show him honor. At this momen
my soul is shaken to the depths. But am I therefore to say, 'Father
spare me this hour of suffering'? No, for it was for the very purpos
28 of suffering that I have been led to this hour. Father, glorify Th
son with the glory that was his with Thee before the universe cam
into being!" Then there came a voice from heaven, saying, "I
glorified him in the past, and I shall glorify him again."
29 Of those who had heard this voice, some said that it was thunder
30 and others, "An angel spoke to him."—"This voice did not com
31 for my sake," said Jesus, "but for yours. The decision concernin
this world is now about to be made. Now the ruler of this worl
32 will be deprived of his sovereignty. And when I have been lifted up
33 from the earth, I shall draw all creatures to me." (He said this t
34 indicate the kind of death that he would die.) Some of the crowd
protested, "We have learned from the Scriptures that the Messiah
will live for all time; how can you say then that the Son of man
35 must first be lifted up? Who is this Son of man?" Jesus answered,
"The light will be with you only a little while longer. Travel whil
you have the light, lest darkness overtake you; for he who must
36 travel in the dark does not know where his path will lead him. As
long as you have the light, put your trust in the light, so that you
may become children of light." After these words he went away
and hid from them.
37 In spite of all the miracles that he had performed before them,
38 they did not believe in him; for in them were to be fulfilled the
words of the prophet Isaiah: "Lord, who has believed our report,
39 and to whom is the arm of the Lord revealed?" They could not
believe for the reason which Isaiah gave in another passage: "He
40 has blinded their eyes and closed their hearts, so that they shall
not see with their eyes and understand with their hearts, and be
41 converted, and so that I shall not be able to heal them." These
were the words spoken by Isaiah when he saw the glorious power of
42 the Messiah and prophesied concerning him. Nevertheless, many of
the leaders of the people believed in Jesus, although they dared not

admit it openly for fear of being put under the ban by the Pharisees;
43 for they valued the praise of men more highly than the praise of
God.
44 Jesus loudly and solemnly affirmed, "Whoever believes in me
45 actually believes not in me, but in Him Who sent me; and whoever
46 understands me understands Him Whose envoy I am. I have come
into the world to be a light, in order that no one who believes in
47 me may remain in the darkness; and if any one were to hear my
words and not heed them, I should not condemn him; for I have
48 not come to condemn the world but to save it. Whoever rejects me
and will not accept my teaching has by this very act pronounced
49 judgment on himself. The teachings I have given him will comprise
his sentence on the last day. I have not proclaimed this doctrine of
my own accord; my Father Who sent me is the One Who directed
me what I should teach and in what words I should present my
50 doctrine. I know that His commission will bring life in the hereafter. Whatever I say, therefore, I speak as I was bidden by my
Father."

CHAPTER 13.

1 It was the eve of the Passover. Jesus knew that the hour had now
come when he was to leave the world and go to the Father. Those
on earth whom he called his own he had always loved, and he con-
2 tinued to love them until his dying breath. They were eating the
meal of the Passover, and already the devil had made Judas, the
3 son of Simon of Cariot, decide to betray his master. Jesus knew
that the Father had given everything into his hands; he knew that
he had come from God and that he was about to return to Him.
4 Nevertheless, he rose from the table, laid aside his outer garment,
5 and taking a linen apron, tied it about his waist. Then he poured
water into a basin and began to wash his disciples' feet, and dry
6 them with the apron that he wore. When he came to Simon Peter,
7 Peter protested, "Lord, do you mean to wash my feet?"—"You
cannot now see the reason for what I am doing," answered Jesus,
8 "but afterwards you will understand." But Peter protested again,
"You shall never wash my feet."—"If you will not let me wash
your feet," said Jesus, "you will be barred from my fellowship."—
9 "Lord," replied Peter, "then wash not only my feet but my hands
10 and my head as well." Jesus answered, "A man who has bathed
need not wash his head, but only his feet, to be entirely clean. You,
11 my disciples, are clean,—but not all of you." For he knew which
12 of them was to be his betrayer. After he had washed their feet he

put on his outer garment again and took his place at the table
Then he said to them, "Do you understand the meaning of what I
13 have just done for you? You call me 'master' and 'lord,' and rightly
14 so, for that is what I am. Now if I, who am your lord and master
have washed your feet, how much more reason there is for you to
15 wash each other's feet. I did it to set you an example, so that you
16 may act as I have acted toward you. I tell you that the servant is
no greater than his master, nor is a messenger greater than he who
17 sent him. If you remember this and act accordingly, you are for-
18 tunate. It grieves me that I cannot say this of all of you. I know the
hearts of those whom I have chosen. But when I made my choice I
had to take into consideration fulfillment of the words of the Scriptures: 'He who eats bread with me has raised his heel against me.'
19 Even now, before this passage of the Scriptures has been fulfilled,
I call it to your attention, so that when it is fulfilled, it may be one
20 more proof to strengthen your faith in me. I tell you that whoever
receives him whom I send receives me, and whoever receives me
21 receives Him Who sent me." After these words his soul was filled
with anguish, and he said, "I must tell you that one of you will
22 betray me." The disciples looked at one another, wondering of
23 whom he could be speaking. One of them, the one especially dear to
24 Jesus, was reclining beside him, and Simon Peter beckoned to him
25 to find out who it was that Jesus meant. This disciple leaned against
26 Jesus' breast and asked him in a low tone, "Lord, who is it?" Jesus
whispered, "The one to whom I shall give this morsel that I am
now dipping into the dish." With these words he dipped the morsel
27 and gave it to Judas of Cariot. When Judas had eaten it, Satan
entered him. Then Jesus said, "Do quickly what you intend to do."
28 None of the others present understood why he said this to him,
29 but because Judas carried the money some of them thought that
Jesus meant to say, "Go quickly and buy the things that we need
for the festival." Others took it that Judas was to give something
30 to the poor. When Judas had eaten the morsel he immediately
left the hall and went out into the darkness of the night.

31 After he had gone, Jesus said, "Now the Son of man is glorified,
32 and God Himself is glorified in him. But God will also glorify him
33 by Himself, and that promptly. My children, I shall be with you
only a little while longer. Then you will look for me, but what I said
to the Jews I now say to you: where I am going you cannot follow.
34 I give you a new commandment: Love one another — and love one
35 another just as I have loved you. By your love for one another
every one shall be able to recognize you as my disciples."

36 Simon Peter now asked him, "Lord, where is it that you are
going?" Jesus answered, "Where I am going you cannot go with
37 me now. You will not follow me until later."—"Lord," Peter insisted, "why can I not go with you now? I am ready to lay down
38 my life for you." Jesus replied, "You say you are ready to lay
down your life for me? I tell you that the cock will not crow before
you have disowned me three times."

CHAPTER 14.

1 Then, again addressing all the disciples, he continued, "Do not
be discouraged. Have confidence in God, and you will also have
2 confidence in me. In my Father's house there are many dwellings.
If it were not so, I would have told you. And because I am going
3 there now, I shall have a place prepared for you; and when I have
been there and prepared a place for you, I shall come back and
4 take you with me, so that you too may be where I am. You know
5 where I am going, and you also know the way there." At this,
Thomas, known as "the Twin" said to Jesus, "Lord, we do not know
6 where you are going; how should we know the way there?"—"I
am the way, the truth, and the life," answered Jesus. "No one comes
7 to the Father except through me. If you really knew me you would
know my Father also. From now on you will know Him, because
8 you have seen Him."—"Lord," said Philip, "show us the Father,
9 and we shall be content. Jesus answered him, "After all this time
that I have been with you, do you not yet recognize me, Philip? He
who has seen me has also seen the Father. Then how can you say,
10 'Show us the Father'? Do you not believe that I am in communion
with the Father, and the Father with me? The words that I spoke to
you I did not speak of my own accord; the Father Himself, Who is
in constant communication with me, speaks and works through me.
11 Yes, you may believe that there is a close communion between me
and the Father, and between the Father and me; and if you are not
willing to believe my words, at least believe because of the deeds
12 themselves. I assure you that whoever believes in me will have the
power to do the same deeds that I do, and even greater deeds; for I
13 am going to the Father. And whatever you ask in my name, I will
15 grant, so that the Father may be honored in the Son. If you love
16 me, abide by my commands. Then I will ask the Father, and He
17 will give you another helper to be with you in the future. That
helper is the spirit-world of truth. The world cannot receive it,
because it neither sees nor knows the spirit-world. But you will know
it, for it will remain with you and enter into communion with you.

18 I shall not leave you fatherless, but I shall come back to you. A
19 little while longer and the world will see me no more. But you will
20 see me; for I shall be living, and you will obtain life too. When
that day comes you will see that I live in close communion with the
Father, and that you live in a like communion with me, and I with
21 you. He who knows my commands and abides by them is he who
loves me; and he who loves me will likewise be loved by my Father.
And I also will love him and will so manifest myself to him that he
22 may be aware of my presence." Judas (not the one from Cariot)
now asked him, "Lord, why will you show yourself only to us, and
23 not to the world?" Jesus answered, "If any one loves me he will
live according to my teachings, and my Father will show His love
24 for Him. I myself will come and take up my abode with him. He
who does not love me does not hold fast to my teachings. True, the
doctrine that you hear from me is not my own, but that of the
25 Father Who sent me, as I have always told you ever since I have
been with you.

26 "After me will come the helper, the holy spirit-world which the
Father will send in my name, to teach you everything else and to
27 recall to you all that I have said. I leave you peace; I give you my
own peace. It is not what the world knows as peace that I give you.
28 Do not be discouraged and despondent. You have heard me tell you
that I am going away but that I am coming back to you. If you
loved me, you would rejoice that I am going to the Father, because
29 the Father is greater than I. Now I have told you of this before it
happens, so that when it does happen you may remain steadfast in
30 your faith. There is not much more that I can say to you, for the
ruler of this world is approaching; but he cannot find anything in
31 me that pertains to him. And I am left at his mercy for the sole
purpose of letting the world know that I love the Father and that I
do everything as the Father has directed me.

CHAPTER 15.

1 "I am the true vine, and my Father is the vine-dresser. He re-
2 moves every one of my branches that does not bear fruit, and He
cleans every bearing branch, so that it may bear even more abundant
3 and better fruit. You are already clean by virtue of my teachings.
4 Remain in me, then, as I will remain in you. Just as a branch cannot bear fruit by itself if it is severed from the vine, so you also can-
5 not bear fruit unless you remain united with me. For I am like the
vine, and you are like its branches. If any one remains united with
me, and I with him, he will bear fruit in abundance. But severed

6 from me, you can do nothing. Whoever severs himself from me is
thrown aside like a branch that is cut off, and withers; and such
withered branches are gathered and thrown into the fire, where they
7 are burned. If you remain united with me and hold fast to my teach-
8 ings, you may ask what you will and it will be given to you. It
would redound to my Father's glory if you were to bear abundant
9 fruit and prove yourselves my true disciples. As the Father has
10 loved me, so I have loved you. Continue in your love for me. If
you abide by my commands you will continue in your love for me,
just as I, obedient to my Father's commands, continue in my love
11 for Him. I have told you this in order that I might find my joy in
12 you and that your own joy might thereby be made perfect. This is
13 my command: that you love one another as I have loved you. He
who has the greatest love is he who lays down his life for his friends;
14 and you are my friends if you do my bidding. I no longer call you
15 my servants, for a servant is not told what his master is doing. I
have called you my friends, because I have made known to you
16 everything that I have heard from my Father. It was not you who
chose me but I who chose you and appointed you to go and bear
fruit, lasting fruit, so that the Father may grant you everything that
17 you ask Him in my name. Above all I earnestly enjoin you, love
one another!

18 "If the world hates you, remember that it hated me before it hated
19 you. If you belonged to the world, the world would love you as its
own; but because you do not belong to the world, but were chosen
20 out of the world by me, it hates you. Do not forget my words to
you: 'The servant is not greater than his master.' If they have
persecuted me, they will persecute you also; and if they have not
21 heeded my words, they will not heed yours. On my account alone
they will take this attitude toward you, for they do not know Him
22 Who sent me. If I had not come and preached to them, they would
not have been guilty of sin; but as it is, they can offer no defence
23 for the sins that they have committed. He who hates me hates my
24 Father also. If I had not done deeds among them such as no one
before me was able to do, they would have incurred no sin; but they
have seen all these deeds with their own eyes, and yet they have
25 hated both me and my Father. Nevertheless, this was bound to
occur in fulfillment of the words of their Law: 'They hated me
26 without cause.' But when the helper comes whom I shall send to
you from the Father, the spirit-world of truth which comes from the
27 Father's kingdom, this will testify for me. And you also are witnesses on my behalf, for you have been with me from the beginning.

CHAPTER 16.

1 "I have told you all this so that you will not falter in your con-
2 viction. For you will be put under the ban, and indeed the time will
come when any one who kills you will think he is doing God a
3 service. They will treat you in this way because they know neither
4 the Father nor me. But I have foretold these things to you so that
you may remember my words when that hour comes. I have not
5 spoken of them previously, because I was still with you; but now
I must speak, because I am going to Him Who sent me. And not one
6 among you asks me, 'Where are you going?'—but your hearts are
7 full of sadness because of what I have told you. But truly, my going
away is for your own good; for unless I go, the helper will not come
8 to you; but if I go, I will send him to you. When he comes he will
open the eyes of the world to sin, to righteousness, and to God's
9 judgment: to sin, which weighs upon them because they do not
10 believe in me; to righteousness, because I, as a pattern of righteous-
11 ness, am going to the Father, and you will see me no more; to God's
judgment, which will then have been passed upon the ruler of this
world.

12 "I have much more to say to you, but you cannot bear it now.
13 But when those spirits of truth have come, they will guide you along
the right path in all matters pertaining to the truth. They will not
speak of their own accord but will tell you only those things which
they themselves hear, and will impart to you whatever may be for
14 your good. They will uphold my honor, for they will take what is
15 mine and communicate it to you. Everything that the Father has is
mine also. That is why I said that they would take what is mine
and communicate it to you.

16 "In a little while you will not see me any more, and a little while
17 later you will see me again; for I am going to the Father." Upon
this some of the disciples asked one another, "What can he mean
when he says 'In a little while you will not see me any more; and a
little while later, you will see me again'? and 'I am going to the
18 Father'? What does he mean by 'In a little while'? We do not
19 understand these words." Jesus saw that they wanted to question
him, and so he said to them, "You are asking each other what I
meant by saying, 'In a little while you will not see me any more;
20 and a little while later you will see me again.' I can tell you only
this: You will weep and lament, while the world will rejoice; you
21 will be sad, but your sadness will be turned into joy. When a
woman is with child she grows anxious as soon as the day of her

confinement comes; but after she has given birth to the child, she
forgets her pains in her joy over having brought a child into the
22 world. So too you are now full of sorrow, but when I see you again
later, your hearts will be filled with a joy that no one can take from
23 you. On that day of rejoicing you will make no request whatsoever
of me; for be assured that the Father will grant whatever you ask
24 for as my disciples. Hitherto you have never asked Him for anything as my disciples. But now ask in this way and you will receive, so that your joy may be complete.
25 "So far I have spoken to you in parables, but the time is coming
when I shall no longer speak to you in parables, but shall teach
26 you in plain words about the Father. Then you will ask of Him as
my disciples, and I shall no longer need to lay your pleas before
27 the Father; for the Father loves you Himself, because you have
loved me and steadfastly believed that I came from the Father.
28 I came into the world, and now I am leaving the world and returning to the Father."
29 His disciples said, "Now you are speaking plainly and not in a
30 parable. And now we understand why it is that you know everything and that no one need even put a question to you. This makes
31 us believe that you did come from God." Jesus answered them,
32 "You believe now? But the time is coming—it has already come
—when you will all be scattered, each of you intent only on his
own welfare, and will leave me alone. Yet I am not alone, for the
33 Father is with me. I have told you this in order that you may strive
for that peace which can be found only in communion with me. In
the world you will indeed have to endure outward distress; but
courage! I have conquered the world."

CHAPTER 17.

1 When he had finished speaking, Jesus looked up to heaven and
prayed: "Father, the hour has come. Glorify Thy Son that Thy Son
2 may glorify Thee. Thou hast given him power over all creation in
order that all whom Thou hast entrusted to him may have life here-
3 after. And the way to the life hereafter is to acknowledge Thee as
the only true God, and Jesus as the Messiah whom Thou hast sent
4 into this world. I have appeared here on earth in behalf of Thy
5 glory; I have finished the work that Thou gavest me to do. And
now, Father, restore to me the glory that I had with Thee before the
6 world existed. I have made known Thy name to these men whom
Thou gavest me from the world. They were Thine, and Thou gavest
7 them to me, and they have obeyed Thy word. Now they know that

everything that Thou hast conferred upon me comes from Thee.
8 For the teachings that Thou hast imparted to me, I have in turn
imparted to them. They have accepted them and have seen in truth
that I came from Thee; and they have the firm conviction that it
9 is Thou Who hast sent me. I pray for them; not for the world, but
10 for those whom Thou hast given me, for they are Thine. All that
is mine belongs to Thee, and all that is Thine to me, and thereby
11 Thou hast glorified me. I am to be in the world no longer, but they
must remain in the world, while I come to Thee. And even though
I shall no longer remain on earth in the flesh, I shall remain on
earth in another way. Holy Father, keep true to Thy teachings those
whom Thou hast given me, that they may be one as we are one.
12 While I was with them, I kept them true to Thy word, and watched
over them. Not one has been lost, except the son of perdition, and
13 this happened in order that the Scriptures might be fulfilled. Now I
am coming to Thee, and I speak these words here on earth only that
14 the joy which is mine may be fully shared by them also. I have im-
planted Thy truth in their hearts. Because they did not come from
15 the world, the world has hated them. I do not pray that Thou wilt
take them out of the world, but that Thou wilt keep them from the
16 Evil One; for they belong to the world as little as I belong to the
17 world. Consecrate them through the truth: Thy word is truth. As
18 Thou didst send me into the world, so have I sent them into the
19 world. For their sakes I consecrate myself, so that by following the
truth they also may be consecrated.

20 "Nor do I pray for them alone, but also for those who come to
21 believe in me through their preaching. Grant that they all may become one, as Thou, Father, art one with me, and I with Thee, so
that they may enter into the same communion with us, and that the
22 world may know that Thou hast sent me. I have given them the
23 glory that Thou gavest me, that they may be one as we are one: I
united with them, and Thou with me, so that they may attain the
highest perfection of unity. By this the world shall know that Thou
didst send me, and that I have loved them as Thou hast loved me.
24 Father, I wish those whom Thou gavest me to be with me where I
am, so that they may witness the glory that Thou hast conferred
upon me; for Thou didst love me before the foundation of the
25 world. O just Father, the world has not known Thee, but I have
known Thee, and these men have also understood that Thou didst
26 send me. I have made known Thy name to them, and I will also make
it known in the future, so that the love with which Thou hast loved
me may remain in them, and I among them.—Rise, and let us go."

CHAPTER 18.

1 When he had spoken these words, Jesus, together with his disciples, left the hall and crossed the brook of Cedron. There was a
2 garden there, which he and his disciples entered. This place was
also known to Judas, who was planning to betray him, for Jesus
3 often went there with his disciples. Judas had had placed at his
disposal a troop of soldiers and the servants of the chief priests,
together with whom he now set out for the same spot, carrying
4 torches, lanterns, and weapons. Knowing everything that lay before him, Jesus came forward and asked them, "For whom are you
5 searching?" — "For Jesus of Nazareth," they answered. "I am he,"
6 said Jesus. His betrayer, Judas, was in their midst. When Jesus
7 said to them, "I am he," they gave way and fell to the ground. Once
more he asked them, "For whom are you searching?" and they re-
8 peated, "For Jesus of Nazareth." — "I have already told you that
I am he," said Jesus. "If I am the man you want, let the others go
9 in peace." This was to fulfill the words he had spoken shortly before: "I have not allowed one of those whom Thou gavest me to be
10 lost." Simon Peter now drew the sword that he had with him and
struck at the high priest's servant with it, cutting off his ear. The
11 servant's name was Malchus. Jesus turned to Peter and said, "Put
up your sword. Am I not to drink the cup that my Father has offered
me?"

12 The troop, which was under the comamnd of an officer, and the
servants of the Jewish leaders now seized Jesus and bound him.
13 They first took him to Hannas, the father-in-law of Caiaphas, who
14 was the high priest for that year. This Caiaphas was the one who
had advised the Jews that it was better for one man to die than for
15 the whole nation to perish. Simon Peter and one other disciple
followed Jesus; the other disciple was acquainted with the high
16 priest and so he went into the high priest's palace with Jesus, while
Peter remained standing outside. Then the disciple who was acquainted with the high priest went out and spoke to the woman at
17 the door, and she allowed Peter to enter. The woman then turned
to Peter and asked, "Are you not one of that man's disciples?" —
18 "I am not," answered Peter. The servants and the attendants had
built a coal fire because of the cold and were warming themselves
by it. Peter also stood by them to warm himself.

19 In the meantime the high priest questioned Jesus about his dis-
20 ciples and his teaching. Jesus answered, "I have preached openly
for all the world to hear. I have constantly taught in the synagogues

and in the temple where all the Jews gather. I have never taught
21 anything in secret. Why do you question me, then? Question those
22 who heard me speak, for they must know what I said." At these
words one of the servants who stood near struck Jesus in the face,
23 exclaiming, "Is that how you answer the high priest?" Jesus said
to him, "If I have spoken improperly, show me where the fault lies;
24 but if I have spoken as I should, why do you strike me?" Then
Hannas sent him, bound, to the high priest Caiaphas.

25 All this while Peter stood by the fire warming himself. The by-
standers asked him, "Are you not one of his disciples, too?" Peter
26 denied it, saying, "I am no disciple of his." Then one of the high
priest's servants, a relative of the servant whose ear Peter had cut
27 off, asked Peter, "Did I not see you in the garden with him?" Again
Peter denied it, and as he did so, the cock crowed.

28 From the palace of Caiaphas Jesus was taken to the governor's
palace. It was early in the morning. The Jews themselves would not
go into the building for fear of being defiled, for they expected to
29 eat the Passover. Pilate therefore went out to them and asked, "What
30 is your charge against this man?" They answered, "If he were not
31 a criminal we would not have brought him to you." Pilate answered, "Then take him and judge him according to your own Law."
—"We have no authority to condemn a man to death and execute
32 him," they cried. This was to fulfill the words in which Jesus had
33 indicated the manner of death that he would die. Then Pilate went
back into the palace, ordered that Jesus be brought in, and asked
34 him, "Are you the king of the Jews?" Jesus answered, "Are you
speaking of your own accord, or have others told you about me?"
35 —"Do you take me for a Jew?" retorted Pilate. "Your own people,
and what is more, their chief priests, have handed you over to me.
36 What are you guilty of?"—"My kingdom does not belong to this
world," said Jesus. "If my kingdom belonged to this world my subjects would have fought for me, and I should not have been de-
37 livered to the Jews. But my kingdom is not an earthly one."—"You
are a king, then?" asked Pilate.—"I am indeed a king," answered
Jesus. "I was born and came into the world for the purpose of testifying to the truth. Every one who comes from the kingdom of
38 truth listens to my voice."—"What is truth?" returned Pilate.
With these words he again went out to the Jews and said to them,
39 "I find no guilt whatever in him. I have instituted among you the
custom of setting free one prisoner at the Passover. If you wish, I
40 will release the king of the Jews for you." At this they all shouted,
"No, not him, but Barabbas!" Barabbas was a highwayman.

CHAPTER 19.

1 Pilate now laid hold of Jesus and struck him with a scourge to
2 signify that he was condemned to death. The soldiers then took him
and wove a crown of thorns and set it on his head. They flung a
3 purple robe over his shoulders, and then they marched up to him
and shouted, "Hail, king of the Jews!" and struck him in the face.
4 Pilate again went out to the Jews and said, "Look, I am having him
brought before you once more to show you that I do not find him
5 guilty." Jesus now came out, wearing the purple robe and the
6 crown of thorns. Pilate called to them, "Here is the man!" No
sooner had the chief priests and their followers laid eyes on him
than they shouted, "Crucify him, crucify him!"—"You may take
him and crucify him yourselves," answered Pilate. "I shall not, for
7 I find no guilt in him."—"But we have a law," answered the Jews,
"and according to our law he must die, for he has called himself
8 the Son of God." When Pilate heard the words "Son of God," his
9 anxiety was greater than before, and going back into the palace he
asked Jesus, "Where do you really come from?" But Jesus made no
10 answer. At this Pilate exclaimed, "What? Will you not even speak
and reply to me? Do you not know that I have the power to have
11 you crucified, and also the power to set you free?" Jesus answered,
"You would have no power over me at all if it had not been given
to you from above. Because you do have that power, the greater
12 the guilt of him who delivered me to you." Pilate was so impressed
by these words that he exerted himself still more to secure the release of Jesus. But the Jewish leaders shouted at him threateningly,
"If you release this man, you are no longer a friend of Caesar's;
for any one who calls himself a king is guilty of disloyalty to
13 Caesar." In the face of these threats Pilate at length gave orders for
Jesus to be led out. He himself sat down in the judge's seat in a
place called the "Marble Pavement," or in Hebrew "Gabbatha."
It was the Day of Preparation for the Passover, at about noon.
14 "There is your king," Pilate called to them. But they only shouted
15 in reply, "Away with him! Away with him! Crucify him!" Pilate
protested, "Am I to crucify your king, then?" But the chief priests
16 answered, "We have no king; we recognize Caesar alone." After this
he handed Jesus over to them to be crucified.

17 They now took Jesus and led him to the garrison, where they
25 placed the cross on his shoulders. Near by stood the mother of Jesus
and his mother's sister, Mary the wife of Cleopas, and Mary of
26 Magdala. When Jesus saw his mother, and by her side his favorite

disciple, he said to his mother, "Woman, that is now your son."
27 Then he said to the disciple, "Son, that is now your mother." And
the disciple led her away from this sorrowful hour to his own house.

18 Jesus carried his cross and arrived at the so-called Place of the
Skulls, which in Hebrew is known as "Golgotha." Here they crucified him, and with him two others, one at his right and one at his
19 left. Pilate had also had an inscription prepared and fastened near
the top of the cross. It read: *Jesus of Nazareth, the King of the*
20 *Jews.* Many of the Jews read this inscription, for the place where
Jesus was crucified was near the city. The inscription was written
21 in the Hebrew, the Greek, and the Latin languages. And so the chief
priests of the Jews said to Pilate, "You should not have written,
'The king of the Jews,' but, 'This man declared that he was the king
22 of the Jews.'" Pilate, however, told them curtly, "What I have
written shall remain written."

23 After they had crucified Jesus, the soldiers took his garments and
divided them into four lots, one for each soldier. There still remained his tunic, a seamless garment woven in one piece from top
24 to bottom. The soldiers said to one another, "Let us not cut this,
but throw lots to decide whose it shall be." Thus they fulfilled the
words of the Scriptures: "They divided my garments among them
and cast lots for my clothing."

28 Jesus knew that so far everything written of him in the Scriptures
had been fulfilled. He now fulfilled the last of these prophecies by
crying out, "I am thirsty." A vessel filled with vinegar was standing
29 there. Some one dipped a sponge in it, fastened it to a hyssop-stalk,
30 and held it to his lips. When Jesus had taken the vinegar, he cried
out, "It is finished!" Then he bowed his head and gave up his spirit.

31 As it was the Day of Preparation, the bodies could not be left on
the crosses over the coming Sabbath, which was an especially high
feast-day. The Jews therefore asked Pilate to allow them to break
the legs of the crucified victims with clubs, and after that to take
32 the bodies from the crosses. So the soldiers came and broke the
legs first of one and then of the other of the men who had been
33 crucified with Jesus. When they came to Jesus and saw that he had
34 already died, they did not break his legs; but one of the soldiers
thrust a lance into his side, and blood and water immediately
35 flowed from the wound. An eyewitness reported this, and his testimony is true. He knows that he has reported truthfully, so that
36 you likewise may believe it. For this too had to take place in fulfillment of the words of the Scriptures: "Not one of his bones shall

37 be broken," as well as in fulfillment of that other Scriptural passage: "They shall look upon him whom they pierced."
38 Joseph of Arimathaea was a disciple of Jesus, but only in secret,
for fear of the Jewish leaders. He now begged Pilate to be allowed
to take the body of Jesus from the cross. Pilate gave his consent,
39 and Joseph went and took the body down from the cross. Nicodemus
also went there (the same Nicodemus who had first visited Jesus at
night) and brought with him a mixture of myrrh and aloes, about
40 a hundred pounds in weight. They took the body and wrapped it in
linen cloth together with the fragrant spices, as is the custom at
Jewish burials.
41 Near the place where the cross stood there was a garden, and in
this garden a new tomb in which no one had ever been buried.
42 There they placed the body of Jesus, out of consideration for the
Jewish Day of Preparation, as the tomb was near at hand.

CHAPTER 20.

1 On the first day after the Sabbath, Mary of Magdala came to the
tomb very early in the morning, when it was not yet entirely light,
2 and saw that the stone at the entrance had been rolled away. Running back to Simon Peter and to the other disciple whom Jesus
dearly loved, she said to them, "They have taken the master from
3 the grave, and we do not know where they have laid him." Peter
4 and the other disciple hurried out and ran toward the tomb, each
trying to outstrip his companion. The other disciple was swifter
5 and reached the tomb first. Stooping forward, he saw the linen
6 cloths lying there, but he did not go into the tomb. Simon Peter,
who had been slower, now came up and went straight into the tomb.
7 He also saw the linen cloths lying there; the cloth that had been
wrapped about the head of the corpse, however, was not among
8 them, but lay folded up in a place by itself. The other disciple,
who had been the first to reach the tomb, now entered, and he too
9 saw and believed. Until then they had not understood the saying
10 of the Scriptures that he must rise from the dead. Then the two
disciples returned home.
11 Meanwhile Mary stood near the grave weeping. As she wept she
12 bent forward and looked into the grave and saw two angels in
white, sitting one at the head and one at the foot of the place where
13 the body of Jesus had lain. The angels said to her, "Woman, why
do you weep? Whom are you seeking?" She answered, "They have
taken away my lord, and I do not know where they have laid him."
14 As she spoke she felt suddenly impelled to look behind her; and

she saw Jesus standing there, but did not know that it was he.
15 Jesus said to her, "Woman, why do you weep? Whom are you
seeking?" Taking him for the gardener, she answered, "Sir, if you
have taken him away, tell me where you have laid him, and I will
16 take him back." Jesus only said, "Mary." She sprang toward him,
exclaiming, "Rabboni!"—a Hebrew word that means "My master!"
17 Jesus said to her, "Do not touch me! I have not yet ascended to the
Father. Go to the brothers and tell them, 'I shall ascend to my
18 Father and your Father, to my God and your God.'" Then Mary
of Magdala hurried away to the disciples and told them that she
had seen the lord, and that he had directed her to inform them of
what he had said to her.

19 It was the evening of the first day after the Sabbath, and the
doors of the house in which the disciples were assembled had been
shut for fear of the Jews. Jesus suddenly came and stood among
20 them, greeting them with the words, "Peace be with you!" He then
showed them the scars in his hands and his side. The disciples were
21 overjoyed at seeing the lord once more. Again he said, "Peace be
22 with you!" and added, "As the Father sent me, so I send you." With
these words he breathed upon them and said, "Receive a holy spirit.
23 If you forgive the sins of others, your own sins will be forgiven you;
but if you harbor resentment against others for their sins, resentment for your own sins will be harbored against you."

24 Thomas, known as the "Twin," who was one of the Twelve, was
25 not with them when Jesus appeared. Afterwards the other disciples
told him, "We have seen the lord." But he answered, "Unless I see
in his hands the mark of the nails and touch a nail-mark with my
own fingers, and put my hand into his side, I will never believe it."
26 Eight days later the disciples were again assembled in the house,
and on this occasion Thomas was with them. Then, although the
doors were shut, Jesus came in to them and stood in their midst,
27 saying, "Peace be with you!" Turning to Thomas, he added, "See,
here are my hands. Touch them with your finger; then put your
28 hand into my side. And do not doubt, but believe." And Thomas
29 exclaimed, "My lord and my master!" Jesus said to him, "Because
you have seen me, you believe. Fortunate are they who do not see
and yet believe."

CHAPTER 21.

1 Afterwards Jesus once more appeared to his disciples by the Lake
2 of Tiberias. It occurred in the following manner. Simon Peter,
Thomas called the "Twin," Nathanael of Cana in Galilee, the two

3 sons of Zebedee, and two other disciples were together. Simon Peter
said to the others, "I am going fishing." They said that they would
go with him, and all went down to the shore and got into their boat.
4 That night, however, they caught nothing. At daybreak Jesus stood
5 on the shore, though his disciples did not know that it was he. He
called to them, "Men, have you any fish?"—"No," they answered.
6 "Throw out your net on the right side of the boat," he advised them,
"and you will make a catch." They threw out their net, and now
they were unable to pull it in because of the quantity of fish that it
7 held. Then the disciple whom Jesus loved dearly said to Peter, "It
is the lord!" When Simon Peter heard that it was the lord, he
quickly put on his outer garment and his belt, for he had been
8 stripped for work, and sprang into the water. The other disciples
followed him with the boat (they were not far from the shore, only
about a hundred yards), dragging the net full of fish after them.
9 When they landed they saw a charcoal fire and a fish broiling on it.
10 There was also some bread there. Jesus called to them, "Bring with
11 you some of the fish that you have just caught." Simon Peter went
aboard the boat again and hauled the net ashore. It held a hundred
and fifty-three large fish, but in spite of this great number the net
12 did not break. Now Jesus said to them, "Come and have breakfast."
But none of the disciples dared to ask him who he was; they well
13 knew that it was the lord. Jesus now took the bread, gave thanks,
14 and divided it among them, and the fish also. This was the third
time that Jesus showed himself to his disciples after rising from the
dead.

15 After they had finished their meal, Jesus asked Simon Peter,
"Simon, son of John, do you love me more than the others do?"—
"Surely you know, lord, that I love you," answered Peter.—"Feed
16 my sheep," Jesus said to him. A second time Jesus asked, "Simon,
son of John, do you love me?" And Peter answered, "You know,
17 lord, that I love you."—"Feed my sheep," Jesus answered. Then
he asked for the third time, "Simon, son of John, do you love me?"
Peter was hurt because Jesus asked him for the third time whether
he loved him, and he answered, "Lord, you know everything, and
you know that I love you." Jesus gave him the same answer: "Feed
18 my sheep." And he added, "I tell you, when you were young you
could put on your own girdle and go wherever you chose. But when
you have grown old you will stretch out your arms, and others will
put a girdle on you and take you to a place where you have no wish
19 to go." He said this to indicate the manner of death by which Peter
20 would glorify God. Then he added, "Follow in my footsteps." Peter

turned and saw the disciple whom Jesus especially loved standing
at his side. It was the same disciple who had leaned on Jesus' breast
21 at supper and asked him, "Lord, who is the traitor?" Glancing at
him now, Peter asked Jesus, "Lord, what will become of this man?"
22 Jesus answered, "If it is my will that he remain until I come, what
concern is that of yours? Only see to it that you walk my way."
23 Because of this saying many of the brothers thought that this disciple
would never die, although Jesus had not said to him, "You shall
never die," but only, "If it is my will that he remain until I come,
what concern is that of yours?"

24 This disciple is the one who testifies to the truth of all these events
and is the author of this account. We know that his testimony is true.

25 Jesus performed many other wonders in the presence of his disciples which are not written down in this book. For if each of them were described in detail, I do not believe that the world would hold all the books that would have to be written. But this account has been written in order that you may believe that Jesus is the Messiah, the Son of God, and that through your belief you may receive the life that he has promised.

The ACTS OF THE APOSTLES

CHAPTER 1.

1 DEAR THEOPHILUS: The first account that I compiled relates
all that Jesus did and taught, from the beginning until the day
2 on which he ascended to heaven. On that day he imparted his last
instructions to the apostles whom he had chosen under the guidance
3 of a holy spirit. He directed them to proclaim the gospel. After his
suffering and death he had given them many proofs that he still
lived, for he had been forty days in visible communication with
4 them and had taught them concerning the kingdom of God. On one
occasion while he was with them he admonished them not to leave
Jerusalem, but to await the fulfillment of the promise that the Father
had given. "This promise," he said to them, "you heard from my
5 own lips. I told you that John baptized only by immersion in
waves of water, but that you were to be baptized by immersion in
the power-waves of a holy spirit. At the end of the few days that
remain between now and Pentecost you will receive these spirits."
6 Those who were present asked him, "Lord, will that be the time
7 when you will restore sovereignty to Israel?" But he answered,
"It is not for you to know the periods of time and the crises fixed
8 by the Father in His omnipotence. You must be content with coming into contact with the holy spirit-world and receiving power from
it. Then you will have sufficient strength to testify on my behalf in
Jerusalem, in all Judaea and Samaria, and indeed to the very ends
of the earth."
9 When he had spoken these words a cloud suddenly enveloped
him from his feet to his head, and he was thereby withdrawn from
10 their sight. While they still stood gazing fixedly as he ascended into
heaven, two men in white garments suddenly appeared before them
11 and said, "Men of Galilee, why do you stand here gazing up toward
heaven? This very Jesus who has been taken away before your eyes
will return to you in the same manner that you have seen him
ascend to heaven."
12 Upon this they returned to Jerusalem from the mountain called
13 Olivet, for it lies only a Sabbath day's journey distant. When they
reached the city they went into the upper room of the house in
which they had been staying. They were Peter, John, James,
Andrew, Philip, Thomas, Bartholomew, Matthew, James the son of

14 Alphaeus, Simon the Zealot, and Judas, the son of James. All were
of one heart and mind, and they devoted themselves to united
prayer, together with their wives and children, as well as with Mary
the mother of Jesus and with his brothers.
15 One day Peter stood up before the disciples of Jesus, who num-
16 bered about a hundred and twenty, and said, "Brothers, the words of
the Scriptures spoken by a holy spirit through the mouth of David
must be fulfilled. I speak of the prophecy concerning Judas, who
17 acted as guide for the captors of Jesus. We counted him one of our
18 number, inasmuch as his mission was the same as ours. With the
wages of his treachery this man had made provision beforehand for
the site of his own burial, the same place where he fell headlong, his
19 bloated body bursting open and pouring out his bowels. All this is
well known to the people of Jerusalem, who therefore call that place
20 Aceldaimach in their tongue, meaning 'the field of blood.' For it is
written in the book of Psalms: 'Let his dwelling-place be vacant,
and let no one occupy it; and another man take over his duties.'
21 This other man must be one of those who were with us constantly
22 while Jesus, the Messiah, went in and out among us, from the time
of his baptism by John until the day on which he was taken from
us. And he must also have been, like us, a witness of his resurrec-
23 tion. Of the men of whom all this is true, we must now choose one."
He then proposed two names: Joseph, called Barnabas, who was
24 surnamed the Just, and Matthias. They now offered this prayer:
"Do Thou O Lord, Who knowest the hearts of all, make known to
25 us which of these two Thou hast chosen for that place in Thy
ministry and apostleship which Judas gave up in order to go where
26 he belonged." The two men were directed to draw. The lot fell to
Matthias, and he was from now on numbered with the twelve
apostles.

CHAPTER 2.

1 The day of Pentecost had come and all had gathered in one place.
2 Suddenly there came from heaven a roaring as of a mighty wind,
3 and filled the whole house in which they sat. Tongues as of fire
appeared before them, and dividing, settled on each one present.
4 Every one was filled with a holy spirit and began to speak in foreign
languages whatever the spirit prompted him to utter.
5 At that time there were living in Jerusalem pious Jews of every
6 nation under heaven. When they heard the roaring sound they assembled in great numbers, and the utmost excitement prevailed
among them, for each one heard his own language spoken by these

7 men. This filled them with amazement, and they asked each other
8 wonderingly, "Are not all these men Galileans? How is it then that
every one of us hears them speaking his own mother tongue?
9 Parthians, Medes, and Elamites, people from Mesopotamia, Syria,
10 and Cappadocia, from Pontus and Asia Minor, from Phrygia and
11 Pamphylia, from Egypt and the district of Lybia near Cyrene;
Roman Jews living among us, as well as Roman non-Jews converted
to Judaism, Cretans and Arabs—we hear them proclaiming God's
12 mighty works in our own languages." All were dumbfounded and
13 asked one another what it could mean. Some, however, said scoffingly, "These men are full of new wine."

14 Peter, who was standing among the eleven, now raised his voice
for all to hear, saying, "You Jews, and all you others who live in
15 Jerusalem, listen to me and mark well what I say. You are mistaken;
these men are not drunk, for it is only nine o'clock in the morning.
16 This is rather the fulfillment of what was foretold by the prophet
17 Joel: 'And it will come to pass in the last days, says God, that I
shall send down upon all mankind a great many of my spirits.
Their sons and daughters will then become instruments of these
spirits, and the young, in a state of clairvoyance, will see visions,
and the old, in a condition similar to sleep, will receive revelations.
18 Upon my servants and upon my handmaidens I will also send down
19 an abundance of my spirits in those days. And I will show wonders
20 in the sky above, and on the earth beneath. The sun shall grow dark
and the moon red as blood before that great day of the Lord will
21 come. And whoever calls on the name of the Lord will be saved.' "

22 "Men of Israel, mark my words! Jesus of Nazareth was a man
whom God sent to us as His envoy and accredited as such by proofs
of divine power, by miracles and signs. You yourselves know all
23 the deeds that God performed among you through him. Now when
this same Jesus was delivered to you in accordance with the decree
and predetermination of God, you seized him and had him cruci-
24 fied and put to death at the hands of the Gentiles. But God raised
him from the depths after he had loosened the fetters of hell, for it
25 was impossible that he should be held fast by the underworld. For
David attributes to him the words: 'I saw my Lord at all times be-
26 fore my eyes; He is on my right hand that I may not falter. Therefore my heart rejoiced and my tongue exulted; for my earthly body
27 will dwell but a short time on earth, in the hope that Thou wilt not
leave my soul in hell or suffer Thy Holy One to know corruption.
28 Thou hast made known to me the ways that lead to life, and Thou
wilt give me the great joy of beholding Thy face again.' "

29 "My dear brothers, I suppose that I may speak quite freely to you
about the patriarch David. He died and was buried and his tomb is
30 to be seen among us to this very day. He was a prophet of God.
He knew that God had sworn to him under oath that out of the fruit
of his loins He would raise up the Messiah in the flesh and seat him
31 on his throne. Because he knew this, he prophesied of the resurrection of the Messiah. He said that his soul would not be left in hell
32 and that his body would not know decay. Now God has actually
33 raised this Jesus from the depths, as all of us have witnessed. Afterward he was uplifted by the right hand of God and received from
his Father the promised power over the holy spirit-world. He has
sent these spirits down here in great numbers, as you yourselves see
34 and hear. For it was not David who ascended to heaven. He himself
35 says, 'The Lord said to my lord, "Sit at my right hand until I make
36 your foes your footstool."' So let all the house of Israel be assured
that the same Jesus whom you crucified is he whom God ordained
as the lord and the Messiah."

37 All who had gathered there were deeply stirred by these words.
Some of them asked Peter and the other apostles, "Brothers, what
38 shall we do? Tell us!"—"Change your inner attitude," answered
Peter, "and let every one of you be baptized as the outward sign of
his faith in the lord Jesus, the Messiah, for the remission of your
sins of apostasy. Then you too will receive the gift of the holy spirit-
39 world. For this promise holds good for every one of us, as well as
for our children and for all others, even to the most remote future.
As many as there may be, the Lord our God will call them all back
to Him."

40 With many other words he bore witness to the truth, ending with
41 the admonition, "Save yourselves from this apostate people!" Those
who believed his words received baptism. Thus on that very day
some three thousand souls were added to the congregation.

42 All the believers in Jerusalem held steadfastly to the teachings of
the apostles and looked upon themselves as one united fellowship,
taking part in the rite of breaking bread and in congregational wor-
43 ship. A feeling of holy awe came over every soul because of the
many signs and wonders performed in Jerusalem by the apostles.

44 All those who had been converted kept loyally together and made
45 common property of everything they owned. Whoever had possessions or stores of provisions sold a part of them and made daily
distribution of the proceeds among the needy, giving to each enough
46 for the day's wants. All continued to worship daily in the temple;
but they also met for divine services in their homes and there cele-

47 brated the breaking of bread. They partook of this meal joyously
and whole-heartedly, praising God and offering prayers for all creation. And the Lord daily added to their fellowship such as were
seeking their salvation.

CHAPTER 3.

1 One day Peter and John went up to the temple. It was about
2 three hours after noon — the hour of prayer. A man who had been
lame from birth was just then being carried by, one who was laid
every day at the so-called "Beautiful Gate" to beg alms of the people
3 who went to the temple. Seeing Peter and John as they were about
4 to enter the temple, he appealed to them for alms. Peter and John
both turned their eyes upon him, and Peter said, "Look at us."
5 The man looked up at them expecting to receive a gift, but Peter
6 said, "Gold and silver I do not have, but what I do have I will give
7 you. In the name of Jesus of Nazareth, rise and walk." Then Peter
took him by the right hand and lifted him up, and the man at once
stood on his feet, for both feet and ankles had been made firm.
8 Full of joy, he began to walk to and fro, and went into the temple
9 with them and praised God. All the people saw how he walked
10 about praising God. They recognized in him the man who had sat
and begged for alms at the "Beautiful Gate" of the temple, and they
were lost in wonder and amazement at the change he had under-
11 gone. When Peter and John made ready to leave the temple, this
man also went out with them and kept close to their side. In what
12 was called the Hall of Solomon every one stood and stared. Then
Peter said to the onlookers, "Men of Israel, why does this astonish
you? Why do you look at us in such amazement, as though it were
13 our own power and piety that had enabled this man to walk? It is
the God of Abraham, of Isaac, and of Jacob, the God of our forefathers, Who by this deed has glorified His servant Jesus — the selfsame Jesus whom you delivered to be condemned, and against whose
release you protested before the tribunal of Pilate, even when Pilate
14 himself recommended it. It was you who withheld pardon from the
holy and righteous one and asked pardon for a murderer instead,
15 leaving the Prince of Life to be executed. But God has raised him
16 from the dead; to this we testify. And because this man before us
believed in the name of Jesus, that name has restored his physical
strength, as you yourselves can see and realize; and the faith inspired by Jesus has given back to him perfect health before your
17 very eyes. Now brothers, we know that you erred through ignorance,
18 as did your rulers. But in this way God brought about the fulfill-

ment of that which He proclaimed long ago through the mouths of
19 all the prophets, concerning the sufferings of His Messiah. Change
your hearts, then, and exert yourselves to the utmost to obtain for-
20 giveness for your sins of apostasy. Then there will come from the
Lord times of rest and refreshment, and He will send Jesus as the
21 Messiah, who has long been ready for you. It was necessary for
heaven to receive him until that age in which all things are restored
to God, as God Himself has proclaimed since the earliest times
22 through the mouths of His faithful messengers. Moses said to our
forefathers, 'The Lord your God will raise up for you a messenger
such as I am from among your brothers. You must heed everything
23 that he will say to you. And every living creature that refuses to
heed that messenger shall be completely exterminated from the
24 people.' Moreover, all the messengers of God, from Samuel on
through the ages that followed, have foretold the days in which we
25 now live. You are the descendants of these messengers of God and
the heirs to the covenant made by God with our forefathers, when
He said to Abraham, 'In one of your descendants all the races of the
26 earth shall be blessed.' You are the first among those on whose behalf God caused His servant to appear. You were to be the first to
be blessed by him, the first to be turned from the path of iniquity;
and so God sent him to you first of all."

CHAPTER 4.

1 While they were thus teaching the people, the priests and the
2 Sadducees came and opposed them, for they could not bear to hear
them address the people in such manner and speak of Jesus as hav-
3 ing risen from the dead. They therefore placed them under arrest,
and as it was late in the afternoon, they held them in custody until
4 the next morning. Many of those who had heard their sermon
nevertheless believed, and the number of Christian men grew to five
thousand.

5 On the following morning the leaders of the people, the elders,
6 and the scribes held a hearing in Jerusalem. The high priest Annas
joined them, as did Caiaphas, John, Alexander, and all those who
7 were reckoned among the high priest's family. They summoned the
apostles and asked them, "By what right and by whose authority
8 could men of your sort venture to do what you did?" At that
moment the power of a holy spirit came over Peter, and he answered,
9 "Leaders of the people and elders of Israel, we are being called
upon to-day to answer to you for a kindness that we showed to a
10 poor cripple. You ask us through whom he was cured. Let it be

proclaimed, then, before you and before all the people of Israel,
frankly and openly, that it is through the power of the name of Jesus
of Nazareth, the Messiah, that this man stands before you sound of
body. To be sure, you crucified this Jesus, but God brought him
11 back from the kingdom of the dead. He is the stone thrown aside
by you builders as useless, the stone that has now become the corner-
12 stone. No such name has been conferred upon any one else, nor has
there been appointed for us men any other name under heaven by
which we may find salvation."
13 When the Council saw how outspoken Peter and John were and
observed that both were simple, uneducated men, they were struck
with amazement. They knew that the two of them were disciples of
14 Jesus. Seeing the man who had been healed standing beside them,
15 they were at a loss what to do or answer next; and so they dismissed
the apostles from the hearing and deliberated among themselves.
16 "What shall we do with these men now?" they asked one another.
"The fact that a miracle has been publicly performed by them is
17 known to every one in Jerusalem. We cannot deny it then. But to
keep the story from spreading, let us forbid them under the severest
penalty even so much as to mention this name in conversation with
18 any one." This proposal met with general assent. They called the
apostles in and gave them strict orders not even to utter the name of
Jesus again, still less to preach about it.
19 But Peter and John answered, "Judge for yourselves whether it
would be right in the eyes of God for us to obey you rather than
20 God; for it is not in our power to give up speaking about the things
21 that we have seen and heard." At this they repeated the warning with
still more serious threats and dismissed them. They were unable to
find any lawful grounds for punishing them, and they were obliged
to consider the great mass of the people, who were going about
22 praising God for the cure that had resulted; for the man who had
been so miraculously healed was over forty years old.
23 After their release Peter and John went back to their congrega-
24 tion and related all that the chief priests and elders had said. Upon
hearing the story and recognizing in it the power of God, the members of the congregation raised their voices to God with one accord
and prayed, "O Lord our God, it is Thou Who hast created heaven
25 and earth and sea, and everything that is in them. Through the
mouth of Thy servant David Thou didst cause a holy spirit to say,
'Why do the unbelievers rage, and the peoples vainly conspire?
26 The kings of the earth rise up, and the rulers plot against the Lord
27 and against His Messiah.' Indeed, within this very city Herod and

Pontius Pilate joined with the unbelievers and with the tribes of
Israel against Thy holy servant Jesus, who was anointed by Thy
28 hand. They did to him everything that Thy hand had foreordained
29 as his destiny in Thy plan of salvation. And now, Lord, consider
their threats, and give Thy servants strength to preach Thy word
30 fearlessly. Stretch forth Thy hand to heal the sick, and grant that
signs and wonders may be performed by the name of Thy holy servant Jesus."

31 When they had prayed, the place where they were assembled was
shaken, and every one without exception was filled with a holy spirit
and boldly proclaimed the word of God to all who were ready to
receive the truth.

33 With mighty manifestations of divine power the apostles bore
witness to the resurrection of the lord Jesus Christ. Great joy had
come upon them all.

32 Many as there were who embraced the faith, they nevertheless
were of one heart and one soul. No distinctions existed among them,
and not one of them looked upon his possessions as his own, but
34 they held all their property in common. Hence there was not a
needy person among them. All who owned lands or houses sold a
35 part of them and put the proceeds at the disposal of the apostles,
36 who made distribution to every one according to his needs. Thus a
certain Joseph, surnamed by the apostles Barnabas (meaning "Son
37 of Consolation"), a Levite of Cyprus, sold a piece of land that he
owned and brought the money and put it at the disposal of the
apostles.

CHAPTER 5.

1 A man named Ananias, in agreement with his wife Sapphira,
2 also sold a piece of land, but he connived with his wife to keep back
a part of the proceeds. The rest of the money he took to the apostles
3 and put at their disposal. But Peter said, "Ananias, why did you
let Satan seduce you into deceiving the holy spirit-world and keep-
4 ing back part of the price of the land? Were you not free to keep
the land? And when you did sell it, could you not do as you chose
with the money? Why did you contrive this scheme? You have not
5 lied to men, but to God." Ananias had no sooner heard these words
than he fell down and expired; and all who heard of it were filled
6 with awe. The younger men at once wrapped his body up and carried it out and buried it.

7 Some three hours later, his wife came in, knowing nothing of
8 what had happened, and Peter asked her, "Tell me, is it true that

you sold the land for this price?" — "Yes," she answered, "that was
9 the price." Peter said to her, "Why did you both conspire to test the
spirit sent by the Lord? Look, the men who have buried your hus-
10 band are at the door, waiting to carry you out also." Then she too
fell down at his feet and died on the spot, and when the young men
returned and saw her body lying there, they carried it out and buried
11 it beside that of her husband. Great fear came over the whole congregation and over every one else who heard the story.

13 All of the faithful met by common consent in the Hall of Solomon, and although none of those of a different creed dared to
14 mingle with them, the people all held them in great esteem. Consequently men and women who learned to believe in the lord kept
joining the congregation in increasing numbers.

12 There were many signs and wonders performed by the hands of
15 the apostles among the people. The sick were carried out into the
streets and laid on beds and pallets, so that when Peter passed, at
least his shadow might fall upon each of them; for this in itself was
16 sufficient to cure any kind of disease one might have. Even from
the surrounding villages the people poured into Jerusalem, bringing with them their sick and those who were possessed by evil
spirits; and all were healed.

17 This aroused the jealousy of the high priest Annas and his whole
18 party, which consisted of the sect of the Sadducees. They ordered
the arrest of the apostles and put them in the state prison, and then
19 each of them went home, well satisfied. But during the night an
angel of the Lord opened the prison-doors, led the captives out, and
20 said, "Go out and show yourselves openly in the temple, and there,
in the presence of all the people, relate in detail everything that has
21 just happened to you." In obedience to his instructions they went
to the temple early in the morning and began to tell their story.
In the meantime the high priest had again assembled his followers.
They had risen very early and called together the High Council and
all of the elders of Israel, and then sent to the prison to have the
22 apostles brought before them. When the servants reached the prison
23 and opened the doors, they did not find the apostles there. They
came back and reported, "We found the prison securely locked and
the guards at the doors, but when we opened it there was no one
24 inside." When the leader of the temple and the chief priests heard
25 this news, they began conjecturing what could have happened. Then
a messenger arrived with the report, "The men whom you sent to
26 prison are now in the temple, addressing the people." The leader
of the temple now went with his men and brought the apostles back

by force, the others not daring to go for fear of being stoned by the
27 people. When they had been brought in and placed before the
28 Council, the high priest asked them, "Did we not expressly forbid
you to preach about this name? Yet you have gone and spread your
doctrine all over Jerusalem and are trying to make us responsible
29 for that man's death." Peter answered, "We owe obedience to God
30 rather than to men. The God of our fathers has raised Jesus, whom
31 you murdered by hanging him on the gallows. But God by the
strength of His right arm has exalted him to be a prince and a redeemer, in order to effect a change of heart among the people of
Israel and thereby make possible deliverance from the sins of apos-
32 tasy. These are facts to which we bear witness; and so too does the
holy spirit-world, which God has given to those who follow Jesus."
33 They were so enraged at these words that they resolved to put
34 them to death. But one of the members of the Council, the Pharisee
Gamaliel, a doctor of the Law who was highly respected by all the
people, rose and ordered the apostles to leave the council-chamber
35 for a short while. Then he addressed the leaders of the people and
the members of the Council in these words: "Men of Israel, consider
36 carefully what you are about to do to these men. A long time ago
a certain Theudas appeared, boasting that he was a man of importance, and he gained about four hundred followers. But he com-
37 mitted suicide and all his followers scattered. After him came Judas
of Galilee, at the time of the census, and attracted many people to
38 him, but he also perished and his followers dispersed. Therefore,
brothers, I advise you to have nothing to do with these men. Let
them alone, and do not soil your hands on them. For if their pro-
jects and accomplishments are the work of men, they will fall of
39 their own weight; but if they are the work of God, nothing that you
or any princes or tyrants can do will hinder them. So keep your
hands away from these men, lest in the end you be found among
those who even fight against God." The Council accepted his advice.
40 They called in the apostles and had them flogged, after which they
dismissed them with strict orders not to utter the name of Jesus
41 again. The apostles went out of the council-chamber, rejoicing that
they had been considered worthy of suffering indignities for the
42 sake of Jesus' name. Not for a single day did they cease to teach
the gospel of Jesus the Messiah, both in the temple and in private
houses.

CHAPTER 6.

1 During the time when the number of the faithful was increasing
in extraordinary measure, great dissatisfaction with the Hebrews

arose among the Greek-speaking members of the congregation. They
complained that the widows among the Greeks were neglected in the
daily distribution of necessities as often as this distribution was
2 made by the Jewish converts. The Twelve therefore called together
all of the faithful and said to them, "It is not proper for us to leave
off preaching the word of God and give our time to administering
3 charities. But in any case, brothers, it is better that you look for
seven trustworthy men among you, men filled with wisdom and a
4 holy spirit, and we will appoint them for this task. We ourselves
will be at the congregation's disposal for the holding of divine
services and will devote ourselves to preaching the word of God."
5 This suggestion found favor with the whole gathering, and they
chose Stephen, a man full of faith and the power of a holy spirit,
Philip, Prochorus, Nicanor, Timon, Parmenas, and Nicolas, the last
being a Gentile from Antioch who had been converted to Judaism.
6 These men now stood up before the apostles, who prayed and laid
their hands on them.

7 The word of the Lord spread constantly, and the number of the
faithful in Jerusalem increased remarkably. A great number of
priests were also won over to the faith.

8 Stephen, a man endowed with high gifts and divine power, performed great signs and miracles among the people by invoking the
9 name of the lord Jesus Christ. At length some of the members of
the synagogues among the Lybians, the Cyrenians, and the Alex-
andrians, as well as among the Cilicians and the Asians, rose in protest against Stephen and engaged him in disputes on religious ques-
10 tions; but they were unable to withstand his wisdom and the holy
spirit which spoke through him in order that his opponents might
11 be publicly refuted. Finding that they could no longer prevail
against the truth, they induced certain men to declare that they had
12 heard Stephen utter blasphemies against Moses and God. In this
way they stirred up the people as well as the elders and the scribes
against him, and they seized him and dragged him before the High
13 Council. They then produced false witnesses who declared, "This
14 man is constantly blaspheming the holy place and the Law. We
have heard him say, for instance, that Jesus of Nazareth will de-
15 stroy this place and change the laws that Moses gave us." In the
meantime all the members of the Council kept their eyes fixed on
Stephen, for they saw his face shine as though an angel were standing among them.

CHAPTER 7.

1 The high priest then asked Stephen, "Are these things actually
2 so?" Stephen answered, "Brothers and fathers, listen to me. The
God of glory appeared to our father Abraham while he was still
3 living in Mesopotamia, before he had settled in Haran, and said to
him, 'Leave your home and your relatives and go into the country
4 that I shall show you.' Then Abraham left the country of the Chal-
deans and made his home in Haran. After his father's death God
removed Abraham into the country that is now yours and that was
5 your fathers' before you. Yet God gave him no property in that
country, not a single foot, but promised to give it in ownership to
him and his descendants later on. God spoke of 'descendants,' even
6 though Abraham was as yet childless. These were God's words:
'Thy descendants shall live as strangers in a strange land, and there
7 they shall be enslaved and oppressed for four hundred years. But
as for the nation that holds them in bondage, I myself,' said God,
'will pass judgment on it. Then they shall leave that country and
8 serve Me in this place.' After that God prescribed for them the rite
of circumcision, in visible token of the Covenant. Then Isaac was
born, and Abraham circumcised him on the eighth day. Isaac became the father of Jacob, and Jacob the father of the twelve patri-
9 archs. Because they were jealous of Joseph, the patriarchs sold him
10 into Egypt; but God was with him and rescued him from all of his
hardships, giving him favor and wisdom in the sight of Pharaoh,
the king, who made him governor over Egypt and the royal house-
11 hold. Then famine and great distress came over the land of Egypt
and over Canaan as well, and our forefathers had nothing to eat.
12 But when Jacob heard that there was grain to be had in Egypt, he
13 sent our fathers into that country for the first time. On their second
visit Joseph made himself known to his brothers, and thus Pharaoh
14 learned of Joseph's parentage. Then Joseph had his father Jacob
and all his relatives, seventy-five souls in all, brought to Egypt.
15 So it came about that Jacob went to Egypt, where he died, and
16 where our fathers also died. Their remains were taken to Sychem
and laid in the tomb that Abraham had bought for a sum of money
from the sons of Hamor in Sychem.

17 "The nearer the time came that was specified in God's promise
to Abraham, the stronger and more numerous did the people be-
18 come in Egypt. At length there came to the throne of Egypt another
19 king who knew nothing about Joseph. This king dealt treach-
erously with our people and brought horrible calamities upon our

fathers, ordering their infants to be thrown into the water so that
20 there might be no further progeny. It was at this time that Moses
was born, a child of uncommon beauty in the eyes of God. For
21 three months he was cared for in his father's house; then his parents
were forced to set him adrift on the river, but the daughter of
22 Pharaoh saved him and brought him up as her own child. Thus
Moses was instructed in all the learning of the Egyptians, and grew
23 up to be a man forceful in word and deed. When he was forty years
24 of age he longed to visit his brothers, the children of Israel. He
saw one of them being grossly mistreated by an Egyptian and came
to his aid, avenging the abused man by killing the Egyptian, whose
25 body he buried in the sands. He assumed that his brothers would
now be convinced that it was by his hand that God intended to de-
26 liver them; but they did not understand. On the following day he
came upon two Hebrews quarrelling and abusing one another. He
tried to make peace between them, and asked, 'What are you doing,
27 brothers? Why are you abusing each other?' But the aggressor
pushed Moses aside and answered, 'Who has made you our ruler
28 and judge? Do you mean to kill me in the same manner that you
29 killed the Egyptian yesterday?' On hearing these words Moses fled.
He lived as an alien in the land of Midian, where two sons were born
30 to him. After another forty years there appeared to him in the
wilderness on Mount Sinai an angel of the Lord in the flame of a
31 thorn-bush. When Moses saw this he marvelled at the sight. As he
32 went up to look more closely, the Lord said to him, 'I am the God
of your fathers, the God of Abraham, Isaac, and Jacob.' Moses began to tremble and dared look no further; but once more the voice
33 of the Lord came to him, and he heard the words, 'Take the shoes
off your feet, for the place where you are standing is holy ground.
34 I have witnessed the distress of my people in Egypt and heard their
groans long enough, and so I have come down to set them free.
35 And now make ready, for I will send you to Egypt.' Thus the selfsame Moses whom his followers had repelled with the words, 'Who
has made you our ruler and judge?' was the man whom God sent
to rule over and deliver them, assisted by the very angel who had
36 appeared to him in the thorn-bush. This was also the angel who led
them out of Egypt and performed the signs and wonders in Egypt
37 and in the Red Sea, and for forty years in the wilderness. And this
Moses was the same Moses who said to the children of Israel, 'God
will raise up among you an envoy such as I am. Give heed to his
38 words.' It was the same Moses who at the general assembly in the
wilderness acted as mediator between the angel who had spoken to

him on Mount Sinai and our fathers; the same Moses who received
39 words of life to give us. But our fathers would not heed him; on
the contrary they thrust him aside, and in their hearts they longed
40 to return to Egypt. They said to Aaron, 'Make gods to lead the way
for us. As for this Moses who led us out of Egypt, we do not know
41 what has become of him.' And in those days they actually made
a calf for an idol and offered sacrifices to it, elated at their own
42 handiwork. Then God turned away from them and allowed them to
sink so low that they worshipped the spirit-hosts of the lowest
spheres. The book of the prophets alludes to this in the words,
'Have you ever offered Me slain beasts or other kinds of sacrifices
during your forty years in the wilderness, you of the house of
43 Israel? No, it was the tabernacle of Moloch and the star-symbol of
the god Rephan that you carried, the idols that you manufactured
to worship. Therefore I shall transport you to the heritage of Baby-
44 lon.' In the wilderness our fathers had the tent of revelation, as
prescribed by Him Who had commanded Moses to build it according
45 to the pattern that he had seen. This tent was carried by our fathers
under Joshua into the territory of the nations that God drove out
46 before them. So it was until the days of David, who found favor
before God and prayed that he might build a dwelling for the God
47 of Jacob. But it was not until the time of Solomon that the dwelling
48 was built. Nevertheless, the Most High does not dwell in structures
49 reared by the hands of men; for as the prophet says, '"Heaven is
my throne, and the earth is my footstool; what house could you
build for Me?" says the Lord; "or where would be My resting-
50 place? Did not My hand create the universe?"'

51 "Stiff-necked and uncircumcised in heart and ears that you are!
You are always resisting the holy spirit-world. Your fathers did so
52 before you, and you do the same. Was there ever a messenger of
God whom they did not persecute? Did they not even kill those
who foretold the coming of the Just One—that just one whose
53 betrayers and murderers you are? True, you looked upon the Law
as instructions from angels of God; but as for obeying it, that you
have never done."

54 At these words they gnashed their teeth at him in rage, but
55 Stephen, filled with the power of a holy spirit, looked steadfastly up
to heaven and beheld the glory of God and saw the lord Jesus stand-
56 ing at the right hand of God. Then he cried out, "I see heaven open-
57 ing, and the Son of man standing at God's right hand." They now
raised a loud outcry, held their ears, and rushed upon him like one
58 man; and they drove him out of the city and stoned him. The wit-

nesses laid down their cloaks at the feet of a young man whose name
59 was Saul. While they were stoning him, Stephen prayed aloud,
60 "Lord Jesus, receive my spirit!" Then he sank upon his knees and
cried out in a voice that carried far and wide, "Lord, do not reckon
this among their sins!" With these words he gave up his spirit.

CHAPTER 8.

1 Saul was fully in accord with Stephen's murder.
From this day there began a period of great persecution and distress for the congregation in Jerusalem, and all except the apostles
were scattered throughout the regions of Judaea and Samaria. The
2 apostles stayed in Jerusalem. Devout men buried Stephen and
lamented loudly over him.

3 As for Saul, he gave full vent to his rage against the congregation of the faithful, entering their homes one by one, dragging off
men and women, and sending them to prison.

4 Those who had dispersed went about the country and preached
5 the gospel. Thus Philip reached the capital of Samaria and preached
6 of the Messiah to its inhabitants. The people came together in great
numbers to hear him and listened to his words with one accord.
7 They also saw the miracles he performed, for amid loud cries unclean spirits came out of many of the possessed, and many of the
8 lame and the halt were healed. On this account there was great
rejoicing in the whole city.

9 There was a man named Simon living there who amazed the
people of Samaria with his sorceries. He assumed the air of a great
10 man, and every one, from the least to the greatest, ran after him,
asserting that he was what they called "the Great Power of God."
11 But he owed his influence over them solely to the fact that for some
12 time he had bewildered them with his sorceries. Now when Philip
preached to the people the gospel of the kingdom of God and the
name of Jesus the Messiah, they accepted his doctrine and received
13 baptism, both men and women. Simon himself was converted and
baptized, and became closely attached to Philip. When he saw
the great signs and wonders that were performed, he was lost in
amazement.

14 When the apostles in Jerusalem heard that the word of God had
15 been accepted in Samaria, they sent Peter and John there. These
two, after their arrival, prayed that the faithful in Samaria might
16 receive holy spirits; for as yet no holy spirit had descended upon
any of them. They had simply been baptized as believers in the

17 lord Jesus Christ. The apostles now laid their hands on them, and
every one of them received a holy spirit.
18 When Simon saw that the holy spirit was bestowed by the laying
on of the apostles' hands, he offered them money and begged them,
19 "Confer this power on me too, so that every one on whom I lay
20 my hands may receive a holy spirit." But Peter said to him, "Go
to destruction with your money—you who think that a gift of God
21 can be bought with money! You cannot lay any claim to this gift
of God or share it at all, for your heart is not upright in His eyes.
22 Change your heart first, and mend your evil ways and pray to the
Lord; perhaps then you will be forgiven for the evil inclinations of
23 your heart. For I see in you a bitter poison and the very essence of
24 evil." Simon answered, "I beg you, pray to the Lord for me yourselves, too, so that none of those failings with which you charge me
may be found in me any more." As he spoke he wept aloud and his
tears flowed without ceasing.

25 After the two apostles had testified to the word of the Lord and
preached in every quarter of the city, they set out for Jerusalem,
spreading the gospel in many Samaritan villages on their homeward
journey.

26 One day an angel of the Lord directed Philip, "Get up, and at
about the noon hour walk along the road that leads from Jerusalem
27 to Gaza. The road is a lonely one." Philip rose and went. Presently
he met an Ethiopian eunuch, who was a court-official and dignitary
of the Ethiopian queen Candace and had charge of her entire
treasure. He had gone to Jerusalem as an act of special worship of
28 God, and was now on his way home. He was sitting in his chariot,
29 reading in the book of the prophet Isaiah. The spirit said to Philip,
30 "Go nearer, and keep close to the chariot." Philip ran toward the
chariot, and hearing the eunuch reading aloud from the book of the
prophet Isaiah, he asked, "Do you understand what you are read-
31 ing?"—"How can I understand it," replied the eunuch, "when I
have no one to explain its meaning to me?" And he asked Philip to
32 get into the chariot and sit beside him. The passage of the Scriptures
which he had been reading was the following: "He was led to the
slaughter like a sheep, and as a lamb is dumb before its shearer, so
33 he does not open his mouth. By his self-abasement the previously
erected barrier has been removed; and who can now tell the number of his spiritual offspring? For his earthly life is at an end."—
34 "Please tell me," the eunuch implored Philip, "whom does the
35 prophet mean by these words? Himself, or some one else?" Philip
now undertook an explanation, beginning with this passage of the

36 Scriptures and proceeding to the gospel of Jesus. As they were
driving along the road conversing, they came to a place where there
was a body of water, and the eunuch said, "Look, here is water.
38 What is there to hinder my being baptized?" He ordered the
charioteer to stop, and both Philip and the court-official went down
39 into the water, and Philip baptized him by immersion. They had
scarcely come out of the water when a holy spirit descended upon
the eunuch. At the same moment, however, a spirit of the Lord
carried Philip away, and the eunuch saw nothing more of him. As
40 the eunuch went on his way rejoicing, Philip found himself in
Azotus. He travelled through this district, preaching the gospel in
every village, until he reached Caesarea.

CHAPTER 9.

1 In the meantime Saul, who in his rage against the disciples of the
lord was still threatening them with death, had gone to the high
2 priest and asked for letters of authority. These he intended to present to the Jewish congregations in Damascus in order that he might
bring to Jerusalem in chains any adherents of the new doctrine who
3 might be found there, whether men or women. As he was on the way
there and approaching the city of Damascus, a light from heaven
4 suddenly shone about him. He fell to the ground and heard a voice
5 calling to him, "Saul, Saul, why do you persecute me?" He asked,
"Who are you, lord?" and the voice answered, "I am Jesus, whom
6 you are persecuting. But get up now, and go to the city. There you
7 will be told what you are to do." His companions stood as though
8 petrified, for they heard the voice but saw no one. Saul rose to his
feet, but when he opened his eyes he could not see, and they had to
9 take him by the hand and lead him to Damascus. For three days he
was blind, and neither ate nor drank.

10 There lived in Damascus a disciple of Jesus named Ananias, who
was clairvoyant and clairaudient. The lord said to him, "Ananias!"
11 and he answered, "I am here, lord." — "Get up," said the lord, "and
go to the street called the Straight Street. There at the house of
Judas ask for a man from Tarsus named Saul. He is at prayer
12 just now, and sees in a vision a man called Ananias coming to him
13 and laying his hand on him to give him back his sight." Ananias
answered, "Lord, I have heard from many sides of the great harm
14 that this man has done to your believers in Jerusalem. Furthermore,
he has been authorized by the high priest to put in chains all those
15 who invoke your name here in this city, too." But the lord answered, "Go without any misgivings, for this man is the instrument

I have chosen to carry my name to the unbelievers and their rulers,
16 as well as to the children of Israel. I will show him how much he
17 must suffer for my sake." Ananias went and entered the house in
question. There he laid his hands upon Saul, saying, "Brother Saul,
the lord, Jesus, who appeared to you on your way here, has sent me
to you. You shall regain your sight and be filled with a holy spirit."
18 Instantly it was as though scales had fallen from Saul's eyes. Once
more he was able to see, and he stood up and received baptism.
19 He ate again and recovered his strength.

For several days he remained among the disciples in Damascus,
20 appearing in the synagogues and preaching that Jesus was the Son
21 of God. All those who heard him were amazed, and asked one another, "Is not that the same man who in Jerusalem furiously persecuted those who confess this name? And did he not come here for
22 the purpose of sending them to the high priest in chains?" But Saul
continued to speak with increasing forcefulness and utterly disconcerted the Jews of Damascus by proving to them that Jesus was the
23 Messiah. After a few days the Jews therefore resolved to put him
24 out of the way; but he learned of their plans, and as the Jews
watched even the city gates day and night in order to lay hands on
25 him, his friends lowered him from the city walls by night in a
26 basket. Thus he returned to Jerusalem. There he tried to join the
disciples, but they were all afraid of him, for no one would believe
27 that he had become a follower of Jesus. Barnabas, however, took
his part and brought him to the disciples, telling them how Saul
had seen the lord on his way to Damascus, and how the lord had
spoken to him; and further how in Damascus he had appeared in
28 public and openly preached in the name of Jesus. Thenceforth he
went freely in and out among them in Jerusalem, and fearlessly
29 preached as a follower of the lord. He also engaged in religious
controversies with the Greek-speaking Jews, and in discussions concerning questions of faith. The result was that they plotted to take
30 his life. When the brothers heard of this, they took him to Caesarea,
and from there sent him to Tarsus.

31 At last the congregations throughout Judaea, Galilee, and
Samaria enjoyed peace and quiet. They perfected themselves inwardly and walked in the fear of the Lord. With the aid of the holy
spirit-world they also made outward progress by increasing the
number of their members.

32 Peter travelled about from community to community, and among
33 others visited the faithful at Lydda. There he found a man named
Aeneas who had been bed-ridden for eight years, for he was com-

34 pletely paralyzed. Peter said to him, "Aeneas, Jesus Christ makes
you well. Get up, and make your bed yourself." At once Aeneas
35 rose to his feet. All the people of Lydda and Saron saw him walking about in good health, and consequently they became converted
to the lord.
36 In Joppa there lived a disciple named Tabitha, which means
"gazelle," a woman who did a great deal of good and gave alms
37 generously. At about this time she became sick and died, and
when her body had been washed, it was laid in an upper room.
38 Lydda was very near Joppa, and so the faithful sent two men there,
for they had heard that Peter was in Lydda. They brought him the
39 message, "Come over to us at once." Peter got up and went with
them, and when he arrived he was led into the upper room. All the
widows came to him in tears and showed him the cloaks and gar-
40 ments that Tabitha had made for them while she was living. Peter
now sent them all out of the room, and knelt down and prayed.
Then he turned to her and said, "Tabitha, rise in the name of our
lord Jesus Christ." She opened her eyes, and when she saw Peter
41 standing beside her, she sat up. Peter gave her his hand and bade
her rise. Then he oalled in the believers and the widows and placed
42 her before them alive. The news spread throughout Joppa like wild-
43 fire, and because of it, many came to believe in the lord. Peter
continued to live in Joppa for some time thereafter, lodging with
a tanner named Simon.

CHAPTER 10.

1 At that time there was living in Caesarea a man by the name of
2 Cornelius, a captain of the so-called Italian Cohort. He and all of
his household were devout and God-fearing, doing many acts of
3 kindness among the people and constantly praying to God. One day
about three hours after noon this man in a clairvoyant state dis-
tinctly saw an angel of the Lord coming toward him. The angel
4 said, "Cornelius." He stared at him and asked in alarm, "What is
it, lord?" The angel answered, "Your prayers and the news of your
good deeds have reached God and have been favorably received.
5 Send men to Joppa at once and have them bring here a certain Simon,
6 surnamed Peter. He lodges at the house of one Simon, a tanner,
7 which stands close to the sea." When the angel who had spoken to
him had gone, Cornelius called two of his servants and a God-
8 fearing soldier from among the men under his command, revealed
to them everything that had taken place, and sent them to Joppa.
9 At about noon on the following day while they were still on the

road and had nearly reached the town, Peter went up to the house-
10 top to pray. Growing hungry, he called for food, and while it was
being made ready he fell into that condition in which the spirit
11 leaves the body. He saw heaven open, and descending from it, a
vessel having the appearance of a large linen sheet being lowered
12 to the earth by cords tied to its four corners. It held all kinds of
four-footed and creeping animals of the earth and birds of the air.
13 Then there came a voice which said to him, "Stand up, Peter; kill
14 and eat." But he answered, "Lord, far be it from me! Never yet
15 have I eaten anything unholy or unclean." Then for a second time
the voice spoke, saying, "What God has cleansed you shall not call
16 unclean!" This was repeated three times; then the vessel was swiftly
drawn up into heaven again.

17 While Peter was still pondering on the meaning of what he had
seen, the men sent by Cornelius had found their way to Simon's
18 house and were now standing at the gate. Calling into the house,
19 they asked whether Simon, surnamed Peter, lived there. Meanwhile
Peter was still trying to unravel the meaning of the vision that he
had seen. And so the spirit said to him, "There are three men below
20 asking for you. Get up, then, and go downstairs, and do not hesi-
21 tate to go away with them, for it was I who sent them." Peter now
went down to the men and said, "I am the man for whom you are
looking. What do you want, and what is it that brings you here?"
22 They told him, "Cornelius the captain, a just, God-fearing man,
highly respected by the whole Jewish population, received a message from God through a holy angel, bidding him call you to his
23 house and hear whatever you have to say to him." Then Peter took
them into the house and saw that they were given food and lodging.
On the following day he set out with them, together with some of
24 the brothers from Joppa. The next day they reached Caesarea,
where Cornelius, together with all his relatives and several intimate
25 friends whom he had invited, was eagerly awaiting them. As Peter
approached Caesarea, one of the servants ran on ahead to announce
his coming, and Cornelius came forward to meet him, falling at his
26 feet and doing him homage. Peter raised him and said, "What are
27 you about? I am only a man like yourself." And so, conversing
with Cornelius, Peter entered the house, where he found a large
28 gathering. He began with the words, "You know that a Jew is forbidden to have dealings with or to visit the people of a Gentile race.
But God has shown me that no one may be called unholy or un-
29 clean, and so when you sent for me, I came without hesitation. And
now tell me, if you will, for what reason you asked me to come."

30 Cornelius answered him, "Three days ago to-day and at this very
time (that is, at about three hours after noon), I was at prayer in
my house when suddenly a man in radiant clothing stood before
31 me and said, 'Cornelius, your prayer has been heard, and God has
32 remembered your charity. Send at once to Joppa, and ask Simon,
surnamed Peter, to come to you. He is lodging with a tanner named
Simon whose house stands near the sea. As soon as he comes here
33 he will tell you what more there is to be told.' I therefore sent to
you immediately and asked you to come to us, and you have been
good enough to do so without delay. And now all of us have met
here to learn from you what God has commanded you to tell us."
34 "Truly," began Peter, "I see now that God is no respecter of
35 persons, but that men of every nation who fear Him and do what
36 is right are acceptable to Him. This truth was revealed by God to
the children of Israel when He sent them the joyful news of peace
37 by Jesus Christ; for he is the lord of all. You have all heard of the
things that took place in Judaea, beginning in Galilee with the bap-
38 tism preached by John. You have heard of Jesus of Nazareth, whom
God anointed with a holy spirit and with power; how he came, a
benefactor to mankind, and healed all those who were in Satan's
39 power, for God was with him. And we can testify to all the deeds
that he did in the country of the Jews and in Jerusalem. They
hanged him on the beam of the cross, and so put him out of the
40 way. But God raised him from the realm of the dead on the third
41 day, and allowed him to make himself visible, not, it is true, to all
the people, but to us, whom God had chosen as witnesses. We ate
and drank with him after he had come back from the kingdom of the
42 dead, and for forty days we were in communication with him. Then
he charged us to proclaim to the people and to testify that it is he
who was ordained by God as the judge of the living and of the spir-
43 itually dead. All the messengers of God bear witness that it is he
through whose name every one who believes in him is released from
the sin of apostasy."
44 As Peter uttered these last words, holy spirits came upon all his
45 hearers. His companions, Jewish believers in Christ, were greatly
astonished to see holy spirits bestowed as a divine gift even upon
46 Gentiles; for they heard them speaking in foreign languages and
47 praising God. But Peter said to them, "Who would dare to take it
upon himself to deny these men baptism, seeing that they have al-
48 ready received a holy spirit in the same way as we did?" He therefore arranged for them to be baptized as followers of Jesus Christ.
They on their part begged him to remain with them a few days
longer.

CHAPTER 11.

1 The apostles and the brothers living in Judaea had heard that
2 even the Gentiles had accepted the word of God, and when Peter
3 came back to Jerusalem they took him to task on that account, "We
hear that you went into the homes of the uncircumcised," they said,
4 "and ate with them." In reply, Peter recounted to them step by step
5 what had taken place. "I was in the town of Joppa," he told them,
"and while I was at prayer, my spirit left my body, and this was
the vision that I saw: a vessel, coming down from above, like a large
sheet of linen being lowered from heaven by its four corners. It was
6 very close to me. I fixed my eyes upon it, and looking carefully,
saw that it held four-footed and creeping beasts, and birds of the
7 air. At the same moment I heard a voice calling to me, 'Stand up,
8 Peter. Kill and eat!' I answered, 'Lord, far be it from me, for never
9 yet has anything common or unclean entered my mouth.' The voice
from heaven then sounded once more and said, 'What God has de-
10 clared clean, you shall not call unclean.' This was repeated three
11 times. Then the whole thing was drawn up into heaven again. At
that very moment there were standing before the house in which I
12 lived three men who had been sent to me from Caesarea. The spirit
now commanded me to accompany them without any hesitation.
These six brothers whom you see here also went with me, and thus
we arrived at the house of the man who had sent the messengers.
13 He told us that he had seen an angel standing before him in his
house and had heard the angel say, 'Send people to Joppa, and have
14 Simon, surnamed Peter, brought to you; from him you will hear
15 words by which you and all your household will be saved.' Scarcely
had I begun to speak there, when holy spirits came upon those men
16 in the same manner as they have also come upon us. Then I remembered the words of the lord when he said, 'John in his baptism immersed you in waves of water, but you shall be immersed in the
17 power-waves of a holy spirit.' Now inasmuch as God bestowed on
those men the same gifts of grace that He bestowed on us when we
first believed in the lord Jesus Christ, who was I to hinder God from
sending holy spirits upon men who put their full faith in Him?"
18 When they heard this they were appeased, and praised God, saying
to one another, "Then God has actually granted even the Gentiles
the grace of changing their hearts, so that they may obtain spiritual
life."

19 When the faithful were scattered in every direction at the time
of the persecution that followed the public appearance of Stephen,

they made their way as far as Phoenecia, Cyprus, and Antioch. As
20 a rule they spoke of the gospel to none but Jews, but among them
were several men from Cyprus and Cyrene, and these, after they
came to Antioch, made mention of the matter to the Greek Gentiles
21 and preached the gospel of the lord Jesus Christ to them. The
power of the Lord was in these men, and a large number of people
22 came to believe, and were converted to the lord. News of this
reached the congregation in Jerusalem, and they commissioned
23 Barnabas to go to Antioch. He went, and when he saw the great
grace of God with his own eyes, he was filled with joy and exhorted
all to remain faithful to the lord with all the devotion of their
24 hearts; for he was a good man, entirely under the guidance of a
holy spirit, and his heart was full of faith and trust in the Lord.
25 Thus a considerable number of new converts were won for the lord.

26 Hearing that Saul was in Tarsus, Barnabas went in search of him.
He found him there and asked him to go with him to Antioch. In
this city they spent a whole year working together with the congregation, and introduced the doctrine of Christ to a considerable number of people. It was also in Antioch that the followers of Christ's
doctrine were first called "Christians."

27 At about this time mediums of the good spirit-world came to
28 Antioch from Jerusalem, to the great joy of the congregation. One
of these mediums, Agapus, spoke at a divine service, and the spirit
controlling him predicted that a great famine would come upon the
whole population of the earth. This famine did in fact occur during
29 the reign of Claudius. The faithful therefore resolved that every one
of them, so far as his means permitted, would contribute to the
30 support of the brothers living in Judaea. This they carried out, and
the funds so collected they sent by Barnabas and Saul to the elders
of the congregation in Jerusalem.

CHAPTER 12.

1 In those days King Herod ordered some of the Christians of
Judaea to be arrested in order that he might vent his hatred upon
2 them. James, the brother of John, he ordered put to death with the
3 sword. When he saw that his manner of dealing with the Christians
pleased the Jews, he proceeded to lay hands on Peter also. This he
4 did during the feast of unleavened bread. He had Peter put in chains
and thrown into prison, and then gave orders for four squads of
soldiers, of four men each, to guard him, intending to bring him to
5 trial before the people after the Easter festival. Peter was therefore

kept under close watch while he was in prison; but the congregation
prayed often and fervently to God for his release.
6 On the night before the trial that Herod intended to hold in the
presence of the people, Peter lay sleeping between two soldiers. He
was bound with two chains, and two men stood guard at the door
7 of his cell. Suddenly an angel of the Lord stood beside Peter, and
the room was filled with a bright light. The angel touched him on
the side, and aroused him, saying, "Get up quickly!" In an instant
8 the chains fell from Peter's wrists, and the angel continued, "Gird
yourself and put on your shoes." Peter did so, and the angel said,
9 "Put on your cloak and follow me." Peter went out of the cell after
the angel, not knowing that what had taken place was actual fact,
10 but believing it to be merely a dream. They walked past the first
guard and the second, and came to the iron gate that led out of
doors. This opened of its own accord, and they stepped outside and
went as far as the next street. Then the angel suddenly vanished
11 from Peter's side. Coming to himself, Peter exclaimed, "Now I
know for certain the Lord has sent His angel and rescued me from
the hand of Herod, and so put an end to the expectation of the
12 Jewish people." Having fully recovered himself, he went to the
home of Mary, the mother of John surnamed Mark, where a large
13 number of people had met for worship. When Peter knocked at the
14 door in the entry, a maid named Rhoda came to answer it, and recognizing his voice, was so overcome with joy that she did not immediately unlock the door but ran back into the house to say that Peter
was standing outside. Some of them replied, "You have lost your
15 wits." And when she insisted that it was Peter, others said, "It may
16 be his angel." Meanwhile Peter continued to knock, and when they
finally opened the door and saw him with their own eyes, they were
17 dumbfounded. He motioned to them with his hand to keep quiet,
and then he went into the house and told them how the Lord had
released him from prison. He asked them to repeat the story to
James and to the other brothers. Then he left the house and went to
another place.

18 When day broke there was great consternation among the sol-
19 diers, for they could not explain Peter's disappearance. Herod had
already sent for him, and when Peter could not be found, he held
an examination of the guards and ordered them to be put to death.
Then he left Judaea for Caesarea and took up his residence there.
20 At that time he was very much embittered against the people of
Tyre and Sidon. They now resolved to send delegates from both
cities to him, and these actually appeared before the king. They

had won over Blastus, the king's chamberlain, and through him con-
trived to make peace; for their cities depended upon the king's
21 dominions for their supplies. On an appointed day Herod donned
his royal robes, seated himself on his throne, and delivered a public
22 address. When he stated that he no longer felt any ill-will toward
the Tyrians and the Sidonians, his hearers shouted applause and
23 cried out, "These are the words of a god, not a man!" At that very
instant an angel of the Lord struck him because he had not given
the honor to God. He stepped down from the throne, and was eaten
alive by worms, so that he died.
24 The word of the Lord steadily gained ground and spread every-
25 where. Barnabas and Saul, who now went by the name of Paul,
fulfilled their task in Jerusalem and went back to Antioch, taking
with them John, whose surname was Mark.

CHAPTER 13.

1 In the congregation at Antioch there were some who were trance-
mediums and others who had the gift of teaching. Among them
were Barnabas and Simeon, surnamed Niger; also Lucius of Cyrene,
Manaes, who had been brought up with Herod the tetrarch, and
2 Saul. One day while they were holding divine service and fasting,
a holy spirit commanded them, "Set aside Barnabas and Saul for
3 the task to which I have called them." After they had fasted and
prayed, they laid their hands on these two.
4 When they had thus been ordained by a holy spirit, they went
down to Seleucia, and from there across the sea to the island of
5 Cyprus. On their arrival in Salamis they proclaimed the word of
the Lord in the synagogues of the Jews, John being with them as
6 their assistant. Thus they travelled over the whole island and came
to Paphos, where there was a Jewish sorcerer named Barjesus, a
7 medium of the evil spirit-world. He had frequent dealings with the
deputy Sergius Paulus, who was a very high-minded man. The
deputy called Barnabas and Saul to him, and requested to hear from
8 them the word of God. The sorcerer Elymas — for so his name is
translated — opposed them and tried to dissuade the deputy from
adopting the faith, although he had heard nothing but good of the
9 men who preached it. Saul, who was also known as Paul, gave him
10 a piercing look, and inspired by a holy spirit, said to him, "You
son of the devil! You enemy of everything good! You who are full
of trickery and deceit! Will you never stop leading men away from
11 the straight path of the Lord? Now, at this very moment, the hand
of the Lord is falling upon you. You shall be blind and for a cer-

tain time see the light of day no more." At once deepest darkness
fell upon the sorcerer's eyes and he groped about for some one to
12 take him by the hand and lead him. When the deputy saw what had
taken place he was amazed, and became a believer; he was pro-
foundly impressed by the power that lay in the doctrine of the Lord.
13 From Paphos Paul and his companions again put to sea and
reached Perga in Pamphylia. Here John left them and went back to
14 Jerusalem. The others went on from Perga to Antioch in Pisidia,
where they entered the synagogue on the Sabbath, and took their
15 seats among the congregation. After the reading of the Law and the
Prophets, the leaders of the synagogue turned to them and said,
"Brothers, if you feel that you have anything of religious interest to
16 lay before the people, you may speak." Then Paul stood up, and
indicated by a gesture that he wished to speak. "Men of Israel," he
17 began, "and all others who fear God, listen to me. The God of our
people Israel chose our forefathers and exalted them before the
people of Egypt where they lived as strangers, until by the might
18 of His uplifted arm He led them out of that country. For forty
19 years He sustained them in the wilderness. He destroyed seven
nations in the country of Canaan, and gave their land to our fathers
20 for their own. All this covered a period of about four hundred and
fifty years. After that He gave them judges as rulers, until the time
21 of the prophet Samuel. From then on they wished to have a king,
and God gave them Saul, the son of Kish, a man of the tribe of
22 Benjamin, who ruled over them for forty years. After Saul had been
dethroned, God raised David to be their king, testifying in regard
to him, 'In David, the son of Jesse, I have found a man after My
23 own heart, who will carry out My will in all things.' From this
man's seed, God, true to His promise, raised a redeemer for Israel.
24 This redeemer is Jesus. His coming had been foretold by John who,
before the public appearance of Jesus, had preached baptism by
water for all Israel. This baptism was to be the outward sign of an
25 inner change of heart. Shortly before the end of his earthly life,
John declared, 'I am not he whom you believe me to be. But after
26 me will come One whose sandals I am not worthy to untie.' Brothers,
sons of Abraham's race, and all you others who fear God, it is to
27 us that the message of this redemption has been sent. But the people
of Jerusalem and their spiritual advisers did not understand the
writings of the prophets which are read on every Sabbath; nevertheless, by condemning the redeemer to death, they contributed
28 toward the fulfillment of those writings. For although they found
that he had committed no offence deserving death, they declared

29 him guilty and delivered him to Pilate for execution. Having thus
fulfilled everything that was written of him, they demanded of Pilate
30 that he be put to death on the cross. As a favor, Pilate permitted
his body to be taken down from the cross and laid in a tomb. But
31 God raised him from the realm of the dead. For many days he was
seen by those who had come to Jerusalem with him from Galilee,
and all of them are now coming forward to bear witness for him to
32 the people. And we also proclaim to you that the glad news God
33 gave to our fathers in their time has now been realized for us, their
children, by the resurrection of our lord Jesus Christ. Indeed it is
written in the second Psalm: 'You are my son; to-day I have begotten you. Ask of Me, and I will give you the nations for your
inheritance and the uttermost parts of the earth for your possession.'
34 And as for God's raising him on high from the spiritually dead,
never again to return to that realm of corruption, this He expressed
in these words: 'I will give you the holiness of David, and his
35 fidelity'; and elsewhere: 'Thou wilt not suffer Thy Holy One to see
36 corruption.' Now David, during his allotted time on earth, served
God's purpose, and then fell asleep and was laid to rest with his
37 fathers. He therefore saw corruption. But the One whom God raised
38 again did not see corruption. So understand, dear brothers, that
through him you are promised release from the sins of apostasy as
soon as you change your inner attitude; sins from which the observance of the Law of Moses could not absolve you and thereby
39 restore you to favor in the eyes of God. But through him every one
40 who believes will find favor with God. See to it, then, that the
41 words of the prophet do not prove true in your case: 'Look, you
scoffers, and die of astonishment, for in your days I shall perform
a work which you will not believe, even though some one were to
explain it to you.'"

42 All of his hearers were silent. As they left the synagogue the
people begged the disciples to speak to them again of these things on
43 the coming Sabbath. When the congregation had dispersed, many
Jews and also many Gentiles who wished to embrace the Jewish
faith, followed Paul and Barnabas. Both spoke to them at greater
length and urged them to remain steadfast in the grace of God. In
this way the word of God was carried everywhere through the town,
44 and hence on the following Sabbath nearly all of the people attended the synagogue and listened to Paul deliver a long sermon
45 about the lord. When the leading Jews saw the great crowds, they
were jealous and contradicted what Paul said; but their arguments
46 consisted mainly of abuse and invective. Then Paul and Barnabas

spoke out boldly and said, "It was to you Jews that the word of God
had to be carried first of all. But since you will have none of it and
thereby pronounce yourselves unworthy of the life hereafter, we now
47 turn to the Gentiles. For these are the orders that the Lord gave us:
'I have made you a light for the Gentiles, so that you may be a
48 means of salvation to the very ends of the earth.'" When the Gentiles heard this they joyfully accepted the word of the Lord, and
49 all who were ready to attain the life hereafter, believed. Thus the
word of the Lord was spread throughout this whole region.
50 The Jews, however, stirred up the most distinguished and highly
esteemed women as well as the leading men of the town, and brought
about such a severe persecution against Paul and Barnabas that they
51 were driven out of this district. Shaking the dust from their feet
to brand their adversaries as refractory, they made their way to
52 Iconium. The hearts of the disciples were full of joy, and they felt
within them the power of a holy spirit.

CHAPTER 14.

1 In Iconium they went straight to the Jewish synagogue and spoke
2 so convincingly that many Jews and Greeks were converted. The
Jewish elders and the authorities of the synagogues instigated the
persecution of those who had adopted the faith, and also stirred up
3 the ill-will of the Gentiles against the brothers. But the Lord soon
granted them a return of peace and quiet. Thus they were able to
remain there for a long time and to speak freely, putting their trust
in the Lord. He Himself bore witness to the grace-bestowing word
of the truth by allowing signs and wonders to be performed by their
4 hands. Then dissension arose among the people of the town, some
taking sides with the Jews, others with the apostles, to whom they
5 were loyally devoted because of the word of God. So it came about
that the Gentiles and the Jews, with the connivance of the author-
6 ities, plotted to fall upon the apostles and stone them. But when the
apostles heard of it, they fled to Lystra and Derbe, towns of Lyca-
7 onia, and into the surrounding districts. There they continued to
preach, and all of the people were deeply impressed with their doc-
8 trine. Paul and Barnabas had taken lodgings in Lystra, where there
lived a man whose legs were powerless and who had been lame from
9 birth and had never been able to walk. This man heard Paul speak,
and his heart was filled with awe. Paul felt that his gaze was being
drawn to this man again and again, and at the same time he could
10 read his thoughts and see that he had faith enough to be cured. And
so he called to him loudly, "In the name of the lord Jesus Christ,

stand erect on your feet and walk about." And the man rose to his
11 feet and walked. When the people saw what Paul had done they
cried out in the Lycaonian tongue, "The gods have come down to us
12 in human form!" Barnabas they called Jupiter, and Paul Mercury,
13 because he was the chief speaker. The priests of Jupiter, who was
the patron god of the city, led garlanded oxen before the gates and
together with the people were about to offer sacrifices to the apos-
14 tles. When Paul and Barnabas heard of it they tore their clothes
15 and ran among the people crying, "Men, what are you about? We
too are only men, with the same human frailties as you. The very
purpose of the gospel that we preach is to turn you from such follies
to the living God, the God who made heaven and earth and the sea
16 and everything in them. In times gone by He let all heathens go
17 their own way, although even then in His goodness He gave proof
of His existence, sending His rain from heaven and fruitful years,
giving food in abundance, and filling your hearts with gladness."
18 Yet for all their protests it was with great difficulty that the apostles
induced the people to desist from offering sacrifices to them and go
quietly to their homes. For some time longer they stayed there and
preached to them.

19 Later certain Jews came from Iconium and Antioch and by publicly haranguing the people persuaded them to turn against the
apostles, in whose preaching they said there was not a word of truth,
nothing but lies. The result was that the people stoned Paul, and
20 thinking that he was dead, dragged him out of the town. But while
the disciples were still gathered about him, he rose and went back
into the town with them, and on the following day he and Barnabas
21 went on to Derbe. There they preached and made many converts,
22 afterwards returning to Lystra, Iconium, and Antioch. In each place
that they visited they encouraged the believers and exhorted them to
remain true to the faith. "It is necessary for all of us," they said,
"to suffer much tribulation before we can enter the kingdom of
23 God." By the laying on of hands they ordained the elders in every
congregation, after which they held a day of fasting, ending with
divine service. Then they commended the faithful to the Lord to
24 whom they had clung so loyally. After this they travelled the length
25 of Pisidia and came to Pamphylia. In Perga they preached the word
of the Lord, and from there they went down into Attalia, preaching
26 to its inhabitants also. From there they sailed back to Antioch,
where they had first been endowed with the grace of God for the
27 work which they had now accomplished. Upon their arrival they
called together the members of the congregation and reported to

them everything that God had done through them as His instruments, and how He had opened the door of faith to the Gentiles also.
28 In this congregation of the faithful they remained a long time.

CHAPTER 15.

1 One day some converted Jews arrived from Judaea and undertook to teach the brothers that unless they were circumcised as
2 Moses had prescribed, they could not be saved. This created a great
disturbance in the congregation, and Paul and Barnabas, together
with their followers, had no little controversy with the new-comers;
for when Paul addressed the congregation, he tried to persuade
them to remain steadfast in the faith which they had previously
held. But the men who had come from Jerusalem advised them to
send some of their members, together with Paul and Barnabas, to
the apostles and elders in Jerusalem, and to let them decide the
3 question. Accordingly they sent a delegation which went by way of
Phoenecia and Samaria, where they told of the conversion of the
Gentiles and thereby aroused great joy among all the brothers.
4 When Paul and Barnabas reached Jerusalem they were received
with great honor by the Christian congregation and by the apostles
and elders, to whom they related everything that God had done
5 through them. Then the men who had challenged them to go to the
elders in Jerusalem got up and opposed them, for several of them
had belonged to the sect of the Pharisees before they had been converted. These men now insisted that every convert should be required to be circumcised and to observe the Law of Moses in all
6 respects. The apostles and the elders met to consider this matter,
7 and after they had discussed it at length, Peter, inspired by a holy
spirit, rose and said, "My dear brothers, you know that a long while
ago the lord chose me from among you as the one from whose lips
the Gentiles were to hear those things which the gospel proclaims
8 as true, and which must therefore be believed. And God, Who
knows our hearts, Himself appeared as a witness for the Gentiles by
giving them the holy spirit-world in the same manner as He gave
9 it to us. He made no distinction between us and them, after their
10 hearts had been purified by the faith. Then why do you now try
to test God and lay upon the necks of the faithful a yoke that neither
11 our fathers nor we were able to bear? It is rather through the grace
of the lord Jesus Christ alone that we come to the faith, finding sal-
12 vation in the same way as they did." Since even the elders accepted
Peter's arguments, the whole assembly held its peace and listened as
Barnabas and Paul told of the signs and wonders that God had

13 worked through them among the Gentiles. When they had finished,
James rose and said to the meeting, "My dear brothers, listen to me.
14 Simon has told us how God Himself was the first to consider taking
15 a people from among the Gentiles to bear His name. This is in
16 agreement with the words of the prophet, for it is written: 'After
this I will return and raise up David's fallen tent. I will rebuild its
17 ruins and cause it to rise anew, so that the rest of mankind may
seek the Lord; likewise all the Gentiles who belong to me as my
18 own people. Thus says the Lord who performs these things. His
19 work is known to the Lord from the beginning.' It is therefore my
opinion that no further burdens should be placed upon those who
20 are converted to God from among the heathens; but we should
write to them to say that they must not pollute themselves by worshipping idols, by unchaste living, or by partaking of blood, and
that they must live according to the motto, 'Do not do to others that
21 which you would not have them do to you.' For ever since the days
of old, Moses has had his preachers in every locality and his writings are read in the synagogues every Sabbath."

22 Then the apostles and the elders, with the assent of the whole
congregation, resolved to choose men from their number and send
them with Paul and Barnabas to Antioch. Those whom they selected
were Judas, surnamed Barsabas, and Silas, both of them leading
men among the brothers. They were to deliver a letter which ran
23 as follows: "We, the apostles and elders, send brotherly greetings
24 to our Gentile brothers of Antioch, Syria, and Cilicia. We have
heard that some of our own number have gone to you and confused
you by their speeches and caused you anxiety. They acted without
25 our authority. Therefore we have unanimously decided to select men
and send them to you. They are coming with your beloved brothers
26 Barnabas and Paul, both of whom have exposed their lives to every
27 danger on behalf of the name of our lord Jesus Christ. We have
sent with them Judas and Silas to bring you our decision by word
28 of mouth. For the holy spirit-world has inspired us with the resolve
to lay upon you no burdens other than the following, which are
29 essential: Abstain from meat offered to idols, from blood, and from
unchastity, and live according to the motto, 'Do not do to others
that which you would not have them do to you.' If you faithfully
observe these rules, all will be well with you and you will have a
holy spirit as your guide. Farewell."

30 A few days later they took their departure, and upon reaching
Antioch, called together the congregation and delivered their letter.
31 When the members read the letter they rejoiced at the encourage-

32 ment it contained. Judas and Silas, who were both mediums, in
fact fully developed instruments of the holy spirit-world, gave the
brothers much consolation and strength with their frequent ad-
33 dresses. For some time they remained in Antioch; then, amid the
fond farewells of the brothers, they took their leave in order to
34 return to those who had sent them. At the last moment, however,
Silas decided to prolong his stay, and Judas went back to Jeru-
35 salem alone. Paul and Barnabas also stayed in Antioch, teaching
and preaching with the assistance of many others.
36 Some time later Paul said to Barnabas, "Let us set out again and
visit every place where we have preached the word of the Lord to
37 see how the brothers there are getting along." Barnabas wanted to
38 take with them John whose surname was Mark; but Paul maintained
that a man who had deserted them in Pamphylia and declined to
go with them into the harvest field of God to which they had been
39 sent, ought not to be taken now. This led to such a sharp dispute
between them that they separated, and Barnabas set sail for Cyprus,
40 accompanied by Mark. Paul chose Silas for his companion and
went off with him, having received the blessings of the brothers,
41 who commended them to the grace of the Lord. They went through
Syria and Cilicia, encouraging the congregations in their faith and
delivering the messages of the elders.

CHAPTER 16.

1 On his travels among the Gentiles of these regions, Paul came to
Derbe and Lystra. Here he found a disciple named Timotheus,
whose mother was a converted Jewess and whose father was a Greek.
2 He had been highly spoken of by the brothers in Lystra and Iconium,
3 and Paul therefore wished to take him as a companion on his travels.
But in deference to the Jews who lived in that district, he first circumcised Timotheus; for it was generally known that his father was
4 a Greek. As they passed through the villages they preached to the
inhabitants and spoke openly of the lord Jesus Christ; at the same
time they communicated the decrees enacted by the apostles and
5 elders in Jerusalem. In this way the congregations grew in strength
and increased daily in the number of their members.
6 While they were travelling through Phrygia and Dalmatia a
holy spirit prevented them from speaking of the word of God to
7 any one in this part of Asia. At length they arrived at the borders
of Mysia and tried to go into Bithynia, but the spirit of Jesus would
8 not permit them, and so, passing through Mysia, they came to Troas.
9 Here there appeared to Paul one night while he was in a state of

clairvoyance, a figure resembling a Macedonian, who stood before
10 him and entreated, "Come over into Macedonia and help us." When
the vision had disappeared, Paul told us of what he had seen by
clairvoyance, and it was our belief that the Lord had called us in
this way to preach the gospel to the people of Macedonia.

11 On the following morning we set sail from Troas and went
12 straight to Samothrace; thence on the next day to Neapolis, and
from there to Philippi, which is the capital of Macedonia and a
13 Roman colony. Here we halted for several days. On the Sabbath
we went outside the gate to the bank of a river, where there appeared to be a place devoted to prayer, and we sat down and con-
14 versed with the women who were gathered there. Among them was
a God-fearing woman named Lydia, a dealer in purple, from the
town of Thyatira. She listened to us attentively, and the Lord
opened her heart so that she accepted the doctrine that Paul ex-
15 pounded. After she had been baptized together with her whole household, she begged us, "If you are convinced that I am a faithful follower of the Lord, come to my house and make it your home." And
she urged us to comply with her request.

16 One day as we were on our way to the same place of worship, we
met a slave-girl through whom a spirit gifted with the power of
divination spoke, and who in this way earned much money for her
17 employers. She followed Paul and us, and cried, "These men are
servants of the Most High, and they are showing you the way to
18 salvation." This she did for many days. At length Paul, full of
annoyance at the spirit that was speaking through her, turned and
said, "In the name of Jesus Christ I command you to come out of
19 her!" And the spirit left her immediately. When the girl's employers saw that the source of income which they had possessed in her
was destroyed, they seized Paul and Silas and dragged them before
20 the city authorities in the market-place, and from there to the magistrates. Here they made the following accusation: "These men are
21 disturbing the peace of the city. They are Jews, and they are teaching customs which we, as Romans, can neither accept nor observe."
22 A large crowd also took sides with them and raised a loud outcry
against the accused. The magistrates ordered them to be stripped
23 and flogged, and they were given many lashes and thrown into
prison. The jailer was instructed to keep them securely guarded,
24 and mindful of his orders, he put them in the innermost part of the
prison and fastened their feet in the stocks.

25 At midnight Paul and Silas were praying and giving praise to
26 God, and their fellow-prisoners were listening attentively, when a

violent earthquake suddenly shook the foundations of the prison.
All the doors burst open, and the chains of all the prisoners were
27 unfastened. The jailer was aroused from his sleep and came at
once. When he saw the doors wide open, he thought that the prisoners had escaped. At this he drew his sword and was about to kill
28 himself, but Paul called to him as loudly as he could, "Do not harm
29 yourself! We are all here!" The jailer called for a light, rushed
into the cell of Paul and Silas, and fell trembling at their feet.
30 Then, after he had secured the other prisoners, he led Paul and
Silas out and turned to them with the question, "Sirs, what must I
31 do to be saved?" They answered, "Believe in the lord Jesus Christ,
32 and you and all of your household will find salvation." They now
33 proclaimed the word of God to him and to his household, and at
that very hour of the night he took them with him and washed their
bruises, and he and his whole household were baptized immediately.
34 Then he took them to his home, set a meal before them, and together
with all of his household rejoiced at having gained faith in God.
35 At daybreak the magistrates met in the market-place to discuss the
earthquake. Fear was written in every face. They sent court-officers
to the prison with instructions to tell the jailer, "Release the men
36 who were committed to your care yesterday." And so the jailer
went to Paul and said to him, "The magistrates have given us
orders to release you. Leave the prison now and go your way in
37 peace." But Paul replied to the officers, "They ordered us to be
flogged in public and thrown into prison without hearing or process
of law, although we are innocent, and Roman citizens. Do they
think now that they are going to get rid of us secretly? By no
38 means! Let them come here themselves and take us out!" The
officers delivered this answer to the magistrates, who became alarmed
39 when they heard that the prisoners were Roman citizens. Accompanied by many friends, they now came to the prison and begged the
two prisoners to leave, excusing themselves by saying, "We did not
realize how matters stood, and we did not know that you were men
of blameless character." Then they led the two prisoners out, but
begged them, "Leave the city. Otherwise the mob may again gather
40 and trump up charges against you before us magistrates." Paul and
Silas therefore left the prison and went to the house of Lydia. Then
they visited the brothers and told them of all the favors the Lord
had shown them, and after giving them some words of encouragement, they left the city.

CHAPTER 17.

1 Going by way of Amphipolis and Appolonia they reached Thessa-
2 lonica, where there was a Jewish synagogue. Paul, as usual, went in,
and on three consecutive Sabbaths expounded his doctrine to the
3 worshippers with the aid of the Scriptures. He quoted various passages by which he proved that it was foreordained that the Messiah
should suffer and be raised from the dead. "This Jesus of whom I
4 am preaching to you," he concluded, "is the Messiah." Some of his
hearers were convinced and became followers of Paul, while many
devout Greeks, among them not a few women of the aristocracy, were
5 drawn to Silas by his preaching. The Jews who remained uncon-
verted, however, gathered a mob of degenerates from the streets and
threw the city into a turmoil. They broke into the house of Jason,
where they hoped to find Paul and Silas and drag them out to the
6 crowd. Not finding them there, they took Jason himself, together
with several of the brothers, before the magistrates, shouting, "These
are the people who have turned the world upside down! Now they
have come here also, and this man Jason has given them shelter.
7 They are all guilty of violating the decrees of Caesar, for they main-
8 tain that another man, Jesus, is king." By these accusations they
succeeded in bewildering the great mass of the people and even the
9 magistrates themselves. At length the magistrates compelled Jason
and his fellow-sufferers to furnish security, and then they let them
10 go. The brothers insisted that Paul and Silas leave for Berea on
that same night. Upon their arrival there they went to the synagogue
11 of the Jews. These Jews were more favorably disposed than those
of Thessalonica and they readily accepted the word of God, searching the Scriptures daily to learn whether everything was as Paul had
12 explained it to them. Many of them believed, but there were also
some who rejected the truth. A number of men and women belong-
13 ing to the foremost Greek circles also embraced the faith. When the
Jews of Thessalonica heard that Paul was in Berea preaching the
word of God, and that the people were accepting it, they too went
14 to Berea and persisted in stirring up its inhabitants. The brothers
therefore urged Paul to leave for Thessaly, while Silas and Tim-
15 otheus remained behind. Paul's companions took him as far as
Athens. He could not enter Thessaly because he had been forbidden
to preach the word of God there. His companions went back and
delivered to Silas and Timotheus Paul's message that they were to
join him as quickly as possible.

16 Paul waited for them in Athens. When he saw idols everywhere

in the city, the spirit by whom he was guided was filled with a holy
17 zeal, and under this impulse Paul discussed religious questions with
the Jews and the Greek converts to Judaism in the synagogue, as
18 well as with those whom he met daily in the public squares. Among
them were also several philosophers of the Epicurean and the Stoic
schools. Some of these asked, "What is that talker trying to make
us believe?" Others said, "He seems to be a herald of deities here-
19 tofore unknown." A few days later they led him up to the Areopagus so that they might question him further. Here they asked
him, "May we know what this new doctrine is that you preach?
20 The things that you tell us sound very strange, and we should like
21 to know precisely what there is to it." For all the Athenians, as well
as the strangers living in Athens, used to spend their entire time
22 telling or listening to the latest news. Then Paul stood up in the
middle of the Areopagus and delivered the following address: "Men
of Athens, from all that I see, you are uncommonly religious people.
23 For as I walked about to look at your sanctuaries I even found an
altar with the inscription, *To an Unknown God.* This God Whom
you worship without knowing who He is, I now proclaim to you.
24 He is the God Who made the universe and everything that is in it.
He is Lord of heaven and earth. He does not dwell in shrines raised
25 by human hands, neither does He allow Himself to be served by
human hands, as if He needed anything; for it is He Who has given
to all creatures life and breath and everything else that they need.
26 He caused all mankind to spring from one forefather and spread
over the face of the earth. At the same time He provided set periods
of time for the different races and fixed the boundaries of their
27 homes. This was done above all things in order that they might
seek that which is divine, groping for it uncertainly at first perhaps,
but in the end actually finding it. Indeed, it is not far from any
28 one of us. For in that which is divine we live, and move, and exist
from day to day. Some of your own people have also expressed the
same thing in the words, 'We too are descended from that which is
29 divine.' Now if we are of divine parentage, we ought not to think
that the divine nature can be likened to images made of gold, silver,
30 or stone, and produced by man's skill and inventive faculty. God
is indeed willing to look with indulgence upon the times when there
was gross ignorance of things divine; but now He calls upon all
31 men, wherever they may be, to change their hearts. For God has set
a day on which He will pass a true judgment upon the whole world
through a man. That man is Jesus. To him He has entrusted the
mission of bringing faith in God to all mankind, inasmuch as He

32 has raised him from the dead." When they heard "resurrection from
the dead," some sneered and others said, "We will hear you further
33 on this subject at another time." So Paul withdrew from them.
34 Several men, however, did join him and embrace the faith, among
them Dionysius, a member of the supreme court, and a woman of
rank named Damaris, as well as others of their acquaintance.

CHAPTER 18.

1 Paul now left Athens and went to Corinth, where he became ac-
2 quainted with a Jew named Aquila. This man was a native of Pontus and had lately come from Italy with his wife Priscilla; for the
Jews had been driven out of Rome by Claudius Caesar and had then
3 emigrated to Achaia. Paul went to see him, and as both men followed the same trade, he made his home with Aquila and the two
4 worked together. On every Sabbath Paul would go to the synagogue
and give religious instructions, in the course of which he would
speak of the name of the lord Jesus and convince not merely Jews
but also Greeks of the truth.

5 Then Silas and Timotheus arrived from Macedonia to join him,
and Paul now devoted himself wholly to preaching the word of
God. In his sermons and detailed explanations of the Scriptures he
6 pointed out to the Jews that Jesus was the Messiah. But when they
stubbornly rejected the truth and grew blasphemous toward him,
Paul shook the dust from his clothes and said to them, "Your blood
be upon your own heads! I am not to blame! Henceforth I shall
7 leave you alone and turn to the Gentiles." He gave up his quarters
with Aquila and went to live with a certain Titus Justus, a devout
8 man whose house adjoined the synagogue. Crispus, the head of the
synagogue, together with his whole household, came to believe in
the Lord, and many of the Corinthian Gentiles who heard the truth
embraced the faith and were baptized, placing their whole trust in
God because of the teaching of our lord Jesus Christ.

9 One night the Lord communicated the following to Paul by
means of a spirit-message: "Have no fear. Speak, do not keep
10 silent, for I am with you. No one shall lay hands upon you and
11 do you harm, for I have a great army of spirits in this city." And so
Paul stayed in Corinth for a year and a half, preaching the word of
God to the people.

12 When Gallio, however, became governor of Greece, the Jews with
one accord rose against Paul and brought him into court before
13 Gallio. With a great uproar they brought against him the accusation, "This man is inducing the people to worship God in a manner

14 contrary to our Law." Paul was about to speak in his own defence,
when Gallio answered the Jews, "If a crime or a serious offence
15 were involved, Jews, I should certainly listen to your charges. But
if it is only a question of words and names and quibbling over what
you call your 'Law,' you must settle it among yourselves, for I will
16 not be a judge of such matters." With these words he turned them
17 out of the court-room. Then all the Greeks surrounded Sosthenes,
the head of the synagogue, and beat him before the judge's bench;
but Gallio took no notice of it.

18 For some time longer Paul remained in Corinth. Then, taking
leave of the brothers, he sailed for Syria, accompanied by Priscilla
and Aquila. Aquila had his hair cut short in Cenchrea, to show
19 that he was under a vow. Paul went to Ephesus, and on the Sabbath
after his arrival he left his companions and visited the synagogue
20 alone, to engage in religious discussions with the Jews. They begged
him to remain longer with them, but he declined and bade them
21 farewell, telling them that he must without fail attend the coming
festival in Jerusalem. "But," he added, "God willing, I shall return
to you." Aquila remained behind in Ephesus, and Paul set out alone
22 and landed at Caesarea. From there he went up to Jerusalem and
23 greeted the congregation, and afterward went down to Antioch. He
spent some time there and then made a journey through Galatia
and Phrygia, exhorting all the believers to remain steadfast.

24 In the meantime a Jew named Apollos had come to Ephesus. He
was a native of Alexandria, a very learned man and uncommonly
25 well versed in the Scriptures. Even before he left his native city,
he had been thoroughly instructed concerning the word of the Lord,
and under the influence of a holy spirit he spoke boldly and with
great fervor. His teachings about Christ were correct in every point,
26 although he knew only the baptism of John. Now he began to appear publicly in the synagogue. When Aquila and Priscilla heard
him speak, they took him to their home and explained God's truths
to him more accurately.

27 It happened that there were in Ephesus certain Corinthians who,
upon hearing his sermons, begged Apollos to go with them to their
native city. He readily consented, and the Christians in Ephesus
now wrote to the believers in Corinth, asking them to give this man
a good reception. Although he arrived in Greece a stranger, he
28 proved of great service to the Christian congregations there. As for
the Jews, he refuted their arguments in a striking manner at public
gatherings, and proved to them from the Scriptures that Jesus was
the Messiah.

CHAPTER 19.

1 Paul had acted upon his own judgment when he decided to go to
Jerusalem, and the spirit therefore directed him to return to Asia
Minor. So it came about that he journeyed overland and reached
2 Ephesus, where he found some of the faithful and asked them, "Did
you receive a holy spirit after you had accepted the faith?" They
answered, "We have not so much as heard of any one's receiving a
3 holy spirit."—"Then how were you baptized?" he now asked
them.—"In the manner that John baptized," they told him.—
4 "John administered baptism only as an outward symbol of a change
of heart," returned Paul; "but at the same time he taught the people
to believe in the one who would come after him, that is, in Jesus
5 Christ." When they heard this, they had themselves baptized as the
followers of the lord Jesus, thus evidencing forgiveness of the sins
6 of apostasy. Then Paul laid his hands on them, and instantly a holy
spirit came upon them. They spoke in foreign languages, and mes-
7 sages were also given in their mother tongue. There were about
twelve men in all.

8 Paul attended the synagogue and for about three months spoke
publicly there with great force, giving religious instruction and
seeking to instill in his hearers the true doctrine concerning the
9 kingdom of God. Many of them, however, stubbornly refused to be
convinced and tried to discredit the new doctrine in the eyes of the
assembled congregation. Paul therefore withdrew from these people, separated the believers from them also, and gave religious instruction daily from eleven o'clock in the morning until four in the
10 afternoon in the hall of a certain Tyrannus. This he did for two
years, until all the inhabitants of the province of Asia, both Jews
11 and Greeks, had heard the word of the Lord. God also made mani-
12 fest certain unusual powers through the hand of Paul; thus, for
example, if one only laid upon sick people articles that had touched
Paul's body, such as handkerchiefs and aprons, their diseases were
cured and the evil spirits driven out.

13 There were also certain vagabond Jewish exorcisers who ventured
to speak the name of the lord Jesus over persons possessed by evil
spirits, pronouncing the incantation, "I adjure you by the Jesus
14 whom Paul preaches." Among them were the seven sons of a certain
15 high priest, Sceuas, who attempted to do the same. Now, as was
their habit, they approached a possessed person and began to invoke the name of Jesus, saying, "We adjure you, in the name of the
Jesus whom Paul preaches, to leave this man." But the evil spirit

answered, "Jesus I know, and Paul I know, but who are you?"
16 Then the man who was possessed sprang upon them, overpowered
two of them, and tore the clothes from their bodies, so that they
17 fled from the house naked and covered with wounds. All the Greeks
and Jews who lived in Ephesus heard of this incident and were
seized with a great fear; but the name of the lord Jesus thereby
18 gained greater prestige from day to day. Many of the converts came
19 to make public confession of their former misdeeds, and some who
had engaged in sorcery brought their books on magic and burned
them before all the people. When the cost of these books was reck-
20 oned it was found to be ten thousand dollars. Thus the belief in
God grew powerfully, spread unceasingly, and became ever more
firmly established.

21 Impelled by a spirit of God, Paul now resolved to go to Macedonia and Greece and then to Jerusalem. He often said, "After I
22 have been there, I must see Rome also." He sent two of his assist-
ants, Timotheus and Erastus, to Macedonia, while he himself stayed
for a while in Asia Minor.

23 At about this time serious trouble arose in Ephesus over the new
24 doctrine. A silversmith named Demetrius was making miniatures in
silver of the temple of Artemis, and in this way brought his work-
25 men large profits. He now called them together and said to them,
26 "Men, you know that we owe our living to our trade. Now as you
can see and hear for yourselves, this man Paul has beguiled the
people not only in Ephesus, but in nearly all Asia, by telling them
27 that gods made by human hands are not gods at all. There is danger,
therefore, not only that our trade will be discredited, but that the
temple of the great goddess Artemis will be completely neglected,
and then she will forfeit the high honor in which she is held all over
28 Asia and throughout the whole world." On hearing this they were
filled with rage, dashed out into the street, and shouted amid great
29 tumult, "Long live Artemis of Ephesus!" Very soon it was rumored
all over the city that a great indignity had been done to Artemis,
and the people with one accord rushed into the theatre, dragging
with them the Macedonians Gaius and Aristarchus, who were Paul's
30 travelling-companions. Paul was ready to go and face the people,
31 but the faithful prevented him, and even some of the highest officials
of the province of Asia, good friends of his, sent messengers to urge
32 him not to venture into the theatre. There confusion reigned, for
the whole assembly was in an uproar, most of those present having
33 no idea why they had come together. A certain Alexander, whom
the Jews pushed to the front, was now chosen from the crowd to go

upon the stage and deliver a speech. He raised his hand to signify
34 that he wished to speak, but when the people saw that he was a Jew,
they all shouted as with one voice for the space of about two hours,
35 "Long live Artemis of Ephesus!" At length the town-clerk signed
to the people that he wished to be heard, and said, "Men of Ephesus,
who is there anywhere in the world who does not know that our
city is the guardian of the shrine of the great Artemis and of her
36 image that fell from heaven? These are facts which no one will
dispute. You ought to keep calm, then, and do nothing rashly.
37 You have brought these men here although they neither rob temples
38 nor blaspheme our goddess. If Demetrius and the others of his craft
believe they have any grievance against them, the courts are open,
and there are governors to look after the matter. Let the contending
39 parties settle their differences before them. If you have any other
complaints to bring, the law requires that they be heard only by the
40 regular assembly. We are in danger of being charged with rioting
because of to-day's happenings, for there are no grounds on which
we can justify this disorderly gathering." With these words he dismissed the assembly.

CHAPTER 20.

1 When quiet had been restored, Paul called together the faithful
and impressed upon them further admonitions. He then took leave
2 of them and set out for Macedonia. After he had visited all the districts there and transmitted numerous messages from the spirit-world
to the faithful, he went to Greece and stayed there for three months.
3 But since the Jews had secretly plotted against him he resolved to
return to Syria. A holy spirit directed him to go by way of Mace-
4 donia. Before he reached Asia Minor he had been joined by Sopater,
the son of Pyrrhus of Berea, by Aristarchus and Secundus of Thessalonica, by Gaius of Derbe, and by Timotheus, Eutychus, and Tro-
5 phimus of Ephesus. These went on ahead of him and waited for him
6 in Troas. We ourselves left Philippi after the Easter celebration,
and met the others in Troas five days later. There we stayed for
7 seven days. On the first day of the week we held divine service, at
which we broke bread. Paul intended to leave on the following day,
and so he held a farewell address which he prolonged until mid-
8 night. Many lamps were burning in the hall where we were gathered.
9 In one of the windows sat a young man named Eutychus who, as
Paul spoke on and on, was overcome with an irresistible drowsi-
ness. Finally he fell fast asleep and dropped from the third story
10 and was taken up for dead. Paul hurried down, fell upon him, and

embraced him. "Do not be alarmed," he said, "for there is still life
11 in him." He then went upstairs again and celebrated the feast of
breaking bread. Afterward, when he himself had eaten, he continued
to converse with those who were present until daybreak. Then he
12 departed. When they had all taken leave of him they took the young
man to his home. He had completely recovered, much to every one's
relief.

13 In the meantime the rest of us had embarked and set sail for
Assos, where we intended to take Paul on board with us. He him-
14 self had so arranged it, choosing to go there alone and on foot. So
he met us again at Assos, and taking him aboard with us, we sailed
15 for Mytilene. From there we continued our voyage and on the following day arrived off Chios. We landed on the island of Samos a
day later and stopped at Trogylium. On the following day we ar-
16 rived at Miletus, for Paul had decided not to land at Ephesus because he feared that he might be detained too long in Asia Minor.
He was hurrying because he wanted to be in Jerusalem on the day
of Pentecost.

17 From Miletus he sent word to the congregations at Ephesus and
18 summoned the elders to him. They came, and he delivered the following address to them: "You yourselves know, my dear brothers,
how from the day on which I set foot in Asia, through more than
19 three years, I have spent my life among you; how I served the Lord
in the midst of nothing but humiliations, tears, and trials resulting
20 from the persecutions by the Jews; how I have neglected no opportunity of teaching you what might be of benefit to you; how I have
21 preached, both in public and in your homes; how I proved to Jews
as well as Greeks the need of changing their hearts and turning to
God and showing faith and confidence in Him with the help of our
22 lord Jesus Christ. And now here I am driven by the spirit to go to
23 Jerusalem. What fate is in store for me there I do not know. I only
know that in every city the holy spirit-world tells me through its
mediums that imprisonment and suffering await me in Jerusalem.
24 But I set no value on my life, and do not care at all by what method
I end my career on earth and my mission on behalf of the truth,
entrusted to me by the lord Jesus, to set forth the gospel of God's
25 grace convincingly to Jews and Greeks alike. And now I must tell
you that I know you will never see my face again — not one of you
among whom I have been going in and out as a preacher of the
26 kingdom of Jesus. To this day my conscience is not burdened with
27 the spiritual death of a single one of you, for I have not failed to
28 proclaim to you God's entire plan of salvation. So keep watch over

yourselves and over the whole flock of which the holy spirit-world
has made you the keepers, so that as shepherds you may lead the
congregation of the lord which he gained possession of with his own
29 blood. For I know that after I have gone, malicious wolves will
30 break in among you and will not spare the flock. Indeed, from
among your own number men will arise and teach false doctrines in
31 order to draw the faithful to them. Be watchful, therefore, and do
not forget that for three years, day and night, I never wearied of
seeking amid tears to win the heart of each one of you for God.
32 And now I commend you to God and to the word of His grace—
to Him Who is strong enough to build you up inwardly and to give
your inheritance to as many of you as have consecrated themselves
33 to God. I have coveted no one's silver, gold, or apparel. You your-
34 selves know that these hands of mine have provided for my own
35 support and for that of my fellow-workers. I have showed all of
you that this is how a man should work and befriend the weak as
well, bearing in mind the words of the lord Jesus Christ: 'He who
gives is happier than he who receives.'"

36 With these words he knelt down and prayed with them all; and
37 they wept aloud, and fell upon Paul's neck and kissed him. They
38 were affected most of all by his saying that they would never see his
face again. Then they accompanied him to the ship.

CHAPTER 21.

1 At our departure we had to tear ourselves from them by force;
then we went aboard and set sail, laying a straight course to Coos,
and on the following day to Rhodes, and thence to Patara and
2 Myra. There we found a ship about to leave for Phoenicia, and
3 going aboard immediately, we put to sea. We sighted Cyprus and
passed to the right of it, holding our course for Syria, and landed
4 at Tyre, where the ship was to discharge her cargo. Here we sought
out the faithful and remained for seven days. The spirit-world,
through the mediums in this congregation, repeatedly warned Paul
5 not to go to Jerusalem. Nevertheless, when the time of our stay was
over, we resumed our voyage. All of the brothers together with
their wives and children escorted us out of the city. On the beach
6 we knelt down and prayed, then took leave of them and went aboard,
while they returned to their homes.

7 Our voyage was nearing its end as we sailed from Tyre to
Ptolomais. There we greeted the brothers and spent a day with
8 them. On the following day we travelled on and reached Caesarea,

9 where we lodged with Philip, one of the seven evangelists. He had
10 four daughters who were mediums. In the course of our stay of
several days with him a medium named Agapus, from Judaea, came
11 to his house. He walked up to us, took Paul's girdle, tied his own
hands and feet with it, and said, "The holy spirit says, 'The man who
owns this girdle will be bound in this way by the Jews in Jerusalem
12 and handed over to the Gentiles.'" When we heard this, both we
and the others who were present begged Paul, earnestly and with
13 tears, not to go to Jerusalem. But he answered, "Why do you weep
and make it so hard for me? I am ready not only to be bound but
14 also to die in Jerusalem for the name of the lord Jesus." Since he
would not be dissuaded, we composed ourselves and said to one
another, "The Lord's will be done."

15 After a few days we made ready for our journey and went up to
16 Jerusalem. Some of the disciples from Caesarea went with us to
show us the way to some one at whose house we might stay as guests.
Under their guidance we arrived at a village and entered the house
of a certain Mnason, a man from Cyprus who had long been a dis-
17 ciple. From there we went on to Jerusalem, and were well received
18 by the brothers there. On the following morning Paul went with us
19 to the house of James, where the elders were assembled. After Paul
had greeted each one individually, he related at length how God had
acted through him in spreading the gospel among the Gentiles.
20 When the elders heard this, they praised God. Then they turned to
Paul and said, "Brother, you know how many thousands there are
in Judaea who have accepted the faith, although they all hold fast
21 to the Law of Moses. Now they have been told that you teach all
the Jews who live among the Gentiles to forsake Moses, and that you
advise them not to circumcise their children or to follow the Jewish
22 ordinances at all. What is to be done? They are certain to hear
23 that you have come, and then they will cause a disturbance. So take
24 our advice. There are four men here who are under a vow. Take
them with you, have yourself purified with them, and pay the cost
of shaving their heads. Then people will see that there is no truth
in the rumors about you, but that on the contrary you keep the Law
25 to the letter. As for the Gentiles who have accepted the faith, the
Jewish converts are not concerned about them; for we sent them a
message in which we stated our opinion that the Gentiles need not
observe the Jewish laws and should only be required to abstain
from the flesh of sacrifices offered to idols, from partaking of blood,
26 and from sexual vice." On the following day, therefore, Paul took
the men, underwent purification with them, and went into the temple.

There he gave notice when the period of purification would end, in
order that the sacrifice might be offered for each one of them.
27 The seven days were almost over when the Jews who had come
from Asia saw Paul in the temple and created a disturbance among
28 the people by rushing upon him and shouting, "Men of Israel, help!
This is the man who preaches to all the world against our people,
against our Law, and against this sacred place. He has even gone
so far as to bring Gentiles into the temple and thus profane this
29 holy place." It happened that they had previously seen him about
the city in company with the Ephesian, Trophimus, and so they
30 thought that Paul had brought him into the temple. Thus the whole
city was thrown into turmoil and a large crowd gathered. Paul was
seized and dragged out of the temple and its doors were immediately
31 shut. The people were on the point of killing him, when the report
reached the commander of the Roman garrison that all Jerusalem
32 was in an uproar. Taking men and officers, he at once marched
rapidly toward the crowd, and when they saw the commander and
33 the soldiers coming they stopped beating Paul. The commander now
went up to him and ordered him to be seized and bound with two
chains. Turning to the crowd, he asked who Paul was and what he
34 had done. Some of the people shouted one thing and some another,
and since the officer could get no reliable information because of the
35 clamor, he commanded that Paul be taken to the barracks. By the
time they arrived at the steps of the barracks Paul had to be literally
36 carried, so menacing was the violence of the mob. For the people
crowded about, demanding his life and shouting, "Down with him!"
37 As Paul was about to be taken into the barracks, he asked the commander, "May I have a word with you?"—"What, do you speak
38 Greek?" returned the commander. "Then you are not the Egyptian
who revolted a short time ago and led four thousand bandits into the
39 desert?" Paul replied, "I am a Jew from Tarsus, a city in Cilicia,
and I beg to be allowed to speak to the people." He gave him per-
40 mission, and Paul stood on the steps and motioned to the people
with his hand. Immediately there was a deep silence. Then he delivered the following speech in the Hebrew tongue:

CHAPTER 22.

1 "Brothers and fathers, listen quietly to the defence that I am
2 going to make before you." When they heard him speaking in
3 Hebrew, they listened in breathless silence, and he continued, "I am
a Jew of Tarsus in Cilicia, although I grew up here in Jerusalem.
At the feet of Gamaliel I learned strict observanec of the laws of

our fathers, and became as zealous on behalf of the traditions of my
4 ancestors as you are to-day. So I persecuted even to the death all
those who adopted this new doctrine as their rule of conduct, and I
5 chained men and women and put them in prison. To this the high
priest and the whole High Council can testify, for I secured from
them credentials with which I set out for Damascus, intending to put
into chains all whom I might find there, and bring them to Jeru-
6 salem for punishment. One day at noon, when I had nearly reached
7 Damascus, a light from heaven suddenly shone around me. I fell to
the ground and heard a voice calling to me, 'Saul, Saul, why do you
8 persecute me?' I answered, 'Who are you, lord?' And the voice said,
9 'I am Jesus of Nazareth, whom you are persecuting.' My companions
saw the light and were terror-stricken, but they could not hear the
10 voice of the one who spoke to me. 'What must I do, lord?' I asked.
The lord answered, 'Get up and go to Damascus. There you will be
11 instructed further concerning your appointed task.' Because of the
glare of that light that had fallen upon me, I could no longer see,
and my companions had to lead me by the hand. In this way I
12 reached Damascus, where a certain Ananias came to me, a man who
conscientiously observed the Law and was highly esteemed by the
13 Jews of that city. Standing before me he said, 'Brother Saul, recover
your sight.' At that instant I regained my sight and saw him stand-
14 ing before me. 'The God of our fathers,' he continued 'has appointed
you to know His will and to see God's Just One and hear from his
15 own lips that you must testify on his behalf and give evidence to all
16 the world of that which you have seen and heard. And now, why
do you hesitate? Stand up and be baptized, and cleanse yourself of
17 your sins by calling upon his name.' After my return to Jerusalem
it happened that while I was praying in the temple my spirit left
18 my body, and I saw Jesus standing before me, and heard him say
to me, 'Make haste and get out of Jerusalem as quickly as possible,
19 for here they will not accept your testimony about me.' I answered,
'Lord, every one in this city knows that it was I who ordered your
followers to be imprisoned and to be flogged in the synagogues;
20 every one knows that it was I who stood by when the blood of your
witness Stephen was shed, and that I gloried in the sight and watched
21 over the clothing of the men who killed him.' But he answered, 'Go,
for I will send you far away to the Gentiles.' "

22 Up to this point they had heard him in silence, but now they
raised a loud outcry and shouted, "Away with such a fellow! Get
him out of the world! He must not be allowed to live any longer!"
23 They roared and threw aside their cloaks and flung dust into the

24 air, until the commander had Paul taken into the barracks, and gave
orders that he should be examined under the lash so as to find out
25 the true reason for this furious outburst against him. He had already
been bound in readiness for the flogging when he asked the officer
who stood by, "Have you the right to flog a Roman citizen, and
26 without judicial sentence?" When the officer heard Paul speaking
of himself as a Roman citizen he hastened to the commander and
said, "Consider what you are about to do, for this man is a Roman
27 citizen." The commander then went to Paul and asked him, "Is it
true that you are a Roman citizen?"—"Yes," answered Paul. The
28 officer replied, "That 'yes' is easily said, but I know how much it
cost me to acquire this citizenship."—"But I was born a Roman
29 citizen," returned Paul. Then they gave up the intended examination, for the commander became alarmed when he found that Paul
was a Roman, and that he had ordered him to be chained. He immediately commanded that the chains be removed.
30 On the following day, in order to learn the whole truth about the
real charges that the Jews were bringing against Paul, the commander ordered him to be brought from his cell, and summoned a
meeting of the chief priests and their whole High Council. Then he
had Paul brought and placed before them.

CHAPTER 23.

1 Paul looked steadily at the members of the High Council and
said, "Brothers, to this day I have lived as I believed right, in my
2 own conscience and in the eyes of God." As Paul uttered these words
the high priest ordered those who stood near him to strike Paul on
3 the mouth, whereupon Paul exclaimed, "God will strike you, you
white-washed wall! Do you sit there to judge me according to the
4 Law, and order me to be struck in violation of the Law?" At this
the men around him said, "Do you dare to insult the high priest of
5 God?" Paul answered, "I did not know, brothers, that he was the
high priest, or I should not have spoken so; for it is written: 'You
6 shall not abuse any ruler of your people.'" Knowing that some of
the Council were Sadducees and others Pharisees, Paul now called
out before the assembly, "Brothers, I am a Pharisee and come from
a Pharisee's family. Because of our hope of a resurrection of the
7 dead, I am here on trial." No sooner had he said this than a violent
dissension arose between the Pharisees and the Sadducees, and the
8 Council was divided into two factions. One was composed of the
Sadducees, who say that there is no resurrection and that there are
neither angels nor spirits; the other faction was composed of the

9 Pharisees, who hold the opposite belief in both matters. A great
clamor arose, and some of the scribes belonging to the Pharisees'
party got up to defend their position. "We find nothing wrong in
this man," they said. "May it not be that a spirit or an angel has
10 actually spoken to him?" The uproar grew louder and louder, and
the commander, fearing that Paul would be torn to pieces, gave his
soldiers orders to go down and take him away from them by force
11 and bring him back to the barracks. On the following night the
lord suddenly stood before Paul and said, "Courage! For as you
have testified on my behalf in Jerusalem, so you shall testify for
me in Rome also."

12 At daybreak the Jews gathered together and swore a solemn oath
13 neither to eat nor to drink until they had killed Paul. More than
14 forty men took part in this conspiracy. They went to the chief priests
and elders and said to them, "We have solemnly sworn to taste no
15 food or drink until we have killed Paul. You and the Council must
ask the commander to give orders that Paul be sent down to you
to-morrow, under the pretext that you wish to look into his case
more closely. We shall be ready to kill him then, even before he
reaches you, and at the risk of our own lives."

16 News of this plot, however, came to the ears of Paul's nephew,
who hurried to the barracks, gained admittance, and told Paul.
17 Paul sent word to one of the officers, "Please take this young man
18 to the commander, for he has something to tell him." The officer
took him and led him to the commander, reporting, "The prisoner
Paul sent for me and asked me to bring this young man to you, be-
19 cause he has something to tell you." The commander then took the
young man by the hand and led him into his private quarters. Here
20 he asked him, "What is it that you have to tell me?" The youth
answered, "The Jews have agreed among themselves to ask you to
send Paul before the Council to-morrow, on the plea that they pro-
21 pose to look more closely into his case. Do not trust them, for more
than forty men will lie in wait for him, all of them bound by a vow
neither to eat nor to drink until they have killed him. They are ready
22 now, and are only waiting for you to give your orders." On hearing
this the commander dismissed the young man with the warning to
23 tell no one of the report he had made. Then he sent for two officers
and instructed them, "By nine o'clock to-night, have two hundred
infantry together with seventy mounted men and two hundred spear-
24 men in readiness to march to Caesarea. Provide mounts to be placed
at Paul's disposal, so that he can be taken in safety to Felix, the
governor, in Caesarea." For the commander feared that the Jews

might carry Paul off and kill him, and that he himself would then
25 be accused of having been bribed by them. He also wrote a letter
26 which read as follows: "Claudius Lysias sends greetings to his ex-
27 cellency the governor Felix. This man had been seized by the Jews
and was in danger of being killed by them, when I came to his
rescue with my troops, for I had heard that he was a Roman citizen.
28 As I wished to know what charges they had to bring against him,
29 I sent him before their High Council, and found that the whole matter resolved itself into questions concerning the Law of Moses and a
certain Jesus, but that no charge could be brought against him to
30 warrant death or imprisonment. It was only with much trouble and
by the use of force that I rescued him from their hands. Then I was
told that certain of the Jews were plotting to make an attempt upon
this man's life, and for this reason I am sending him to you forth-
with, and have told his accusers to lay the case before you. Farewell."
31 In obedience to their orders, the soldiers took Paul with them,
32 and on the same night escorted him as far as Antipatris. At daybreak
33 they allowed him to go on, escorted only by the cavalry. When they
reached Caesarea, the letter was delivered to the governor, and Paul
34 was taken before him. After he had read the letter, the governor
asked Paul, "To which province do you belong?" Paul answered,
35 "To Cilicia." The governor said, "I will give you a hearing as soon
as your accusers have also arrived." Then he gave orders for Paul
to be confined in the palace of Herod.

CHAPTER 24.

1 A few days later the high priest Ananias arrived in Caesarea with
several elders and a certain attorney named Tertullus, and they laid
2 before the governor the charges against Paul. Paul was summoned
before them, and Tertullus began the prosecution. "Most noble
Felix," he said, "it is thanks to you that we enjoy perfect peace. It
is thanks to your wise forethought that the condition of the people
of this country has been bettered in every way by thorough-going
3 reforms in all districts. All this we gratefully acknowledge.
4 "And now, not wishing to take up more of your time than I must,
I shall ask that with your accustomed kindness you grant us a brief
5 hearing. We have found that this man here is a menace to society,
for he stirs up unrest among the Jews all over the world and is the
6 ringleader of the sect of the Nazarenes. He even went so far as to
try to desecrate the temple. We caught him and were about to judge
7 him according to our Law. But Lysias, the commander, intervened
with a strong force of soldiers, ordering him to be taken out of our

8 hands and carried away, and referring his accusers to you. Examine
him yourself, so that you may form your own personal opinion concerning the different charges which we are bringing against him."
9 The Jews joined in the attack and confirmed everything that Tertullus had said.

10 The governor beckoned to Paul to defend himself, and he now
made the following reply: "For many years past you have been a
just judge to the people of this country. This I know, and am there-
11 fore the more ready to defend myself. As you may ascertain for
yourself, it is only twelve days since I arrived in Jerusalem. I went
12 there only to worship in the temple. I was never seen speaking to
any one there, still less stirring up the people, whether in the temple
13 or in the synagogues or anywhere else in the city. My accusers are
therefore unable to prove a single one of their charges against me.
14 To be sure, I do frankly confess to you that I worship the God of
my fathers according to a creed which they call heresy. This creed
consists in accepting as true that which is written in the Law and the
15 prophets. From this I derive the same hope which they themselves
place in God, namely that all, both the just and the unjust, shall in
16 time return to Him. For this reason I also try never to do anything
that might weigh on my conscience as a wrong to God or man.
17 "Now, after an interval of several years, I came to bring alms to
the people of my race and to make offerings in the temple, and on
18 the same occasion I underwent purification. I was thus engaged
when they found me. I was not accompanied by a crowd, still less
19 by a riotous mob. It was rather that certain Jews from Asia Minor
20 instigated a riot and directed it against me. They are the men who
ought to have appeared before you and declared what charges they
had against me. Or let the men who are here state of what crime
21 they were able to convict me before the High Council. My crime
must have consisted in that one sentence that I uttered as I stood
among them: 'It is because I say that the dead will be raised that I
am on trial before you to-day.'"

22 Felix suspended judgment in the case. He was well acquainted
with the doctrines of the new creed, and so he said to the Jews,
"When the commander Lysias comes, I will render my decision in
23 this matter." He then gave orders to the officer to keep Paul in
custody, but to treat him with consideration and not to hinder the
prisoner's friends from doing him kindnesses or visiting him.
24 A few days later Felix himself came with his wife Drusilla, who
was a Jewess. She had begged to be allowed to see Paul and hear
him speak, and in order to please her Felix sent for Paul and had

25 him lecture about his belief in Christ. When Paul at the same time
took occasion to speak of righteousness, of self-control, and of the
coming judgment of God, Felix became very thoughtful and dismissed him with the words, "This is enough for to-day. You may
26 go, and if I should find time again, I will send for you." All the
while he harbored the secret hope that Paul would pay him a sum
of money to be set free; and for this reason he often sent for him
27 and conversed with him. After two years, Felix was succeeded in
office by Porcius Festus; but in order to please his wife Drusilla,
he left Paul in prison.

CHAPTER 25.

1 Three days after Festus had assumed the governorship he went
2 from Caesarea to Jerusalem. Here the high priest and the leading
Jews came to him and told him of the action that was pending
3 against Paul, and begged him to grant them the favor of sending
Paul to them at Jerusalem; for they intended to waylay him on the
4 journey and kill him. Festus answered that Paul was in confinement in Caesarea and that he himself was going there before long.
5 "Any men of standing among you who are competent to act in such
matters," he added, "are welcome to go with me, and there they
can bring their accusations against the man if he has committed
any offence."
6 After spending some eight or ten days among them, Festus went
back to Caesarea. On the day following his arrival he held a hearing
7 and summoned Paul. When he appeared, the Jews who had come
from Jerusalem crowded about him, bringing against him many
8 grave charges, for which, however, they could offer no proof. In
reply Paul defended himself by saying that he had in no way what-
9 ever trespassed against the Jewish Law, the temple, or Caesar. But
Festus, eager to ingratiate himself with the Jews, asked him, "Are
you willing to go up to Jerusalem and stand trial there, in my
10 presence, on these charges?" Paul answered, "I am on trial here in
Caesar's court, and it is here that I should be judged. I have done
11 the Jews no wrong, as you yourself well know. If I were in the
wrong and had done anything to deserve death, I should not refuse
to die. But since there is not a word of truth in the accusations
which these men are bringing against me, no one has the right to
12 sacrifice me as a favor to them. I appeal to Caesar." Then Festus
conferred with his councillors and pronounced the following decision: "You have appealed to Caesar. To Caesar you shall be
taken."

13 A few days later King Agrippa and Bernice came to Caesarea to
14 pay a visit to Festus, and in the course of their visit of several days,
Festus spoke to the king of Paul's case. "There is a man here," he
15 said, "who was left in prison by Felix. While I was in Jerusalem
the chief priests and the elders of the Jews came to see me about him
16 and demanded that he be sentenced. I told them that the Romans
are not in the habit of delivering a man to death as a favor to any-
body, before the accused has been brought face to face with his accusers and had the opportunity of defending himself against the
17 accusation. And so they came here with me, and on the very next
day I held a hearing at which I ordered the man to be brought in.
18 His accusers appeared against him, but were unable to charge him
19 with any serious crime such as I had expected. All that they could
bring up against him hinged upon questions dealing with particular
forms of worship and a certain Jesus who is dead and who Paul
20 maintains is alive. It is not within my province to inquire into such
matters, and I therefore asked Paul whether he was willing to go to
21 Jerusalem and be tried there for the crimes laid against him. But
Paul entered an appeal and demanded to be held in custody until
the ruler himself should decide his case. So I ordered him to be kept
22 in custody until I could send him to Caesar." Agrippa now said to
Festus, "I wish that I could hear that man myself." Festus answered, "You shall hear him to-morrow."

23 On the following day Agrippa and Bernice appeared with great
pomp, and entered the audience-room attended by officers of high
rank and the prominent men of the city. At the order of Festus Paul
24 was brought in, and Festus rose and delivered the following speech:
"King Agrippa and all others who are present, you see here before
you the man concerning whom the whole Jewish population of
Jerusalem and also of this city has appealed to me, loudly demand-
25 ing that he no longer be allowed to live. Nevertheless, I am certain
that he has done nothing that deserves death, and since he himself
26 has appealed to Caesar, I have determined to send him. But I have
nothing definite to write to my lord the emperor about him. For
this reason I have had him appear before you all, and especially
before you, King Agrippa, so that after he has had a hearing I may
27 have something on which to base my report; for it seems to me
unreasonable to send a prisoner to the higher court without being
able to state the crime with which he is charged."

CHAPTER 26.

1 Then Agrippa turned to Paul and said, "You are permitted to
speak for yourself." Paul raised his hand to show that he was about
2 to begin, and made the following reply: "I consider myself fortunate, King Agrippa, to be allowed to defend myself before you
3 to-day against all the accusations of the Jews; for you are thoroughly acquainted with all the religious customs and questions of
the Jews. For this reason I ask you to hear me with patience.
4 "The life that I have led from my childhood among the people
5 of my race in Jerusalem is well known to all the Jews, for they have
known me from my earliest days. If they were willing to do so, they
would have to testify that I belonged to the sect of the Pharisees,
6 the strictest party that our Jewish religion knows. To-day I am on
trial for cherishing the hope that all the promises God made to our
7 fathers will be fulfilled. It is the same hope that all the twelve
tribes of our people wish to see realized. To this end they devote
themselves day and night to the worship of God. On account of this
9 hope, O king, I am accused by the Jews. It is true that at one time
I too was hostile to the name of Jesus the Nazarene and considered
10 it my duty to combat him in every way possible. I opposed him in
Jerusalem. I obtained from the high priest a warrant on the strength
of which I put many of the Christians in prison. In every case in
11 which the death-penalty was imposed I voted in its favor. In all the
synagogues I had the followers of Christ flogged until they blasphemed his name. Even in the more remote cities I persecuted them
relentlessly.
12 "Thus it happened that one day I set out for Damascus with the
13 authority and on the commission of the chief priests. While I was
on my way there, O king, at about noon I saw a radiant light from
heaven, brighter than the sun, suddenly beam on me and my com-
14 panions. We fell to the ground, all of us, and I heard a voice calling
to me in the Hebrew tongue, 'Saul, Saul, why do you persecute me?
15 It will go hard with you if you kick against the goad.' I asked, 'Who
are you, lord?' The voice answered, 'I am Jesus of Nazareth whom
16 you are persecuting. But get up and stand on your feet, for I have
appeared to you in order to make you my servant. You shall testify
to that which you have just now witnessed and to that which you
17 will witness in the future as often as I shall appear to you. I hereby
choose you from among the people of the Jews and the Gentiles, in
18 order to send you to both. You shall open their eyes so that they
may turn from darkness to light, and from the power of Satan to

God. They shall obtain forgiveness for their sins of apostasy, and
receive their inheritance together with those who are consecrated by
faith in me.'
19 "Tell me, O King Agrippa, how could I refuse obedience to this
20 heavenly vision? So it was that I preached first to the people of
Damascus and Jerusalem, then throughout Judaea, and then to the
Gentiles, calling upon all to change their hearts and turn to God,
21 and to perform works worthy of such a change of heart. Because of
22 this the Jews seized me in the temple and tried to kill me, but with
the help of God I have remained alive to this day, and am testifying
to the truth before high and low. Nevertheless, I teach nothing but
23 that which the prophets and even Moses himself foretold, namely
that the Messiah would have to suffer, and that he would be the first
to rise from the realm of the dead and show both Jews and Gentiles
the way to the light. Why do you think it incredible that God should
lead the spiritually dead back to life again?"
24 At these words Festus exclaimed in a loud voice, "Paul, you are
25 out of your mind! Too much study is driving you mad." Paul
answered, "I am not out of my mind, noble Festus. The words that
26 I speak are words of truth, and they arise from clear thinking. The
king knows this very well, too, and to him above all others I speak
freely. I am certain that none of these things is unknown to him,
27 for they were not done in a corner. King Agrippa, do you believe
28 the prophets? I know that you do believe them." Agrippa replied
to Paul, "Before long you will succeed in making a Christian of
29 me."—"Would to God," replied Paul, "that sooner or later not
only you but all who hear me to-day might become as I am, except
for my chains!"
30 Then the king rose, together with the governor and Bernice and
31 the others who were present; and as they went away they discussed
the matter among themselves and agreed, "This man is doing nothing
32 that deserves death or imprisonment." And Agrippa said to Festus,
"This man might have been set at liberty if he had not appealed to
Caesar."

CHAPTER 27.

1 The governor therefore decided to send Paul to Caesar, and the
day was set for our sailing for Italy. Paul and several other prisoners were handed over to an officer of the imperial regiment named
2 Julius. We went aboard a ship from Andramythium bound for the
seaports of Asia Minor, and set sail. A Macedonian from Thessa-
3 lonica named Aristarchus went with us. On the following day we

touched at Sidon. Julius treated Paul very considerately, allowing
him to visit his friends in Sidon and permitting them to provide him
4 with such things as he might need on the voyage. As we continued
our voyage we were forced by head-winds to sail along the eastern
5 shore of Cyprus. Then we sailed along the coast of Cilicia and
6 Pamphylia and in fifteen days came to Myra in Lycia. There the
officer found a ship from Alexandria bound for Italy, and put us on
7 board her. After a slow and troublesome passage we arrived off
Cnidus, but head-winds prevented our landing there, and so we con-
8 tinued along the coast of Crete toward Cape Salmone. Passing this
point with difficulty, we arrived at a place called Fairhaven, not far
9 from the city of Lasea. In the meantime the season was far advanced; the great feast-day was past, and the time was approaching
10 when sailing would become dangerous. Paul warned the ship's
officers, "Gentlemen, I foresee that to proceed further will mean
danger and heavy loss, not only to the cargo and the ship, but also
11 to our own lives." But the officer had greater faith in the pilot and
12 the captain than in Paul, and as the harbor did not seem to be a
good place to winter in, the majority decided to continue the voyage
and, if possible, to reach the Cretan port of Phoenix and winter
there; for this harbor was well protected against the southwest and
northeast winds.

13 Just at that time a south wind sprang up, and all believed that
they could safely carry out their purpose. We weighed anchor and
14 sailed close along the shores of Crete, but before long a violent wind
called the Euroclydon (meaning an east-northeast wind) came down
15 upon us from the island. Our ship, unable to head into the wind,
16 was allowed to run before it, and ran under the lee of a small island
17 called Clauda. With great trouble we saved our life-boat, hoisted it
aboard, and tried to secure it by fastening it with ropes. As it was
feared that we might be thrown upon the Syrtis shoals, the sails
18 were taken in and the ship was allowed to drift. We suffered ter-
ribly from the storm. On the following day a part of the cargo was
19 thrown overboard, and on the third day we had to do the same with
20 the ship's gear. For days we could see neither sun nor stars, and
the storm showed no sign of abating. Finally we lost all hope of
21 being saved, and no one cared to eat any longer. Then Paul stood
up among them and said, "Gentlemen, you ought to have listened to
me and not sailed from Crete; then you would have been spared all
22 this hardship and loss. But be that as it may now, I beg you to take
heart, for not one of you will lose his life; only the ship will be
23 lost. For last night there stood before me a messenger of the God

24 to Whom I belong and Whom I serve, and said, 'Have no fear, Paul.
You shall appear before Caesar; and see, God has granted you the
25 lives of all your fellow-travellers.' So take courage, gentlemen, for
I have full faith in God and believe that everything will be as He
26 said. But we are to be driven ashore on some island."

27 It was now the fourteenth night that we had been tossed about on
the Adriatic Sea. At about midnight the crew discovered that land
28 was near, for when they took soundings they found twenty fathoms
of water, and on sounding again shortly afterwards they found fif-
29 teen fathoms. Fearing that they might be driven upon rocks they
dropped four anchors from the stern and anxiously waited for day-
30 light. The crew now tried to desert the ship, lowering the life-boat
31 on the pretext of throwing out anchors ahead. Then Paul said to the
officer and his soldiers, "Unless these men are kept on board, you
32 cannot be saved." The soldiers immediately cut the life-boat adrift.
33 When day broke Paul urged every one to take food. "For the past
fourteen days," he said, "what with work and worry, you have eaten
34 hardly anything. I am advising you for your own good when I say,
eat something; your own safety depends on it. Not one of you will
35 lose a hair of his head." With these words he took bread, offered a
prayer in the presence of all, then broke the bread and after dividing
36 some among us, began to eat. At this they all plucked up courage
37 and likewise took food for themselves. There were in all two hun-
38 dred seventy-six of us on board. Strengthened by the food they had
taken, they lightened the ship by throwing overboard her cargo of
39 grain. When daylight finally came they could not recognize the
land. All that they could see was a bay and a beach upon which
40 they proposed to run the ship ashore if possible. The cables were
therefore cut and allowed to fall into the sea; at the same time the
lashings of the steering-oars were undone, the foresail was set to the
41 wind, and they headed for the beach. The ship at once struck a shoal
and ran aground. The bow was driven deeply into the sand and became wedged fast, while the stern was soon broken to pieces by the
42 beating of the waves. For fear that the prisoners might try to escape
43 by swimming away, the soldiers intended to kill them. But the officer, because he wanted to save Paul, prevented his men from carrying out their plan, and ordered all who could swim to jump over-
44 board and get to land. Of the rest some were obliged to make their
way to the shore on planks and others on pieces of wreckage. In
this way all succeeded in getting safely to land.

CHAPTER 28.

1 After we had reached safety we learned that we were on the island
2 of Malta. The natives showed us the greatest kindness, and as we
were dripping wet and shaking with cold they kindled a fire and
3 arranged a place where each of us could warm himself. Paul gathered a bundle of sticks and laid them on the fire, and as he did so,
an adder crawled out because of the heat and fastened on his hand.
4 When the natives saw the snake hanging from his hand they said to
one another, "This man must be a murderer, for the goddess of
vengeance will not let him live, although he has been saved from
5 the sea." But Paul shook the adder off into the fire, and was none
6 the worse. They had expected that his hand would swell and that
he would suddenly fall dead; but when they had watched for some
time in intense expectation without seeing anything unusual happen
to him, they changed their minds and took him for a god.
7 Not far from here lay the estate of the most prominent man of
the island, Publius by name. He took us in, and for three days
8 looked after us and showed us every courtesy. At that time his father
was suffering from fever and dysentery. Paul went to the sick man's
9 bedside, prayed and laid his hands on him, and cured him. When
this became known, all of the other sick people of the island came
10 to him and were healed. During the rest of our stay they showed
us many honors, and when we sailed they supplied us with everything that we needed.
11 After three months we put to sea in a vessel from Alexandria
12 which had wintered at the island. It was named *The Dioscuri.* We
13 landed at Syracuse and stayed there three days. Then making a wide
circuit, we sailed to Rhegium. On the following day a south wind
14 prevailed, and we made Puteoli in two days. There we found some
of the brothers who asked us to spend a week with them, and from
15 there we went to Rome. The brothers of that city had heard of our
coming, and went out as far as Forum Appii and Tres Tabernae to
meet us. When Paul saw them he thanked God and took new courage.
16 After we reached Rome the officer delivered his prisoners to the
commander of the imperial guards. Paul, however, was allowed to
occupy rented lodgings by himself, with the soldier who was detailed
to guard him.
17 Three days later Paul invited the heads of the Jewish congregations to meet at his lodgings. When they arrived he said to them,
"My dear brothers, although I have committed no offence whatever
against our people or the customs of our fathers, I was carried away

18 from Jerusalem a prisoner and handed over to the Romans. They
were willing to let me go after they had examined me, for they
could find nothing against me to warrant my being put to death.
19 But the Jews raised objections and shouted, 'Down with this enemy
of our people!' Consequently I was obliged to appeal to Caesar. I
did this, not because I wanted to accuse my people before the court
20 of appeals, but to escape the death penalty. I have been anxious to
see you and have asked you to come here to me, only that I might
tell you this; for it is solely because of that which represents the
21 hope of Israel that I wear these chains." They answered, "We have
had no written report of your case from Judaea, and no one of our
faith has come to us from there to tell us anything against you,
22 either of his own knowledge or from hearsay. We think it would be
well, however, if you would tell us something further concerning
your belief. So far as this sect of Christians is concerned, we only
23 know that it meets with opposition everywhere." So they fixed a day
and at the appointed time came to his lodgings in even greater numbers than before. From early in the morning until late in the evening he explained to them in detail the doctrine of God's kingdom,
telling them at the same time of his own personal experiences. He
tried to prove to them from the Law of Moses and the writings of
24 the prophets that Jesus was the Messiah. Some of them were con-
25 vinced by his arguments, others rejected them. The meeting broke
up amid great dissension, and Paul's parting words were these: "It
was a striking speech that was addressed to your fathers by a holy
26 spirit when he said through the prophet Isaiah: 'Go and say to these
people, "You shall hear again and again but not understand; you
27 shall look again and again but not see; for the hearts of this people
have become hardened. Their ears are dull of hearing, and their
eyes they keep closed, so that they may not see with their eyes and
hear with their ears and understand with their hearts and be con-
28 verted, and so that I may not heal them."' Understand, then, that
the salvation of God has been sent to the Gentiles. They will listen
29 to it." After Paul had spoken these words the Jews went away,
quarrelling vehemently among themselves.

30 For two full years Paul lived at his rented lodgings. There he
31 received all who went to see him, both Jews and Gentiles, teaching
them the doctrine of the kingdom of God and the truth concerning
Jesus, quite openly and unmolested.

The Epistle of Paul the Apostle to the ROMANS

CHAPTER 1.

1 I, PAUL, am sending you this letter. As a servant of Jesus Christ
I was called to be an apostle and was charged with the task
2 of proclaiming the gospel of God. This is the same gosepl which
God had made known in the past through His prophets in the sacred
3 Scriptures. It concerns His Son, who was descended in body from
4 David, but who as a Son of God was chosen to return to God from
the realm of the spiritually dead, by virtue of a divine power. This
power was conferred upon him by God's spirit-world, which brought
5 him to the perfection of obedience to God. This is our lord Jesus
Christ. Through him we have received heavenly gifts and apostleship, in order that we may labor among the Gentiles throughout the
world, teaching men to believe in His name and to follow His doc-
6 trine. You also are numbered among them; you also are called to
7 be followers of Jesus Christ. To all in Rome who are beloved of
God and whom He has called to dedicate their lives to Him, I send
my greeting. May grace and peace be granted to you by God our
Father and by our lord Jesus Christ.

8 First, I thank my God through Jesus Christ because of you all,
9 for all the world is praising your faith. The God whom I serve by
preaching the gospel of His Son under the guidance of the spirits
10 assigned to me is my witness that I think of you constantly, and
that I pray to Him unceasingly to grant me the happiness, if He so
11 wills, of being allowed to visit you. I earnestly long to see you in
12 order to bring you some spiritual gift to strengthen your faith; or
rather that when I am with you we may derive spiritual benefit on
13 both sides, I from your faith and you from mine. As you perhaps
already know, dear brothers, I have often intended to visit you, but
I have always been prevented. And yet I am eager to bring to
maturity some spiritual fruit among you as well as among the rest
of the Gentiles.

14 The truth is that I am in duty bound to serve Greeks and bar-
15 barians, the wise and the ignorant alike. For this reason it is my
16 wish to preach the gospel among the Romans also. I am not ashamed

of this gospel, inasmuch as it harbors a divine power which brings
salvation to all who accept it sincerely. This applies first of all to
17 the Jews, but also to the Gentiles. For in the gospel it is revealed
that we gain favor with God by means of a faith that leads to trust.
As it is written in the Scriptures: "Every one who does my will in
every respect, will have life as a result of his confident faith."

18 On the other hand, there is also revealed the penalty which, according to a higher divine law, rests on every ungodliness and every
wrong-doing of men who in their wickedness tread the truth under-
19 foot. For such truths concerning God as can be known by men lie
plainly before their eyes. God has indeed displayed them openly.
20 Since the creation of the universe, the qualities of God which are
invisible to human eyes are plainly visible in His works; above all,
21 His eternal and divine power. There is accordingly no excuse for
those who, although they could have recognized God, would not acknowledge His existence or give Him thanks; who deceived themselves by their false conclusions and so shrouded their God-estranged
22 hearts in darkness; who professed themselves to be wise, but in
23 reality were fools; who set the images of mortal men, of birds, of
four-footed animals, and of creeping things in the place of the
24 glorious and everlasting God. And so God gave them over to the vile
inclinations of their hearts, so that they sank into the mire of im-
25 morality and shamefully dishonored their own bodies. They branded
the truth of God's existence as a lie and paid homage to and worshipped the creature rather than the Creator — may He be blessed
26 for ever: Amen. For this reason God gave them over to the lowest
of passions. Their women exchanged the natural relations of sex
27 for the unnatural; their men did likewise, and inflamed with lust
for one another, they abandoned all natural relations with women.
Men committed acts of shame with men, and paid the penalty for
their perversion in their own bodies.

28 In the measure that they spurned acknowledgment of God, He
allowed them to fall into depravity, so that they gave themselves up
29 to all kinds of infamous actions and were filled with wrong-doing,
wickedness, greed, and vice of every kind; with envy, murderous
30 desires, quarrelsomeness, deceit, and spite. They became scandal-
mongers, slanderers, enemies of God, brutal and arrogant, boasters,
31 inventive in evil, disobedient to parents, faithless and unscrupulous,
32 devoid of love and mercy. They were very well acquainted with the
decree of God that those who practise such vice are deserving of
spiritual death; yet they not only behaved so themselves, but ap-
plauded others who did the like.

CHAPTER 2.

1 Therefore if you, whoever you may be, should act the part of
judge over such men, there would be no excuse for you. In pronouncing your fellow-man guilty you condemn yourself; you, the
2 judge, commit the self-same offences. But we know that God alone
3 can judge such evil-doers justly. If you, O man, pronounce judgment on those who commit such sins, even though you are as guilty
as they, do you suppose that you will escape the punishment of God?
4 Or do you so despise His wealth of goodness, patience, and forbearance that you fail to consider that God in His mercy is willing to
5 allow you time for repentance? If your heart remains hard and
impenitent, you are storing up for yourself punishment upon punishment, which will fall upon you on the day when God's sentence
6 is carried out and His judgment vindicated as just. Then He will
7 give every one the due reward of his deeds: life hereafter to those
who sought honor, glory, and immortality by persevering in their
8 endeavor to do good; bitter punishment to those who out of selfishness set themselves against the truth that they knew and gave way
9 to every evil impulse. Misery and tormenting anguish will overtake
the soul of every one who does evil—of the Jew first, but also of
10 the Gentile; on the other hand, glory and honor and peace will
11 come to him who does good—to the Jew first, but also to the
12 Gentile; for outward rank means nothing to God. Whoever, then,
has sinned without knowing the Law of Moses will sink into spiritual death without being subjected to the Law of Moses; and whoever has sinned in spite of his knowledge of the Law of Moses will
13 be punished according to that Law. For it is not knowledge of the
Law that renders man pleasing to God; it is by obedience to the
14 Law that he finds favor in His sight. Accordingly, if the Gentiles,
although they know nothing of the Law of Moses, instinctively fulfill the requirements of that Law, then in their case, since they do
15 not possess the Law of Moses, their own instinct becomes law. By
this they show that the essence of the Law of Moses is written on
their hearts by nature. Their conscience, therefore, together with the
Law of Moses, will at some time arise to testify for or against them,
because their own convictions either warned them against or sanc-
16 tioned what they did. That will be on the day when God judges the
secret hearts of men — and judges them, as my gospel teaches,
through Jesus Christ.

17 Assuming, then, that you are proud to call yourself a Jew; that
you feel secure in the Law; that you boast that yours is the true

18 faith and that you know God's will; that your knowledge of the
Law would enable you in every instance to determine what is
19 right; that you would presume to be a guide to the blind, a light
20 for those who sit in darkness, an instructor of the ignorant, a teacher
of the young, because you have the substance of knowledge and
21 truth and the letter of the Law in black and white; but assuming
further that while teaching others you neglect to teach yourself;
that you yourself steal while telling others that it is wrong to steal;
22 that you tell others that adultery is forbidden, when you yourself
are an adulterer; that you picture idols as an abomination while
23 you profane the temple of the true God, — would you not then be a
person who on the one hand boasts of possessing the divine Law and
on the other shamefully dishonors God by breaking that Law?
24 Would not these words from the Scriptures apply to you: "Because
of you, the name of God is blasphemed among the Gentiles"?

25 Circumcision will only be of benefit to you if you keep the Law
of Moses. If you are a violator of the Law your circumcision is of
26 as little avail as if it did not exist. If, however, an uncircumcised
man obeys the Law, should not his uncircumcision be counted as
27 circumcision? Indeed, the physically uncircumcised who abides by
the Law will be your judge, if in spite of the Law of Moses and in
28 spite of your circumcision you transgress the Law. For he is not
a Jew who is but outwardly one, neither does circumcision consist
29 in the outward removal of flesh. The true Jew is rather he who is
one inwardly, and true circumcision is not that which is performed
according to the letter of the Law, but that which is performed in
the heart by a spirit of God. Whoever is so circumcised wins the
recognition not of men but of God.

CHAPTER 3.

1 What advantage then has the Jew over the Gentile? What value
2 is there in circumcision? Well, quite a large one in every respect.
First, the Jews have the advantage of having been entrusted with
3 God's promises. Certainly you may object that many of the Jews
proved faithless. But can their faithlessness offset the faithfulness of
4 God? Assuredly not, for the saying, "God is truthful, while all men
are liars," will for ever remain true; just as it is also written in the
Scriptures, "Thou shalt be found right where Thy promises are con-
5 cerned and remain victorious when Thy cause is judged." On the
contrary, our own wrong-doing sets off God's right-doing so much
the more plainly. Then what are we to conclude? That God is un-

just because he inflicts punishment? — if I may so express myself in
6 human fashion. By no means does He thereby act unjustly, for how
7 then could God be the judge of the whole universe? Now if God's
truthfulness reflects His glory the more brightly because of my own
8 untruthfulness, how can I still be condemned as a sinner? In that
case, are not certain slanderers right in ascribing to us the doctrine
that we ought to do evil in order that good may come of it? People
who make such a statement justly undergo the sentence of God.
9 What, then, is the truth of the matter? Do we Jews as such occupy
a superior position? Have we not already been forced to make the
sweeping accusation that Jews as well as Gentiles, without exception,
10 are under the rule of the sin of apostasy? Indeed, it says in the
11 Scriptures: "There is none faithful to God, no, not one. There is
12 none that rightly understands, none that sincerely seeks God. They
have all strayed from the right way, all together become debased.
13 There is none that does good, no, not one. Their throat is an open
tomb, their tongues speak falsehood and deception, adders' poison
14 is concealed under their lips. Their mouth is full of cursing and
15 bitterness. Their feet are swift when it is a matter of shedding blood.
16 Devastation and calamity mark their path, and they do not know
17 the way of peace. There is no reverence for God among them." —
18 Now we know that all these words are addressed by the Law of
19 Moses to those who are in possession of this Law. Thus every mouth
must be silent, and the whole universe must confess itself guilty
20 before God. It is therefore impossible for any creature to find favor
in the sight of God by the outward observance of the Law. For the
sole purpose of the Law is to impart consciousness of sin.

21 The way to win favor with God without observing the Law has
now been disclosed, a way at which the Mosaic Law and the prophets
22 have already hinted. This favor in the sight of God is obtained
only through faith in Jesus Christ, and it will be shared without
23 distinction by all who have such faith. For all committed the sin
of apostasy and as a result were barred from the glory of God.
24 But they will be restored to God's favor — through no merit of their
own, to be sure, but by God's mercy — through the redemption that
25 has its foundation in Jesus Christ. It was he whom God destined as
the mediator in the reconciliation, because of the loyalty he manifested in the face of his bloody death. For by this death he was to
prove his loyalty to God so that he might be pardoned for the short-
26 comings of which even he was guilty at the time when God withheld His aid in order to test his constancy during those critical
hours. Thus in the end he was to prove himself entirely worthy of

God's favor, and secure favor in the eyes of God for all who remain
loyal to Jesus Christ.
27 Have we a single reason for boasting, then? It is out of the
question. Is there any standard of conduct prescribed by the Law,
or merit in its observance, to give us ground for boasting? No.
28 There is but one standard: that of faith. From this we conclude that
man finds favor with God by remaining true to his faith regardless
29 of outward observance of the provisions of the Law. Or is God a
God of the Jews only, and not of the Gentiles also? Certainly of
30 the Gentiles also. For there is only one God. This one God will
look with favor upon the circumcised only by reason of their faith,
31 and likewise on the uncircumcised solely because of their faith. Do
we then overthrow the Law of Moses by our doctrine of faith? Far
from it; we are merely assigning to the Law its proper place.

CHAPTER 4.

1 In view of the foregoing, what shall we answer if we are asked
2 what our earthly forbear Abraham received from God? Had he
obtained God's favor by observing the Law, he would have had
reason to boast. But in the eyes of God he had no such reason.
3 For what do the Scriptures say? "Abraham believed God, and this
faith was accounted to his credit so that he obtained favor with God."
4 If a man does a piece of work, the wages that he earns are paid him
5 not as a special favor but as a debt which is lawfully due him. But
if he does no work, but simply places his faith in One Who can bring
the godless into the path of godliness, his faith is accounted so
6 highly that he thereby gains favor with God. This is the thought
expressed by David when he describes the good fortune of the man
7 on whom God looks with favor, regardless of his works. He says,
"Fortunate are they whose trespasses are forgiven and whose sins
8 of apostasy are covered. Fortunate is the man to whom the Lord no
9 longer imputes the sin of apostasy." Now is it only the circumcised whom David calls fortunate, or the uncircumcised as well?
We say: Abraham's faith was accounted so highly that he thereby
10 gained favor in the sight of God. When was his faith so accounted?
Was it after he was circumcised, or before? It was not after but be-
11 fore his circumcision. He received the outward token of circumcision
merely as a seal of God's favor, which he obtained by virtue of his
faith as an uncircumcised man. Thus he was to become the father
of all those who might come to believe as uncircumcised persons,
and whose faith is likewise so highly accounted that they thereby
12 gain favor in the eyes of God. As to the circumcised, Abraham is to

be regarded as their father only if they not merely have bodily circumcision but also walk in the paths of faith that were trodden by
13 our father Abraham as an uncircumcised man. It was not through
the Law of Moses that Abraham or his seed received the promise
that he should inherit all the universe, but in consequence of God's
14 favor, which he had obtained by his faith. If only those who
have the Law of Moses were to be heirs, faith would have no mean-
15 ing at all and the promise would be void. For the Mosaic Law as
such carries with it only punishment; and where no law exists, there
16 can be no transgression of law. Therefore that promise was made
conditional upon faith alone, and, what is more, offered as a gift
of grace, so that the promise might hold good for all of Abraham's
descendants; not merely for those who are subject to the Law of
Moses, but also for those who have only the faith of Abraham, who
17 is thus father of us all. Of him it is written, "I have appointed you
the father of many nations." He avowed his faith before the face
of the God Who can bring back the spiritually dead to spiritual life,
18 and Who can call into being that which does not yet exist. When
according to human opinion there was no longer ground for hope,
Abraham, in his faith, clung firmly to the hope that he would become the father of many nations, because he had been told, "So
19 countless shall your descendants be." He was so unshakable in his
faith that he, a man nearly a hundred years old, did not even take
into consideration the fact that his body was now impotent and that
20 Sarah's womb could no longer conceive. He never permitted him-
21 self to be led into unbelief by doubting the promises of God, but
grew stronger and stronger in his faith, giving honor to God and
standing firm in the conviction that God was able to do what He
22 had promised. For this reason his faith was so highly accounted
23 that through it he won God's favor. But it was not only for his sake
that it is written that his faith was so highly accounted, but for our
24 sakes as well. For our own faith shall be accounted in like manner
if we believe in Him Who raised our lord Jesus from the kingdom
25 of the spiritually dead. He had been delivered up to that realm
because of the sins of our apostasy, and he was brought back from
it in order to reconcile us with God.

CHAPTER 5.

1 Now that we have become reconciled with God by faith, let us
2 preserve that peace with the help of our lord Jesus Christ. Through
him we have access to the spiritual gifts that are now our permanent possession, and may rejoice in the hope of attaining the

3 glory of God. Not only this, but we may be proud even of our
4 sufferings, for we know that suffering develops constancy; that constancy shows our trustworthiness; that trustworthiness is the basis
5 of our hope; and that this hope does not deceive us; for the love of
God has been poured into our hearts by a holy spirit that has been
6 given to us. Moreover, Christ died for us wretched men at a time
7 when we were still enemies of God. Now there is scarcely a person
alive who will be ready to die for a good man; at the most, men
8 will venture their lives for those who have been kind to them. But
God shows his love for us by this, that Christ died for us while we
9 were still estranged from God. How much more then, now that
through his blood we have become reconciled to God, shall we be
entirely freed by it from the consequences of our former condition.
10 If the way was cleared for our reconciliation with God by the death
of His Son at a time when we were still enemies of God, how much
more shall we find our final salvation in living communion with
11 Him as soon as that reconciliation is completed. And not only this,
but we may glory in the communion with God imparted to us by
Jesus Christ our lord, inasmuch as it was through him that we have
attained perfect reconciliation with God.

12 Therefore, as the sin of apostasy from God came into God's
creation through a single individual, and in consequence of this
apostasy the spiritual death of separation from God likewise stepped
in, so this spiritual death also affected all mankind; for they had all
13 fallen away from God. It follows that the sin of apostasy was in the
world even before the Law of Moses. But we become conscious that
14 something is a sin only if there is a law that forbids it as sin. Thus
the Prince of Death reigned from the time of Adam to that of Moses
over all who had committed the same sin of apostasy that Adam had
committed. This Prince of Death is thus the antitype of the Prince
who was to come later.

15 But the analogy between apostasy and pardon does not hold in every respect; for if on the one hand the transgression of one individual brought upon many the spiritual death of separation from God, on the other hand the pardon of God proved itself considerably richer, as did also the gift of mercy which was given to the many in the incarnation of Jesus Christ.

16 There is also a difference in the consequences of the fall brought about by one individual and the gift of pardon likewise conveyed by one individual. For in the first case the deliberate act of the one carried with it the death-sentence of separation from God, while in the second case the gift of pardon brought to the many who had

shared in the fall the decree that the spiritually dead may return to
spiritual life.
17 Again, if the Prince of Death could establish a kingdom for himself by his one act of apostasy, for which he alone was responsible,
how much more will those who enjoy God's abundant mercy and
friendship build a kingdom in the realm of spiritual life through the
merit of one, namely Jesus Christ.
18 Therefore just as the apostasy which was brought about by one
led to a death-sentence for all apostates, so in consequence of one's
loyalty to God a decree was issued for all apostates which again
19 endows them with life. For just as the many became enemies of God
through the disobedience of one, so the many will again be reconciled with God through the obedience of one.
20 The one purpose of later adding the Law of Moses, was to make
outwardly clear the excess of sin. But where sin prevailed to over-
21 flowing, the mercy of God prevailed in yet greater abundance. As
the sin of apostasy from God led to the founding of a kingdom under
the rule of the Prince of Death, so also pardon was to lead the
apostates back by the way of righteousness to the kingdom of the
life beyond, through Jesus Christ our lord.

CHAPTER 6.

1 Now what shall we conclude from the foregoing? Shall we say,
"Let us continue in the sin of apostasy so that pardon may abound
2 the more"? Far from it. How could we continue to live in the
3 sin of apostasy when we have completely renounced this sin? Or
do you not know that all of us who by virtue of our baptism are in
communion with Jesus Christ, by the same baptism also shared
4 death with him? — by the same baptism descended with him into the
grave of spiritual death, so that in communion with him we might
be raised by his Father's glorious power from the realm of the
5 spiritually dead and travel the paths of a new life? For if we were
members of his body when he descended into the realm of death,
then we must also be members of his body after his return from the
6 realm of death. We know that our old selves were crucified with
Jesus in order that the body of sin might be destroyed and that
7 henceforth we might not be slaves to sin; for he whose sinful self
is once dead, is freed from the sin of apostasy and is a friend of God.
8 Now if we died with Christ as members of his spiritual body, then
we have the firm assurance that we shall also share spiritual life
9 with him. We know that Christ after his return from the realm of
spiritual death need go there no more, for the Prince of Death has

10 no further dominion over him. His descent to the spiritually dead
was required but once, because of the sin of apostasy. But now, after
11 his return to spiritual life, he lives only for God. The same must
be true of you also. You must look upon yourselves as men who
because of their sin of apostasy from God were numbered among
the spiritually dead, but who now in communion with Jesus Christ
12 live only for God. Then let the sin of apostasy from God no longer
dominate your mortal body, again making you slaves to this sin;
13 do not put your members at the service of ungodliness as instruments of wrong-doing, but put yourselves at the service of God,
as befits men who have returned from the realm of the spiritually
14 dead to the realm of spiritual life. For the phrase "sin of apostasy"
no longer has any meaning in your case; you are no longer bound
by the Law, but allow yourselves to be guided by the impulse of
15 love. What follows then? Shall we sin because we are no longer
constrained by the Law but are impelled by love for God? God for-
16 bid. Do you not know that you are the servants of him whom you
obey — either servants of the sin of apostasy, which results in spirit-
17 ual death, or servants who obey the impulse to do right? Thanks to
God, the time is past when you were servants of the sin of apostasy.
To-day you whole-heartedly obey the teachings as they have been
18 laid before you. Ever since you were freed from the slavery of the
19 sin of apostasy you entered into the service of righteousness — if I
may use this purely human expression that I have chosen because of
your human weakness. As in the past you have given your members
to unclean and ungodly practices and thereby made yourselves ungodly, so henceforth use your members in the cause of righteous-
20 ness, as people who have dedicated their lives to God. When you
were servants of the sin of apostasy the performance of good deeds
21 played no part in your lives. And what fruit had you to show
in those days? Was it not fruit of which you are ashamed to-day?
The end of all that is the spiritual death of separation from God.
22 But now that you are freed from the sin of apostasy and have become God's children again, you can produce fruit that will sanctify
23 you and finally result in the life hereafter. For the wage that
the sin of apostasy pays is the spiritual death of separation from
God; but that which God gives as a gift of mercy is a life hereafter
in communion with Christ Jesus our lord.

CHAPTER 7.

1 It is well known to you, my brothers, — for I am speaking to
people familiar with the Law — that every precept of the Law is

2 valid only during man's earthly lifetime. Thus, for example, according to the Law a woman is bound to her husband only during
his lifetime. If he dies, the provision of the Law under which he
3 made her his wife becomes void. While her husband was alive she
would have been branded as an adulteress if she had given herself
to another man; but once her husband is dead, the Law regards her
union with him as severed. Hence she commits no adultery by be-
4 coming another man's wife. So too, my brothers, you, as members
of the body of Christ, are dead to him to whom you were formerly
bound by law; you are therefore free to belong to another — to
him who was brought back from the realm of the spiritually dead,
5 so that in him we might bring forth fruit to God. So long as
we lived under the sway of our baser natures, we knew from the
precepts of the Law of Moses that our baser passions were sinful;
but in spite of this we allowed them full play in our members and
6 by so doing made ourselves servants of the Prince of Death. Now,
however, we are freed from that precept of the Law which bound us
to the Prince of Death, for we are dead in the eyes of him to whom
we were previously bound; hence we are free to enter the service of
a new master, the service of a spirit of God. The old order, the
observance of the letter, no longer exists for us.

7 What conclusion shall we draw then? That the Law of Moses is
sinful? God forbid. To be sure, if it had not been for that Law I
should not have recognized the sinful as "sin"; neither should I have
known the evil desire to be evil, if the Law had not said, "You shall
8 not have evil desires." For sin took this prohibition as its starting-
point and aroused in me one base desire after another; for where
9 there is no law, we are not conscious of the sin in sinful acts. At
one time, before the Law of Moses was in force, I lived as I chose,
unconcerned; but when the commandments and the prohibitions
10 came, the sinfulness within me came to life as conscious sin. But in
consequence I suffered spiritual death. The very commandment
ordained to bring me spiritual life in my case proved the cause of
11 spiritual death. My conscious sin arose from the fact that the commandment existed and I was beguiled into its violation; and thus,
by reason of my violation, the commandment was the cause of my
12 spiritual death. The Law of Moses, accordingly, is in itself holy, and
13 the commandment is holy, just, and good. Then was it a good thing
that brought about my spiritual death? No. That was brought about
by sin, knowingly committed. My hidden sinful inclination brought
about my spiritual death, in that it led me to sin knowingly in consequence of this commandment, which in itself is good. Thus the

commandment was destined to make us conscious of our excessive
sinfulness.
14 We know that the law of Moses came from God's spirit-world.
15 But I am worldly-minded and sold to the rule of sin. I cannot therefore understand my own behavior, for I do not do the good deeds
that I am eager to do, and I do commit the evil that is hateful to
16 my better self. Now if when I break the Law I do what my better
nature detests, I thereby prove that the intention of the Law is
17 wholly good. Therefore it is not my true self that is guilty of my
18 evil-doing, but my inherent sinfulness. I know that within me — that
is, within my baser self — there is nothing good. True, the desire to
do good is present in me, but I have not the strength to carry out
19 my good intentions; for I leave undone the good that I should like
20 to do, and do the evil that I should gladly leave undone. Now if I do
that which I do not care to do, it is not my true self that is the
21 offender, but a sinful inclination that has lodged within me. This,
then, is the experience that I have had with the Law: "I should like
22 to do what is right, but the things that I do are not right. My better
23 self assents to what the Law of God requires of me, but then I per-
ceive in my members quite another law, which conflicts with the
dictates of my better nature and brings me under subjection to the
law of sin that prevails in my members. My better self, therefore,
would rather serve the Law of God, but my baser nature obeys the
24 law of sin." What an unhappy man I am! Who will deliver me
25 from the slavery of this spiritual death? The mercy of God will do
so through Jesus Christ, our lord.

CHAPTER 8.

1 Thus there can be no further question of condemnation for those
2 who are in communion with Christ Jesus; for the laws governing
the spirit-world that lives in communion with Christ Jesus have
freed me from the laws governing the realm of the spiritually dead
3 who are separated from God by the sin of apostasy. For that which
the Law of Moses could not accomplish because it was too weak in
the face of the lusts of the flesh, God has accomplished. He sent
His own Son, clothed in an earthly body like that of other sinful
mortals. He sent him because of the sin of apostasy, and through
him doomed to destruction the dominion which this sin held over all
4 that was earthly, so that the precepts of the Law of Moses might be
fulfilled among us who do not live according to earthly desires, but
5 as a spirit of God directs. For the worldly-minded are only intent
upon the things of the world, but those who are guided by a spirit

6 of God are intent upon that toward which the spirit directs them. The
craving that obeys the impulse of the flesh brings with it spiritual
death; but striving for that toward which the spirit-world of God
7 urges us brings true life and peace. Worldly ambition is therefore
hostile to God, for it is not and cannot be in harmony with divine
8 law. Hence the worldly-minded cannot find favor with God. You
9 do not belong to the worldly-minded, but to those who allow themselves to be guided by God's spirits; for such spirits have taken
up their abode among you. Whoever does not harbor a spirit sent
10 by Christ, does not belong to Christ. But if Christ is in communion
with you, your spirit possesses spiritual life because of your faithfulness to God, though your body may still belong to the realm of
11 death because of the sin of apostasy. Now if the spirit-world of Him
Who raised Jesus from the dead has taken up its abode among you,
He Who delivered Jesus Christ from the realm of death will also
impregnate your bodies, which are still under that kingdom's
dominion, with the radiation of life, through His spirit-world that
has come to dwell among you.

12 Therefore, brothers, we no longer owe it to the desires of the
13 flesh to live as they would have us live; for if you were to live according to those desires, you would suffer spiritual death. But if,
with the help of one of God's spirits, you kill everything within you
14 that springs from sinful desires, then the true life will be yours; for
those who accept the guidance of one of God's spirits are children
15 of God. The spirit whom you have received is not one to enslave you
and make you fear him, but a spirit who will make you children of
God, so that we may joyously exclaim with him, "Abba! Dear
16 Father!" Thus the spirit-world of God, together with our own
17 spirit, arises to testify that we are children of God. But if children,
we are also heirs, for we are heirs of God and co-heirs with Christ,
provided that we have shared in his suffering in order to be able to
share in his glory also.

18 It is my belief that the sufferings here on earth cannot be com-
19 pared with the glory that will be revealed to us hereafter. All
creation longingly awaits this revelation of the glory that is to be
20 conferred upon the children of God. The material creation was made
subject to destruction, not of its own free will but by the will of Him
21 Who ordained its subjection, and ordained it in the hope that this
creation might free itself from the bondage of corruption, and so attain to that liberty which consists in the glory of being God's chil-
22 dren. For we know that to this hour the whole material creation
23 sighs and awaits the pangs of a new birth, just as we do. For not

only creation, but we ourselves, who already possess the first-fruits
of communication with God's spirit-world, sigh inwardly as we wait
24 to be released from our body. For it was by our confident hope that
we were saved. But a hope that one sees realized is a hope no
longer; for what need is there of hoping further if the fulfillment is
25 already at hand? But when we hope for something as yet unfulfilled,
26 we await its fulfillment with patience. In this point too the spirit-
world of God helps us, with regard for our human frailty. We do
not even know what to pray for, or in what manner, but God's spirit-
world itself comes to our aid with prayerful sighs that cannot be
27 expressed in human words. And He Who searches our hearts knows
the wishes of this spirit-world; He knows that it is interceding be-
28 fore God with its pleas on behalf of seekers after God. We know
that everything works together for the good of those who love God,
so that they may achieve their high ends — for the good of those
29 who are ready to be called in accordance with the divine plan. For
God decreed that those whom he knew to be fitted for the first rank
should be the first to be conformed to the image of His Son, who
30 was thus to be the first-born among many brothers. Those whom He
so foreordained He also called, and those whom He called He made
His friends, and those whom He made His friends He glorified.

31 Now what but this can we conclude from these facts: "If God is
32 for us, who can be against us? If He did not spare even His own
Son but gave him up for us all, will He not in His mercy give us
33 everything else?" Who could arise to accuse God's elect? God Him-
34 self? No, for He makes them His friends. Who would condemn
them? Christ? But it was Christ who died for them; and what is
more, he returned from the kingdom of death for their sakes, and
35 also sits at the right hand of God and intercedes for us. Then who
can separate us from the love of Christ? Can distress and tribulation? Persecution or hunger or nakedness? Danger of death, or
36 the executioner's axe? The Scriptures tell us: "For Thy sake we
are in daily peril of our lives; we are accounted as sheep for the
37 slaughter." But we shall overcome all these sufferings with the help
38 of him who loved us so dearly. For I am certain that neither death
nor life, nor Satan's angels nor his other powers and forces, neither
39 present nor future events, nor the powers of the earth, the air, or
the deep, nor anything else in creation will be able to separate us
from the love of God which has been manifested in Jesus Christ our
lord.

CHAPTER 9.

1 What I am telling you now is the truth. I call Christ Jesus to
witness that I do not lie; moreover, my own conscience, under the
2 influence of a holy spirit, testifies that my soul is heavy with sorrow
3 and incessant pain. I myself would willingly be banished from my
fellowship with Christ in the place of my brothers, men of my own
4 earthly race, who are Israelites. Once they were God's people; they
witnessed the glorious deeds of God; with them He made His
covenant; to them He gave the Law, the true form of worship, the
5 promises; theirs were the patriarchs, and from them was descended
the mortal body of Christ; for this may the God Who rules over
all be praised for ever!

6 Do not understand me to say that the promises given by God no
longer hold good. For not all who are bodily descended from Israel
7 are true Israelites, and not all are children of God because they
trace their ancestry back to Abraham. The promise was rather,
8 "Your descendants shall be named for Isaac alone"; that is, "Those
who are descended from Abraham in the flesh are not thereby children of God; the only ones reckoned as true descendants of Abraham
9 are those who are such by virtue of God's promises." One promise
10 runs, "At this time I will come, and Sarah will have a son." But
this was not the only promise. Another was given to Rebecca when
11 she was with child by our father Isaac. Before her twin children
were born, and hence before they could have done either good
12 or evil, she was told, "The older shall serve the younger." Thus
God sought to show that He predetermines the order of succession
at His pleasure, not waiting to see what deeds shall be accomplished,
13 but exercising His own choice. It is also written in the Scriptures,
"Jacob I loved, but I was not concerned about Esau."

14 Now what are we to infer from this? That God permits Himself
15 to be guided by injustice? Assuredly not, for He had said to Moses,
"I will be gracious to whom I choose, and I will have compassion
16 upon whom I choose." Thus the choice is guided not by the wishes
and the efforts of the one who is to be chosen, but wholly by God's
17 mercy. This is confirmed by the Scriptural passage that says with
reference to Pharaoh, "I have raised you from the deep for the very
purpose of showing my power in you and making my name known
18 throughout the earth." Hence God is gracious to those to whom He
wishes to be gracious, and abandons to their obstinacy those whom
he wishes to abandon.

19 You will protest, "Then how can He censure any one? For who
20 could resist His will?" O wretched man, who are you to call God to

account? Shall the thing created say to the creator, "Why have you
21 made me like this?" Has not the potter full power over his clay?
May he not shape from the same lump one vessel for lofty use and
22 another for lowly? Shall we protest because God, however often
He wished to pronounce sentence and manifest His power, nevertheless patiently tolerated those vessels that were to be reshaped by
23 punishment and were already marked for destruction — tolerated
them in order that He might thereby show the wealth of His glory
in the vessels designed for His mercy and prepared beforehand to
24 share in this glory? He has called us ourselves to be such vessels
of mercy, not only from among the Jews, but also from among the
25 Gentiles. Thus He says in Hosea, "Those who were not my people I
shall call my people, and the one whom I did not love I shall call
26 my beloved; and in the very place where it was said to them, 'You
are not my people,' they will be called the children of the living
27 God." And Isaiah exclaims concerning Israel, "Though the number
of the children of Israel be as the sands of the sea, nevertheless they
28 shall all be saved, down to the last remnant; for the Lord will fulfill
His promise in its entirety; at the same time He will choose the
shortest path in accordance with His just plan, so as to carry out
29 His promise as quickly as possible." Isaiah had also declared, "If
the Lord of hosts had not left us a seed, we should have been like
Sodom and met the same fate as Gomorrha."

30 What follows, then? The Gentiles, who did not strive for God's
favor, became His friends, although only by reason of their faith.
31 On the other hand, Israel, though careful to observe the Law that
was devised to secure God's friendship, has not reached the goal set
32 by the Law of Moses. Why not? Because they did not believe, but
merely relied upon outward observance of the Law. They stumbled
33 against the stumbling-block of which it is written, "Behold, I lay
in Sion a stone that will arouse their enmity and a rock that they
will turn away from; but whoever puts his faith and confidence in
it will not be disappointed."

CHAPTER 10.

1 Dear brothers, it is my heart's desire and my constant prayer
2 to God that Israel may be saved. For one thing I am bound to give
them credit: they display zeal for God. Unhappily they do so with-
3 out true understanding. They do not know in what true righteousness before God consists, and they strive to set their own standards
in this respect. That which God demands of them as right, they re-
4 ject. The end and aim of the Law of Moses is only to lead us to

Christ; and only those who believe in Christ find favor with God.
5 For this reason Moses writes that only those of their number will
receive spiritual life who fulfill the requirements for righteousness
6 imposed upon them by the Law of Moses. But the righteousness that
consists in faith is indicated in the following words: "Do not say in
your heart, 'Who will go up into heaven?'—that is, to bring Christ
7 down; or, 'Who will go down into the world below?'—that is, to
8 bring Christ up from the kingdom of the dead." And what do the
Scriptures answer? "The fulfillment of the promise is close to you;
it is in your mouth and in your heart,"—that is, the promise of the
9 faith which we preach. If you confess with your mouth that Jesus
is the lord, and believe in your heart that God raised him from the
10 kingdom of the dead, you will be saved. For man believes with his
heart in order thereby to obtain God's friendship, and makes ac-
11 knowledgment with his mouth in order thereby to be saved. Do not
the Scriptures say, "No one who puts his trust in him will be dis-
12 appointed"? On this score there is no distinction between Jews and
Gentiles. All have the same Lord, Who is bountiful to all who call
13 upon Him for help; for whoever calls upon the name of the Lord
will be saved. But how shall those who do not believe in Him call
14 to Him for help? And how shall they believe in Him of Whom they
have not yet heard? And how shall they hear of Him unless some
15 one comes and preaches about Him? And how can people preach unless they have been commissioned by God? As it is written, "How welcome are those who bring tidings of peace and news of good things!"
16 Not all, however, have heeded this good news; for Isaiah says,
17 "Lord, who has believed our words?" Thus faith comes from
hearing the truth, and the truth is preached at the instance of
18 Christ. Now let me ask you, "Have they perhaps not heard the
truth?" Indeed they did, for "their sound carried over all the earth
19 and their words to the end of the world." Let me ask further, "Did
Israel not understand?" Israel understood, for Moses, as the first
witness, says, "I will make you jealous of a nation that is not considered a nation of God, and provoke your anger against a nation
20 that is ignorant of God." Isaiah further says, "I have been found
by those who did not seek me and made known to those who did not
21 ask after me." But of Israel he says, "All day long I have stretched
out my arms in vain to a disobedient and rebellious people."

CHAPTER 11.

1 And now I ask, "Has God rejected the people whom He once
chose for His own?" By no means. I am an Israelite myself, a

physical descendant of Abraham and a member of the tribe of
2 Benjamin. Then God has not rejected the people whom He once
chose for His own. Do you not know what the Scriptures relate in
the story of Elijah? How he appealed to God and complained of
3 Israel, "Lord they have killed Thy prophets and torn down Thine
4 altars. I alone am left, and they seek my life also." What was the
answer that God sent through His spirit-world? "I have reserved
for myself," He said, "seven thousand men who have not knelt down
5 before the goddess Baal." In like manner there has now been left
6 a remnant, selected by grace; and if by grace, then not on account
of the deeds performed under the Law, for otherwise grace could
7 not enter into the question. How do things really stand, then?
Israel has not obtained what it has been seeking up to this very day;
the elect, indeed, have obtained it, but the rest remain hardened,
8 as the Scriptures say, "God has permitted a spirit of stupor to take
possession of them, permitted them to have eyes with which they
were unable to see, and ears with which they could not hear, even
9 to this very day." And David says, "Let their planchette be a snare
10 and a trap to them, a pitfall and a retribution. Let their eyes remain
darkened, and let Him bow their necks completely."

11 Now I ask, "Have they stumbled and fallen to their utter destruction?" Decidedly not; but in consequence of their fall, salvation has come to the Gentiles, so that the Jews might thereby be
12 spurred to emulation. But if their downfall was a blessing to the
world, and if their reduction to a small remnant of the faithful was a
spiritual gain for the Gentiles, how great will be the blessing when
13 all of the Jews have been saved.—I say this to you because you
are Gentiles. As an apostle to the Gentiles I take pride, in the
14 exercise of my apostleship, in using your salvation to urge this man
or that of my own race to emulation, and in thus saving them
15 also. For if their rejection leads the rest of the world to reconciliation with God, what will their readmission to God's people
16 be but a restoration of the spiritually dead to life? If the first loaf
is dedicated to God, so is the whole mass of the dough. If the root
17 is dedicated to God, so also are the branches. Even if some of the
branches have been broken off, and you, a Gentile, a wild olive shoot,
have been grafted in their place and received a share in the root
18 and the fruitfulness of the cultivated olive tree, do not look down
upon the broken branches. If you do, remember that it is not you
19 who support the root, but the root that supports you. Now you may
protest, "But the branches were broken off so that I might be grafted
20 in." Quite right, but it was only because of their unbelief that they

were broken off, and you stand in their place only by virtue of your
21 faith. Do not pride yourself on that account, but beware, for if God
did not spare the natural branches of the tree, He will surely not
22 spare you. Then consider both God's goodness and His severity:
severity toward those who deserted Him, goodness toward you while
you remain in His love; otherwise you too will be pruned away.
23 And the others will be grafted in again as soon as they abandon
24 their unbelief. God is well able to graft them in again. If you were
taken from an olive tree which is wild by nature, and grafted, contrary to nature, upon a cultivated tree, how much more readily will
the branches which naturally belong there be grafted upon their own
25 native tree. Brothers, I should not like to leave you in ignorance of
the mystery concealed here, for fear that your conceit might lead
you to false conclusions concerning this point: Hardness of heart
has come over a part of Israel, and will last until all of the Gentiles
26 have been gathered into God's community. Afterwards Israel also
will obtain salvation, as it is written, "The deliverer will come from
27 Sion; he will free Jacob from his ungodliness. And by my removal
of their sins of apostasy the covenant that I have made with them will
28 be verified." Hence, because they reject the gospel they are indeed
enemies of God, which is to your advantage; but because of having
been chosen, they are still loved by God for the sake of their fathers.
29 For God's election and call cannot be revoked. Just as you were
30 once disobedient to God, but have now obtained His mercy because
31 of the disobedience of the Israelites, so they are still disobedient to
Him Who had mercy on you; but in time they too will find mercy.
32 For God has confined them all together because of their disobedience in the past, in order that afterward He may pardon them all.
33 Oh, how vast is the wealth of God's knowledge and wisdom! How
34 incomprehensible are His plans, how inscrutable His ways! For who
has known the mind of the Lord, or who has been His counsellor?
35 Or who has given Him anything first and therefor had to be re-
36 paid? Everything is from Him and through Him, and everything
will return to Him. Glory to Him for ever! Amen.

CHAPTER 12.

1 I admonish you, my dear brothers, to dedicate your earthly lives
as a living, consecrated, and acceptable offering to God in return
for the mercy that He has shown you. That would be a divine
2 service which your own reason must commend. Do not shape your
lives as you see the men of to-day shaping theirs, but change them
in accordance with your new inner attitude. Then you will under-

stand what God requires of you; then you will be able to judge what
3 is to be regarded as good and acceptable to God. For by virtue of
the gift of grace bestowed upon me I admonish every one of you not
to esteem himself more highly than he ought, but to cherish a
modest opinion of himself and to lay claim to only such measure
of understanding in matters of faith as God has actually allotted to
4 him. For just as our bodies have many members and not all members
5 have the same task, so we faithful ones, though many in number,
are but one spiritual body in Christ; and in relation to one another
6 we are merely members of this body. So likewise the spiritual gifts
7 apportioned to us by the grace of God widely differ. For example,
if one is gifted to the extent that a spirit of God speaks through
him, this gift is in proportion to the degree and quality of his faith.
If some one has an office to fill in the congregation, let him devote
8 himself solely to this office. If some one has the gift of explaining
spiritual truths, let him perform the duties of the teacher. Let him
who has the gift of bringing consolation to others seek to console
his fellow-men. Let him who is in the position to do acts of charity
do so without presumption. Let him who has been appointed leader
display due zeal. Let him who is charged with dispensing alms per-
9 form his duty cheerfully. Let your love be sincere. Abhor that
10 which is evil, cling to that which is good. Let your brotherly affection for one another be hearty. Strive to excel in showing your
11 esteem for one another. Do not slacken in your zeal. Cherish a
12 fervent love for the spirit that has been allotted to you. Be servants of the Lord. Let your hope be an occasion for joy. Be stead-
13 fast in the midst of suffering. Pray without ceasing. Relieve the
14 needy among God's faithful ones. Dispense hospitality freely. Bless
those who persecute you; bless, instead of cursing them. Rejoice
with those who are happy, and sympathize with those who weep.
15 Live in harmony with one another. Harbor no thought of pride, but
16 befriend the lowly. Do not be among those who think they know
17 everything better than others. Do not repay evil with evil. Think
18 well of all men. Insofar as it lies within your power, seek to live in
19 peace with all of your fellow-men. Do not avenge yourselves, beloved, but let your anger cool; for it is written, "'Vengeance is
20 mine; I will repay,' says the Lord." On the contrary, if your enemy
is hungry, give him his fill to eat, and if he is thirsty, give him
drink; for by so doing you will heap coals of fire upon his head.
21 Do not let yourself be overcome by evil, but overcome evil with
good.

CHAPTER 13.

1 Render obedience to all the spirit-powers charged with your guidance, for there is no spirit-power placed over you that does not
come from God, and those at hand have been appointed by God.
2 Hence any one who resists such a power opposes the will of God and
3 thereby incurs punishment. These rulers are therefore not to be
feared by those who do good, but only by evil-doers. If you wish to
be among those who need not fear this power, do that which is good
4 and you will earn its praise; for it is assigned to you as a servant of
God for the accomplishment of good. But if you do evil, you have
every reason to fear it; for it does not bear the sword of punishment
in vain, and as God's servant is charged with executing sentence
5 upon evil-doers. Be obedient, therefore, not only for fear of punishment but because your own conscience urges you to obedience.
6 Bring good fruits to maturity also, for these powers are God's min-
7 isters and stay with you constantly for this very purpose. Give all of
them their due. If one demands a sacrifice, offer it. If another demands the performance of a good deed, do it. If a spirit leads you to
fear something, then fear it. If one of them points out something as
8 valuable, regard it so. Insofar as you observe the commandment to
love one another, you will fail in your duty to no one. He who loves
9 his fellow-man has thereby fulfilled the entire Law. For the commandments, "You shall not commit adultery, you shall not kill, you
shall not steal, you shall not covet," and all other such commandments of God are comprehended in the one saying, "You shall love
10 your neighbor as yourself." Love does not wrong a neighbor, there-
11 fore love is the fulfillment of the Law. Keep this rule before you in
all critical moments; for the hour is at hand when you must arouse
yourselves from sleep; salvation is nearer to us now than it was
12 when we first learned to believe. The night is nearly over, and the
day is about to break; so let us throw aside the deeds of darkness
13 and clothe ourselves in the deeds of light. Let us walk honorably,
like men who go about in broad daylight, not indulging in revelry
and drunkenness, in lewdness and excess, in quarrelling and jeal-
14 ousy. But clothe yourselves with the spiritual garment of our lord
Jesus Christ; and when the baser passions of human nature arise to
drag you down again, do not yield.

CHAPTER 14.

1 Befriend the man who is still weak in faith, and do not argue
2 controversial matters with him. One man believes that he may eat
food of any kind, while another, still weak of faith, believes that

3 only vegetables may be eaten. The man who eats food of every sort
with an untroubled conscience must not smile in disdain at him who
cannot do the same. And he who abstains from certain food must
not sit in judgment over the one who considers all food permissible
4 and whom God has chosen as His servant. How can you presume to
judge some one else's servant? Whether a servant stands or falls,
it concerns no one but his master; but he will stand, for his Master
5 is well able to support him. Again, some men think one day better
than another, while others consider all days alike. In such matters
6 let every one decide for himself. Whoever considers one day better
than another does so to please the Lord, and whoever holds that all
days are equal likewise does so to please the Lord. Whoever makes
no distinction in the matter of food acts out of love for the Lord,
for he returns thanks at his meals; and whoever does make a distinction also acts out of love for the Lord, for he too returns thanks
7 at meals. Not one of us lives and not one of us dies for himself
8 alone. If we live, our life is consecrated to the cause of God; and
if we die, our death likewise serves His cause. Whether we live or die,
then, we are at all times members of the spiritual body of the lord;
9 for Christ descended into the realm of the spiritually dead and returned to the kingdom of spiritual life to the end that he might
prove himself lord of both the spiritually dead and the spiritually
10 living. Now how can you presume to judge your brother, or how
dare you despise your brother? We shall all one day stand before
11 the throne of God, for it is written, "As I live, says the Lord, every
12 knee will bow to Me, and every tongue will confess God." Every
one of us will therefore have to render his own account.

13 Let us cease judging one another, then; let us rather take care
not to put a stumbling-block in our brother's way, or give him any
14 cause to sin. I know with certainty, for it was the lord who taught
me, that nothing is unclean in itself. But if any one considers it
15 unclean, then for him it is unclean. And so if by reason of your
choice of food you endanger your brother's conscience, you are not
keeping to the path of love. Do not, for the sake of a dish of food,
16 bring ruin upon him for whom Christ died. Do not speak ill of
17 that which is good in our eyes. The kingdom of God does not lie in
what we eat and drink, but in doing right under the guidance of a
holy spirit and thereby obtaining true inward peace and happiness.
18 For whoever recognizes in this the duty that he owes to Christ finds
19 favor with God and honor among men. Let us earnestly strive for
those things which make for peace and faithfully observe every-
20 thing that contributes to our mutual inner upliftment. Do not let a

trifling question as to the lawfulness of food wreck God's work of
salvation. As I have said, everything is indeed clean; but if any
21 one eats what his conscience forbids, for him it is sin. In such cases
you do well to eat no meat and to drink no wine and abstain from
everything which might offend your brother or give him occasion
22 to sin or merely to indulge a weakness. You have your own convictions in certain matters: good, then keep them to yourself; let them
be known to God alone. Happy is the man who has nothing with
23 which to reproach himself when he examines his conscience. But he
who eats a certain food despite his conscience has pronounced sentence upon himself; for he was not convinced that he might eat that
food. Every act committed without a firm conviction of its lawfulness, is sin.

CHAPTER 15.

1 We who are strong ought to bear with the infirmities of our
weaker brothers. But at the same time we are not permitted to do
2 everything that we should like to do. Each one of us must rather
take his neighbor into consideration, doing only that which seems
3 good in his eyes and thus serves for his edification. Not even Christ
did that which was most pleasing to him as a man, but, as the
Scriptures say of him, "The reproaches of those who reproach Thee
4 fall upon me." Such words as these, set down in the Scriptures in
times past, were written for our instruction, so that by reason of the
persistence and encouragement which we draw from the Scriptures,
5 we might steadfastly cling to hope. May God, Who is the source of
all constancy and encouragement, grant you the grace to live in
6 harmony with one another, as Christ commands us. If you are of
one heart and one soul among yourselves, you can praise the God
7 and Father of our lord Jesus Christ as with one mouth. Therefore
give each other your hands as Christ gave us his hand in order to
8 lead us back into the glory of God. I maintain that Christ became
the servant of the nation of the circumcised in order that God's
truthfulness might be proved, for thereby the promises given to the
9 fathers were fulfilled. But at the same time the Gentiles were to
praise God for His mercy to them, as it is written in the Scriptures,
"Therefore I will extol Thee among Gentiles and sing praises to Thy
10 name." Again, it is written, "Rejoice, you Gentiles, with His people
11 Israel;" and yet again, "Praise the Lord, all you Gentiles, and let
12 all nations extol Him." And Isaiah says, "There will be a growth
from the root of Jesse — one who will rise to reign over the Gentiles.
13 The nations will set their hopes on him." May God, on Whom alone

we rest our hope, fill you with the highest measure of joy and peace,
so that hope may abound within you, by the aid of a holy spirit.

14 I myself am convinced, dear brothers, that your will is of the
best; that you possess the necessary knowledge of the truth in every
15 respect and so are able to instruct one another. If I have written
to you in spite of this, my brothers, — and in some parts of my letter
I have spoken rather plainly — I did so only in order to refresh
your memory on certain points. In so doing I fulfill the task as-
16 signed to me by the grace of God. For I am to work among the
Gentiles as a servant of Jesus Christ and to be a priest of God's
gospel among them, so that the Gentiles may become an offering
17 acceptable to God, sanctified by the aid of a holy spirit. Now if I
have reason to be proud of my work for the cause of God, it is only
18 because I am in communion with Jesus Christ. For I should not
dare speak of any success, were it not Christ who achieved it through
me in order to recall the Gentiles to obedience to God by word and
19 deed, by performing signs and wonders, by the power of a holy
spirit. In this way I have preached the gospel of Jesus Christ in
20 its entirety from Jerusalem to Illyricum and far beyond. In so
doing I have made it a point of honor not to preach the gospel
where Christ's name was already known; for I was unwilling to
21 build where others had laid the foundation. I was guided rather by
the words of the Scriptures: "Those who have been told nothing
about him shall know him, and those who have had no knowledge of
22 him shall hear about him." That is also the reason why I have so
23 often been prevented from visiting you. But now my presence in
these parts is no longer needed, and as for many years I have been
24 longing to visit you, I will come to you on my journey to Spain.
I therefore hope to pay you a visit as I pass through, and to have
you see me off on my journey as soon as my longing for you has
been at least partly satisfied by my stay with you.

25 I am now on the point of leaving for Jerusalem in order to render
26 a service to those who have dedicated their lives to God. The congregations of Greece and Macedonia have resolved to take up a contribution for the poor belonging to the congregation of the faithful
27 of Jerusalem. They considered that they owed them this help, as
indeed they do; for if the Gentiles who are converted to Christianity
have received spiritual gifts from the Jewish converts, they are in
28 duty bound to assist them in turn with their material goods. When
I have settled this matter of business and delivered the sum contributed, I shall set out on my journey to you, and from you proceed

29 on my way to Spain. I know that when I arrive I shall bring with
me an abundance of Christ's blessings.
30 And now, brothers, I beg you by our lord Jesus Christ and by
the love that God's spirit-world cherishes toward you, stand by me
31 in my struggles by praying to God that I may escape from the persecution of the unbelievers in Judaea, and that the fact that it is I
who bring the contribution may not arouse the displeasure of the
32 faithful in Jerusalem. Then, God willing, I may come to you with
33 a joyful heart, and take a rest among you.—The peace of God be
with you all! Amen.

CHAPTER 16.

1 I am introducing to you our sister Phoebe, who is in the service
2 of our congregation at Cenchrea. Receive her as a member of
Christ's communion, as befits the faithful, and assist her in all
matters in which she may require your help; for she too has already
3 given assistance to many, including myself. Greet Prisca and Aquila,
my fellow-workers in the cause of Christ Jesus, as well as the whole
4 congregation that meets at their house. They have risked their own
lives to save mine. Thanks are due them for this, not only from me
5 but from all of the Christian congregations of Gentiles. Greet my
beloved Epaenatus, the first in Asia Minor to become a follower
6 of Christ. Greet Mary, who has labored so faithfully for you. Greet
7 Andronicus and Junias, my fellow-countrymen and fellow-prisoners,
who are held in high honor by the apostles, and who were converted
8 to belief in Christ before I was. Greet Ampliatus, my beloved in the
9 Lord; Urbanus, our fellow-worker in the service of the lord, and my
10 beloved Stachys. Greet Apelles, who is a tried servant of Christ.
11 Greet the brothers in the household of Aristobulus. Greet my fellow-countryman Herodian. Greet those of the household of Nar-
12 cissus who belong to Christ. Greet Tryphaena and Tryphosa, who
are zealous in the Lord's service. Greet the beloved Persis, who has
13 been a faithful worker for the Lord. Greet Rufus, one of the Lord's
14 chosen, and his mother, whom I regard as my mother also. Greet
Asyncritus, Phlegon, Hermes, Patrobas, Hermas, and the brothers
15 who meet with them. Greet Philologus and Julias, Nereus and his
sister Olympias, as well as all the faithful who meet at his house.
16 Greet one another with a holy kiss.
17 Now, brothers, I implore you, beware of those who cause dissensions and difficulties by opposing the doctrine which you have
18 received from us. Avoid them. Such men do not serve Christ our
lord, but their own gluttony; and by their spirit-messages they de-

19 ceive the hearts of the simple. It is generally known that you are
very willing to listen to such messages, and although your obedience
in such matters pleases me, it is my earnest wish that you do not
neglect caution in your striving after the good, and that you re-
20 main untouched by evil. The God of peace will soon tread Satan
beneath your feet.
21 Timotheus, my fellow-worker, and Lucius, Jason, and Sosipater,
my fellow-countrymen, as well as all the Christian congregations,
22 send their greetings. I, Tertius, who write this letter, greet you in
23 the Lord. Gaius, my host, who is also the host of the whole congregation, sends his greetings to you, as does Erastus, the city treas-
24 urer, and our brother Quartus. May the grace of our lord Jesus
Christ be with you all. Amen.
25 There is One Who has the power to strengthen you in the faith
— the faith that I have preached to you, the faith that Jesus Christ
himself proclaimed, the faith that is a revelation of the mystery
26 that has lain hidden in past ages but has now been disclosed through
writings set down by mediums at the direction of God, the Ruler of
all ages, in order that all nations might give ear to the proclama-
27 tion of the faith. To Him, the only wise God, be honor through
Jesus Christ, now and for ever. Amen.

The First Epistle of Paul the Apostle to the CORINTHIANS

CHAPTER 1.

1 PAUL, who by the will of God was chosen as an apostle of Jesus
2 Christ, and our brother Sosthenes send this letter to the church
of God in Corinth — to those who have consecrated themselves to
fellowship with Jesus Christ and who have been called to holiness,
and to all of every rank and vocation who call themselves by the
3 name of our lord Jesus Christ, their lord and ours. May grace and
love be granted to you by God, our Father, and the lord Jesus Christ.
4 I constantly thank God for the grace which God has bestowed
5 upon you through Jesus Christ; by your fellowship with him you
have been enriched in every way — in knowledge and in under-
6 standing of every sort, and in the measure in which your testimony
7 on behalf of Christ has gained in strength, so that now you need be
second to none in regard to any spiritual gift, and may await with
8 serenity the appearance of our lord Jesus Christ. He will strengthen
you to the last, so that you may be found blameless on the day of
9 the coming of our lord Jesus Christ. Faithful indeed is God, by
Whom you were called to fellowship with His Son Jesus Christ,
our lord.
10 My dear brothers, I beg you in the name of our lord Jesus Christ,
agree in your teachings. Let no divisions arise among you. Restore harmony by showing the same attitude and the same faith.
11 I say this, brothers, because I have been told by Chloe's people that
12 disputes are prevalent among you. For example, you are in the
habit of saying, "I am a follower of Paul," "I, of Apollos," "I, of
13 Cephas," "And I, of Christ." Has Christ been divided? Was it Paul
who was crucified for you? Was it in the name of Paul that you
14 were baptized? I thank God that I baptized none of you except
15 Crispus and Gaius. So no one can declare that I baptized him in
16 my name. Oh yes, it occurs to me that I also baptized the household
17 of Stephanas, but no one else, so far as I can remember. Christ did
not send me out to baptize, but to preach the gospel. It is true that
I do not preach it in high-sounding words of worldly wisdom, lest
18 the cross of Christ be desecrated. For to those who are on the way

to destruction the story of the cross seems foolishness. But to those
of us who have been saved from destruction it is a divine power.
19 As we read in the Scriptures, "I will put to shame the wisdom of the
sages and will turn into foolishness the knowledge of the wise."
20 What has become of the wise, the learned, the orators of these times?
21 Has not God branded the wisdom of this world as folly? The world,
because of its own "wisdom," did not recognize God in His true
wisdom; therefore God resolved, by means of a gospel that sounds
22 like foolishness, to save those who believe in it. While the Jews ask
23 for miraculous signs and the Greeks demand worldly wisdom, we
preach a Christ hung on a cross, who is a stumbling-block to the
24 Jews and a fool to the Gentiles. But to those who have been called
to believe, be they Jews or Gentiles, we preach Christ as the power
25 of God and the wisdom of God. For God's folly, as it is called, is
still far wiser than the so-called wisdom of men; and what is called
God's weakness is still far stronger than the so-called strength of
26 men. Look about you, brothers, at those in your own ranks who
have been called to salvation. You will find among them not many
who are wise in the eyes of the world, not many who are powerful,
27 not many of noble birth. God has rather chosen what the world
28 calls foolish in order to shame the wise; and it is what the world
calls base and contemptible, indeed what the world counts as nothing
at all, that God has chosen in order to destroy that which looms
29 large in the eyes of the world. For no mortal shall boast of his
30 own accomplishments before God. You owe it to Him alone that
you are in fellowship with Christ Jesus, whom God made for us a
spirit of wisdom, of righteousness, of sanctification, and redemption,
31 so that in accordance with the words of the Scriptures, he who
boasts shall boast only of what he has accomplished through the
power of the Lord.

CHAPTER 2.

1 For my part, brothers, when I came to you, I did not come
preaching God's mystery to you in high-sounding, learned phrases.
2 I was determined to appear before you as one who knew nothing
3 but Jesus Christ, and Jesus Christ the crucified. I impressed you
4 as a physically weak, timid, and very nervous man; and the things
that I said and preached I did not lay before you in fascinating
words of human wisdom, but it was God's spirit-world and God's
5 power that spoke through me. For your faith was not to be based
on human wisdom, but on a divine power.
6 And yet, that which we express is true wisdom, although only

in the eyes of those who are ripe for it. It is not the wisdom of this
7 world or of its rulers, who are indeed far from being wise. We proclaim the mysterious plan conceived by God in His wisdom, a plan
which has hitherto been concealed, but which God established be-
8 fore time began in order to lead us back to glory. This plan was
known to none of the rulers of this world, for otherwise, they
9 would not have crucified the lord of glory. We preach that which the
Scriptures express in the words, "No eye has seen and no ear has
heard and no human heart has divined the things that God has
10 prepared for those who love Him." But to us God has revealed
them through His spirit-world; for the spirit-world of God fathoms
11 everything, even the depths of divinity. What human being knows
his fellow-man's innermost thoughts? Not one. Only the spirit that
dwells in man knows his true inner nature. So too only the spirit-
12 world of God knew God's thoughts and plans. Now we have not
received one of the evil spirits that rule the world, but a spirit that
comes from God, so that we may know what God in His grace has
13 bestowed upon us. We preach about this also, not with words taught
by human wisdom, but in such words as a spirit of God teaches us;
thus we deliver the spirit's message in the same words in which the
14 spirit gave it to us. True, a worldly-minded man does not accept
what comes from a spirit of God, for he looks upon communication with God's spirit-world as madness. Neither is he fit to understand it correctly, for only those who know the laws governing
15 spirit-communication can properly judge it. But any one who is in
communication with the world of spirits can judge of these things
correctly, although such people, to be sure, are not understood by
16 the worldly-minded. For what worldly-minded man has ever known
the thoughts of the Lord, so that he was able to teach those who
communicate with God's spirits? But we, by our spirit-communication, know the thoughts of the Lord.

CHAPTER 3.

1 Even I myself, brothers, could not speak to you as to people who
are in communication with the spirit-world of God, but only as
to people whose whole manner of thought is worldly. So far as
2 Christ's gospel was concerned you were infants; I dared give you
only milk, not solid food, for you were not yet able to digest it;
3 and even now you cannot digest it, for you are still too worldly-
minded. As long as envy, strife, and dissensions prevail among you,
you reveal your lower nature and in no way differ from the general
4 run of men. For if one of you says, "I am a follower of Paul," and

another, "I am a follower of Apollos," are you not men of the
5 ordinary stamp? Who, pray, is Paul, and who is Apollos? Only
servants of Christ by whom you were led to faith. To each of them
6 fell the task allotted to him by the Lord. I attended to the planting,
and Apollos the watering, but it was God Who granted the growth.
7 Therefore neither he who plants nor he who waters is of any con-
8 sequence, but only God Who grants the growth. The one who plants
and the one who waters are of equal rank; but each will be specially
9 rewarded according to his special accomplishment. For we are
10 God's helpers; you are God's field and God's building. In accordance with the gift of grace bestowed upon me by God, I, as an expert
master-builder, have laid the foundation among you. Some one else
is now building upon it. Every one, whoever he may be, must build
11 with the utmost care. I have laid the foundation for all time; it is
12 Jesus Christ, and no one may lay a new foundation beside this. But
what kind of building each man will erect on this foundation—
whether of gold, silver, precious stones, or of wood, hay, or straw—
13 will appear later in every case. The value of every one's work will
14 be revealed on the day when it is tried by fire. If the structure built
15 upon it remains unharmed by the fire, he will be rewarded; but if
his work is destroyed by the flames, he will suffer punishment. He
himself will be saved, to be sure, but only to be tried by fire anew.

16 Do you not know that you are a spiritual temple of God, and that
17 the spirit-world of God dwells among you? If any one destroys
that temple of God, God will destroy him, for the temple of God is
18 consecrated to God, and therefore so are you. Let no one be deceived by hollow phrases. If any one is looked upon as a wise
man by the world of our day, let him first become a fool, for only
19 then will he become wise. The wisdom of this world is folly in the
eyes of God. It is written, "He catches those who are called wise
20 in the net of their own craftiness." And again, "The Lord knows
the thoughts of those who are called wise, and knows that they are
21 foolish." Then let no one boast about men. You are indeed lord
22 over everything—over Paul and Apollos and Cephas—over the
whole world, over life and death, present and future—over all this
23 you are lord; but Christ is lord over you, and God is Lord over
Christ.

CHAPTER 4.

1 So let all men look upon us as nothing other than servants of
2 Christ and stewards of the divine mysteries. Beyond that, only see
3 to it that each steward is found faithful. It is, of course, the least of

my cares how I am judged by you or by any human tribunal; in-
4 deed I even refrain from judging myself. I am not aware of any
unfaithfulness on my part, although this does not mean that I stand
innocent in the sight of God; for it is the lord who really judges
5 me. Therefore never judge anything prematurely, but wait until the
lord comes. He will bring to light the things that lie hidden in darkness, and lay bare the inmost thoughts of our hearts. Then every one
will be granted the recognition that he merits before God.
6 In what I have just said to you, brothers, I meant to show you
as in a mirror what has happened in your congregation in reference
to myself and Apollos. The lesson that you should learn from what
is here set down is that no one may consider himself superior to
his fellows, and that you must not take one man's part against an-
7 other. For who gives you precedence? And what do you own that
you have not received? But if you have received it, why do you boast
8 and thus give the impression that you have not received it? Are you
by chance already in full possession of the truths concerning salvation? Is spiritual wealth already at your disposal? Do you look
upon yourselves as kings in the realm of God and no longer in need
of our help? Would to God you were in your kingdom, so that we
9 might share the kingship with you. For it seems that God has chosen
to exhibit us apostles at the very end, as is the custom with gladiators
doomed to death, so that we may be made a spectacle to the world
10 and to angels and to men. In everything pertaining to the cause of
Christ you look upon us as fools and upon yourselves as wise; you
regard us as weak and yourselves as strong; you are honored, and
11 we are despised. Such is our folly that to this very hour we suffer
hunger and thirst; we are ill-clad; we allow ourselves to be struck
12 with fists; we wander about without a home, toil with our hands to
earn our daily bread, bless those who curse us, bear persecution with
13 patience, speak kindly to those who insult us; yes, because of our
folly we are to this day like the scum of the earth and the dregs of
humanity.
14 I do not write this to make you blush for shame but to warn you
15 as beloved children of mine. For though you may have many thousand teachers to instruct you concerning Christ, you do not have
many fathers. With regard to your life in communion with Christ I
16 am your father, by virtue of the gospel I preached. I beg of you,
therefore, as my children to try to resemble me as your father, just
17 as I strive to become like Christ. For this reason I have sent to you
Timotheus, my faithful son beloved in the Lord, so that he may recall to your memory the methods that I use to spread the doctrine

18 of the lord Jesus everywhere, in every congregation. On the assump-
tion that I would not come to you, some of you have taken to
19 speaking arrogantly; but God willing, I shall visit you shortly.
Then I shall soon find out from these boasters the true extent, not
20 of their oratory, but of their power. For the kingdom of God does
21 not manifest itself in talk, but in power. Now which do you prefer:
that I come to you with a rod, or with love and in a spirit of
gentleness?

CHAPTER 5.

1 It is reported on all sides that unchastity prevails among you,
and unchastity of a sort unknown even among the Gentiles; for one
2 of your number has sexual intercourse with his father's wife. Do
you still feel proud of yourselves? Should you not rather grieve,
and see to it that such an evil-doer is removed from your number?
3 I, who am present with you in spirit if not in body, have passed
judgment upon this man who has offended so outrageously, exactly
4 as if I were there in person. My sentence runs, "In the name of our
lord Jesus, and in your presence and in the presence of my spirit,
5 in the power and by the authority of our lord Jesus Christ, we
consign this man to Satan for the destruction of his vile passion, so
that his spirit may be saved on the day of the lord Jesus Christ."
6 Now you indeed have cause to feel proud, have you not? Do you
not know that a little leaven leavens the entire mass of the dough?
7 Get rid of the old leaven, so that you may become a new mass of
dough with no leaven in you any more. For Christ was sacrificed
8 for us as our Passover lamb; therefore let us celebrate the festival
not with the old leaven of wickedness and unchastity, but with the
unleavened bread of purity and truth.

9 In my last letter I wrote that you should not associate with the
10 licentious. By that I did not mean that you should have no dealings
at all with the unchaste anywhere in the whole world, or with the
dishonest and robbers or idolators that are to be found everywhere;
11 in that case you would have to leave the world altogether. I meant
to say in that letter that you should not associate with any one who
bears the name of a brother Christian and nevertheless is unchaste or
dishonest, an idolator, a slanderer, a drunkard, or a robber; you
12 should not even eat in the company of such a person. For why should
I be so concerned about those who are not of the Christian faith as
to admonish them also? You do not admonish even those who be-
13 long to your own number. As for the outsiders, God will bring

their failings home to them. In short, see to it that that wicked person is banished from your midst.

CHAPTER 6.

1 If one of you has a legal dispute with a brother in faith, can he
still find it in his heart to go to law before non-Christian judges
2 instead of before the faithful? Do you not know that the faithful
will sit in judgment over the world? If the judgment of the world
is entrusted to you, are you not competent to decide trifling mat-
3 ters now? Further, do you not know that we shall judge even
angels? Are we not capable, then, of judging worldly matters?
4 Then if you have legal questions concerning worldly matters to
settle, will you actually choose for your judges men who have no
5 standing whatever in your congregation? It is to your shame that I
am forced to say this to you. Is there really not one man of sound
judgment among you who is able to decide a dispute between
6 brothers? As it is, brother sues brother before worldly judges, and
what is worse, before unbelievers.

7 It is a moral defect in you that you go to law with one another
at all. Why do you not rather suffer wrong? Why do you not sooner
8 allow yourselves to be defrauded? Instead, you yourselves do wrong
and take advantage of others, even of members of your brotherhood.
9 Do you not stop to reflect that those who do wrong will not inherit
the kingdom of God? Do not deceive yourselves; neither the unchaste nor the idolatrous, nor adulterers, nor libertines and sodom-
10 ites, nor thieves, nor cheats, nor drunkards, nor slanderers, nor rob-
11 bers will inherit the kingdom of God. You were once people of
that stamp. But you were washed clean, you became faithful, you
obtained favor with God through the power of the name of the lord
Jesus and through the spirit-world that our God sent to you.

12 All things are lawful for me, but not all things are good for me.
All things are lawful for me, but I must not allow myself to be
13 mastered by anything. Food is for the stomach, and the stomach is
for food; but the day will come when God will separate us from
stomach as well as food. The body is not meant for immorality, but
to serve the lord as an instrument; for the lord has need of your
14 body as an instrument. And the same God Who raised the lord from
15 the realm of the dead will also raise us by His power. Do you not
know that your bodies are instruments of Christ? Am I to make
these instruments of Christ the instruments of a harlot? God for-
16 bid. Do you not stop to think that he who has dealings with a harlot
becomes one with her in body? For it is said, "The two shall be-

17 come one flesh." But he who forms a connection with the lord is
18 one with him in spirit. Therefore avoid unchastity. Every other sin
that man commits affects that which is apart from his body, but he
19 who commits unchastity makes his own body the object of sin. Have
you already forgotten that your body is a temple for the holy spirit-
world which dwells among you and which you have received from
20 God? You are not your own masters, then, for you were bought at
a high price. So contribute to the glory of God with your body.

CHAPTER 7.

1 Now as for the particular matters you mentioned in your letter
to me, I have this to say: It is commendable for a man to have no
2 intercourse with women; but to guard against immorality, let every
3 man have his own wife and every woman her own husband. Let the
husband perform his marital duty to his wife, and the wife hers to
4 her husband. In this respect the wife's person is not her own to do
with as she pleases, but her husband's; in the same way the hus-
5 band's person is not his own, but his wife's. Do not deny one another intercourse, except for a fixed time and by common consent,
for the purpose of devoting yourselves to prayer; afterwards resume
the conjugal relation, so that Satan may not take advantage of a
6 longer period of abstinence to tempt you. All this I offer by way
7 of concession, and not as a command; for if it lay with me, all men
would be the same as I in this respect; but every one has his special
gift of God — one in this way, another in that way.

8 To the unmarried and the widowed my advice is this: they do
9 well to remain single, as I am. But if they find it beyond their
strength to abstain, let them marry; for it is better to marry than to
10 be consumed by the fire of passion. To the married, my command
— no, not mine, but the lord's — is that a wife shall not separate
11 herself from her husband. If she has already separated, let her
either remain unmarried or be reconciled to him. On the other hand,
neither must the husband put his wife away.

12 As for the remaining points that I should like to touch upon
concerning this matter, I am expressing merely my personal opinion,
not speaking on behalf of the lord. If any brother is married to a
non-Christian woman, and she is willing to continue living with
13 him, he may not put her away. Similarly a Christian woman whose
husband is a non-Christian may not leave him if he consents to live
14 with her. For a non-Christian husband is led to God by his union
with a Christian wife, and a non-Christian wife is led to God by her
union with our Christian brother; moreover, since your children by

themselves know nothing of God, in this way they are led to God.
15 But if the non-Christian party desires separation, let it be so. In such
cases the Christian brother or sister is no longer bound by matri-
monial union; for it is to a life of peace that God has called us.
16 And how do you know, Christian wife, whether you will save your
non-Christian husband? And you, Christian husband, whether you
17 will save your non-Christian wife? But however this may be, let
every one lead his life as the lord has allotted, and as God has
called him.

18 This rule I lay down for all congregations: If a man who has
been circumcised is called to the faith, he is not to require circumcision of the rest also; and if a Gentile is called, he need not first
be circumcised. Circumcision has no importance, and the lack of
19 it is likewise unimportant. The one thing that matters is the keeping
20 of God's commandments. Let every one remain in the station that
21 he held when he was called. If you were a slave when you were
called, do not fret over your slavery; but if you have a chance to
22 become free, then choose freedom. For the slave who enters into
fellowship with the Lord because he was called is the Lord's freed-
man. In like manner a free man who is called becomes a servant of
23 Christ. You were bought dearly; do not become the servants of
24 men. Every one, brothers, should therefore remain in the condition
of life in which he was when he was called, as long as God so wills.

25 Concerning the unmarried, I have no message from the lord, but
I shall merely give my personal opinion as that of a man in whom
you may have confidence after all the mercy the Lord has shown
26 him. My opinion is this. Because of the present distress, it is ad-
27 visable for every one to remain as he is. If you are bound to a
woman by marriage, do not seek to break the bonds. If you are
28 free, remain unmarried. Of course you commit no sin if you do take
a wife. And a single woman does not sin if she marries. None the
less, those who marry take upon themselves worldly troubles, such
29 as I should like to spare you. There is just one thing that I will add,
brothers: it will not be long before those who have a wife must live
30 as though they had none; those who would weep must hold back
31 their tears; the joyous must restrain their mirth; those who buy
must realize that they will not keep what they have bought, and
those who have worldly connections must live as though they were
32 utterly ignorant of such connections. For the present order of things
will undergo a complete transformation, and I should like you to
be free from all needless cares when that time comes. Then the
unmarried will think only of the cause of the Lord and how best to

33 please Him, while he who is married must also be concerned about
worldly matters and consider the wishes of his wife, thus carrying
34 a load on both shoulders. Widows who do not remarry and young
women who remain single will likewise care only for the cause of the
Lord, so as to stand before Him holy in body and in spirit. But a
married woman has her worldly cares and must defer to the wishes
35 of her husband. All this I say to you by way of advice for your own
good, without wishing to fetter you in any way. My only purpose
in advising you is that you may become blameless and faithful followers of the Lord whom nothing can divert from him.

36 If a father should consider it a disgrace for his daughter to pass
the marriageable age unwed—and if it is therefore necessary—
then let him do as he pleases. He commits no sin. Let him give her in
37 marriage. But if he has any set convictions in the matter and there
are no strong objections against it, so that he is free to accomplish
his own will, and if after due deliberation he has decided not to give
38 his daughter in marriage, he will do well. In short, he who gives his
daughter in marriage does well; but he who does not give his
39 daughter in marriage does better. A wife is bound by the bond of
matrimony as long as her husband lives; after his death she is free
to marry whom she will, only he must be a follower of the Lord.
40 But she would be happier if she were to remain unmarried. That is
my personal belief, and I think that I also have a spirit of God.

CHAPTER 8.

1 I now come to your question as to the lawfulness of eating meat
offered to idols. No doubt all of us are well informed in this matter, but knowledge by itself leads to conceit, while love leads o
2 spiritual edification. And whenever any one thinks that he has acquired a certain amount of knowledge his understanding is far from
3 being as thorough as it should be. But any one who loves God is
4 endowed by Him with true knowledge. Now as to eating meat that
has been offered to the "gods," we know that in reality there are no
5 gods in the universe, and that there is only One who is God. For
although there may be many in the super-terrestrial as well as the
terrestrial spheres who have themselves called "gods,"—and indeed
6 there are many such "gods" and many such "lords"—for us Christians there is but One Who is God, namely the Father, in Whom
everything originates and to Whom we shall all return; and there is
but one lord, namely Jesus Christ, through whom all things came
7 into being and through whom we shall return to God. But not every
one has this knowledge. There are many who are so wedded to their

former idolatry, that to this day they eat the food offered to idols as
something unlike ordinary food. They thereby stain their conscience,
weak as it is.
8 The eating of food in no way affects our standing with God. We
may abstain from a certain food and be none the better, or we may
9 eat it and be none the worse. But be careful that your freedom in
the choice of food does not became a stumbling-block to the weak.
10 For if a weak person sees a brother who possesses the true knowledge
take a meal in an idol's temple, will he not thereby be emboldened
to eat meat that has been offered to idols, although his feeble con-
11 science may tell him that he must not? Thus a weak person will
suffer spiritual harm from an act that is permissible for you by
reason of your knowledge — and yet he is your brother, for whom
12 Christ died. If you thus wrong your brothers and wound their weak
13 consciences, you sin against Christ. Therefore if the meat that I eat
causes my brother to sin, I would rather abstain from meat for all
time in order to give my brother no cause for sin.

CHAPTER 9.

1 Am I not a free man? Am I not an apostle? Have I not seen our
lord Jesus? Are not you, as a Christian congregation, my work?
2 Even though I may not be an apostle in the eyes of others, surely I
am an apostle to you; for you, as a congregation of the Lord, are
3 the seal of my apostleship. My answer to those who would sit in
4 judgment over me is this: Are we not entitled to be supplied with
5 food and drink free of charge? Have we not the right to take a
Christian wife with us on our travels, as do the other apostles, even
6 the lord's brothers, and Cephas? Or are we two — I and Barnabas
— the only ones who have no right to leave off earning our living
7 by the work of our hands? What man performs military service at
his own expense? Who works in a vineyard without eating its fruit?
8 Who tends a herd without drinking the milk of the herd? Am I
speaking from a purely human standpoint? Does not the Law say
9 the same? For it is written in the Law of Moses, "You shall not
10 muzzle the ox that treads out the corn." Is it only for oxen that God
is concerned, or do His words rightly apply to us? It was undoubt-
edly on our account that these words were written, because he who
plows must hope to harvest, and he who threshes must hope to share
11 in the crop. Now if we have scattered the spiritual seed among you,
is it too much for you to allow us a share in your worldly posses-
12 sions? If others share your possessions, have not we a still better
right to do so? True, we have never availed ourselves of that right,

but have paid for our support out of our own means, so as to put
13 no hindrance in the way of the gospel. Do you not know that those
who serve in the temple draw their livelihood from the revenues of
the temple, and that those who serve at the altar have their share of
14 the altar-gifts? So likewise the lord has commanded that those who
15 preach the gospel should earn their living from it. For my own part
I have not availed myself of any of these rights, nor have I written
this in order to claim such rights for myself from now on, for I
16 would rather die than be deprived of this one boast of mine. There
is nothing for me to boast of in the fact that I preach the gospel,
for I am inwardly driven to do this, and it would be a woeful thing
17 for me if I did not preach it. But if I do this gladly, my own inner
joy is my reward, whereas if I were to undertake the work of the
18 gospel unwillingly, what reward would there be to induce me to
preach the gospel without charge and to forego the right to main-
19 tenance to which my preaching entitles me? Although I am indebted
to no one in this way, yet I have made myself a servant of every one,
20 in order that I might win over all the more. When I was among
Jews, I lived like the Jews in order to win over Jews; if they were
strict observers of the Law, so was I, although the Law no longer
21 interests me. I did this only in order to win them over also. When
I was among those who knew nothing of the Law of Moses, I lived
like a man who knows nothing about it; although, to be sure, not
like a man heedless of all divine law, but like one guided by the law
of Christ. Thus I sought to win those who were without the Law
22 of Moses. Among the weak I was weak, so as to win over the weak.
I have been everything to every one, in order to save all of them.
23 For the sake of the gospel I am ready to do everything, so that I
may share in its blessings.

24 Do you not know that in a foot-race all the contestants run, but
25 only one receives the prize? Run in such a way that you will win
the prize. And every one who enters an athletic contest first im-
poses upon himself strict abstinence in everything. These men do
so to win perishable wreaths, but the wreath that we have in prospect
26 is imperishable. For my part I run with my eye on a fixed goal,
27 and when I fight I do not beat the air; I keep my body in strict
subjection and make it my servant, in order that I, who preach the
glory of God's kingdom to others, may not forfeit that glory myself.

CHAPTER 10.

1 For I should not like to leave you in ignorance, brothers, of what
actually occurred in the case of our fathers. They were all under

2 the protection of the cloud; all had passed through the sea; all had
been baptized in the cloud and in the sea as followers of Moses;
3 all had eaten the same food, prepared for them by God's spirit-
4 world; and all had drunk the same drink, offered by spirit-hands;
for they drank from a spiritual Rock that was with them at all times,
5 and that Rock was Christ. But in spite of all this, most of them did
not gain favor with God, for they were struck down in the wilder-
6 ness. This was to warn us not to set our hearts on what is evil, as
7 they did. Do not become idolators, like some of them, of whom it
is written, "The people sat down to eat and drink at the feasts of
8 the idols and rose up to perform their dances." And let us not
practise unchastity as many of them did, so that twenty-three thou-
9 sand fell on a single day. Nor let us tempt Christ as some of them
10 did, in punishment for which they were killed by serpents. And do
not murmur, as a number of them did, with the result that they met
11 their death under the sword of the avenging angel. All these things
happened to them by way of warning, and were written down as a
warning for us who live on the boundary line between two eras.
12 Therefore let him who thinks he stands firmly take care that he does
13 not fall. As yet you have been faced with no temptation beyond
that of the ordinary human life. And God is faithful; even in the
future He will not allow you to be tempted beyond your strength;
as soon as temptation assails you He will provide a way of escape,
so that you may be saved.

14 Above all things, my beloved, shun idolatry. I am speaking to
15 men of discernment, so judge for yourselves whether I am right in
16 what I am about to say. The cup of blessing which we bless, is it not
the symbol of fellowship with the blood of Christ? The bread
which we break, is it not the symbol of fellowship with the body
17 of Christ? Just as it is but one loaf of bread, so we, although
many, are but one spiritual body; for we all share in that one loaf
18 and in that one cup. Look at Israel in the flesh! Are not those who
19 eat of the sacrifice in communion with the altar? Need I explain
in detail what meaning there is in the offerings to idols or in the
20 idols themselves? I should like to point out just this: the heathens
offer their sacrifices to the evil spirits and not to God. But I am not
21 willing for you to enter into communion with the evil spirits. You
cannot at the same time drink the cup of the lord and the cup of
the evil spirits; you cannot at the same time be guests at the table
22 of the lord and at the table of the evil spirits. Or do we intend to
provoke the lord to jealousy? Are we by chance stronger than he?

23 Everything is indeed lawful, but not everything is of benefit.

Everything is lawful, but not everything contributes to spiritual
24 growth. Every one should consider the welfare of others, and not
25 merely his own. You may eat whatever is sold in the meat-market
26 with a clear conscience without asking where it comes from, for the
27 earth and everything in it is the Lord's. If an unbeliever invites you
to a meal and you consent to go, have no scruples about eating what
28 is set before you. But if some one tells you, "This is sacrificial
food," then refrain from eating it, out of consideration for the one
29 who told you; for it is now a matter of conscience. When I say conscience, I mean the other man's conscience, not yours. For why
should I let my freedom of conscience be restricted by another
30 man's scruples? If I for my part eat and give thanks, why should I
let others speak ill of me because of food for which I thank God?
31 So whether you eat or drink, or whatever you do, do it all for the
32 glory of God. Give no offence to either Jew or Gentile or the church
33 of God. I too live so as to please all men in all points, not aiming
at my own advantage but at that of my fellow-men generally, so that
they may be saved.

CHAPTER 11.

1 Follow my example, as I follow the example set by Christ.
2 Brothers, I appreciate your remembering me at all times and fol-
3 lowing the instructions that I gave you. Above all I should like you
to keep the following precept well in mind: Christ is the head of
every man; the woman's head is man, and Christ's head is God.
4 Any man who wears his hair long and allows it to hang loose while
a spirit of God is praying or proclaiming a divine message through
5 him, dishonors him who is his head; and every woman dishonors
him who is her head if she does not wear her hair bound around her
head while a spirit of God is uttering a prayer or a message through
6 her, for in that case she is on a level with a harlot. If a woman will
not bind her hair firmly on her head, let her have her hair cut off;
but if she is ashamed to have her hair cut short, or her head shaved,
7 let her wind it about her head. A man, however, should not wear
his hair long and wound about his head, because he is the image
8 and reflection of God; but woman is the reflection of man. For man
9 is not sprung from woman, but woman from man. And man was not
created for the sake of woman, but woman for the sake of man.
10 On this account a woman should wear a crown of hair on her head,
11 for the sake of the messengers of God who speak through her. And
here I might remark that in a Christian community a man and his
12 wife and a woman and her husband form one unit. For although
woman springs from man, man is also born of woman, and every-

13 thing, male and female, comes from God. Now tell me yourselves,
is it not unfitting for a spirit to pray to God through a woman while
14 she sits with her hair dishevelled? Does not your natural instinct
15 teach you that long, flowing hair disfigures a man, whereas long hair
is a woman's glory, provided that it is neatly wound about her
6 head like a head-dress? If any one nevertheless persists in holding
a contrary opinion, I can only say to him that we are not acquainted
with any such custom, and neither are the churches of God.

17 And now I have something to say that does not reflect credit upon
you. Your meetings for divine service are not improving you, but
18 rather making you worse. First of all, I hear that when you meet
for worship quarrels are prevalent among you, and I believe there
19 is some truth in the report. To be sure, there must always be dis-
agreement so that it may be made clear which of you are on the
20 right road. But to come to the actual facts: when you meet in this
way, such a thing as a "lord's supper" no longer enters into the
21 question. As it is, every one of you before receiving the "lord's
supper" eats the food that he has brought with him from home.
Thus it happens that one goes hungry while another eats and drinks
22 to excess. Can you not eat and drink enough at home? Have you so
little reverence for the congregation of God, and do you mean to
humiliate the needy by your behavior? What shall I say? Shall I
praise you? You surely deserve no praise on this score.

23 That which I have told you in the past concerning the celebration
of the lord's supper I received from the lord himself. I told you
that on the night when the lord was betrayed he took a piece of
24 bread, gave thanks, broke the bread, and said, "This is the symbol
of my body, which is broken for you. Do this in memory of me."
25 In the same way he took the cup, after he had eaten, and said,
"This cup is the symbol of the new covenant in my blood; when-
26 ever you drink it, do so in memory of me." As often as you eat the
bread and drink from the cup in this manner, you proclaim the
27 lord's death until he comes back. Whoever, therefore, eats the bread
or drinks from the cup of the lord in an unworthy manner, sins
28 against the body and the blood of the lord. Hence let every one
examine himself, and only then let him eat the bread and drink from
29 the cup; for he who eats and drinks unworthily, brings a sentence
upon himself by his eating and drinking, because he does not show
30 due reverence for the body of the lord. This is also the reason why
so many among you are spiritually weak and ailing, and not a few
31 have already met spiritual death. If we were to sit in judgment over
32 ourselves, there would be no need of our being judged at all. But

if we have yet to be judged by the lord, we shall be punished with a
view to our correction, so that we shall not be condemned along
33 with the world. And so, brothers, wait for one another when you
34 meet for the celebration of the lord's supper. If any one is hungry,
let him eat at home, so that your celebration of the lord's supper
may not result in your punishment. The details I will settle when
I come.

CHAPTER 12.

1 With respect to spirit-communication, brothers, I wish you to have
2 a clear understanding. You know that at the time when you were still
heathens you entered into communication with the hideous spirits
3 of the abyss as often as you were impelled to do so. I will therefore
give you a rule by which you can distinguish between the spirits:
No spirit from God who speaks through a medium will call Jesus
accursed; and no spirit can speak of Jesus as his lord unless he
belongs to the holy spirits.

4 Spiritual gifts vary widely, but it is the same spirit-world of God
5 that bestows them all. The services rendered in the Christian congregation also vary, but here again it is the same lord who allots
6 them. Moreover, there are various effects produced by the spiritual
power, but it is the same God Who acts as the source of power in
every instance and with every medium.

7 Each medium is given manifestations of the good spirit-world for
8 the common good alone. Thus God's spirit-world endows one with
words of wisdom; another is endowed with the gift of discernment
9 under the operation of the same spirit-world; another, with understanding of doctrinal truths, by the same spirit-world; another is
10 given the gift of healing by the same spirit-world; another, power
over evil spirits; another, the gift of becoming a medium through
whom the mother tongue of the spectators is spoken; another is
endowed with the ability to discriminate between good and evil
spirits; another becomes a medium through whom spirits can speak
in foreign languages; another, a medium through whom foreign
11 languages can be translated into the mother tongue. All these gifts
are bestowed by one and the same spirit-world, which selects for
each the gift that he is suited for and dispenses it in such measure
as the spirit-world sees fit.

12 The human body is considered a whole, and yet has many members; but all the members of this one body, in spite of their number,
form but a single body. So it is with the spiritual body of Christ.
13 For through baptism we were all immersed in the one spirit-world

that belongs to Christ, and so became one spiritual body with him,
whether Jews or Gentiles, slaves or freemen: one and the same
14 spirit-world was poured out upon us. The human body does not
15 consist merely of one member, but of many. If the foot should say,
"Because I am not a hand, I do not belong to the body," would it
16 therefore not be a member of the body? And if the ear should say,
"Because I am not an eye, I do not belong to the body," would it
therefore not belong to the body? If the whole body were nothing
17 but eye, where would hearing be? If the whole body were nothing
18 but ear, where would our sense of smell be? As it is, God has given
to each member its proper place in the body according to His own
19 plan. If the whole body were but a single member, how could we
20 still speak of a body? But as it is, there are many members, while
21 there is only one body. Hence the eye cannot say to the hand, "I
have no need of you," nor can the head say to the feet, "I have no
22 need of you." On the contrary, the members of the body that seem
23 the feeblest are as necessary as the others. And to the very members
of the body that we consider less honorable, we pay special attention; and those members which we regard with a certain feeling of
shame we clothe with more care than we think necessary for the
members which we may expose without offending our sense of
24 modesty. Yes, God has thus arranged the members of the body,
providing for the least respected members a more important func-
25 tion, in order that there may be no conflict between the members of
the body, but that the members may look after one another's needs
26 in perfect harmony. And if one member suffers, all the members
suffer together with it; and if one member is honored, all the others
rejoice with it.

27 All of you together with Christ form one spiritual body, and each
28 one of you is a member of it. Among the members to whom God
has assigned their place in the congregation come first of all the
apostles; second, the mediums who speak in their mother tongue;
third, those endowed with the gift of teaching; then those who have
the power to cast out evil spirits; then those who have been endowed
with the power of healing; then such as have received the gift of
bringing spiritual help to others; then those who are gifted in administering the external affairs of a congregation; then the mediums
who speak in various foreign languages; then the mediums through
whom foreign languages are translated into the mother tongue of
29 the congregation. Do you suppose that all are apostles? Are all
speaking-mediums for the mother tongue? Do all have the gift of
30 teaching? Do all have the power to drive out evil spirits? Do all

have the gift of healing? Are all mediums for foreign languages?
Are all mediums for the translation of foreign languages into the
31 mother tongue of the congregation? Try to outdo one another in becoming more and more perfect in your several gifts. And now let me
show you a way that leads to a specially high degree of perfection.

CHAPTER 13.

1 If I could speak all the languages of men and of God's spirit-
messengers, but had no love, I should be like resounding brass or
2 a tinkling bell. And if I were a speaking-medium, and knew all
mysteries, and had all knowledge, and were so strong in faith that
I could move mountains, but had no love, all this would be of no
3 value to me. And if I distributed all that I have to the poor, and
gave up my body to be burned, but had no love, it would be of no
4 benefit to me. Love is full of patience and kindness; love knows no
5 envy; it does not boast or proudly put itself above others. Love
never acts inconsiderately, knows no selfishness, does not permit
itself to be provoked to bitter words, and harbors no grudge for the
6 wrong it suffers; does not rejoice in the triumph of injustice, but is
7 glad when the truth is victorious; does not expose the faults of
others, but seeks to excuse them; believes only the best, never aban-
8 dons hope, never loses courage. Love never dies, even though the
speech of God's spirits through mediums, be it in their mother
tongue or in foreign languages, may cease, and even though the
9 knowledge gained through clairvoyance may vanish. For the truths
of God are revealed to us in part by our own gifts of clairvoyance
and clairaudience, and in part by spirits using human trance-
10 mediums; but once we have become spiritually mature, our knowl-
11 edge will no longer be "in part, and in part." When I was a child
I spoke like a child, had the outlook of a child, and judged like a
child; but since I have reached the full maturity of manhood, I
12 have laid aside childish ways. Thus at present we still see truths as
in a mirror and in images difficult to understand; but sometime we
shall see them in their reality. Now I know only partial truths, but
afterwards I shall know everything as fully as I have been known by
13 God's spirit-world. Now these three gifts remain at our disposal:
faith, hope, and love; but the greatest of these is love.

CHAPTER 14.

1 Exert yourself to the utmost to obtain love. Also be eager, of
course, to enter into communication with God's spirits. Above all,
strive to become instruments through which God's spirits speak to

2 you in your mother tongue. For if a spirit speaks in a language
unknown to those present, he cannot make himself understood by
these people, but only by God. He therefore remains incomprehensible to every one, for the spirit uses words whose meaning is
3 hidden from his hearers. But if he speaks in their mother tongue,
this conduces to their edification, admonishment, and consolation.
4 A spirit speaking in a foreign language derives spiritual benefit
from it for himself alone, while one who speaks in the mother
5 tongue of his hearers edifies the whole congregation. I wish that
you had all progressed so far in your development as mediums that
spirits could speak through every one of you in a foreign language;
but it would please me even better if they could speak through you
all in your mother tongue. For a spirit who speaks to you in your
own language is of greater service to you than one who speaks in a
foreign language—unless, indeed, he also interprets that foreign
language into your own, so that the congregation may derive spirit-
6 ual benefit from it. Suppose, brothers, that I were to come to you
as one through whom God's spirit-world speaks in foreign languages; what good would I do you? Unless I could speak to you in
such a way as to reveal to you truths hitherto unknown, or unless
by virtue of my gift of clairvoyance, or as a speaking-medium or a
teacher, I could impart the gospel to you in your mother tongue,
7 my coming would be to no purpose. It would be the same as it is
with lifeless musical instruments. If, for example, the sounds given
out by a flute or a harp are such that no melody can be distinguished, how is one to recognize the air that is being played on the
8 flute or harp? The same applies to the trumpet. If one hears
nothing but unintelligible sounds blown on it, how can the call to
9 arms be recognized? It is the same in your case also. If a medium
should speak in a foreign language, how could you understand what
10 he was saying? It would all be spoken to the air alone. There are
ever so many languages in the world, and not one of them is in
itself unintelligible. But it is unintelligible to me, if I do not know
11 the meaning of the words in these languages. Then if some one
speaks to me in these languages I cannot understand him, nor can
12 he understand me. Therefore in your earnest endeavor to communicate with the spirit-world you should be intent on reaching a great
13 number of the most diverse of God's spirits. Thus a person who is a
speaking-medium for foreign languages should also ask for a spirit
14 able to translate foreign languages. For supposing that I, a medium,
were to pray in a foreign language, the spirit speaking through me
would, it is true, utter the words of the prayer, but my own spirit

15 would get no benefit from it. What value would such a prayer have?
I may indeed be glad to pronounce the words of the prayer spoken
by one of God's spirits, but it concerns me even more to understand
their meaning and thus be enabled to participate in the prayer myself. I should be glad to praise God in the words of one of His
16 spirits, but also to understand the words of praise myself. Suppose
that you were to offer a prayer of thanksgiving as the medium of a
spirit speaking a foreign language; how should simple folk, ignorant of foreign tongues, who sit there listening to you, say
"Amen" at the conclusion of your prayer? For they do not under-
17 stand what you have said. Without a doubt the prayer that you have
offered is beautiful in itself, but it in no way benefits the other peo-
18 ple. I am, God be thanked, a better medium for speaking in foreign
19 languages than any of you; but when I am conducting the service
I would rather speak five words that I understand, in order thereby
to teach others, than many thousand words in a foreign language.
20 Brothers, do not act like inexperienced children in judging such
matters. In evil be ignorant as children, but in other matters show
21 the understanding of mature men. In the Law of Moses it is written:
"'In foreign languages and with the lips of foreigners I will speak
to this nation; but even then they will not listen to me,' says the
22 Lord." From this it follows that speaking in foreign languages is a
23 proof, not for believers, but for unbelievers. Suppose that the whole
congregation were gathered in one place, all speaking in foreign
languages, and that people came there who knew nothing of communicating with spirits and did not believe in it; would they not
24 say that you had lost your wits? But if you as mediums were speaking your own language, and an unbeliever or a person inexperienced
in such things came to you, he would be furnished with proof of
25 spirit-communication, and his doubts would be dispelled; the secrets
of his heart would be laid bare; he would fall on his face and praise
God and acknowledge that a messenger from God was actually in
your midst.

26 Then how shall you proceed, brothers? In this way. Whenever
you have met for worship, each one of you receives something from
the spirit-world; with one it is a song of praise, with another a
lesson, with a third a revelation, with a fourth an address in a foreign language, and with a fifth the translation of that address. All
27 this is for your edification. If a foreign language is to be spoken,
let two spirits, or at the most, three, be permitted to speak, one at a
time, and let one spirit translate the addresses into the mother tongue
28 of the hearers. If no spirit is present who can translate the foreign

language, let the other spirit forego his address also, and offer a
29 silent prayer to God instead. Even addresses in the mother tongue
should be limited to two or three, and those present should discuss
30 what they have heard. If any one attending the service is suddenly
31 given an inspiration, the speaking-medium should be silent; for the
speaking-mediums all have sufficient opportunity to teach and en-
32 courage the whole congregation. The spirits manifesting themselves
33 through the speaking-mediums will obey the mediums, for God is
not a God of disorder but of harmony. Thus I teach in all the congregations of the faithful.

36 But perhaps you suppose that the word of God proceeded first
from you, or that you were the first to receive it and therefore know
37 everything better? If any one considers himself a speaking-medium
or otherwise in communication with the world of spirits, let him
assure himself by inquiring of God's spirit-world that what I am
38 writing to you is a command of the lord. But if he disregards it, he
39 too will be disregarded in the future by God's spirit-world.—Therefore, brothers, earnestly endeavor to become instruments of the
40 spirit-world for speech in your own language. Nevertheless, do not
try to prevent the spirits from speaking in foreign languages altogether, but let everything be done decorously and in perfect order.

34 Let the women keep silent at the meetings of the congregation;
for their mission is not to speak but to subordinate themselves, as
35 the Law of Moses prescribes. If they wish information on any point,
let them ask their husbands at home; for it does not become a
woman to begin a discussion at a religious gathering.

CHAPTER 15.

1 Once more, brothers, I shall refer to the gospel which I have
2 preached to you. You have accepted it, you are convinced of its
truth, and you will be saved by it, if you will hold fast to the doctrine that I have proclaimed to you. If you do not, your conversion
3 to the faith has been to no purpose. One of the first doctrines that
I preached to you, and one of the first that I myself received, was
that Christ died for our sins of apostasy, as it had been foretold of
4 him in the Scriptures. He was buried, and on the third day he was
5 raised, as the Scriptures likewise foretold, and he appeared to Peter
6 and then to the eleven. After that he was seen by more than five
hundred of the faithful at one time; most of them are alive to this
7 day, although some have died. Afterwards he was seen by James,
8 and then by all the apostles. Last of all he appeared to me also—
9 I being born out of due time, so to speak; for I am the least of the

apostles and really do not deserve the name of apostle, because I
10 persecuted the church of God. But by God's grace I became what
I now am; and the grace that He showed me was not in vain, for I
have done more work than all the rest. To be sure, it was not my
own strength that enabled me to do this, but the grace of God which
11 stood by me. Of course, it makes no difference whether it was I who
preached the gospel to you or they; we all preached the same truth,
and this truth is what you have accepted.

12 Now if it is preached that Christ was raised from the dead, how
can some of you maintain that there is no resurrection of the dead?
13 If there is no such thing as the resurrection of the dead, then even
14 Christ has not risen. But if Christ has not risen, then both our
15 preaching and our belief are empty illusions. Then we have testified
falsely concerning God, since we bore witness that He raised Christ,
16 while in reality He did not raise him; for if the dead do not rise,
17 then Christ did not rise either. And if Christ did not rise, your faith
18 is futile, you are still in your sins of apostasy, and all those who
19 have died believing in Christ are lost. If it is only in this life that
we may build our hope on Christ, we are the most pitiable of all
men.

20 But the truth is that Christ did rise from the dead, the first of
21 those who have fallen asleep. For because the spiritual death of
man was brought about by a man, the resurrection of the spiritually
22 dead was brought about by a man. For just as all died the spiritual
23 death in common with Adam, so all will return to spiritual life in
common with Christ, each in his turn. Christ was the first; then
come those who belong to him, as often as he appears to make his
24 selection; the last ones will come when he surrenders the kingdom
to God, the Father, after having terminated every other rule and all
25 authority and power hostile to God. For Christ must reign as king
26 until God has put all enemies under Christ's feet. The last enemy
to be overthrown will be the Prince of Death; for the Scriptures
27 say, "Until He has put everything under his feet." When the time
comes for Christ to say, "Everything is overcome," we must obvi-
ously make an exception in the case of Him Who subjected every-
28 thing to Christ. But when Christ has overcome everything, then
Christ himself as the Son will subject himself to the One Who made
everything subject to him, so that God may be everything to every
one.

29 Why do some people have themselves baptized on behalf of the
dead? If the dead do not rise at all, why do they have themselves
30 baptized for them? And we ourselves — why should we court dan-

31 ger every hour? My life is in danger daily — I swear it by the pride
which I take in you and to which our lord Jesus Christ has given
32 me the right. If I fought with wild beasts in Ephesus like the
ordinary person, what good could it do me? If no one can escape
from the kingdom of the spiritually dead, then let us eat and drink,
33 for to-morrow we die. Do not be misled. Bad company ruins good
34 morals. Be wide awake, and do not relapse into your former sins.
Unfortunately there are some of you who do not yet have the true
knowledge of God. To your shame I must say this.

35 But, some one will ask, how do the dead rise? What kind of a
36 body do they have? Foolish man! Just consider the earthly seed
that you sow in the ground. Must it not first perish in the earth
37 before new life sprouts from it? And the seed that you put in the
ground is by no means the same as the plant that later springs from
38 it. You sow the bare seed, be it of wheat or any other grain; but
God gives the plant such body as He pleases — in fact gives each
kind of seed its own characteristic body.

39 Not all earthly creatures have the same material body. There is
one kind of material body for men, another for four-footed animals,
40 another for birds, another for fish. Moreover, there are celestial
41 bodies and terrestrial bodies. The radiance of the sun is one thing,
that of the moon another, and that of the stars another. And one
42 star differs from another in radiance. So is it with the resurrection
of the dead. That which is sown perishes; that which grows out of
43 it does not perish. That which is sown is unsightly; that which
springs into life is glorious. That which is sown is sick and feeble;
44 that which springs into life is sound and strong. That which is sown
is an astral body; that which springs into life is a spiritual body.
45 This is the meaning of the Scriptures also, in the passage, "The first
man Adam was made a living being with an astral body;" the last
46 Adam was made a life-giving spirit. It is not the spiritual body that
comes first, however, but the astral, and then the spiritual body.
47 The first man is from the earth, and therefore earthly; the second
48 man is from heaven, and therefore heavenly. As the earthly man
was, so are all who are earthly; and as the heavenly was, so are all
49 who are heavenly. And as we have borne the outward form of
earthly man, so we shall also bear the outward form of the heavenly.
50 Let me impress upon you this one thing, brothers: earthly flesh
and blood cannot inherit the kingdom of God, for the perishable
51 can never have a part in the imperishable. Now I am going to tell
you something that has hitherto been unknown to you: None of us
will remain in the kingdom of the spiritually dead for ever, but we

52 shall all undergo the transformation into the spiritual body. In a
moment, in the twinkling of an eye, at the last trumpet-call, this
transformation will take place. The trumpet will sound, and the
spiritually dead will rise to eternal life; and we too shall be trans-
53 formed. For it is destined that this perishable creature be clothed
54 in the imperishable, and this mortal shall put on immortality. And
when this perishable creature has been clothed in the imperishable,
and this mortal in immortality, then we shall see the fulfillment of
55 the words of the Scriptures, "The Prince of Death was trodden in
56 the dust until the victory was won. Where, O Prince of Death, is thy
57 sceptre now? Where, O Prince of Death, is thy victory?" Thanks
be to God, Who granted us victory through Jesus Christ, our lord!
58 Therefore, brothers, show yourselves steadfast and immovable, and
always and in all places work for the lord's cause. You know that
your work will not go unrewarded if it is done in fellowship with
the lord.

CHAPTER 16.

1 Now with regard to the collection for the faithful, follow the same
2 rules that I laid down for the congregations of Galatia. On the first
day of each week let every one put aside something at home and in
this way save as much as his circumstances permit, so that there
3 may be no need of taking up a collection when I arrive. After my
arrival, I will send such men as you may think fit to Jerusalem with
4 your gifts and furnish them with letters of introduction. If it should
5 be worth my while to go there myself, they shall go with me. I shall
come to you, however, after I have visited Macedonia; I am merely
6 going to pass through Macedonia. I shall be among you for
some time, it may be for the whole winter, so that you may accom-
7 pany me when I continue my journey. This time I do not wish to
pay you a hasty visit in passing, but hope to make a longer stay
8 with you, if the Lord so wills. I shall remain here in Ephesus until
9 Pentecost, for I have been offered an opportunity to render exten-
sive and effective service in this place. To be sure, there are also
plenty of opponents.

10 If Timotheus comes to you, see to it that he is able to appear
among you without fear, for he is working for the cause of the Lord
11 just as I am. Let no one slight him, then. Afterwards send him on
his way in peace, so that he may return to me, for I am expecting
12 him with the other brothers. As for our brother Apollos, I might
tell you that I have urged him to go to you with the brothers; but at
present he is quite unwilling to take the journey. He intends to go,
however, as soon as a good opportunity offers.

13 Be watchful, be steadfast in faith, act like men, be strong. Let
14 everything you do be done in love. There is still one thing, brothers,
15 to which I should like to draw your attention. You know that the
households of Stephanas and Fortunatus were the first in Greece to
adopt the faith and devote themselves to the service of the faithful.
16 So put yourselves under the guidance of such people, and of any
one at all who energetically supports the cause and works hard.
17 I am glad that Stephanas and Fortunatus and Achaicus are with
18 me, for they have made up for your absence, and their presence
has been a great spiritual comfort to me, as well as to you. You
should appreciate men of this sort.

19 The congregations of Asia Minor greet you. Aquila and Prisca
send you their hearty greetings in the Lord, as do the members of
20 the congregation that meets at their house. All of the brothers greet
you. Greet one another with a holy kiss.

21 And my greeting, which I, Paul, write to you in my own hand,
22 is this: "If any one does not love the lord, let him be banished from
23 all communion with him. May our lord come. The grace of the
24 lord Jesus Christ be with you. My love is with you all in Christ
Jesus. Amen."

The Second Epistle of Paul the Apostle to the CORINTHIANS

CHAPTER 1.

1 PAUL, who by God's will became an apostle of Jesus Christ,
and Timotheus our brother, send greetings to the congregation
2 in Corinth and to all the faithful everywhere in Greece. Grace and
peace to you from God our Father and from the lord Jesus Christ.
3 Praise and glory be to the God and Father of our lord Jesus
4 Christ. He is the Father of mercy and the God of all comfort. He
comforts us in all our distress, so that we too may offer to those
who are in any trouble the same consolation that we receive from
5 God. As the sufferings that Christ endured come upon us in liberal
measure, so through Christ we are also granted consolation in the
6 same liberal measure. And so though trouble may befall us, even
this trouble will contribute to your consolation; and if we are con-
soled, this too will contribute to your own consolation and salvation; for you can win your salvation by remaining constant in the
7 midst of the same sufferings that we also have to endure. Hence we
are full of hope for you, knowing that as you share our sufferings,
you will share our comfort in equal measure also.

8 We do not wish to conceal from you, brothers, the trials that
beset us in Asia Minor. They were so excessively hard and un-
9 bearable that we despaired of escaping with our lives. Indeed, in
our mind's eye we could picture the execution of the death-sentence.
This was to teach us not to rely on ourselves, but on God, Who
brings back to life those who are already reckoned among the dead.
10 He on Whom we rested our hope delivered us from this frightful
11 peril and will deliver us again, because you too offer prayers to Him
on our behalf, so that on account of our deliverance prayers of
thanksgiving may rise from the lips of the many whose faces have
been turned heavenward in supplication for our safety.

12 Our one boast is in the testimony of our conscience that we have
led lives of uprightness and purity acceptable to God; that in the
world, and above all in our dealings with you, we have not acted
according to principles of worldly wisdom but as the grace of God
13 has directed us. But in writing this to you we are writing nothing
that you do not already know well and admit to be true; I hope that

14 you will become thoroughly acquainted with us, for hitherto you
have been only partially acquainted with us. On the day when the
lord Jesus comes, we shall then reflect glory upon you, and you
upon us.
15 Relying on this confidence in you, I had intended to visit you
16 before now, and so to afford you a double pleasure; for at first I
intended to go by way of Corinth to Macedonia and from there return to you, after which I meant to have you give me an escort to
17 Judaea. Now did I act thoughtlessly in forming this plan? Do I
make my decisions on the impulse of the moment, as worldly men
18 do, now saying, "Yes," and a moment later, "No"? God is my witness that when we make you a promise we do not mean "yes" and
19 "no" in the same breath. For the Son of God, Jesus Christ, who has
been preached to you by us—that is, by me, Silvanus, and Timotheus—was not one of those who say "yes" now and later change
it to "no," but once having said "yes," he made his "yes" good.
20 Thus in him all of God's promises have become a "yes" of fulfillment. Hence it is also through him that we have the "Amen" for
21 which we praise and glorify God. And it is God Who unites us
22 with you ever more firmly in our fellowship with Christ; it is God
who gave us spiritual anointment and set His seal upon us and sent
His spirit into our hearts as a pledge.
23 Now if in spite of my promise I have not yet come to you in
Corinth, it was only for the sake of sparing you—as surely as there
24 is a God Who may take my life if I do not speak the truth. We did
not wish our coming to give the impression that we were trying to
pose as masters over your religious convictions. All that we intended
was to contribute to your joy. In the matter of faith, you have
already gained a firm footing.

CHAPTER 2.

1 On turning the matter over in my mind I resolved not to pay you
another visit at a time at which my coming would cause you pain.
2 For if I grieve you, who would there be to gladden me? Only the
3 very ones whom I myself saddened. And this is the very reason why
I have written you this letter, so that when I come I may not be
grieved again and again by those who ought to be a source of joy
to me. I am justified, I presume, in my confidence that my joy is a
4 joy to you all. For I have written to you in great affliction and
anguish of heart and with many tears, not for the purpose of griev-
ing you, but so that you might know the abundance of love that I
5 bear you. If a certain person has given cause for grief, he has not

grieved me so much as a part—not to say all—of your congrega-
6 tion. The majority of the members of the congregation have in-
7 flicted punishment on this person; let that suffice. Indeed, you
should now show him every kindness and encourage him, so that
8 excessive remorse may not drive him to despair. I therefore recom-
9 mend that he be treated lovingly; for in my last letter I had it in
mind to ascertain whether you were willing to render absolute obedi-
10 ence. Now if you forgive this man, I forgive him too; for I have
forgiven everything for your sakes in the sight of Christ, whenever
11 I had anything to forgive. We must certainly not let ourselves be
beguiled by Satan, whose wiles we know only too well.
12 When I came to Troas to preach the gospel of Christ, I did indeed find every door open to the cause of the Lord; but under the
13 influence of the spirit allotted to me, I enjoyed no peace of mind because I did not find my brother Titus there. I therefore took leave
14 of the congregation in Troas and went into Macedonia. For this I
thank God, Who always triumphs over us through the power of Christ,
and Who allows the true knowledge of Him to rise everywhere like
15 a spiritual fragrance because of our deeds; we are a fragrance shed
by Christ for the glory of God upon those who will be saved as well
16 as upon those who are going to perdition. To the latter, this fragrance will be like the odor of decay that prevails in the kingdom
of spiritual death; to the others it will be like the breath of life
that is wafted in the kingdom of spiritual life. And who is fit to
17 perform such deeds? Assuredly we are, since we do not, like the
others, seek commercial profit from proclaiming the word of God,
but preach the gospel unselfishly, at the behest of God and in the
sight of God, as servants of Christ.

CHAPTER 3.

1 Are we once more beginning to recommend ourselves? Do we,
like some people, need letters of recommendation to you or from
2 you? You are our letter of recommendation, written upon our
3 hearts, for all men to recognize and to read as such. It is manifest
that you are a letter of Christ, written by us as servants of Christ,
not with ink, but with a spirit of the living God; not on tablets of
stone, but on tablets of the human heart.
4 Such is the faith in God that we have acquired through Christ,
5 that we do not rely upon ourselves at all in judging any matter;
on the contrary, our ability to form judgments derives from God.
6 He also enables us to act as the ministers of a new covenant, expressed not in letters but in the activity of a spirit. For the letter was

7 to lead to spiritual death, but the spirit to spiritual life. Now the
service that led to spiritual death and was engraved upon stone shed
such a brilliant light that the Israelites could not look at the face
of Moses on account of its radiance, although it afterward faded.
8 Then should not the service of the spirit shine with an even greater
9 radiance? For if the service that resulted in the sentence of condemnation was invested with so great a glory, how much brighter
will be the glory of a service that results in the winning of God's
10 favor? Indeed, the glory of the letter that appeared in those times
will in comparison be quite overshadowed by the matchless glory of
11 the service of the spirit. For if transient radiance was so glorious,
12 how much more glorious will be the radiance that endures? In
reliance upon this great hope we speak with the utmost frankness.
13 We do not do as Moses did, who covered his face for fear that the
Israelites might mark the disappearance of that transient radiance.
14 In spite of this, their hearts remained hardened, for to this very day
they still have the veil there whenever the Scriptures of the Old
Testament are read to them. Nor will this veil be lifted; for it can
15 only be removed by belief in Christ. Yes, to this day a veil rests
16 upon their souls whenever Moses is read; but as soon as Israel is
17 converted to the lord the veil will be removed. For the lord is the
spirit, and where the spirit of the lord is, there is true freedom.
18 Therefore as soon as we allow the glory of the lord to be reflected
in ourselves with the countenance of our spirit unveiled, we shall
be changed into his image, ascending to glory stage by stage, and
in such degree as will be brought about by a spirit of the lord.

CHAPTER 4.

1 For this service of the spirit we are indebted to the mercy of
2 God. Hence we know no despondency. We have renounced the
subterfuges that the fear of men carries with it. We do not dis-
semble, neither do we falsify the word of God. We state the truth
openly and so conduct ourselves that every one may speak his mind
3 concerning us with a good conscience in the sight of God. And
if the truth that we preach is obscure, it is obscure only to those
4 who are on the road to destruction, for the "god of this world" has
darkened the minds of the unbelievers; hence the light of the gospel
of the glory of Christ, who is an image of God, cannot illuminate
5 them. That which we preach is not our own doctrine but the doctrine
of Jesus Christ our lord, and we look upon ourselves only as your
6 servants in the cause of Jesus. For the God Who said, "Let light
shine out of darkness," has made light shine into our hearts as well,

so that by means of this light others may come to a knowledge of
the glory of God, under the guidance of Jesus Christ.
7 But we carry this treasure in fragile vessels, so as to show that
the extremely great power with which we are endowed can come only
8 from God and not from ourselves. And so although we are hard
pressed on every side, we are never crushed; though frightened, we
9 do not despair; though persecuted, we are not abandoned to our
10 persecutors; though struck down, we are not destroyed. All along
the road of our earthly life we have to bear suffering like that which
Jesus had to endure to the day of his death, so that the life-giving
11 power of Jesus may be manifested in our earthly life. And although
we always escape with our lives, we are always in danger of death
for the sake of Jesus, so that the life-giving power of Jesus may be
12 manifested in this flesh of ours that is doomed to death. In us everything that signifies "death" is trying its powers; in you, everything
13 that signifies "life." We possess the same spirit of faith of which
it is written, "I believed, and so I spoke." We also believe, and so
14 we speak. Moreover, we are sure that He Who raised Jesus will also
raise us who are in communion with Jesus and set us together with
15 you at Jesus' side. For it is all done for your benefit. The manifestations of grace shall constantly increase until they finally glorify
God in the highest degree with the ever-growing number of those
16 who offer thanks to God for them. And so we never lose heart.
Though our outer man may be tormented to death, our inner self
17 grows stronger day by day. For our present afflictions, momentary
and slight, will procure for us in the other world a measure of
18 glory that exceeds all human understanding. Let us therefore direct
our vision not toward that which we see with our corporeal eyes,
but toward that which we cannot see. For what is now visible to us
perishes, but that which is invisible endures for all time.

CHAPTER 5.

1 We know that after this earthly tent that has served as our dwelling has been taken down, we shall receive a dwelling from God—
a house not built by human hands, but kept in readiness for us in
2 the heavenly spheres for all time. And the reason for our sighing
is that we long to enter the shelter of our heavenly abode, and that
3 after our earthly dwelling has been demolished we shall not find
4 ourselves homeless in the beyond. But so long as we must dwell in
this earthly tent we sigh under a heavy burden. It is because we
do not wish to be divested piece by piece of our earthly garments,
but to be clothed at once in the heavenly, so that everything con-

5 nected with spiritual death may be absorbed by spiritual life. The
One Who gives us the strength to reach this goal is God; indeed He
has already given us one of His spirits as its guaranty.
6 So we are full of good cheer at all times. True, we know that so
long as we are clothed in base substance we must live far away
7 from the lord; but we walk the way of faith, not of sight. We are
8 confident, nevertheless, and should prefer to believe that we have
already cast off the earthly side of our natures, and hence can find
9 our home near the lord. But be this as it may, whether we are far
from the lord or near him, we look upon ourselves as in honor
10 bound to lead lives that are pleasing in his sight. How far we have
really progressed in this way must appear when we all stand before
the tribunal of Christ; on that day every one will receive the form
of astral body that he deserves according to his deeds, good or bad.
11 In our efforts to "win men over to us" we are conscious at all
times of the fear of the Lord. Our actions are plain in the sight of
12 God; plain also, I hope, in the sight of your better selves. By this
we are not trying to recommend ourselves to you again, but merely
to give you reason to be proud of us, so that you may have a fitting
answer to make to those who glory only in external things and not in
13 the inward reality. For when we speak on behalf of God's cause we
have, in the eyes of such people, "lost our wits"; but when we speak
14 on your behalf they call us "quite rational." And yet we are guided
in everything by our love of Christ, always mindful of this truth:
"This one died for all; hence we had all been condemned to spiritual
15 death. He died for all, so that those who come to life will no longer
live for themselves, but devote their lives to him who died for them
and rose from the realm of the spiritually dead for their sakes."
16 Therefore human failings are hereafter of no moment in our eyes;
and although we knew Christ as a man with human weaknesses, this
17 no longer enters into the question. If any one lives in communion
with Christ, he thereby becomes an entirely new creature; his old
18 self is gone, and a new one has taken its place. All this is the work
of God, Who reconciled us to Himself through Christ and charged
19 us with the task of arranging for the reconciliation. As it was God
Who reconciled the universe to Himself through Christ, no longer
counting the one-time apostasy of His creatures against them, so it
is the same God who has charged us with the mission of spreading
20 the knowledge of this reconciliation. We appear, therefore, in
Christ's stead as his envoys, in such a way that you may regard it
as the summons of God when we say to you, "On Christ's behalf we
21 beg you, be reconciled with God." For our sakes God made a sin-

ner of the One who knew nothing of the sin of apostasy, so that in fellowship with him we might win favor in the sight of God.

CHAPTER 6.

1 As fellow-workers of yours we should like to warn you to see to
2 it that you have not received the mercy of God in vain. For it is
written, "At your appointed time I have heard you, and upon a day
set for your salvation I have helped you." See, now is your favor-
3 able time; this is the day set for your salvation. Take care, therefore, that you give no one reason to sin, so that our religion may
4 not be overwhelmed with abuse. Rather let us show ourselves to be
true servants of God, bravely bearing all vicissitudes, patiently en-
5 during suffering, privation, and anxiety; constant under wounds and
imprisonment, despite riots and flogging, sleeplessness and hunger;
6 constant in purity and true knowledge of God, in forbearance and
kindness, under the guidance of a holy spirit and in unfeigned love;
7 constant in preaching the truth amid manifestations of God's power
and with the aid of weapons of offence and defence acceptable to
8 God, whether this yields us honor or scorn; whether men speak well
9 of us or ill; whether we are called deceivers, although we speak the
truth, or are treated like people whose acquaintance is not desired,
although they are very well known. Let us bear it like people who
apparently are doomed to death daily and nevertheless remain alive;
10 tempted by the Evil One, yet never forsaking God; forced to endure
much suffering, yet always cheerful; poor themselves, but enriching
many; having nothing, yet possessing everything.

11 My beloved Corinthians! Out of the fulness of our hearts we
12 have just given free rein to our words; but although you fill no
small space in our affections, there is little room for us in your own.
13 Repay one good turn with another! I speak to you as though you
14 were my children: "Open your hearts too." Do not yoke yourselves
with unbelievers, for what does loyalty to God have in common
with godlessness? Or what bond is there between light and dark-
15 ness? What harmony can prevail between Christ and Belial? What
16 has the believer to do with the unbeliever? What agreement is there
between the temple of God and the temple of the idols? For we are
a temple of the living God, as He Himself has told us in the words,
" 'I will dwell with them and walk among them; I will be their
17 God, and they shall be My people. Therefore go forth from their
midst and separate from them,' says the Lord." And further, "Touch
18 nothing that is unclean, and I will receive you." And again, " 'I will

be a Father to you, and you shall be my sons and daughters,' says
the Lord Almighty."

CHAPTER 7.

1 On the strength of these promises of God, my beloved, let us keep
ourselves unsullied in body and mind and become completely hal-
2 lowed in the fear of God. Give us a place in your hearts; we have
wronged no one, we have harmed no one, we have imposed on no
3 one. I do not say this by way of reproach, for as I have just declared, we carry you in our hearts and are ready to live and die with
4 you. I have full faith in you; I am very proud of you; I am fully
comforted, and my heart is overflowing with joy in spite of all outward trouble.
5 For after we arrived in Macedonia our bodies had no rest; on all
sides we met suffering and distress; assault from without, tempta-
6 tions within. But God, Who always befriends the oppressed, con-
7 soled us by the coming of Titus. And not only by his coming, but
also by the consolation that he brought from you. He told of your
longing for me, of your distress on my account, and of your deep
love for me, so that my heart was filled to the brim with joy.
8 Although I grieved you with my former letter, I do not regret
it now. At first I did regret it, for I saw that you were deeply pained
9 by that letter, although it was only for a short time. Now I am
glad, not because you were pained, but because on that account you
were made to repent; for your sorrow was such as God intended
you to have, so that you should suffer no harm from our letter.
10 Sorrow such as God wills produces repentance that results in reform, which no one has reason to regret; but sorrow such as the
11 world knows leads to spiritual death. Reflect how great a zeal this
very God-given sorrow aroused in you; and not only was your zeal
aroused but you begged for forgiveness, you were dissatisfied with
yourselves, you were awed, you yearned to become better men, you
strove for goodness, you punished the guilty. In every way you
showed that you had undergone spiritual purification as a result of
12 this affair. My letter, then, was not written to you for the sake of
those who had done wrong, nor for the sake of those who had suffered wrong, but to give you an opportunity of displaying zeal
13 for your soul's welfare in the sight of God. From this I have derived great comfort, and to our comfort there has been added an
exceedingly great joy. This was the joy that we shared with Titus,
14 for he gained great spiritual refreshment from all of you. If I have
often spoken to him highly of you in the past, I have not been put

to shame on your account now; for the praise that I then bestowed
in the hearing of Titus has now proved true, as indeed everything
15 that I told you has also proved true. His affection for you is all the
greater when he remembers how obedient you all were, and how
16 you received him with fear and trembling. As for me, I rejoice that
I can rely on you in every way.

CHAPTER 8.

1 Now dear brothers, we are going to tell you of the manifestations
of God's grace that were given to the congregations of Macedonia.
2 In spite of their severe ordeals of suffering, an abundance of spiritual joy has been bestowed upon them. Because of this joy they displayed such generosity that in spite of their poverty a great wealth
3 of gifts was collected. I can bear witness that they have contributed
4 to the utmost of their ability, and beyond. Of their own accord
they begged us as a favor to allow them to share in our labor of
5 love on behalf of the faithful. Not only did they give as much as we
could have expected, but they gave themselves, as it were, chiefly
out of love for the Lord, but partly out of love for us, as indeed is
6 according to God's will. This has prompted us to ask Titus to complete the collection of charitable gifts among you that he began in
7 the past. Now just as you have excelled in every respect — in sincerity of faith, in power of preaching, in your understanding of the
gospel, in your zeal for the good, and in your demonstration of love
8 for us — may you now excel all others in this work of love. I do not
mean this as a command; I only wish to test the sincerity of your
love for your neighbors by pointing out the zeal displayed by others.
9 For you know the kindness of our lord Jesus Christ, who although
he was rich, became poor out of love for you so that you might be
10 enriched by his poverty. I feel that you are in honor bound to lend
a helping hand in this matter, for not only were you the first to begin the collection a year ago, but also the first to urge that a collec-
11 tion be made. So finish now the work that you began. Your good
will at that time inspired you to take this work in hand; let it now
inspire you to complete the task — only so far as your means per-
12 mit, of course. Every gift willingly given, in accordance with the
13 giver's means, is a good deed; no one is asked to give beyond his
means, for the help that you afford others must not leave you your-
14 self in need. The aim is to strike a balance, so to speak; whatever
you have beyond the average, according to the standard of these
times, must serve to bring up to the average those who are below it.

Thus they receive a material gain and you suffer a material loss.
15 In this way is established the equality of which it is written, "He
who gathered much had no surplus, and he who gathered little, had
no lack."
16 Thanks be to God Who has filled the heart of Titus with a zeal
17 for you as great as my own. Titus not only acceded readily to my
wish that he should go to you, but of his own accord chose an earlier
day for his departure, in order to reach you as quickly as possible.
18 We have given him as a companion a brother whose fame as a
19 preacher of the gospel has spread to every congregation. He has
also been chosen by the congregations to be my travelling-com-
panion when I deliver the charitable gifts that are being collected by
20 us for the glory of God and in token of our good will. This measure
was taken to avoid all danger of ultimately arousing any one's
suspicion against us, however unjustly, in view of the liberal dona-
21 tion collected by our efforts. Thus provision has been made for
honest administration—honest not only in the sight of the Lord,
22 but also in the sight of men. To these two we have added from the
ranks of our brothers a third, whose zeal I have had many and
varied opportunities to put to the test. In this matter, however, he
will be even more zealous, because he has absolute confidence in you.
23 Now whether or not you consider Titus as my companion and fellow-worker, or our other two brothers as delegates of the congrega-
24 tions here, it will redound to the honor of Christ if you show them
all your love, and thereby prove to these congregations that you are
truly deserving of the praise that we have bestowed upon you in
their hearing.

CHAPTER 9.

1 As to the manner in which the work of love on behalf of the
faithful is to proceed, there is nothing further that I need to say to
2 you. I know your willingness and speak highly of it to the Macedonian congregations, pointing out to them that in Greece every one
was ready to begin the collection a year ago; and it was this men-
3 tion of your zeal that spurred most of them on to a like effort. For
this reason I have sent the brothers from here to convince themselves with their own eyes that my praise of you on this score has
not been unjustly bestowed, but that you have actually made all
4 arrangements, just as I had said. Now if members of the Macedonian
congregations were to visit you in my company and on their arrival
find you utterly unprepared, I should be put to shame because of

my confident reports about you — to say nothing of the shame that
5 you yourselves would feel. I have therefore thought it expedient to
advise the brothers to go to you in advance of me and get ready
your promised contribution in due time and on a scale large enough
to be of real service, and not as though it had been painfully wrung
6 from misers. Remember this: "He who sows sparingly will reap
sparingly, and he who sows bountifully will reap bountifully."
7 Let every one give as his heart bids him, but not grudgingly or
8 under compulsion; for God loves a cheerful giver. And God is able
to reward you abundantly for every gift, so that you will always
have enough for yourselves and ample means besides to assit in any
9 good work. The Scriptures say, "He distributed freely, he gave to
the poor; by doing right he secures his reward for all time."
10 He Who furnishes the sower with seed and thereby provides the
bread that you eat will also amply provide you with seed and mul-
11 tiply the fruits of your righteousness, leaving you so well supplied
with everything that you will be able to dispense charity freely, and
12 your charity will cause men to give thanks to God. The service that
is rendered by this act of devotion on your part not only remedies
the neediness of the faithful, but carries with it a rich blessing
by reason of the many prayers of thanksgiving that rise to God.
13 In this service they will recognize your true merit, and will praise
God for your acknowledgment and observance of the gospel of
Christ and for the benevolence you show to them and to all men
14 by your charity. They will remember you in their prayers, for they
feel drawn to you because of the grace of God that has been so
15 exceedingly active in you. Thanks be to God for His unutterably
great gift!

CHAPTER 10.

1 By the meekness and gentleness of Christ I personally make this
appeal before you — I, the selfsame Paul who you say is humble
enough in your presence, but full of self-confidence when he is at a
2 distance. I beg of you not to force me to be self-assertive on my
next visit; for I propose to be quite outspoken toward certain
people. I mean those who believe that our lives are directed by
3 quite worldly motives. Although we do mingle in worldly affairs,
we do not fight the battles that we are obliged to fight after the
4 manner of worldly people; for our weapons are not those of the
world. They are the weapons of God for the destruction of spiritual
5 strongholds. With them we overcome all false objections and other
mental obstacles raised against the knowledge of God. With them

we reduce to captivity the faulty reasoning of men and bring it un-
6 der subjection to the teachings of Christ. Moreover, we keep these
weapons ready to punish any disobedience on your part too, as soon
as you have gone so far as to surrender fully and absolutely to the
demands of Christ's doctrine.

7 Look at the facts as they actually lie before you. If any one is
certain that he really belongs to Christ, let him think twice and re-
8 member that we too are followers of Christ as well as he. Indeed,
if I were to boast that I have a higher standing on this score than
others, I should have no reason to be ashamed of this pride, for it
would be justified in view of the divine power with which the Lord
has endowed me in order to erect a new spiritual building among
9 you, but not for the destruction of that which has been erected. But
I shall rather refrain from this boast, for I do not wish to give the
10 impression that I am trying to intimidate you with my letters. To
be sure, my opponents say, "He may be stern and peremptory in his
letters, but when he appears in person he is a weakling; and as a
11 speaker he amounts to nothing." To those who make such a statement, let me say this: We shall deal with you just as forcefully in
your presence as we have dealt with you in letters during our ab-
12 sence. True, we have no desire to compare or class ourselves with
those who set themselves up as patterns. We seek within our own
hearts the standard by which we measure ourselves, and we compare
13 what we are with what we ought to be. So we shall never lay claim
to more glory than is our due. God has determined the sphere of
14 our labors, and we shall act accordingly. You also come within its
bounds, so that we are not extending our sphere unduly when we
include you; for you cannot say that you do not belong to it. We
were the ones who came to preach the gospel of Christ to you, and
15 indeed we were the first to do so. We do not seek recognition for
ourselves where others have done the work. To this we should not
be entitled. But we do cherish the hope that we shall be able to
widen our field of work considerably, as soon as the religious zeal
16 that has been awakened in you has increased. Then we will go into
the regions that lie beyond you to preach the gospel there. But we
shall never seek to gain reputation in a field in which others have
17 labored successfully before us. If any one seeks glory, let him seek
18 it of the Lord! For no one is accepted on his own recommendation
but only on the recommendation of the Lord.

CHAPTER 11.

1 I wish you would be indulgent with me if I appear to speak
2 rather foolishly. You will bear with me, will you not? If I betray
warmth in speaking to you, it is because I am pleading the cause of
God. I feel as though I had persuaded you to betroth yourselves to
a single bridegroom, Christ, and that I must now present you to
3 him as a chaste maiden. But at the same time I tremble for fear that
the old serpent, which beguiled Eve with its cunning, may lead you
to abandon the simplicity and purity with which you have hitherto
4 clung to Christ. You are already calmly permitting that serpent to
approach you in any shape whatsoever and to preach to you a Christ
other than the Christ whom we have been preaching; or you admit
to your presence spirits of quite another kind than those you have
previously admitted; or you accept a gospel unlike any that you
5 have heard in the past. We do not think ourselves in any way in-
6 ferior to the "excellent apostles"; and although as a speaker I may
have no "eloquence", I am not lacking in knowledge; of this I have
7 given you ample proof. Have I committed a sin, perhaps, by lowering myself in order to exalt you when I preached the gospel of God
8 to you without any compensation from you? I have exploited other
congregations, taking pay from them solely to give you my services
9 gratuitously. When I lived among you I was a burden to no one,
not even when I suffered want, for the brothers who came from
Macedonia supplied my needs. At all times I have avoided becoming
10 a burden to you, and shall do likewise in the future. As surely as
I am in fellowship with Christ, no one in Greece shall detract from
11 my reputation on this score. Why do I say this? Is it because I feel
12 no love for you? God knows the love that I bear you. No; I intend
to proceed in the future as I have done in the past, so that I may
cut the ground from under the feet of those who are doing everything
possible in order to be recognized as apostles equal to us on the
13 score of the efficiency in which they take such pride. Apostles
indeed! False apostles is what they are, full of guile and deceit,
14 wearing only the mask of Christ's apostles. We need not wonder at
this, for Satan himself assumes the form of an angel of light.
15 Therefore it is not strange that his helpers should appear disguised
as faithful ministers of God. But their end will correspond to their
deeds.

16 I repeat, let no one take me for a fool; but if you must do so,
then please be patient with this fool, and let me boast a little, as
17 others do. What I am now going to say I shall not present in the

way that the lord would speak; for now I am indeed playing the part
of a fool — now that boasting seems to be the order of the day.
18 Seeing that so many boast of their worldly merits, I shall do the
19 same; for you like to put up with fools, you who are so clever!
20 Without a murmur you allow fools to enslave you, to take your
21 money, to deceive you, to lord it over you, to browbeat you. To my
shame I confess it: fools like ourselves were not strong enough to
do these things. But whatever else any one may pride himself on,
22 I do the same — to continue speaking in this foolish vein. Are they
proud of being Hebrews? I too am a Hebrew. Of being Israelites?
I too am an Israelite. Of being descended from Abraham? I too
23 am his descendant. Of being servants of Christ? Then I — to give
free rein to foolishness — am a head servant; for I have worked
much harder than they, received beatings beyond measure, been
24 imprisoned often, and faced death time and again. Five times I have
been given forty lashes by the Jews; only one missed the mark.
25 Three times I was beaten with rods, and once I was stoned. Three
times I suffered shipwreck and have been adrift at sea a night and a
26 day. Add to this my many toilsome journeys and the dangers that
I faced from rivers and robbers, dangers from Jews and Gentiles,
dangers in cities, in the desert, and at sea, dangers at the hands of
27 treacherous Christian brothers. What sufferings and hardship have
I not had to endure! How many sleepless nights I have passed, what
hunger and thirst I have suffered! How often have I lacked the
barest necessities, shivered with cold and had nothing to put on.
28 And there are many other things of the same kind. Then there is
the daily pressure of business, and my concern for all the congre-
29 gations. For who is weak without my suffering with him? Whose
30 faith is in danger without my being distressed on his account? If
31 I must boast, I will boast of that which shows my weakness. The
God and Father of our lord Jesus Christ — may He be blessed for
32 ever — knows that I am speaking the truth. When I was in Damascus
the governor under King Aretas placed a guard over the city to
33 arrest me, but I was lowered in a basket through an opening in the
city wall, and so escaped from his clutches.

CHAPTER 12.

1 Since I am compelled to boast, though there is little to be gained
by it, I shall speak of the visions and revelations given to me by the
2 Lord. I know a disciple of Christ who fourteen years ago was taken
to the spheres of the third heaven. Whether his spirit remained in

his body or whether it was released from his body I cannot tell—
3 God knows. All that I know about this man is that he was caught
up into the sphere of Paradise and there heard words that human
4 tongues cannot utter. As I have said, whether his spirit remained
connected with his body or whether it was released from it, I cannot tell; God alone knows. I am proud to be the man who has ex-
5 perienced this. Of my purely human self I do not boast, for I should
6 have nothing to show but failings and infirmities. But if I were to
boast of other things I should not be a fool to do so, for I should
be telling the truth. But I will refrain, so that no one will take me
7 for more than that which he sees or hears that I am. And in order
to keep me from priding myself upon my abundance of revelations,
an angel of Satan was given to me on my journey through life, a
8 thorn in the flesh, to belabor me. Three times I have implored the
9 Lord in prayer to rid me of this angel, but the Lord answered, "My
grace is sufficient for you; for my power is most effective where
there is the greatest weakness." So I will gladly boast of my infirmity, so that the power of the Lord may produce its effect in me.
10 That is why I am cheerful in spite of all the infirmities, abuse,
tribulation, persecution, and distress that I have to bear for Christ's
sake. For in the hour of my weakness, I am strong.

11 There, now I have played the fool. But you forced it upon me
by failing to stand by me as I deserved. For although I myself am
nothing, nevertheless I am in no way inferior to the "peerless apos-
12 tles." You have certainly had abundant proof of my apostleship in
all that I have suffered, in spirit-manifestations, in miraculous cures,
13 and in my power over the evil spirits. Can you mention a single
point in which you are inferior to the other congregations, apart
from the fact that I did not make myself a burden to you? And this
injustice you have no doubt forgiven me.

14 Here I am now making ready to visit you for the third time, and
even this time I shall not be a burden to you. It is you that I long
for, and not your money. Children are not bound to provide for
15 their parents, but the parents for their children. I will gladly give
up what is dearest to me and sacrifice even myself, if by so
doing I can save your souls. I love you too much, you love me too
16 little.—Perhaps you will admit that I was not a burden to you;
but, being a "crafty man," as you say, I outwitted you. Is that true?
17 Did I exploit you through any one whom I have sent to you? I
18 asked Titus to go to you and sent our brother to accompany him.
Has Titus exploited you? Do we not both walk in the same spirit,
in the same footsteps?

19 You may again think that I am trying to defend myself before
you. By no means! I speak only as a servant of Christ in the sight
of God; and everything that I say to you, my loved ones, is for
20 your edification. For I fear that when I come I shall not find you
as I would have you, and that you will not find me as you would
have me. I fear that I shall find among you dissension and jealousy,
bitterness and rivalry, slander and gossip, arrogance and disorder.
21 Perhaps God will again have me suffer great humiliations at your
hands upon my arrival. I shall no doubt be grieved over many
who have sinned and not repented, but persisted in leading impure,
unchaste, and dissolute lives.

CHAPTER 13.

1 This, then, will be my third visit to you. Every case is to be de-
2 cided upon the testimony of two or three witnesses. I warned you
at the time of my second visit, and I warn you again now before I
come, both those who have sinned and all the rest as well. If I
3 come now, I shall spare no one. You ask for proof that Christ is
speaking through me; you shall have it. Christ will not be weak in
4 dealing with you but will exhibit his power among you. For although he was a weak mortal when he was crucified, now that he
lives as a spirit he possesses power from God. So we too are weak
as mortals, just as he was, but we shall show you that like him we
5 possess spiritual life, and with him, a power from God. Examine
yourselves, not me, to see whether you are firm in faith. Judge yourselves! If you do not know in your own hearts whether Christ is in
6 communion with you, you are not true Christians. I trust you will
7 find that we are not false Christians. But we pray to God that you
may do no evil. Our prayer for you is not intended to make us
appear as true Christians, but only to lead you into the path of
8 goodness, whether you look upon us as true Christians or not. For
we can do nothing against the truth; we can only act in accordance
9 with the truth. Indeed, we rejoice in your strength, even if you think
of us as weaklings. Allow yourselves to be led into the right path;
that is all that we ask.

10 I write this to you before my coming, in order that I may not
have to deal severely with you on my arrival. I have the authority
to do it. The Lord bestowed it upon me. But I received it for building up, not for tearing down.

11 And now, farewell, brothers. Strive for perfection. Give heed to
our admonitions. Preserve harmony, live in peace, and the God of

12 love and of peace will be with you. Greet one another with the holy
kiss. All the faithful send you their greetings.
13 The grace of our lord Jesus Christ and the love of God and communion with His spirit-world be with you all. Amen.

The Epistle of Paul the Apostle to the GALATIANS

CHAPTER 1.

1 I PAUL, am writing this letter to you. It was not by men that I
was chosen as an apostle, nor do I exercise my apostleship at
the bidding of any man, but only at the bidding of Jesus Christ and
of God the Father, Who raised Jesus from the kingdom of the spirit-
2 ually dead. I join all the brothers who are with me in sending
3 greetings to the congregations of Galatia. Grace be to you and peace
4 from God our Father and from the lord Jesus Christ, who on account
of the sin of our apostasy from God sacrificed himself in order to
5 deliver us from an age in which the Evil One reigns supreme. For
such was the will of our God and Father; may He be praised for
ever. Amen.
6 I am astonished that you have so quickly forsaken Him Who
called you to share in the communion of grace with Jesus Christ,
7 and that you have turned to another gospel. But there can be no
other gospel. To be sure, there are people who confuse you by seek-
8 ing to pervert the gospel of Christ. But even though we or a messenger from the beyond were to preach to you a gospel other than
that which we have hitherto preached to you, let him be banished
9 from your midst. What I have just said, let me repeat: if any one
should preach to you a gospel other than that which you have re-
received, let him be banished from your midst.
10 Am I now seeking to "gain favor with men," perhaps, or with
God? Am I trying to please men? If I were trying to please men,
I could be no servant of Christ.
11 Let me tell you, brothers, that the gospel that I have preached is
12 not the work of man. I did not receive it from a human being, nor
did I learn it through human instruction, but it was imparted to me
through a revelation of Jesus Christ.
13 You have heard of my former conduct in Judaism. You know
that as a Jew I relentlessly persecuted the church of God and tried
14 to destroy it. I distinguished myself among the men of my own age
by my Jewish fanaticism, and was notoriously zealous on behalf of
15 the traditions inherited from my fathers. But from the day of my
birth, God in His goodness had determined for me my true mission

16 in life; and when He considered that the moment had come to reveal His Son to me, so that I might carry the gospel to the Gentiles,
17 I made my decision regardless of worldly considerations. I did not
go to Jerusalem to those who had been called to the apostleship
much earlier than I, but went rather to Arabia and from there
18 back to Damascus. Three years later I went to Jerusalem to meet
19 Cephas. I remained with him a fortnight. At that time I saw none
20 of the other apostles except James, the lord's brother. That which
I state here is the whole truth. I swear before God that I am not
21 lying. After that I went into the regions of Syria and Cilicia, but
22 to the Christian congregations of Judaea I was unknown. They had
23 only heard it said of me, "Our former persecutor is now preaching
24 the faith that he once tried to destroy." And they praised God for
the change of heart that had taken place in me.

CHAPTER 2.

1 After fourteen years I again went to Jerusalem. Barnabas ac-
2 companied me, and I took Titus with me also. This journey was
undertaken as the result of a revelation. I told them of the gospel
that I preach among the Gentiles, but I spoke of it only in private
to those who were at the head of the congregation. I merely wished
to see whether in their eyes I was following or had followed the
3 right path with my work. But no attempt was made to persuade
4 even my companion Titus, a Gentile, to undergo circumcision. It is
true that certain false brothers had made their way into the congregation there; they gained admission for the sole purpose of spying
out the extent of the liberty that is ours under the doctrine of Jesus
Christ, for they wanted to bring us back into the old bondage of the
5 Law of Moses. But in order that the teachings of the gospel might
be preserved for you in all their purity, we did not yield to their
6 wishes for a moment. No further obligations were imposed on me
by those who were in authority in the congregation there. Besides,
I do not care how high their standing in the congregation was; God
7 takes no account of a man's outward rank. In short, these had no
fault to find with my work, but on the contrary were convinced that
I had been entrusted with preaching the gospel among the Gentiles,
8 just as Peter among the Jews. For God, Who had endowed Peter
with the power of exercising his apostleship among the Jews, had
9 endowed me with the same power among the Gentiles. And because
they had seen the gift of grace that had been bestowed upon me,
the so-called "pillars of the church," James, Cephas, and John, held

out their hands to me and Barnabas as their co-workers, with the
understanding that we should work among the Gentiles and they
10 among the Jews. Only, we were to remember the poor among the
converted Jews, and I did my best to comply with their wishes on
this score.
11 Now one day Peter came to Antioch. On this occasion I was
obliged to oppose him openly, as he had placed himself in the wrong
12 by his conduct. For before the emissaries sent out by James arrived,
Peter would eat with the Gentile Christians according to their customs; but when the converted Jews arrived he began to draw back
and hold aloof from the Gentile converts out of fear of the others,
13 who taught the need of circumcision. All the other converted Jews
joined in this hypocrisy, so that even Barnabas was led to participate
14 in the sham. When I saw that their conduct was not at all in accordance with the true teachings of the gospel, I said to Cephas in
the presence of all, "If you, a Jew, observe the customs of the Gentiles instead of those of the Jews, how can you hope to compel the
Gentile converts by your example to observe the Jewish customs?"
15 It is true that by birth we are Jews and not sinners of heathen de-
16 scent; but we know that man does not become acceptable in the eyes
of God by observing the provisions of the Law, but by faith in
Jesus Christ. For this reason we have adopted the belief in Jesus
Christ in order that we might win God's favor by this faith in Christ
and not by virtue of observing the Law; for no creature can win the
17 favor of God by observance of the Law. To be sure, hard as we
may strive to win favor with God in fellowship with Christ, sins will
be found in us too; but is Christ therefore a servant of sin? Never.
18 But if I try to restore that which I demolished, I thereby acknowl-
19 edge that I have transgressed. I for my part consider myself dead
to the Mosaic Law by reason of the Mosaic Law, in order that I may
20 have life in God. As a member of Christ's body I was crucified with
Christ, hence I no longer live my own life, but I live as a member
of Christ. The life that I am now leading on earth is therefore in
reality simply a life of faith in the Son of God who loved me and
21 sacrificed himself for me. I dare not reject the grace that God has
thus conferred upon me; for if favor with God could be attained by
the outward observance of the Law, then Christ would have died in
vain.

CHAPTER 3.

1 O you foolish Galatians! Who has bewitched you — you to whom
the crucifixion of Christ in its significance for yourselves was so

2 clearly set forth? This is all that I wish to ask you: Was it as the
result of outward observance of the Law that you gained communication with God's spirit-world, or was it the result of adopting the
3 faith? You see how foolish you are. Having laid the foundation for
a new life under the guidance of a spirit of God, do you now seek
4 to complete the structure with pure worldliness? Was it in vain
that you witnessed such powerful spirit-manifestations? Was it
5 really all in vain? Does He Who allows the spirit-world to communicate with you and through it develops such marvellous powers
within you do this because of your observance of the Law, or because of your faith?

6 It is the same with you as it was with Abraham. Abraham believed God, and his faith was so highly esteemed that he found favor
7 with God because of it. By this you may know that those who have
8 faith are the true children of Abraham. The Scriptures, foreseeing
that the Gentiles would obtain salvation only by faith, foretold this
in the promise given to Abraham: "In you all nations shall be
9 blessed." Thus all who have the faith of Abraham share in the
10 blessing conferred upon Abraham, while all who seek salvation by
outward observance of the Law come under a curse. The curse runs
thus in the Scriptures: "Cursed is every one who does not faithfully
carry out all the precepts that are written in the book of the Law."
11 That no one can obtain the favor of God by observing the written
Law is manifest from the words, "He who has found favor with God
12 will have spiritual life in consequence of his faith." However, the
written Law has nothing to do with faith, but teaches, "He who has
13 obeyed these statutes is thereby assured of life upon earth." Christ
has redeemed us from the curse pronounced by the Law by taking
the curse upon himself; for it is written, "Cursed is every one who
14 hangs on a tree." Thus the blessing promised to Abraham was to
be conferred upon the Gentiles in Jesus Christ; and we were to receive this blessing through God's spirit-world by virtue of our faith.

15 Brothers, I shall take an example from human life. When a
man has made his will and duly signed it as required by law, no
16 one else may afterwards cancel that will or add to it. Now these
divine promises were given to Abraham and to his descendant. It
does not say to his descendants, as if there were many, but speaks of
one descendant only; for the Scriptures say, "to your descendant."
17 This descendant is Christ. What I mean to say is this: a decree
solemnly pronounced by God cannot be annulled by a law enacted
four hundred and thirty years later, so as to render the promise void.
18 For if the promised inheritance were dependent upon the later Law,

it would no longer be bequeathed under the promise. But God
granted it to Abraham by a promise, as an act of grace.
19 Under these circumstances, does the Law of Moses still have
meaning? Yes, for it was given as a supplement in order to define
transgression more clearly until such time as the descendant came,
to whom the promise refers. The Law was transmitted by messengers
of God, who came at the instance of one who wished to mediate be-
20 tween two parties. Now a mediator does not act only for one side;
21 but God belongs only to one side. Then does the Law conflict with
the promise of God? By no means. True, such a conflict would exist
if an external law had been given which could produce spiritual life;
for in such a case the favor of God would actually be obtained by the
22 observance of outward provisions of the Law. But according to the
Scriptures everything was placed under the dominion of the sin of
apostasy, so that the promised salvation through faith in Jesus Christ
23 might be given to those who accept this faith. But before the faith
came, the precepts of the Law made us feel as if we were in prison,
and weighed down with chains we awaited the day when the faith
24 should be revealed to us. Thus the Law of Moses became a school-
master for us, leading us in strict discipline to Christ, so that by
25 faith in him we might attain the favor of God. But now, having accepted the faith, we are no longer under the tutelage of a school-
26 master. You are all children of God by virtue of your faith, and you
27 are in spiritual fellowship with Jesus Christ; for by baptism you
have become spiritually merged with Christ, and his spiritual gar-
28 ment envelops you. In this spiritual fellowship there is no distinction between Jew and Gentile, slave and freeman, man and woman.
29 In your spiritual fellowship with Christ Jesus you are all equal.
And if you belong to Christ, you are true descendants of Abraham;
on the strength of the promise you are his heirs.

CHAPTER 4.

1 Let me add something further. So long as an heir is a minor,
there is little outward distinction between him and a servant of the
2 household, although he is the lord of all the property. He is rather
under the care of guardians and trustees until the time fixed by his
3 father. So it is with us. We too were minors and were held in
4 bondage by those spirit-powers which rule the world. But when the
time of our majority came, God sent His Son. This Son was born of
5 a woman and likewise made subject to the Law, so that he might ransom those who were under the same bondage of the Law, and so that
6 it might be possible for us to become children of God. Now since you

are God's children, God has sent into your hearts the spirits be-
7 longing to His son, who call aloud, "Father." Therefore you are
no longer a servant but a child; and if you are a child of God, you
are also an heir of God by virtue of your spiritual fellowship with
Christ.

8 At that time, to be sure, when you did not yet know God, you
9 served gods who were really no gods at all. But now you have
come to know the true God; and what is more, you are recognized
by God as His children. Then how can you turn back to the weak
and paltry spirit-powers of the depths, and consent to be enslaved by
10 them again? You are again observing the days, months, seasons,
11 and New Year's Days that have been dedicated to these spirits. I
am almost afraid that my labor with you has been in vain.

12 Brothers, I earnestly beg you once more, become as I am, so that
I may see my likeness in you. — You have never done me any harm;
13 far from it. Do you remember how I first preached the gospel to
14 you while I was ill? How you felt neither fear nor loathing of my
physical malady, but welcomed me like a messenger of God, indeed
15 like Christ himself? What blessed happiness it gave you! I can
bear witness that if it had been possible you would have plucked
16 out your eyes and given them to me. And now have I become your
17 enemy because I have told you the truth? I know that others are
seeking your favor, but to no good purpose. They would be only
too glad to come between you and me in order that you might bestow your affection elsewhere. But you should employ your zeal first
18 and last in attaining the higher gifts. It would be an excellent thing
for you to strive after nothing but the highest at all times, and not
19 only when I am with you. You are my children, for whom I must
suffer anew the pangs of childbirth until I have again made you such
20 that the form of Christ is reflected in you. How happy I should be if
I could be with you at this moment! I should gladly alter my tone
in speaking to you face to face; for in writing I am at a loss to
express my thoughts otherwise than I do.

21 Tell me, you who are so eager to live under the Law of Moses,
22 do you not read the Law? It is written there that Abraham had
23 two sons, one by a slave and the other by a free woman. His son
by the slave was of normal issue, but his son by the free woman was
24 born contrary to nature's law, by virtue of a promise. All this has
an allegorical meaning. These two women represent a twofold
declaration of God's will. The one is that which was proclaimed
from Mount Sinai, imposing bondage on those for whom it was
25 meant; it is symbolized by Hagar, for Mount Sinai is called Hagar

in the Arabian language and has the same spiritual significance as
the Jerusalem of to-day; for this city is also held in bondage to-
26 gether with her children. But the Jerusalem on high in the spirit-
27 world is the free woman, and she is the mother of us all. For it is
written: "Rejoice, childless woman, you who have hitherto born no
children. Break forth into exultation, you who know no birth-pains.
For the unwed woman will have many children, more than she who
28 is wed." You, brothers, are children of the promise, like Isaac. But
29 just as in those days the son who was born in the ordinary way
persecuted him who was born according to the promise given by
30 one of God's spirits, so it is now. What do the Scriptures say? "Put
away the slave-woman and her son, for the slave-woman's son shall
31 not be heir with Isaac, the son whom I gave you." So then, brothers,
we are not children of a slave, but of a free woman.

CHAPTER 5.

1 Christ freed us so that we might avail ourselves of our liberty.
Stand fast, then, and do not let yourselves be placed under the yoke
2 of bondage again. Mark, it is I — Paul himself — who assure you
that if you undergo circumcision, Christ will be of no further value
3 to you. Again and again I testify to every man who submits to the
rule of circumcision that he thereby binds himself to observe the
4 Law of Moses in full. All of you who seek the favor of God through
compliance with the Law of Moses are thereby severed from com-
5 munion with Christ; you have forfeited God's gift of grace. For
we derive our hope of winning favor in God's eyes from the con-
6 fident faith which was taught us by a spirit from God. But to those
who live in spiritual communion with Christ Jesus it is of no importance whether they are circumcised or not; what is important is
simply faith, but only a faith that manifests itself in works of love.
7 You ran so well at the start! Who has impeded you in your race,
8 so that you now refuse to obey the truth? It is only obedience, not
disobedience, that comes from Him Who called you to the truth.
9 A little leaven alters the appearance of the whole mass. I for my
10 part am confident in the Lord that you are wholly of my belief.
If any one tries to lead you astray, he will pay the penalty for it,
11 whoever he may be. Brothers, if it were true that even I preach the
necessity of circumcision, then why should I still be persecuted?
12 For then the offence that is implicit in the cross would be eliminated.
The best thing would be for those who try to upset you to be elim-
13 inated too. For you have been called to liberty, brothers; only do

not misuse this liberty as a license for earthly desires, but serve
14 one another with deeds of love. For the whole Law is summed up
15 in the command, "You shall love your neighbor as yourself." But if
you bite and gnaw at each other, take care that one is not entirely
devoured by the other.

16 So I warn you, let one of God's spirits be your guide through
17 life, and then you will not yield to the baser passions. For the
natural cravings conflict with the spirit-world of God, and the spirit-
world of God conflicts with the natural cravings. The two are always at war; whatever you do, therefore, you cannot do it without
18 a struggle. Be guided by a spirit from God; then the Law of Moses
19 need no longer concern you. But if you allow your bodily desires
to guide you, the deeds arising from them will soon come to light:
20 unchastity, indecency and debauchery, idolatry and witchcraft, enmity, strife, jealousy and anger, treachery, discord and dissension,
21 envy, murder, drunkenness, gluttony, and the like. I have already
spoken to you of these sins, and I again point out that no one who
22 commits them can inherit the kingdom of God. In contrast to these
consider the fruits that God's spirit-world produces among you:
23 love, joy, peace, patience, amiability, kindness, faithfulness, gentleness, and self-control. Not one of them conflicts with the Law of
24 Moses. All who belong to Christ in spirit have crucified all worldly
25 ambition together with their passions and desires. Now if we have
obtained spiritual life through a spirit from God, let us also conduct
26 our lives in accordance with the instructions of that spirit. Let us
not in our vain ambition provoke one another to quarrels, or envy
one another.

CHAPTER 6.

1 Brothers, if any one thoughtlessly does wrong, you, as men under the guidance of a spirit from God, should set him right in a
spirit of gentleness; and at the same time let every one watch him-
2 self in case he too is tempted. Bear one another's burdens, and so
3 fulfill the law of Christ. And if any one should consider this beneath
him because he is something out of the ordinary, when in reality he
4 is nothing, he is deceiving himself. Let every one scrutinize his own
conduct; then he will not boast even to himself, much less give him-
5 self airs in front of others. For every one has a heavy enough load
to bear in his own burden.

6 He who receives instruction in divine truth must share all his
worldly possessions with the one who gives him instruction.

7 Make no mistake. God does not let Himself be mocked, for what
8 a man sows, he will also reap. He who sows on the field of his
worldly desires will reap destruction; but he who sows on the field
prepared by God's spirit-world will reap from that spirit-world life
9 in the beyond as his reward. Let us not weary of doing good, then,
10 for in due time we shall reap, if we do not sit with folded hands. So
then, whenever the opportunity offers, let us do good to all men,
especially to our fellow-believers.
11 See in what large letters I now write you these closing words in
12 my own hand: All those who consider themselves people of consequence because of their worldly standing try to make you undergo circumcision so that they may escape persecution on account of
13 the doctrine of Christ crucified. For these people themselves, in
spite of their circumcision, do not abide by the Law of Moses. They
urge circumcision on you only that they may boast of your belong-
14 ing at least outwardly to their number. Far be it from me to glory
in anything except in the cross of our lord Jesus Christ, by which
15 the world was crucified for me, and I for the world. For in our
fellowship with Christ Jesus, neither circumcision nor the lack of it
is of any importance whatsoever; it is only spiritual rebirth that
16 counts. On all who are willing to live according to this rule, may
peace and divine mercy rest; for they are the true Israel of God.
17 Henceforth let no one cause me further suffering, for I bear on
my body the marks of suffering of the lord Jesus.
18 May the grace of our lord Jesus Christ be with your spirit,
brothers. Amen.

The Epistle of Paul the Apostle to the EPHESIANS

CHAPTER 1.

1 PAUL, an apostle of Christ Jesus by the will of God, sends greetings to the faithful in Ephesus who also remain true to Jesus
Christ.
2 Grace and peace to you from God our Father and from the lord
Jesus Christ.
3 Praised be the God and Father of our lord Jesus Christ! Because
of our fellowship with Christ He has bestowed on us all manner of
4 heavenly gifts through His spirit-world. It was He Who had chosen
us in fellowship with Christ, before the creation of the universe, to
5 lead lives holy and blameless in His eyes; for in His love He had
predestined us to return to Him as His children through Jesus Christ.
6 Such was His purpose, and this He accomplished, so that praise and
honor are due Him for the loving mercy He has shown us in His
7 beloved Son, through whose blood we have obtained redemption and
8 deliverance from the sin of our apostasy. The merciful love of God
that has been bestowed upon us has been amply proved by His
having endowed us with the fullness of wisdom and understanding,
9 and revealed to us the mystery of His plan of salvation. This was
10 the plan of salvation that He intended to carry into effect: When the
gradual upward progress of the universe should have run through
the full number of appointed cycles, He proposed to unite everything
in the terrestrial and super-terrestrial spheres under the leadership
11 of Christ — the same Christ in whose fellowship we too have been
called to salvation. To this end we were predestined by God, Who
12 accomplishes every purpose conceived by His own will; in fact we
were now to serve for the glorification of His divine might — we who
in an earlier existence had already put our hope in Christ. You also
13 belong to his fellowship. You heard in the message of the truth
the good news of your salvation. You believed, and your faith
was sealed by the holy spirit-world which had been promised to you
14 and which is the first instalment, so to speak, of our inheritance in
God's spirit-kingdom, until after our final salvation, when the full
heritage will be ours for the glorification of the power of God.
15 Hence, having heard of your faith in the lord Jesus and of the

16 love that you cherish toward all the faithful, I have not ceased to
17 thank God and to remember you continually in my prayers. I pray
to the God of our lord Jesus Christ, the Father of glory, that he may
give you a spirit of wisdom and insight, and so enable you to under-
18 stand His divine nature. May He open your spiritual eyes so that
you may see what hope is yours by virtue of His call, and how rich
in His glory is the inheritance that you will share with His faithful,
19 and also how vast is His power, as manifested in us who believe in
20 Him. We witness in ourselves the same operation of His might and
power that He demonstrated in Christ when He raised him from the
kingdom of the spiritually dead and seated him at His right hand
21 in heaven's highest sphere, and exalted him above all sovereignty
and power and might and dominion, and above everything that bears
22 any name whatever, not only in this age but in time to come. God
has put everything under his rule and has made him the supreme
23 head of the church. By "church" is meant his spiritual body, which
he will restore in its entirety by reuniting with himself the whole
universe with all its parts.

CHAPTER 2.

1 You also were spiritually dead in consequence of your apostasy
2 and your other sins, in which you lived throughout the ages, since
this world began. You were under the rule of the Prince of Darkness,
that spirit who even now exerts his power over all who persist in
3 disobedience. Once we too were numbered among them. We had
all, at one time, turned away from God and become subservient to
our baser natures, doing as our sinful desires bade us and as our
corrupted minds directed. Like all the others, we were in the position of children against whom the divine judgment has been pro-
4 nounced. But God is rich in mercy. Because of His great love for
5 us who were spiritually dead as the result of our apostasy, He
raised us, together with Christ, from the realm of the spiritually
6 dead to the kingdom of spiritual life. Thus you also have been
saved by His grace. God raised us as members of Christ's spiritual
7 body, and together with him removed us to the heavenly spheres,
wishing to make known to the age that has now dawned the infinite
bounty of His grace, through the goodness that He shows us as
8 members of Christ. It is to His grace alone that you owe your salvation after having adopted the faith. Your salvation is not what
9 you deserve, then, but purely a gift of God. It is not the reward for
10 your deeds, so that no one can boast of his salvation. For we are
simply the work of His hands. He has made us members of Christ's

spiritual body in order that as such we might bear good fruit. Long
ago in past ages God's provident hand was at work on us, that we
might be able to bear good fruit in our present life.
11 Remember, then, that once you were not outwardly reckoned
among the people of Israel, but were called uncircumcised, to distinguish you from those who had received the circumcision that is
12 performed on the body by hand. Do not forget that in those days
you were not yet members of Christ; that you had no rights as citizens of Israel; you were strangers to the covenants and their prom-
13 ises; you lived in the universe without hope and without God. But
now you who were once severed from Christ have entered into
14 closest fellowship with him by virtue of Christ's bloody death. For
he has become our peacemaker. He has united the two hostile kingdoms, bridging by his human incarnation the deep gulf that sepa-
15 rated them. He has repealed the law that divided them, together
with its unalterable precepts, and so enabled both adversaries to be
remade into one new man in his own person and thus restore peace.
16 By his death on the cross he sought again to reconcile both with
God, making them members of one and the same spiritual body, and
so ending the former enmity through the union of the two in his
17 own person. Then he came and preached the joyful news of peace,
to those who, like you, had been remote from him as well as to those
18 who had already drawn near him. Thus by his mediation on behalf
of both — of you and ourselves — the path to the Father has once
more been laid open; and this path consists in one and the same
19 fellowship with God's spirit-world. Now you are no longer strangers
and aliens, but fellow-citizens of the saints and members of the
20 household of God. You are stones in the spiritual edifice that is
founded upon the teachings of the apostles and mediums of God's
spirit-world. In this building Christ Jesus himself is the corner-
21 stone. By him the whole edifice is welded together and rises higher
and higher into a holy temple, which is the spiritual fellowship
22 with the lord. You too are being built into this temple as a spiritual
abode for God.

CHAPTER 3.

1 To this end I, Paul, who bear chains for the sake of Christ, am
2 coming as his envoy to you Gentiles. No doubt you have heard of
3 the dispensation of God's grace, given to me for your benefit —
namely, the revelation of the mystery of which I have already writ-
4 ten you in brief. Read again what I wrote to you on this matter,
so that you may understand my knowledge of the mystery of Christ's

5 person — a mystery that was not revealed to the sons of men of
earlier times. It is only now revealed by a spirit to his faithful
6 apostles and the mediums of his spirit-world. It is this: The Gentiles
have equal rights in the inheritance of God's kingdom, and are equal
members of Christ's spiritual body, and participate in the promises
7 given to those who live in communion with Christ Jesus. Such is
the gospel of which I have become a minister, and for which I labor
according to the gift of grace that was given to me through the
8 exercise of his power. Upon me, the least of all the faithful, this
grace was bestowed: I am to preach to the Gentiles the good news
9 of Christ's boundless wealth of mercy; I am to enlighten them fully
as to its bearing on the mystery which from time out of mind has
10 been hidden with God, the Creator of all things. In this way the
princes and potentates in the spheres of the beyond are to learn of
the infinitely manifold wisdom of God through the revelations given
11 in the Christian congregations. Such was the purpose of God, conceived before the beginning of time and accomplished in Christ
12 Jesus, our lord. In our fellowship with him we have been filled with
a great joy, and by virtue of our confident faith in him we are
13 travelling toward our complete liberation. So I beg you not to lose
courage because of the hardships that I endure for your sake; in-
14 deed, they redound to your glory. For this reason I bend my knees
15 before the Father of our lord Jesus Christ, in Whom all that is
known as fatherhood in the beyond and on earth has its source.
16 May He, out of the wealth of His power, grant you grace to receive
inner strength through the action of the spirits with which He has
17 endowed you; then, because of your faith, Christ will be able to
dwell in your hearts, for love will then be deeply rooted in you,
18 and in love you will have a firm foundation. Hence you will be able,
together with all the faithful, to grasp the meaning of the breadth
19 and the length, the depth and the height of spiritual life, and to
know the love of Christ, the vastness of which baffles our imagina-
tion; in this way you will once more attain the utter perfection with
which you yourselves were once clothed by God.
20 Now to Him Who by the action of His power within us is able to
do all things in an infinitely greater measure than we can ask for
21 or even conceive, to Him be the glory offered in the congregation and
through Christ Jesus, throughout all generations and ages. Amen.

CHAPTER 4.

1 So, as one who feels that he is bound to the lord by unbreakable
bonds, I appeal to you to live a life worthy of the summons that has

2 been issued to you. Walk in humility, gentleness, and patience.
3 Bear with one another's weaknesses lovingly. Above all, seek to
4 preserve spiritual unity through the bond of peace; let there be but
one spiritual body and but one spirit ruling that body, just as there
5 is but one hope to which you are called; but one lord, one faith,
6 one baptism; one God and Father of all, supreme over all, and more
perfect than all, and in the closest communion with us all.

7 To each of us a gift of grace has been given in the measure that
8 Christ has thought best to grant us; for as the Scriptures say, "He
has ascended on high, he has made captives of those who were in
captivity and distributed gifts to men."

9 As for the phrase, "He has ascended on high," what can this mean
except that he had first descended into spheres lower than the earth?
10 He who descended into the depths of hell is the same who ascended
far above all spheres, in order to restore the whole universe to the
11 perfection that it once had. It is also he who has designated some
to be apostles, others to be speaking-mediums in their mother tongue,
others to be travelling evangelists, and others to be leaders and
12 teachers of the congregations; thus the faithful are to gain that inner
development that qualifies them for the work of the ministry and
for aiding in the gradual upbuilding of the spiritual body of Christ,
13 until we all shall have attained the great unity of faith and the
knowledge of the Son of God, and become a perfect man, having the
14 full measure of growth in which Christ is our pattern. For we are
no longer to remain half-grown children, allowing ourselves to
be tossed to and fro and driven hither and thither like the waves of
the sea by every wind of treacherous human doctrine with its artful
15 misguidance. We must rather remain faithful to the true doctrine,
and little by little make all creatures, through love, spiritual mem-
16 bers of him who is our spiritual head, Christ. For through him the
spiritual body is fitted and joined together as a whole. In this structure each member has its duty to perform according to the strength
with which it is endowed as a part of the whole. Thus each member
helps to build up the spiritual body, until the spiritual edifice of
Christ is completed, reared on the foundation of love.

17 Therefore, I urge and implore you in the name of the Lord, do
not live like the unbelievers, whose minds are set upon the vanities
18 of the world. They grope in the dark, and can no longer see clearly.
They are estranged from life in God, because on account of the
hardness of their hearts they no longer have any knowledge of God.
19 Having lost all moral sense they abandon themselves to every excess. As men who have lost all hope of higher things they commit

20 every sort of wantonness and debauchery. You have not learned
21 such behavior from the teachings of Christ. You have heard what
Christ teaches, and you have been fully instructed that this doctrine
22 was borne out in the life of Jesus himself; that in consequence of
your recent conversion you must lay aside your old selves — those
natures that worked their own ruin by indulging in the baser crav-
23 ings which have proved to be nothing but a delusion; that you are
now formed anew by the spirit of knowledge that has been given to
24 you, and that you must put on your new self — the nature that was
once created in God's image, faithful, pure, and truth-loving.
25 Banish falsehood from your hearts, then, and be truthful in your
dealings with each other. For we stand in the same relation to one
26 another as the members of the body. If you give way to an outburst
27 of rage, do not let it lead you into sin. Do not let the sun go down
upon such an angry mood, for fear that you may give the devil a
28 hold over you. Let him who has been a thief give up stealing and
industriously apply himself to work, so as to earn his worldly possessions with his own hands. Then he will be able to contribute
29 something to the needy. Let nothing of a corrupting nature escape
your lips, but only speak when that which you have to say will serve
for edification in the faith, so that you may thereby bring benefit to
30 your hearers. Do not grieve the holy spirit-world which has been
given to you by God and is your pledge that the day of your com-
31 plete salvation is at hand. Shun all bitterness, all anger and resentment, all blustering and cursing, together with everything else that
32 is evil. Be kind and affectionate to one another, and forgive one another, just as God forgave you when He made you spiritual members
of Christ.

CHAPTER 5.

1 Pattern yourselves after God, then, as His beloved children, and
2 lead lives of love, just as Christ loved us and gave himself up for
3 us as an offering with which God was very greatly pleased. Never
make unchastity or impurity of any kind or greed the subject of your
conversation, as is proper for those who have dedicated their lives
4 to God. Indulge in no indecorous behavior, no idle talk, no loose
jesting, for these things do not become you. Rather express the
5 thanks which you owe to God. For of this you are certain, that
no unchaste or immoral or covetous persons (who in reality are
nothing but idolators) can have any share in the kingdom of Christ
6 and God. Let no one deceive you with empty words, for it is because of such sins that God's punishment is inflicted upon those who

7 refuse to obey God. See to it that you are not numbered among
8 these people. At one time, it is true, you were darkness, but now
9 you are light, as members of Christ's spiritual body. Live like children of light, then, for the fruits that light ripens within you are
10 goodness, uprightness, and truthfulness. Weigh everything that you
11 do, and consider whether it is acceptable to the Lord. Take no part
12 in the fruitless doings of those who walk in darkness; rather, reprove
them openly, for the things that they do in secret are such that the
13 very mention of them makes us blush for shame. By expressing our
disapproval we bring such matters to the light; and that which the
14 light shines on becomes light itself. Thus it is said, "Awake, you
sleeper, and come forth from the realm of the spiritually dead, and
you will enter into the radiance of Christ."

15 Pay careful attention, then, to the lives you lead. Do not behave
thoughtlessly, but like men who deliberate upon every step that
16 they take. Make the most of every moment, for we are living in evil
17 days. Do not act like fools, but try to learn what the Lord's will is.
18 Do not drink wine to excess; that leads to debauchery. Instead of
19 this, be filled with a holy spirit; then your heart will overflow with
hymns of praise and thanksgiving and spiritual songs, in which you
20 will glorify and extol the Lord and at all times give thanks to your
God and Father in the name of our lord Jesus Christ for all the
benefits you receive.

21 Serve one another out of reverence for Christ. Let the wives be
22 submissive to their husbands, as they would be to the Lord, for the
23 husband is the head of his wife, just as Christ is the head of the
24 church and the protector of the spiritual body. Just as the church is
subject to Christ, therefore, so let the wives be subject to their hus-
25 bands in every respect. Let the husbands on their part love their
26 wives as Christ loves the church, having offered himself as a sacrifice for it so as to consecrate it to God by washing it clean in the
27 water of his teachings. Thus he placed the church beside him like
a bride, radiant in the glory of her beauty, with no spot or wrinkle
28 or any such flaw, but holy and without a blemish. So too it is the
duty of men to love their wives as they love themselves; for he who
29 loves his wife thereby shows the greatest love to himself. There is
no one who hates his own self; on the contrary, every one gives the
30 best care and attention to his own person, just as Christ does with
us, his church, for we are members of his spiritual body, flesh of his
31 flesh and bone of his bone. For this reason a man will leave his
father and mother and cling to his wife, and the two will be like a
32 single living being. This is a great mystery. I for my part contend

that the same mystery exists in the relationship between Christ and
33 the church. Be this as it may, let every man among you love his
wife as he loves himself; likewise let the wife love her husband and
treat him with respect.

CHAPTER 6.

1 Children, obey your parents, for this is the will of God. "Honor
2 your father and your mother"—that is the only commandment that
3 carries with it the promise, "that it may be well with you and that
you may live long on earth."

4 And you fathers, do not arouse bitterness in the hearts of your
children, but train them in a manner suited to children and give
them the right understanding of the Lord's teachings.

5 Servants, obey your temporal masters, not in fear and trembling
6 but with singleness of heart, as you would serve Christ. Do not be
eye-servants, seeking only to please men, but show yourselves ser-
7 vants of Christ, doing God's will from the heart. Do your duty as
servants with as much good will as if it were for the Lord, and not
8 merely for men. You know that every one will be properly rewarded
by the Lord for all the good that he accomplishes, whether he be a
slave or a freeman.

9 And you who are masters, deal likewise with your servants. Leave
off threatening them. You know that their Master and yours dwells
in heaven, and that with Him there is no partiality.

10 In conclusion I beg of you, increase your spiritual power in
the fellowship of the Lord day by day with the aid of the strength
11 that flows into you from His source of power. Put on the whole
armor of God, so that you may withstand the wily attacks of Satan.
12 For you have to struggle not only against enemies of flesh and blood,
but also against supernatural powers and forces, against the spirits
of darkness that rule this world, and against the manoeuvres of the
13 evil spirits in the spheres beyond. So put on the whole armor of
God, that you may be strong enough to offer resistance on the "day
14 of the evil spirits," and do your utmost to stand firm. Be prepared
for all emergencies—your loins girt with the truth, wearing the
15 coat of mail of uprightness, and your feet shod with readiness to
16 preach the gospel of peace. Above all, take up the shield of faith,
for with this you will counteract all the fiery darts of the Evil One.
17 Put on your head the helmet of salvation, and take in your right
18 hand the sword of the spirit—the word of God. In every entreaty
and prayer make your supplication with the help of a spirit of God.

Take care that you persevere in prayer and remember to pray for
19 all the faithful. Pray for me also, that I may be endowed with the
gift of speech and that I may open my lips in order to preach the
mystery of the gospel with greater eloquence; for in this respect
20 I perform my duty as elder with great timidity. I should like to
acquire greater ease and thus be able to speak as I ought to speak.
21 Now in order that you may learn about my condition and my
work, Tychicus, a beloved brother and a faithful servant in the cause
22 of the Lord, will report everything to you. I have sent him to you
for the sole purpose of informing you of our condition here and
cheering your hearts.
23 Peace to all the brothers, and love and faith, from God the Father
24 and the lord Christ Jesus. Grace be with all who love our lord Jesus
Christ with unchanging devotion. Amen.

The Epistle of Paul the Apostle to the PHILIPPIANS

CHAPTER 1.

1 PAUL and Timotheus, servants of Christ Jesus, send greetings to
all the faithful in Philippi who belong to Christ, as well as to
2 the bishops and their fellow-workers. Grace be with you and peace
from God our Father and from the lord Jesus Christ.
3 As often as I think of you I thank our Lord and include you all
4 in every prayer I make. When I pray thus, I am always filled with
5 a great joy, for I remember the help that you have given me in
6 preaching the gospel from the very first day until now. I am confident, moreover, that He Who has begun so good a work in you will
7 have completed it on the day of the coming of Christ Jesus. It is
natural for me to cherish this good opinion of you all, for I have
borne your image in my heart from the moment when you all showed
so much sympathy for me by your deeds of love, both on the occasion of my imprisonment and defence, and in your support of the
8 gospel. God is my witness how much I long for you all in the
9 heartfelt love of Christ Jesus. And it is my one prayer that your love
from day to day may grow to overflowing, by reason of the knowl-
10 edge that you have gained and the deeper spiritual perception that
enables you to make the right decision in every crisis; then on the
day of the coming of Christ you will be found flawless and irre-
11 proachable, filled with the fruits of faithfulness to God, which are
brought to ripeness through Jesus Christ to the glory and praise of
God.
12 And now, brothers, I must tell you that so far as spreading the
13 gospel is concerned, my affairs have taken a turn for the better. It is
known among the whole Imperial Guard and elsewhere that I am
14 being kept in prison for the sake of Christ. Hence the majority of
the brothers, relying on the help of the Lord, have taken new courage from my captivity and now venture to preach the word of God
15 with increasing boldness. Some, to be sure, preach the doctrine of
Christ with hearts full of malice and envy; others, in good faith.
16 These preach out of love for the cause of God, knowing that I am
17 imprisoned because I have defended the gospel. The self-seeking
preachers of Christ's doctrine, however, do not do so with pure

intentions, but are all too well aware that they thereby add grief to
18 my captivity. After all, what does it matter? In either case Christ
19 is preached, whether or not from ulterior motives. At this I rejoice,
and shall continue to rejoice, for I know that my present state, by
virtue of your intercession and with the help of the spirit sent by
20 Jesus Christ, will contribute to my salvation. I cherish the firm belief and live in the glad hope that I shall not be put to shame in any
way. On the contrary, Christ will be glorified before all the world
by the bodily sufferings that I must undergo, just as in the past,
21 whether my life is spared or whether I die. If I live, my life is con-
22 secrated to Christ; if I must die, my death will be my gain. If my
life on earth is spared, it will mean that I shall continue my fruitful
23 labors. Which of the two I should choose, I cannot tell. One seems
as much to be desired as the other. On the one hand, I greatly long
to be freed from this body and to be united with Christ; how much
24 better this would be for me! On the other hand, for your sakes it is
25 more important that my life should be spared. For this reason I am
confident that I shall remain with you and labor among you, so as
26 to further your progress and your joy in the faith. Then when I
come back to you, your hearts will overflow with joy on account of
my deliverance, for it is the cause of Christ Jesus that is at stake.
27 Let the lives that you lead before the world be worthy of the
gospel. In case I should come, I wish to see with my own eyes —
and if I cannot come, I wish to be informed by you — whether you
are all ruled by one and the same spirit; whether you stand shoulder
to shoulder, inspired by one purpose, in your fight for faith in the
28 gospel, and remain undaunted by your adversaries. Your fearless-
ness spells perdition for them, but for you it is a token of salvation,
29 and a token that comes from God. For where the cause of Christ is
concerned, you have been given the grace not only to believe in
30 Christ but also to suffer for him. You face the same conflict which
you saw in my case, and which, as you hear, I am still waging.

CHAPTER 2.

1 Now if there is any virtue in an admonition offered in the name
of Christ; in a kindly word of encouragement; in the feeling of
2 spiritual fellowship; in affection and mutual sympathy; then, I
entreat you, make my joy complete by being of one mind and harboring the same feeling of love, by being one in heart and soul, by
3 pursuing the same ends, doing nothing out of selfishness or vain
4 ambition, but every one in all humility cherishing a greater regard
5 for others than for himself, with an eye not only to his own interest

6 but also to that of his fellow-man. Take the same attitude that Jesus
Christ adopted. Although he appeared godlike in his spiritual form,
he did not consider it self-deprivation to humble himself before God.
7 Indeed, he divested himself of his own nature, assumed the outward
form of a servant, and became just like other men; in his life on
8 earth he was found to be like an ordinary human being. He humbled
himself through his obedience, even to the point of death—death
9 on the cross. Therefore God exalted him above everything and gave
10 him a name above all other names, so that at the name of Jesus
every knee will bend in the spheres of heaven and earth and hell,
11 and every tongue will confess, "Christ Jesus is the lord." And by
this confession God the Father will be glorified.
12 Therefore, my beloved, heed my admonitions as you have done
in the past; heed them not only as you did when I was among you,
but even more scrupulously now in my absence, and work at your
13 salvation with fear and trembling. For it is God Who gives you such
strength as He deems necessary, not only to will, but to accomplish.
14 Do everything without murmuring and disputing. Become pure and
15 flawless, children of God who live without guile or reproach in the
midst of a dishonest and apostate race of men. You must be their
16 light-bearers, holding forth to the world the life-giving truth. Then
you will contribute to my glory on the day when Christ appears, and
I shall know that I have not run my race in vain nor wasted my
17 labor. Even if I am to offer my blood as a sacrifice for having
brought the faith to you by my service as priest, I am glad of it and
18 heartily rejoice with all of you. This should be an occasion for rejoicing among you too, so that your joy may combine with my own.
19 If Christ Jesus so wills, I hope to send Timothy to you shortly,
so that my mind too may be set at rest when I have heard from him
20 how you are faring. I have no like-minded helper who will look
21 after your best interests as well as he. All the others, I am sorry to
say, think only of themselves and not of the cause of Jesus Christ.
22 But you are already acquainted with his confirmed faithfulness, and
you know that in preaching the gospel he has helped me like a son
23 helping his father. So I hope to send him as soon as my own affairs
24 are sufficiently settled. But I trust to the Lord that I myself shall
25 soon be able to come, too. I feel obliged to send back to you
my brother and fellow-worker and fellow-combatant Epaphroditus,
26 whom you sent to me with a gift for my support, for he has been
homesick for you all and has been deeply distressed because he
27 heard that you had learned of his illness. He was in fact so sick
that we feared he would die, but God had mercy on him, and not

only on him but also on me, to save me from having one sorrow
28 after another. So I had a double reason for sending him home
quickly: first, that you might have the joy of seeing him again, and
29 second, that I might be relieved of anxiety on his account. Receive
him as a servant of the Lord, then, with a hearty welcome, and hold
such men in esteem, for he was near death for the sake of Christ's
30 work. He risked his very life by rendering me in your stead and in
full measure the services that you were unable to render.

CHAPTER 3.

1 So then, my brothers, rejoice in the Lord. I never weary of writing this same thing over and over again, and it helps to fortify you
inwardly.
2 Beware of these dogs, these ill-intentioned fellow-workers, and
3 of this mania for circumcision. For we carry the mark of true circumcision on us, serving God as we do under the guidance of one
of His spirits and glorying in our fellowship with Christ Jesus. We
are not concerned with marks that appear outwardly on the body;
4 otherwise I myself would have reason to boast. If any one thinks he
5 can rely on outward distinction, it is surely I, for I was circumcised
on the eighth day, I am of the race of Israel, belong to the tribe of
Benjamin, am a Hebrew by birth, and as regards the interpretation
6 of the Law, belonged to the party of the Pharisees. In my religious
fanaticism I became a persecutor of the church of God, and as for
righteousness according to the letter of the Law, there was not one of
7 its precepts which I did not fulfill in every particular. But all these
things which I then considered so valuable, now in looking back I
8 regard as a hindrance to the cause of Christ. Indeed, I reckon
everything unprofitable beside the priceless knowledge I have of
my lord Jesus Christ, for whose sake I gave up all those things. I
think them no better than the mud in the street. It was only Christ
9 whom I wanted to win. Once I had entered into communion with
him, of what further value to me was my former "righteousness",
which lay in the observance of the Jewish Law? For thenceforth I
had that inner rightness which springs from faith in Christ, and
10 which God gave me as a recompense for my faith. By virtue of this
faith I learn to know him, I witness in myself the power of his resurrection and the happiness of sharing his sufferings and dying as
11 he died, in order thus some day to attain like him the resurrection
12 from the dead. For I myself am not one of those who have entirely
reached the goal or already won favor in the eyes of God; but I

pursue that goal and strive to reach it. That is why I was drawn
13 by Christ into fellowship with him. Brothers, although I do not contend that I have reached the goal, nevertheless I can say one thing: I
try to forget what lies behind me, and I stretch out my hand toward
14 that which lies ahead; I race toward the goal for the prize that
awaits us above and consists in being called back into the house of
God our Father, which we are to reach in fellowship with Christ.
15 Let all of us who wish to be counted among the mature strive for
the same end; and if you hold a different opinion on any point,
16 God will enlighten you on that point also. Only, let us continue to
follow the same rule by which we guided our lives in the faith at
the outset.
17 Follow my example, brothers, and observe the behavior of those
18 who have taken us as the model. Unhappily many of them lead lives
that stamp them as enemies of the cross of Christ. I have spoken to
you of these people more than once, and this time I do so with
19 tears. Their end is destruction; their god is their belly; the things
of which they should be ashamed they boast of, and their whole end
20 and aim is their worldly well-being. And yet we are enrolled as
citizens of a heavenly kingdom, and from there we expect the lord
21 Jesus Christ to come as our deliverer. He will change the body of our
low condition until it resembles his own body of light. This transformation will be effected by the power through which he reunites
all creatures as members of his body.

CHAPTER 4.

1 My brothers, you whom I love so dearly and for whom I long,
you who are my joy and my crowning glory, cling faithfully to the
Lord.
2 I beg Evodia and Syntyche to work together harmoniously in the
3 service of the Lord. And I beg you also, my faithful fellow-worker,
to be helpful to them both, for they stood by me in my battle for
the gospel, together with Clement and my other fellow-workers,
whose names are recorded in the book of life.
4 Be joyous at all times while you work in the service of the Lord;
5 again and again I shall say to you, be joyous. Let the good that is
6 in you be evident to all men. The Lord is always near you. Have
no anxiety, but whatever life brings you, make your wishes known
7 to God with supplications and prayers of thanksgiving. Then the
peace of God, which is greater than men can understand, will enfold
your hearts and minds like a protecting wall in the power of Christ
Jesus.

8 Finally, to sum up everything in a single sentence: whatever is
true, whatever is precious, whatever is just, pure, lovely, harmless,
9 virtuous, or praiseworthy to know—strive for these things. Also
practise in your daily lives what you have learned and received from
me, what you have heard me say and what you have seen me do; and
the God of peace will be with you.
10 During my work in the Lord's service it has been a great joy to
me to witness the revival of your care for me. To be sure, you have
always had my welfare at heart, but you lacked the opportunity for
11 practical demonstration of your interest. Not that I need complain of
want, for I have learned to make a little suffice, in whatever situation
I may find myself. I know how to get along under the most straitened
circumstances, and I also know how to live in the greatest prosperity.
12 I know the secret of adapting myself to every turn of fortune and
to every condition in life; whether I eat my fill or go hungry,
13 whether I possess everything in abundance or suffer want, I find all
14 the power that I need in Him Who strengthens me. And now you
have had the kindness to show your sympathy to me in my trouble.
15 You yourselves know, my dear Philippians, that in the early days
of preaching the gospel, when I had left Macedonia, no other congregation was on terms of giving and receiving with me; you were
16 the only ones. Even when I was in Thessalonica you contributed to
17 my support more than once. Not that I care about your money; what
I am concerned about is the constant accumulation of interest in
18 your account with God. You have paid your debt to me, and more
than paid it. I am provided for beyond my needs, now that I have
received what you sent to me by Epaphroditus. It is a sweet per-
19 fume, a welcome and acceptable sacrifice in the eyes of God. My
God will abundantly and gloriously provide for all your needs,
20 according to His boundless wealth, in Christ Jesus. Glory for ever
to God our Father. Amen.
21 Greetings to all the faithful as members of the communion with
Christ Jesus. The brothers who are with me send their greetings to
22 you. All the faithful greet you, especially those who are members of
the Imperial Court.
23 The grace of the lord Jesus Christ be with you all. Amen.

The Epistle of Paul the Apostle to the COLOSSIANS

CHAPTER 1.

1 PAUL, an apostle of Jesus Christ by the will of God, and our
2 brother Timothy send their greetings to the devoted and faithful
brothers at Colossae who are in fellowship with Christ Jesus. Grace
be with you and peace from God our Father.
3 We thank God the Father of our lord Jesus Christ whenever we
4 pray for you. We have heard of your faith in Christ Jesus and of the
5 love you cherish for all the faithful. We thank God for the hope of
the riches that have been laid up for you in the heavenly spheres.
You first heard of these riches at the time when the word of the truth
6 was revealed to you through the preaching of the gospel. This
gospel has been scattered throughout the whole universe like a seed
that propagates itself by bearing fruit. This was also the case with
you from the day on which you first heard the gospel and learned
of the grace of God that was bestowed upon you in the proclamation
7 of the truth. You learned of it through our dear fellow-servant
Epaphras, who has worked among you in our place as a faithful
8 follower of Christ. It is he who has told us of the love that was
awakened in you under the influence of a holy spirit.
9 Since the day we heard of this we therefore pray for you continually. We implore God to fill you with the knowledge of His
10 will; to endow you through His spirit-world with the wisdom and
insight necessary to enable you to live a life worthy of the Lord and
pleasing to Him in every way; to make you fruitful in all kinds of
11 good deeds, and let your knowledge of God increase; to equip you
with the necessary strength, which His glorious might enables Him
to bestow, so that you may preserve your steadfastness and endur-
12 ance to the fullest degree. Then you will be able joyfully to give
thanks to the Father, Who has fitted you to share the heritage of the
13 faithful in the kingdom of light; Who has delivered us from the
power of the kingdom of darkness, and restored us to the kingdom
14 of His beloved Son. In fellowship with him we have obtained redemption, which consists in the forgiveness of the sins of apostasy
15 from God. He is the image of the invisible God, the first-born of all
16 creation. For in him were created all things in the non-terrestrial

and terrestrial spheres, the visible and the invisible, be they high
princes of heaven or other powers, rulers, or forces; all were cre-
17 ated through him and for spiritual fellowship with him. He was the
first of all creatures to come into being, and in him everything
18 created was merged into a spiritual whole. Hence he is the head
of that spiritual body known as the "church." It was also he who
led the return of the spiritually dead, inasmuch as he was the first
to come back from the kingdom of the spiritually dead. Indeed,
19 he was destined to be foremost in everything; for in God's plan of
salvation it was provided that God would reincorporate all of
20 Christ's apostate members in him. As soon as Christ should have
sealed the covenant of peace with the blood he shed upon the cross,
God proposed to reconcile all things with Himself, both the things
of this earth and those of the other worlds.

21 You also at one time were among those who were banished from
God's kingdom, and were subjects of the kingdom hostile to Him,
by reason of the character that found expression in your evil deeds.
22 But now you are again reconciled with God, because Christ sacrificed
his earthly body through his death on the cross in order to present
23 you to God, holy, flawless, and blameless—provided, of course,
that you cling immovably to the faith and do not allow yourselves
to be dissuaded from the hope derived from the gospel that you have
heard. That gospel has been proclaimed to all creation, and I, Paul,
am also one of those who preach it.

24 I am glad now that I am permitted to suffer for you; glad to offset
by my bodily afflictions any lack of suffering on the part of the
church as Christ's spiritual body, in comparison with the sufferings
25 that Christ endured. For I have become a servant of the church by
virtue of the stewardship with which God has entrusted me, and as
such it is my duty to preach to you the word of God in its entirety.
26 It is my task to reveal to you the mystery which has been hidden
in all previous ages and generations, and which has only now been
27 disclosed to His faithful ones. To them God chose to make known
the wealth in store for the Gentiles in this glorious mystery of God
—the meaning of Christ's fellowship with you and of the hope of
28 glory that you possess through him. It is Christ whom we preach,
impressing his truth upon the hearts of all and instructing all men
in every field of the true wisdom. Thus we mean to enable all of
them to regain their original perfection as members of Christ's body.
29 This is also the reason why I exert myself to the utmost, and try to
fight with all the strength with which he endows me and which is
so powerfully active in me.

CHAPTER 2.

1 For I wish you to know what a hard battle I have to fight for you
and for the congregation of Laodicea, as well as for all those who
2 do not know me personally. My object in telling this is to inspire
their hearts with new courage and unite them more and more closely
with one another in love. Then you will witness in yourselves the
full spiritual wealth that lies in such union. You will understand
3 the mystery of God; and this mystery is Christ. In him all the
4 treasures of wisdom and knowledge lie hidden. I say this only to
prevent you from being deceived by any one's powers of persuasion.
5 For although I am absent from you in body, my spirit is with you,
and I rejoice as I look upon your close ranks and on the strong
bulwark of your faith in Christ.

6 So just as you have received the image of the lord Jesus Christ in
7 your hearts, follow his example in your way of life. Take root in
him, build yourselves up in him, grow firm in the faith as it was
taught to you, and at the thought of Christ let your heart overflow
8 with gratitude. See to it that no one captivates you with so-called
science or with foolish and misleading theories which are based on
human traditions and derived from the evil powers that rule the
world, but have nothing in common with the teachings of Christ.
9 For in Christ we find only that which proceeds from God — and
find it in as high a degree of perfection as can be accorded to any
10 creature. You also, if you are in communion with him, possess his
complete doctrine, for he is lord over all the spirit-forces and all
11 spiritual powers. Because you belong to him, you too have received
a circumcision, not one performed by hand, but one that consists in
stripping your daily lives of worldliness; that is the circumcision
12 conferred by Christ. It was accomplished by your descent with him,
through immersion in baptism, into the tomb of the lower world,
and by your ascent with him from the depths in consequence of your
faith in the same power of God that raised him from the kingdom
13 of the spiritually dead. You too once inhabited the kingdom of the
dead, owing to your desertion from God and your want of spiritual
circumcision, but God has restored you, in communion with Christ,
14 to spiritual life, after having pardoned all your trespasses. He had
previously cancelled the bond of indebtedness that stood against us;
for it contained stipulations that raised an impassable barrier to our
salvation. Thus He had removed that barrier, nailing the bond to
15 the cross. He had disarmed the powers and authorities of hell, ex-

posed them to open disgrace, and triumphed over them in the person of Christ.

16 Therefore let no one find fault with you for your choice of food
and drink, or for your failure to attach any importance to the ob-
17 servance of festivals, new moons, and Sabbaths. All this is but the
shadow of what is to come. The principal thing is to belong to
18 Christ. Do not let yourselves be defrauded of your prize by any of
those men who parade their humility and their veneration for the
angels; who attach great importance to their visions and fall so
19 utterly under the sway of their own worldly notions, but who do
not hold to Christ as the head under which the whole spiritual body
is connected and held together by joints and sinews, and thus accomplishes its divinely ordained growth.

20 If you, as members of Christ, have wholly freed yourselves from
the spirit-powers that rule the world, why do you still submit to its
21 regulations as though you still belonged to the world? Such rules,
for example, as "Do not touch this," "Do not eat that," "Do not
22 handle this." According to human laws and doctrines, whoever
23 breaks these rules takes the road to ruin. It is true that all such
regulations pass for wisdom, acquire the standing of religious precepts, and are regarded as a sign of humility and a means of keeping the body in subjection; but they have no real value whatever,
and serve only to make man's baser nature swell with pride.

CHAPTER 3.

1 Now since you have risen with Christ from the depths, seek the
things that are above, where Christ sits enthroned at the right hand
2 of God. Strive for what is heavenly, not what is earthly. For you
3 are dead to the things of this world, and your new life in fellowship
4 with Christ lies hidden in God. When Christ, to whom you owe your
spiritual life, appears, then you too will appear as his members,
radiant in glory before all the world.

5 So put to death the worldly inclinations within you: the inclination toward unchastity, immorality, unnatural intercourse, evil de-
6 sires, and greed, which are nothing less than idolatry. Because of
this idolatry God's punishment is imminent and will be visited upon
7 the children of disobedience. You yourselves were numbered among
them at one time when you lived in the sins I have named, but now,
8 away with it all! Away with anger, bitterness, and malice. Away
with the abuses and foul language in which you once indulged.
9 Away with lying to one another. You are supposed to have laid aside

10 your old selves with all their misdeeds, and to have put on your new
selves which must be built up anew, step by step, until they reflect
11 the whole image of him who created them. In this respect there is
no distinction between male and female, Greek and Jew, circumcised and uncircumcised, barbarian and Scythian, slave and freeman. Christ is one and all and in communion with all.

12 As God's elect, faithful to Him and beloved by Him, clothe yourselves in tender mercy, kindness, humility, gentleness, and patience.
13 Be forbearing with each other, and forgive each other if any one
thinks that he has a grievance against another. As the Lord has
14 forgiven you, so must you forgive. Above all things, bear love in
15 your hearts, for love is the bond of union. Let the peace of Christ
dwell in your hearts as your most treasured possession, for it was
for this that you were called to be members of one and the same
spiritual body.

16 Learn to be grateful. Let the teachings of Christ fill you in all
their wealth, so that you may teach and instruct one another in
every field of knowledge. Praise and glorify God with thankful
hearts in psalms, hymns, and songs with which God's spirits will
17 inspire you. Whatever you say or do, let it be in the name of Jesus;
through him offer your prayers of thanksgiving to God the Father.

18 Wives, obey your husbands so far as is consistent with the teach-
19 ings of the lord; husbands, love your wives, and do not be harsh
20 with them. Children, obey your parents at every point, for this is
21 in keeping with the lord's teaching. Fathers, refrain from irritating
22 your children, so that they will not weary of you. Servants, render
obedience to your temporal masters in all respects, not with eye-
service, for the sake of finding favor with men, but whole-heartedly
23 out of reverence for the Lord God. By so doing you will perform
your tasks of your own accord, as if it were for the Lord and not for
24 men; you know that you will be rewarded for it by the Lord with
25 your share of inheritance, for you serve Christ the lord. But whoever does wrong in these matters will be punished accordingly. No
partiality will be shown.

CHAPTER 4.

1 Masters, allow your servants that which is fair and just. Remember that you also have a Master in heaven.

2 Persevere in prayer, but also be inwardly attentive while you
3 pray. Pray for us, too, so that God may open every door to our
preaching; then we shall be free to proclaim without hindrance the

4 mystery of Christ, for whose sake I am in chains, and I myself shall
be able to explain it as I should.
5 Use wisdom in dealing with unbelievers, and always be careful
6 to choose the most favorable moment. Let your speech be gentle
and kindly at all times, never indulging in idle gossip. Learn how
to give every one the right answer.
7 Tychicus will report to you in detail concerning my personal
affairs. He is my beloved brother and a faithful helper and fellow-
8 worker in the service of the Lord. I am sending him to you for the
express purpose of letting you know how we are getting along and
9 of thus cheering your hearts. With him I am sending Onesimus, a
faithful and beloved brother and a fellow-countryman of yours.
Both will inform you exactly how matters stand here.
10 Aristarchus, my fellow-prisoner, sends his greetings, as does
Mark, the cousin of Barnabas, whom you have already been asked
11 to receive kindly as soon as he comes to you. And so does Jesus,
surnamed Justus. These three are the only converted Jews who have
become fellow-workers on behalf of the kingdom of God, and they
12 have been a great comfort to me. Your fellow-countryman Epaphras
sends his greetings. He is a servant of Christ Jesus who is at all
times zealous for you in his prayers, so that as far as possible you
may be perfect and firmly convinced Christians in everything that
13 accords with the will of God. I must testify that he exerts himself
to the utmost on your behalf and on behalf of the brothers in
14 Laodicea and Hieropolis. Luke, our beloved physician, greets you,
15 and so does Demas. Greet the brothers in Laodicea, and Nymphas
16 and the congregation that meets at his house. After this letter has
been read to you, see that it is also read to the congregation at
Laodicea; in return, the letter that was sent to the Laodiceans is to
17 be turned over to you and read to your congregation. Give this
message to Archippus: "See that you faithfully perform the duties
of the office that you have assumed in the service of the Lord."
18 I, Paul, write my greeting to you here in my own hand· "Remember my fetters. Grace be with you. Amen."

The First Epistle of Paul the Apostle to the THESSALONIANS

CHAPTER 1.

1 PAUL, Sylvanus, and Timothy send their greetings to the congregation in Thessalonica which is in communion with God the
Father and with the lord Jesus Christ. Grace be with you and peace
from God our Father and from the lord Jesus Christ.
2 We constantly give thanks to God for all of you and remember
3 you in our prayers, mindful at all times of your energetic life in the
faith, your zealous work in the exercise of neighborly love, and the
steadfastness of the hope you have placed in our lord Jesus Christ
4 because of your faith in God, our Father. We know, brothers beloved
5 by God, that you have been chosen, for our gospel was presented to
you not merely in words, but also in signs of divine power and
with the manifestations of a holy spirit, the result of which was full
6 conviction. You know how careful we were to set you an example
by our conduct while we lived among you, and how you became
imitators of us and of the lord; how, in spite of the grave suffering
that it brought, you accepted our doctrine with a cheerfulness that
7 only a holy spirit can inspire. Thus you became a pattern for all
8 believers in Macedonia and in Greece, and from you the word of the
Lord not only spread throughout Macedonia and Achaia, but the
news of your faith in God travelled in every direction, so that there
9 was no need for us to speak of it anywhere. For everywhere the
people of their own accord tell what a welcome you gave us, and
how you were converted from idolatry to the worship of the true
10 God, in order to serve this living and only true God and to wait
for the coming from heaven of His Son, whom He raised from the
kingdom of the spiritually dead. That Son is Jesus, who rescues us
from the coming judgment.

CHAPTER 2.

1 You yourselves know, brothers, that our first visit to you was not
2 without results. As you are aware, we had previously met with
suffering and ill-treatment in Philippi; nevertheless, through confidence in our God we found the courage to deliver God's joyful
3 message to you, though with great difficulty. Our sermons were

not inspired by idle fancies or by impure intentions or any ulterior
4 motives. No, since God has found us worthy to be entrusted with
the preaching of the gospel, we preach with Him alone in mind;
it is not men whom we seek to please, but only God, Who tests our
5 hearts. Therefore we never resorted to flattery, as you know, or to
6 any designs for enriching ourselves, as God is our witness. Nor did
7 we seek honors from men, either among you or elsewhere. As envoys of Christ we might have laid claim to special consideration, yet
we lived among you in utter simplicity and innocence, like a nurse
8 taking care of the children entrusted to her. Such was our devotion
to you that we were ready not only to carry God's gospel to you,
but to lay down our lives gladly for your sake; so dear were you to
9 us. You may remember, brothers, how we toiled and labored,
working day and night to earn our living so as not to be a burden
to any of you, and preaching the gospel of God to you in between.
10 You are witnesses, and so is God, to the conscientiousness, fairness,
11 and blamelessness of our behavior toward you believers; you know
how we admonished and encouraged each of you, like a father with
12 his children, and implored you to lead lives worthy of the God Who
has called you back to His kingdom and His glory.

13 We also thank God daily for your acceptance of His word on the
strength of our preaching, not taking it for the word of man, but
for what it really is, the word of God. And such, it shows itself active
14 in you because you believe in it. Therefore, brothers, your lot is
the same as that of the congregations of God in Judaea that are in
union with Christ Jesus. You have to suffer the same persecution at
the hands of your countrymen that they underwent at the hands of
15 the Jews — the very Jews who killed the lord Jesus and the prophets
and persecuted us, too; who displease God and are hostile to the
16 whole Gentile world; and who try to prevent us from carrying the
message to the Gentiles so that they too may obtain salvation. Thus
day by day they fill up the measure of their sins, until finally the
chastisement of God falls upon them.

17 For a short time, brothers, we were separated from you, but al-
18 though you were out of sight, you were not out of mind. We longed
all the more keenly to see you again, and we therefore resolved to
visit you. As for myself, Paul, I have tried again and again to carry
19 out my intention, but Satan has succeeded in preventing me. For
who is our hope, our joy, and our crown of glory? Will it not also
be you on the day when our lord Jesus Christ appears and you stand
20 in his presence? Indeed, then you will be our glory and our joy.

CHAPTER 3.

1 So, when we could endure it no longer, we decided that I should re-
2 main alone in Athens, and we sent Timothy to you. He is our brother
and fellow-worker in the service of God, a preacher of the gospel
of Christ. He was chosen for the task of fortifying and encouraging
3 you in your faith, so that none of you might falter in the face of our
4 present troubles. As you yourselves know, suffering is the lot of all
of us. Even when we were with you we repeatedly predicted that
suffering was in store for us; and it has come true, as you know.
5 When I could bear it no longer, I sent a messenger to you to find
out about your faith. I was afraid that the tempter might have succeeded with his temptations, and that as a result our work might
6 have been in vain. Now Timothy has just returned to us from his
visit with you and brought a good report concerning your faith and
your love. He tells us that you always think kindly of us, and that
7 you long for us as keenly as we long for you. So we are again freed
8 from all worry and anxiety on the score of your faith. Now that we
know that you are firmly united with the Lord, we have been given
9 new life. Indeed, we cannot thank the Lord enough for all the joy
10 that you have made us feel in the presence of God. We will earnestly
pray to Him night and day to grant that we may see you again.
11 Then, if there should be something lacking here and there in your
12 faith, we might supply the want. May our God and Father as well
as our lord Jesus open our way to you. May the Lord grant you
love in overflowing abundance for one another and for all men,
13 such love as we cherish for you. May he strengthen your hearts
that they may shine in immaculate holiness before our God and
Father when our lord Jesus comes again with all his saints. Amen.

CHAPTER 4.

1 Finally, brothers, we beg and exhort you in the name of the lord
Jesus, to follow our instructions concerning the way that you must
live in order to please God. It is true that you are doing this, but
2 perhaps you might do so even more perfectly. You remember the
3 message that we gave you, spoken through us by the lord Jesus: "It
4 is God's will that you should be sanctified. Abstain from unchastity;
let each man have intercourse with none but his own wife, chastely
5 and honorably, and not only to satisfy his lust, as is the way with
6 the heathens who have no knowledge of God. Let no one overreach
and take advantage of his brother in matters of business, for the

Lord will inflict due punishment for such sins." To all this we had
already drawn your attention and given evidence of the truth of our
7 words. God has not called us to immorality but to holiness. Hence,
8 whoever disregards our warning disregards not man, but God—
the God Who sent you His holy spirit-world.
9 As for brotherly love, we have no need to write you about this
subject, for you have been taught by God Himself to love one an-
10 other. And indeed you do love all the brothers all over Macedonia.
Nevertheless, brothers, we urge you to perfect yourselves still fur-
11 ther in this respect. Moreover, it should be a matter of pride with
you not to meddle with the affairs of others, but to look after your
own and to earn your living by the work of your hands. These
12 admonitions, too, we have given you before. We remind you of
them because we wish you to appear blameless in the eyes of the
Gentiles and not depend upon any one for your support.
13 Now so far as the departed are concerned, we intend not to
leave you in ignorance of their fate, so that you may not abandon
14 yourselves to grief as do those who have no hope. For as surely as
we believe that Jesus descended into the kingdom of the dead and
rose again, so surely will God through Jesus lead on high, together
15 with Jesus, those who have fallen asleep. For this we can tell you
on the authority of the lord: We who possess spiritual life and abide
by it until the coming of the lord shall have no advantage over those
16 who have fallen asleep; for when the summons is issued, when the
voice of an archangel and the trumpet of God sound, the lord himself will descend from heaven, and those who have departed this
life in communion with Christ will be the first to be led on high.
17 Then we, in so far as we possess spiritual life, shall be drawn together with them into Christ's spirit-world and shall hasten amid
hosts of spirits to meet the lord; and then we shall be with the lord
18 for ever. So console one another by calling these words to mind.

CHAPTER 5.

1 As to the period and the hour, brothers, I have no need to write
2 you. As you yourselves well know, the day of the lord will come
3 like a thief in the night. When people are saying, "Peace and
safety prevail now," destruction will unexpectedly fall upon them,
just as birth-pangs come suddenly upon a pregnant woman, and
4 they will not be able to escape. But with you, brothers, let it never
5 be night, lest that day surprise you like a thief; for you are all
children of light, with whom it is always day. You have nothing
6 to do with night and darkness. Then we dare not lie down to sleep

7 as the others do, but we must be watchful and sober; for those who
8 sleep, sleep at night, and those who get drunk, do so after dark. Let
us, with whom it should always be day, remain sober; let us put on
the armor of faith and of love, and helmet ourselves with the hope
9 of our salvation. For God has not destined us for His punishment,
but to gain the salvation that is ours through our lord Jesus Christ,
10 who died for us in order that we might share spiritual life in com-
11 munion with him, whether we are now awake or asleep. With this
in mind, uplift one another and aid in one another's spiritual growth,
as indeed you are now doing.

12 Brothers, I have one more request to make of you. Learn to appreciate those who labor for the good of your congregation and who
are placed over you as guardians and shepherds of your souls in the
13 service of the Lord. Show them special affection in return for the
tasks that they have to perform among you. Live in peace and harmony with them at all times.

14 And then, brothers, we urge you to warn the unruly, encourage
15 the timid, support the weak, and be patient with all. See to it that
no one repays evil with evil, but strive to do nothing but good to
16 one another and to every one else. Always be cheerful. Pray con-
17 stantly, and thank God under all conditions; for this is what God
18 requires of you who live in fellowship with Christ Jesus. Do not
19 make it impossible for God's spirits to communicate with you. Do
20 not disdain the utterances of spirits through mediums, but test all
21 that they say and adhere to that which proves to be good. Keep away
22 from any kind of spirit-communication that has even the appearance
of evil.

23 May the God of peace sanctify you completely. May you be found
altogether pure in spirit, soul, and body on the day when our lord
24 Jesus Christ appears. He Who has issued His call to you is faithful,
and He will also carry it into effect.

25 Brothers, include us in your prayers, too.

26 Greet all the brothers with a holy kiss.

27 In the name of the Lord I adjure you to have this letter read to
all our brothers in the faith.

28 The grace of our lord Jesus Christ be with you. Amen.

The Second Epistle of Paul the Apostle to the THESSALONIANS

CHAPTER 1.

1 PAUL, Sylvanus, and Timothy send their greetings to the congregation at Thessalonica which is in communion with God our
2 Father and with the lord Jesus Christ. Grace be with you and peace
from God the Father and from the lord Jesus Christ.
3 On your account, brothers, we are bound always to thank God.
This thanksgiving is fully justified, for your faith deepens from day
to day, and with every one of you brotherly love is growing in a
4 way to make us feel proud of you before other congregations. We
are proud of your steadfastness, proud of your faithfulness to God
despite all of the persecution and suffering that you have to endure.
5 This is proof that God's choice is made justly, for it is only after
you have shown your readiness to suffer for the sake of His kingdom
6 that you are accounted worthy of it. On the other hand, He will
likewise employ His standard of justice in bringing trouble upon
7 those who have troubled you, as well as in granting rest and relief
8 to you who, like ourselves, have suffered persecution. That will be
on the day when the lord Jesus is revealed from heaven together with
his hosts in a blaze of fire, in order to repay those who ignored God
and those who refused obedience to the gospel of our lord Jesus.
9 These will have to be punished with a destiny of long duration and
full of calamities. They will be banished from the presence of
the lord and from the splendor of his mighty kingdom on the day
10 when he comes to be glorified in his saints. On that day he will be
marvelled at by all who came to believe in him because they accepted as true the testimony that we ourselves have given you con-
11 cerning him. Mindful of that day, we constantly pray for you that
our God may find you worthy of your calling, and that by endowing
you with His strength He may help you to carry out to the best of
12 your ability every good resolution and every act of faith, so that the
name of our lord Jesus may be glorified in you, and you in him,
through the love of our God and our lord Jesus Christ.

CHAPTER 2.

1 Now as to the reappearance of our lord Jesus Christ, before whom
2 we shall all be gathered, I beg you, brothers, do not permit your-

selves to lose your spiritual poise so quickly and to be disturbed,
either by any message from a spirit or by anything that we may say
3 or write to the effect that the day of the lord is at hand. Let no one
mislead you in any way on this point, for that day will not come
until there has been a breaking away from the truth; the Man of
4 Sin, the Son of Destruction, must be revealed as such. He is that
enemy who opposes and looks down upon everything that relates to
the true God and the true worship. He seats himself in God's temple
5 and acts as if he himself were God. Do you not remember that I
6 repeatedly spoke to you of this while I was with you? You also
know what it is that still restrains him, until the moment for him
to throw aside his mask arrives; for even now his forces are secretly
7 at work to enact laws contrary to the law of God. But this secret
activity will continue only until he who opposes open activity is
8 taken out of the way. Then he who is working to abolish the law of
God will appear in the open. May the lord Jesus, through his spirits
of truth, defeat him and render him powerless on the day when the
9 lord's return becomes manifest to all men. The appearance of this
enemy of the law of God is to be ascribed to the activity of Satan,
and is attended by every kind of false manifestation, sign, and won-
10 der, and by all the deception of the Evil One. The ones who suc-
cumb to him are those who are bound for destruction, because they
have not opened their hearts to the love of the true doctrine of
11 Christ, which could have saved them. For this reason God afflicts
them with a powerfully effective delusion, so that they put their faith
12 and confidence in falsehood. The result will be that all who did not
believe the truth but found their pleasure in that which violates the
law of God will be sentenced by God.

13 As to all of you, brothers beloved by the Lord, we owe sincere
thanks to God because He chose you for salvation from the beginning. It will be bestowed upon you by a spirit of sanctification and
14 by virtue of your belief in the truth. God called you to it through
the gospel that we have preached to you so that you might share the
glory of our lord Jesus Christ.

15 So then, brothers, stand firm and hold fast to the teachings that
16 you have received from us by word of mouth or by letter. May our
lord Jesus Christ himself and God our Father, Who in His love has
called us to Himself again and again throughout past ages, and Who
in His goodness has held before our eyes the glorious goal of our
17 hope, comfort your hearts and grant you strength for every good
accomplishment in deed and word.

CHAPTER 3.

1 Lastly I beg you to remember us in your prayers, so that the
word of the Lord may be spread quickly and triumph as it did
2 among you; further, so that we may be freed from our evil-minded
3 and godless adversaries, for not all men are open to the faith. But
God is faithful; He will strengthen you and keep you from the Evil
4 One. We are firmly confident in the Lord that you will follow our
5 counsel, both now and in the future. May the Lord direct your hearts
toward the love of God and the steadfastness that Christ possessed.
6 Brothers, on the authority of the lord Jesus Christ we advise you
to shun every brother in faith who leads an irregular life instead of
7 following the teachings that you have received from us. You yourselves know in which respects you should be guided by our example;
8 for we did not live irregularly while we were with you. We did not
accept bread from any one as a gift, but worked hard at our trade
9 day and night so as not to become a burden to any of you. Not that
we had no right to free support, but we wanted to give you an ex-
10 ample to follow. While we were with you we lived according to the
11 rule, "He who will not work, shall not eat." And now we are sorry
to hear that some of you are leading irregular lives, doing no serious work, but wandering around, making a show of being busy.
12 Such as these we earnestly enjoin in the name of Jesus Christ to
remain at home, attending to their work and thereby earning their
living.

13 As for yourselves, brothers, never weary of doing good. If any
14 one should fail to obey the instructions that are given in this letter,
consider him a marked man; stop associating with him, so that he
15 may feel ashamed; do not treat him as an enemy, however, but
earnestly reprove him as you would a brother.

16 May the Lord of peace grant you peace continually, whatever
may be your lot in life. The Lord be with you all.

17 I, Paul, am writing this greeting in my own hand. Let these
18 characters serve to authenticate every one of my letters. This is how
I write: "May the grace of our lord Jesus Christ be with you all.
Amen."

The First Epistle of Paul the Apostle to TIMOTHY

CHAPTER 1.

1 PAUL, who by the will of God our Deliverer and of Christ Jesus
2 our hope, became an apostle of Jesus Christ, sends greetings to
Timothy, his true son in the faith. Grace, mercy, and peace be with
you from God the Father and from our lord Christ Jesus.
3 When I went to Macedonia I asked you to stay in Ephesus, to
make it clear to certain people that they must teach no doctrine that
4 deviates from the truth, and that they must not devote themselves to
the study of meaningless tales and endless genealogies. Such studies
as these centre in hair-splitting research, rather than in the erection
5 of God's spiritual edifice, which consists of faith. What we aim at
in our preaching is the love that springs from a pure heart and a
6 clear conscience and true faith. Some have lost sight of this goal and
7 are wasting effort with their interpretations. They would like to be
regarded as experts in the Law, but they do not have the slightest
understanding of the terms that they use or the things of which they
8 speak with so much assurance. We are well aware that in itself the
Law of Moses is excellent, if it is observed in the spirit in which it
9 was enacted. We must bear in mind, however, that laws are not
made for the people who have the right moral attitude, but for the
lawless and rebellious; for the godless, and like sinners; for those
to whom nothing divine or human is sacred; for those who lay
10 violent hands on their fathers and mothers; for murderers, forni-
cators, sodomites, slave-dealers, liars, perjurers; and for all those
11 whose actions are contrary to the sound doctrine laid down in that
glorious gospel of the blessed God, with the preaching of which I
have been entrusted.
12 With all my heart I thank our lord Jesus Christ, who has given
me the necessary strength, for the trust that he displayed in me when
13 he called me into his service. I had previously been a blasphemer
of his name, a persecutor of his congregation, a wanton transgressor;
but I obtained mercy, for I had acted in ignorance, since at that
14 time I knew nothing of the true faith. Like a mighty flood the waves
of the Lord's grace swept into my life, bringing with them the
powers of faith and love which are active in the fellowship of Christ

15 Jesus. It is a true statement, and should be gratefully accepted by
every one, that Christ Jesus came into the world to save those who
16 had committed the sin of apostasy from God. I myself am one of
the worst of them, but for this very reason I obtained mercy, because
Christ Jesus chose to show all his forbearance in my case first of all.
I was to serve as an example for all who were to believe in him
and attain the salvation to come.
17 To the King of all the ages, the immortal, invisible and only God,
be honor and praise for ever. Amen.
18 I am sending these instructions to you, my dear son Timothy,
because of messages from God's spirits concerning you. According
19 to these messages you are to fight the good fight to the end, clinging
unshakably to the faith, and keeping a clear conscience. Certain
people have simply thrown aside what is known as a "clear con-
20 science," and their faith has been wrecked. Among these are Hymenaeus and Alexander; I have been forced to let them become instruments of the powers of Satan, at whose hands they will become so
worn that they will stop abusing others.

CHAPTER 2.

1 Now first of all I must advise you that supplications, prayers,
2 intercessions, and thanksgivings are to be offered for all men, even
for kings and all persons in authority, so that we may lead a life of
3 peace and quiet in all piety and devotion. This is good and accept-
4 able to God our Deliverer; for it is His will that all men should be
5 saved and attain to full knowledge of the truth. For there is but one
6 God and but one mediator between God and man. This mediator is
Christ Jesus, by virtue of his human incarnation; and he gave himself as a ransom for all. This truth was preached in every place
7 where conditions seemed favorable. I too was ordained as a herald
and an apostle of the truth, and in fact was chosen to instruct the
Gentiles in matters pertaining to the faith and the truth. What I am
saying is the truth, not a falsehood.
8 It is my wish that wherever men meet for worship, the hands that
they lift in prayer shall be clean and their hearts free from the
blemish of strife and contention.
9 I likewise request that the women who attend divine service be
appropriately dressed; let modesty and propriety be their ornaments, not elaborately dressed hair, nor gold, pearls, nor expensive
10 garments. Let them dress as befits women who are destined to preach
11 the true worship by displaying good behavior. Let a woman learn

12 the truth by listening quietly and in submissive silence. I will have
no woman serve as a teacher or in any other way assume authority
13 over men; rather, let her cultivate a quiet reserve. For Adam was
14 created first, then Eve. And Adam was not deceived, it was the
woman who was deceived and committed the sin of apostasy.
15 Woman will obtain salvation by giving birth to children, provided
that in all humility she continues in the true faith and in a holy
way of life.

CHAPTER 3.

1 There is a popular saying, "Whoever aspires to office aims at an
2 excellent life-task." To qualify for the office of bishop, a man must
be above reproach; in addition, he must be married and must always have been faithful to his wife; he must be sober, judicious,
3 honorable, hospitable, and competent to teach others; he must not
be among those who indulge excessively in wine and hence easily
become quarrelsome, but must rather be gentle and peaceable and
4 free from avarice. He must be able to govern his own household
in exemplary fashion, and with the utmost dignity teach his children
5 obedience. For if a man cannot rule his own family, how shall he
6 be able to supervise God's congregations? He must not be a recent
convert, for fear that he may fall a victim to his conceit and resort
7 to measures inspired by the devil. Moreover, he must bear a good
name among the unbelievers, so that he will not be slandered by
them and fall into the snares of the devil.
8 Let his helpers also be men who command respect; not double-
9 dealers, not addicted to drinking, and not greedy for low gains, but
men who carry within pure hearts the mystery that their faith has
10 disclosed to them. They too should first be tested and assume their
11 office only if they have been found blameless. Their wives must also
be persons held in esteem, not prone to gossip, but earnest and reli-
12 able in every way. The deacons, too, must be married men who have
always been true to their wives; they must set an example in the
training of their children and in the management of their house-
13 holds. By faithfully discharging the duties of their office they will
win the respect and confidence of their community and will be free
to act boldly on behalf of the faith in Jesus Christ.
14 Although I hope to visit you shortly, I am writing these things
15 to you in case my coming is delayed. From this letter you are to
learn how to conduct God's household. Any congregation in which
God's power manifests itself and makes it a pillar and bulwark of
16 the truth, is a member of God's household. In it we publicly con-

fess how great is the mystery concealed in our religion, that mystery which came down to us as a human being, which attained to perfection in the spirit, which appeared to the apostles, which was preached in the spirit-world that is estranged from God, which the universe relies on, and which was led on high in glory.

CHAPTER 4.

1 God's spirit-world expressly declares that in later times many
will fall away from the true faith, turning to spirits of deceit, and
2 spreading doctrines inspired by demons. They will be led to do so
by the hypocritical demeanor of lying preachers who stamp their
3 own consciences with the brand of guilt. These men will forbid
marriage and require abstinence from certain foods which God has
created for believers and for all who have come to a full knowledge
4 of the truth to partake of with thanksgiving. For everything created
by God is good; nothing can be considered forbidden, if it can be
5 partaken of with a prayer of thanks to God; for it has been sanctified by the word of God that created it, as well as by your prayer.
6 Lay this before your congregation and you will be an excellent
servant of Christ; for you drank in the truths of the faith and their
wonderful interpretation with your mother's milk, and you have
7 faithfully observed all of them. So reject the worthless fables of old
8 women, and train yourself in true godliness. For the mortification
of the body is of little avail, but genuine godliness is of the highest
value, for it carries within it the spiritual life of the present and
9 the future. We may safely rely on the truth of our doctrine. It
10 therefore deserves to be accepted by every one. For the reason why
we endeavor to guide our lives by it is that we have set our hope on
God, the source of all life. He is the Deliverer of all men. He saves
them in the order of sequence in which they attain faith in Him.
11 This is the doctrine which it is your task to proclaim and teach.
12 Let no one slight you because of your youth. In everything that you
do and say, set an example for the believers — an example of love,
an example of faith, and an example of purity.
13 Continue with your reading of the Scriptures and with your ex-
14 hortations and teachings bearing on them until I come. Do not neglect this gift with which you have been endowed in a special measure.
It was conferred upon you when the elders laid their hands on you
15 at the bidding of a message brought by spirits. Employ it to the
fullest extent. Make this your chief concern, so that the results of
16 your work may be evident to all. Above all things, see to it that the
conduct of your own life harmonizes with your teachings. Stand

loyally by your congregation, for by so doing you will make certain of your own salvation as well as that of your hearers.

CHAPTER 5.

1 Do not rebuke an older man harshly, but speak to him as you
would speak to your father. Treat the younger men like brothers,
2 the older women like mothers, and the younger women like sisters,
3 all with perfect propriety. Provide means of support for widows
4 who are alone in the world and who are in real want; but if a widow
has children or grandchildren, they should be taught that the first
duty of religion is to take care of their own family and to repay
their parents and grandparents for the benefits that they have re-
5 ceived from them; for this is pleasing in the sight of God. A widow
who is truly needy and alone in the world puts her trust in the Lord,
6 and night and day she is engaged in constant prayer; but a widow
who lives in luxury is spiritually dead even before she experiences
corporeal death.

7 So lay down the following rules for the members of your congregation, in order that they may incur no reproach:

8 Whoever fails to provide for his own relatives, especially for the members of his own household, has denied the faith and is worse than an infidel.

9 Let no widow be enrolled among the workers in the service of the
congregation unless she is at least sixty years of age and has been
10 faithful to her husband during her married life. She must have a
reputation for being dutiful in the performance of good works, in
rearing her children, in showing hospitality, in acts of humility, and
in relieving those who are in distress; in short, for her zeal in all
good work.

11 Refuse to enroll the younger widows as workers in the service of
the congregation, for as soon as their carnal desires estrange them
12 from the cause of Christ they want to marry, and thus they incur the
reproach of having betrayed the confidence that was placed in them.
13 At the same time they become careless in their work; not only that,
but they begin to gossip, meddle with the affairs of others, and talk
14 about that which does not concern them. It is therefore my wish
that the younger widows remarry, bear children, look after their
households, and give none of our opponents cause to speak ill of
15 them. For some of these widows have later on been ensnared by
Satan.

16 If any Christian, man or woman, has widows among his relatives,
he is to provide for them. They are not to be supported by the congregation, which is sufficiently burdened as it is with helping widows
who really need its aid.
17 The elders who distinguish themselves above others in the discharge of their duties are to be regarded as deserving of double compensation, especially if they are active as both preachers and
18 teachers; for the Scriptures say, "You shall not muzzle the ox when
he is treading the grain;" and further, "A workman deserves his
wages."
19 Do not consider any accusation against an elder unless it is con-
20 firmed by two or three witnesses. If an elder has done wrong, reprimand him in the presence of the whole congregation, so that fear
may prevent the others from committing similar offences.
21 I adjure you before God and Christ Jesus, as well as before God's
chosen messengers, to carry out these instructions impartially. Do
not, however, dispose of any case in a manner resembling the sum-
22 mons of a court of law. Do not be too ready to lay your hands on
any one, and do not become an accomplice in the guilt of others.
23 Keep yourself pure. Rid yourself of the habit of drinking nothing
but water; take some wine daily for your stomach-complaint and
your fainting-spells.
24 There are people who sin openly and therefore require public
condemnation. With others their sins become known only in the
25 course of time. So also there are good works that become publicly
known; and even those of which this is not true cannot remain hidden for ever.

CHAPTER 6.

1 Let all who are servants in the households of others remember that
their masters are entitled to be treated with proper respect; otherwise they will bring disgrace to the name of God and to our doc-
2 trine. If they have Christians for masters they should not show them
less respect because these are their brothers in the faith. On the
contrary, let them serve them all the more faithfully, because it is
their beloved fellow-Christians who profit by such service.
3 These are the directions and instructions that you are to lay before your congregation. Whoever departs from the sound doctrine
of our lord Jesus Christ and our religion to teach otherwise is
4 deluded and ignorant; he is afflicted with a craving for splitting
hairs and for sophistry, all of which leads to ill-will, dissension,
mutual affronts, and false conclusions of the most mischievous kind;

5 in short, to such constant friction as is common between men who
have ceased to think clearly and who have turned aside from the
6 truth. Such men look upon religion only as a profitable business.
It is true that religion may also be a source of income in a good
sense, if one seeks to derive from it only that which is necessary to
7 sustain life; for we bring nothing into the world, and it is equally
8 certain that we take nothing with us when we leave it. If we have
9 food and clothing, let us be content with that. Those who are eager
to be rich fall into the temptations and snares of Satan; they become the victims of many foolish and harmful desires which usually
10 plunge men into the worst corruption. For the love of money is the
root of all evil. The craving for wealth has led many astray from
11 the faith and has caused them much anguish of soul. Therefore, if
you aspire to be a man after God's heart, spurn all these things and
let the goal of your endeavor be purity of soul, genuine piety, faith,
12 love, steadfastness, and patience. Fight the good fight of the faith,
and strive for the life hereafter, for it is to this that you have been
called and for this purpose you made your glorious confession of
faith before many witnesses.

13 In the presence of God, Who leads everything back to spiritual
life, and of Christ Jesus, who made his glorious confession before
14 Pontius Pilate, I charge you to keep your office free from all blem-
15 ish and reproach until the coming of our lord Jesus. His coming
will be brought about by that Most Exalted and only Sovereign,
16 at the time that He has fixed — He, the King of kings and Lord of
lords; He Who alone possesses immortality; He Who dwells in an
unapproachable light; He Whom no human being has ever seen
or can see; He to Whom honor and power belong for ever. Amen.

17 Impress upon those who have earthly riches that they must not
be overbearing, nor fix their hopes on so uncertain a thing as wealth.
They must put their trust in God alone, the source of all life, Who
18 gives us an abundance of everything for our enjoyment. Let the
wealthy do good and strive to become rich in good works; let them
be generous and charitable, and thus amass for themselves an ex-
19 cellent treasure for the future. In this way they will assure themselves of a life that can really be called life.

20 My dear Timothy, guard the treasure that has been entrusted to
you. Ignore idle talk and the objections raised by what is called
21 "science." Many who call themselves "learned" have strayed into
paths that lie far away from the truths taught by the faith.

The grace of God be with you. Amen.

The Second Epistle of Paul the Apostle to TIMOTHY

CHAPTER 1.

1 PAUL, who by the will of God became an apostle of Christ Jesus,
in order to preach the gospel of the spiritual life that lies in the
2 fellowship with Christ Jesus, sends greetings to his beloved son
Timothy. May grace, mercy, and peace be granted to you by God
the Father and by Christ Jesus our lord.

3 I thank God Whom I have served from my childhood with a good
4 conscience that I can always remember you in my prayers. Day
and night I long to see you again, for I cannot forget the tears that
5 you shed when we parted. Besides, it would fill me with new joy
if your unfeigned faith could exert its power upon me from near at
hand—a faith that animated your grandmother Lois and your
mother Eunice, and belongs, I am convinced, to you as well.

6 For this reason I would admonish you to rekindle the gift of God
7 that you received on the day when I laid my hands on you; for God
has not given us a spirit of timidity but a spirit of strength, love,
8 and prudence. Do not be ashamed to testify on our lord's behalf;
and do not be ashamed of me, who am in chains for the lord's sake.
Rather, accept your share of the sufferings that the preaching of the
9 gospel entails. God will give you the strength for it. It is God Who
has saved us and called us to salvation through a life of holiness. This He has done not because of our own works, but in accordance with the decision of His free will, and on account of the grace
10 bestowed upon us ages ago through Jesus Christ. In the appearance
on earth of Christ Jesus as our Savior this grace has become appar-
ent to all. It is he who has taken away the power that the Prince
of Death once had over us. Through this joyful news he has caused
11 the light of an imperishable life to rise before our eyes. And I have
been appointed to act among the Gentiles as a herald, an apostle,
and a teacher of this joyful news.

12 This is why I must endure all these sufferings; but it is no disgrace, for I know who it is whom I have believed and trusted, and
I am confident that he is able to hold his protecting hand over that
which was committed to my charge, until the day of reckoning.

13 On the basis of the sound doctrine that you have learned from
me, set an example to all; an example of faith in Christ Jesus and
14 of love for him. Guard the glorious treasure that has been entrusted
to you; you will receive strength for this task from a holy spirit,
such as is allotted to every one of us.
15 You know that every one in Asia Minor has abandoned me, not
16 excepting Phygelus and Hermogenes. May the Lord show especial
mercy to the family of Onesiphorus, for he often comforted me and
17 was not ashamed of my imprisonment. When he arrived in Rome
18 he searched eagerly for me and found me. The Lord God grant that
on the day of judgment he may find mercy before Christ the lord.
You yourself know best of all what a great service he did me in
Ephesus.

CHAPTER 2.

1 Now, my dear son, become ever more proficient in the use of the
2 gift that Christ Jesus has bestowed on you. As for that which you
have heard from me and for the truth of which you have had so
many proofs, confide them only to such of the faithful as are able
3 to teach them to others in the right way. As for yourself, endure
4 your hardships like a true soldier of Christ Jesus. No soldier can
be troubled with the cares of earning his daily bread; otherwise he
would not be able to attend to the duties required of him by his
5 commander. And if a man wants to win the victor's wreath, it is not
enough for him merely to be present at the contest; he must com-
6 pete according to the rules. The farmer who tills the field in the
7 sweat of his brow has the first right to its fruits. Try to grasp the
meaning of my words; the lord will give you full understanding to
8 that end. Always keep in mind the truth that Jesus Christ, begotten
as a man of the seed of David, was raised from the kingdom of the
9 spiritually dead. Such is the gospel that I proclaim. For its sake I
must undergo suffering, even to the extent of being imprisoned like
10 an ordinary criminal. But God's word cannot be imprisoned; so I
cheerfully endure all my troubles for the sake of the elect, in order
that they also may share the salvation that is obtained in fellowship
with Christ Jesus, and thus enter the glory of the future.
11 So much is true beyond all doubt: "If we die with Christ, we shall
12 also live with him; if we remain constant in suffering, we shall reign
13 with him; if we deny him, he will deny us in turn; if we prove faithless to him, he will still be faithful to us; for he cannot be faithless
to himself."
14 Remind all the people of this and again earnestly admonish them

before the Lord not to let themselves be drawn into controversies
about words. This benefits no one and only bewilders the audience.
15 Take the greatest pains to show God that He may rely on you; that
you are a workman who has no need of being ashamed of his work,
but that you are able to present the word of the truth correctly, both
16 in content and in form. Avoid empty phrases; they are worthless,
for they only further the mistaken religious opinions held by the
17 people. Phrases of this kind spread among them with the swiftness
of wild-fire sweeping over a parched meadow. Among these phrase-
18 makers are Hymenaeus and Philetus, who have strayed far from the
truth, and maintain that the resurrection has already taken place.
By so doing, they destroy the faith of some.

19 Nevertheless, the foundation of faith laid by God remains unshaken. It bears the inscription certified by His seal, "The Lord
knows His own"; furthermore, "Let every one who calls upon the
name of the Lord refrain from iniquity."

20 In every prominent household there are vessels not only of gold
and silver, but also of wood and of clay. The first are used when
special honor is to be shown; the others, for common, everyday
21 purposes. Now if any one keeps himself unsullied by all that is
low, he will be among the vessels which the master of the house uses
to confer a special honor; he will be like a consecrated vessel prized
by the master of the house and used on every great occasion.

22 Shun the evil passions of youth. Strive to do right, hold fast to
faith and trust in God and love, and keep peace with those who
23 invoke the Lord with pure hearts. Take no part in foolish and child-
24 ish controversies. As you know, they serve only to bring on quarrels,
and a servant of the Lord should not quarrel. He should be gentle
with every one, always able to give good counsel, and not quick to
25 resent another's contradiction. Let him correct his opponents gently;
if he does this, perhaps God will finally work a change of heart in
26 them and they will come to knowledge of the truth. Then they may
come to their senses again and free themselves from the snares in
which Satan has caught them in order to bend them to his own will.

CHAPTER 3.

1 Mark this, toward the end of every age evil conditions will pre-
2 vail. Men will grow selfish and eager for money; in their boastful-
ness and conceit, they will scoff at everything noble and sacred;
they will be disobedient to their parents, ungrateful, and indifferent
3 to God. There will be no love and no loyalty among them; like devils
in human form they will revel in excess and licentious behavior;

4 their love of goodness will be extinguished; and in place of reverence for God there will be treachery and base flattery, arrogance
5 and self-indulgence. Nevertheless, they will cling to the outward
form of religion from habit; but not a trace of the inner power of
6 religion will be perceptible in them. Keep away from such people,
for some of them make their way into families and captivate those
women who are heavily laden with sin and who are the sport of
7 every conceivable passion; women who constantly desire to learn
something new, but who are never able to arrive at the real knowl-
8 edge of the truth. People of this stamp oppose the truth in the same
manner as Jannes and Jambres opposed Moses in their day. They
9 are unsound of mind, and untrustworthy in matters of faith; but
they will be unmasked before all the world, just as were those others
whom I mentioned.

10 But you have been a faithful follower of mine in every respect:
in doctrine, in your whole life and endeavor, in faith and patience,
11 in love and constancy, in persecutions and sufferings such as I also
have had to endure in Antioch, Iconium, and Lystra. And what
persecutions I had to endure! But the Lord has delivered me from
12 all of them. Such persecutions will be the lot of every one who
13 chooses to lead a godly life in fellowship with Christ. That is taken
care of by the wicked and the seducers of the people, who grow
worse day by day; they are deceivers who are themselves deceived.

14 Hold fast to that which you have learned and of which you have
15 become fully convinced. You know who your teacher was. You
have also been familiar with the Scriptures from childhood; from
them you can derive the wisdom that will show you the way to sal-
16 vation through faith in Jesus Christ. Every Scripture that is inspired
by a spirit of God can always be used for teaching others and for
17 proving the truth; one can also use it as a means of improving
and perfecting others until they become men after God's own heart,
ready for any good deed, and also persevering.

CHAPTER 4.

1 Now I adjure you in the name of God and of Christ Jesus, who
will judge both the living and the spiritually dead when he returns
2 and appears as king: Proclaim the truth; but you yourself must decide whether the moment is opportune or not. Produce the evidence
of the truth. If you are obliged to reprimand and admonish, do so
3 with the utmost gentleness and patience. To be sure, the time will
come when sound doctrine will no longer be accepted. People will
select preachers to suit their own taste, and in great numbers, only

4 to provide a feast for their ears. They will close their ears to the
truth and turn to empty oratory.
5 Go about your work calmly and resolutely. Accept suffering
quietly. Fulfill your task as an evangelist, and be thorough in the
performance of your other duties to the congregation.
6 As for me, there are already indications that my life must be
sacrificed and that the moment of my departure from this world is
7 near at hand. I have fought a good fight for God on the battlefield
of life; I have run my course and reached the goal; I have kept my
8 faith and my trust in God; last of all there now awaits me the victor's crown that is destined for those who have won merit in the
eyes of God. This the lord, the just judge, will give me on that day
on which the prizes are awarded. But it is not only to me that such
a prize will be given, but to all who have longed with great love
for the lord's return.
9 Come to me soon, for Demas has forsaken me. He could no longer
10 resist his love for what this world offers him. He has gone to Thessa-
11 lonica. Crescens has gone to Galatia, and Titus to Dalmatia. Only
Luke is with me. Fetch Mark, and bring him with you, for he can be
12 of great service to me. I have sent Tychicus to Ephesus. In Troas
13 I left my travelling-cloak with Carpus. Bring it with you when you
come; also the books, but above all, the parchment rolls.
14 Alexander the smith has been very malicious toward me. The
15 Lord will requite him accordingly. You too must be on your guard
16 against him, for at my first hearing in court he contradicted my
declaration most violently. No one testified in my favor; all de-
17 serted me. May it not be held against them! Nevertheless, the Lord
stood by me and gave me strength, that my speech in my own defence might carry complete conviction and be heard by all the
18 Gentiles. Thus I fortunately escaped the lion's jaws. The Lord will
also deliver me from all spiteful persecution in the future and bring
me safely into his heavenly kingdom. May he be praised and honored for ever. Amen.
19 Give my greetings to Prisca and Aquila and to all of the house-
20 hold of Onesiphorus. Erastus stayed in Corinth. I left Trophimus
21 in Miletus because he was ill. Make haste and come to me before
winter sets in. Eubulus, Pudes, Linus, Claudia, and all of the
brothers send their greetings.
22 May the lord Jesus Christ be your spiritual guide. Farewell, and
peace be with you. Amen.

The Epistle of Paul the Apostle to
TITUS

CHAPTER 1.

1 I, PAUL, am the writer of this letter. I have been ordained as an
apostle of Christ, to carry the faith to God's chosen ones and to
teach them the worship of the true God, in order that they may have
2 the hope of the life to come — a life which God, Who cannot lie,
3 foretold ages ago; He has fulfilled His word at the time that He
appointed, and is causing the fulfillment of His word to be proclaimed through the preaching with which I, among others, have
been entrusted at the command of God our Deliverer.
4 This letter is for you, dear Titus, my spiritual son and my equal
in rank by virtue of your adoption of the same faith that I profess.
Grace and peace be with you from God the Father and from Christ
Jesus our Redeemer.
5 I left you in Crete to settle everything that I was forced to leave
unfinished. It was to be your task to go from place to place, ordain-
ing elders in the congregations according to the instructions that I
6 gave you. These were as follows. In choosing elders, you must consider none but married men who are above reproach and have always been faithful to their wives; men whose children are of the
faith and are not open to the charge of licentiousness and insub-
7 ordination. Clearly, any man who is entrusted with the supervision
of a congregation must be blameless in his position as the steward
of God; neither presumptuous nor quick-tempered, nor addicted to
8 drinking and quarreling, nor ruled by love of vile money. He must
rather be hospitable, charitable, thoughtful, just, God-fearing, and
9 chaste. He must hold fast to the true text of the divine doctrine, so
that he may be able to teach sound doctrine to others and refute any
10 who may challenge it. For there are many who cannot refrain from
raising objections and who, in so doing, speak nonsense and thus
bewilder others. The chief offenders on this score are those who
11 were formerly Jews. Their mouths must be stopped, because for the
sake of vile gain they teach things that are not true and thereby
12 throw entire families into a turmoil. Even one of their own people,
a prophet, has said of them, "Cretans are always liars, vicious as
13 beasts, and lazy gluttons." It is a true statement. Therefore, correct
them sharply, so that they may adopt the sound faith and abandon
14 their belief in Jewish traditions and lay no weight on man-made
15 ordinances that deviate from the truth. To the pure, all things are

pure, but to those who are stained with guilt and to unbelievers,
16 nothing is pure, for their minds and consciences are polluted. They
may indeed profess to acknowledge a God, but in all their acts they
disown Him. They do what they ought to abominate; they refuse to
be obedient, and they are strangers to good deeds of any kind.

CHAPTER 2.

1 Let everything that you preach to your congregation accord with
2 sound doctrine. Thus, give the elderly men to understand that they
must not drink wine to excess, that they must be dignified and dis-
creet in their deportment, and grow stronger and stronger in faith,
in love for one another, and in constancy.
3 In the same way impress it upon the older women that they must
be like priestesses in their demeanor; that they must not indulge in
gossip or drink wine to excess, but that they must give others les-
4 sons in goodness. They should induce the younger women to love
5 their husbands and children with all their hearts; to be modest, virtuous, home-loving, and helpful, and to submit to their husbands,
so that they may not discredit the cause of God.
6 Exhort the young men likewise to control themselves in every
7 respect. Above all, set them a good example. Let your teaching dis-
8 play a pure character and personal dignity; let the substance of
your lectures accord with sound doctrine, so that no exception can
be taken to them and so that all your opponents may be put to shame
because they can find nothing evil to repeat about us.
9 Teach servants that they must obey their masters and fulfill all
duties to their satisfaction; that they must not oppose them, or em-
10 bezzle, but that they must show themselves worthy of the confidence
placed in them. By observing these rules they will reflect credit in
every way upon the doctrine of God our Deliverer.
11 For the grace of God that brings salvation to all men has ap-
12 peared. It induces us to lay aside ungodliness and worldly passions,
and to lead pure, godly, and pious lives here on earth, at the same
13 time keeping our eyes fixed upon the lofty goal of our hopes and
awaiting the hour when the glory of the great God will appear,
14 together with the glory of our redeemer Jesus Christ, who sacrificed
himself for us in order to deliver us from all ungodliness and so to
purify us that we might be his chosen people — a people filled with
the sole desire of doing good.
15 Make these truths the subject of your sermons and use them as
the foundation of your instructions. Speak of them with the utmost
forcefulness, giving no one occasion to look down upon you.

CHAPTER 3.

1 Remind the members of your congregation that they must submit to the powers and authorities of God's spirit-world; that they
2 must obey their commands and be ready for any good work; that
they must abuse no one, but be peaceable and conciliatory, treat-
3 ing all men with gentleness on every occasion. For we too were
once deluded and disobedient and strayed from the right path; we
were enslaved by various lusts and passions; our lives were filled
with wickedness and spite; we were full of hatred, and each was
4 the bane of the other. Then appeared the kindness and love of God
5 our Deliverer toward man. He saved us not because of our doing
right but only out of His compassion for us; He cleansed us in the
water of spiritual regeneration and made new men of us through
6 the operation of a holy spirit poured upon us in rich abundance of
7 power through Jesus Christ our redeemer. By virtue of the redeemer's service of love we were again to obtain the favor of God
and have the hope of inheriting the life hereafter.

8 The teachings that I impart to you are true. I wish that you
would live in complete accordance with them, so that those who have
faith in God may strive to excel in good deeds. This would be an
9 excellent thing and would bring a blessing upon the people. But
avoid foolish research and questions of ancestry, controversial matters and quarrels over the provisions of the Law of Moses, for
10 such things are useless and not worth the time spent on them. If
any one should stir up dissension in the congregation by discussing
these matters, warn him more than once, and if your warning is not
11 heeded, expel him from the congregation. Such men as that have
strayed from the right path, as you know; they sin, because their
own conscience condemns them.

12 As soon as I send Artemas or Tychicus to you, come to me immediately at Nicapolis, for I have decided to spend the winter there.
13 Provide Zenas, the lawyer, and Apollos with everything they need
14 to continue their journey so that they may lack nothing. This is also
an opportunity for the people of your congregation to learn how to
excel in good deeds by supplying the most pressing needs of others,
in order that they may not be altogether lacking in the fruits of
neighborly love.

15 All who are with me send their greetings to you. Greet all who
love us as fellows in faith.

The grace of the Lord be with you all. Amen.

The Epistle of Paul the Apostle to PHILEMON

1 PAUL, an apostle of Christ Jesus, and Timothy, our brother, send
their greetings to you, Philemon, our beloved brother and fel-
2 low-worker, as well as to our sister Appia and our comrade Archip-
3 pus, together with the congregation that meets at your house. Grace
be with you and peace from God our Father and from the lord
Jesus Christ.

4 I thank God as often as I remember you in my prayers, for I have
5 heard so much in praise of your faithfulness to God and of the love
that you bear in your heart for the lord Jesus and for all the faith-
6 ful. I pray that your membership in the Christian brotherhood may
spur you on to further efforts to discover any good work that we
7 might perform between us on behalf of Christ Jesus. Indeed, we are
indebted to your love, my dear brother, for great joy and consolation, because by you the hearts of the faithful have been relieved of
many a care.

8 Now since I am a servant of Christ, I feel that I need have no
scruples about giving you orders as to what is the proper thing to
9 do; but I prefer to appeal to you in all kindness. I, Paul, an old
10 man, and besides that a prisoner for the sake of Christ Jesus, appeal
to you on behalf of my dear son Onesimus, whose spiritual father
11 I became during my imprisonment. At one time he was of little value
12 to you, but now he is worth a great deal both to you and to me. I
am sending him to you; receive him as you would receive my own
13 heart. I should have liked to keep him with me so that he might
serve me in your stead during the imprisonment that I have to suf-
14 fer because I preach the gospel. But I was unwilling to do anything
without your knowledge, so that this act of neighborly love on your
part might not have the appearance of compulsion but arise from
15 your own free will. It may well be that he was separated from you
for a time only in order that you might have him as your own for
16 life, no longer as a slave but as something more — a brother whom
I especially love and cherish. How much more he must mean to you
to whom he now belongs both as a man and as a fellow-Christian!
17 Now if you look upon me as one of your own family, so to speak,

18 receive him as you would receive me. If he has wronged you in any
19 way or owes you anything, put that down to my account. I, Paul,
give you the written statement, "I will repay it." I should not like
to remind you that you, in your capacity as a Christian, are in-
20 debted to me. Yes, dear brother, allow me to impose on you a little
because of your allegiance to the lord. Grant this heartfelt wish of
mine for the sake of Christ.
21 Confident that you will comply with my request, I have written
this to you. Indeed, I know that you are ready to do even more than
22 I ask. At the same time prepare to receive me as your guest, too;
for I hope that in answer to your prayers, I shall be restored to you.
23 Epaphras, who shares captivity with me for the sake of Christ
24 Jesus, greets you, as do my fellow-workers Mark, Aristarchus,
Demas, and Luke.
25 May the grace of our lord Jesus Christ be with your spirit. Amen.

The Epistle of Paul the Apostle to the HEBREWS

CHAPTER 1.

1 ON many occasions and in various ways God in times past spoke
2 to our fathers through the prophets. Finally in our own day
He has spoken to us through a son whom He appointed to rule over
the universe and by whom He also caused the ages to be determined.
3 In him is reflected God's glory, and he is the image of God's true
being. He accomplishes everything in obedience to God's word of
power. Through him God effected our purification from the sins
of apostasy and then seated him at His almighty right hand in the
4 kingdom of heaven. He is as far above the angels as the name that
5 he inherited is superior to theirs. For when did God ever say to one
of His angels, "You are my son; to-day I myself have begotten
you"? And again, "I will be his Father, and he shall be My son"?
6 And when, under the new order, He introduced the first-born into
the world once more, He said, "Let all the angels of God do homage
7 to him." Of His angels He says, "He makes the spirit-world His
8 messengers, and flames of fire His servants." But of His son He
says, "God is your throne for ever; the sceptre of the royalty with
9 which He invests you is a sceptre of justice. To please God has been
your heart's desire, and you have scorned to become an apostate
from Him. Therefore God, Who is also your God, has anointed you
with the oil of gladness and has placed you above your fellows."
10 And further, "You, lord, in the beginning laid the foundation of the
earth, and all the spheres under heaven are the work of your hands.
11 They will pass away again, but you will outlast everything. They
12 all will grow old like a garment, and you will change those spheres
as an old mantle is changed for a new one; so those spheres will
be exchanged for new ones. But you will always remain the same,
13 and your years will have no end."—And when did He ever say to
an angel, "Sit at My right hand until I make your enemies my foot-
14 stool"? Are not all angels simply ministering spirits sent out to help
those who are to regain the salvation that is theirs by inheritance?

CHAPTER 2.

1 Let us therefore give more earnest attention to the things that we
have just heard, so that they may never fade from our memory.

2 Thus, if the message proclaimed through God's angels was absolutely true, and if every transgression or violation thereof met with
3 the punishment that it deserved, how much less shall we escape
punishment if we neglect such a glorious gospel, which was first
preached by the lord himself and then confirmed to us by those who
4 had personally heard him. In addition, the testimony of these ear-
witnesses was vouched for by God Himself, Who corroborated it with
signs and wonders and other manifestations of divine power, as well
as by the bestowal upon individual witnesses of a holy spirit in
such measure as He saw fit.

5 It was not to angels that He gave the sovereignty over the future
6 kingdom of which we are speaking. One writer has told who the
sovereign of that kingdom is in the words, "What is man, that Thou
art mindful of him, or any son of man, that Thou regardest him?
7 And yet Thou hast made one, as a son of man, inferior to the angels
for a little while. Then Thou didst crown him with glory and honor,
making everything subject to him as king, and appointing him lord
over the works of Thy hands."

8 Now if we are told here that God subjected everything to him,
this expressly means that He exempted nothing from subjection to
him. As yet, to be sure, we can see that not everything has been
9 brought into subjection to him. Nevertheless, we see that it is Jesus
who for a short time was made lower than the angels, and that it is
he who by his sufferings and his death earned the crown of glory
and honor, and that by God's mercy he tasted death for every one.
10 For God's plan of salvation provided that through suffering he for
whom and through whom the universe was created should be made
perfect; he, who had once brought so many children to glory; he,
11 who shall now lead the apostate children back to salvation. For he
who leads the way to sanctification and those who are led to sanctification all have the same Father. For this reason he is not ashamed
12 to call them his brothers in saying, "I will declare Thy name to my
brothers; in the midst of the congregation I will proclaim Thy
13 praise." And elsewhere, "I will put all my trust in Him." And
again, "See, here am I, and here are the children whom God has
14 given me." Now since he had clothed the children in bodies of flesh
and blood, he could not do otherwise than share the same lot. Thus
he was to be enabled to suffer the death of the body in order to wrest
the power from him who rules over the spiritually dead, namely,
15 the devil. He was to restore to freedom all those who throughout all
the periods of their earthly existence lived under the spell of fear
16 of the Prince of Death and were thus held in slavery by him. Hence

he was by no means to take up the cause of angels, but to bring help
17 to the true descendants of Abraham. He was therefore obliged to become like his brothers in all respects, so that he might be a merciful
and faithful high priest for all creatures who wish to return to God.
He was to build the bridge over which the hosts of those who had
18 committed the sin of apostasy might return. As one who himself
was sorely tempted to commit that sin, he is especially fitted to help
those who are assailed by the same temptation.

CHAPTER 3.

1 Therefore, devoted brothers and comrades on the journey to the
heavenly home to which you are recalled, cast your eyes upon the
2 envoy and high priest of our creed, Jesus, who kept faith with
his Creator, just as Moses also was found faithful in everything
3 pertaining to his service in the tabernacle of God. But let Jesus be
deemed worthy of far greater honor than was Moses; for the builder
4 of a sanctuary enjoys more honor than the sanctuary itself. Every
building has its builder, and the builder of the universe is God.
5 Moses was indeed faithful as a servant, appointed to perform all
the duties in the house of God and to repeat faithfully the words
6 spoken by God. But Christ, as the Son of God, was appointed
steward over God's house. And we are that house of God, if we
only keep our hope in God with confidence and pride to the end.
7 Therefore heed the words of a holy spirit: "To-day, when you hear
8 His voice, do not harden your heart, as they did at Marah, and as on
9 the day when your fathers were tempted in the desert and undertook
to put Me to the test at Massa, although for forty years they had
10 witnessed My wonders. Therefore I was angry with that generation
11 and said, 'In their hearts they are always astray. They have been
unwilling to acknowledge My ways, and so I have sworn in My
wrath: Truly, it shall be a long time before they enter My rest!'"
12 See to it, brothers, that there is no one among you whose heart
has been corrupted by unbelief which has led him to forsake God,
13 the source of all life. Rather encourage one another daily, so long
as the word "to-day" still has meaning for you, so that none of your
hearts may be hardened by the delusion of the sin of apostasy.
14 For we have been made companions of Christ, provided that we
preserve our faith in him to the end.
15 If we are told, "To-day, when you hear His voice, do not harden
16 your hearts as they did at Marah," then let me ask who the people
of those days were who heard His voice and yet hardened their

17 hearts? Were they not all who had followed Moses out of Egypt?
And who were the people with whom He was angry for forty years?
Were they not those who had fallen away from Him, and whose
18 bodies dropped dead in the wilderness? And who were the people
to whom He had sworn that they would not enter His rest for a long
19 time? Were they not those who had refused Him obedience? So
we see that it was because of their unbelief that they could not enter
into rest.

CHAPTER 4.

1 But the promise that all shall enter His rest still stands. Then
let us make it our anxious concern that none of us may even give
2 the appearance of lagging behind; for that joyful message was sent
to us no less than to them. True, they did not profit by the message,
3 for although they heard it they were lacking in faith. We, however,
shall enter the rest by virtue of our faith; for it is written, "I swore
in My wrath that they shall not enter My rest for a long time."
4 Now God's work was over when He completed the creation, for
somewhere it is written of the seventh day, "God rested from all His
5 work on the seventh day." But our passage reads, "It will be a long
6 time before they enter My rest." Then there are some who still have
to enter the rest: those who in times past did not enter, in spite of
7 the joyous message, because of their unbelief. Therefore God once
more sets a certain day—a "to-day"—by long afterwards proclaiming through David, as I have already quoted, "To-day, when
8 you hear His voice, do not harden your hearts." For if Joshua had
led them into rest, God would not have spoken of another and a
9 later day. From this it follows that there is still a Sabbath-rest
10 awaiting God's people; for he who has entered God's rest is at rest
from his own labors, just as God is from His.

11 Let us endeavor then to enter that rest, so that no one may serve
12 like them as a warning example by reason of his disobedience. For
the word of God is life and strength, and sharper than any two-edged
sword. It penetrates until it severs soul and spirit, bone and marrow
from each other, and bares all the thoughts and inclinations of our
13 hearts to the scrutiny of our conscience. Nothing in all creation is
hidden from God. Everything lies bare and open before the eyes of
Him to Whom we shall have to render an account.

14 Now since in Jesus, the Son of God, we have an exalted high
priest who has passed through all the spheres, let us profess true
15 loyalty to him. For in him we have, not a high priest who has no
sympathy with our weaknesses, but one whose experience in the

temptations that beset him was similar to ours in every respect. Only he did not commit the sin of apostasy.

16 So let us approach the throne of grace with great confidence, in order that we may obtain mercy and find grace to help us in the hour of need.

CHAPTER 5.

1 For every high priest who is chosen from among men for this
office, administers his office before God on behalf of the people for
2 whose sins he must offer gifts and sacrifices to God. Since he himself is beset by weakness of every kind, he can be lenient with those
who have sinned from lack of the true knowledge and so have gone
3 astray. For this reason he must make the same offerings for his own
4 sins as for the sins of the people. No one can take upon himself the
dignity of high priesthood of his own accord. Only God can call
him to it, as He called Aaron.

5 So even Christ did not at his own instance assume the office of
6 high priest, but received it from Him Who said to him, "You are
My son; to-day I have begotten you;" and Who says elsewhere,
7 "You are for ever a priest of the order of Melchisedec." In the days
of his earthly life, Christ, with bitter cries and many tears sent up
fervent prayers to Him Who could save him from the spiritual death
of apostasy. His prayers were heard because of his faithfulness to
8 God. But although he was a son of God, even he first had to learn
obedience through the sufferings that he was obliged to undergo.
9 After he had attained perfection he became the author of the future
10 salvation that awaits all who now obey him; for he was named by
God as a high priest of the order of Melchisedec.

11 On this point I still have a great deal to say, but it is too hard
to make these things clear to you. Your power of understanding is
12 not sufficient for it. In view of the time you have had, you ought
now to be teachers of the truths of salvation. Instead of this you
yourselves are again in need of a teacher to instruct you in the first
principles of the divine truths. Like infants, you are in need of milk,
13 not of solid food. Any one who is restricted to a diet of milk in
spiritual matters is too inexperienced to be entrusted with the whole
14 truth; he is still an infant. The solid food of the whole truth is only
for those who are spiritually mature, and who by reason of their
long spiritual exercise have acquired a fine faculty of spiritual perception that enables them to tell whether a doctrine is true or false.

CHAPTER 6.

1 However, for the present let us not consider the fundamentals of
Christ's doctrine, but pass on to spiritual maturity. Accordingly, we
shall not begin by laying anew the foundations of the faith; that is,
the doctrine of change of heart and abandonment of the dead works
2 of the Law, the doctrine of belief in one God, of baptism, of the
laying on of hands, of the resurrection of the spiritually dead, and
3 of the judgment to take place at the close of every era. This we can
4 do later, if God permits it at all. For if any one has ever received
the inner light and tasted the heavenly gift, has been endowed with
5 a holy spirit, received the glorious messages of God, and thus felt
6 the powers of the future life — and in spite of this falls away again,
it is impossible to bring him back once more; he is one of those
who in their hearts crucify the Son of God anew and publicly put
him to shame.

7 A piece of land that drinks in the frequent rains falling upon it
and yields a good harvest to those who till it, turns the heaven-sent
8 blessing to good account; but if it bears nothing but thorns and
thistles it is not worthy of the blessing, and a curse hangs over it
which will only be dispelled when the field is cleared by being
burned.

9 But concerning you, beloved, even though we have used the foregoing example, we are convinced that you will choose the better
part and that you will hold fast to that which leads to salvation.
10 For God will not be so unjust as to forget your good deeds and the
love you have shown for His cause by the great services that you
have rendered and are still rendering to the faithful.

11 It is my most earnest desire that each one of you may show the
same zeal with regard to approaching the goal of your hope, until
12 you have finally reached it. You must never slacken in that zeal.
Take as your model those who by their faith and constancy have
obtained the heritage that was promised to them.

13 When God made a promise to Abraham He swore by Himself,
14 since He could swear by none greater, and said, "Truly, I will bless
15 you abundantly and greatly increase your numbers." Relying upon
this oath, Abraham patiently waited until he obtained what had
been promised to him.

16 When men swear, they swear by something greater than themselves. The oath signifies to them such confirmation of their state-
17 ment as must end all dispute. In a far greater measure God wished

to hold out to those to whom He had given His promise the prospect of its certain fulfillment, by pledging Himself to it with an
18 oath. Thus, because of these two unalterable facts, the promise and
the oath, which precluded the possibility of a lie on the part of God,
we were to acquire unshakable trust and faith; the hope of the ful-
19 fillment of the promise was to afford us a safe refuge. In this hope
we were to have a strong and reliable anchor for our soul — an
anchor whose cable reaches behind the veil of the beyond, where
20 Jesus has gone ahead of us for our sakes — he who was made a
high priest for all time and whose rank was typified by Melchisedec.

CHAPTER 7.

1 For this Melchisedec was king of Salem and a priest of the Most
High God. He had gone out to meet Abraham, who was returning
from his victory over the kings, and had given him his blessing,
2 whereupon Abraham gave him a tenth of all the booty. The name
of Melchisedec means "king of justice," and inasmuch as he was the
3 king of Salem, we may also call him "king of peace." Neither his
father nor his mother nor his ancestors are mentioned, neither the
beginning nor the end of his life. He may therefore be likened to
4 the Son of God, in that he remains a priest for ever. Moreover, consider the greatness of this man. The patriarch Abraham gave him a
5 tenth of his spoils. Now only the descendants of Levi, who fill the
priestly offices, may lawfully receive tithes from the people, that is
to say, from their own brothers, although they too are flesh and
6 blood descendants of Abraham. But Melchisedec, while in no way
related to them through descent, nevertheless received the tithe from
Abraham and blessed him who had already received God's prom-
7 ises. Now it is beyond dispute that the lesser man can be blessed
8 only by his superior. Moreover, in the case of Levi's descendants
mortal men receive the tithe, but in the case of Melchisedec, it was
9 received by one of whom it is testified that he lives. Through Abraham, so to speak, even Levi the receiver of tithes paid tithes to
10 Melchisedec; for Levi was not yet begotten by the patriarch when
11 Melchisedec and Abraham met. Now if perfection could have been
achieved through the Levitical priesthood to which the people were
bound by the Law, what need was there of another priest of the
12 standing of Melchisedec, and not of the standing of Aaron? For if
a change is to be made in the priesthood, there must needs be a
13 change in the priestly law also. For he to whom all this applies
belonged to another tribe, no member of which ever entered the

14 priesthood. As is well known, our lord came from the tribe of
Judah, a tribe from which no priest could be taken under any of the
15 rules laid down by Moses. And the matter becomes perfectly clear
through the fact that there was to arise a priest of quite another
16 order, namely the order of Melchisedec; hence one who would not
be a priest according to the Law, which prescribes a given lineal
descent for the priesthood, but a priest by virtue of the power of
17 indestructible life residing in him. For the words of the promise
are, "You are a priest for ever, of the order of Melchisedec."

18 This abolishes a hertofore valid law because it was proved in-
19 effectual and therefore useless. The Law really made nothing perfect, but it did open the way for the hope of something better — the
20 hope of drawing nearer and nearer to God. And this promise of
something better was not given without an oath. Previous priests
21 had been ordained without any oath on the part of God, but when
this one was ordained, God swore, "The Lord has sworn and will not
regret it: You are a priest for ever, with the rank of Melchisedec."
22 In these words, Jesus became the mediator of a better covenant;
23 and whereas in times past there were many who held the priestly
24 office, because death prevented them from continuing to serve, we
now have but one, who lives for ever and thereby holds an office
25 that is never handed over to a successor. For this reason he is able
to obtain complete salvation for those who try to reach God through
him; for he lives for ever, and it is his mission to intercede on their
behalf.

26 For we have such a high priest — and such we needed — as is
holy, innocent, blameless, free from all sin, and exalted far above
27 the earthly spheres; one who does not need, as did the high priests
of former times, to bring daily offerings, first for his own sins and
then for the sins of the people. This he did once for all when he
28 offered himself upon the altar. For the Law makes high priests of
men who are beset by weaknesses; but the words of the oath, that
was rendered after the Law had been introduced, appoint as high
priest a son who has attained to perfection for all time.

CHAPTER 8.

1 The sum and substance of what has been said is this. We have
a high priest who has been seated in heaven at the right of the throne
2 of God's Majesty; he is the high priest of the saints and of the true
3 tabernacle, set up by the Lord God Himself and not by man. For
as it is the duty of every high priest to offer gifts and sacrifices, he

4 too must have something to bring to the altar. If he were on earth,
he would not be admitted to the priesthood at all, for on earth there
are already priests who make the offerings prescribed by the Law
5 of Moses — men who serve only an image and shadow of the heavenly sanctuary, in accordance with the directions that Moses received when he was about to build the tabernacle. "See to it,"
said the Lord, "that you make everything according to the pattern
that was shown to you on the mountain."

6 But now he has received a ministry all the more excellent in that
he is the mediator of a better covenant, which was lawfully estab-
7 lished on the basis of better promises. I say a better covenant, because if the first one had been perfect, there would have been no
8 need of a second one to take its place. But God finds fault with the
men of the first covenant in these words: "Know that the time will
come, says the Lord, when I will make a new covenant with the
9 house of Israel and with the house of Judah, not a covenant like
that which I made with their forefathers, in the days when I took
them by the hand in order to lead them out of the land of Egypt; for
they did not abide by that covenant, and so I had no more to do
10 with them," says the Lord. "Now this is the covenant that I shall
make with the house of Israel after that time: I will put my laws
into their minds and write them upon their hearts; then I will once
11 more be their God, and they shall again be My people. Then no one
need teach his neighbor or his brother, saying to him, 'Know the
Lord.' For every one will know Me, from the least among them to
12 the greatest; for I will be merciful to their misdeeds and no longer
remember their sins of apostasy and their ungodliness."

13 By saying, "a new covenant," He has declared the first one obsolete. And whatever is obsolete and has outlived its usefulness is
ready to be discarded.

CHAPTER 9.

1 It is true that the first covenant also had its regulations for wor-
2 ship and its earthly sanctuary. A tabernacle was built, its antechamber containing a candlestick and the table with the showbread;
3 this part of the tabernacle was called the sanctuary. Behind the
second veil lay the part of the tabernacle known as the Holy of
4 Holies. In it was the golden incense-altar and the ark of the covenant, which was completely overlaid with gold. The ark contained
a golden jar of manna, Aaron's rod that once budded, and the tab-
5 lets of the covenant. Above it were the two cherubim of glory, over-

shadowing the cover of the ark, — but at present I shall not speak
6 in detail of the meaning of these things. Such, then, was the arrangement of the tabernacle. Only the antechamber might be entered by
7 the priests in the performance of their ceremonial duties. The second chamber could be entered by none but the high priest, and by
him but once a year and not without blood; for this he was obliged
8 to offer for his own short-comings and those of the people. Thus the
holy spirit-world clearly signified that the way into the Holy of
Holies was not open so long as the antechamber of the tabernacle
9 was still standing. This antechamber is a symbol of the former age,
in which offerings were made of gifts and sacrifices, which were
nevertheless unable to clear the conscience of the one who wor-
10 shipped in that manner. For these ordinances, like those relating to
food and drink and to various ablutions, referred to purely external
observances and were to be valid only until they should be replaced
by something better.

11 Now when Christ had been made a high priest in order that he
might administer the heavenly possessions that he had won, he
passed through a greater and more perfect tabernacle, not built by
human hands; that is to say, not belonging to this material creation.
12 He entered the heavenly sanctuary, not taking the blood of goats and
calves, but his own blood, and that but once; for by this one act he
13 secured everlasting deliverance. For if the blood of goats and bulls
and the ashes of a heifer do in a measure sanctify those who are
touched with them, and do so by purifying the radiation of their
14 bodies, how much more will the blood of Christ, who by the power
of a holy spirit offered himself as a flawless sacrifice to God, purify
our consciences so that we may no longer act like the spiritually
15 dead, but serve God as the source of all life? For this same reason
he was able to act as mediator in an entirely new relationship between the two kingdoms. His death was necessary in order that
those who had fallen away from God might be delivered from the
consequences of their apostasy, which they had brought upon themselves under the earlier order of things. Nevertheless, this was to
apply only to those who receive with faith the message proclaiming
to them that they have been called home to take possession once
more of the heavenly heritage bequeathed to them untold ages ago
16 by the law of God. For where a testament is set forth as its maker's
17 last will, the death of the testator first must be established; for a
will becomes valid only after the testator's death; it is not in force
18 while he is alive. Hence, not even the first bequest of salvation was
19 instituted without blood. For when Moses had announced to all the

people every precept of the Law, he took the blood of calves and
goats, together with water and purple wool and hyssop, and sprinkled
20 the scroll of the Law and all the people, saying, "This is the blood
21 of the legacy that God has bequeathed to you." He sprinkled even
the tabernacle and all the utensils of worship with the blood in the
22 same manner. According to the Law of Moses almost everything is
thus purified with blood, and without sprinkling with blood there is
23 no deliverance. It was therefore necessary that everything symbolical of the sanctuaries in heaven should be purified in the manner
described; but for the heavenly sanctuaries themselves, better offer-
24 ings than these must be found. Christ has not entered a sanctuary built by human hands, for the sanctuary on earth is only an
image of the true sanctuary. He has entered heaven itself, in order
25 to intercede before God for our salvation. Nor is he required to
offer himself again and again, as the high priest is obliged to enter
the Holy of Holies every year with blood that is not his own; for
26 otherwise Christ would have to suffer over and over again, as long
as the world endures. As it is, he has appeared but once, to pay
tribute for all time, and thus to atone for the sin of apostasy from
27 God by the sacrifice of himself. And just as it is an established fact
that men underwent spiritual death but once and that thereupon
28 their fate was decided once for all, so it is also certain that it was
necessary for Christ to offer himself but once in order to undo the
sin of apostasy committed by the many, and that if he later appears
to those who have eagerly awaited his coming as their savior, it will
not be because of the sin of apostasy.

CHAPTER 10.

1 The Law of Moses gives but a shadowy image of the future blessings of salvation, not their reality, and therefore cannot, on the
strength of the yearly offering of sacrifices, bestow perfect salvation
2 on those who participate in the sacrifice. Otherwise men would long
ago have ceased to make offerings, because the worshippers, having
3 once been purged, would no longer be conscious of sin. But as it is,
the yearly offerings are a reminder of the existence of the sins of
4 apostasy, for the blood of bulls and goats cannot possibly take away
5 such sins. Therefore when the Messiah came into the world he said,
"Thou hast not desired sacrifice and offering, but I shall prepare a
6 body for myself. In burnt offerings and sacrifices for sin Thou hast
7 had no pleasure; so I said, 'See, here am I. In the scroll of the book
8 it is written of me that I do Thy will, O God.'" First he said, "Thou

hast not desired sacrifice and offering and burnt offerings and sacrifices made for sin, nor hast Thou taken any pleasure in them."
And yet these offerings are made in obedience to the Law of Moses.
9 He then continues, "I have come to do Thy will." He thereby does
away with the first in order that from now on the second alone may
10 be valid. Thus, by virtue of his performance of this will of God,
we are again consecrated to God, because Jesus Christ has offered
11 his blood for us, once for all time. Every ordinary priest stands
at the altar daily and presents the same offerings — offerings which
12 can never deliver us from the sin of apostasy. Christ, however,
brought but a single sacrifice and then seated himself for ever at
13 the right hand of God, henceforth to await the time when all of his
14 enemies are subjected to him. For by a single offering he has for
ever achieved the result that those who strive to be sanctified shall
15 obtain final salvation. The same truth is also attested by a holy
16 spirit, for after the words, "This shall be the new order of things
that I will establish among them after those days," the Lord continues, "I will put My laws into their hearts and write them in their
17 consciences, and I will no longer remember their sins and violations
18 of the Law." Now, where these have been forgiven, there is no further need of an offering in atonement for the sins of apostasy.

19 Thus, brothers, we have the joyful confidence that we shall be
able to enter the heavenly Holy of Holies by virtue of the offering
20 of the blood of Jesus. That is the new way of life which he has laid
open to us through the veil, that is to say, through his human in-
21 carnation. Now we have a high priest appointed to govern the king-
22 dom of God. Let us draw near to him with a sincere heart and full
assurance of faith, for we have rid our hearts of the consciousness
23 of guilt and bathed our spiritual bodies in pure water. Let us hold
unwaveringly to the hope that we profess, for he who promised to
24 bring about the fulfillment of our hope is trustworthy. Let us be
intent on rousing one another to neighborly love and good deeds.
25 Let us not absent ourselves from common worship, as is already the
habit of some, I regret to say. Let us rather exhort one another to attend, and all the more so as you see the day of the lord approaching.

26 For if we deliberately sin again after we have been initiated into
the full knowledge of the truth, there is no other sacrifice left to us
27 by which we can atone for those sins. Nothing is left but to await
a fearful sentence and a fire that is eager to consume God's adver-
28 saries. Any one who wantonly violated the Law of Moses had to die
29 without mercy on the testimony of two or three witnesses. How
much heavier will be the sentence pronounced upon him who has

trodden the Son of God underfoot; who has considered as worthless
the blood to which you owe both the new order of salvation and
your own sanctification; and who has ridiculed the spirit-world that
30 God's love sent to him? For we know Who said, "Vengeance is
mine, I will repay;" and Who said further, "The Lord will judge
31 His people." It is a fearful thing, then, to fall into the hands of the
living God.

32 Recall the early days of your conversion, when after receiving
33 enlightenment you endured many a hard siege of suffering, now by
having to undergo abuses and insults to your own persons, now by
sympathizing with the fate of others who met with similar experi-
34 ences; for you openly displayed your compassion for those who had
been thrown into prison, and when you were deprived of your own
belongings, you were filled with joy; for you knew that you had a
greater treasure to call your own, a treasure that no one can take
35 from you. Do not now throw aside that former joyful confidence of
36 yours. It carries with it a great reward. It is absolutely necessary
that you should remain constant if you are ready to do the will of
37 God and receive the promised blessings. "It will be but a short, a
very short time, until he who is to come will appear, and he will not
38 delay his coming. Whoever has won favor in My eyes by his trust
and faith, will obtain spiritual life; but if any one loses courage and
39 draws back, My heart will take no pleasure in him." But we know
nothing of that faintheartedness that entails destruction, but hold
fast to the faith and confidence by which our spiritual life is raised
to perfection.

CHAPTER 11.

1 Faith is a confident trust in the things we hope for, and a firm
2 belief in things that cannot be seen with our physical eyes. It was
3 through such faith that the men of old won renown. Through faith
we know that the worlds and their stages of development came into
being at the word of God, and that everything we now see before us
4 was created out of the invisible. Because of his faith, Abel offered to
God a more valuable sacrifice than Cain's, and it was testified of
him that because of his faith he had found favor with God. God
Himself gave this testimony at the time of the offering. And although
Abel died a long time ago, he is spoken of to this day just on account
5 of his faith. Because of his faith Enoch was translated from the earth
in order that he might not see death; he was no longer to be found
on earth, because God had taken him away. For before he was

6 taken, he had been assured that God was pleased with him. Without
faith it is indeed impossible to please God, for he who wishes to
approach God must first believe that there is a God, and that He
7 will reward those who seek Him. Because of his faith, Noah was
warned through spirit-messages of things that he could not yet see.
He received the messages with faith and built the ark to save his
family. By this rescue he showed that the punishment of his unbelieving fellow-men was just, and he obtained God's favor, which,
8 according to a divine law, is always the fruit of faith. By faith
Abraham obeyed the call of God that required him to go out into
a country which he was to receive as a heritage. He went without
9 knowing where he was going. By faith he settled as an alien in the
land that God had named to him. He lived there in tents together
10 with Isaac and Jacob, who were co-heirs to the same promise; for
he was looking forward to the heavenly city with its firm founda-
11 tions, whose builder and designer is God Himself. By faith even the
barren Sarah received strength to conceive in spite of her age, because she firmly believed in Him Who had given her the promise of
12 motherhood. Thus there sprang from this one man, following his
death, a posterity as numerous as the stars in heaven and the sand
13 on the seashore, which no one can count. All these died in the faith
without having obtained the fulfillment of the promise; they had
only seen that fulfillment from afar and greeted it joyously. They
14 confessed that they were only aliens and strangers on earth. But
whoever declares himself an alien shows that he is trying to reach
15 his own true fatherland. If they had been thinking of the earthly
fatherland that they left, it would have been possible for them to
16 return to it; but they longed for a better country, for the heavenly
one. Hence God does not object to being called their God, for it was
17 He Who prepared a heavenly fatherland for them. When Abraham
was put to the test he was ready, by reason of his faith, to sacrifice
18 Isaac; he was willing to offer up his only son, although he had
received the promise that said of Isaac, "Through Isaac your de-
19 scendants shall be reckoned." His one thought was that God had the
power to raise the dead; and it was precisely because he surrendered
20 him that his son was restored to him. By reason of his faith Isaac
21 blessed Jacob and Esau, even with reference to future events. By
faith Jacob, in the hour of his death, blessed each of the sons of
Joseph, and leaning upon the head of his staff, he prayed over them.
22 By faith Joseph, as he lay dying, spoke of the departure of the
Israelites from Egypt, and made arrangements for the removal of
23 his bones. By faith Moses was kept hidden by his parents for three

months after his birth, because they saw the divine beauty of the
child and had no fear of the royal edict. When Moses was grown
up and saw the humiliation inflicted on his brothers, it was by his
24 faith that he killed the Egyptian. On account of his faith, after he
attained manhood he scorned to be known as the son of Pharaoh's
25 daughter. He chose to undergo privations with God's people rather
26 than to derive any passing advantage from this false report. He
considered it greater wealth than all the treasures of Egypt to be
allowed to endure the contempt heaped upon the Messiah; for he was
27 paying heed only to the reward to come. Upheld by his faith he set
out from Egypt, unafraid of the king's anger. He felt strong enough
28 for this because it was as if he saw the Invisible before him. On the
strength of his faith he instituted the Passover and had the door-
posts sprinkled with the blood of the lamb, so that the avenging
29 angel might not touch Israel's first-born. By faith the Israelites
passed through the Red Sea as though it were dry land, while the
Egyptians were drowned when they ventured to attempt the same
30 thing. Faith caused the walls of Jericho to collapse after the be-
31 siegers had marched around them for seven days. As a result of her
faith, the harlot Rahab escaped death when her unbelieving fellow-
townsmen perished, for she had given the spies a friendly welcome.
32 Why need I cite further examples? Time would fail me if I were
to tell of Gideon and Barak, of Samson and Jephthah, of David and
33 Samuel and the rest of the prophets. By faith these men conquered
kingdoms, administered justice, obtained the fulfillment of prom-
34 ises, shut the mouths of lions, quenched the fury of fires, and escaped the edge of the sword. When they were overcome by faintness,
they revived. In warfare they were victorious and put to flight the
35 armies of foreign nations. Women were given back their dead
through resurrection; others submitted to torture and scorned to be
released by ransom, that they might obtain a better resurrection.
36 Still others allowed themselves to be taunted and flogged, and en-
37 dured chains and imprisonment besides. They were stoned, racked,
sawed in two, and put to death with the sword. They wandered about
clad in sheepskins and goatskins, enduring hardships, privations,
38 and maltreatment. Men of whom the world was not worthy, were
forced to seek refuge in deserts and mountains, in caves and dens.
39 All of them, though they won renown because of their faith, failed to
40 obtain in this life the fulfillment of God's promise; for out of regard for us, God has provided something better for them, something
which they were not to obtain without us.

CHAPTER 12.

1 Since we see around us such a great host of witnesses to the faith,
let us too lay aside everything that inwardly weighs us down. Let
2 us lay aside the sin that so tightly ensnares us. Let us run with
endurance the race that has been prescribed for us, fixing our
eyes upon Jesus, who laid the first stone for the edifice of our faith,
and is also responsible for its completion. Mindful of the joy that
awaited him as the fruit of victory, he endured death on the cross,
thinking nothing of the attendant disgrace. Afterward, however, he
3 was allowed to seat himself at the right of the throne of God. Think
of the immeasurable hostility that he was forced to endure at the
hands of sinners; then you will not so easily weary of your own
4 battle and grow discouraged. For up to this point, your fight against
5 sin has not cost a drop of your blood. Have you quite forgotten the
admonition addressed to you as God's children? "My child, do not
despise the Lord's chastisement, and do not become discouraged
6 when He inflicts suffering upon you; for whomever the Lord loves
He chastises, and He punishes with the rod every child whom He
7 regards as His own." Endure your sufferings; they are an essential
part of your discipline, for God treats you as one treats children.
8 Where is the child who is not chastised by his father? If you were
spared such chastisement as falls to the lot of all children, you would
9 be bastards and not legitimate children. Furthermore, we have been
chastised by our fathers, who are only the fathers of our bodies, and
have loved them notwithstanding. Then should we not far more submit with love to the Father of our spirit, and thus obtain spiritual
10 life? Besides, our earthly fathers used to punish us for trifling
things, according to the mood of the moment, but God does it only
for our true inner good, so as to enable us to share in His own holi-
11 ness. All chastisement, to be sure, seems disagreeable and painful
at first; but in the end it bears as fruit for those who are inwardly
strengthened by such chastisement the peace that lies in the consciousness of God's friendship.

12 So lift up your faltering hands! Strengthen your feeble knees!
13 Straighten the paths on which your feet must travel, so that the lame
14 may not lag still further behind, but rather be healed. Make an
effort to live in peace with all, and to attain that measure of holiness
15 without which no one shall see the Lord. Let one pay heed to the
other, so that no one may make frivolous use of God's gifts, and no
root may send forth a shoot of mutual bitterness through which
16 calamity results and many are contaminated; further, that none of

you may enter into dealings with the world of evil spirits and fall
away from God, as Esau did, who sold his birthright for a single
17 meal. You know how he was afterwards rejected when he claimed
the first-born's blessing on the basis of his right as such; for he
found no way to change his inner attitude, hard as he tried with
tears to undo the past.

18 For you have not come to a mountain that you can touch with
your hand, or to a blazing fire, or to overcast skies, darkness, and
19 tempest, or to the sound of a trumpet or to that thunderous voice at
which those who heard it implored that they might be spared all
20 further words; for they could not bear the tremor that this voice
sent through their bones as it called, "Even an animal that touches
21 the mountain will be killed by falling stones." So awe-inspiring
was the manifestation that even Moses said, "I am beside myself
22 with fear and trembling." You, however, have come to Mount Zion,
to the city of the living God, to the heavenly Jerusalem, to a festal
23 gathering of myriads of God's holy messengers, to the congregation
of the first-born registered in heaven; to a Judge, the God of all;
to the spirits of men faithful to God who have already reached their
24 goal in the beyond; and to Jesus, who acted as mediator of the new
order of salvation through his purifying blood that cried louder
25 to heaven than the blood of Abel. See to it that you are not among
those who refuse to listen to His voice. For if there was no escape
for those who were unwilling to listen to the voice of Him Who made
Himself known to them on earth, how much less shall we escape if
we turn a deaf ear to the voice of Him Who speaks to us from the
26 celestial spheres. In those days His voice shook the earth, but now
He has given the promise, "Once more I shall shake not only the
27 earth, but also the heavenly bodies." The words "once more" indicate the transformation of that which will be shaken because it is
transitory by nature, as distinguished from that which is lasting and
28 therefore cannot be shaken. Therefore, let us be heartily thankful
that we shall receive a kingdom that cannot be shaken. In view of
this kingdom let us serve God as best we can, in reverence and holy
awe; for our God is a consuming fire.

CHAPTER 13.

1 Let nothing impair your love of your fellow-men. Do not neglect
2 the duties of hospitality, for in the fulfillment of these duties some
3 have entertained God's messengers without knowing it. Remember
those who are in prison as if you were one of them, and those who
suffer bodily distress as if your own bodies were undergoing the

4 same. Let marriage be held in honor among you and the marriage
relation kept sacred, for the unchaste and adulterous will meet with
5 God's punishment. Let your life be free from avarice. Be content
with what you have, for God Himself has said, "I will never deny
6 you my help, and never forsake you." Hence we can say with all
confidence, "The Lord is my helper, and I need not be afraid. What
can men do to me?"

7 Do not forget your leaders, who proclaimed the word of God to
you. Always think of the end of their earthly careers and follow the
8 example of their faith. Jesus Christ is the same yesterday and to-
9 day and for ever. Amen. Therefore do not be led astray by all sorts
of fantastic doctrines. It is best to have one's heart firmly established in the grace of God and unconcerned about the laws relating
to food; for those who have scrupulously regulated their daily lives
by such laws have derived no spiritual benefit whatsoever from it.
10 We too have an altar at which those who still adhere to the offerings
11 of the Jewish temple may not eat; for the bodies of the beasts whose
blood is brought into the Holy of Holies by the high priest as a
12 sin-offering must be burned outside the camp. For this reason Jesus
also, in order to cleanse the people from the sin of apostasy with
13 his own blood, suffered death outside the city gate. Then let us go
out to him from the camp of the Jews and take his disgrace upon
14 ourselves; for we have no fixed abode here, but seek that which has
15 been provided for us in time to come. Let us, through Jesus, lay a
daily offering of praise to our God upon the altar — an offering
which consists of the spiritual fruit that falls from the lips of those
who praise the name of God.

16 Do not forget to do good for others and let them share your
17 belongings, for such sacrifices are pleasing to God. Obey your
leaders and submit to their guidance, for theirs is the duty of watching over your souls and one day rendering an account concerning
you. May they be able to do so gladly and not with grief, for that
would be a misfortune for you.

18 Pray for us too, for we are sure that we have a good conscience,
since we have tried to lead a life pleasing to God in every respect.
19 I urge this all the more, so that I may be restored to you the sooner.

20 May the God of peace, Who brought back from the kingdom of
the spiritually dead our lord Jesus Christ — that great shepherd who
with his blood founded a new order of salvation for all time —
furnish you with every good gift so as to enable you to do His will.
21 May He effect in all of us through Jesus Christ that which is pleasing
in His sight. Honor to Him for ever and ever! Amen.

22 I beg you, brothers, accept these words of admonition with a good
grace. They are but a small portion of my letter to you.
23 I might also tell you that our brother Timothy has been released
again. As soon as he comes I shall visit you and bring him with
me.
24 Greet all your leaders and all the faithful. The Christians of
Italy send you their greetings.
25 Grace be with you all. Amen.

The Epistle of James the Apostle

CHAPTER 1.

1 JAMES, a servant of God and of the lord Jesus Christ, sends greetings to the twelve congregations that live scattered among the
heathens.
2 Welcome it joyfully, brothers, if you must pass through the most
3 varied temptations, for you can show your constancy only when
4 your faith is put to the test. This you know. But let your constancy
be of such a high order that you may be regarded as men who stand
perfect and leave nothing to be desired in any respect.
5 If any of you should be wanting in wisdom, let him ask it of
God, Who gives to all men unconditionally and without reproach.
6 His prayer will therefore be answered, but it must be offered in faith
and confidence and without the slightest doubt; for a man who harbors doubt is like a wave of the sea tossed hither and thither by the
7 wind. Such a person need not expect to receive anything from the
8 Lord, for he is one of those who have two souls in one body and in
all that they do are for ever trying to carry water on both shoulders.
9 If a brother has a humble station in life let him inwardly take
10 pride in his exalted place before God. If he is among those who
possess earthly riches, it will redound to his honor to reflect in all
humility that his wealth will pass away like a flower in the garden.
11 The sun rises higher and higher and scorches the garden with its
heat; the petals of the flowers fall to the ground and the lovely
appearance of the garden vanishes. So too does the wealth of the
rich vanish under life's vicissitudes.
12 Fortunate is the man who stands the test, for if he endures trial,
he will receive the crown of spiritual life that the Lord has promised to those who love him.
13 Let no one who is tempted to do evil, say, "I am being tempted
by God." For as God Himself cannot be tempted to do evil, neither
14 does He tempt any one. In every one temptation arises rather from
15 his own evil passions, by which he is enticed and allured. Once the
evil passions have gained man's assent, they breed the sin of apos-

tasy from God; and if this sin develops to maturity, it results in the
spiritual death of separation from God.

16 Cherish no illusions on this point, my dear brothers: only gifts
17 that are good and gifts that are perfect come from above, for they
spring from the Father of all that is light. With Him there is no
variation, no waxing and waning of darkness; He casts no shadow.
18 Of His own free will He caused us to be spiritually reborn by the
word of truth, and among His earthly creatures we were destined to
be, as it were, His spiritual first-born.

19 Bear the following in mind, too, beloved brothers. Let every one
20 be quick to listen, but slow to speak or to be roused to anger; for
21 an angry man does not do what is right in God's eyes. So cast out of
your hearts every base inclination and the last traces of evil.
Nurture tenderly the plant of the divine truth, which has the power
22 to save your souls. Do not be content with simply hearing the
23 truth, but live accordingly; otherwise you deceive yourselves. For
whoever merely hears the truth but does not put it into practice is
24 like a man who glances in a mirror to find out how he looks, and
after looking at himself goes away and never gives his appearance
25 another thought. But whoever has looked into the perfect law of true
liberty and perseveringly practises what he has seen in it, does not
belong among the forgetful hearers, but among those who accomplish good. Whoever acts thus may be called fortunate.

26 If any one thinks that he is serving God, but does not bridle his
tongue, he is greatly deceived, for his way of "serving God" is
27 worthless. In the eyes of God the Father, true and faultless worship
is to care for orphans and widows in their distress, and to keep one's
self unstained by the world.

CHAPTER 2.

1 Brothers, do not make an outward display of your faith in the
glory of our lord Jesus Christ for the sake of winning men's favor.
2 Suppose there should come to your gathering a man decked with
golden rings and elegant clothes, and together with him a poor man
3 meanly clad, and you were to turn your eyes upon the one with
elegant clothes and say to him, "Sit here in this fine chair," but tell
the poor man, "Stand over there," or, "Take a seat on that foot-
4 stool." Would you not, in your hearts, be assigning a higher rank
to one than to the other? Would you not, in your own minds, be
acting the part of judges who allow themselves to be influenced by

5 entirely wrong opinions? Listen to me, my dear brothers; has not
God chosen the very ones whom the world looked upon as poor to
be rich in faith and to inherit the kingdom of heaven which He has
6 promised to those who love Him? But in the case that I have described you would have treated the poor with contempt. Again, are
not the rich the very ones who try to oppress you and hale you be-
7 fore the courts? Are not they the ones who deride the glorious
8 name you bear? The Scriptures contain this royal command: "You
shall love your neighbor as yourself." If you really fulfill this law,
9 you do right. But if you allow yourselves to be influenced by men's
outward rank, you commit a sin, and you will be branded as trans-
10 gressors of the Law. If any one observes all the rest of the Law
but breaks only a single one of its precepts, he has thereby violated
11 the whole Law; for He Who said, "Do not commit adultery," also
said, "Do not kill." Now if you do not commit adultery, but do
commit murder, you have transgressed the Law as a whole.

12 In everything that you say and do, behave like men who are one
day to be judged by a law that is free from all man-made provi-
13 sions. This law will show no mercy to those who have shown no
mercy to their fellow-men. Only the merciful will triumph before
that tribunal.

14 What good does it do, brothers, for any one to say that he has
faith, if he can show nothing in the way of good deeds? Can his
15 faith alone save him? Suppose a brother or a sister had no clothes
16 and lacked daily food. If one of you said to them, "Go in peace!
See that you procure warmth and food," but you yourself gave
nothing to relieve their bodily needs,—what good would that do
17 them? So faith, if it can show no deeds, is dead in itself. Now some
18 one might say, "You have faith, and I deeds." My answer to him is,
"Show me your faith without deeds, and I will show you my faith
19 manifested in deeds." Do you believe that there is but one true God?
20 Good; but even the devils hold this belief—and tremble. Does this
prove to you, thoughtless man, that faith without good deeds is
21 worthless? When our father Abraham was willing to sacrifice his
son Isaac upon the altar, was it not by that very act that he gained
22 favor in the sight of God? In him you see faith working hand in
hand with deeds and finding its natural expression in the deeds.
23 Thus were fulfilled the words of the Scriptures, "Abraham believed
God and thereby gained favor in His eyes, and was called God's
24 friend." You see, then, that man pleases God with good deeds and
25 not by faith alone. Did not the harlot Rahab likewise gain favor
with God by what she did—by sheltering the scouts at her home

26 and sending them off in freedom by another road? Hence, just as
the body without the spirit is dead, so faith without deeds is dead

CHAPTER 3.

1 Brothers, you should not come forward in such great numbers
as teachers of the gospel. Remember, we who engage in that work
2 have a much greater responsibility to bear. We all have many faults,
but any one who never makes a slip in speech is a perfect man;
3 for he is able to bridle his whole person. If we succeed in putting
a bit into a horse's mouth to make him obey us, we thereby gain
4 control over his whole body. Again, consider ships; large as they
are, and strong as are the winds by which they are driven, they can
be guided by a very small rudder wherever the helmsman chooses.
5 So, too, the tongue is but a very small member of the body, and yet
it can boast of having accomplished great things. Consider, further,
how small a fire can be and how great the forest that it can set
6 ablaze. The tongue is such a fire, too, and it conceals within itself a
world of mischief. Of all our members it is the one that proves
itself capable of covering the whole body with burns. It throws the
torch between the spokes of the nations' wheel of fortune and draws
7 its fuel from the pools of hell. Every kind of four-footed beasts, of
birds, of reptiles, and of marine animals is tamed and has always
8 been tamed by mankind, but no man can tame another's tongue. It
can become an uncontrolled and disastrous thing, filled with deadly
9 poison. And yet it is with the tongue that we praise and glorify the
Lord and Father; but with it we also curse men, who were made in
10 the image of that selfsame God. Blessing and cursing — both stream
11 from the same mouth. Such things ought not to be, my brothers. Is
there a spring that yields both sweet and bitter water from the same
12 outlet? No spring can give both fresh and salt water at once. Or
can a fig tree, my brothers, bear olives, or a vine, figs?

13 Let him among you who wishes to be considered wise and dis-
cerning show with due modesty, as befits the wise, the deeds that
14 his conversion has prompted. But if you carry bitter envy and
enmity in your hearts, make no outward display of your so-called
Christianity, and do not lie so shamelessly in the face of the truth.
15 Such wisdom is surely not from above; it is a worldly wisdom, in-
16 spired by base passions, a devilish wisdom. For wherever jealousy
and enmity prevail, there you will find dissension and every other
17 evil. But the wisdom that comes from above manifests itself first
of all in purity of character, and then makes men peaceable, gentle,

obedient, and rich in mercy and in other good fruits; it rids them
18 of scepticism and hypocrisy. The seed from which God's friendship
is to spring forth can be sown only in the garden of peace and is
destined only for those who perform acts of peace.

CHAPTER 4.

1 Why do quarrels and disputes prevail among you? Is it not because of those passions of yours that war against you in your mem-
2 bers? You covet, and you do not receive; in spite of all your envy
3 and jealousy you do not reach your goal. You fight and struggle,
and still you do not reach it, because you do not pray. And if you
pray without receiving that for which you ask, it is because you pray
4 with the evil desire for a further indulgence of your passions. O
victims of passion! Do you not know that friendship with the world
spells enmity with God? Accordingly, whoever chooses to be a
5 friend of the world makes himself God's enemy. Or do you think
that the Scriptures speak idly when they say that the spirit-world
that has taken up its abode among us jealously yearns to be our sole
6 possessor and therefore offers us all the greater love? Hence the
Scriptures say, "God resists the proud, but gives His love to the
7 humble." Place yourselves under God's guidance, then. Resist the
devil, and he will flee from you. Draw nearer to God, and He will
8 draw nearer to you. Cleanse your hands, you sinners, and purify
your hearts, you double-minded. Realize your need, mourn and
9 lament. Let your laughter be turned into weeping and your joy into
10 sorrow. Humble yourselves before the Lord, and He will lift you
11 up. Do not speak ill of one another, brothers. He who speaks ill
of a brother, or condemns him, also condemns the Law; he con-
stitutes himself as its judge. And if you constitute yourself as judge
of the Law, it is self-evident that you do not abide by the Law; for
12 you are sitting in judgment over the Law itself. There is but one
Lawgiver, and He alone can be the judge. It is He Who has the
power to save and to condemn to destruction. Who are you then to
aspire to be a judge — a judge of your fellow-men?

13 And now a word to you who say, "To-day or to-morrow we shall
go to such and such a city, stay there for a year, engage in business,
14 and earn money." Do you know what to-morrow will bring, or what
your life will be to-morrow? You are but a vapor, which is seen
15 for a short time and then vanishes. You ought rather to say, "If the
16 Lord so wills, and we are still alive, we shall do this or that." But
as it is, you boast of your ambitious plans. All such boasting is

17 inspired by the Evil One. Therefore if any one knows how he can
do good and fails to do it, his omission will be counted against him
as a sin.

CHAPTER 5.

1 Now as to you rich men, weep and wail over the distress that
2 will come upon you. Your wealth will have moldered, your clothes
3 will have been eaten by moths. Your gold and silver will have
rusted, and their rust will testify against you and consume that
which is ungodly within you as with fire. To the end of your days
4 you will have sought to amass treasure. See how the wages that you
have withheld from the laborers who reaped your fields cry to
heaven from your houses; and the plaintive cries of your reapers
5 have reached the ears of the Lord of hosts. You have revelled in
luxury on earth; you have fattened your hearts as if you were pre-
6 paring them for the day of slaughter. As judges you have condemned
and delivered to death him who was within his rights; for any resistance against you has been impossible.

7 Be patient, therefore, brothers, until the coming of the lord. See,
it is thus that the farmer also waits for the precious fruit of his
fields, allowing it time to receive both the early and the later rain.
8 So you too must have patience and keep stout hearts, for the com-
9 ing of the lord is at hand. Therefore do not complain of each other
so much, brothers, lest you be made to answer to the judge for your
complaints. Remember that the judge is already standing at the
10 door. Take as examples of suffering and constancy, brothers, the
11 prophets who have spoken at the Lord's command. Observe, we call
them fortunate because they remained steadfast. You have heard of
the steadfastness of Job, and you know what goal the Lord had in
view for him. From this you can see that the Lord abounds in compassion and is full of mercy.

12 Above all things, brothers, when you make a promise, swear
neither by heaven nor by the earth, nor by anything else. Let your
"yes" remain "yes," and do not change it into a "no"; otherwise
you would play the role of a hypocrite.

13 If any one among you is in trouble, let him pray; if all is well
with him, let him sing songs of praise and thanksgiving to God.
14 If one of you is sick, let him send for the elders of the congregation
and let them pray over him, anointing him with oil in the name of
15 the Lord. The prayer that is offered in faith and confidence will aid
the sick man, and the Lord will restore him. If he has committed

16 sins, they will then be forgiven. So confess to one another the mutual
wrongs that you have committed, and pray for one another, so that
you may be cured of your sicknesses. The persistent prayer of one
17 who is faithful to God has a great power. Elijah was a man like
ourselves; he prayed fervently that no rain might fall, and for three
18 years and six months there was no rain in his country. He prayed
again, and the sky yielded rain, and the earth brought forth its fruit.
19 My brothers, if any one of you has strayed from the path of the
20 truth and another brings him back into it, be assured that he who
brings a sinner back from the error of his way will save that sinner's
soul from spiritual death, and cover up a host of his own sins.
Amen.

The First Epistle of Peter the Apostle

CHAPTER 1.

1 PETER, an apostle of Jesus Christ, sends greetings to the elect
who live as aliens in Pontus, Galatia, Cappadocia, Asia Minor,
2 and Bithynia, and who have been chosen in accordance with God's
plan of salvation, through the power of a holy spirit, to attain obedience to God and the purification effected by the blood of Jesus
Christ. May grace and peace be yours in abundance.
3 Praised be the God and Father of our lord Jesus Christ; for in
the greatness of His mercy He has restored to us, through the return
of Jesus Christ from the kingdom of the spiritually dead, the hope
4 of a new life, an everlasting, perfect, and indestructible heritage,
5 which awaits you in the spheres of heaven. By reason of your faith
you are shielded by a power of God, so that the salvation held in
readiness for you may be revealed to you at the end of your allotted
6 space of time. Let this thought fill your hearts with rejoicing, even
7 though for a brief time it may be necessary for you to be subjected
to many outward trials. That is to prove the genuine quality of
your faith; it must be found far more precious than perishable gold,
which is tested by fire. May your test redound to your praise and
honor and glory on the day when Jesus Christ appears before you.
8 You have never seen him, and yet you love him; even now you
cannot see him, but you put your faith and trust in him, and in this
9 trust you acclaim him with an inexpressible, glorious joy, fixing
your eyes upon the goal of your faith, which is the salvation of your
10 souls. The prophets who foretold the grace to be bestowed upon us
11 inquired into and studied this salvation. They tried to discover the
time and circumstances indicated by the spirit speaking through
them when he referred to the sufferings that God's anointed would
have to endure, as well as to the great glory that was to follow his
12 sufferings. Then it was made known to them that they as instruments of God had been chosen to predict what did not apply to the
men of their own times, but to the men of your day. It is the same
that has now been proclaimed to you as the gospel by those who
likewise received their message from a holy spirit, sent to them
from heaven. Even the angels are eager to gain a deeper insight
into this gospel.
13 Therefore, gird up the loins of your spirit; abstain from every-

thing that might harm you, and set all your hopes on the gift of
14 grace that will be yours at the coming of Jesus Christ. Be obedient
children of God. Do not allow yourselves any longer to be ruled
by those passions that you once harbored in the days of your spirit-
15 ual ignorance. Rather become holy in your way of life, after the
16 pattern of the Holy One Who called you; for it is written, "Be holy,
17 because I am holy." And if you call Him your Father, Who without regard of person will judge every one by his deeds, then may a
holy awe direct your footsteps on your brief earthly pilgrimage.
18 You know that it was not with perishable gold or silver that you
were redeemed from the bondage into which you had been brought
by the base apostasy in which you yourselves participated, follow-
19 ing the example set by your fathers. You were redeemed by the
precious blood of Christ, who was led like an innocent, spotless lamb
20 to the slaughter. Even before the foundation of the universe he was
predestined for this fate, but for our sakes he has appeared in these
21 later times, so that through him we might attain to belief in God—
belief in the same God Who raised him again from the kingdom of
the spiritually dead and crowned him with glory, that you too might
acquire faith and confidence and the hope of returning to God.

22 You have consecrated your souls to God by obeying the doctrine
of truth which teaches you genuine, unfeigned love of your neighbors. But see that the love for one another that springs from a pure
23 heart is above all things constant. You have been reborn, not from
a seed that perishes, but from an imperishable seed, the word of
24 God, Who is the source of all life and Who lives for ever. But all
earthly things are like a garden, and all earthly glory perishes like
flowers in a garden. The garden becomes parched and the petals of
25 the flowers fall; but the word of God endures for ever, and it is
this word that has been preached to you as the gospel.

CHAPTER 2.

1 Away, then, with all that is evil! Away with insincerity! Away
2 with hypocrisy, envy, and every kind of slander! Be like new-born
babes, craving the unadulterated milk that is offered to you in the
word of God. With this nourishment you will grow until you are
3 ripe for salvation. You have already had a taste of the lord's good-
4 ness since you entered into communion with him. He is the stone
of life. Mankind, to be sure, has rejected him as worthless; but
5 before God he is a choice and precious gem. Through him you yourselves become life-giving stones which are used to build a spiritual

house; you become a holy priesthood that offers spiritual sacrifices — sacrifices that are pleasing to God because they are offered
6 in fellowship with Jesus Christ. For the Scriptures say, "Behold,
I lay in Zion a choice and precious cornerstone. He who con-
7 fidently believes in him will not be disappointed." To you who
believe and trust in him he is therefore a stone to be honored; but to
those who do not believe and trust in him he is the stone that the
8 builders rejected as worthless; to them he has become the corner-
stone, and hence a guard-stone which one runs against and a rock
on which one is dashed to pieces. They are dashed against the stone
because they will not obey the word of God; and this disobedience
9 is ordained for them in their fate. But you are a chosen band, a
royal priesthood, a congregation consecrated to God, a people won
over to God. Yours is the task of proclaiming the mighty power of
Him Who called you back from the realm of darkness into His
10 wonderful kingdom of light. Once you were known as a "people
without a God," but now you are called "God's people;" then you
were "men excluded from God's mercy," but to-day you are those
who are "included in God's mercy."

11 My beloved, I beseech you, as people who have no real home or fatherland on this earth, to abstain from that into which your earthly passions would seduce you; for worldly lust is an enemy of the soul.

12 Lead good lives among the Gentiles, so that those who to-day brand you as evil-doers may witness your noble deeds and because of them glorify God on the day when His eye rests with merciful love even upon them.

13 Submit to every ordinance that is made by man at the instance
of the lord, whether it be issued by the lord himself as king and
14 supreme authority, or by his subordinate leaders, sent by him to
reprimand evil-doers and to bestow praise upon those who do good.
15 For it is the will of God that by doing good you should silence those
who repeat foolish tales about you because they know no better.
16 Be among those who are truly free; not free in the sense that you
use your freedom as a cloak for wickedness, but free insofar as you
serve none but God.

17 Be courteous to every one, love your neighbors, fear to offend God, and render the king the honor due him.

18 You who are servants, take pains to follow the instructions of
your masters — not only of kind and considerate masters but also
19 of those who are ill-tempered; for if any one patiently endures un-
20 merited suffering out of regard for God, he will obtain his reward.

Indeed, what credit would it be to you if you endured in patience
only such troubles as resulted by way of punishment for your faults?
But if in spite of your good life you must undergo sufferings, and if
21 you bear them patiently, you may expect a reward from God. For
suffering is inseparable from your calling. Even Christ suffered for
you and thereby set you an example. You must follow in his foot-
22 steps. He did not commit the sin of apostasy from God, nor was
23 any falsehood against God ever found upon his lips. When he was
reviled, he did not revile in turn, nor did he threaten those who tortured him, but committed everything to Him Who will judge justly.
24 In his own body he bore the sins of our apostasy to the cross, in
order that we might become dead to that life of sin and enter upon
a new life, a life pleasing to God. By his death-wounds you your-
25 selves have been healed. For in the past you too wandered about
like sheep without a shepherd; but now you have come back to the
shepherd and guardian of your souls.

CHAPTER 3.

1 Now as to you, wives, be obedient to your husbands. By this
means men who are indifferent to the word of truth may be converted to the cause of God by the good conduct of their wives with-
2 out oral preaching, when they see what God-fearing and pure lives
3 they lead. Give no thought to outward adornment, to the elaborate
braiding of your hair, to the wearing of golden ornaments and
4 finery. Let yours be rather an inner adornment, the imperishable
adornment of a gentle and tranquil spirit, which in the sight of God
5 is very precious. This was the adornment worn in the past by
6 devout women who set their hopes on God. They too were obedient
to their husbands. Sarah obeyed Abraham and called him "lord."
You are her spiritual daughters if you endeavor to do right. In so
doing there is no need for you to cower or cringe before your
husbands.

7 And you husbands, be true companions to your wives as members
of the weaker sex. Show them the consideration due them, for they
were chosen, together with you, to inherit the gracious gift of the
life hereafter. Otherwise there could be no such thing as joint
8 prayer among you. Finally, live in harmony with one another; be
full of sympathy and neighborly love; be compassionate and hum-
9 ble; do not return evil for evil, or abuse for abuse. On the contrary, make others happy; consider this as your mission. Then you
10 yourselves will inherit happiness, for it is written, "If any one

wishes to have a happy life and enjoy good days, let him keep his
11 tongue from evil and his lips from lies and deceit; let him refrain
from evil and do good; let him seek what conduces to peace, and
12 make it his aim to further peace; for the eyes of the Lord are upon
the faithful and His ears are open to their prayer, but His face is set
against those who do wrong."
13 And who can harm you if you make strenuous efforts to do good?
14 But even if you should suffer because of your faithfulness to God,
you would be fortunate. Have no fear of their threats, then, and do
15 not be dismayed by them. Dedicate your hearts to Christ the lord;
then you will always be ready to give the right answer to any one
who asks you to account for the hope that you cherish in your
16 hearts. But answer gently and cautiously, according to the best of
your knowledge and belief, so that those who cast suspicion on your
17 Christian way of living may be ashamed. It is better to suffer for
18 doing good, if God so wills, than to suffer for doing wrong. Even
Christ in his day suffered death for our sins of apostasy — he, the
faithful, on behalf of the unfaithful — in order that he might lead
us back to God. Only his body was put to death; his spirit was
19 raised to the heavenly life. As a spirit he descended to the spirits
20 in the prisons of Satan and preached to them. They had once been
disobedient, in the days of Noah, when God in His forbearance
continued to withhold His punishment and commanded the building
of the ark, in which only a few souls, eight in all, were saved from
21 the flood with the aid of the flood. This event is symbolical of your
own case, for now you too are saved by the water of baptism.
Baptism is not the outward removal of stains from the body, but
the outward token of an upright heart, ready to do the will of God.
This is made possible by the resurrection of Jesus Christ, who has
ascended to heaven and is seated at the right hand of God, and to
whose rule angels, authorities, and powers are subject.

CHAPTER 4.

1 Now since Christ, the man, suffered so much for your sake, arm
yourselves with the same courage, to suffer in turn for him; for
whoever is ready to undergo bodily sufferings for his sake is rid
2 of the sin of apostasy. He will no longer spend the remainder of
his earthly life in the service of human passions, but in accordance
3 with the will of God; for the time of your subjection to the will of
the unbelievers has lasted long enough — the time when you gave
yourselves over to excess and the indulgence of your passions,
to drunkenness, gluttony, carousals, and all the other disgraceful

4 doings connected with idolatry. To-day the unbelievers are surprised
that you no longer wallow with them in the mire of debauchery;
5 and because you no longer do so, they abuse you. But they will have
to render an account for this to Him Who has the power to judge
6 the living and the spiritually dead. For this very reason the gospel
was preached to the spiritually dead, that although as men they
suffer punishment in the body, as spirits they might be brought
back to the life with God.

7 The ultimate goal of all has drawn near. Therefore act with
calm judgment in all circumstances, and even in your prayers avoid
8 everything that is excessive. Above all things, love one another
9 deeply, for love covers a host of sins. Practise hospitality toward
10 each other, and do so ungrudgingly. Let each serve the other with
the gift that he has received, so that you may prove good stewards
11 of the manifold gifts of God. If some one is a speaking-medium,
look upon his words as the oracles of God. If one of you has a gift
for rendering helpful services to others in the congregation, let him
exercise his gift to the full extent of the ability that God has conferred upon him for that purpose; and so in every case let it be your
sole aim to glorify God, in fellowship with Jesus Christ. Praise be
to God, and to Him belongs all power for ever and ever. Amen.

12 My dear friends, do not be surprised at the fire of suffering that
comes to test you, as though something extraordinary were happen-
13 ing to you. Rather, rejoice that in this way you are allowed to
share in Christ's sufferings. Then, when his glory is once revealed
14 before your eyes, you will also rejoice and exult. If you are reviled
because of Christ, you are to be called fortunate; for a spirit of
glory and power, a spirit that comes from God, rests on you. This
spirit is blasphemed by those who revile you, but by you he is held
15 in due honor. The suffering of which I am speaking is utterly unlike
that which has to be endured by a murderer, a thief, or any other
kind of evil-doer, or even by men who meddle with things that do
16 not concern them. For if a man suffers only because he is a follower
of Christ, let him not be ashamed, but praise God that he can be
17 called a Christian. For the time has come for the judgment to begin
with those who belong to God's people; and if it begins with us,
what will be the final fate of those who gave no credence to the
18 gospel of God? Again, if the faithful can scarcely obtain salvation,
19 what will become of the ungodly and the apostate? So let all who
suffer through fulfilling God's will commit their souls to the keeping
of the faithful Creator by the performance of good deeds.

CHAPTER 5.

1 Finally, as an elder and a witness to the sufferings of Christ, and
also as a participant in the glory that is soon to be revealed, I ex-
2 hort those among you who are elders to be good shepherds of the
flock of God that has been placed in your keeping. Watch over it,
not because you are forced to do so by your sense of duty, but
willingly, for the sake of God; not for vile money, but for love of
3 the cause. Do not tyrannize over the congregations allotted to you,
4 but serve as examples to your flock in every respect. Then when the
chief Shepherd comes, you will be rewarded with an unfading wreath
of glory.

5 And now a word to you younger people. Obey the elders. Serve
one another, and put on the garment of humility; for God resists
6 the proud, and bestows His grace on the humble alone. Submit
humbly, therefore, to the mighty hand of God, and in due time He
7 will raise you up. Lay all your burdens in His hands, for He cares
8 for you. Be cautious and watchful, for your enemy the devil is
prowling about like a hungry lion, looking for some one to devour.
9 Resist him with your strength of faith, for you know that your
brothers throughout the world have the same experience of suffer-
10 ing. The God Who is the giver of every good gift and Who has
called you back to His eternal glory through Jesus Christ, will
Himself furnish you, after you have suffered for a brief time, with
11 His own gifts, and will support, strengthen, and fortify you. His is
the glory and the power for ever. Amen.

12 By the hand of Silvanus, a faithful brother of ours, as I am convinced, I have written you this brief letter for the purpose of in-
fusing you with new courage and testifying to you that the faith
that you now hold to is God's true way of grace.

13 Your sister-congregation of Babylon, chosen by God like yourselves, sends greetings to you, and so does my son Mark.

14 Greet one another with the kiss of love.

Peace be to all of you who are in fellowship with Christ Jesus. Amen.

The Second Epistle of Peter the Apostle

CHAPTER 1.

1 SIMON PETER, a servant and apostle of Jesus Christ, sends greetings to those who under the just rule of our God and our
2 redeemer Jesus Christ have attained the same faith as we. May
grace and peace be yours in greater abundance, the farther you
progress in your knowledge of God and of our lord Jesus Christ.
3 He has given us all that lay within the power bestowed upon
him by God, in order to procure for us spiritual life and the true
worship of God. This gift became ours after we had recognized Him
4 Who called us back to His own glory and supreme joy. Through
Him we also received those great and precious promises by virtue of
which you shall again become members of the household of God
from which you came. But first you must have escaped from the
corruption that entered God's creation as a result of evil passion.
5 Therefore be zealously intent upon supplementing faith with virtue,
6 virtue with true self-knowledge, true self-knowledge with self-
mastery, self-mastery with steadfastness, steadfastness with the love
7 of God, the love of God with neighborly love, neighborly love with
8 love for all creatures. If these virtues exist and increase in you,
that is a proof that your knowledge of our lord Jesus Christ has not
9 been unsuccessful and unproductive for you. But whoever lacks
these virtues suffers from spiritual blindness; he has grown short-
sighted; he has become so forgetful that he no longer remembers
10 having been cleansed from his former sins. Therefore, brothers,
bend all your efforts toward safely reaching the goal of your calling
and election by means of good deeds. If you do this you can never
11 miss the right path. On the contrary, the road to the heavenly
kingdom of our lord and savior Jesus Christ will lie wide open to
you.
12 For this reason I am anxious to remind you of these truths again
and again, even though you already know them and are firmly
13 grounded in the truth that has been imparted to you. But as long
as I live in this earthly tent I nevertheless consider it my duty to
14 keep on stirring you up by recalling these truths to your mind. For
I know that my tent on earth must soon be put away, as our lord
15 Jesus Christ has shown me. Now I am eager to do my share toward

making you remember these truths at all times, even after I am
16 gone. It is not as though we had followed fables of our own in-
vention when we told you of the mighty return of our lord Jesus
Christ; on the contrary, we were eyewitnesses of his glorification.
17 The honor of his glorification was conferred upon him by God the
Father. It occurred at the time when there came to him from the
sublime glory of God the voice saying, "This is My beloved Son
18 with whom I was well pleased." These words from heaven sounded
19 in our ears when we were with him on the sacred mountain. Spoken
as they were by the Spirit of God, we consider them absolutely
trustworthy, and you yourselves would do well to cling to them
steadfastly; they serve as a lamp shining in a dark place, until the
20 day dawns and the morning star rises in your hearts. You must
understand first of all that no utterance by a spirit of God can be
21 interpreted according to mere human opinion; for no such utterance
ever resulted from the human will; it is only by God's command
that men have spoken as instruments of a holy spirit.

CHAPTER 2.

1 It is true that among the people of Israel untruthful spirits also
spoke through men, just as there will also be among you mediums
through whom low spirits will proclaim false doctrines. In this way
they will create disastrous divisions; they will not acknowledge as
their lord him who redeemed them, and consequently they will fall
2 early victims to spiritual destruction. There will be many who will
follow them in their immoral ways. Men of this stamp will be to
blame for the evil repute into which the way of the truth will fall.
3 Out of greed they will impart to you false spirit-messages and so
lure money from your pockets. With them the doom that has
always followed hard upon such doings will not be delayed, and
4 disaster will quickly overtake them. For God did not spare even
the fallen angels, but drove them down into hell, into the caverns
of darkness, where they will be kept until they turn their hearts to
5 God again. Neither did God spare the earliest people. When they
became ungodly, He sent the flood to overwhelm them, saving only
the eight members of Noah's household, because Noah had preached
6 uprightness to his fellow-men. He reduced the cities of Sodom and
Gomorrha to ashes, and thus executed sentence upon their inhabitants, who were to serve as a warning example to any who might
7 turn to ungodliness in the future. He saved only the faithful Lot,
who had suffered much from the immoral conduct of the wicked;

8 for the corruption that this God-fearing man was forced to witness
daily among his neighbors had caused his devout soul the deepest
9 anguish. Thus the Lord knows how to rescue the godly from trials,
and to keep the ungodly under punishment until the day when they
10 manifest a change for the better. He proceeds in this manner especially with those who seek to satisfy their base lust by sins against
nature, and who acknowledge no master. Presumptuous and in-
solent as they are, they do not hesitate to blaspheme the high powers
11 of heaven, whereas the angels of God, who are far above them
in power and might, do not utter a word of reproach against them
12 before the Lord. Such men are like wild brutes, created to be
captured and killed. They pour out their scorn upon everything
that they do not understand. Accordingly, like the beasts, they will
perish and be destroyed and so receive the punishment that their
13 wickedness deserves. They find their pleasure in dissipation day
after day; and it is a shame and a disgrace how they get the best of
14 you with their deceptions on such occasions. Their eyes are on the
watch for nothing but opportunities to commit adultery and are
insatiable in sinning. They are skilled in seducing weak souls, and
their hearts are set wholly on material gain — accursed children
15 that they are! They have abandoned the right way and gone astray,
following in the footsteps of Balaam, the son of Bosor, who for love
16 of money also allowed himself to be led into wrong-doing and was
rebuked for his misdeed. A dumb beast of burden spoke to him with
17 human voice and so checked the prophet's folly. These people are
like wells without water; they are like wisps of vapor driven before
18 the tempest. For them the deepest darkness is held in readiness.
With high-sounding, meaningless words they take advantage of weak
moments of physical craving to lure into new debauchery those who
19 have but recently escaped from the company of profligates. They
promise them "freedom," but they themselves are slaves of corruption; for whoever has been overcome by another in battle becomes
20 his slave. Any one who has escaped from the pollution of the world
through his knowledge of the lord and savior Jesus Christ, but
afterwards is again ensnared by such people and falls a victim to
21 their seductions, is in a worse state than he was before. It would be
better for him never to have learned the way of righteousness at all
than to withdraw from the holy mission entrusted to him after hav-
22 ing acquired such knowledge. Such persons offer proof of the
adage, "The dog returns to what he has vomited, and the sow that
has washed wallows in the mire again."

CHAPTER 3.

1 This is the second letter that I have written to you, dear friends.
2 I have written both of them for the purpose of recalling to your
minds the correct interpretation of the words spoken in the past by
the true prophets, as well as of the teachings of your apostles, who
received them from the lord and redeemer himself.
3 First of all, bear in mind that the close of every era will be
marked by the appearance of scoffers who have an inborn craving
to sneer at everything lofty, because they allow themselves to be al-
4 together guided by base instincts. These people will ask in derision,
"Where is his promised coming? For since the passing of our forefathers, things have been just as they were from the beginning of the
5 world." Persons who speak thus do not know that ages ago the
heavenly bodies and the earth were condensed from a vaporous con-
6 dition to a solid by God's spirits and at His command. In this way
7 the nebulous character of the universe disappeared. But the heavenly bodies and the earth will remain in their present state only
until the day on which they are dissolved by fire, as that same God
has ordained. That will be on the day when the godless undergo an
inward change and turn to God.
8 But do not overlook this one thing, dear friends, that with the
Lord one day is like a thousand years, and a thousand years are like
9 one day. The Lord is not slow to fulfill His promise, as some men
think; He shows forbearance with you, for He is unwilling that
even one should be lost, but wishes all to have a change of heart.
10 The day of the Lord will come like a thief in the night; on that
day the heavenly bodies will vanish amid roaring and hissing; the
elements of which they are composed will be dissolved in the flam-
ing heat, and the earth, together with all the works of man, will
11 be consumed in the fire. Now if all these things are to be dissolved,
think how it behooves you to lead lives that are holy and pleasing
12 to God. You long for the coming of the day of God and would
gladly hasten its arrival — the day that will cause the heavenly
bodies to be dissolved in fire and the elements to melt in the heat
13 of the flames. According to the promise, we may then expect new
heavenly bodies and a new earth, where every one will perform the
will of God.
14 Therefore, dear friends, in view of these things, make every effort
to be found by the Lord pure and spotless and at peace with God.
15 Look upon the Lord's forbearance as the means to your salvation.
Of these matters our beloved brother Paul has already written

16 to you with the wisdom that has been bestowed upon him. And in
all of his other letters he speaks similarly in the passages that refer
to these things. There are some things in his letters, of course, that
are hard to understand. People who have not progressed far in the
knowledge of the truth and become well grounded in it often mis-
interpret these passages to their own destruction. They do the same
with the rest of the Scriptures.
17 Be on your guard then, dear friends, since you have been warned,
Do not be led astray by idle fancies arising from the errors of god-
18 less people, so that you may not lose your firm stand; but grow
in the grace and knowledge of our lord and savior Jesus Christ.
To him be the glory from now until an appointed day in a future
era. Amen.

The First Epistle of John the Apostle

CHAPTER 1.

1 I AM writing to you to tell you of him who is the Word of Life;
of the events in his career from the beginning; of that which we
ourselves heard from him; of that which we ourselves saw with
our own eyes, of that which we observed in him, and which was so
2 close to us that we could touch it with our hands. In this way we
ascertained that in him the true life was actually made manifest.
We saw it before our eyes and therefore can bear witness to it and
tell you of the life that awaits us hereafter. The bearer of this life
3 was with the Father, and came down to us. It is what we have seen
in him and heard from him that we are proclaiming to you, so that
you also may become our fellows in faith. By this fellowship of
faith we are closely united with the Father and with His Son Jesus
Christ.

4 We write this to you in order that your joy may be complete.

5 Now this is the message that we heard from him and that we wish
to deliver to you: "God is light, and in Him there is no dark shadow
6 whatsoever." Hence if we declared that we were in fellowship with
Him, and still travelled the dark paths of sin, we should be liars and
7 our actions would be at odds with the truth. But if we walk in the
path of light in which He Himself lives, we are in communion with
Him, and the blood of His Son Jesus Christ cleanses us from all
8 sin. If we were to assert that we had committed no sin we should
9 grossly deceive ourselves, and the truth would not be in us; but if
we confess our sins to Him we may rely on it that He will keep His
10 promise to forgive our sins and cleanse us of all wrong-doing. If
we were to maintain that we had not sinned we should brand Him
as a liar, and His word of truth would have found no place in our
hearts.

CHAPTER 2.

1 My dear children, I am writing this to you so that you may refrain from sinning. But even if any one does relapse into sin, we
have an advocate with the Father; it is Jesus Christ, with whom God
2 is well pleased. It is he who has delivered us from the consequences
of the sin of apostasy, and not us alone, but the whole universe.
3 Our only proof that we rightly know him lies in our faithful ob-
4 servance of his teachings. If any one says, "I know him," but does

not abide by his doctrine, he deceives himself, and the truth is not
5 in him. But in any one who practises his teachings, the love of God
has indeed reached the state of perfection. Moreover, this is the
sign by which we may know whether we shall be united with Him;
6 for whoever says that he is already united with Him must live as
Jesus lived.

7 My dear friends, this is no new doctrine that I am writing to you
but an old one, and one which you accepted from the beginning.
8 This old doctrine is the truth that you have just heard. But in one
sense I am sending you a new doctrine. It runs thus: "That which
proved true in his case applies to you also: the darkness must yield,
9 and the ray of the true light must shine." He who says that he is
in the light and nevertheless harbors hatred of his fellow-man in his
10 heart, is still in the darkness. But he who loves his fellow-man
lives perpetually in the light and is in no danger of stumbling.
11 Whoever hates his fellow-man lives in darkness; he gropes around
in the dark and does not know how to find the right path, for the
darkness has blinded his eyes.

12 I am writing to you, my children, because your sins are forgiven
13 you for his name's sake. And I am writing to you, fathers, because
you have attained to knowledge of him who was the first to come
14 into existence. I am writing to you, young men, because you have
overcome him who brings destruction into the world. Do not love
15 the world or what is in the world. He who loves the world has no
16 love for the Father; for everything that the world calls its own —
the physical craving for sensual pleasure, the covetous desire of the
eyes, and the boast of wealth — belongs not to the Father but to
17 the world. The world with its lusts is passing away, but he who does
the will of God will endure for ever.

18 Dear children, the last age of the world has dawned. You have
heard that antichrist is coming, and indeed there are many antichrists already. From this we know that the final era has begun.
19 These antichrists have sprung from our midst, although in reality
they never belonged to us. If they had really belonged to us, they
would have remained with us; but they have served to make it clear
20 to all that not every one among us really belongs to us. You, however, are among those who have received the spiritual anointment
of truth at the hands of the Holy One, and are therefore initiated
into the whole truth.

21 I have not written to you as though you were ignorant of the
truth, but precisely because you do know it and because you know
that no lie can come from the truth.

22 Who is the liar whom I have in mind? None other than he who
23 denies that Jesus is the Messiah. Such a man is antichrist, denying
alike the Father and the Son; for whoever denies the Son also disowns the Father, and whoever professes belief in the Son is also in communion with the Father. Let that which you accepted as the
24 truth in the beginning remain in you permanently. If the truth that
you heard from the beginning remains in you, then you yourselves
25 will remain in communion with the Son and the Father. This is the
message that he himself brought us, the message of the life hereafter.

26 I am writing this to you with an eye to those who would gladly
27 lead you astray. But as for you, the spiritual anointment that you
received from Him will remain with you permanently, and you need no further teaching; indeed, this very anointment teaches you everything, and what it teaches is the truth and no lie. And hold faithfully to that which it has taught you.

28 Once more I say to you, my children, hold fast to it. Then when
Christ appears, we can look forward to his coming with confidence,
29 and we need not be ashamed in his presence. Inasmuch as you know
that he has found favor in the sight of God, you may be sure that every one who performs deeds that are pleasing to God is a child of God.

CHAPTER 3.

1 Think what great love the Father showed for us in allowing us
to be called His children once more, and actually to be His children.
And because the world has not learned to know God, it also has
2 no desire to have anything to do with us as His children. My dear
friends, we are already God's children, although as yet there are no
outward signs to show the full import of this relationship. We
know, however, that when He becomes visible to our eyes we shall
3 be like Him and therefore shall see Him as He is. Every one who
rests this hope on Him will strive to become holy, because He is
4 holiness itself. But whoever commits the sin of apostasy separates
5 himself from God, for apostasy is separation. And you know that
Jesus appeared on earth in order to banish the sin of apostasy from
6 the world; for the sin of apostasy does not rest upon him. Accord-
ingly, whoever remains in communion with him does not belong to the apostates, but whoever commits the sin of apostasy has never experienced contact with him or known him.

7 Let no one deceive you, my children. Only he who does God's
8 will is pleasing to God, as Jesus himself is pleasing to God. Whoever forsakes God belongs to the kingdom of Lucifer; for the devil

was the first to desert and the ringleader of all apostates. This is
the reason why the Son of God appeared on earth, that he might
deliver those whom the devil held in bondage by having led them
9 into apostasy. No one reborn of God commits the sin of apostasy,
because a divine spark continually remains in him. He can never
again wholly separate himself from God, for he is united with Him
10 by the bond of rebirth. This is the sign by which you may know
who are God's children and who are the devil's: any one who does
not love God is not one of God's children; neither is he who does
not love his neighbor.
11 The first thing that you were taught was this: "Love one an-
12 other." We must not be like Cain, who came from the Evil One's
kingdom and killed his brother. And why did he kill him? Because
his own deeds were inspired by the Evil One and his brother's by
13 God. Then do not think it strange, brothers, if the world hates you.
14 We know that we have worked our way out of the realm of spiritual
death into the realm of spiritual life, because we love our fellow-
15 men. He who does not love his fellow-man still belongs to the kingdom of spiritual death. Every one who hates his fellow-man is a
fratricide; and you know that no fratricide can gain permanent
16 possession of the life to come. We know what true love is from the
fact that he laid down his life for us. Accordingly, we too must lay
17 down our lives for our fellow-men. If a man has worldly possessions and sees his fellow-men in want, but closes his heart to them,
18 how can love for God dwell in him? My dear children, we must not
manifest our love only in fine words on the tongue, but by deeds,
19 as divine truth teaches us. From this we shall know whether our
actions are guided by the truth. We must acquire a firm conviction
20 on this point, in all honesty before God. If our conscience condemns
us, a higher judge, the omniscient God, sits in judgment over us.
21 If our conscience acquits us, however, we may appear before God
22 with confidence, and whatever we ask of Him, we shall receive from
Him, because we keep His commands and do what is pleasing in
23 His sight. And this is His command, that we believe in the name
24 of His Son Jesus Christ and love one another as he taught us. Whoever obeys God's commands will remain in communion with God,
and God in communion with him. And that God is in communion
with us we know by the spirit-world that He has granted to us.

CHAPTER 4.

1 My dear friends, do not believe every spirit, but test the spirits
to learn whether they come from God. For many false spirits have

emerged from the abyss and gone out into the world, and are
2 speaking through human mediums. This is how you can find out
whether a spirit comes from God: every spirit who confesses that
3 Jesus Christ appeared on earth as a man, comes from God, while
every spirit who seeks to destroy belief in Jesus as our lord in-
carnated does not come from God, but is sent by the adversary of
Christ. You have been told that such spirits would come, and they
are already appearing in the world.

4 My children, you belong to God, and you have overcome the
messengers of Christ's adversary; for He who is in communion with
5 you is more powerful than he who holds sway in the world. Those
adversaries belong to the world; therefore they speak through their
mediums on worldly matters only, and the worldly-minded give
ear to them.

6 We belong to God; therefore he who believes in God listens to
our words. He who does not belong to God does not listen to what
we say to him. These, then, are the ways by which we can distinguish the spirits of truth from the spirits of falsehood.

7 My dear friends, let us meet one another in love, for love is of
divine origin, and every one who loves God is a child of God and
8 possesses the true conception of God. He who is lacking in love has
9 no understanding of God's nature, for God is love. The love of God
was manifested among us men by His sending into the world His
Son — the only one whom He Himself had called into existence —
10 so that through him we might obtain spiritual life. His love for us
was not occasioned by our having loved God first; on the contrary,
He loved us first, and that is why He sent His Son to deliver us from
the sin of apostasy.

11 Dear friends, if God's love for us was so great, it is our duty in
12 turn to show love for one another. No human being has ever seen
God. If we love one another, God remains in communion with us,
and only then does our love for Him become complete in our hearts.
13 That God is in communion with us, and we with Him, we recognize
14 from the fact that He has sent us spirits from His kingdom. For we
have seen with our own eyes and can testify that the Father has sent
15 His Son to be the Savior of the universe. If any one confesses that
Jesus Christ is the Son of God, God is in communion with him,
16 and he with God. We have perceived the love that God cherishes
for us and placed all our trust in it.

17 God is love; and he who continues in love remains united with
God, and God with him. Our love attains the height of perfection
when we reach the point at which we can await the day of judgment

with the utmost confidence; for just as Christ lived in the world
spotless and pure, so must we ourselves live in this world in the
same way.
18 Where love prevails, fear is unknown. Perfect love dispels all
fear. Fear is to be found only where punishment threatens. There-
19 fore any one who feels fear has not yet attained perfect love. We
love God because He first loved us. Any one who says that he loves
20 God, and yet hates his fellow-man, is a liar; for how can any one
who does not love his neighbor whom he sees with his physical eyes,
21 love God Whom he cannot see? It is from God that we have received the command that he who would love God must love his
fellow-man also.

CHAPTER 5.

1 Whoever believes that Jesus is the Messiah is one of God's chil-
2 dren; and whoever loves the Father, loves His children also. By
loving God and obeying His commands we know that we love God's
3 children. True love for God consists in obeying His commands.
4 His commands are not burdensome; for all who are called "children of God" overcome the power of the world with ease. What
5 gives us our victory over the powers of the world is our faith. The
only one who triumphs over the powers of the world is he who
6 believes that Jesus is the Son of God. Jesus Christ came to us as
the Son of God, with the testimony of water and blood; not with the
testimony of water alone, but water and blood both bore witness to
7 him. Moreover, the Spirit of God appeared as an unimpeachable
8 witness on his behalf, because this Spirit is truth itself. Thus we
have three witnesses for him, the Spirit, the water, and the blood;
9 and these three agree in their testimony. If we accept the testimony
of men as authentic, how much more highly must we regard the
testimony of God! And such testimony is available in the words
10 with which God testified to us concerning His Son. Consequently,
whoever believes in the Son of God can defend his faith by appeal-
ing to God's testimony; but whoever does not believe even the testimony of God, brands God as a liar. Such is the case with him who
11 refuses to believe God's own testimony on behalf of His Son. This
testimony also contains the truth that God has restored to us the life
hereafter, and that this life is to be found only in communion with
12 His Son. Accordingly, he who is in close communion with the Son
has spiritual life, and he who lacks this communion with the Son
of God also lacks spiritual life.
13 I have written this to you so as to make you aware that you will

obtain life in the beyond only if you believe in the name of the Son
14 of God. Our hearts are filled with great confidence in God; it is
because we know that He listens to our prayers whenever we ask
15 Him for anything that is in accordance with His will. And if we
know that He listens to every one of our prayers, we may be certain
that the requests we make of Him will actually be granted.
16 If any one sees his fellow-man commit a sin which does not lead
to the spiritual death of apostasy, he should pray for him. In this
way he will impart to him spiritual strength; but, as I have said,
only if it is not a sin that leads to spiritual death. There is one such
"deadly sin." This is not the sin I mean when I urge you to pray
17 for sinners. People usually call everything "sin" that is against the
will of God, but there is one sin that carries spiritual death with it.
18 We know, however, that no one who is a child of God commits such
sin; his relationship to God protects him against it, and the Evil
19 One is not able to lay hands on him. We know that we belong to
God, but that the world is entirely under the power of the Evil One.
20 Furthermore, we know that the Son of God came to earth to bring us
true understanding, so that we might know the true God. And we
are in communion with the true God, since we are in communion
with His Son Jesus Christ. It is he who teaches the truth and grants
life in heaven.
21 My children, keep away from communication with evil spirits.
Amen.

The Second Epistle of John the Apostle

1 As elder I am sending this letter to the elect lady and her children of whom I am truly fond. And not only I am fond of them,
2 but so are all who have attained to knowledge of the truth — that
truth which dwells among us and which will remain united with us
3 for all time to come. — Grace, mercy, and peace be with you from
God the Father and from the lord Jesus Christ, the Son of the
Father, with whom you are united by truth and peace.
4 It gave me great happiness to learn that your children conduct
their lives according to the true doctrine, as the Father has com-
5 manded us. And now, dear lady, I beg leave to give you this precept, which to be sure is not new, but was among the first we
6 received, namely, that we should love one another. Love is mani-

fested by our obeying God's commands in our daily lives. That is
the chief command, as you have heard from the beginning; observe it, then.
7 Many deceitful spirits have gone out into the universe, all of them
denying that Jesus Christ has appeared on earth in human form.
Every spirit who makes such denial is a liar and an enemy of Christ.
8 Take care that you do not forfeit what you gained with great effort,
9 and that you reap your full reward for it. Whoever fails to heed
this admonition and hold fast to the doctrine of Christ severs his
connection with God; but whoever remains true to Christ's doctrine
10 is in communion with both the Father and the Son. If any one
should come to you as a teacher and fail to bring this doctrine,
11 refuse him admittance to your house and bid him no welcome; for
whoever welcomes such a person becomes an accomplice in all the
evil that he does.
12 There is much more that I should like to write to you, but I am
unwilling to commit it to paper and ink. I hope instead that I
shall be able to visit you personally. Then we can speak face to
face, and our joy will be all the greater.
13 The children of your elect sister send their hearty greetings.—
The grace of God be with you. Amen.

The Third Epistle of John the Apostle

1 As elder I am sending this letter to the beloved Gaius, for whom
I bear true affection.
2 Dear friend, I wish you above all things prosperity and bodily
health in the same measure in which you prosper spiritually.
3 It has afforded me great happiness every time that the brothers
have come to us and reported favorably of you, telling us that you
are living according to the doctrine of the truth, as is indeed the
4 case. Nothing makes me happier than to hear that my children live
according to the true doctrine.
5 Dear friend, your services to your brothers, strangers to you
6 though they were, are a splendid proof of your faith. They have
testified to your love in the highest terms before the whole congregation. You will do a good deed if you make it possible for them to
continue on their journey in a manner worthy of God's cause; for
7 they set out for the sake of Christ's name, and they accept no help

8 from the non-Christians. Hence it becomes our duty to help these
men; in so doing we assist in spreading the truth.
9 I wrote a letter to the congregation, but Diotrephes, who aspires
10 to be its leader, will have nothing to do with us. And so upon my
arrival I shall call him to account for his conduct in casting suspicion on us with his evil reports, and, not content with that, in
refusing to entertain the brothers himself and forbidding others to
do so, even expelling from the congregation all who are so inclined.
11 Dear friend, do not imitate evil, but good. He who does good
is a child of God; he who does evil has no understanding of God.
12 Demetrius is well spoken of by all, even by Him who is the truth
itself. We also testify in his favor, and you know that our testimony
is true.
13 There are many other things that I wish to tell you, but I prefer
14 not to commit them to writing. I hope to see you shortly, and then
we can speak of all these matters face to face.
15 Peace be with you. The friends send their greetings. Greet all
of the friends who are with you, each one personally. Amen.

The Epistle of Jude the Apostle

1 JUDE, a servant of Jesus Christ and a brother of James, sends this
letter to the chosen who remain constant in their love of God the
2 Father and in their loyalty to Christ Jesus. May God's mercy, peace,
and love be with you in an ever increasing measure.
3 Dear friends, it is my heart's desire to write to you concerning
our common salvation. At the same time I feel constrained to urge
you by letter to fight for the faith which has been bestowed once
4 for all upon those who are devoted to God. For there have crept in
among you certain people for whom the judgment written down in
times long past holds good: "Ungodly men who misuse God's gifts
in licentious living; men who deny God, our only Sovereign, as
well as our lord Jesus Christ."
5 I wish to remind you, though you have already heard all these
things, that while the Lord saved the people of Israel from the yoke
of the Egyptians, He afterward allowed those who would not be-
6 lieve, to perish; furthermore, that He has had the angels who would
not confine themselves to the domain assigned to them but ex-
ceeded their proper authority, fettered in darkness with unbreakable chains, until the coming of that great day on which they will
7 experience a change of heart; that Sodom and Gomorrha, together
with the surrounding cities whose inhabitants had similarly devoted
themselves to lewdness and the indulgence of unnatural desires,
stand as a warning example, for they are forced to endure a punishment by fire that continues throughout long ages.
8 In like manner these dreamers also pollute their own bodies,
they own no master, and they blaspheme high heavenly powers.
9 And yet the archangel Michael did not dare to revile even the devil
when he contended with him for the body of Moses and fell into a
dispute with him. He simply said, "May the Lord demand strict
10 obedience of you." These people, however, scoff at everything they
do not understand. But they are well-versed in manifesting the lower
instincts which they have in common with brute animals, and in so
11 doing they bring ruin upon themselves. Woe to them! They have
travelled the path of Cain; through avarice they have allowed themselves to be ensnared by the error of Balaam; and as a result of a
12 revolt like Korah's they have fallen a prey to destruction. These are
the ones who are a blemish upon your feasts of brotherly love,

where they carouse together unabashed, and meanwhile set themselves up as shepherds of the congregation. They are like clouds of
mist driven before the wind; like leafless trees in the autumn, with-
13 out fruit, doubly dead, and uprooted; like wild sea-waves, foaming
out their own shame; like wandering stars for which utter darkness
14 is reserved throughout a vast period of time. It is of them that a
spirit of God said through Enoch, the seventh in descent from
15 Adam, "Truly, the Lord comes in the midst of His holy myriads to
sit in judgment upon all, and to punish all the godless for all the
godless deeds that they have committed and for the defiant words
16 that godless sinners have spoken against Him." These are the mal-
contents who are for ever dissatisfied with their lot and who are the
slaves of their own moods; men who talk arrogantly, but flatter
people to their faces when their own interests are at stake.

17 But you, dear friends, must remember the words that were spoken
18 in the past by the apostles of our lord Jesus Christ when they said,
"At the end of the era there will appear scoffers who will follow all
the paths of ungodliness in accordance with the dictates of their
19 own passions." They are the men who cause divisions; sensual
men, who have not received a holy spirit.

20 But you, dear friends, must build up your spiritual edifice on
the foundation of your thoroughly sanctified faith; pray under the
21 guidance of a holy spirit; be constant in your love for God, and live
in the expectation that you will obtain the life hereafter through
22 the mercy of our lord Jesus Christ. There are some who are tormented by doubts. Have pity on them, snatch them from these
23 flames, and save them. Others also are deserving of your pity, but
be on your guard, and do not even touch the clothes that they have
polluted with the sins of the flesh.

24 There is One Who can keep you from stumbling and give you
the strength to appear, blameless and exultant, before the radiant
25 glory of His eyes. To Him, the only God, Who is our Deliverer
through our lord Jesus Christ, be glory and majesty, might and
power, as in time immemorial, so also now and for ever. Amen.

THE REVELATION OF JOHN

CHAPTER 1.

1 THE following is a revelation that comes from Jesus Christ. God
gave it to him in order that he might show His servants events
that are destined to occur in rapid succession. Christ then sent his
2 angel, and through him communicated it to his servant John. Thus
John became a witness of God's plan of salvation, in respect to the
past as well as the future, so far as he gained insight into them as
a result of Jesus Christ's communication.
3 Fortunate is he who reads the words of this revelation of God,
and fortunate are those who hear them read and take them to heart;
for the critical moment has arrived for every one.
4 John sends greetings to the seven congregations of Asia Minor.
Grace be with you and peace from Him Who is, was, and will be
the essence of all being, and from the seven spirits who stand be-
5 fore His throne, and from Jesus Christ the faithful witness, the first-
born from the kingdom of the spiritually dead, and the sovereign
over the kings of the earth. To him who loves us and who through
6 his blood delivered us from the sin of apostasy, and exalted us to
be kings and priests in the kingdom of his God and Father — to him
be glory and power throughout the ages. Amen.
7 See, he is coming with his hosts of spirits, and every eye will
behold him, even the men who exposed him to every indignity; and
on his account all the spirits of the earthly spheres will lament.
That is a positive certainty.
8 "I am the Alpha and the Omega — the beginning and the end,"
says God the Lord. "I am the essence of all being, was so, and
shall be so for ever — I in Whom all power is united."
9 I, your brother John, your companion in the sufferings as well
as in the royal dignity and the steadfastness of Christ Jesus, had been
carried to the island called Patmos for proclaiming the word of God
10 and testifying on behalf of Christ Jesus. Then — it was on a Lord's
day — my spirit was withdrawn from my body, and I heard behind
11 me a voice, powerful as the sound of a trumpet, which said, "Write
what you see in a book and send it to the seven congregations: to
Ephesus, Smyrna, Pergamum, Thyatira, Sardis, Philadelphia, and
12 Laodicea." I turned to see whose voice it was that spoke to me, and
13 when I looked around I saw seven golden candlesticks, and in the

midst of them some one who resembled a man. He wore a garment
14 that hung to his feet, and around his breast was a golden belt. His
head and his hair were white as snow-white wool. His eyes shone
15 like flames of fire. His feet were like the gold-ore that is brought
to a glow in the furnace. His voice sounded like the rush of many
16 waters. In his right hand he held seven stars. From his mouth issued
a sharp, two-edged sword, and his face shone like the sun when it
shines with all its strength.

17 When I saw him, I fell at his feet like a dead man. Then he laid
his right hand upon me and said, "Do not be afraid. I am the first
18 and the last. Once I too belonged to the kingdom of the spiritually
dead; but see, now I possess spiritual life for ever. I have the keys
19 of the Prince of Death and of his kingdom of death. Write down
what you have seen and what it means, as well as what will be shown
to you afterwards.

20 "The mysterious image of the seven stars that you saw in my
right hand and of the seven golden candlesticks means this: The
seven stars are the apostles of the seven congregations, and the seven
candlesticks are the congregations themselves.

CHAPTER 2.

1 "To the apostle of the congregation in Ephesus write: 'These are
the words of him who holds the seven stars in his right hand and
2 who walks about among the seven golden candlesticks: I know your
deeds, your hard work, and your steadfastness. I know that you
cannot tolerate the evil-minded. You have put to the test those who
falsely call themselves apostles, and have shown them to be liars.
3 You have remained steadfast and have suffered for my name's sake,
4 and still not lost courage. But I have one fault to find with you:
5 the love that you first felt has abated. Just think of the height from
which you have fallen. Mend your ways and show by your deeds
that you are once more what you were in the beginning. Otherwise
I shall come to you suddenly and remove the candlestick from its
6 place, unless you change your attitude. I grant it in your favor, certainly, that the practices of the Nicolaitans are as revolting to you
7 as they are to me. Let him whose ear is open to these words, hear
what the spirit says to the congregations: I will allow him who
conquers to eat from the tree of life that stands in the Paradise
of my God.'

8 "To the apostle of the congregation in Smyrna write: 'These are
the words of the first and the last — who descended to the spiritu-

9 ally dead and returned to the kingdom of spiritual life: I know
your doings, your distress, and your poverty. But in reality you are
rich. I also know that you are reviled by those who call themselves
Jews, although they are not true Jews but a synagogue of Satan.
10 Do not be afraid of the sufferings that await you. Mark, Satan pro-
poses to throw some of you into prison in order to seduce you into
apostasy. For ten days you will have to bear this hardship. Be
faithful until death, and I will give you the victor's crown of life.
11 Let him whose ear is open to these words hear what the spirit says
to the congregations: He who conquers shall be spared another
separation from God.'

12 "To the apostle of the congregation in Pergamum write: 'These
13 are the words of him who has the sharp two-edged sword: I know
your doings and I know where you live, namely where Satan has
erected his throne. But you hold fast to my name; you did not disown your belief in me even in the days when my faithful witness
14 Antipas was killed in your city, the residence of Satan. But I have
some fault to find with you. You have people in your congregation
who follow the advice once given by Balaam when he counselled
Balac to induce the children of Israel to take part in the sacrifices
to the idols and in the attendant immorality, thus seducing them into
15 the sin of apostasy. You also have in your congregation adherents
16 of the Nicolaitans who teach a similar doctrine. You must make a
change here, or I will soon come to you and fight them with the
17 sword of my mouth. Let him whose ear is open to these words hear
what the spirit says to the congregations: To him who conquers I
will give some of the hidden manna, and I will give him a white
stone with a new name written on it, a name known to no one except
him who receives it.'

18 "To the apostle of the congregation in Thyatira write: 'These
are the words of the Son of God, who has eyes like flames of fire,
19 and whose feet are like gold-ore: I know your doings, your love,
your faith, your helpfulness, and your steadfastness. I know that of
late your good deeds have been even more numerous than at first.
20 But the one fault that I have to find with you is that you grant too
much license to that woman Jezebel. She professes to be a good
medium and delivers discourses, but she seduces my servants into
practising idolatry and eating the meat of offerings sacrificed to
21 idols. I gave her a specified time in which to reform, but she will
22 not abandon her dealings with the world of evil spirits. Mark, I
will cast her upon a sick-bed and plunge into great distress those
who join in her idolatry, unless they forsake the ways of this

23 woman. I will cause her children to die. Then all the congregations will know that I am he who searches men's innermost hearts,
and I will repay every one in your congregation according to his
24 deeds. But to you others in Thyatira who are not followers of this
doctrine and who will have nothing to do with the so-called "pro-
fundities of Satan," I say, I shall lay no further burden upon you;
25 but hold fast to that which you have, until I come.

26 " 'To him who conquers and continues to perform my work to
27 the end, I will give power over the evil spirits; he shall drive them
before him with a rod of iron, and shatter them as one shatters a
28 potter's vessels. This is the same power that I received from my
29 Father. And I will give him the morning star. Let him whose ear is
open to these words hear what the spirit says to the congregations.' "

CHAPTER 3.

1 "To the apostle of the congregation in Sardis write: 'These are
the words of him who has the seven spirits of God and the seven
stars: I know your doings. You have the reputation of being spiritu-
2 ally alive, but you are spiritually dead. Rise up from the spiritually
dead, and give new strength to the others of the congregation who
are on the point of spiritual death. I find that what you are doing
3 will not pass muster in the sight of my God. Remember the way in
which you received and heard the gospel; live accordingly, and
change your heart. But if you do not choose to awaken to spiritual
life again, I will come like a thief, and you shall not know at what
4 hour I am going to overtake you. Nevertheless, there are a few
members of your congregation in Sardis who have kept their garments unsoiled. They shall walk with me clothed in white, for they
deserve to do so.

5 " 'He who conquers shall be clothed in a white garment; I will
not again erase his name from the Book of Life, but will acknowledge him before my Father and His angels.

6 " 'Let him whose ear is open to these words, hear what the spirit
says to the congregations.'

7 "To the apostle of the congregation in Philadelphia write: 'These
are the words of him who is holy and true, and who has the key of
David—who opens that which no one can close, and who closes
8 that which no one can open: I know your doings. See, I have
thrown open before you a door that no one can close. It is true that
your strength is slight, but you have held fast to my teachings and
9 have not denied my name. Mark, this is what I am going to do.

I will have the people from Satan's synagogue who call themselves
Jews but are not Jews (they are liars) go to you and fall at your
10 feet and learn that I have given you a place in my heart. Because
you have held steadfastly to my teachings I also will protect you,
and save you from the hour of trial which will come upon the whole
11 world so as to put to the test all the inhabitants of the earth. I shall
come soon. Hold fast to what you have, so that no one may rob
you of your crown.

12 " 'I will make him who is victorious a pillar in the temple of my
God, and he shall never lose his place there. Upon his forehead I
will write the name of my God and the name of the city of my God,
the new Jerusalem which comes down out of heaven from the place
where my God is enthroned. I will also write my own name, my
new name, upon his forehead.

13 " 'Let him whose ear is open to my words, hear what the spirit
says to the congregations.'

14 "To the apostle of the congregation in Laodicea, write: 'These
are the words of him who is the Amen, the faithful and true witness,
15 the first of all that God created: I know your doings; I know that
you are neither cold nor hot. I wish that you were either cold or
16 hot! But because you are lukewarm and neither cold nor hot, there
17 is nothing left for me to do but to spit you out of my mouth. You
say, "I am rich. I myself have amassed these riches, and I need
nothing further." And all the while you do not know that it is you
who are so wretched and pitiable, so poor and blind and naked.
18 Therefore I advise you to buy from me gold that has been refined
in the fire, so that you may be truly rich. Buy white garments to
put on, so that the whole world may not see the shame of your
nakedness; and buy salve to put on your eyes, so that you may see
19 clearly again. I rebuke and chastise all whom I love. So renew your
20 zeal and alter your ways. See, I stand at the door and knock. If any
one listens to my voice and opens the door to me, I will go in and
dine with him, and he with me.

21 " 'I will allow him who conquers to take a seat on my throne beside me; for I also have conquered, and I was allowed to sit with
my Father on His throne.

22 " 'Let him whose ear is open to these words, hear what the spirit
says to the congregations.' "

CHAPTER 4.

1 Then I had this vision: I saw a door open in heaven, and the
voice that I heard before, loud as the sound of a trumpet, said,

"Come here, and I will show you what must take place in the
2 future." Immediately my spirit left my body. And behold, there
3 was a throne in heaven, and seated upon the throne One who had
the gleam of jasper and carnelian. The throne itself was surrounded
4 by a rainbow as radiant as an emerald. Around the throne were
twenty-four other thrones, on which I saw twenty-four elders sitting.
They were clothed in white garments and wore golden crowns on
5 their heads. Out of the throne came lightning, voices, and thunder.
Seven torches burned before the throne; they are the seven spirits
6 of God. The space before the throne was like a sea of crystal. Standing in a circle before the throne were four living creatures which
7 were covered with eyes before and behind. The first creature was
like a lion, the second like a bull, the third had the face of a man,
8 and the fourth was like a flying eagle. Each of the creatures had
six wings, all alike, and these wings were covered with eyes, on the
inside as well as on the outside. Day and night they exclaim without ceasing, "Holy, holy, holy is God the Lord Almighty, Who was,
9 Who is, and Who will be." Whenever these creatures render praise,
honor, and thanks to Him Who is seated on the throne and lives for
10 ever, the twenty-four elders fall down before Him Who sits upon
the throne, and worship Him Who lives for ever, and lay down
11 their crowns before the throne, exclaiming, "Thou art worthy, Lord
our God, to possess glory and honor and power, for Thou hast
created all things; all things were as Thou wouldst have them, and
all things were fashioned according to Thy will."

CHAPTER 5.

1 In the right hand of Him who sat upon the throne I saw a scroll,
covered with writing on the inside and sealed on the outside with
2 seven seals. Now I saw a mighty angel who called in a loud voice,
3 "Who is worthy to open the scroll and to break its seals?" But no
one was found, either in heaven or on earth or under the earth, who
4 was able to open the scroll and look into it. Then I began to weep
aloud because no one was found worthy to open the scroll or look
5 into it; but one of the elders said to me, "Do not weep. See, the
lion of the tribe of Judah, the scion of David, has won the victory.
He can therefore open the scroll and break its seven seals."

6 Then I saw a Lamb standing between the throne and the four
beings and in the midst of the elders. It seemed to have been
slaughtered. It had seven horns and seven eyes; these are the seven
spirits of God whose duty it is to work as God's messengers in the
whole earthly creation.

7 The Lamb went and took the scroll from the right hand of Him
8 Who sat on the throne; and when it had taken the scroll, the four
creatures and the twenty-four elders fell down before the Lamb.
Each had a harp and golden vessel full of incense—a symbol of
9 the prayers of the faithful. They sang a new song, and the words
were these: "You are worthy to take the scroll and to break its seals,
for you have allowed yourself to be slaughtered, and with your blood
you have redeemed for God men from every tribe and tongue, people
10 and nation. You have made them kings and priests for the cause of
our God, and they shall rule in the earthly spheres."
11 Again I looked, and I heard the voices of many angels surrounding the throne and the four creatures and the elders. Their
12 number was ten thousand times a thousand, and they cried with a
loud voice, "The Lamb that offered itself to be slaughtered is worthy
of receiving power and riches, wisdom and strength, honor, glory,
13 and praise." And I heard every creature in heaven, on earth, under
the earth, and in the sea, yes, everything that lives in them, say,
"Praise and honor, glory and power for ever to Him Who sits on
14 the throne and to the Lamb." And the four creatures said, "Amen,"
while the elders fell down and worshipped.

CHAPTER 6.

1 After that I saw the Lamb break the first of the seven seals, and
I heard one of the four creatures call with a voice like thunder,
2 "Come and see!" Then I beheld a white horse, and seated upon it
a rider carrying a bow. He was given a crown of victory, and he
went forth from conquest to conquest.
3 Now the Lamb broke the second seal, and I heard the second
4 creature call, "Come and see!" And a second horse appeared, red
as fire. It carried a rider also, and he was given power to take peace
from the earth, so that men would slaughter one another. He was
also given a sword.
5 When the Lamb broke the third seal, I heard the third creature
call, "Come and see!" Then a black horse appeared, and its rider
6 held a pair of scales in his hand. And I heard a voice from the
midst of the four creatures say, "A measure of wheat for a silver
coin; but do not harm the oil and the wine."
7 The Lamb then broke the fourth seal, and I heard the fourth
8 creature call loudly, "Come and see!" I looked and saw an ash-
colored horse. Upon it sat a rider whose name was Death, and the
inhabitants of the kingdom of death were his followers. They were

given power to kill a fourth part of the people of the earth with the
sword, with hunger and pestilence, and with the wild beasts of the
earth.

9 When the Lamb broke the fifth seal, I saw under the altar the
souls of those who had been slain on account of the word of God
and on account of the testimony which they had offered on behalf
10 of the Lamb and to which they adhered. They cried with a loud
voice, "How long, O Lord, holy and true, wilt Thou wait before
Thou sittest in judgment and avengest our blood on the inhabitants
11 of the earth?" Then each of them was given a white robe, and they
were told to wait in patience a little while longer, until the number
of their fellow-servants and their brothers who were to be killed
like themselves, should be complete.

12 Next I saw the Lamb open the sixth seal, and there was a mighty
earthquake. The sun became black as sackcloth of hair; the full
13 moon looked like blood; the stars of the sky fell to earth as a fig
14 tree sheds its unripe fruit when shaken by a gale. The sky vanished
like a scroll that is rolled up, and every mountain and hill was
15 moved out of its place. The kings of the earth, the dignitaries and
the generals, the rich and the mighty, every slave and every freeman,
16 hid in caves and among the rocks of the mountains. And they
called to the mountains and the rocks, "Fall on us and hide us from
the face of Him Who sits on the throne, and from the anger of the
17 Lamb. For the great day of their punishment has come, and who
can stand the test?"

CHAPTER 7.

1 After that I saw four angels standing at the four ends of the
earth and holding fast the four winds of the earth, so that no wind
2 might blow on the land or on the sea or on any tree. And I saw
another angel ascending from the east and carrying the seal of the
living God in his hand. He called in a loud voice to the four angels
who had been given power to bring disaster upon land and sea,
3 "Do no harm to the land or to the sea or to the trees, until we have
marked the servants of our God by setting a seal upon their fore-
4 heads." I heard the number of those on whom the seal was set; the
full number of those who were sealed in this way was a hundred
and forty-four thousand, and they belonged to every tribe of the
5 children of Israel. Twelve thousand were from the tribe of Judah;
twelve thousand were from the tribe of Reuben; twelve thousand
6 were from the tribe of Gad; twelve thousand were from the tribe of

Aser; twelve thousand were from the tribe of Nepthali; twelve
7 thousand were from the tribe of Manasseh; twelve thousand were
from the tribe of Simeon; twelve thousand were from the tribe of
8 Levi; twelve thousand were from the tribe of Issachar; twelve
thousand were from the tribe of Zebulon; twelve thousand were
from the tribe of Joseph; and twelve thousand were from the tribe
of Benjamin.

9 After this I saw a great host whom no one could count: men of
every nation and race and people and tongue; they stood before the
throne and before the Lamb, clothed in white garments and hold-
10 ing palm-branches in their hands. They exclaimed with a loud
voice, "Our salvation is in the hand of our God and of the Lamb."
11 And all the angels gathered around the throne and around the
elders and the four creatures. They fell upon their faces before the
12 throne and worshipped God, saying, "Amen! Praise and glory,
wisdom and thanksgiving, honor, power, and might be to our God
for ever. Amen!"

13 Then one of the elders said to me, "Who are these, clothed in
14 white garments? Where have they come from?" I answered, "Sir,
you know." He replied, "They are those who on their way through
great trials have washed their robes and made them white in the
15 blood of the Lamb. Therefore they may stand before the throne of
God and serve Him day and night in His temple; and He Who sits
16 upon the throne will live among them. They shall no longer know
hunger or thirst. The sun's rays shall no longer scorch them, nor
17 shall they be struck by any burning heat, for the Lamb that stands
in front of the throne will be their shepherd and will lead them to
the fountains of life; and God Himself will wipe away all tears
from their eyes."

CHAPTER 8.

1 When the Lamb broke the seventh seal, there was silence in
2 heaven for about half an hour. I saw that the seven angels who
stood before God were given seven trumpets.

3 Then came another angel and stood at the altar with a golden
censer. He was given a great quantity of incense to be offered upon
the golden altar before the throne as a symbol of the prayers of all
4 the saints. And the cloud of smoke rose before God from the hand
5 of the angel as a symbol of the prayers of the faithful. Then the
angel took the censer, filled it with embers from the altar, and threw
them upon the earth. At this there was a loud outcry; flashes of
lightning followed, and peals of thunder, and the earth shook.

6 The seven angels who held the seven trumpets now made ready
to blow them.
7 The first angel blew, and there followed hail and fire mingled
with blood, and this was hurled upon the earth. A third of the
earth's surface was burned, and a third of the trees, and all of the
green grass was burned.
8 Then the second angel blew, and it was as though a great mountain glowing with fire were hurled into the sea. A third of the sea
9 was turned into blood, and a third of all the creatures living in the
sea perished, and a third of the ships was destroyed.
10 Then the third angel blew, and a great star, blazing like a torch,
11 fell from heaven and struck a third of the rivers and springs. The
name of this star is Wormwood; and a third of the waters turned
into wormwood, and many people died from drinking the water, because it had turned bitter.
12 The fourth angel blew, and a third of the sun, a third of the
moon, and a third of the stars were so violently shaken that a third
of them was darkened. Consequently a third of the day had no
light, and it was the same with the night.
13 After this I saw an eagle flying high up in the sky, and heard it
call with a loud voice, "Woe, woe, woe to the inhabitants of the
earth, because of the trumpet-blasts of the three angels who are yet
to blow."

CHAPTER 9.

1 Now the fifth angel blew, and I saw a star which had fallen from
heaven to earth. He was given the key to the mouth of the pit.
2 He opened the mouth of the pit with it, and smoke rose from the
pit like the smoke of a great furnace. The sun and all the air were
3 darkened by the smoke from the pit. Out of the smoke came locusts
upon the earth, and they were given such power as scorpions have
4 on the earth. But they were commanded to do no harm to the grass
of the earth or to any green thing or any tree, but only to those
human beings who did not bear the seal of God on their foreheads.
5 The locusts were furthermore commanded not to kill people, but
to torment them for five months. The torment that they caused was
6 like the torment undergone by a man stung by a scorpion. In those
days men will seek death, but will not find it; they will long for
7 death, but death will flee from them. The locusts had the appearance
of horses armed for battle. On their heads were crowns that looked
as though they were made of gold. Their faces were like human
8 faces; their hair was as long as women's hair, and their teeth were

9 like lions' fangs. They wore breastplates like iron mail, and the
sound of their wings was like the noise of many chariots when their
10 horses are rushing to battle. And they have tails and stings like
scorpions, and in their tails lies the power to torture men for five
11 months. The king who rules over them is the angel of the abyss,
whose name is Abaddon in the Hebrew tongue, and Apollyon in
the Greek.

12 The first woe is past; two woes are yet to come.

13 Then the sixth angel blew his trumpet; and I heard a voice from
14 the four corners of the golden altar that stands before God say to
the sixth angel who held the trumpet, "Release the four angels who
15 are bound at the great river Euphrates." Then the four angels who
had stood ready for the hour and the day and the month and the
16 year to destroy a third of mankind, were unbound. The hosts of
their horsemen numbered two hundred million; I heard this num-
17 ber. And this is how the horses and their riders looked in my vision:
They wore coats of mail that were fiery-red, hyacinth-blue, and
sulphur-yellow. The heads of the horses were like lions' heads, and
18 out of their mouths poured fire, smoke, and brimstone. A third
of mankind was killed by these three plagues: by the fire, the
19 smoke, and the brimstone that issued from the horses' mouths; for
their strength lies in their mouths and in their tails. Their tails look
20 like serpents and have heads with which they inflict harm. Nevertheless, the rest of mankind, who were not killed by these plagues,
did not repent of their evil ways. They persisted in worshipping evil
spirits and their images — images made of gold, silver, brass, stone
21 or wood, which therefore can neither see nor hear nor move. These
people did not mend their ways, but continued to murder, to com-
pound poison, to practise sexual vice, and to steal.

CHAPTER 10.

1 Then I saw another mighty angel descend from heaven wrapped
in a cloud. A rainbow was above his head, his face was like the
2 sun, and his feet were like pillars of fire. He held a small book
open in his hand. Setting his right foot upon the sea and his left
3 foot upon the land, he cried out in a voice as loud as the roar of a
lion. When his cry had died away, seven thunders uttered their
4 voices. As soon as the seven thunders had spoken, I was about to
write down what they had uttered, but I heard a voice from heaven
saying to me, "Seal up what the seven thunders have uttered, and
do not write it down."

5 The angel whom I had seen standing on the sea and on the land
6 now raised his right hand to heaven and swore this oath by Him
Who lives for ever, Who created the heavens and all that is in them,
the earth and all that is on it, and the sea and all that it contains:
7 "From now on the conception of time will cease, but the days when
the voice of the seventh angel is raised, and the moment when he
prepares to blow his trumpet, will mark the end of God's mysterious
plan of salvation, which He imparted to His servants the prophets
as joyful news."
8 Then the voice that I had heard from heaven spoke to me again
and said, "Go and take the small open book from the hand of the
9 angel who stands on the sea and on the land." I went to the angel
and said to him, "Give me the small book," and the angel answered,
"Take it and eat it. It will be bitter in your stomach, but in your
10 mouth it will be as sweet as honey." I took the book from the
angel's hand and ate it. And it was as sweet as honey in my mouth,
11 but when I had eaten it, it turned bitter in my stomach. Then some
one said to me, "There are still other messages from the world of
spirits which you must proclaim, messages that relate to many
peoples and nations, tongues and kings."

CHAPTER 11.

1 Now I was given a reed like a measuring-rod, and the angel came
to me and said, "Go and measure the temple of God and the altar,
2 and count the number of those who worship there. But leave out
the court that lies outside of the temple; do not measure that, for
it was set aside for the unbelievers. They will walk about the holy
3 city in derision for forty-two months. And I will grant my two witnesses the grace to appear for one thousand, two-hundred and sixty
4 days as prophets, clothed in sackcloth. They are the two olive-trees
and the two candlesticks that stand before the Lord of the earth.
5 If any one tries to harm them, fire comes out of their mouths and
consumes their enemies; every one who tries to harm them must
6 perish in this way. They have power to close the heavens so that no
rain falls during the days on which they speak as prophets. They
also have the power to turn water into blood and to scourge the
7 earth with every sort of plague as often as they wish. When they
have offered complete proof for the truth, the beast will ascend from
the abyss and make war on them. He will overcome them and kill
8 them. Their corpses will be left to lie unburied in the street of the
great city that is known in the spirit-world as Sodom; it is the city
9 in which our lord also was crucified. Men of all races and tribes,

tongues and nations will see their bodies lying there for three days
10 and a half, and will not allow them to be put in a tomb. The inhabitants of the earth will rejoice over their death; they will be
jubilant and in their joy send gifts to one another, for these two
prophets had prepared torments for the inhabitants of the earth.
11 But after three days and a half the breath of life from God entered
them again. They rose to their feet, and great fear fell upon all
12 who saw them. I heard a loud voice from heaven calling to them,
"Come up here." And they ascended to heaven in a cloud, while
13 their enemies looked on. At the same moment there was a violent
earthquake. A tenth of the city fell, and seven thousand of the leading people were killed by the earthquake. Those who were spared
were seized with terror and gave glory to the God of heaven.
14 The second woe was past, and the third followed closely upon it.
15 The seventh angel blew his trumpet, and loud voices were heard
in heaven saying, "The sovereignty of the universe has passed to
our Lord and His Anointed, and He will be King for ever and ever.
Amen."
16 Then the twenty-four elders who sit upon their thrones before
17 God fell upon their faces and worshipped God, saying, "We thank
Thee, O Lord God Almighty, Who art and wert and wilt be the
essence of all life, because Thou hast recovered Thy mighty power
18 and resumed Thy full sovereignty. The unbelievers were full of
bitterness, but Thy punishment has overtaken them. The time has
come for the spiritually dead to stand judgment, and for Thy servants — the prophets and the faithful and all who honor Thy name,
from the least to the greatest — to receive their reward, and for the
devastators of the earth to be destroyed."
19 Then the temple of God in heaven was opened, and the ark of
His covenant was seen inside His temple. Voices sounded, lightning
flashed, thunder pealed, and a great torrent of hail fell.

CHAPTER 12.

1 A wonderful sight appeared in heaven: a woman, clothed with the
sun, who had the moon under her feet and a crown of twelve stars
2 on her head. She carried a child in her womb; the birth-pangs came
3 upon her, and she cried aloud with the pain of delivery. Then another sight suddenly appeared in heaven: a great, fiery-red dragon
4 with seven heads and ten horns and seven crowns on its heads. Its
tail swept a third of the stars out of the heavens and hurled them
to the earth. And the dragon took its stand before the woman who
was about to be delivered, in order to devour the child as soon as

5 it was born. She gave birth to a child, a son, who was to shepherd
all unbelievers with a rod of iron; and her child was taken up to
6 God and to His throne. The woman herself fled into the wilderness,
where a place has been prepared for her by God, in which she will
receive care for one thousand two hundred and sixty days.
7 War broke out in heaven, Michael and his angels fighting with
8 the dragon, and the dragon and his angels offering resistance. But
their strength was not great enough, and it was impossible for them
9 to maintain any place in heaven. So the great dragon, that old
serpent called the "Devil" and "Satan," the seducer of the whole
universe, was hurled down into the earthly spheres, and his angels
were thrown down with him.
10 And I heard a loud voice in heaven calling, "The salvation, the
might, and the rule of our God and the power of His Anointed have
now appeared; for the accuser of our brothers, who accused them
11 before God day and night, is overthrown. They have prevailed over
him by the blood of the Lamb and by the testimony that they
offered on behalf of the truth; their lives were not so dear to them
12 that they were not ready to die for the truth. Therefore rejoice, O
heavens, and all who dwell in them. But woe to you, O Earth, and
to you, O Sea; for the devil has come down to you full of rage,
well knowing that his time is short."
13 Now when the dragon saw that he was thrown down to the earthly
spheres, he pursued the woman who had given birth to the child.
14 Then the woman was given the two wings of a great eagle, so that
she might fly to her place in the wilderness where she receives care
for a year and two years and half a year, safe from the eye of the
15 serpent. Then the dragon vomited forth water after the woman like
16 a river, so as to sweep her away with this river; but the earth came
to the rescue of the woman by opening its mouth and swallowing the
17 river that the dragon had poured out of his mouth. So the dragon
was enraged at the woman and went off to make war on the rest of
her descendants—the descendants who obey God's commands and
testify on behalf of Jesus.
18 Then I was placed on the seashore.

CHAPTER 13.

1 As I stood there I saw a beast rising out of the sea. He had ten
horns and seven heads, ten crowns on his horns, and blasphemous
2 names on his heads. The beast that I saw was like a panther; his
paws were like those of a bear, and his mouth was like that of a

lion. The dragon gave him his power, his throne, and great author-
3 ity. One of his heads seemed to me to have been fatally wounded;
but the wound that threatened to cause death was healed. All the
4 world looked up to the beast in wonder, and paid homage to the
dragon for having conferred this power on the beast. The same
homage was paid to the beast himself, and people said, "Who is
5 the beast's equal, and who can contend with him?" The beast was
endowed with the power to utter arrogant sayings and blasphemies
with his mouth, and was permitted to do so for a period of forty-
6 two months. He opened his mouth in blasphemies against the name
and the temple of God and against those who dwell in the temple of
heaven. He also had the power to make war on the faithful and to
7 conquer them. He was given authority over all tribes and peoples
8 and tongues and nations. He will be worshipped by all the inhabitants of the earth whose names are not entered in the Book of Life
of the Lamb — the Lamb that had offered himself for sacrifice from
the foundation of the world.

9 Let him whose ear is open to these words, listen: He who leads
10 others into captivity must himself be led into captivity; and he who
kills with the sword must himself die by the sword. Here remember the steadfastness and the faith of the true worshippers of God.

11 I now saw another beast rising from the earth. He had two horns
12 like a ram, but he spoke like a dragon. He exercises all the power
of the first beast in his presence, and causes the inhabitants of the
earth to worship the first beast, whose deadly wound had been
13 healed. He also performs great wonders; he is even able to draw
14 fire down from heaven in the sight of men. By these miracles that he
is able to perform in the sight of the beast, he leads the earth's inhabitants astray, and induces them to make an image of the first
beast — the beast that had been wounded with a sword and came
15 back to life. He was given the power to endow the image of the
first beast with a spirit, so that the image of the beast spoke; and
he succeeded in having every one who would not worship the image
16 put to death. In addition he makes all men, high and low, rich and
poor, freemen and slaves, make a mark on their right hands or
17 on their foreheads. No one can buy or sell unless he bears this
mark, which is either the name of the beast or the number corre-
18 sponding to his name. It requires wisdom to understand this. Let
him who has the right understanding calculate the number of the
beast, for it is the number of a man, and it amounts to six hundred
and sixty-six.

CHAPTER 14.

1 Then I saw the Lamb standing on Mount Sion. With him were a
hundred and forty-four thousand who had the name of the Lamb
2 and the name of his Father written on their foreheads. I heard a
voice from heaven like the roar of a great waterfall and like a
mighty peal of thunder. At the same time the voice that I heard
sounded to me like the voice of harpists singing to the accompani-
3 ment of their harps. It sounded like a new song that was sung before the throne and the four creatures and the elders, and no one
could sing that song except the hundred and forty-four thousand
who had been redeemed from among the inhabitants of the earth.
4 They are men who have not been defiled by women but who have
preserved their chastity. They follow the Lamb wherever he goes.
They have been ransomed from among mankind as the first-fruits
5 for God and for the Lamb. No falsehood has ever been found on
their lips, for they are without blemish.

6 Then I saw another angel flying across the sky. He had a message to proclaim that concerned a certain era, and this message was
7 addressed to all nations and tribes and tongues and races. He called
in a loud voice, "Be fearful of offending God, and give Him glory,
for the hour of judgment has come! Worship Him Who made
8 heaven and earth and the sea and the springs of water." He was
accompanied by another angel who called, "The great Babylon is
fallen, fallen, the city that made all nations drink the fiery wine of
9 its idol-worship!" A third angel followed and cried with a loud
voice, "Whoever worships the beast and his image and allows his
10 mark to be put on his forehead or his hand, shall be made to drink
of the wine of God's wrath, which will be poured unmixed into the
cup of His punishment. He shall be tormented with fire and brim-
11 stone before the eyes of the angels and of the Lamb. The smoke
from the place of his torment rises from one age to another. The
worshippers of the beast and his image, and those who bear the
mark of his name, have no rest day or night."

12 How great the contrast between this and the steadfastness of the
true worshippers, who faithfully observe God's commands and hold
13 fast to their loyalty to Jesus! — And I heard a voice from heaven
saying, "Write: Fortunate from now on are the dead who depart this
life in fellowship with the Lord. Yes, says the spirit, they will rest
from their afflictions, for what they have done will go with them."

14 Then I saw a white cloud, and seated on it one who resembled
a man. He had a golden crown on his head and a sharp sickle in his

15 hand. Another angel came out of the temple and called loudly to
him who sat on the cloud, "Fall to with your sickle and begin to
reap, for the harvest time has come. The harvest of the earth is
16 over-ripe." Then he who sat on the cloud swung his sickle over
the earth, and the earth was reaped.

17 Then another angel came out of the temple of heaven, and he
18 also carried a sharp sickle. And still another angel came from the
altar. It was he who had power over the fire, and he called loudly
to the angel who had the sharp sickle, "Fall to with your sharp
sickle and reap the fruit of the vine of the earth, for its grapes are
19 fully ripe." The angel swung his sickle over the earth, reaped the
clusters from the vine of the earth, and threw the grapes into the
20 great winepress of God's punishment. The winepress was trodden
outside the city, and blood flowed out of it and rose as high as the
horses' bridles, for a space of two hundred miles.

CHAPTER 15.

1 I saw another great and marvellous sign in heaven: seven angels
who were in charge of the last seven plagues with which God's
punishment was completed.

2 I saw something that resembled a sea of crystal mingled with
fire. Standing by the sea of crystal I saw those who had gained the
victory over the beast and his image and the number of his name.
3 They held harps of God in their hands, and they were singing the
song of Moses the servant of God, and the song of the Lamb: "Great
and marvellous are Thy works, Lord God Almighty. Just and true
4 are Thy ways, Thou King of Nations. Who shall not fear to offend
Thee, and who shall not glorify Thy name? Thou alone art holy.
Yes, all nations will come and worship before Thee, for Thy destined ways have been found just."

5 After that I looked and saw the sanctuary of the tabernacle in
6 heaven open, and out of the sanctuary came the seven angels with
the seven plagues. They were clothed in dazzling white linen, and
7 wore golden belts about their breasts. One of the four creatures gave
the seven angels seven golden vessels filled with the punishment of
8 the God Who lives for ever; and the sanctuary was filled with
smoke from the glory of God and from His power. No one could
enter the sanctuary until the seven plagues of the seven angels had
run their course.

CHAPTER 16.

1 Then I heard a loud voice from the temple calling to the seven
angels, "Go and pour out the seven vessels of God's punishment
upon the earth."
2 The first angel went and poured out his vessel upon the earth,
and immediately malignant ulcers broke out on the people who bore
the mark of the beast and worshipped his image.
3 The second angel poured out his vessel into the sea, and the sea
became like the blood of slain men, and every creature that lived in
the sea died.
4 Then the third angel poured out his vessel into the rivers and
5 the sources of water. They also were turned into blood, and I heard
the angel of the waters say, "O Lord, Thou holy One! Thy sentence
6 is and has ever been just, for the guilty have shed the blood of
saints and prophets, and for this Thou hast given them blood to
drink. This is the punishment that they deserve."
7 And I heard the angel of the altar say, "Yes, almighty Lord and
God, Thy sentence is founded upon the truth and accords with
justice."
8 The fourth angel now poured out his vessel upon the sun; and
9 the sun was given power to destroy men with its fiery glow; men
were consumed by a fierce wave of heat and died with curses on
their lips against the God Who has the power to send such plagues,
instead of repenting and acknowledging Him as their God.
10 The fifth angel emptied his vessel upon the throne of the beast,
and his kingdom was plunged into darkness. Men gnawed their
11 tongues for pain, but continued to blaspheme the God of heaven
because of their torments and because of their ulcers, and they did
not abandon their wicked ways.
12 Then the sixth angel poured out his vessel upon the great river
Euphrates, and its waters were dried up, leaving the way open for
13 the kings approaching from the east. And I saw coming out of the
mouth of the dragon and out of the mouth of the beast and out of
the mouth of the false prophet three unclean spirits in the shape of
14 frogs. They are the spirits of devils, which are able to perform
marvellous signs. They go out and seize upon the kings of the
whole earth, so as to incite them to join in battle on that great day
15 when the Almighty God rises against them. Mark, God will come
unexpectedly, like a thief; fortunate, then, is he who is watchful and
keeps his clothing ready, so that he need not go naked and let people
16 see his shame. — And those devils assembled the kings at a place
called in Hebrew Armageddon.

17 The seventh angel now poured out his vessel into the air, and a
loud voice came out of the temple of heaven from the throne, crying,
18 "It is finished." Then came flashes of lightning, accompanied by
cries and peals of thunder. There was a mighty earthquake, such
as had never been since men lived on the earth—so violent and
19 fearful was this earthquake. As a result, the great dominion fell
apart and was broken into three. The cities of the unbelievers fell;
and God did not forget to give to the great empire of Babylon the
20 cup filled with the fiery wine of His punishment. Every island van-
21 ished, and mountains were no longer to be found. A violent hail-
storm, each stone weighing a pound, fell upon men from heaven;
but they blasphemed God because of the plague of hail, for such a
plague is frightful.

CHAPTER 17.

1 Then one of the seven angels who had the seven vessels came to
me and said, "Come, I will show you the sentence to be executed
2 upon the great harlot who is enthroned beside many waters, and
with whom the kings of the earth have carried on illicit intercourse,
and on whose wine of lewdness the earth's inhabitants have been
3 made drunk." My spirit left my body, and the angel led me into a
wilderness, where I saw a woman sitting on a scarlet beast. This
beast was covered with blasphemous names, and had seven heads
4 and ten horns. The woman was clothed in purple and scarlet and
richly adorned with gold, precious stones, and pearls. In her hand
was a golden cup filled with idolatrous abominations and with the
5 filth of all the harlotry of the earth. On her forehead was written a
name, the meaning of which is a mystery. It was, "Babylon the great
—the mother of harlots and of the abominations of the whole
6 earth." I saw the woman drunk with the blood of the faithful and
the blood of the witnesses of Jesus, and at the sight of her I was
7 filled with utter astonishment. Then the angel turned to me and
said, "Why are you so astonished? I will give you an explanation
of the mysterious woman and of the beast on which she is sitting and
8 which has the seven heads and the ten horns. The beast that you
saw was here in times past, but is no longer to be seen. But it will
rise again from the abyss, and will also withdraw again into the
region of the damned. Those inhabitants of the earth whose names
are not recorded in the Book of Life, which has been kept since the
foundation of the universe, will marvel when they see that the beast
9 was here, then vanished, and then reappears. Intelligence must be
coupled with wisdom in order to understand this. The seven heads

are the seven hills on which the woman is enthroned. They also
10 signify seven kings. Five of them have fallen into the abyss, one is
still here, and the other has not yet come; and when he does come
11 he will remain only a short time. The beast that was here in times
past and is now gone, is the eighth king, but nevertheless belongs
12 to the seven and will sink back again into perdition.—The ten
horns that you saw are ten kings who have not yet been invested
with their royal office. They will receive royal power at the same
13 time as the beast, but only for an hour. They are all of one mind
and will place at the disposal of the beast all the resources that they
14 command. They will make war upon the Lamb, but the Lamb
will overcome them; for the Lamb is the lord of lords and the king
of kings. It is for this very purpose that his fellow-combatants were
15 called and chosen and numbered among his faithful." Then the
angel continued, "The waters beside which you saw the harlot en-
16 throned are tribes and nations and tongues. The ten horns that
you saw will, together with the beast, hate the harlot and rob and
despoil her and strip her naked, and then they will devour her flesh
17 and burn her with fire. For God has put it into their minds to carry
out His decree and with this aim unanimously to resolve to lend the
beast the resources at their command, until the words of God are
18 fulfilled. The woman whom you saw is the powerful organization
that controls the kings of the earth."

CHAPTER 18.

1 After that I saw another angel come down from heaven. He had
2 vast power, and the earth was lighted with his radiance. He called
out with a mighty voice, "Babylon the great is fallen, fallen. She
has become the haunt of devils, the stronghold of all impure spirits,
and the gathering-place for every unclean and loathsome animal.
3 For all the infidels have drunk the fiery wine of her lewdness; the
kings of the earth have carried on illicit intercourse with her, and
the merchants of the earth have grown rich through her unbridled
luxury."

4 I heard another voice from heaven cry, "Depart from her, my
people, so that you may not share the guilt of her sins and be
5 stricken with the plagues that are visited upon her. For her sins are
heaped as high as heaven, and God has not forgotten her criminal
6 deeds. Pay her back for what she has done to you, and give her
double for the harm that she has inflicted. Mix her a double draught
7 of poison in the cup that she has brewed for you. In the same
measure in which she has excelled in vain ambition and debauchery,

mete out to her torment and sorrow. Because she says in her heart,
'I am enthroned as a queen, I am no widow and shall never know
8 sorrow,' all the plagues in store for her shall overtake her in one
day. Death, sorrow and famine shall befall her, and in the end she
shall be utterly consumed by fire; for the Lord God Who has pro-
9 nounced this sentence upon her is well able to carry it out. The
kings of the earth will weep and lament over her when they see the
smoke of her burning, for they carried on illicit intercourse with her
10 and took part in her revels. They will stand far off for fear of
sharing her punishment, and will break out into the lament, 'Alas,
alas, you great city of Babylon, you mighty city! In a single hour
11 judgment has overtaken you.' The merchants of the earth will likewise weep and mourn over her, for no one will buy their merchan-
12 dise any more — their wares of silver and gold, their precious stones
and pearls, fine linen and purple, silk and scarlet, all the fragrant
citron wood, and all the vessels of ivory as well as of all sorts of
13 costly wood, of brass, iron, and marble; and their cinnamon and
ointments, perfumes, myrrh and frankincense, wine and oil, fine
flour and wheat, cattle and sheep, horses and chariots, and the
14 bodies and souls of men. Even the fruit that your soul longs for
has been taken from you for ever. All your splendor and finery
15 have vanished, assuredly never to be found again. The merchants
who trade in these wares and have grown rich from her will stand
far off, weeping and wailing for fear of her punishment, and ex-
16 claim, 'Alas, alas, you great city! You who clothed yourself in fine
linen, in purple and scarlet, and were richly adorned with gold and
17 precious stones and pearls! Oh, that a single hour should have
demolished such wealth!' And every pilot and master of coasting-
vessels, every sailor and all who trade by sea, stood far off, and
18 when they saw the smoke of her conflagration they cried, 'Where
is there a city as great as this?' They threw dust on their heads and
19 exclaimed, weeping and wailing, 'Alas, alas, for that great city
whose prosperity enriched all who had ships on the sea! In a single
20 hour she has been laid waste!' — Rejoice over her, heaven! Rejoice, saints and apostles and prophets! For God has executed upon
her the sentence that she deserved on your account."

21 Then a strong angel lifted up a stone as large as a millstone and
hurled it into the sea, saying, "Thus shall the great city of Babylon
22 be thrown down and found no more. The sound of minstrels and
singers, of flutes and trumpets, shall never be heard in you again,
and no craftsman of any craft whatever shall be found within your
23 walls. The noise of the mill shall be heard there no more. No lamp

shall shed its light in you, no rejoicing of bridegroom and bride
shall be heard in you. For your merchants were the great men of
the earth, because all nations were blinded by your magic splendor.
24 In you was found the blood of the prophets and the faithful, and
of all those who were slain on earth."

CHAPTER 19.

1 Then I heard a sound like the loud exultation of a great host,
shouting in heaven, "Hallelujah! Salvation, glory, and power be-
2 long to our God. His judgments are true and just. He has sentenced
the great harlot who drove the earth to perdition with her lewdness,
3 and has called her to account for the blood of His servants." And
again their cry went up, "Hallelujah! The smoke from her rises
4 throughout many ages!" Then the twenty-four elders and the four
creatures prostrated themselves and exclaimed in homage to God,
5 Who was seated upon the throne, "Amen! Hallelujah!" And a voice
sounded from the throne, saying, "Praise our God, all of you who
are His servants and all, both small and great, who reverence Him!"
6 Then I heard a sound like the exultation of great hosts, and like
the roar of many waters and the peal of mighty thunder, saying,
"Hallelujah! The Lord our God, the Almighty, has resumed His
7 reign. Let us rejoice and exult and give honor to Him, for the
wedding of the Lamb has come, and the bride has made herself
8 ready. She has been allowed to clothe herself in shining white
linen." For the linen signifies the favor that the faithful have gained
in the eyes of God.
9 Then he said to me, "Write, 'Happy are they who have been
invited to the wedding-banquet of the Lamb.'" And he continued,
10 "These are truly the words of God." I fell at his feet to worship
him, but he said to me, "Not that! I am only a fellow-servant of
yours and of your brothers who have the testimony of Jesus. Worship God alone." For those who have the testimony of Jesus are the
ones through whom a spirit of God manifests itself.
11 After that I saw the heavens open and beheld a white horse.
Mounted upon it was a rider who bore the name "Faithful and
True." His judgments are made in accordance with the laws of
12 justice, and executed in accordance with those same laws. His eyes
flashed like flames of fire. On his head were many crowns. He had
names which were written on these crowns, and he alone could read
13 them, no one else. He was dressed in a robe that had been dipped
14 in blood. He is called "The Word of God." The hosts of heaven,
15 clothed in shining white linen, followed him on white horses. The

breath of his mouth shaped itself into a sharp sword with which he
is to conquer the enemies of God. He will drive them before him
with an iron rod, as a shepherd drives his flock. It is he who treads
the winepress in which the fiery wine of the judgments of almighty
16 God are made. On the part of the robe that covered his thigh was
written the name, *King of Kings and Lord of Lords.*

17 Then I saw an angel standing in the sun, who cried with a loud
voice to all the birds that flew high in the air, "Come and gather
18 for a great banquet of God. You shall eat the flesh of kings, the
flesh of commanders, the flesh of the mighty, the flesh of horses and
their riders, the flesh of men of every kind, freemen and slaves, small
19 and great." Then I saw the beast and the kings of the earth at the
head of their armies, gathered to give battle to him who was mounted
20 on the white horse and to his army. In this battle the beast was
overpowered, and with him the false prophet who had worked
miracles before the beast and seduced those who had marked themselves with the sign of the beast and worshipped his image. Both
of them were thrown alive into the lake of fire that burns with brim-
21 stone. The rest were killed with the sword that issued from the
mouth of the rider of the white horse; and all the birds gorged
themselves on the flesh of the fallen.

CHAPTER 20.

1 Now I saw an angel come down from heaven with the key to
2 the lower regions and a large chain in his hand. He seized the
dragon, that old serpent, the Devil or Satan, bound him for a thou-
3 sand years, threw him into the lower regions, and locked and sealed
the entrance so that he might no longer deceive the nations, until
the thousand years were over. After that he must be released for
a short time.

4 Then I saw thrones on which were seated judges invested with
the power of holding court. Moreover I saw the souls of those who
had been put to death because of their testimony on behalf of Jesus
and for the sake of the word of God. They had not worshipped the
beast and his image, nor placed his mark on their foreheads or
hands. All of them received spiritual life, and ruled with Christ
5 throughout the thousand years. But the rest of the spiritually dead
did not attain to spiritual life until the thousand years had run their
6 course. This is the first spiritual resurrection. Fortunate and holy
is he who shares in the first resurrection. Over such the Prince of
Death cannot exert his power for a second time; they will be priests

of God and of Christ, and rule with him as kings throughout the
thousand years.
7 When the thousand years have expired, Satan will be released
8 from his prison; he will go out and deceive the nations as far as the
four corners of the earth — Gog and Magog — and assemble them
9 for battle. They are as numerous as the sands of the sea. They then
went up to the higher earthly spheres and surrounded the camp of
the faithful and the beloved city; and fire fell upon them from
10 heaven and consumed them. Their seducer, the devil, was thrown
into the lake of fire and brimstone in which are also the beast and
the false prophet. There they will be tortured day and night until
the remotest future.
11 Then I saw a great white throne, and Him Who sat upon it. The
earth and the sky fled before His face, and there was no place for
12 them any longer. I saw the dead, great and small, standing before
the throne. Books were opened, and then another book called the
Book of Life was opened; and the spiritually dead were judged by
13 their deeds as recorded in the books. The sea had been made to give
up the dead that it concealed; the Prince of Death and the kingdom
of death had surrendered their dead, and every one of them was
14 judged by his deeds. The Prince of Death and his subjects were
thrown into the lake of fire; thus they returned to the place of the
15 spiritually dead, the lake of fire. And every one whose name was not
recorded in the Book of Life was thrown into the lake of fire.

CHAPTER 21.

1 Now I saw a new heaven and a new earth, for the former heaven
and the former earth had passed away. The sea had also vanished.
2 And I saw the holy city come down out of heaven from God, like
a bride adorned for her marriage with the bridegroom.
3 At the same time I heard a loud voice calling from the throne,
"That is the dwelling-place of God with men. He will live among
them; they will be His people, and God Himself will be among
4 them. He will wipe away all the tears from their eyes. There will
be no more death, no grief, no lamentation, no pain; for now, and
5 for the first time, all these things are past." And He Who sat upon
the throne said, "See, I am making everything anew." Then He continued, "Write down everything. You may rely on these words, for
6 they are the truth." He spoke to me again and said, "I am He, I
the Alpha and the Omega, the beginning and the end. I will let the
7 thirsty drink from the fountain of life. He who is victorious shall

inherit all these things; I will be his God, and he shall be My child.
8 But cowards and unbelievers, the impure and the murderers, the
unchaste and the compounders of poison, the idolators and all the
liars, shall suffer the punishment that they deserve in the burning
lake of fire and brimstone. For them this signifies spiritual death
anew."

9 Then one of the seven angels who carried in their hands the
seven vessels filled with the last seven plagues, came and said to
me, "Come and I will show you the bride, the wife of the Lamb."
10 At once my spirit left my body, and the angel took me to a great,
high mountain, and showed me the holy city, Jerusalem, coming
11 down out of heaven from God, adorned with the glory of God. It
shone with a light as radiant as that of the most precious stone, as
12 of crystal-clear jasper. It had a great, high wall with twelve gates,
and at the gates stood twelve angels. On the gates were inscribed
13 names, which were the names of the twelve tribes of Israel. Three
gates opened to the east, three to the north, three to the south, and
14 three to the west. The wall of the city had twelve foundation-stones,
and on these were written the names of the twelve apostles of the
Lamb.

15 He who talked with me had a golden reed for a measuring-rod
16 with which to measure the city and its gates and its wall. The city
was laid out in a quadrangle, its length equal to its width. He
measured the city with his reed and found that its length was fifteen
17 hundred miles, and its width and height the same. Then he measured the wall, which was two hundred and sixteen feet according to
the human standard—the standard which the angel also used.
18 The material of the wall was jasper, while the city itself was of gold
19 as pure as the most transparent glass. The foundation-stones of the
wall were made of every kind of precious stone. The first founda-
tion-stone was of jasper, the second of sapphire, the third of chalce-
20 dony, the fourth of emerald, the fifth of sardonyx, the sixth of
carnelian, the seventh of chrysolite, the eighth of beryl, the ninth of
topaz, the tenth of chrysoprase, the eleventh of jacinth, and the
21 twelfth of amethyst. The twelve gates were twelve pearls, each gate
consisting of a single pearl. The streets were pure gold, as transparent as the clearest glass.

22 I saw no temple in the city, for the Lord God Almighty is its
23 temple, and so is the Lamb. And the city did not need either sun
or moon for illumination, for the glory of God illumined it, and the
24 Lamb was its light. The nations will walk in the light of this city,
and the kings of the earth will bring their own glory and splendor

25 into it. The gates will never be shut by day, for there is no night
26 there. Whatever is precious in the eyes of the nations will be taken
27 into the city; but nothing unclean may enter it, and no one who is a
slave to idolatry and falsehood, but only those who are recorded in
the Lamb's Book of Life.

CHAPTER 22.

1 Then the angel showed me a river of the water of life, clear as
2 crystal, flowing out of the throne of God and of the Lamb. In the
middle of the streets of the city and on both banks of the river stood
trees of life, bearing twelve kinds of fruit, one kind for every month.
The leaves of these trees serve for the healing of the nations.
3 Nothing that lies under a curse will be found there. The throne
of God and of the Lamb will be in the city. God's servants will serve
4 their Lord and see His face, and His name will be written on their
5 foreheads. Since there will be no night there, neither lamplight nor
sunlight is necessary. God the Lord will give them light, and they
will rule as kings for all the future.
6 Then the angel said to me, "You may rely on these words, for
they are the truth. The Lord and God of those spirits who manifest
themselves through human instruments has sent His angel on this
occasion also, to show God's servants events that must occur in close
7 succession. Mark, I am coming soon! Fortunate is he who keeps in
his heart the words of this book imparted by one of God's spirits."
8 I, John, am the one who heard and saw all these things. And
after I had heard and seen them, I fell at the feet of the angel who
9 had shown me all of them, and was about to worship him. But he
said to me, "You must not do that. I am only a fellow-servant of
yours and of your brothers the prophets and of those who abide by
the words of this book. Worship God alone."
10 Then the angel continued, "Do not conceal the truths in this book
which have been given to you by one of God's spirits; for the time
11 of their fulfillment is at hand. Let the sinner keep on sinning and
the guilty add to his guilt; let the faithful continue to live according
to God's will, and God's follower continue to walk in the path that
12 leads to God. Mark, I am coming soon, and I have with me the
reward that I will bestow. I will requite every one according to the
work he has accomplished.
13 "I am the Alpha and the Omega, the first and the last, the be-
14 ginning and the end. Fortunate are they who wash their robes in
order that they may claim a share in the tree of life and be able to

15 enter the gates of the city. Outside will remain the dogs and the
compounders of poison, the lewd and the murderers, the idolators
and all who love and practise falsehood.
16 "I, Jesus, have sent my angel to tell you these things for the
benefit of the congregations. I am the root and the scion of the
house of David; I am the bright morning star.
17 "And the spirit and the bride say, 'Come.' And whoever hears it
shall answer, 'Come.' Let every one who is thirsty come. And any
one who desires the water of life may come; it shall be his for the
asking.
18 "I warn every one who hears the words of this book as pronounced by one of God's spirits, that if any one adds anything to
19 them God will add to him the plagues described in this book; and if
any one removes any of the words of God's spirit that are contained
in this book, God will remove from him his share in the tree of life
and in the holy city described in this book.
20 "He who testifies to the truth of the contents of this book says,
'Yes, I am coming soon.'"
Amen! Come, lord Jesus!
21 The grace of the lord Jesus Christ be with all the faithful. Amen.

CPSIA information can be obtained at www.ICGtesting.com
Printed in the USA
LVOW041013010312

270574LV00005B/2/A

9 780974 807324